**Literature** Online

Textbook Internet resources are just a click away!

STEP 1 Go to glencoe.com

STEP 2 Connect to resources by entering **QuickPass**™ codes.

LOG ON ▶ **Literature** Online

GL27534u1 — Enter this code with appropriate unit numbers.

STEP 3 Access your Online Student Edition, handheld downloads, games, and more:

Literature and Reading Resources

- Author Search
- Literature Classics
- Big Question Web Quests
- Literary and Text Elements eFlashcards and Games
- Interactive Reading Practice

Selection Resources

- Audio Summaries
- Selection Quizzes
- Selection Vocabulary eFlashcards and Games
- Reading-Writing Connection Activities

Vocabulary and Spelling Resources

- Academic and Selection Vocabulary eFlashcards and Games
- Multi-Language Glossaries
- Spelling Games

Writing, Grammar, and Research Resources

- Interactive Writing Models
- Writing and Research Handbook
- Graphic Organizers
- Sentence-Combining Activities
- Publishing Options

Media Literacy, Speaking, Listening, and Viewing Resources

- Media Analysis Guides
- Project Ideas and Templates
- Presentation Tips and Strategies

Assessment Resources

- End-of-Unit Assessment
- Test-Taking Tips and Strategies

Program Consultants

Jeffrey D. Wilhelm, Ph.D.

Douglas Fisher, Ph.D.

Kathleen A. Hinchman, Ph.D.

David G. O'Brien, Ph.D.

Taffy Raphael, Ph.D.

Cynthia Hynd Shanahan, Ed.D.

Acknowledgments

Grateful acknowledgment is given authors, publishers, photographers, museums, and agents for permission to reprint the following copyrighted material. Every effort has been made to determine copyright owners. In case of any omissions, the Publisher will be pleased to make suitable acknowledgments in future editions.

Acknowledgments continued on page R73.

PHOTO CREDITS: COVER Bloomimage/CORBIS, (bkgd)Ryan McVay/Getty Images; **GA13** Image 100/PunchStock; **GA22** Edwin Tennison, Confederate Army soldier, Private Collection, Peter Newark Military Pictures/The Bridgeman Art Library; **GA23** (cw from top) Joel W. Rogers/CORBIS, Ron Chapple Stock/CORBIS, James Randklev/Getty Images, (bkgd)W. Cody/CORBIS; **GA24** (t)Courtesy, American Antiquarian Society, (c)Courtesy of Hargrett Rare Book & Manuscript Library/University of Georgia Libraries, (bl)Jupiter Unlimited, (br)Dorling Kindersley; **GA25** (t)Bettmann/CORBIS, (cl)General Research & Reference Division, Schomburg Center for Research in Black Culture, The New York Public Library, (cr)CORBIS, (b)Courtesy United States Government; **GA26** (tl)Terry Kay, (bkgd) Jim Richardson/CORB, (b)Jeremy Swinborne/Shutterstock; **GA27** (t)CORBIS, (c)AP Images, (bl)Chepe Nicoli/Shutterstock, (br)Courtesy United States Government; **GA28** All About Jewish Theatre www.jewish-theatre.com; **GA28–GA29** Getty Images; **GA29** ©Warner Bros. Courtesy Everett Collection; **GA32** SuperStock/SuperStock; **GA34** Richard Hamilton Smith/CORBIS; **GA35** North Wind Picture Archives/Alamy Images; **GA36** John Hawkins/FLPA/Minden Pictures/Getty Images; **GA38** SuperStock/SuperStock; **GA39** Images.com/CORBIS; **GA40** Getty Images; **GA41** ImageState/Alamy Images; **GA43** Chuck Franklin/Alamy Images; **GA49** Bettmann/CORBIS; **GA51** CORBIS; **GA52** David Brooks/CORBIS; **GA58** Dinah Mite Activities; **GA59** Creatas/PunchStock.

Glencoe

The **McGraw·Hill** Companies

Send all inquiries to:
Glencoe/McGraw-Hill
8787 Orion Place
Columbus, OH 43240-4027

ISBN: 978-0-07-880753-4
MHID: 0-07-880753-0

Printed in the United States of America.

2 3 4 5 6 7 8 9 058/055 14 13 12 11 10 09

Program Consultants

Senior Program Consultants

Jeffrey D. Wilhelm, Ph.D. Jeffrey Wilhelm is Professor of English Education at Boise State University and Director of the Boise State Writing Project. He specializes in reading and adolescent literacy and does research on ways to engage readers and writers. A middle and high school teacher for thirteen years, Wilhelm is author or coauthor of eleven books, including the award-winning works *You Gotta BE the Book* and *Reading Don't Fix No Chevys.*

Douglas Fisher, Ph.D. Douglas Fisher is Professor of Language and Literacy Education at San Diego State University. He is also Director of the award-winning City Heights Educational Pilot, a project for improving urban adolescent literacy. Fisher has published many articles on reading and literacy and has coauthored *Improving Adolescent Literacy: Strategies That Work.*

Program Consultants

Kathleen A. Hinchman, Ph.D. Kathleen Hinchman is Professor and Chair, Reading and Language Arts Center, School of Education, Syracuse University. A former middle school English and reading teacher, Hinchman researches social perspectives toward literacy. She is coauthor of three books on reading and literacy, including *Principled Practices for a Literate America: A Framework for Literacy and Learning in the Upper Grades.*

David G. O'Brien, Ph.D. David O'Brien is Professor of Literacy Education at the University of Minnesota and a former classroom teacher. O'Brien's research explores reading in content areas as well as ways to motivate learners to engage in school-based literacy tasks. He is conducting studies on the use of technology-based literacy, using computers and related technology.

Taffy Raphael, Ph.D. Taffy Raphael is Professor of Literacy Education at the University of Illinois at Chicago (UIC). She does literacy research on upper elementary and middle school students and has coauthored several books, including *Book Club: A Literature-Based Curriculum* and *Book Club for Middle School.* She has received the International Reading Association (IRA) Outstanding Educator Award and is in the IRA Hall of Fame.

Cynthia Hynd Shanahan, Ed.D. Cynthia Hynd Shanahan is Professor in the Reading, Writing, and Literacy program at the University of Illinois at Chicago (UIC). She is also a consultant with the Center for Literacy at UIC. Hynd Shanahan has been a classroom teacher and has taught reading instruction to elementary-level through college-level teachers. She has authored a chapter in the book *Engaged Reading,* edited by John T. Guthrie and Donna Alverman.

Advisory Board

Georgia Teacher Advisory Board

Georgia Performance Standards

Reading and Literature

ELA7R1 **The student demonstrates comprehension and shows evidence of a warranted and responsible explanation of a variety of literary and informational texts.**

For literary texts, the student identifies the characteristics of various genres and produces evidence of reading that:

a. Distinguishes between the concepts of theme in a literary work and the author's purpose in an expository text.

b. Interprets a character's traits, emotions, or motivations and gives supporting evidence from a text.

c. Relates a literary work to information about its setting or historical moment.

d. Analyzes recurring and similar themes across a variety of selections, distinguishing theme from topic.

e. Identifies events that advance the plot and determines how each event explains past or present action(s) or foreshadows future action(s).

f. Analyzes characterization (dynamic and static) in prose and plays as delineated through a character's thoughts, words, speech patterns, and actions; the narrator's description; and the thoughts, words, and actions of other characters.

g. Explains and analyzes the effects of sound, form, figurative language, and graphics in order to uncover meaning in literature:

   i. Sound (e.g., alliteration, onomatopoeia, internal rhyme, rhyme scheme)

   ii. Figurative language (e.g., simile, metaphor, personification, and hyperbole)

   iii. Graphics (e.g., capital letters, line length, word position).

h. Identifies and analyzes how an author's use of words creates tone and mood, giving supporting evidence from text.

i. Identifies and analyzes similarities and differences in traditional literature from different cultures.

For informational texts, the student reads and comprehends in order to develop understanding and expertise and produces evidence of reading that:

a. Analyzes common textual features to obtain information (e.g., paragraphs, topic sentences, concluding sentences, introduction, conclusion, footnotes, index, bibliography).

b. Identifies and uses knowledge of common graphic features to draw conclusions and make judgments (e.g., graphic organizers, diagrams, captions, illustrations).

c. Applies knowledge of common organizational structures and patterns (i.e., logical order, cause and effect relationships, comparison and contrast, transitions).

d. Recognizes and traces the development of the author's argument for and against an issue.

e. Identifies evidence used to support an argument.

f. Understands and explains the use of a simple device by following technical directions.

ELA7R2 **The student understands and acquires new vocabulary and uses it correctly in reading and writing.**

The student

  a. Determines the meaning of unfamiliar words using context clues (e.g., contrast, cause and effect, etc.).

  b. Uses knowledge of Greek, Latin, and Anglo-Saxon roots and affixes to determine the meaning of unfamiliar words.

  c. Identifies and explains idioms and analogies in prose and poetry.

  d. Determines word meanings through the use of definition, example, restatement, or contrast.

ELA7R3 **The student reads aloud, accurately (in the range of 95%), familiar material in a variety of genres, in a way that makes meaning clear to listeners.**

The student

  a. Uses letter-sound knowledge to decode written English and uses a range of cueing systems (e.g., phonics and context clues) to determine pronunciation and meaning.

  b. Uses self-correction when subsequent reading indicates an earlier miscue (self-monitoring and self-correcting strategies).

  c. Reads with a rhythm, flow, and meter that sounds like everyday speech (prosody).

Reading Across the Curriculum

ELA7RC1 **The student reads a minimum of 25 grade-level appropriate books or book equivalents (approximately 1,000,000 words) per year from a variety of subject disciplines. The student reads both informational and fictional texts in a variety of genres and modes of discourse, including technical texts related to various subject areas. .**

ELA7RC2 **The student participates in discussions related to curricular learning in all subject areas.**

The student

  a. Identifies messages and themes from books in all subject areas.

  b. Responds to a variety of texts in multiple modes of discourse.

  c. Relates messages and themes from one subject area to those in another area.

  d. Evaluates the merits of texts in every subject discipline.

  e. Examines the author's purpose in writing.

  f. Recognizes and uses the features of disciplinary texts (e.g., charts, graphs, photos, maps, highlighted vocabulary).

ELA7RC3 **The student acquires new vocabulary in each content area and uses it correctly.**

The student

  a. Demonstrates an understanding of contextual vocabulary in various subjects.

  b. Uses content vocabulary in writing and speaking.

  c. Explores understanding of new words found in subject area texts.

ELA7RC4 **The student establishes a context for information acquired by reading across subject areas.**

The student

   a. Explores life experiences related to subject area content.

   b. Discusses in both writing and speaking how certain words and concepts relate to multiple subjects.

   c. Determines strategies for finding content and contextual meaning for unfamiliar words or concepts.

Writing

ELA7W1 **The student produces writing that establishes an appropriate organizational structure, sets a context and engages the reader, maintains a coherent focus throughout, and provides a satisfying closure.**

The student

   a. Selects a focus, an organizational structure, and a point of view based on purpose, genre expectations, audience, length, and format requirements.

   b. Writes texts of a length appropriate to address the topic or tell the story.

   c. Uses traditional structures for conveying information (e.g., chronological order, cause and effect, similarity and difference, and posing and answering a question).

   d. Uses appropriate structures to ensure coherence (e.g., transition elements).

   e. Supports statements and claims with anecdotes, descriptions, facts and statistics, and specific examples.

ELA7W2 **The student demonstrates competence in a variety of genres.**

The student produces a narrative (fictional, personal, experiential) that:

   a. Engages readers by establishing and developing a plot, setting, and point of view that are appropriate to the story (e.g., varied beginnings, standard plot line, cohesive devices, and a sharpened focus).

   b. Creates an organizing structure appropriate to purpose, audience, and context.

   c. Develops characters using standard methods of characterization.

   d. Includes sensory details and concrete language to develop plot, setting, and character (e.g., vivid verbs, descriptive adjectives, and varied sentence structures).

   e. Excludes extraneous details and inconsistencies.

   f. Uses a range of strategies (e.g., suspense, figurative language, dialogue, expanded vocabulary, flashback, movement, gestures, expressions, tone, and mood).

   g. Provides a sense of closure to the writing.

The student produces writing (multi-paragraph expository composition such as description, explanation, comparison and contrast, or problem and solution) that:

a. Engages the reader by establishing a context, creating a speaker's voice, and otherwise developing reader interest.
b. Develops a controlling idea that conveys a perspective on the subject.
c. Creates an organizing structure appropriate to purpose, audience, and context.
d. Develops the topic with supporting details.
e. Excludes extraneous and inappropriate information.
f. Follows an organizational pattern appropriate to the type of composition.
g. Concludes with a detailed summary linked to the purpose of the composition.

The student produces technical writing (business correspondence: memoranda, emails, letters of inquiry, letters of complaint, instructions and procedures, lab reports, slide presentations) that:

a. Creates or follows an organizing structure appropriate to purpose, audience, and context.
b. Excludes extraneous and inappropriate information.
c. Follows an organizational pattern appropriate to the type of composition.
d. Applies rules of Standard English.

The student produces a response to literature that:

a. Engages the reader by establishing a context, creating a speaker's voice, or otherwise developing reader interest.
b. Demonstrates an understanding of the literary work.
c. Organizes an interpretation around several clear ideas, premises, or images from the original work.
d. Supports a judgment through references to the text and personal knowledge.
e. Justifies interpretations through sustained use of examples and textual evidence from the literary work.
f. Provides a sense of closure to the writing.

The student produces a multi-paragraph persuasive essay that:

a. Engages the reader by establishing a context, creating a speaker's voice, and otherwise developing reader interest.
b. States a clear position or perspective in support of a proposition or proposal.
c. Describes the points in support of the proposition, employing well-articulated, relevant evidence.
d. Excludes information and arguments that are irrelevant.
e. Creates an organizing structure appropriate to a specific purpose, audience, and context.
f. Anticipates and addresses readers' concerns and counter-arguments.
g. Provides a sense of closure to the writing.

ELA7W3	**The student uses research and technology to support writing.**
	The student
	a. Identifies topics, asks and evaluates questions, and develops ideas leading to inquiry, investigation, and research.
	b. Gives credit for both quoted and paraphrased information in a bibliography by using a consistent and sanctioned format and methodology for citations.
	c. Includes researched information in different types of products (e.g., compositions, multimedia presentations, graphic organizers, projects, etc.).
	d. Documents sources.
	e. Uses electronic media to locate relevant information.
ELA7W4	**The student consistently uses the writing process to develop, revise, and evaluate writing.**
	The student
	a. Plans and drafts independently and resourcefully.
	b. Uses strategies of note taking, outlining, and summarizing to impose structure on composition drafts.
	c. Revises manuscripts to improve the organization and consistency of ideas within and between paragraphs.
	d. Edits writing to improve word choice after checking the precision of the vocabulary.

Conventions

ELA7C1	**The student demonstrates understanding and control of the rules of the English language, realizing that usage involves the appropriate application of conventions and grammar in both written and spoken formats.**
	The student
	a. Identifies and writes simple, compound, complex, and compound-complex sentences correctly, punctuating properly, avoiding fragments and run-ons, adding or deleting modifiers, combining or revising sentences.
	b. Identifies and writes correctly punctuated adjective and adverb clauses.
	c. Uses standard subject-verb and pronoun-antecedent agreement.
	d. Identifies and uses verb tenses consistently (simple and perfect).
	e. Demonstrates correct usage of comparative and superlative forms of adjectives and adverbs.
	f. Demonstrates appropriate comma and semicolon usage (compound, complex, and compound-complex sentences, and split dialogue).
	g. Distinguishes differences in meaning and spelling of commonly confused homonyms.
	h. Produces final drafts/presentations that demonstrate accurate spelling and the correct use of punctuation and capitalization.

Listening/Speaking/Viewing

ELA7LSV1 **The student participates in student-to-teacher, student-to-student, and group verbal interactions.**

The student

a. Initiates new topics in addition to responding to adult-initiated topics.

b. Asks relevant questions.

c. Responds to questions with appropriate information.

d. Confirms understanding by paraphrasing the adult's directions or suggestions.

e. Displays appropriate turn-taking behaviors.

f. Actively solicits another person's comments or opinions.

g. Offers own opinion forcefully without domineering.

h. Responds appropriately to comments and questions.

i. Volunteers contributions and responds when directly solicited by teacher or discussion leader.

j. Gives reasons in support of opinions expressed.

k. Clarifies, illustrates, or expands on a response when asked to do so.

l. Employs a group decision-making technique such as brainstorming or a problem-solving sequence (e.g., recognizes problem, defines problem, identifies possible solutions, selects optimal solution, implements solution, evaluates solution).

m. Develops an outline that highlights the important issues discussed.

ELA7LSV2 **The student listens to and views various forms of text and media in order to gather and share information, persuade others, and express and understand ideas. The student will select and critically analyze messages using rubrics as assessment tools.**

When responding to visual and oral texts and media (e.g., television, radio, film productions, and electronic media), the student:

a. Analyzes the effect on the viewer of image, text, and sound in electronic journalism.

b. Identifies the techniques used to achieve the effects studied in each instance.

When delivering and responding to presentations, the student:

a. Gives oral presentations or dramatic interpretations for various purposes.

b. Organizes information to achieve particular purposes and to appeal to the background and interests of the audience.

c. Shows appropriate changes in delivery (e.g., gestures, vocabulary, pace, visuals).

d. Uses language for dramatic effect.

e. Uses rubrics as assessment tools.

f. Responds to oral communications with questions, challenges, or affirmations.

g. Uses multimedia in presentations.

What Are the Georgia CRCT Grade 7 Tests?

The Georgia Criterion-Referenced Competency Tests (CRCT) measure how well students have met the Georgia Performance Standards (GPS) in five content areas: Reading, English/Language Arts, Mathematics, Science, and Social Studies. The skills and strategies you will learn in *Glencoe Literature* can help you get ready for the Georgia CRCT Reading and English/Language Arts Tests.

How Can I Prepare for The Tests?

Pages GA12–GA21 of this textbook include a section called Countdown to the CRCT Reading and English/Language Arts Tests. The Reading and English/Language Arts Tests contain passages and questions that are similar to the multiple-choice questions on the Grade 7 CRCT Reading and English/Language Arts Tests.

How Does *Glencoe Literature* Help Me Prepare for The Tests?

Your textbook contains several opportunities to help you prepare for the tests every day. Take advantage of these so you don't need to cram before the test.

- The **Countdown to CRCT** section gives you practice with the kinds of questions you will find on the CRCT Reading and English/Language Arts Tests.

- The **After You Read** pages following many of the reading selections contain multiple-choice questions that allow you to practice evaluating, interpreting, and using other critical thinking skills and reading strategies. These pages also include vocabulary and grammar features.

- The **Assessment** at the end of every unit helps you prepare for the multiple-choice format of the tests.

Test-Taking Tips

Before a game, professional athletes get ready by developing a positive attitude. They clear their minds, pump-up their confidence, and picture themselves performing well. You can apply similar strategies to prepare for the CRCT tests. Here are some tips to help you succeed:

- Go to bed early the night before the test. Eat a good breakfast in the morning.

- Read all test directions carefully. Listen carefully if test directions are read aloud. Ask questions about directions that you don't understand.

- Relax. Most people get nervous when taking a test. It's natural. Just do your best.

- Compare the numbers for test items with the numbers on your answer sheet. Be sure your answers are in the right place.

Multiple-Choice Items

A multiple-choice item on the CRCT Reading and English/Language Arts Tests usually includes an incomplete sentence or a question with four responses. You then choose the response that best completes the sentence or answers the question. Use this checklist to help you answer multiple-choice items.

☑ Read each question carefully and think of your own answer before you choose one of the printed answer choices.

☑ Read all of the answer choices for a question before you mark an answer. You might find a better choice if you keep reading.

☑ Eliminate any responses that are clearly wrong. Then focus your attention on the responses that may be correct.

☑ Answer questions you are sure about first. If you do not know the answer, skip it and go back to that question later.

Test Practice Workbook

A *Georgia State Assessment and Practice Workbook* is available to help you prepare for the grade 7 CRCT tests. The workbook explains how the Reading and English/Language Arts Tests are scored, provides test-taking strategies, and includes a practice test with passages and questions similar to those on the test.

Accidents Happen

Esther decided that she wanted to do something special on her mother's birthday. As soon as she got home from school, she set to dusting the apartment. "Mother will surely be surprised when she returns home from work," Esther thought. She lifted her mother's favorite vase and carried it to the kitchen table to dust it, as she had done many times before. But this time, she tripped over one of Blink's toys, and the vase slipped from her hands and shattered on the tile floor.

Esther stared at the pieces of her mother's favorite vase that lay scattered across the kitchen floor. It had all happened so innocently.

As soon as her mother arrived home, Esther burst into tears and confessed what had happened. She stood in the kitchen with tears streaming down her cheeks, waiting for her punishment. But Esther's mother smiled and gave her daughter an <u>affectionate</u>, warm hug.

ELA7R2.d

1. What is a synonym for the word *affectionate* as used in this passage?

   A. strong

   B. phony

   C. flat

   D. loving

ELA7R1.b

2. Which of the following words BEST describes Esther?

   A. clumsy

   B. thoughtful

   C. impatient

   D. studious

ELA7R1.f

3. Why does Esther's mother hug her at the end of the story?

   A. She is happy that Esther broke the vase.

   B. She is so angry that she does not know what else to do.

   C. She appreciates Esther's honesty and forgives her.

   D. She is very upset with Esther.

ELA7R1.a

4. What is the purpose of this passage?

   A. to entertain readers by telling a story

   B. to persuade readers to help with household chores

   C. to inform readers about the dangers of being careless

   D. to explain the proper way to clean an apartment

ELA7W2.f

1. Francis wants to use a metaphor to describe his friend's smile. Which of the following sentences contains a metaphor?

   A. Her smile showed her kindness.

   B. Her smile warmed her friends like summer day.

   C. Her smile was like no other.

   D. Her smile was a magnet

ELA7C1.e

2. What change should be made to the underlined words in the sentence below?

   Ricardo is tall, but Eva is <u>most tall</u>.

   A. Change *most tall* to *taller*.

   B. Change *most tall* to *more tall*.

   C. Change *most tall* to *tallest*.

   D. Change *most tall* to *most tallest*.

ELA7C1.f

3. How should the punctuation be corrected in the sentence below?

   The game was scheduled for Friday afternoon therefore, the team left class early.

   A. Add a comma after *scheduled*.

   B. Add a semicolon after *afternoon*.

   C. Remove the comma after *therefore*.

   D. Add a comma after *team*.

Use the paragraph below to answer question 4.

Ginger Rogers

[1]After appearing in her first high school play, Ginger Rogers knew she wanted a life on the stage. [2]Her mother was a newspaper reporter and wrote movie scripts. [3]From the age of 14 to 17, Rogers worked in vaudeville. [4]She loved stage work so much that she tried out for a Broadway play.

ELA7W2.e

4. Which sentence should be removed from the paragraph above?

   A. sentence 1

   B. sentence 2

   C. sentence 3

   D. sentence 4

ELA7C1.a

5. What is the structure of the sentence below?

   I like to dance, but I don't dance often, although I have plans to take dance lessons in the fall.

   A. simple

   B. compound

   C. complex

   D. compound-complex

The Crow and the Pitcher

A crow perishing with thirst saw a pitcher and, hoping to find water, flew to it with delight. When he reached it, he discovered to his grief that the pitcher contained only a little water at the bottom. Because the pitcher was tall and very narrow, the crow could not possibly get the water. He tried everything he could think of, but all his efforts were <u>in vain</u>. At last he collected as many stones as he could carry and dropped them one by one with his beak into the pitcher. <u>Kerplunk</u>! Finally, he brought the water within his reach, thus saving his life.

ELA7R1.a

1. What of the following sentences BEST states the theme of this passage?

   A. Crows, like people, need water.

   B. Great need can lead to creative thinking.

   C. A deep pitcher is not a good place to store water.

   D. Some things are not worth the trouble.

ELA7R2.a

2. In this passage, the phrase *in vain* means that the crow's efforts were

   A. useless.

   B. done with pride.

   C. too late.

   D. not right.

ELA7RC1.f

3. Which word BEST describes the crow's character?

   A. considerate

   B. unfriendly

   C. studious

   D. persistent

ELA7R1.g/i

4. In this passage, the word *kerplunk* is an example of

   A. onomatopoeia.

   B. alliteration.

   C. rhyme.

   D. hyperbole.

ELA7W2.g

1. Which sentence BEST concludes the paragraph?

> Each year in October there is an exciting balloon festival in Albuquerque, New Mexico. Brightly colored gas and hot air balloons fill the sky. These balloons carry passengers in the gondola, or basket.

  A. These magnificent balloons are truly a sight to see!

  B. The balloons cost a lot of money.

  C. Other cities host similar festivals.

  D. Where is Albuquerque, New Mexico?

ELA7C1.g

2. What is the meaning of the underlined word in the sentence below?

> My teacher wanted to be certain that the rules were <u>fair</u> to everyone.

  A. light in color

  B. just

  C. market

  D. beautiful

ELA7C1.h

3. Which of the following sentences contains a punctuation error?

  A. Traveling the Mediterranean, the Minoans became seafarers.

  B. Ships, you might imagine, were invented thousands of years ago.

  C. The Egyptians, the inventors of sails, built wooden barges.

  D. The first packet ship a small one, did not travel very fast.

ELA7W2.f

4. Which of the following sentences uses a metaphor?

  A. Those words were music to my ear.

  B. Her anger was like an approaching storm.

  C. I could eat a horse.

  D. My little sister is as bright as the sun.

Majestic Mountains!

As I began my climb up the sloping mountain, the cold bit sharply through my clothing. However, the cold was somehow necessary to appreciate the view of the Arctic mountains. I could taste the crisp air as it flowed into my mouth and nostrils. Everything seemed to stand still as I climbed. I was struck by the <u>solitude</u>. Eventually I stopped moving and took in the frozen, tranquil scene. To the right, puffy clouds drifted over the immense mountains, which were so much greater than I. To the left was a view that stretched to the end of the world. I wished that I could get a picture of all the untouched arctic beauty, but I didn't have a camera. The only pictures I took that day were the ones that I keep in my head.

ELA7R1.h

1. Which of the following sentences BEST describes how the author feels about the scene that is described in the passage?

   A. The author thinks it is too cold to be on the mountain.

   B. The author is filled with a feeling of awe.

   C. The author thinks that it is a dangerous risk to take.

   D. The author is excited to be hiking for the first time.

ELA7R2.b

2. What is the meaning of *solitude* as used in this passage?

   A. comforting

   B. rocky

   C. isolation

   D. crowded

ELA7R1.c

3. Which of the following would LEAST likely be found in the setting of this passage?

   A. snow-capped mountain peaks

   B. puffy clouds

   C. an Arctic fox

   D. a highway

ELA7R1.h

4. Which of the following BEST describes the tone of the passage?

   A. joyful

   B. fearful

   C. serious

   D. pessimistic

ELA7C1.c

1. Which sentence below contains a pronoun or pronouns that agree with the antecedent?

   A. Every student should finish their project by next week.

   B. If a person cannot attend the meeting, you must notify the club secretary.

   C. When someone notices a problem, he or she should say something.

   D. The winner should present their ticket and claim their prize.

ELA7C1.b

2. Which of the following sentences is punctuated correctly?

   A. My new blue dress which I will wear to the dance is in my closet.

   B. Joe went to the game early, because he wanted to get a good seat.

   C. When everyone arrived the host made the announcement.

   D. John Williams, who wrote the music for the movie, was presented with an award.

Use the outline below to answer question 3.

Taking Care of the Earth

  I. Taking Care of the Air
   A. Industry
   B. Outdoor Burning
   C. Contaminants in the Air

  II. _____
   A. Water Use at Home
   B. Keeping Waterways Clean
   C. Contaminants in Water

ELA7W4.b

3. Which of the following heads should be used for topic II?

   A. Taking Care of the Ocean

   B. Taking Care of Pollution

   C. Taking Care of the Water

   D. Taking Care of the Earth

ELA7W2.d

4. Which of the following sentences contains vivid verbs?

   A. Joann was ready for the big event.

   B. Joann had a great coach.

   C. Joann sprinted for fifty yards.

   D. Joann got a first-place award.

BUS SCHEDULE Route 3
Eastbound Route

Hamilton E. Holmes Station	West Lake Station	Martin Luther King & Whitehouse	Alabama & Broad
7:25 A.M.	7:34 A.M.	7:42 A.M.	7:55 A.M.
8:25 A.M.	8:34 A.M.	8:42 A.M.	8:55 A.M.
8:55 A.M.	9:04 A.M.	9:13 A.M.	9:27 A.M.
9:25 A.M.	9:35 A.M.	9:44 A.M.	9:58 A.M.
9:55 A.M.	10:05 A.M.	10:14 A.M.	10:58 A.M.

Points of Interest
Apex Museum (Martin Luther King & Whitehouse)

Docents provide information about the contributions African Americans have made in the United States and around the world.

ELA7RC2.f

1. Based on the schedule, what time should you arrive at Alabama & Broad if you board the bus at the Hamilton E. Holmes Station at 9:25 A.M.?

   A. 9:35 A.M.

   B. 9:44 A.M.

   C. 9:58 A.M.

   D. 9:27 A.M.

ELA7RC2.f

2. Based on the schedule, how long do you have to wait for the next bus if you miss the 8:34 A.M. bus at West Lake Station?

   A. 9 minutes

   B. 30 minutes

   C. 40 minutes

   D. 60 minutes

ELA7RC3.a

3. Based on the schedule, which is the closest in meaning to the word *docents*?

   A. doctors

   B. museum guides

   C. college professors

   D. cashiers

ELA7C1.e

1. Which sentence is written correctly?

   A. Carlos is the tallest of the three boys.

   B. Carlos is the taller of the three boys.

   C. Carlos is the most tall of the three boys.

   D. Carlos is the most tallest of the three boys.

ELA7W2.d

2. Which of the following BEST supports the main idea of the sentence below?

   > The Appalachian Trail runs more than twenty-one hundred miles in the eastern United States through the Appalachian Mountains.

   A. Oaks, firs, and pines grow on mountains.

   B. My brother and I will be going on our first camping trip next year.

   C. Fall is a beautiful time of year.

   D. The trail passes through fourteen states.

ELA7C1.h

3. In the sentence below, what change should be made to correct the capitalization error?

   > "Nobody tell Frank about the party on Thanksgiving Day," Maria said. "it's a surprise."

   A. Use a capital *P* in *party*.

   B. Use a small letter *d* in *day*.

   C. Use a capital *I* in *it's*.

   D. Use a capital *S* in *surprise*.

ELA7C1.f

4. Which sentence below is written correctly?

   > Friday was my favorite day of the week, we had no homework.

   A. Friday was my favorite day of the week; we had no homework.

   B. Friday was my favorite day of the week we had no homework

   C. Friday was my favorite day of the week, we had no homework.

   D. Friday was my favorite day of the week "we had no homework."

Georgia Authors

Many well-known American writers were born in Georgia or lived there. Georgia writers have written about the state's landscapes. They have written about major events in its history, from frontier life to the civil rights movement. Georgia writers have also written about the experience of growing up. As you read, take notes on how Georgia's literature shows the experiences of young people and a sense of time and place.

Looking Ahead

The following selections appear in your textbook. The writers of these selections are either from Georgia or have important ties to the state.

Historical Overview

- The earliest literature in what is now the state of Georgia was the spoken myths and folktales of the Native Americans of the Southeast.
- The first writings were the letters and journals of explorers and settlers.
- In the 1800s, Georgia literature included humorous stories and lyric poetry.
- Georgia authors wrote about the Civil War and its effects.
- In the twentieth century, Georgia authors often wrote about social problems such as poverty and racism.
- Georgia authors today come from many different ethnic groups.

LITERARY GEORGIA

Lake Sidney Lanier

Capitol Building

Atlanta

Georgia Douglas Johnson born (c.1877)
W.E.B. Du Bois begins teaching (1897)
Margaret Mitchell born (1900)
Martin Luther King Jr. born (1929)
Alfred Uhry born (1936)
Gone with the Wind premieres (1939)
Pat Conroy born (1945)
Toni Cade Bambara teaches (1978)

Etowah Mounds

Lake Sidney Lanier

Chattahoochee R.

Athens
Judith Ortiz Cofer begins teaching (1984)

■ *Stone Mountain*

★ **ATLANTA**

Augusta
Augustus Baldwin Longstreet born (1790)
Frank Yerby born (1916)

Moreland
Erskine Caldwell born (1903)

Eatonton
Joel Chandler Harris born (1845)
Alice Walker born (1944)

Sparta
Jean Toomer researches *Cane* (1921)

Macon
Sidney Lanier born (1842)

Columbus
Carson McCullers born (1917)

Savannah
Flannery O'Connor born (1925)

Chattahoochee R.

Plains
Jimmy Carter born (1924)

Albany
Ray Charles born (1930)

Marshes of Glynn

Okefenokee swamp

Thomasville
Bailey White born (1950)

TRY IT

Use the information on the map to make a timeline of Georgia authors. What is the earliest event? What is the most recent? What ten-year period has the most events?

In Their Own Words

Augustus Baldwin Longstreet | *Georgia Scenes* (1835)

Longstreet wrote humorous stories about frontier life. Here he describes Georgia girls at a dance.

"Let the reader [imagine] a lady beginning a strut at her own place, and ending it (precisely as does the turkey-cock) three feet nearer the gentleman opposite her; then giving three sparrow-hawk bobs, and then waddling back to her place like a duck; and he will have a pretty correct idea of their dancing."

Eliza Frances Andrews
The War-Time Journal of a Georgia Girl (1865)

In late 1864, General Sherman's Union troops cut a path of destruction across Georgia. Eliza Andrews fled her family home.

"Jan. 1, Wednesday.—While I was ill, home was the one thought that haunted my brain, and if I ever do get back, I hope I will have sense enough to stay there. I don't think I ever suffered so much in all my life, and dread of the Yankees raised my fever to such a pitch that I got no rest by night or day. I used to feel very brave about Yankees, but since I have passed over Sherman's track and seen what devastation they make, I am so afraid of them that I believe I should drop down dead if one of the wretches should come into my presence."

Timeline

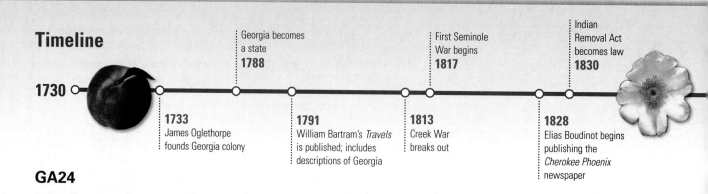

1730

1733
James Oglethorpe founds Georgia colony

Georgia becomes a state
1788

1791
William Bartram's *Travels* is published; includes descriptions of Georgia

1813
Creek War breaks out

First Seminole War begins
1817

1828
Elias Boudinot begins publishing the *Cherokee Phoenix* newspaper

Indian Removal Act becomes law
1830

Sidney Lanier | "The Raven Days" (1868)

Lanier mourns the destruction caused by the Civil War.

Our hearths are gone out, and our hearts are broken,

And but the ghosts of homes to us remain,

And ghostly eyes and hollow sighs give token

From friend to friend of an unspoken pain.

W. E. B. Du Bois | *The Souls of Black Folk* (1903)

Du Bois produced his landmark collection of essays while teaching at Atlanta University

"To be a poor man is hard, but to be a poor race in a land of dollars is the very bottom of hardships."

Georgia Douglas Johnson
"Youth" (1918)

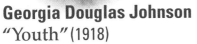

Johnson compares the passing of youth to the movement of a sundial's shadow.

The dew is on the grasses, dear,

The blush is on the rose,

And swift across our dial-youth,

A shifting shadow goes.

The primrose moments, lush with bliss,

Exhale and fade away,

Life may renew the Autumn time,

But nevermore the May!

Respond and Think Critically

1. Which of the passages on pages GA24–25 affects you the most strongly? Why?

2. What do Andrews's journal and Lanier's poem tell you about the effect of the Civil War on Georgia?

3. A sundial is an old time-keeping device that uses the shadow cast by a pointer on a dial to show the hours of the day. Why do you think Johnson compares youth to a sundial?

1861
Civil War begins; Georgia secedes from the Union

1868
Atlanta becomes state capital

1908
Eliza Frances Andrews's *The War-Time Journal of a Georgia Girl* is published

1917
United States enters World War I

1835
Augustus Baldwin Longstreet's *Georgia Scenes* is published

1864
Union forces capture Atlanta; March to the Sea follows

1868
Sidney Lanier writes "The Raven Days"

1903
W.E.B Du Bois's *The Souls of Black Folk* is published

1923
Jean Toomer's *Cane* is published

1930

Born in 1938, Terry Kay grew up on a farm in Hart County in northeastern Georgia. He attended high school in Royston. After college, he worked on newspapers and in advertising. His first novel, *The Year the Lights Came On,* was published in 1976. It describes the effect of bringing electric power to rural Georgia after World War II. The novel was based on Kay's youth in Royston. In 2006, Kay was inducted into the Georgia Writers Hall of Fame.

Terry Kay | *The Year the Lights Came On* (1976)

"It had stopped raining on Monday, but it was a gray morning and there was a fine, chilling mist, part fog. Wesley and I went to the corn crib after breakfast and began to shuck corn, stacking the ears in neat, yellow pyramids. It was hateful work, and frightening. My father always kept a king snake in the corn crib. King snakes love to feast on rats, but king snakes are not poisonous. It didn't matter. We knew that somewhere, warm and cozy under the heat of corn shucks, a king snake was curled, waiting. Garry absolutely refused to go near the corn crib, and, once, my sister Frances had accidentally sat on a king snake and she gave a horrible description of snake fangs sinking into flesh.

Corn shucking was a wet-day ceremony, the always-something-else job. But there was one consolation, one promise: if we worked long enough to achieve my father's predetermined goal of the number of bushels needed, we would be permitted to fish the swollen streams that fed into Beaverjam Creek. When it rained, catfish rallied by schools at the mouth of those streams, gobbling away at the fresh supply of land food washed into the inlets."

Timeline

Margaret Mitchell's *Gone with the Wind* is published; wins Pulitzer Prize
1936

Carson McCullers's first novel is published
1940

Flannery O'Connor's first collection of short stories is published
1955

Martin Luther King Jr. receives the Nobel Peace Prize
1964

1930

1939
Film of *Gone with the Wind* premieres in Atlanta

1941
United States enters World War II

1963
Martin Luther King Jr. delivers "I Have a Dream" speech

Jimmy Carter | *An Hour Before Daylight* (2001)

Former president Carter pictures how his hometown of Plains looked on a busy Saturday during his childhood in the 1920s and 1930s.

"Despite its small size, Plains was a major trade center for its own citizens and for all the farm families in the western half of Sumter County. Hundreds of customers would crowd into the stores, and many more would use this trading day to assemble on the only sidewalk, to meet with their friends or just to relish the electric atmosphere."

Cynthia Kadohata | *Kira-Kira* (2004)

Kadohata and her family moved from Iowa to Georgia in search of work. She based her Newbery Medal–winning novel on this experience.

"We rode our bicycles—Sam rode with me on mine. It was a lovely late-summer day. I love the days at the end of summer. Each day before the regular school year started became more and more precious.

The wind blew hard. Decaying magnolia petals drifted on the streets as we road. We headed south toward Mr. Lyndon's mansion—white with white pillars. We liked to see his house. My father always said it was his dream house. It was even in a book at the library, about Georgia mansions from the pre–Civil War days."

TRY IT

Write a short list of questions that you would like to ask Terry Kay, Jimmy Carter, or Cynthia Kadohata about the experience that he or she describes in one of these passages.

Jimmy Carter is elected U.S. president
1976

Alice Walker wins Pulitzer Prize for fiction
1983

Film of *Driving Miss Daisy* is released; wins Academy Award as Best Picture
1989

Jimmy Carter receives the Nobel Peace Prize
2002

2010

1979
Ray Charles performs "Georgia on My Mind" for legislature; later adopted as state song

1987
Alfred Uhry's play *Driving Miss Daisy* is produced; wins Pulitzer Prize

2000
Georgia Writers Hall of Fame opens

2004
Cynthia Kadohata's *Kira-Kira* is published; wins Newbery Medal

Literature on Film:
Driving Miss Daisy

The two main characters in Alfred Uhry's *Driving Miss Daisy* are an elderly woman and an African American man hired to drive her car. The action of the play covers 25 years, from 1948 to 1973. Over that period, understanding, respect, and friendship slowly grow between Daisy Werthan and her driver Hoke Colburn.

Meet Alfred Uhry

Alfred Uhry was born in Atlanta in 1936. His family lived in the well-to-do area of Druid Hills. After college, he taught school while trying—and at first failing—to write a successful play. After many years of work in the theater, Uhry scored his biggest hit in 1987 with *Driving Miss Daisy.* This play is the first of Uhry's "Atlanta Trilogy." The two other plays focus on life in Georgia in the early twentieth century.

The Civil Rights Movement: *Before and After*

During the period covered by *Driving Miss Daisy,* the civil rights movement changed life in the South. When the play opens, African Americans there still faced unjust laws that denied them good schools. Laws limited how African Americans could use trains and buses and how they could use hotels, theaters, and restaurants. Laws kept black people from voting. Miss Daisy's driver Hoke has himself been a victim of a poor education. In the following passage, she asks him to find a name on a tombstone, and he is forced to admit that he can't read. (She later helps him learn.)

DAISY. I told you it's over on the other side of the weeping cherry. It says Bauer on the headstone.

HOKE. How'd that look?

DAISY. What are you talking about?

HOKE. (Deeply embarrassed.) I'm talkin' bout I cain' read.

DAISY. What?

HOKE. I cain' read.

DAISY. That's ridiculous. Anybody can read.

HOKE. Nome. Not me.

In the mid-1950s, under the leadership of Martin Luther King Jr., the civil rights movement arose. Through his powerful speeches and writing, Dr. King inspired a campaign of peaceful protest. The goal was to end the laws that had limited opportunities for African Americans and to gain them better schools and voting rights. By the time *Driving Miss Daisy* ends in 1973, huge strides were made in reaching these goals.

Hoke (Morgan Freeman) helps Daisy (Jessica Tandy) tend a grave.

Stage and Film Versions

Uhry based his play on the relationship between his strong-willed grandmother and her dignified African American driver. The play is set in Druid Hills, the area in which Uhry grew up. *Driving Miss Daisy* opened off-Broadway in New York City in April 1987, and soon became a hit. At first the play was only going to run for five weeks in a small theater. But the play soon moved to a larger theater where it ran for three years. The original cast included Atlanta native Dana Ivey as Daisy Werthan and Morgan Freeman as her driver Hoke Colburn. Ivey won an Obie Award as Best Actress. Uhry won the 1988 Pulitzer Prize for Drama.

A movie version of *Driving Miss Daisy* was released in 1989. Uhry wrote the screenplay— though he had never written for the movies before. Morgan Freeman repeated his role as Hoke. Eighty-year-old actress Jessica Tandy played Daisy. *Driving Miss Daisy* was shot in Druid Hills and other areas of Atlanta. Daisy's house in the movie was one in which Uhry had actually played as a child. The film was a hit, winning the Academy Award for Best Picture. Both Jessica Tandy and Alfred Uhry also won Oscars.

Respond and Think Critically

1. Why do you think it was so difficult for Hoke to admit that he couldn't read?

2. How was location shooting used to make the film version accurate?

3. What do you think the image of Daisy in this scene from the film shows about her character?

Book Overview

UNIT ONE

Whom Can You Count On? 1

Reading Skills and Strategies: Identify Sequence, Analyze Plot, Make Inferences About Characters, Analyze Setting, Interpret Plot Events

Literary Elements: Narrator and Point of View, Plot, Setting, Character, Characterization, Description, Theme

Writing Product: Narrative

Vocabulary: Word Usage, Context Clues, Synonyms and Antonyms

Grammar: Action and Linking Verbs, Main and Helping Verbs, Verb Tenses

UNIT TWO

Why Do You Read? 171

Reading Skills and Strategies: Monitor Comprehension, Recognize Author's Purpose, Analyze Evidence, Analyze Text Structure, Distinguish Fact and Opinion

Literary Elements: Author's Purpose, Text Structure, Text Features

Writing Product: Functional Document

Vocabulary: Context Clues, Word Usage, Synonyms and Antonyms

Grammar: Present Perfect Tense, Past Perfect Tense, Future Tense, Irregular Verbs, Infinitives, Participles and Participial Phrases

UNIT THREE

What Makes Life Good? 349

Reading Skills and Strategies: Interpret Meaning, Analyze Style, Interpret Imagery

Literary Elements: Line and Stanza, Imagery, Style, Rhyme, Rhythm and Meter

Writing Product: Response to Literature

Vocabulary: Context Clues, Word Usage, Synonyms and Antonyms

Grammar: Nouns, Pronouns and Antecedents, Indefinite Pronouns, Subject Pronouns and Object Pronouns, Comparative and Superlative Adjectives

UNIT ONE

WHOM Can You Count On?

BQ Explore the **BIG** Question

Part 1 *Friends and Family*

Part 2 Me, Myself, and I

Part 3 Extraordinary Individuals

UNIT TWO

WHY Do You Read?

BQ Explore the **BIG** Question

Part 1 *For Fun*

Part 2 *For Information*

Part 3   *For Understanding*

UNIT THREE

WHAT Makes Life Good?

BQ Explore the **BIG** Question

Part 3 · *Love and Friendship*

Part 2 *Persuasive Ideas*

> ### Comparing Literature

Writing Workshop

Speaking, Listening, and Viewing Workshop

Unit Challenge

UNIT FIVE

HOW Can You Become Who You Want to Be?

BQ Explore the **BIG** Question

Part 1   *Positive Actions*

Part 2   *Courage and Confidence*

Part **3** *People Who Lend a Hand*

UNIT SIX

WHY Share Stories?

BQ Explore the **BIG** Question

Part 1 · *Entertainment*

Part 2 · *Messages and Lessons*

Selections by Genre

Fiction

Poetry

Drama

Folktales, Fables, and Myths

Graphic Story

Song Lyrics

Speech

Nonfiction

Features

Perspectives

Award-winning nonfiction book excerpts and primary source documents

TIME

High-interest, informative magazine articles

Genre Focus

Unit Challenge

Independent Reading

Assessment

Skills Workshops

How to Use *Glencoe Literature*

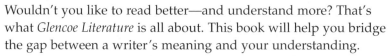

Consultant's Note

People read for enjoyment, to help themselves think, to solve problems, and to get work done. Their reading is often organized around "inquiry" questions. These questions help them explore how what they learn can help make a difference in the real world.

—Jeffrey Wilhelm

Wouldn't you like to read better—and understand more? That's what *Glencoe Literature* is all about. This book will help you bridge the gap between a writer's meaning and your understanding.

The next few pages will show you some of the ways *Glencoe Literature* can help you read, think, and write better.

What's in it for you?

Every unit in *Glencoe Literature* is built around a **Big Question,** a question that you will want to think about, talk about, maybe even argue about, and finally answer. The unit's reading selections will help you come up with your answers.

Organization

Units contain:

- A **Unit Opener** that introduces and helps you explore the unit's Big Question. A short reading selection uses the themes of the unit's **Parts** to guide you through ways of approaching the Big Question.

- **Literature selections** such as short stories, poems, plays, and biographies.

- **Informational texts** such as nonfiction; newspaper, online, and magazine articles; textbook lessons; and interviews.

- A **Genre Focus** that guides you through the features of a main genre from the unit.

- **Functional documents** such as signs, schedules, letters, and instructions.

- A **Comparing Literature** feature that gives you a chance to compare and contrast pieces of writing.

- A **Writing Workshop** to help you express your ideas about the Big Question through a specific form of writing.

- A **Speaking, Listening, and Viewing Workshop** to help you make oral presentations and become a better listener.

- A **Unit Challenge** where you'll answer the Big Question.

Reading and Thinking

As an active reader, you'll use *Glencoe Literature* to develop your reading and thinking skills.

BEFORE YOU READ sets the stage for the selection and previews the skills and strategies that will guide your reading.

MEET THE AUTHOR introduces you to the real-life story of the writer whose work you will read and write about. · · · · · · · · · · · · · · · · ·

The **LITERARY ELEMENT** and the **READING SKILL** or **STRATEGY** give you the basic tools you will use to read and analyze the selection. · · · · · · · · · · · ·

As you read the **LITERATURE SELECTIONS**, you will see that parts of the text are highlighted in different colors. On the side of the page are color-coded questions that help you think about and understand the selection. · · · · · · · · · · · · · · ·

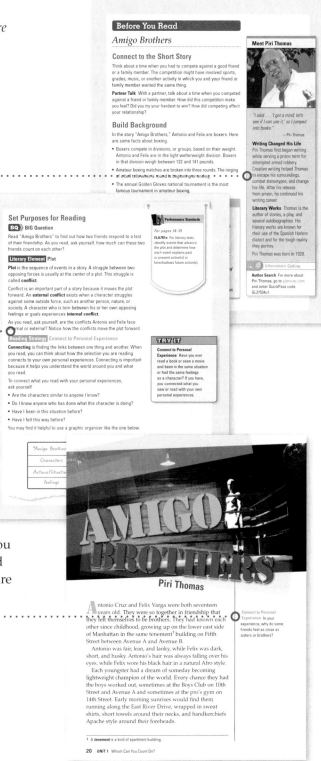

VOCABULARY A new vocabulary word is in **bold** type when it first appears in the reading selection.

VOCABULARY The word and its pronunciation, part of speech, and definition appear at the bottom of the same page.

FOOTNOTES Selection footnotes explain words or phrases that you may not know to help you understand the story.

VISUAL VOCABULARY Some vocabulary words are explained with the help of a picture.

BIG QUESTION These side notes help keep you focused on the unit's Big Question as you read.

Sample page 27:

tops, covered with mats, serving as resting tables. Antonio thought he caught a glimpse of Felix waving to him from a room at the far end of the corridor. He waved back just in case it had been him.

The fighters changed from their street clothes into fighting gear. Antonio wore white trunks, black socks, and black shoes. Felix wore sky blue trunks, red socks, and white boxing shoes. Each had dressing gowns to match their fighting trunks with their names neatly stitched on the back.

The loudspeakers blared into the open windows of the school. There were speeches by dignitaries, community leaders, and great boxers of yesteryear. Some were well prepared; some **improvised** on the spot. They all carried the same message of great pleasure and honor at being part of such a historic event. This great day was in the tradition of champions emerging from the streets of the lower east side.

Interwoven with the speeches were the sounds of the other boxing events. After the sixth bout, Felix was much relieved when his trainer Charlie said, "Time change. Quick knock-out. This is it. We're on."

Waiting time was over. Felix was escorted from the classroom by a dozen fans in white T-shirts with the word FELIX across their fronts.

Antonio was escorted down a different stairwell and guided through a roped-off path.

As the two climbed into the ring, the crowd exploded with a roar. Antonio and Felix both bowed gracefully and then raised their arms in acknowledgment.

Antonio tried to be cool, but even as the roar was in its first birth, he turned slowly to meet Felix's eyes looking directly into his. Felix nodded his head and Antonio responded. And both as one, just as quickly, turned away to face his own corner.

Bong—bong—bong. The roar turned to stillness. "Ladies and Gentlemen, *Señores y Señoras.*"[16]

Connect to Personal Experience If you had to face a good friend in a competition, would you look him or her in the eyes or look away? Why?

16 *Señores y señoras* (sen yōr´ ās ē sen yōr´ əs) is Spanish for "ladies and gentlemen."

Vocabulary
improvised (im´ prə vīzd´) v. invented, composed, or did without preparation

Amigo Brothers **27**

Sample page 21:

While some youngsters were into street negatives, Antonio and Felix slept, ate, rapped, and dreamt positive. Between them, they had a collection of *Fight* magazines second to none, plus a scrapbook filled with torn tickets to every boxing match they had ever attended, and some clippings of their own. If asked a question about any given fighter, they would immediately zip out from their memory banks divisions, weights, records of fights, knock-outs, technical knock-outs, and draws or losses.[2]

Each had fought many bouts representing their community and had won two gold-plated medals plus a silver and bronze medallion. The difference was in their style. Antonio's lean form and long reach made him the better boxer, while Felix's short and muscular frame made him the better slugger. Whenever they had met in the **ring** for sparring sessions,[3] it had always been hot and heavy.

Now, after a series of elimination bouts,[4] they had been informed that they were to meet each other in the division finals that were scheduled for the seventh of August, two weeks away—the winner to represent the Boys Club in the Golden Gloves Championship Tournament.

The two boys continued to run together along the East River Drive. But even when joking with each other, they both sensed a wall rising between them.

One morning less than a week before their bout, they met as usual for their daily work-out. They fooled around with a few jabs at the air, slapped skin, and then took off, running lightly along the dirty East River's edge.

Antonio glanced at Felix who kept his eyes purposely straight ahead, pausing from time to time to do some fancy leg work while throwing one-twos followed by upper cuts to an imaginary jaw. Antonio then beat the air

Visual Vocabulary
A boxing **ring** is a square area, bounded by ropes, in which boxing matches take place.

Plot Given the details in the story so far, what kind of conflict do you think is developing?

2 A *knock-out* is when a boxer falls to the ground and does not stand up within a certain amount of time. In a *technical knock-out* (TKO), the boxer is judged to be physically unable to go on fighting. A TKO can be called by an official, the fighter, or the fighter's coach. A *draw* is when a fight is so close that neither boxer can be called the winner.
3 *Sparring sessions* are practice fights.
4 *Elimination bouts* are fights in a tournament; the winners advance to fight again, but the losers are eliminated from competition.

Amigo Brothers **21**

Sample page 23:

"If it's fair, *hermano,* I'm for it." Antonio admired the courage of a tug boat pulling a barge five times its welterweight[8] size.

"It's fair, Tony. When we get into the ring, it's gotta be like we never met. We gotta be like two heavy strangers that want the same thing and only one can have it. You understand, don'tcha?"

"*Sí,* I know." Tony smiled. "No pulling punches. We go all the way."

"Yeah, that's right. Listen, Tony. Don't you think it's a good idea if we don't see each other until the day of the fight? I'm going to stay with my Aunt Lucy in the Bronx. I can use Gleason's Gym for working out. My manager says he got some sparring partners with more or less your style."

Tony scratched his nose pensively.[9] "Yeah, it would be better for our heads." He held out his hand, palm upward. "Deal?"

"Deal." Felix lightly slapped open skin.

"Ready for some more running?" Tony asked lamely.

"Naw, bro. Let's cut it here. You go on. I kinda like to get things together in my head."

"You ain't worried, are you?" Tony asked.

"No way, man." Felix laughed out loud. "I got too much smarts for that. I just think it's cooler if we split right here. After the fight, we can get it together again like nothing ever happened."

The amigo brothers were not ashamed to hug each other tightly.

"Guess you're right. Watch yourself, Felix. I hear there's some pretty heavy dudes up in the Bronx. *Suavecito,*[10] okay?"

"Okay. You watch yourself too, *sabe?*"[11]

BQ BIG Question
Do you think that it will be possible for Antonio and Felix to remain friends after the fight?

8 *Hermano* (ār män´ ō) is Spanish for "brother." A professional *welterweight* boxer weighs between 141 and 147 pounds
9 *Pensively* means "in a thoughtful or sad way."
10 *Suavecito* (soo äv´ vä sē´ tō) is American Spanish slang for "take it easy" or "be cool."
11 *Sabe* (sä´ bā) means "You know?"

Amigo Brothers **23**

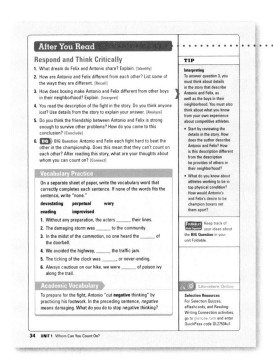

Wrap up the selection with **AFTER YOU READ**. Explore what you have learned through a wide range of reading, thinking, vocabulary, and writing activities.

Vocabulary

VOCABULARY WORDS may be new to you or seem difficult, but they are important words. Vocabulary words from each selection are introduced on the **BEFORE YOU READ** page. Each word is accompanied by its pronunciation, its part of speech, its definition, and the page number on which it first appears. The vocabulary word is also used in a sample sentence. The first appearance of each vocabulary word is highlighted in the literature selection.

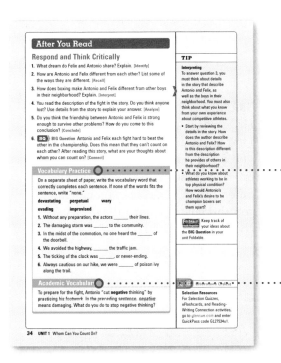

VOCABULARY PRACTICE On the **AFTER YOU READ** pages, you will be able to practice using the vocabulary words in an exercise. This exercise will show you how to use a vocabulary strategy to understand new or difficult words.

ACADEMIC VOCABULARY Many of the **AFTER YOU READ** pages also introduce you to examples of academic vocabulary. These are words that you come across in your schoolwork. You will be asked to use these words to answer questions.

Organizing Information

FOLDABLES For every unit, you'll be shown how to make a **Foldable** that will help you keep track of your thoughts about the Big Question. See page R8 for more about Foldables. ....

GRAPHIC ORGANIZERS In *Glencoe Literature*, you will use different kinds of graphic organizers to help you arrange information. These graphic organizers include, among others, Venn diagrams, compare and contrast charts, cluster diagrams, and chain-of-events charts.

Writing Workshops

Each unit in *Glencoe Literature* includes a Writing Workshop. The workshop walks you through the writing process as you work on an extended piece of writing related to the unit.

- You will use helpful strategies to meet writing goals.

- You will learn tips and polish your critical thinking skills as you analyze workshop models.

- You will focus on mastering specific aspects of writing, including organization, grammar, and vocabulary.

- You will use a writing plan to guide the structure and content of your writing.

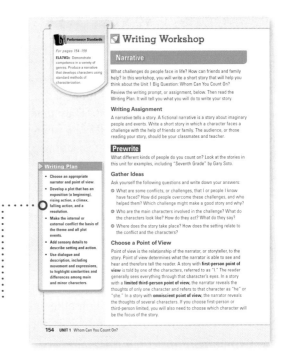

Assessment

Following each unit, you will be tested on the literature, reading, and vocabulary skills you learned. This test will give you the practice you need to succeed while providing an assessment of your understanding of the unit objectives.

Reading and Thinking with Foldables®

by Dinah Zike, M.Ed., Creator of Foldables®

Foldables® are three-dimensional interactive graphic organizers for taking notes and organizing your ideas. They're also fun! You will fold paper, cut tabs, write, and manipulate what you have made in order to organize information; review skills, concepts, and strategies; and assess your learning.

Using Dinah Zike's Foldables in Reading and Literature Classes

Use Foldables before, during, and after reading selections in *Glencoe Literature.*

- Before you read: Your unit Foldable will help you focus on your purpose for reading by reminding you about the Big Question.

- During reading: Your unit Foldable will help you stay focused and engaged. It will also help you track key ideas and your thoughts about each selection to help you answer the Big Question. Using the Foldable will also encourage you to use higher level thinking skills in approaching text.

- After reading: Your Foldable will help you review your thoughts from your reading and

analyze, interpret, and evaluate various aspects of the Big Question. Your Foldable notes will also help you with your unit challenge. These notes stimulate rich group discussions and inquiry as well.

FOLDABLES
Study Organizer

As you read, you'll make notes about the Big Question. Later, you'll use these notes to complete the Unit Challenge. See pages R8–R9 for help with making Foldable 1. This diagram shows how it should look. ○···

> Become an active reader. Track and reorganize information so that you can better understand the selection.

1. Make one page for each selection. At the end of the unit, you'll staple the pages together into one Foldable.

2. Label the front of the fold-over page with the selection ○···········
title.

> Practice reading and following step-by-step directions.

3. Open the fold-over page. On the right side, write the label My Purpose for Reading.

4. Open the Foldable all the way. At the top center, write the label The Big Question.

Selection
title
here

> Use the illustrations that make the directions easier to follow.

Be Computer Safe and Smart

Cyber Safety

As you explore the *Glencoe Literature* program, you will have many opportunities to go online. When you use the Internet at school or at home, you enter a kind of community—the cyber world. In this online world, you need to follow safety rules and to protect yourself. Here are some tips to keep in mind:

- ☑ Be a responsible cyber citizen. Use the Internet to share knowledge that makes people's lives better. Respect other people's feelings and do not break any laws.

- ☑ Beware of cyber bullying. People can be hurt and embarrassed by comments that have been made public. You should immediately tell your teacher or counselor if you feel threatened by another student's computer postings.

- ☑ Do not give out personal information, such as your address and telephone number, without your parents' or guardians' permission.

- ☑ Tell your teacher, parent, or guardian right away if you find or read any information that makes you feel uneasy or afraid.

- ☑ Do not e-mail your picture to anyone.

- ☑ Do not open e-mail or text messages from strangers.

- ☑ Do not tell anyone your Internet password.

- ☑ Do not make illegal copies of computer games and programs or CD-ROMs.

Words To Know

cyber world the world of computers and high-tech communications

cyber safety actions that protect Internet users from harm

cyber ethics responsible code of conduct for using the Internet

cyber bully a person who uses technology to frighten, bother, or harm someone else

cyber citizen a person who uses the Internet to communicate

LOG ON ▶ Literature Online

For more about Internet safety and responsibility, go to glencoe.com.

Reading Handbook

The What, Why, and How of Reading

You'll need to use the skills and strategies in the following chart to respond to questions and prompts in the selections. As you begin a new lesson, look carefully at the **Reading Skills** or **Strategies** on the **Before You Read** pages. Then find those skills or strategies in this chart and read about what they are, how to use them, and why they're important. The more you refer to the chart, the more these active reading strategies will become a natural part of the way you read.

What is it?	Why is it important?	How to do it
Preview Previewing is looking over a selection before you read.	Previewing lets you begin to see what you already know and what you'll need to know. It helps you set a purpose for reading.	Look at the title, illustrations, headings, captions, and graphics Look at how ideas are organized. Ask questions about the text.
Skim Skimming is looking over an entire selection quickly to get a general idea of what the piece is about.	Skimming will tell you what a selection is about. If the selection you skim isn't what you're looking for, you won't need to read the entire piece.	Read the title of the selection and quickly look over the entire piece. Read headings and captions and maybe part of the first paragraph to get a general idea of the selection's content.
Scan Scanning is glancing quickly over a selection in order to find specific information.	Scanning helps you pinpoint information quickly. It saves you time when you have a number of selections to look at.	As you move your eyes quickly over the lines of text, look for key words or phrases that will help you locate the information you're looking for.
Predict Predicting is taking an educated guess about what will happen in a selection.	Predicting gives you a reason to read. You want to find out if your prediction and the selection events match, don't you? As you read, adjust or change your prediction if it doesn't fit what you learn.	Combine what you already know about an author or subject with what you learned in your preview to guess what will be included in the text.
Set a Purpose Setting a purpose for reading is deciding why you are reading.	Setting a purpose for reading helps you decide on the reading strategies you use with a text.	Ask yourself if you are reading to understand new information, to find specific information, or to be entertained.

What is it?	Why is it important?	How to do it
Clarify Clarifying is looking at difficult sections of text in order to clear up what is confusing.	Authors often build ideas one on another. If you don't clear up a confusing passage, you may not understand main ideas or information that comes later.	Go back and reread a confusing section more slowly. Look up words you don't know. Ask questions about what you don't understand. Sometimes you may want to read on to see if further information helps you.
Question Questioning is asking yourself whether information in a selection is important. Questioning is also regularly asking yourself whether you've understood what you've read.	When you ask questions as you read, you're reading strategically. As you answer your questions, you're making sure that you'll get the gist of a text.	Have a running conversation with yourself as you read. Keep asking: Is this idea important? Why? Do I understand what this is about? Might this information be on a test later?
Visualize Visualizing is picturing a writer's ideas or descriptions in your mind's eye.	Visualizing is one of the best ways to understand and remember information in fiction, nonfiction, and informational text.	Carefully read how a writer describes a person, place, or thing. Then ask yourself: What would this look like? Can I see how the steps in this process would work?
Monitor Comprehension Monitoring your comprehension means thinking about whether you're understanding what you're reading.	The whole point of reading is to understand a piece of text. When you don't understand a selection, you're not really reading it.	Keep asking yourself questions about main ideas, characters, and events. When you can't answer a question, review, read more slowly, or ask someone to help you.
Identify Sequence Identifying sequence is finding the logical order of ideas or events.	In a work of fiction, events are usually presented in chronological (time) order. With nonfiction, understanding the logical sequence of ideas in a piece helps you follow a writer's train of thought. You'll remember ideas better when you know the logical order a writer uses.	Ask yourself what the author is trying to do: Tell a story? Explain how something works? Present information? Look for clues or signal words that might point to time order, steps in a process, or order of importance.
Connect Connecting means linking what you read to events in your own life or to other selections you've read.	You'll "get into" your reading and recall information and ideas better by connecting events, emotions, and characters to your own life.	Ask yourself: Do I know someone like this? Have I ever felt this way? What else have I read that is like this selection?

What is it?	Why is it important?	How to do it
Summarize Summarizing is stating the main ideas of a selection in your own words and in a logical sequence.	Summarizing shows whether you've understood something. It teaches you to rethink what you've read and to separate main ideas from supporting information.	Ask yourself: What is this selection about? Answer who, what, where, when, why, and how? Put that information in a logical order.
Determine Main Idea Determining an author's main idea is finding the most important thought in a paragraph or in a selection.	Finding main ideas gets you ready to summarize. You also discover an author's purpose for writing when you find the main ideas in a selection.	Think about what you know about the author and the topic. Look for how the author organizes ideas. Then look for the one idea that all of the sentences in a paragraph or all the paragraphs in a selection are about.
Respond Responding is telling what you like, dislike, or find surprising or interesting in a selection.	When you react in a personal way to what you read, you'll enjoy a selection more and remember it better.	As you read, think about how you feel about story elements or ideas in a selection. What's your reaction to the characters in a story? What grabs your attention as you read?
Review Reviewing is going back over what you've read to remember what's important and to organize ideas so you'll recall them later.	Reviewing is especially important when you have new ideas and a lot of information to remember.	Filling in a graphic organizer, such as a chart or diagram, as you read helps you organize information. These study aids will help you review later.
Interpret Interpreting is when you use your own understanding of the world to decide what the events or ideas in a selection mean. It's more than just understanding and remembering the facts.	Every reader constructs meaning on the basis of what he or she understands about the world. Finding meaning as you read is all about you interacting with the text.	Think about what you already know about yourself and the world. Ask yourself: What is the author really trying to say here? What larger idea might these events be about?
Infer Inferring is when you use your reason and experience to guess what an author does not come right out and say.	Making inferences is a large part of finding meaning in a selection. Inferring helps you look more deeply at characters and points you toward the theme or message in a selection.	Look for clues the author provides. Notice descriptions, dialogue, events, and relationships that might tell you something the author wants you to know.

What is it?	Why is it important?	How to do it
Draw Conclusions Drawing a conclusion is using a number of pieces of information to make a general statement about people, places, events, and ideas.	Drawing conclusions helps you find connections between ideas and events. It's another tool to help you see the larger picture.	Notice specific details about characters, ideas, and events as you read. Can you make a general statement on the basis of these details? For example, do a character's actions lead you to conclude that he or she is kind?
Analyze Analyzing is looking at separate parts of a selection in order to understand the entire selection.	Analyzing helps you look critically at a piece of writing. When you analyze a selection, you'll discover its theme or message, and you'll learn the author's purpose for writing.	To analyze a story, think about what the author is saying through the characters, the setting, and the plot. To analyze nonfiction, look at how the writer has organized main ideas. What do those ideas suggest?
Synthesize Synthesizing is combining ideas in order to reach a new understanding.	Synthesizing helps you move to a higher level of thinking. Creating something new of your own goes beyond remembering what you learned from someone else.	Think about the ideas or information you've learned in a selection. Ask yourself: Do I understand something more than the main ideas here? Can I create something else from what I now know?
Evaluate Evaluating is making a judgment or forming an opinion about something you have read. You can evaluate a character, an author's purpose , or the reliability of information in an article or text.	Evaluating can help you become a wise, sensible reader. Many selections,—especially text you read online—require careful judgments about an author's qualifications and about the reliability of information presented.	As you read, ask yourself: Is this character realistic and believable? Is this author qualified to write on this subject? Is this author biased? Does this author present opinions as facts?

WHOM Can You Count On?

THE BIG Question

> Some say we are responsible for those we love. Others know we are responsible for those who love us.
>
> —NIKKI GIOVANNI

FOLDABLES®
Study Organizer

Throughout Unit 1, you will read, write, and talk about the **BIG Question**— "Whom Can You Count On?" Use your Unit 1 **Foldable,** shown here, to keep track of your ideas as you read. Turn to the back of this book for instructions on making this **Foldable.**

My Purpose for Reading   The Big Question   My Thoughts

WHOM Can You Count On?

There are people in the world you can count on. You turn to these people for help and support. You may count on your family members or elders. You probably depend on your teacher or a best friend. You may not realize that you count on other people, too—such as the farmers who grow your food or the postal workers who deliver your mail. Sometimes, you also have to rely on yourself.

As you read this unit, think about the people you count on:

○ Friends and Family

○ Me, Myself, and I

○ Extraordinary Individuals

What You'll Read

In this unit, you'll focus on reading **fiction,** such as short stories, folktales, and fables. Works of fiction tell stories about imaginary characters and events. By reading fiction, you share in the characters' discoveries about themselves, the world, and life. The fiction and other types of writing in this unit will help you find answers to the Big Question.

What You'll Write

As you explore the Big Question, you'll write notes in your Unit **Foldable.** Later, you'll use these notes to complete two writing assignments related to the Big Question.

1. **Write a Fictional Narrative**

2. **Choose a Unit Challenge**

   ○ **On Your Own Activity: Create a Chart**

   ○ **Group Activity: Write a Handbook**

What You'll Learn

Literary Elements

narrator and point of view

plot

setting

narrative poetry

short story

fable

character

description

characterization

theme

Reading Skills and Strategies

identify cause-and-effect relationships

connect to personal experience

identify sequence

summarize

visualize

analyze plot

make inferences about characters

analyze setting

distinguish fact and opinion

interpret plot events

preview

determine main idea and supporting details

Fish Cheeks

Amy Tan

I fell in love with the minister's son the winter I turned fourteen. He was not Chinese, but as white as Mary in the manger. For Christmas I prayed for this blond-haired boy, Robert, and a slim new American nose.

When I found out that my parents had invited the minister's family over for Christmas Eve dinner, I cried. What would Robert think of our shabby *Chinese* Christmas? What would he think of our noisy *Chinese* relatives who lacked proper American manners? What terrible disappointment would he feel upon seeing not a roasted turkey and sweet potatoes but Chinese food?

On Christmas Eve I saw that my mother had outdone herself in creating a strange menu. She was pulling black veins out of the backs of fleshy prawns. The kitchen was littered with appalling[1] mounds of raw food: A slimy rock cod with bulging fish eyes that pleaded not to be thrown into a pan of hot oil. Tofu,[2] which looked like stacked wedges of rubbery white sponges. A bowl soaking dried fungus back to life. A plate of squid, their backs crisscrossed with knife markings so they resembled bicycle tires.

And then they arrived—the minister's family and all my relatives in a clamor[3] of doorbells and rumpled

Set a Purpose for Reading
Read "Fish Cheeks" to see who Amy Tan learns to count on.

BQ BIG Question
Why is Amy nervous about counting on her family?

---

1 **Appalling** means "shocking" or "horrifying."

2 **Tofu** (tō′ fōō) is a protein-rich food made from soybeans and used in soups, salads, and stir fries.

3 A **clamor** is a loud, continuous noise.

Christmas packages. Robert grunted hello, and I pretended he was not worthy of existence.

Dinner threw me deeper into despair. My relatives licked the ends of their chopsticks and reached across the table, dipping them into the dozen or so plates of food. Robert and his family waited patiently for platters to be passed to them. My relatives murmured with pleasure when my mother brought out the whole steamed fish. Robert grimaced.[4] Then my father poked his chopsticks just below the fish eye and plucked out the soft meat. "Amy, your favorite," he said, offering me the tender fish cheek. I wanted to disappear.

At the end of the meal my father leaned back and belched loudly, thanking my mother for her fine cooking. "It's a polite Chinese custom to show you are satisfied," explained my father to our astonished guests. Robert was looking down at his plate with a reddened face. The minister managed to muster up a quiet burp. I was stunned into silence for the rest of the night.

After everyone had gone, my mother said to me, "You want to be the same as American girls on the outside." She handed me an early gift. It was a

BQ **BIG Question**
What do you think of Amy's reactions to her relatives?

---

4 Robert *grimaced,* or twisted his face, showing his displeasure.

miniskirt in beige tweed. "But inside you must always be Chinese. You must be proud you are different. Your only shame is to have shame."

And even though I didn't agree with her then, I knew that she understood how much I had suffered during the evening's dinner. It wasn't until many years later—long after I had gotten over my crush on Robert—that I was able to fully appreciate her lesson and the true purpose behind our particular menu. For Christmas Eve that year, she had chosen all my favorite foods.

BQ **BIG Question**
In what way is Amy's mother supportive of her?

BQ **BIG Question**
Whom has Amy learned to count on?

Asian Woman with Hair Comb. Todd Davidson. **View the Art** What words would you use to describe the woman in this artwork? Do the same words apply to the story's narrator?

After You Read

Respond and Think Critically

1. Use your own words to describe the most important events of the Tans' Christmas Eve dinner. **[Summarize]**

2. Why is Amy so upset about entertaining Robert's family? Explain. **[Interpret]**

3. Compare your family's holiday traditions with Amy Tan's. What foods does your family prepare, and what traditions do you follow? **[Compare]**

4. In addition to the miniskirt, what gift does Amy's mother give Amy? Explain. **[Analyze]**

Writing

Write a Summary Write a one-paragraph summary about the selection. You may want to begin your summary with this topic sentence:

Amy Tan was embarrassed when _____.

In your summary, use your own words to explain the story's main ideas and important details. Your summary should also tell what you think is the meaning of the story.

Getty Images

GA Performance Standards

For page 6

ELA7W2g Produce writing that concludes with a detailed summary linked to the purpose of the composition.

LOG ON ▶ **Literature** Online

Unit Resources For additional skills practice, go to glencoe.com and enter QuickPass code GL27534u1.

Part 1

Friends and Family

In the Cool of the Evening, 1994. Jessie Coates. Acrylic on masonite. Private Collection.

BQ ▸ **BIG Question   Whom Can You Count On?**

What does the painting *In the Cool of the Evening* show about the family relaxing on the front porch? Why do you enjoy getting together with family members or friends you can count on?

Before You Read

The Wise Old Woman

Connect to the Folktale

Think about the role an older person, such as a grandparent, has had in your life.

Quickwrite Freewrite for a few minutes about what you have learned from that person. Explain how what you have learned has influenced your way of thinking.

Build Background

Folktales from around the world often follow a similar pattern. They begin with a dreamlike "once upon a time" or "in a land far away" that helps listeners or readers be carried away by the often fantastic events of the story.

- Characters are quickly introduced, and conflict appears early in the story. The characters are often in direct contrast to each other: one is very good and the other is terribly evil.

- Three events, riddles, or wishes often carry the plot along to the frequent conclusion of "happily ever after."

Vocabulary

haughtily (hô′tə lē) *adv.* in a way that shows too much pride in oneself and scorn for others (p. 10). *"The other team doesn't stand a chance against us," Lindsay said haughtily.*

banished (ban′ishd) *v.* forced to leave a country or community (p. 10). *The king banished anyone who went against his ruling.*

commotion (kə mō′shən) *n.* noisy confusion (p. 14). *The musician's appearance at the stage door caused a commotion among the fans.*

commended (kə mend′ed) *v.* expressed approval of (p. 15). *The teacher commended the student on a job well done.*

undoubtedly (un dou′tid lē) *adv.* without a question, definitely (p. 15). *This film is undoubtedly one of the best I've seen.*

Meet Yoshiko Uchida

"Although it is important for each of us to cherish our own special heritage . . . above everything else, we must all celebrate our common humanity."

—Yoshiko Uchida

Writer and Folktale Collector Yoshiko Uchida was born in California, but her parents taught her to love the folktales from their home country of Japan. As an adult, she traveled to Japan to collect folktales. Japanese culture became very important to her writing.

Literary Works Uchida published fiction, nonfiction, and folktale collections. She once expressed the hope that "all children, in whatever country they may live, have the same love of fun and a good story."

Yoshiko Uchida was born in 1921 and died in 1992.

 Literature Online

Author Search For more about Yoshiko Uchida, go to glencoe.com and enter QuickPass code GL27534u1.

Set Purposes for Reading

BQ BIG Question

This folktale tells the story of a wise old woman in trouble. As you read, ask yourself, who can the wise old woman count on in a time of need?

Literary Element Narrator and Point of View

In literary works, the **narrator** is the person who tells the story. **Point of view** is the narrator's relationship to the story. In a story using **first-person point of view,** the narrator is a character in the story. The reader sees everything through that character's eyes. In a story with a **limited third-person point of view,** such as "The Wise Old Woman," the narrator is outside the story and reveals the thoughts and feelings of only one character. In a story with an **omniscient point of view,** the narrator is outside the story and may reveal any kind of information, along with the thoughts of several characters.

As you read, ask yourself, how do the narration and point of view affect details of characters and events?

Reading Skill Identify Cause-and-Effect Relationships

In a **cause-and-effect relationship,** one event or action causes another event or action. For example, a character does something wrong (cause) and then feels guilty about what he or she did (effect). The character may then try to correct the wrong that was done (a new effect caused by the character's feeling of guilt).

Identifying cause-and-effect relationships helps readers understand the reasons why events happen and why characters act in certain ways.

To identify cause-and-effect relationships,

- think about the connection between events or actions and the resulting outcomes
- ask yourself why things happen in the story and how events affect characters
- look for words and phrases, such as *because, so, since, if . . . then,* and *as a result of,* that signal cause and effect

As you read, use a graphic organizer like the one below to keep track of cause-and-effect relationships. Add more boxes, as needed, to show chains of causes and effects.

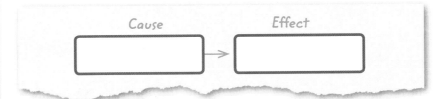

Cause → Effect

GA Performance Standards

For pages 8–17

ELA7R1h For literary texts, identify and analyze how an author's use of words creates tone and mood.

TRY IT

Identify Cause-and-Effect Relationships Think about a decision that you made in the last day or two. What caused you to make that decision? What was the result? How might things be different if you had made another choice?

The Wise Old Woman

Adapted by Yoshiko Uchida

Many long years ago, there lived an arrogant and cruel young lord who ruled over a small village in the western hills of Japan. "I have no use for old people in my village," he said **haughtily.** "They are neither useful nor able to work for a living. I therefore decree¹ that anyone over seventy-one must be **banished** from the village and left in the mountains to die."

Landscape, Mid-Edo. Ike Gyokurano. Hanging scroll, ink and colors on silk, 44 1/8 x 19 3/16 in. Gift of the Asian Art Foundation of San Francisco, The Avery Brundage Collection. Asian Art Museum of San Francisco.

---

1 When you *decree,* you make an official rule or decision.

Vocabulary

haughtily (hô´tə lē) *adv.* in a way that shows too much pride in oneself and scorn for others

banished (ban´ishd) *v.* forced to leave a country or community

"What a dreadful decree! What a cruel and unreasonable lord we have," the people of the village murmured. But the lord fearfully punished anyone who disobeyed him, and so villagers who turned seventy-one were tearfully carried into the mountains, never to return.

Gradually there were fewer and fewer old people in the village and soon they disappeared altogether. Then the young lord was pleased.

"What a fine village of young, healthy and hardworking people I have," he bragged. "Soon it will be the finest village in all of Japan."

Now there lived in this village a kind young farmer and his aged mother. They were poor, but the farmer was good to his mother, and the two of them lived happily together. However, as the years went by, the mother grew older, and before long she reached the terrible age of seventy-one.

"If only I could somehow deceive the cruel lord," the farmer thought. But there were records in the village books and everyone knew that his mother had turned seventy-one.

Each day the son put off telling his mother that he must take her into the mountains to die, but the people of the village began to talk. The farmer knew that if he did not take his mother away soon, the lord would send his soldiers and throw them both into a dark dungeon to die a terrible death.

"Mother—" he would begin, as he tried to tell her what he must do, but he could not go on.

Then one day the mother herself spoke of the lord's dread decree. "Well, my son," she said, "the time has come for you to take me to the mountains. We must hurry before the lord sends his soldiers for you." And she did not seem worried at all that she must go to the mountains to die.

"Forgive me, dear mother, for what I must do," the farmer said sadly, and the next morning he lifted his mother to his shoulders and set off on the steep path toward the mountains. Up and up he climbed, until the trees clustered close and the path was gone. There was no longer even the sound of birds, and they heard only the

Identify Cause-and-Effect Relationships What has caused the disappearance of old people in the village?

Narrator and Point of View What does the narrator reveal to readers? What does this information tell you about the point of view of the story?

soft wail of the wind in the trees. The son walked slowly, for he could not bear to think of leaving his old mother in the mountains. On and on he climbed, not wanting to stop and leave her behind. Soon, he heard his mother breaking off small twigs from the trees that they passed.

"Mother, what are you doing?" he asked.

"Do not worry, my son," she answered gently. "I am just marking the way so you will not get lost returning to the village."

Standing Beauty, 1851. Ando Hiroshige. Hanging scroll, ink and color on paper, 91.5 x 27.7 cm. The British Museum, London.

View the Art Notice the woman's posture and expression. What qualities might she have in common with the old woman in this story?

The son stopped. "Even now you are thinking of me?" he asked, wonderingly.

The mother nodded. "Of course, my son," she replied. "You will always be in my thoughts. How could it be otherwise?"

At that, the young farmer could bear it no longer. "Mother, I cannot leave you in the mountains to die all alone," he said. "We are going home and no matter what the lord does to punish me, I will never desert you again."

So they waited until the sun had set and a lone star crept into the silent sky. Then in the dark shadows of night, the farmer carried his mother down the hill and they returned quietly to their little house. The farmer dug a deep hole in the floor of his kitchen and made a small room where he could hide his mother. From that day, she spent all her time in the secret room and the farmer carried meals to her there. The rest of the time, he was careful to work in the fields and act as though he lived alone. In this way, for almost two years, he kept his mother safely hidden and no one in the village knew that she was there.

Then one day there was a terrible commotion among the villagers for Lord Higa of the town beyond the hills threatened to conquer their village and make it his own.

"Only one thing can spare you," Lord Higa announced. "Bring me a box containing one thousand ropes of ash and I will spare your village."

The cruel young lord quickly gathered together all the wise men of his village. "You are men of wisdom," he said. "Surely you can tell me how to meet Lord Higa's demands so our village can be spared."

But the wise men shook their heads. "It is impossible to make even one rope of ash, sire," they answered. "How can we ever make one thousand?"

"Fools!" the lord cried angrily. "What good is your wisdom if you cannot help me now?"

And he posted a notice in the village square offering a great reward of gold to any villager who could help him save their village.

BQ **BIG Question**

How does the farmer count on his mother? Do you think the mother is counting on her son to spare her?

But all the people in the village whispered, "Surely, it is an impossible thing, for ash crumbles at the touch of the finger. How could anyone ever make a rope of ash?" They shook their heads and sighed, "Alas, alas, we must be conquered by yet another cruel lord."

The young farmer, too, supposed that this must be, and he wondered what would happen to his mother if a new lord even more terrible than their own came to rule over them.

When his mother saw the troubled look on his face, she asked, "Why are you so worried, my son?"

So the farmer told her of the impossible demand made by Lord Higa if the village was to be spared, but his mother did not seem troubled at all. Instead she laughed softly and said, "Why, that is not such an impossible task. All one has to do is soak ordinary rope in salt water and dry it well. When it is burned, it will hold its shape and there is your rope of ash! Tell the villagers to hurry and find one thousand pieces of rope."

The farmer shook his head in amazement. "Mother, you are wonderfully wise," he said, and he rushed to tell the young lord what he must do.

"You are wiser than all the wise men of the village," the lord said when he heard the farmer's solution, and he rewarded him with many pieces of gold. The thousand ropes of ash were quickly made and the village was spared.

In a few days, however, there was another great **commotion** in the village as Lord Higa sent another threat. This time he sent a log with a small hole that curved and bent seven times through its length, and he demanded that a single piece of silk thread be threaded through the hole. "If you cannot perform this task," the lord threatened, "I shall come to conquer your village."

The young lord hurried once more to his wise men, but they all shook their heads in bewilderment.[2] "A needle cannot bend its way through such curves," they moaned. "Again we are faced with an impossible demand."

Identify Cause-and-Effect Relationships Why does the lord give the farmer gold?

---

2 *Bewilderment* means "confusion."

commotion (kə mō′shən) *n.* noisy confusion

"And again you are stupid fools!" the lord said, stamping his foot impatiently. He then posted a second notice in the village square asking the villagers for their help.

Once more the young farmer hurried with the problem to his mother in her secret room.

"Why, that is not so difficult," his mother said with a quick smile. "Put some sugar at one end of the hole. Then, tie an ant to a piece of silk thread and put it in at the other end. He will weave his way in and out of the curves to get to the sugar and he will take the silk thread with him."

"Mother, you are remarkable!" the son cried, and he hurried off to the lord with the solution to the second problem.

Once more the lord **commended** the young farmer and rewarded him with many pieces of gold. "You are a brilliant man and you have saved our village again," he said gratefully.

But the lord's troubles were not over even then, for a few days later Lord Higa sent still another demand. "This time you will **undoubtedly** fail and then I shall conquer your village," he threatened. "Bring me a drum that sounds without being beaten."

"But that is not possible," sighed the people of the village. "How can anyone make a drum sound without beating it?"

This time the wise men held their heads in their hands and moaned, "It is hopeless. It is hopeless. This time Lord Higa will conquer us all."

The young farmer hurried home breathlessly. "Mother, Mother, we must solve another terrible problem or Lord Higa will conquer our village!" And he quickly told his mother about the impossible drum.

His mother, however, smiled and answered, "Why, this is the easiest of them all. Make a drum with sides of paper and put a bumblebee inside. As it tries to escape, it will

Identify Cause-and-Effect Relationships Why do you think the old woman finds Lord Higa's challenges so easy?

Vocabulary
....

commended (kə mend′ ed) *v.* expressed approval of

undoubtedly (un dou′ tid lē) *adv.* without a question, definitely

buzz and beat itself against the paper and you will have a drum that sounds without being beaten."

The young farmer was amazed at his mother's wisdom. "You are far wiser than any of the wise men of the village," he said, and he hurried to tell the young lord how to meet Lord Higa's third demand.

When the lord heard the answer, he was greatly impressed. "Surely a young man like you cannot be wiser than all my wise men," he said. "Tell me honestly, who has helped you solve all these difficult problems?"

The young farmer could not lie. "My lord," he began slowly, "for the past two years I have broken the law of the land. I have kept my aged mother hidden beneath the floor of my house, and it is she who solved each of your problems and saved the village from Lord Higa."

He trembled as he spoke, for he feared the lord's displeasure and rage. Surely now the soldiers would be summoned[3] to throw him into the dark dungeon. But when he glanced fearfully at the lord, he saw that the young ruler was not angry at all. Instead, he was silent and thoughtful, for at last he realized how much wisdom and knowledge old people possess.

"I have been very wrong," he said finally. "And I must ask the forgiveness of your mother and of all my people. Never again will I demand that the old people of our village be sent to the mountains to die. Rather, they will be treated with the respect and honor they deserve and share with us the wisdom of their years."

And so it was. From that day, the villagers were no longer forced to abandon their parents in the mountains, and the village became once more a happy, cheerful place in which to live. The terrible Lord Higa stopped sending his impossible demands and no longer threatened to conquer them, for he too was impressed. "Even in such a small village there is much wisdom," he declared, "and its people should be allowed to live in peace."

And that is exactly what the farmer and his mother and all the people of the village did for all the years thereafter. 🎐

---

3 To *summon* means "to send for or request the presence of someone."

Narrator and Point of View
How does the point of view affect your understanding of the farmer's thoughts and feelings?

Identify Cause-and-Effect Relationships What has caused the village lord to change his mind about the old people in the village?

After You Read

Respond and Think Critically

1. Name the three demands from Lord Higa and describe the wise old woman's solutions. **[Recall]**

2. Why do you think the wise men of the village are unable to solve Lord Higa's problems? Explain. **[Infer]**

3. What point does this folktale make about people who have power over others? Support your answer. **[Interpret]**

4. **Literary Element** **Narrator and Point of View** How might this story be different if it were told from the old woman's point of view? **[Analyze]**

5. **Reading Skill** **Identify Cause-and-Effect Relationships** Use your cause-and-effect graphic organizer to help you explain why the farmer goes against the lord's decree. Describe the effect of his decision. **[Analyze]**

6. **BQ** **BIG Question** Think about how the farmer depends on his mother, and how his mother depends on him. What are the qualities of someone who can be counted on? **[Connect]**

Vocabulary Practice

Respond to these questions.

1. Whom would you describe as behaving **haughtily**—a friendly person or an arrogant person?

2. Whom would you **banish** from a club—a member who never pays the fees or a member who volunteers to help out with events?

3. Whom would you **commend** after giving a test—a student who scored well or a student who failed?

4. Where would you be likely to hear a **commotion**—a library or a crowded stadium?

Writing

Write a Journal Entry Put yourself in the village lord's place on the day he realizes who is responsible for saving the village. As the lord, what might you think about your previous beliefs and actions? Describe your thoughts and feelings in a journal entry.

TIP

Interpreting
Here are some tips to help you interpret the moral or lesson of the story.

- Start by thinking about the village lord's decree. How do the villagers respond to it?

- Who is responsible for solving the challenges and saving the village?

- What lesson does the lord learn from the experience?

FOLDABLES **Study Organizer** Keep track of your ideas about the **BIG Question** in your unit Foldable.

Literature Online

Selection Resources
For Selection Quizzes, eFlashcards, and Reading-Writing Connection activities, go to glencoe.com and enter QuickPass code GL27534u1.

Before You Read

Amigo Brothers

Connect to the Short Story

Think about a time when you had to compete against a good friend or a family member. The competition might have involved sports, grades, music, or another activity in which you and your friend or family member wanted the same thing.

Partner Talk With a partner, talk about a time when you competed against a friend or family member. How did this competition make you feel? Did you try your hardest to win? How did competing affect your relationship?

Build Background

In the story "Amigo Brothers," Antonio and Felix are boxers. Here are some facts about boxing.

- Boxers compete in divisions, or groups, based on their weight. Antonio and Felix are in the light welterweight division. Boxers in that division weigh between 132 and 141 pounds.

- Amateur boxing matches are broken into three rounds. The ringing of a bell tells when a round is beginning or ending.

- The annual Golden Gloves national tournament is the most famous tournament in amateur boxing.

Vocabulary

devastating (dev′əs tāt′ing) *adj.* causing a lot of pain, damage, or destruction; overwhelming (p. 22).
The devastating drought ruined most of the farmer's crops.

wary (wār′ē) *adj.* cautious; on the alert (p. 24). *The mail carrier was wary of the large, barking dog.*

perpetual (pər pech′o͞o əl) *adj.* constant; unceasing (p. 26).
The perpetual rocking motion of the ship made Anthony ill.

improvised (im′prə vīzd′) *v.* invented, composed, or did without preparation (p. 27). *Without a recipe, we improvised as we made the stew.*

evading (i vād′ing) *adj.* keeping away or avoiding (p. 32). *Evading the rain, we hurried to take shelter during the storm.*

Meet Piri Thomas

"I said . . . 'I got a mind; let's see if I can use it,' so I jumped into books."

—Piri Thomas

Writing Changed His Life
Piri Thomas first began writing while serving a prison term for attempted armed robbery. Creative writing helped Thomas to escape his surroundings, combat stereotypes, and change his life. After his release from prison, he continued his writing career.

Literary Works Thomas is the author of stories, a play, and several autobiographies. His literary works are known for their use of the Spanish Harlem dialect and for the tough reality they portray.

Piri Thomas was born in 1928.

LOG ON ▶ **Literature** Online

Author Search For more about Piri Thomas, go to glencoe.com and enter QuickPass code GL27534u1.

Set Purposes for Reading

BQ BIG Question

Read "Amigo Brothers" to find out how two friends respond to a test of their friendship. As you read, ask yourself, how much can these two friends count on each other?

Literary Element Plot

Plot is the sequence of events in a story. A struggle between two opposing forces is usually at the center of a plot. This struggle is called **conflict.**

Conflict is an important part of a story because it moves the plot forward. An **external conflict** exists when a character struggles against some outside force, such as another person, nature, or society. A character who is torn between his or her own opposing feelings or goals experiences **internal conflict.**

As you read, ask yourself, are the conflicts Antonio and Felix face internal or external? Notice how the conflicts move the plot forward.

Reading Strategy Connect to Personal Experience

Connecting is finding the links between one thing and another. When you read, you can think about how the selection you are reading connects to your own personal experiences. Connecting is important because it helps you understand the world around you and what you read.

To connect what you read with your personal experiences, ask yourself

- Are the characters similar to anyone I know?
- Do I know anyone who has done what this character is doing?
- Have I been in this situation before?
- Have I felt this way before?

You may find it helpful to use a graphic organizer like the one below.

"Amigo Brothers"	My Connections
Characters	
Actions/Situations	
Feelings	

GA Performance Standards

For pages 18–35

ELA7R1e For literary texts, identify events that advance the plot and determine how each event explains past or present action(s) or foreshadows future action(s).

TRY IT

Connect to Personal Experience Have you ever read a book or seen a movie and been in the same situation or had the same feelings as a character? If you have, you connected what you saw or read with your own personal experiences.

AMIGO BROTHERS

Piri Thomas

Antonio Cruz and Felix Varga were both seventeen years old. They were so together in friendship that they felt themselves to be brothers. They had known each other since childhood, growing up on the lower east side of Manhattan in the same tenement[1] building on Fifth Street between Avenue A and Avenue B.

Antonio was fair, lean, and lanky, while Felix was dark, short, and husky. Antonio's hair was always falling over his eyes, while Felix wore his black hair in a natural Afro style.

Each youngster had a dream of someday becoming lightweight champion of the world. Every chance they had the boys worked out, sometimes at the Boys Club on 10th Street and Avenue A and sometimes at the pro's gym on 14th Street. Early morning sunrises would find them running along the East River Drive, wrapped in sweat shirts, short towels around their necks, and handkerchiefs Apache style around their foreheads.

Connect to Personal Experience In your experience, why do some friends feel as close as sisters or brothers?

---

1 A *tenement* is a kind of apartment building.

While some youngsters were into street negatives, Antonio and Felix slept, ate, rapped, and dreamt positive. Between them, they had a collection of *Fight* magazines second to none, plus a scrapbook filled with torn tickets to every boxing match they had ever attended, and some clippings of their own. If asked a question about any given fighter, they would immediately zip out from their memory banks divisions, weights, records of fights, knock-outs, technical knock-outs, and draws or losses.[2]

Each had fought many bouts representing their community and had won two gold-plated medals plus a silver and bronze medallion. The difference was in their style. Antonio's lean form and long reach made him the better boxer, while Felix's short and muscular frame made him the better slugger. Whenever they had met in the **ring** for sparring sessions,[3] it had always been hot and heavy.

Now, after a series of elimination bouts,[4] they had been informed that they were to meet each other in the division finals that were scheduled for the seventh of August, two weeks away—the winner to represent the Boys Club in the Golden Gloves Championship Tournament.

The two boys continued to run together along the East River Drive. But even when joking with each other, they both sensed a wall rising between them.

One morning less than a week before their bout, they met as usual for their daily work-out. They fooled around with a few jabs at the air, slapped skin, and then took off, running lightly along the dirty East River's edge.

Antonio glanced at Felix who kept his eyes purposely straight ahead, pausing from time to time to do some fancy leg work while throwing one-twos followed by upper cuts to an imaginary jaw. Antonio then beat the air

Visual Vocabulary

A boxing **ring** is a square area, bounded by ropes, in which boxing matches take place.

Plot Given the details in the story so far, what kind of conflict do you think is developing?

---

2   A **knock-out** is when a boxer falls to the ground and does not stand up within a certain amount of time. In a **technical knock-out** (TKO), the boxer is judged to be physically unable to go on fighting. A TKO can be called by an official, the fighter, or the fighter's coach. A **draw** is when a fight is so close that neither boxer can be called the winner.

3   **Sparring sessions** are practice fights.

4   **Elimination bouts** are fights in a tournament; the winners advance to fight again, but the losers are eliminated from competition.

with a barrage of body blows and short **devastating** lefts with an overhand jaw-breaking right.

After a mile or so, Felix puffed and said, "Let's stop a while, bro. I think we both got something to say to each other."

Antonio nodded. It was not natural to be acting as though nothing unusual was happening when two ace-boon buddies[5] were going to be blasting each other within a few short days.

They rested their elbows on the railing separating them from the river. Antonio wiped his face with his short towel. The sunrise was now creating day.

Felix leaned heavily on the river's railing and stared across to the shores of Brooklyn. Finally, he broke the silence.

"Man, I don't know how to come out with it."

Antonio helped. "It's about our fight, right?"

"Yeah, right." Felix's eyes squinted at the rising orange sun.

"I've been thinking about it too, *panin*. In fact, since we found out it was going to be me and you, I've been awake at night, pulling punches[6] on you, trying not to hurt you."

"Same here. It ain't natural not to think about the fight. I mean, we both are *cheverote*[7] fighters and we both want to win. But only one of us can win. There ain't no draws in the eliminations."

Felix tapped Antonio gently on the shoulder. "I don't mean to sound like I'm bragging, bro. But I wanna win, fair and square."

Antonio nodded quietly. "Yeah. We both know that in the ring the better man wins. Friend or no friend, brother or no . . . "

Felix finished it for him. "Brother. Tony, let's promise something right here. Okay?"

> **Connect to Personal Experience** Have you ever had a difficult subject to discuss with a friend? How did you handle it?

---

5 Here, *ace* means "best" and *boon* means "merry," so ace-boon buddies are best friends who share fun and good times.

6 *Panin* (pä′nēn) is American Spanish slang for "pal" or "buddy." *Pulling punches* means holding back on the strength of a punch.

7 *Cheverote* (che ve rō′tā) is American Spanish for "really cool; fine."

devastating (dev′əs tāt′ing) *adj.* causing a lot of pain, damage, or destruction; overwhelming

22   UNIT 1 Whom Can You Count On?

"If it's fair, *hermano*, I'm for it." Antonio admired the courage of a tug boat pulling a barge five times its welterweight[8] size.

"It's fair, Tony. When we get into the ring, it's gotta be like we never met. We gotta be like two heavy strangers that want the same thing and only one can have it. You understand, don'tcha?"

"*Si*, I know." Tony smiled. "No pulling punches. We go all the way."

"Yeah, that's right. Listen, Tony. Don't you think it's a good idea if we don't see each other until the day of the fight? I'm going to stay with my Aunt Lucy in the Bronx. I can use Gleason's Gym for working out. My manager says he got some sparring partners with more or less your style."

Tony scratched his nose pensively.[9] "Yeah, it would be better for our heads." He held out his hand, palm upward. "Deal?"

"Deal." Felix lightly slapped open skin.

"Ready for some more running?" Tony asked lamely.

"Naw, bro. Let's cut it here. You go on. I kinda like to get things together in my head."

"You ain't worried, are you?" Tony asked.

"No way, man." Felix laughed out loud. "I got too much smarts for that. I just think it's cooler if we split right here. After the fight, we can get it together again like nothing ever happened."

The amigo brothers were not ashamed to hug each other tightly.

"Guess you're right. Watch yourself, Felix. I hear there's some pretty heavy dudes up in the Bronx. *Suavecito*,[10] okay?"

"Okay. You watch yourself too, *sabe?*"[11]

BQ BIG Question

Do you think that it will be possible for Antonio and Felix to remain friends after the fight?

---

8   *Hermano* (ār män′ō) is Spanish for "brother." A professional *welterweight* boxer weighs between 141 and 147 pounds

9   *Pensively* means "in a thoughtful or sad way."

10   *Suavecito* (soo äv′vā sē′tō) is American Spanish slang for "take it easy" or "be cool."

11   *Sabe* (sā′bā) means "You know?"

Tony jogged away. Felix watched his friend disappear from view, throwing rights and lefts. Both fighters had a lot of psyching up[12] to do before the big fight.

The days in training passed much too slowly. Although they kept out of each other's way, they were aware of each other's progress via the ghetto grapevine.

The evening before the big fight, Tony made his way to the roof of his tenement. In the quiet early dark, he peered over the ledge. Six stories below the lights of the city blinked and the sounds of cars mingled with the curses and the laughter of children in the street. He tried not to think of Felix, feeling he had succeeded in psyching his mind. But only in the ring would he really know. To spare Felix hurt, he would have to knock him out, early and quick.

Up in the South Bronx, Felix decided to take in a movie in an effort to keep Antonio's face away from his fists. The flick was *The Champion* with Kirk Douglas, the third time Felix was seeing it.

The champion was getting the daylights beat out of him. He was saved only by the sound of the bell.

Felix became the champ and Tony the challenger.

The movie audience was going out of its head. The champ hunched his shoulders grunting and sniffing red blood back into his broken nose. The challenger, confident that he had the championship in the bag, threw a left. The champ countered with a dynamite right.

Felix's right arm felt the shock. Antonio's face, superimposed on the screen, was hit by the awesome force of the blow. Felix saw himself in the ring, blasting Antonio against the ropes. The champ had to be forcibly restrained. The challenger fell slowly to the canvas.

When Felix finally left the theatre, he had figured out how to psyche himself for tomorrow's fight. It was Felix the Champion vs. Antonio the Challenger.

He walked up some dark streets, deserted except for small pockets of **wary**-looking kids wearing gang colors.

Connect to Personal Experience How does Felix's connection to the character in the movie help him prepare for the fight with Antonio?

---

12 *Psyching* (sī′ king) *up* means getting emotionally ready for a task.

Vocabulary

wary (wār′ē) *adj.* cautious; on the alert

Vinny Pazienza, 1996. Bill Angresano. Oil on canvas, 24 x 20 in. Big Fights Boxing Memorabilia, NY.

Despite the fact that he was Puerto Rican like them, they eyed him as a stranger to their turf. Felix did a fast shuffle, bobbing and weaving, while letting loose a torrent of blows that would demolish whatever got in its way. It seemed to impress the brothers, who went about their own business.

Finding no takers, Felix decided to split to his aunt's. Walking the streets had not relaxed him, neither had the fight flick. All it had done was to stir him up. He let himself quietly into his Aunt Lucy's apartment and went straight to bed, falling into a fitful sleep with sounds of the gong for Round One.

Antonio was passing some heavy time on his rooftop. How would the fight tomorrow affect his relationship with Felix? After all, fighting was like any other profession. Friendship had nothing to do with it. A gnawing doubt crept in. He cut negative thinking real quick by doing some speedy fancy dance steps, bobbing and weaving like mercury.[13] The night air was blurred

---

13 **Mercury** is a metal that is liquid at room temperature and moves about as if it were alive.

with **perpetual** motions of left hooks and right crosses. Felix, his *amigo* brother, was not going to be Felix at all in the ring. Just an opponent with another face. Antonio went to sleep, hearing the opening bell for the first round. Like his friend in the South Bronx, he prayed for victory, via a quick clean knock-out in the first round.

Large posters plastered all over the walls of local shops announced the fight between Antonio Cruz and Felix Vargas as the main bout.

The fight had created great interest in the neighborhood. Antonio and Felix were well liked and respected. Each had his own loyal following.

Antonio's fans had unbridled[14] faith in his boxing skills. On the other side, Felix's admirers trusted in his dynamite-packed fists.

Felix had returned to his apartment early in the morning of August 7th and stayed there, hoping to avoid seeing Antonio. He turned the radio on to *salsa*[15] music sounds and then tried to read while waiting for word from his manager.

The fight was scheduled to take place in Tompkins Square Park. It had been decided that the gymnasium of the Boys Club was not large enough to hold all the people who were sure to attend. In Tompkins Square Park, everyone who wanted could view the fight, whether from ringside or window fire escapes or tenement rooftops.

The morning of the fight Tompkins Square was a beehive of activity with numerous workers setting up the ring, the seats, and the guest speakers' stand. The scheduled bouts began shortly after noon and the park had begun filling up even earlier.

The local junior high school across from Tompkins Square Park served as the dressing room for all the fighters. Each was given a separate classroom with desk

Plot Antonio and Felix continue to deal with their internal conflicts the night before the fight. How does Antonio get ready? How does Felix get ready?

Connect to Personal Experience How do you think Felix feels at this point in the story?

---

14 Here, ***unbridled*** means "uncontrolled."

15 ***Salsa*** is a lively Latin American dance music that uses elements of rhythm and blues, jazz, and rock.

perpetual (pər pech′ oo əl) *adj.* constant; unceasing

tops, covered with mats, serving as resting tables. Antonio thought he caught a glimpse of Felix waving to him from a room at the far end of the corridor. He waved back just in case it had been him.

The fighters changed from their street clothes into fighting gear. Antonio wore white trunks, black socks, and black shoes. Felix wore sky blue trunks, red socks, and white boxing shoes. Each had dressing gowns to match their fighting trunks with their names neatly stitched on the back.

The loudspeakers blared into the open windows of the school. There were speeches by dignitaries, community leaders, and great boxers of yesteryear. Some were well prepared, some **improvised** on the spot. They all carried the same message of great pleasure and honor at being part of such a historic event. This great day was in the tradition of champions emerging from the streets of the lower east side.

Interwoven with the speeches were the sounds of the other boxing events. After the sixth bout, Felix was much relieved when his trainer Charlie said, "Time change. Quick knock-out. This is it. We're on."

Waiting time was over. Felix was escorted from the classroom by a dozen fans in white T-shirts with the word FELIX across their fronts.

Antonio was escorted down a different stairwell and guided through a roped-off path.

As the two climbed into the ring, the crowd exploded with a roar. Antonio and Felix both bowed gracefully and then raised their arms in acknowledgment.

Antonio tried to be cool, but even as the roar was in its first birth, he turned slowly to meet Felix's eyes looking directly into his. Felix nodded his head and Antonio responded. And both as one, just as quickly, turned away to face his own corner.

Bong—bong—bong. The roar turned to stillness.

"Ladies and Gentlemen, *Señores y Señoras*."[16]

16 *Señores y señoras* (sen yôr′ ās ē sen yôr′ əs) is Spanish for "ladies and gentlemen."

Vocabulary

improvised (im′prə vīzd′) *v.* invented, composed, or did without preparation

Connect to Personal Experience If you had to face a good friend in a competition, would you look him or her in the eyes or look away? Why?

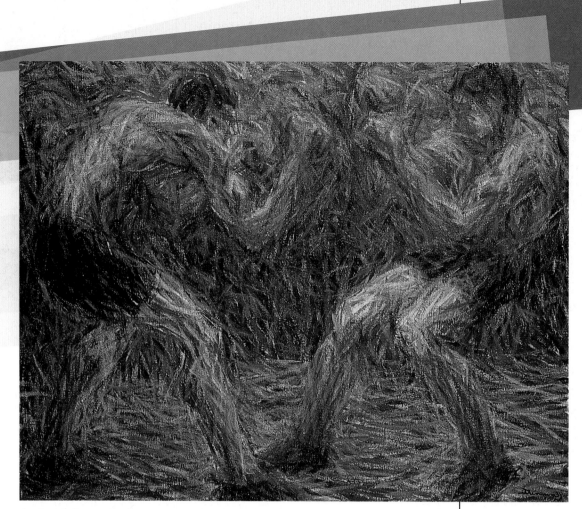

Boxing. G. Cominetti. 75.3 x 92 cm. Private Collection.

View the Art How does this artwork show the action of a boxing match?

The announcer spoke slowly, pleased at his bilingual[17] efforts.

"Now the moment we have all been waiting for—the main event between two fine young Puerto Rican fighters, products of our lower east side.

"In this corner, weighing 134 pounds, Felix Vargas. And in this corner, weighing 133 pounds, Antonio Cruz. The winner will represent the Boys Club in the tournament of champions, the Golden Gloves. There will be no draw. May the best man win."

---

17 A *bilingual* person can use two languages.

The cheering of the crowd shook the window panes of the old buildings surrounding Tompkins Square Park. At the center of the ring, the referee was giving instructions to the youngsters.

"Keep your punches up. No low blows. No punching on the back of the head. Keep your heads up. Understand. Let's have a clean fight. Now shake hands and come out fighting."

Both youngsters touched gloves and nodded. They turned and danced quickly to their corners. Their head towels and dressing gowns were lifted neatly from their shoulders by their trainers' nimble fingers. Antonio crossed himself. Felix did the same.

BONG! BONG! ROUND ONE. Felix and Antonio turned and faced each other squarely in a fighting pose. Felix wasted no time. He came in fast, head low, half hunched toward his right shoulder, and lashed out with a straight left. He missed a right cross as Antonio slipped the punch and countered with one-two-three lefts that snapped Felix's head back, sending a mild shock coursing through him. If Felix had any small doubt about their friendship affecting their fight, it was being neatly dispelled.[18]

Antonio danced, a joy to behold. His left hand was like a piston pumping jabs one right after another with seeming ease. Felix bobbed and weaved and never stopped boring in.[19] He knew that at long range he was at a disadvantage. Antonio had too much reach on him. Only by coming in close could Felix hope to achieve the dreamed-of knockout.

Antonio knew the dynamite that was stored in his *amigo* brother's fist. He ducked a short right and missed a left hook. Felix trapped him against the ropes just long enough to pour some punishing rights and lefts to Antonio's hard midsection. Antonio slipped away from Felix, crashing two lefts to his head, which set Felix's right ear to ringing.

Bong! Both *amigos* froze a punch well on its way, sending up a roar of approval for good sportsmanship.

Plot How does the conflict between Felix and Antonio advance the plot?

---

18 To *dispel* something is to make it go away or disappear.

19 Here, *boring* means drilling, making a hole. *Boring in* with punches is to punch hard and fast.

Felix walked briskly back to his corner. His right ear had not stopped ringing. Antonio gracefully danced his way toward his stool none the worse, except for glowing glove burns, showing angry red against the whiteness of his midribs.

"Watch that right, Tony." His trainer talked into his ear. "Remember Felix always goes to the body. He'll want you to drop your hands for his overhand left or right. Got it?"

Antonio nodded, spraying water out between his teeth. He felt better as his sore midsection was being firmly rubbed.

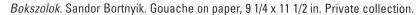

Bokszolok. Sandor Bortnyik. Gouache on paper, 9 1/4 x 11 1/2 in. Private collection.

Felix's corner was also busy.

"You gotta get in there, fella." Felix's trainer poured water over his curly Afro locks. "Get in there or he's gonna chop you up from way back."

Bong! Bong! Round two. Felix was off his stool and rushed Antonio like a bull, sending a hard right to his head. Beads of water exploded from Antonio's long hair.

Antonio, hurt, sent back a blurring barrage of lefts and rights that only meant pain to Felix, who returned with a short left to the head followed by a looping right to the body. Antonio countered with his own flurry, forcing Felix to give ground. But not for long.

Felix bobbed and weaved, bobbed and weaved, occasionally punching his two gloves together.

Antonio waited for the rush that was sure to come. Felix closed in and feinted[20] with his left shoulder and threw his right instead. Lights suddenly exploded inside Felix's head as Antonio slipped the blow and hit him with a pistonlike left, catching him flush on the point of his chin.

Bedlam[21] broke loose as Felix's legs momentarily buckled. He fought off a series of rights and lefts and came back with a strong right that taught Antonio respect.

Antonio danced in carefully. He knew Felix had the habit of playing possum when hurt, to sucker an opponent within reach of the powerful bombs he carried in each fist.

A right to the head slowed Antonio's pretty dancing. He answered with his own left at Felix's right eye that began puffing up within three seconds.

Antonio, a bit too eager, moved in too close and Felix had him entangled into a rip-roaring, punching toe-to-toe slugfest that brought the whole Tompkins Square Park screaming to its feet.

Rights to the body. Lefts to the head. Neither fighter was giving an inch. Suddenly a short right caught Antonio squarely on the chin. His long legs turned to jelly and his arms flailed out desperately. Felix, grunting like a bull,

Plot What type of conflict are Felix and Antonio facing at this point in the story?

---

20 To *feint* is to make a movement intended to fool an opponent.

21 Noisy uproar and confusion is *bedlam.*

threw wild punches from every direction. Antonio, groggy, bobbed and weaved, **evading** most of the blows. Suddenly his head cleared. His left flashed out hard and straight catching Felix on the bridge of his nose.

Felix lashed back with a haymaker, right off the ghetto streets. At the same instant, his eye caught another left hook from Antonio. Felix swung out trying to clear the pain. Only the frenzied screaming of those along ringside let him know that he had dropped Antonio. Fighting off the growing haze, Antonio struggled to his feet, got up, ducked, and threw a smashing right that dropped Felix flat on his back.

Felix got up as fast as he could in his own corner, groggy but still game. He didn't even hear the count. In a fog, he heard the roaring of the crowd, who seemed to have gone insane. His head cleared to hear the bell sound at the end of the round. He was very glad. His trainer sat him down on the stool.

In his corner, Antonio was doing what all fighters do when they are hurt. They sit and smile at everyone.

The referee signaled the ring doctor to check the fighters out. He did so and then gave his okay. The cold water sponges brought clarity to both *amigo* brothers. They were rubbed until their circulation ran free.

Bong! Round three—the final round. Up to now it had been tic-tac-toe, pretty much even. But everyone knew there could be no draw and that this round would decide the winner.

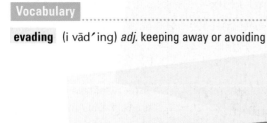

This time, to Felix's surprise, it was Antonio who came out fast, charging across the ring. Felix braced himself but couldn't ward off the barrage of punches. Antonio drove Felix hard against the ropes.

The crowd ate it up. Thus far the two had fought with *mucho corazón.*[22] Felix tapped his gloves and commenced his attack anew. Antonio, throwing boxer's caution to the winds, jumped in to meet him.

Both pounded away. Neither gave an inch and neither fell to the canvas. Felix's left eye was tightly closed. Claret[23] red blood poured from Antonio's nose. They fought toe-to-toe.

The sounds of their blows were loud in contrast to the silence of a crowd gone completely mute.

Bong! Bong! Bong! The bell sounded over and over again. Felix and Antonio were past hearing. Their blows continued to pound on each other like hailstones.

Finally the referee and the two trainers pried Felix and Antonio apart. Cold water was poured over them to bring them back to their senses.

They looked around and then rushed toward each other. A cry of alarm surged through Tompkins Square Park. Was this a fight to the death instead of a boxing match?

The fear soon gave way to wave upon wave of cheering as the two *amigos* embraced.

No matter what the decision, they knew they would always be champions to each other.

BONG! BONG! BONG! "Ladies and Gentlemen. *Señores* and *Señoras.* The winner and representative to the Golden Gloves Tournament of Champions is . . ."

The announcer turned to point to the winner and found himself alone. Arm in arm the champions had already left the ring. 🔔

Connect to Personal Experience If you were in the crowd, how would you feel watching two best friends try to defeat each other for the title?

BQ BIG Question
Can Antonio and Felix still count on each other at the end of the fight?

---

22 They fought with "great heart." Pronunciation: ***mucho corazón*** (mo͞o´cho̅ kō rə zōn´)

23 ***Claret*** (klar´it) is a dark, purplish-red color.

After You Read

Respond and Think Critically

1. What dream do Felix and Antonio share? Explain. **[Identify]**

2. How are Antonio and Felix different from each other? List some of the ways they are different. **[Recall]**

3. How does boxing make Antonio and Felix different from other boys in their neighborhood? Explain. **[Interpret]**

4. You read the description of the fight in the story. Do you think anyone lost? Use details from the story to explain your answer. **[Analyze]**

5. Do you think the friendship between Antonio and Felix is strong enough to survive other problems? How do you come to this conclusion? **[Conclude]**

6. **BQ** **BIG Question** Antonio and Felix each fight hard to beat the other in the championship. Does this mean that they can't count on each other? After reading this story, what are your thoughts about whom you can count on? **[Connect]**

Vocabulary Practice

On a separate sheet of paper, write the vocabulary word that correctly completes each sentence. If none of the words fits the sentence, write "none."

devastating   **perpetual**   **wary**

evading   **improvised**

1. Without any preparation, the actors _____ their lines.

2. The damaging storm was _____ to the community.

3. In the midst of the commotion, no one heard the _____ of the doorbell.

4. We avoided the highway, _____ the traffic jam.

5. The ticking of the clock was _____, or never-ending.

6. Always cautious on our hike, we were _____ of poison ivy along the trail.

Academic Vocabulary

To prepare for the fight, Antonio "cut **negative** thinking" by practicing his footwork. In the preceding sentence, *negative* means damaging. What do you do to stop negative thinking?

TIP

Interpreting

To answer question 3, you must think about details in the story that describe Antonio and Felix, as well as the boys in their neighborhood. You must also think about what you know from your own experience about competitive athletes.

- Start by reviewing the details in the story. How does the author describe Antonio and Felix? How is this description different from the description he provides of others in their neighborhood?

- What do you know about athletes working to be in top physical condition? How would Antonio's and Felix's desire to be champion boxers set them apart?

 FOLDABLES **Study Organizer** Keep track of your ideas about the **BIG Question** in your unit Foldable.

 Literature Online

Selection Resources
For Selection Quizzes, eFlashcards, and Reading-Writing Connection activities, go to glencoe.com and enter QuickPass code GL27534u1.

Literary Element Plot

Standards Practice ELA7R1e

1. What is the external conflict that drives the plot of "Amigo Brothers"?

    A   Felix and Antonio do not want to harm their friendship.

    B   Antonio is not as good a fighter as Felix.

    C   Felix and Antonio must fight each other in the division finals.

    D   Felix does not want to fight Antonio.

Review: Narrator and Point of View

As you learned on page 9, in **limited third-person point of view,** the narrator reveals the thoughts of only one character. In **omniscient point of view,** the thoughts of several characters are revealed.

Standards Practice ELA7R1f

2. Whose thoughts and feelings are revealed in the story?

    A   only Antonio's

    B   only Felix's

    C   both Antonio's and Felix's

    D   the spectators' at the fight

Reading Strategy Connect to Personal Experience

3. Why is connecting to personal experience an effective reading strategy? How did it better your understanding of the story? Explain.

Grammar Link

Action and Linking Verbs A **verb** is a word that expresses action or a state of being.

An **action verb** is a word that expresses action, or something that can be done. Action verbs tell what the subject of a sentence *does.* For example:

The fighter **threw** a punch to his opponent's head.

In the preceding sentence, the fighter (the subject) threw (the action verb) a punch.

A **linking verb,** or state-of-being verb, connects the subject of a sentence with a noun or with a descriptive word or phrase. Linking verbs connect the subject with words that tell what the subject *is* or *is like.* For example:

He **was** a talented boxer.

In the preceding sentence, the linking verb *was* connects the subject (he) with words that tell what the subject is like (a talented boxer).

Practice Look for two or three sentences in "Amigo Brothers" that have action and linking verbs. Write down the sentences and identify the action verb or the linking verb in each.

Speaking and Listening

Literature Groups Antonio and Felix faced an ordeal that threatened their friendship. In order to remain friends, they decided to train for their fight separately. With your group, discuss other solutions they could have chosen. Make a list of the solutions. For each solution, write down details from the text that support the solution. Discuss why the solutions might have worked.

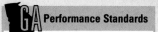 **Performance Standards**

For pages 36–37

ELA7C1a Identify and write simple, compound, complex, and compound-complex sentences correctly, combining sentences.

Grammar Workshop

Sentence Combining

Too many short sentences can make writing sound choppy or boring. In "Amigo Brothers," Piri Thomas uses varied sentence structure to create a lively and more personal style. Here are some ways you can combine sentences.

Prepositional Phrases

You can use a **prepositional phrase,** a group of words that begins with a preposition and ends with a noun or a pronoun.

> **Original:** Antonio wiped his face. He wiped his face with his short towel.
>
> **Combined:** Antonio wiped his face <u>with his short towel</u>.

Appositives

You can use an **appositive,** a noun or a pronoun placed next to another noun or pronoun to give additional information about it. An **appositive phrase** is an appositive plus any words that modify it.

> **Original:** Felix was his *amigo* brother. Felix was not going to be Felix at all in the ring.
>
> **Combined:** Felix, <u>his *amigo* brother</u>, was not going to be Felix at all in the ring.

Coordinating Conjunctions

You can use **coordinating conjunctions** to join words or groups of words with equal grammatical weight in a sentence. You can use coordinating conjunctions to form **compound sentences,** sentences that contain two or more simple sentences. Coordinating conjunctions include *and, but, so, or, nor, for,* and *yet.*

> **Original:** The scheduled bouts began shortly after noon. The park had begun filling up even earlier.
>
> **Combined:** The scheduled bouts began shortly after noon <u>and</u> the park had begun filling up even earlier.

Subordinating Conjunctions

You can use **subordinating conjunctions** to join two clauses, making one dependent upon (subordinate to) the other. They include words such as *after, although, as, because, if, since, when,* and *while.* Subordinating conjunctions introduce subordinate clauses, which have a subject and a predicate but can't stand alone as a sentence.

Tip

Watch out! Sometimes a preposition will have a compound object: two nouns or a noun and a pronoun.

Tip

Watch out! When two main clauses are connected by a coordinating conjunction, the first main clause often ends with a comma. Also, sometimes a semicolon is used instead of a coordinating conjunction to join main clauses.

You can use subordinating conjunctions to form **complex sentences,** sentences that contain a main clause and one or more subordinate clauses.

> **Original:** The two climbed into the ring. The crowd exploded with a roar.
>
> **Combined:** <u>As</u> the two climbed into the ring, the crowd exploded with a roar.

You can also use coordinating conjunctions with subordinating conjunctions to make **compound-complex sentences,** sentences with more than one main clause and at least one subordinate clause.

> **Original:** The bell rang. The crowd silenced. The announcer began to speak.
>
> **Combined:** After the bell rang, the crowd silenced and the announcer began to speak.

Adjective Clauses

You can use an **adjective clause,** a group of words with a subject and a predicate that modify a noun or a pronoun. Adjective clauses often begin with *who, whom, whose, that,* or *which.*

> **Original:** It seemed to impress the brothers. They went about their own business.
>
> **Combined:** It seemed to impress the brothers, <u>who went about their own business.</u>

TRY IT: Sentence Combining

Write a sentence that combines the sentences.

1. *Antonio's long reach made him a better boxer.*
   Felix's muscular frame made him a better slugger.

   Coordinating conjunction: *but*

2. *The referee watched.*
   Antonio charged toward Felix.

   Subordinating conjunction: *while*

3. *The bell rang.*
   The referee pried Antonio and Felix apart.
   Both boxers went to their corners.

   Subordinating conjunction: *as*
   Coordinating conjunction: *and*

Tip

Helpful Hint Using subordinating conjunctions is very helpful when you want to tell *how, when, where, why,* or *under what conditions* the action occurs.

Tip

Watch out! When a subordinate clause appears at the beginning of a sentence, a comma is used to separate it from the main clause.

 Literature Online

Grammar For more grammar practice, go to glencoe.com and enter QuickPass code GL27534u1.

Rikki-tikki-tavi

Connect to the Short Story

The mongoose in this story bravely protects a family from a pair of dangerous snakes. Think about a time when you protected someone or someone protected you.

Partner Talk With a partner, talk about a time when you were responsible for someone. How did you care for the person? What skills did you use? How did you feel as you were caring for the person?

Build Background

This short story tells of the adventures of several animals native to India.

- A mongoose is a small mammal known for its ability to kill snakes. Mongooses grow to an average length of only about sixteen inches, but their lightning speed makes them fearsome enemies of snakes.

- The king cobra is one of the largest poisonous snakes in the world. It can reach sixteen feet in length, and its venom is deadly.

- The tailorbird actually sews! It punches holes in several leaves and then weaves leaf stems or stolen thread through the holes to form its nest.

Vocabulary

restless (rest′lis) *adj.* nervous, unable to keep still (p. 40). *Anxious before the test, Diego seemed restless as he paced the room.*

cultivated (kul′tə vā′tid) *adj.* prepared for growing plants and free from weeds (p. 43). *Mrs. Li tended her flower beds until they were neatly cultivated.*

cowered (kou′ərd) *v.* crouched or drawn back in fear (p. 43). *The cat cowered at the sight of the huge dog.*

valiant (val′yənt) *adj.* brave; courageous (p. 51). *The firefighters made a valiant attempt to control the blaze.*

Meet Rudyard Kipling

Nobel Prize Winner Rudyard Kipling was born to English parents in Bombay, India. Though Kipling was sent to live in England at age five, India made a deep impression on him. Kipling returned to India at age seventeen to work as a journalist. He began to travel widely and publish stories and poems about Indian culture under English rule.

Literary Works Kipling is the author of novels, poetry, and short story collections including *The Jungle Book.* In 1907, Kipling became the first British writer to win the Nobel Prize in Literature.

Kipling was born in 1865 and died in 1936.

 Literature Online

Author Search For more about Rudyard Kipling, go to glencoe.com and enter QuickPass code GL27534u1.

Set Purposes for Reading

BQ BIG Question

As you read, ask yourself, who is the family in the story able to count on for protection?

Literary Element Setting

Setting is the time and place in which the events of a story occur. Setting includes values, traditions, and customs that are connected to the time and place of the story.

Writers use setting to create atmosphere, or mood. For example, a writer may use a stormy night and a run-down house to create a gloomy setting for a mystery story. Concrete details, such as "an abandoned house in the middle of a dense Kentucky forest," and sensory details, such as "the damp, poorly lit hallway," can help to create a vivid picture.

Try forming a picture in your mind of the house and garden in the story. As you read, ask yourself, which details in the story help me to visualize the house and garden?

Reading Skill Identify Sequence

Identifying sequence means understanding the order, or sequence, of events in a story. The events in a story usually take place in chronological order, or time order. Identifying sequence as you read will help you stay involved with the story. Identifying sequence can also help you understand how one event in the story is related to past or future events in the story.

To identify sequence, look for signal words that help you identify the order in which events occurred. Words and phrases such as *meanwhile, before, after, later, first, then, earlier, next, eventually,* and *last* tell you when something happened. You may find it helpful to use a timeline like the one below.

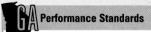

GA Performance Standards

For pages 38–58

ELA7R1e For literary texts, identify events that advance the plot and determine how each event explains past or present action(s) or foreshadows future action(s).

> **TRY IT**
>
> **Identify Sequence** With a partner describe how you get ready for school in the morning, using such words as *first, next, then,* and *last.*

Rikki-tikki-tavi

Rudyard Kipling

Mungos fasciatus, November 1836. Edward Lear. Watercolor on paper. 36.4 x 53.4 cm. ©The Right Honorable Earl of Derby. Private Collection.

*T*his is the story of the great war that Rikki-tikki-tavi fought single-handed, through the bathrooms of the big **bungalow** in Segowlee cantonment.[1] Darzee, the tailorbird, helped him, and Chuchundra, the muskrat, who never comes out into the middle of the floor, but always creeps round by the wall, gave him advice; but Rikki-tikki did the real fighting.

He was a mongoose, rather like a little cat in his fur and his tail, but quite like a weasel in his head and his habits. His eyes and the end of his **restless** nose were pink; he could scratch himself anywhere he pleased, with any leg, front or back, that he chose to use; he could fluff up his tail till it looked like a bottle brush, and his war cry, as he scuttled[2] through the long grass, was *"Rikk-tikk-tikki-tikki-tchk!"*

1 In India, a *cantonment* was a British military "town," where servicemen and their families lived in separate bungalows, or cottages.

2 *Scuttled* means moved with short, rapid steps.

Vocabulary

restless (rest′lis) *adj.* nervous, unable to keep still

Visual Vocabulary

Bungalow is an Anglo-Indian variation of the Hindu word *bangala*. In India, it is a one-story house, usually with a wide porch.

One day, a high summer flood washed him out of the burrow where he lived with his father and mother, and carried him, kicking and clucking, down a roadside ditch. He found a little wisp of grass floating there, and clung to it till he lost his senses. When he revived, he was lying in the hot sun on the middle of a garden path, very draggled[3] indeed, and a small boy was saying: "Here's a dead mongoose. Let's have a funeral."

"No," said his mother: "let's take him in and dry him. Perhaps he isn't really dead."

They took him into the house, and a big man picked him up between his finger and thumb and said he was not dead but half choked; so they wrapped him in cotton wool and warmed him, and he opened his eyes and sneezed.

"Now," said the big man (he was an Englishman who had just moved into the bungalow), "don't frighten him, and we'll see what he'll do."

It is the hardest thing in the world to frighten a mongoose, because he is eaten up from nose to tail with curiosity. The motto of all the mongoose family is "Run and find out"; and Rikki-tikki was a true mongoose. He looked at the cotton wool, decided that it was not good to eat, ran all round the table, sat up and put his fur in order, scratched himself, and jumped on the small boy's shoulder.

"Don't be frightened, Teddy," said his father. "That's his way of making friends."

"Ouch! He's tickling under my chin," said Teddy.

Rikki-tikki looked down between the boy's collar and neck, snuffed at his ear, and climbed down to the floor, where he sat rubbing his nose.

"Good gracious," said Teddy's mother, "and that's a wild creature! I suppose he's so tame because we've been kind to him."

"All mongooses are like that," said her husband. "If Teddy doesn't pick him up by the tail, or try to put him in a cage, he'll run in and out of the house all day long. Let's give him something to eat."

Setting Which details in this paragraph help you visualize the setting of Rikki's adventure?

---

3 Rikki-tikki was *draggled,* or wet and dirty.

They gave him a little piece of raw meat. Rikki-tikki liked it immensely, and when it was finished he went out into the **veranda** and sat in the sunshine and fluffed up his fur to make it dry to the roots. Then he felt better.

"There are more things to find out about in this house," he said to himself, "than all my family could find out in all their lives. I shall certainly stay and find out."

He spent all that day roaming over the house. He nearly drowned himself in the bathtubs, put his nose into the ink on a writing table, and burned it on the end of the big man's cigar, for he climbed up in the big man's lap to see how writing was done. At nightfall he ran into Teddy's nursery to watch how kerosene lamps[4] were lighted, and when Teddy went to bed Rikki-tikki climbed up too; but he was a restless companion, because he had to get up and attend to every noise all through the night and find out what made it. Teddy's mother and father came in, the last thing, to look at their boy, and Rikki-tikki was awake on the pillow. "I don't like that," said Teddy's mother; "he may bite the child."

"He'll do no such thing," said the father. "Teddy's safer with that little beast than if he had a bloodhound to watch him. If a snake came into the nursery now—"

But Teddy's mother wouldn't think of anything so awful.

Early in the morning Rikki-tikki came to early breakfast in the veranda, riding on Teddy's shoulder, and they gave him banana and some boiled egg; and he sat on all their laps one after the other, because every well-brought-up mongoose always hopes to be a house mongoose someday and have rooms to run about in, and Rikki-tikki's mother (she used to live in the general's house at Segowlee) had carefully told Rikki what to do if ever he came across Englishmen.

Then Rikki-tikki went out into the garden to see what was to be seen. It was a large garden,

Identify Sequence What are the events of Rikki-tikki's first day at the house?

Tent Hanging. Early 18th century, Mughal (Jaipur?). Cotton quilt embroidered in silk. Victoria and Albert Museum, London.
View the Art How might the characters in "Rikki-tikki-tavi" have used a tent hanging? What do you think would have been its original use?

---

4 A *kerosene lamp* burns a liquid fuel made from petroleum.

only half **cultivated,** with bushes as big as summer houses of roses, lime and orange trees, clumps of bamboos, and thickets of high grass. Rikki-tikki licked his lips. "This is a splendid hunting ground," he said, and his tail grew bottle-brushy at the thought of it, and he scuttled up and down the garden, snuffling here and there till he heard very sorrowful voices in a thornbush.

It was Darzee, the tailorbird, and his wife. They had made a beautiful nest by pulling two big leaves together and stitching them up the edges with fibers, and had filled the hollow with cotton and downy fluff. The nest swayed to and fro, as they sat on the brim and cried.

"What is the matter?" asked Rikki-tikki.

"We are very miserable," said Darzee. "One of our babies fell out of the nest yesterday, and Nag ate him."

"H'm!" said Rikki-tikki; "that is very sad—but I am a stranger here. Who is Nag?"

Darzee and his wife only **cowered** down in the nest without answering, for from the thick grass at the foot of the bush came a low hiss—a horrid cold sound that made Rikki-tikki jump back two clear feet. Then inch by inch out of the grass rose up the head and spread hood of Nag, the big black cobra, and he was five feet long from tongue to tail. When he had lifted one third of himself clear of the ground, he stayed balancing to and fro exactly as a dandelion tuft balances in the wind, and he looked at Rikki-tikki with the wicked snake's eyes that never change their expression, whatever the snake may be thinking of.

"Who is Nag?" he said. "*I* am Nag. The great god Brahm put his mark upon all our people when the first cobra spread his hood to keep the sun off Brahm as he slept. Look, and be afraid!"

He spread out his hood more than ever, and Rikki-tikki saw the spectacle mark on the back of it that looks exactly like the eye part of a hook-and-eye fastening. He was afraid for the minute; but it is impossible for a mongoose

Setting Which details of the setting contribute to the mood of Nag's entrance?

Vocabulary

cultivated (kul′tə vā tid) *adj.* prepared for growing plants and free from weeds

cowered (kou′ərd) *v.* crouched or drawn back in fear

to stay frightened for any length of time, and though Rikki-tikki had never met a live cobra before, his mother had fed him on dead ones, and he knew that all a grown mongoose's business in life was to fight and eat snakes. Nag knew that too, and at the bottom of his cold heart he was afraid.

"Well," said Rikki-tikki, and his tail began to fluff up again, "marks or no marks, do you think it is right for you to eat fledglings[5] out of a nest?"

Nag was thinking to himself, and watching the least little movement in the grass behind Rikki-tikki. He knew that mongooses in the garden meant death sooner or later for him and his family, but he wanted to get Rikki-tikki off his guard. So he dropped his head a little and put it on one side.

"Let us talk," he said. "You eat eggs. Why should not I eat birds?"

"Behind you! Look behind you!" sang Darzee.

Rikki-tikki knew better than to waste time in staring. He jumped up in the air as high as he could go, and just under him whizzed by the head of Nagaina, Nag's wicked wife. She had crept up behind him as he was talking, to make an end of him; and he heard her savage hiss as the stroke missed. He came down almost across her back, and if he had been an old mongoose, he would have known that then was the time to break her back with one bite; but he was afraid of the terrible lashing return stroke of the cobra. He bit, indeed, but did not bite long enough, and he jumped clear of the whisking tail, leaving Nagaina torn and angry.

"Wicked, wicked Darzee!" said Nag, lashing up as high as he could reach toward the nest in the thornbush; but Darzee had built it out of the reach of snakes, and it only swayed to and fro.

Rikki-tikki felt his eyes growing red and hot (when a mongoose's eyes grow red, he is angry), and he sat back on his tail and hind legs like a little kangaroo, and looked all around him, and chattered with rage. But Nag and Nagaina had disappeared into the grass. When a snake misses its

King Cobra meets his Match from "Nature's Kingdom." Susan Cartwright. Gouache on paper. Private collection.

Identify Sequence What happens just before Rikki-tikki jumps in the air?

---

5 *Fledglings* are young birds that haven't yet grown the feathers needed to fly.

stroke, it never says anything or gives any sign of what it means to do next. Rikki-tikki did not care to follow them, for he did not feel sure that he could manage two snakes at once. So he trotted off to the gravel path near the house, and sat down to think. It was a serious matter for him.

If you read the old books of natural history, you will find they say that when the mongoose fights the snake and happens to get bitten, he runs off and eats some herb that cures him. That is not true. The victory is only a matter of quickness of eye and quickness of foot—snake's blow against mongoose's jump—and as no eye can follow the motion of a snake's head when it strikes, that makes things much more wonderful than any magic herb. Rikki-tikki knew he was a young mongoose, and it made him all the more pleased to think that he had managed to escape a blow from behind. It gave him confidence in himself, and when Teddy came running down the path, Rikki-tikki was ready to be petted.

But just as Teddy was stooping, something flinched[6] a little in the dust, and a tiny voice said: "Be careful. I am death!" It was Karait, the dusty brown snakeling that lies for choice on the dusty earth; and his bite is as dangerous as the cobra's. But he is so small that nobody thinks of him, and so he does the more harm to people.

Rikki-tikki's eyes grew red again, and he danced up to Karait with the peculiar rocking, swaying motion that he had inherited from his family. It looks very funny, but it is so perfectly balanced a gait[7] that you can fly off from it at any angle you please; and in dealing with snakes this is an advantage. If Rikki-tikki had only known, he was doing a much more dangerous thing than fighting Nag, for Karait is so small, and can turn so quickly, that unless Rikki bit him close to the back of the head, he would get the return stroke in his eye or lip. But Rikki did not know: his eyes were all red, and he rocked back and forth, looking for a good place to hold. Karait struck out. Rikki jumped sideways and tried to run in, but the wicked little dusty gray head lashed

BQ BIG Question

How does Rikki-tikki prove himself to be someone on whom this family can count?

---

6 *Flinched* means drew back, as from something painful, dangerous, or unpleasant.

7 A *gait* is a particular manner of moving on foot.

Rikki-Tikki-Tavi, illustration from 'The Jungle Book' by Rudyard Kipling. Andre Collot. Published in Paris, 1937. Color lithograph. Bibliotheque Nationale, Paris. Archives Charmet.

within a fraction of his shoulder, and he had to jump over the body, and the head followed his heels close.

Teddy shouted to the house: "Oh, look here! Our mongoose is killing a snake"; and Rikki-tikki heard a scream from Teddy's mother. His father ran out with a stick, but by the time he came up, Karait had lunged[8] out once too far, and Rikki-tikki had sprung, jumped on the snake's back, dropped his head far between his forelegs, bitten as high up the back as he could get hold, and rolled away. That bite paralyzed Karait, and Rikki-tikki was just going to eat him up from the tail, after the custom of his family at dinner, when he remembered that a full meal makes a slow mongoose, and if he wanted all his strength and quickness ready, he must keep himself thin.

He went away for a dust bath under the castor-oil bushes, while Teddy's father beat the dead Karait. "What

Identify Sequence Reread the last two paragraphs. Which signal words help you identify the sequence of events?

---

8 When Karait **lunged,** he made a sudden forward movement.

is the use of that?" thought Rikki-tikki. "I have settled it all"; and then Teddy's mother picked him up from the dust and hugged him, crying that he had saved Teddy from death, and Teddy's father said that he was a providence,[9] and Teddy looked on with big scared eyes. Rikki-tikki was rather amused at all the fuss, which, of course, he did not understand. Teddy's mother might just as well have petted Teddy for playing in the dust. Rikki was thoroughly enjoying himself.

That night, at dinner, walking to and fro among the wineglasses on the table, he could have stuffed himself three times over with nice things; but he remembered Nag and Nagaina, and though it was very pleasant to be patted and petted by Teddy's mother, and to sit on Teddy's shoulder, his eyes would get red from time to time, and he would go off into his long war cry of *"Rikk-tikk-tikki-tikki-tchk!"*

Teddy carried him off to bed and insisted on Rikki-tikki sleeping under his chin. Rikki-tikki was too well bred to bite or scratch, but as soon as Teddy was asleep he went off for his nightly walk round the house, and in the dark he ran up against Chuchundra, the muskrat, creeping round by the wall. Chuchundra is a broken-hearted little beast. He whimpers and cheeps all the night, trying to make up his mind to run into the middle of the room, but he never gets there.

"Don't kill me," said Chuchundra, almost weeping. "Rikki-tikki, don't kill me."

"Do you think a snake-killer kills muskrats?" said Rikki-tikki scornfully.

"Those who kill snakes get killed by snakes," said Chuchundra, more sorrowfully than ever. "And how am I to be sure that Nag won't mistake me for you some dark night?"

"There's not the least danger," said Rikki-tikki; "but Nag is in the garden, and I know you don't go there."

"My cousin Chua, the rat, told me—" said Chuchundra, and then he stopped.

Identify Sequence What happens just before Rikki-tikki meets Chuchundra?

---

9 A *providence* is a blessing from God or nature.

"Told you what?"

"H'sh! Nag is everywhere, Rikki-tikki. You should have talked to Chua in the garden."

"I didn't—so you must tell me. Quick, Chuchundra, or I'll bite you!"

Chuchundra sat down and cried till the tears rolled off his whiskers. "I am a very poor man," he sobbed. "I never had spirit enough to run out into the middle of the room. H'sh! I mustn't tell you anything. Can't you *hear*, Rikki-tikki?"

Rikki-tikki listened. The house was as still as still, but he thought he could just catch the faintest *scratch-scratch* in the world—a noise as faint as that of a wasp walking on a windowpane—the dry scratch of a snake's scales on brickwork.

"That's Nag or Nagaina," he said to himself; "and he is crawling into the bathroom sluice.[10] You're right, Chuchundra; I should have talked to Chua."

He stole off to Teddy's bathroom, but there was nothing there, and then to Teddy's mother's bathroom. At the bottom of the smooth plaster wall there was a brick pulled out to make a sluice for the bath water, and as Rikki-tikki stole in by the masonry curb where the bath is put, he heard Nag and Nagaina whispering together outside in the moonlight.

"When the house is emptied of people," said Nagaina to her husband, "*he* will have to go away, and then the garden will be our own again. Go in quietly, and remember that the big man who killed Karait is the first one to bite. Then come out and tell me, and we will hunt for Rikki-tikki together."

"But are you sure there is anything to be gained by killing the people?" said Nag.

"Everything. When there were no people in the bungalow, did we have any mongoose in the garden? So long as the bungalow is empty, we are king and queen of the garden; and remember that as soon as our eggs in the melon bed hatch (as they may tomorrow), our children will need room and quiet."

Setting How do details of the setting help you visualize the action of the story?

---

10 Here, the *sluice* is a drainpipe.

"I had not thought of that," said Nag. "I will go, but there is no need that we should hunt for Rikki-tikki afterward. I will kill the big man and his wife, and the child if I can, and come away quietly. Then the bungalow will be empty, and Rikki-tikki will go."

Rikki-tikki tingled all over with rage and hatred at this, and then Nag's head came through the sluice, and his five feet of cold body followed it. Angry as he was, Rikki-tikki was very frightened as he saw the size of the big cobra. Nag coiled himself up, raised his head, and looked into the bathroom in the dark, and Rikki could see his eyes glitter.

"Now, if I kill him there, Nagaina will know; and if I fight him on the open floor, the odds are in his favor. What am I to do?" said Rikki-tikki-tavi.

Nag waved to and fro, and then Rikki-tikki heard him drinking from the biggest water jar that was used to fill the bath. "That is good," said the snake. "Now, when Karait was killed, the big man had a stick. He may have that stick still, but when he comes in to bathe in the morning he will not have a stick. I shall wait here till he comes. Nagaina—do you hear me? I shall wait here in the cool till daytime."

There was no answer from outside, so Rikki-tikki knew Nagaina had gone away. Nag coiled himself down, coil by coil, round the bulge at the bottom of the water jar, and Rikki-tikki stayed still as death. After an hour he began to move, muscle by muscle, toward the jar. Nag was asleep, and Rikki-tikki looked at his big back, wondering which would be the best place for a good hold. "If I don't break his back at the first jump," said Rikki, "he can still fight; and if he fights—O Rikki!" He looked at the thickness of the neck below the hood, but that was too much for him; and a bite near the tail would only make Nag savage.

"It must be the head," he said at last; "the head above the hood; and when I am once there, I must not let go."

Then he jumped. The head was lying a little clear of the water jar, under the curve of it; and, as his teeth met, Rikki braced his back against the bulge of the red earthenware to hold down the head. This gave him just one second's

Identify Sequence What steps does Nag plan to take to get rid of Rikki-tikki?

purchase,[11] and he made the most of it. Then he was battered to and fro as a rat is shaken by a dog—to and fro on the floor, up and down, and round in great circles; but his eyes were red, and he held on as the body cartwhipped[12] over the floor, upsetting the tin dipper and the soap dish and the fleshbrush, and banged against the tin side of the bath. As he held, he closed his jaws tighter and tighter, for he made sure he would be banged to death, and, for the honor of his family, he preferred to be found with his teeth locked. He was dizzy, aching, and felt shaken to pieces when something went off like a thunderclap just behind him; a hot wind knocked him senseless, and red fire singed his fur. The big man had been wakened by the noise, and had fired both barrels of a shotgun into Nag just behind the hood.

Rikki-tikki held on with his eyes shut, for now he was quite sure he was dead; but the head did not move, and the big man picked him up and said: "It's the mongoose again, Alice; the little chap has saved *our* lives now." Then Teddy's mother came in with a very white face, and saw what was left of Nag, and Rikki-tikki dragged himself to Teddy's bedroom and spent half the rest of the night shaking himself tenderly to find out whether he really was broken into forty pieces, as he fancied.[13]

When morning came he was very stiff, but well pleased with his doings. "Now I have Nagaina to settle with, and she will be worse than five Nags, and there's no knowing when the eggs she spoke of will hatch. Goodness! I must go and see Darzee," he said.

Without waiting for breakfast, Rikki-tikki ran to the thornbush where Darzee was singing a song of triumph at the top of his voice. The news of Nag's death was all over the garden, for the sweeper had thrown the body on the rubbish heap.

"Oh, you stupid tuft of feathers!" said Rikki-tikki angrily. "Is this the time to sing?"

BQ BIG Question
Why does Rikki-tikki protect Teddy and his parents?

---

11 In this context, **purchase** is an advantageous position for applying force.

12 Rikki's body is being thrown about like a whip (**cartwhipped**) as the cobra lashes.

13 **Fancied** means "imagined" or "pictured mentally."

"Nag is dead—is dead—is dead!" sang Darzee. "The **valiant** Rikki-tikki caught him by the head and held fast. The big man brought the bang-stick, and Nag fell in two pieces! He will never eat my babies again."

"All that's true enough; but where's Nagaina?" said Rikki-tikki, looking carefully round him.

"Nagaina came to the bathroom sluice and called for Nag," Darzee went on; "and Nag came out on the end of a stick—the sweeper picked him up on the end of a stick and threw him upon the rubbish heap. Let us sing about the great, the red-eyed Rikki-tikki!" And Darzee filled his throat and sang.

"If I could get up to your nest, I'd roll all your babies out!" said Rikki-tikki. "You don't know when to do the right thing at the right time. You're safe enough in your nest there, but it's war for me down here. Stop singing a minute, Darzee."

"For the great, the beautiful Rikki-tikki's sake I will stop," said Darzee. "What is it, O Killer of the terrible Nag?"

"Where is Nagaina, for the third time?"

"On the rubbish heap by the stables, mourning for Nag. Great is Rikki-tikki with the white teeth."

"Bother my white teeth![14] Have you ever heard where she keeps her eggs?"

"In the melon bed, on the end nearest the wall, where the sun strikes nearly all day. She hid them there weeks ago."

"And you never thought it worthwhile to tell me? The end nearest the wall, you said?"

"Rikki-tikki, you are not going to eat her eggs?"

"Not eat exactly; no. Darzee, if you have a grain of sense you will fly off to the stables and pretend that your wing is broken, and let Nagaina chase you away to this bush! I must get to the melon bed, and if I went there now she'd see me."

Identify Sequence Why is it important for Darzee to fly to the stables before Rikki-tikki goes to the melon bed?

---

14 ***Bother my white teeth*** is a British way of saying, "Don't concern yourself with my teeth."

Vocabulary

valiant (val′yənt) *adj.* brave; courageous.

Darzee was a featherbrained little fellow who could never hold more than one idea at a time in his head; and just because he knew that Nagaina's children were born in eggs like his own, he didn't think at first that it was fair to kill them. But his wife was a sensible bird, and she knew that cobras' eggs meant young cobras later on; so she flew off from the nest, and left Darzee to keep the babies warm, and continue his song about the death of Nag. Darzee was very like a man in some ways.

She fluttered in front of Nagaina by the rubbish heap and cried out, "Oh, my wing is broken! The boy in the house threw a stone at me and broke it." Then she fluttered more desperately than ever.

Nagaina lifted up her head and hissed, "You warned Rikki-tikki when I would have killed him. Indeed and truly, you've chosen a bad place to be lame in." And she moved toward Darzee's wife, slipping along over the dust.

"The boy broke it with a stone!" shrieked Darzee's wife.

"Well! It may be some consolation to you when you're dead to know that I shall settle accounts with the boy. My husband lies on the rubbish heap this morning, but before night the boy in the house will lie very still. What is the use of running away? I am sure to catch you. Little fool, look at me!"

Darzee's wife knew better than to do *that*, for a bird who looks at a snake's eyes gets so frightened that she cannot move. Darzee's wife fluttered on, piping sorrowfully, and never leaving the ground, and Nagaina quickened her pace.

Rikki-tikki heard them going up the path from the stables, and he raced for the end of the melon patch near the wall. There, in the warm litter about the melons, very cunningly hidden, he found twenty-five eggs, about the size of a bantam's eggs, but with whitish skin instead of shell.

"I was not a day too soon," he said; for he could see the baby cobras curled up inside

Rikki-Tikki-Tavi, illustration from 'The Jungle Book' by Rudyard Kipling. Published in Paris, 1930. Louis Joseph Soulas. Bibliotheque Nationale, Paris. Archives Charmet.

the skin, and he knew that the minute they were hatched they could each kill a man or a mongoose. He bit off the tops of the eggs as fast as he could, taking care to crush the young cobras, and turned over the litter from time to time to see whether he had missed any. At last there were only three eggs left, and Rikki-tikki began to chuckle to himself, when he heard Darzee's wife screaming:

"Rikki-tikki, I led Nagaina toward the house, and she has gone into the veranda, and—oh, come quickly—she means killing!"

Rikki-tikki smashed two eggs, and tumbled backward down the melon bed with the third egg in his mouth, and scuttled to the veranda as hard as he could put foot to the ground. Teddy and his mother and father were there at early breakfast; but Rikki-tikki saw that they were not eating anything. They sat stone-still, and their faces were white. Nagaina was coiled up on the matting by Teddy's chair, within easy striking distance of Teddy's bare leg, and she was swaying to and fro singing a song of triumph.

"Son of the big man that killed Nag," she hissed, "stay still. I am not ready yet. Wait a little. Keep very still, all you three. If you move I strike, and if you do not move I strike. Oh, foolish people, who killed my Nag!"

Teddy's eyes were fixed on his father, and all his father could do was to whisper, "Sit still, Teddy. You mustn't move. Teddy, keep still."

Then Rikki-tikki came up and cried: "Turn round, Nagaina; turn and fight!"

"All in good time," said she, without moving her eyes. "I will settle my account with *you* presently. Look at your friends, Rikki-tikki. They are still and white; they are afraid. They dare not move, and if you come a step nearer I strike."

"Look at your eggs," said Rikki-tikki, "in the melon bed near the wall. Go and look, Nagaina."

The big snake turned half round and saw the egg on the veranda. "Ah-h! Give it to me," she said.

Rikki-tikki put his paws one on each side of the egg, and his eyes were blood-red. "What price for a snake's egg? For a young cobra? For a young king cobra? For the

Identify Sequence Why does Rikki-tikki destroy the eggs before they hatch?

last—the very last of the brood?[15] The ants are eating all the others down by the melon bed."

Nagaina spun clear round, forgetting everything for the sake of the one egg; and Rikki-tikki saw Teddy's father shoot out a big hand, catch Teddy by the shoulder, and drag him across the little table with the teacups, safe and out of reach of Nagaina.

"Tricked! Tricked! Tricked! *Rikk-tck-tck!*" chuckled Rikki-tikki. "The boy is safe, and it was I—I—I that caught Nag by the hood last night in the bathroom." Then he began to jump up and down, all four feet together, his head close to the floor. "He threw me to and fro, but he could not shake me off. He was dead before the big man blew him in two. I did it. *Rikki-tikki-tck-tck!* Come then, Nagaina. Come and fight with me. You shall not be a widow long."

Nagaina saw that she had lost her chance of killing Teddy, and the egg lay between Rikki-tikki's paws. "Give me the egg, Rikki-tikki. Give me the last of my eggs, and I will go away and never come back," she said, lowering her hood.

"Yes, you will go away, and you will never come back; for you will go to the rubbish heap with Nag. Fight, widow! The big man has gone for his gun! Fight!"

Rikki-tikki was bounding all round Nagaina, keeping just out of reach of her stroke, his little eyes like hot coals. Nagaina gathered herself together and flung out at him. Rikki-tikki jumped up and backward. Again and again and again she struck, and each time her head came with a whack on the matting of the veranda, and she gathered herself together like a watchspring. Then Rikki-tikki danced in a circle to get behind her, and Nagaina spun round to keep her head to his head, so that the rustle of her tail on the matting sounded like dry leaves blown along by the wind.

He had forgotten the egg. It still lay on the veranda, and Nagaina came nearer and nearer to it, till at last, while Rikki-tikki was drawing breath, she caught it in her mouth, turned to the veranda steps, and flew like an

Identify Sequence What events lead up to Nagaina taking back her egg from Rikki-tikki?

---

15 A **brood** is all of the young of an animal that are born or cared for at the same time.

arrow down the path, with Rikki-tikki behind her. When the cobra runs for her life, she goes like a whiplash flicked across a horse's neck.

Rikki-tikki knew that he must catch her, or all the trouble would begin again. She headed straight for the long grass by the thornbush, and as he was running Rikki-tikki heard Darzee singing his foolish little song of triumph. But Darzee's wife was wiser. She flew off her nest as Nagaina came along, and flapped her wings about Nagaina's head. If Darzee had helped they might have turned her; but Nagaina only lowered her hood and went on. Still, the instant's delay brought Rikki-tikki up to her, and as she plunged into the rathole where she and Nag used to live, his little white teeth were clenched on her tail, and he went down with her—and very few mongooses, however wise and old they may be, care to follow a cobra into its hole. It was dark in the hole; and Rikki-tikki never knew when it might open out and give Nagaina room to turn and strike at him. He held on savagely and struck out his feet to act as brakes on the dark slope of the hot, moist earth.

Then the grass by the mouth of the hole stopped waving, and Darzee said: "It is all over with Rikki-tikki! We must sing his death song. Valiant Rikki-tikki is dead. For Nagaina will surely kill him underground."

So he sang a very mournful song that he made up all on the spur of the minute, and just as he got to the most touching part the grass quivered again, and Rikki-tikki, covered with dirt, dragged himself out of the hole leg by leg, licking his whiskers. Darzee stopped with a little shout. Rikki-tikki shook some of the dust out of his fur and sneezed. "It is all over," he said. "The widow will never come out again." And the red ants that live between the grass stems heard him, and began to troop down one after another to see if he had spoken the truth.

Rikki-tikki curled himself up in the grass and slept where he was—slept and slept till it was late in the afternoon, for he had done a hard day's work.

"Now," he said, when he awoke, "I will go back to the house. Tell the coppersmith, Darzee, and he will tell the garden that Nagaina is dead."

BQ BIG Question
Whom can Rikki-tikki count on to help him catch up with Nagaina? Who fails him?

Setting How does the setting of the final battle increase the suspense?

The coppersmith is a bird who makes a noise exactly like the beating of a little hammer on a copper pot; and the reason he is always making it is because he is the town crier to every Indian garden, and tells all the news to everybody who cares to listen. As Rikki-tikki went up the path, he heard his "attention" notes like a tiny dinner gong; and then the steady "*Ding-dong-tock! Nag is dead—dong! Nagaina is dead! Ding-dong-tock!*" That set all the birds in the garden singing, and the frogs croaking, for Nag and Nagaina used to eat frogs as well as little birds.

Setting How does the setting and mood of the story change after Nagaina is killed?

When Rikki got to the house, Teddy and Teddy's mother (she still looked very white, for she had been fainting) and Teddy's father came out and almost cried over him; and that night he ate all that was given him till he could eat no more, and went to bed on Teddy's shoulder, where Teddy's mother saw him when she came to look late at night.

"He saved our lives and Teddy's life," she said to her husband. "Just think, he saved all our lives!"

Rikki-tikki woke up with a jump, for all mongooses are light sleepers.

"Oh, it's you," said he. "What are you bothering for? All the cobras are dead; and if they weren't, I'm here."

Rikki-tikki had a right to be proud of himself; but he did not grow too proud, and he kept that garden as a mongoose should keep it, with tooth and jump and spring and bite, till never a cobra dared show its head inside the walls. 🐾

After You Read

Respond and Think Critically

1. What is Rikki-tikki's "great war"? Describe Darzee and Chuchundra. Explain how they help Rikki-tikki. [Recall]

2. How does Kipling call attention to Rikki-tikki's bravery? List two incidents in the story that illustrate Rikki-tikki's courage. [Analyze]

3. Why do you think Kipling starts the story with an account of the rescue of Rikki-tikki? Explain. [Interpret]

4. Compare the characters of Nag and Nagaina. Which one is more sympathetic, or likeable? Use examples from the story to support your answer. [Compare]

5. How does the family count on Rikki-tikki's cleverness? [Evaluate]

6. **BQ** **BIG Question** What traits or characteristics make Rikki-tikki someone to be counted on? Explain. [Connect]

TIP

Interpreting
Writers include details in the beginning of a story to introduce the characters and foreshadow later events. To answer question 3, think about what the family does for Rikki-tikki at the beginning of the story. Then, consider how Rikki-tikki repays them later.

FOLDABLES Study Organizer Keep track of your ideas about the **BIG Question** in your unit Foldable.

Daily Life and Culture

Colonial India

The story takes place in India during the late 1800s, a time when the British ruled India. Many British government officials had administrative jobs there. They lived, with their families, in large, elegant bungalows. The British official was the *sahib,* or master, of the house. The official's wife was the *memsahib.*

The cottages of Indian servants surrounded the main house. A typical British family could have as many as 25 servants. Indians served as cooks, maids, butlers, gardeners, tailors, and nannies for the children.

The British brought improvements to India, including railroads, a telegraph system, and a postal system. However, British rule was unfair to the vast majority of Indians. The best housing and jobs were reserved for the British. Indians were not allowed to advance to high positions in the colonial government or to become officers in the army.

Group Activity Discuss the following questions with your classmates.

1. Review the information about colonial India presented above. How does the information that you just read influence your impressions of the family in the story? Explain.

2. What aspects of life in colonial India do you see reflected in the story? Explain.

Literary Element Setting

1. Given the setting, what advantages does Rikki-tikki have in his fight with Nag and Nagaina?

2. How might this story be different if it were set in another time or place? Explain what the setting contributes to the story.

Review: Plot

As you learned on page **19, plot** is the sequence of events in a story. The plot often centers on a **conflict,** or central struggle between opposing forces. Conflict is an important part of a story because it moves the plot forward.

Standards Practice ELA7R1e

3. The conflict in the story is
   A   Nag's internal struggle.
   B   Rikki's internal struggle.
   C   an external struggle between the cobras and Rikki.
   D   an external struggle between Rikki and the family.

Reading Skill Identify Sequence

Standards Practice ELA7R1e

4. What event happened before Rikki killed Karait?

   A   Rikki met Nag at night and killed him.
   B   A British family rescued Rikki.
   C   Karait bit Teddy.
   D   Nagaina tried to save her last egg from Rikki.

Vocabulary Practice

Choose the sentence that uses the vocabulary word correctly.

A. Hakim hid during the storm because he was a **cowered**.

B. Hakim, terrified during the storm, **cowered** under his blanket.

A. Aisha was **restless** and paced from room to room.

B. Aisha was **restless** and calmly read a book during the long afternoon.

A. The soup was half **cultivated** before Maria added the salt.

B. Maria's garden was mulched and fully **cultivated** by the end of April.

A. Ella was **valiant**, protecting her younger sister from the vicious dog.

B. Ella was **valiant**, running with her younger sister from the tiny kitten.

Academic Vocabulary

Rikki-tikki-tavi's life with the British family **ensured** that a cobra would never again live inside the garden walls.

In the preceding sentence, *ensured* means "made sure or certain." Think about Rikki's plan to kill Nag. Where did he have to strike Nag to kill him? Then fill in the blank for this statement:

Rikki ensured his attack would kill Nag by _____.

Respond Through Writing

Summary

Report Story Events In "Rikki-tikki-tavi," Kipling relates the events of a "great war" in nature. Write a summary of the story, reporting on the events in the story.

Understand the Task When you summarize, you explain the main idea and the most important details in your own words. You probably summarize all the time—when you tell a friend about a movie, a book, or what happened in class yesterday. Writing a summary of something you read or heard can help you understand and remember the most important information.

Prewrite Think of the main, or most important, ideas. State them in your own words. Include important details. Leave out minor or unimportant details. Refer to the timeline you created as you read to help you pick out the most important ideas and details of the story.

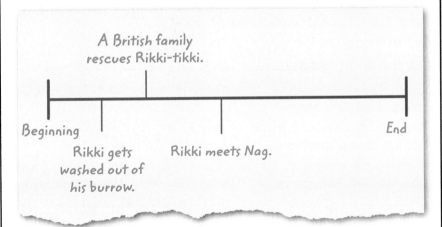

Draft Before you begin drafting, highlight the most important ideas and details on your timeline. Delete any unimportant events. Review sequence words, such as *then, next, after, meanwhile,* and *before,* to use in your summary.

Revise After you have written your first draft, read it to determine whether the events occur in the same order as in the story. Rearrange your summary as needed.

Edit and Proofread Proofread your paper, correcting any errors in spelling, grammar, and punctuation. Review the Grammar Tip in the side column for information on verb tense.

 **Performance Standards**

For page 59

ELA7W2b Produce a response to literature that demonstrates an understanding of the literary work.

> ## Grammar Tip

Verb Tense
Practice using the **literary present** verb tense in your summary. For example:

Rikki moves into a new territory where cobras live.

Keep the verb tense consistent in your summary. If you use more than one tense, readers will be confused about when events happen. You can use the literary present tense to discuss an author, too. For example:

Kipling uses descriptive details to help readers picture the setting.

The Highwayman

Connect to the Poem

Think about people you rely on and people who rely on you. If someone is counting on you, how far do you go to help that person? Do you value others' safety as much as your own? Explain.

Quickwrite Freewrite for a few minutes about the sacrifices you are willing to make for those who count on you.

Build Background

"The Highwayman" is about a thief who robs coaches in eighteenth-century England.

- In eighteenth-century England, many landowners became wealthier than they had ever been. Yet poverty and crime remained widespread.

- Thousands of poor, unemployed men were forced by the British government to serve for life as soldiers.

- By the eighteenth century, horse-drawn coaches traveled regularly on English roads.

- A highwayman is a roadside robber, especially one on horseback. In England, from the seventeenth century to the nineteenth century, highwaymen would stop coaches by gunpoint and demand that passengers surrender their money and other valuables. Highwaymen who were caught were usually severely punished.

- Some highwaymen became popular, at least among those who were never robbed. A few highwaymen became legends in their time, inspiring songs, poems, and stories in the popular newspapers of the time. One of them, Jonathan Wild, became the hero of a novel and an opera in the eighteenth century.

Meet Alfred Noyes

Popular Poet Alfred Noyes was one of the most popular British poets of the early twentieth century. Because he became a successful poet while still in his twenties, Noyes was able to pursue a full-time career as a poet. Many other British poets at that time were modern in their writing styles, but Noyes wrote traditional poetry in the manner of the great nineteenth-century Romantic poets.

Literary Works Noyes wrote more than fifty books, including novels, short stories, and poetry.

Alfred Noyes was born in 1880 and died in 1958.

Literature Online

Author Search For more about Alfred Noyes, go to glencoe.com and enter QuickPass code GL27534u1.

Set Purposes for Reading

BQ BIG Question

As you read the poem, ask yourself, how do the highwayman and his love, Bess, show their support for each other?

Literary Element Narrative Poetry

The purpose of **narrative poetry** is to tell a story. Narrative poems share many of the narrative elements of short stories, including **plot** and **setting.** The plot is the sequence of events in the poem. The time and place in which the action occurs make up the setting.

Plot and setting are important elements of narrative poetry because they help create a vivid story. The plot of "The Highwayman" twists and turns as it moves towards an eerie ending. Details about the setting help readers visualize the action and sense the atmosphere, or mood, of the poem.

As you read, ask yourself, how do details of plot and setting help to shape the story told in the poem?

Reading Strategy Summarize

When you **summarize** a poem, you state the main ideas and important details of the poem in your own words. You omit unimportant details, so that the summary is much briefer than the piece it is summarizing. Summarizing helps you remember, organize, and explain a series of events. Summarizing shows that you understand the main message of what you have read.

To summarize, decide what's most important as you read. Ask the basic questions: *who, what, when, where, why,* and *how.* Using your own words, write your answers to these questions in a logical order. Leave out examples and unimportant details. You may find it helpful to use a graphic organizer like the one below.

Who	
What	
When	
Where	
Why	
How	

GA Performance Standards

For pages 60–69

ELA7R1h For literary texts, identify and analyze how an author's use of words creates tone and mood.

TRY IT

Summarize When a friend asks you to tell him or her about a movie you have seen, you summarize the events in the movie to explain it to him or her. With a partner, summarize the plot of a book you have read recently or a movie or television show you saw recently.

The Highwayman

Alfred Noyes

PART 1

The wind was a torrent° of darkness
    among the gusty trees.
The moon was a ghostly galleon° tossed upon
    cloudy seas.
The road was a ribbon of moonlight over the purple
    moor,°
And the highwayman came riding—
5   Riding—riding—
The highwayman came riding, up to the old inn door.

He'd a French cocked hat on his forehead, a bunch of
    lace at his chin,
A coat of the claret velvet, and breeches of brown
    doeskin.
They fitted with never a wrinkle. His boots were up
    to the thigh.
10 And he rode with a jewelled twinkle,
        His pistol butts a-twinkle,
His rapier hilt° a-twinkle, under the jewelled sky.

Over the cobbles he clattered and clashed in the dark
    inn yard.
He tapped with his whip on the shutters, but all was
    locked and barred.
15 He whistled a tune to the window, and who should
    be waiting there
But the landlord's black-eyed daughter,
        Bess, the landlord's daughter,

Narrative Poetry What do you learn about the setting from the first few lines of the poem?

---

1 A **torrent** is a strong rush of anything (usually water) flowing swiftly and wildly.

2 A **galleon** (gal′yən) is a large sailing ship of the fifteenth to seventeenth centuries.

3 A **moor** is an area of open, rolling, wild land, usually a grassy wetland.

12 A **rapier** is a long, lightweight sword, and the **hilt** is its handle.

Moon Landing, 1977. Jamie Wyeth. Oil on canvas, 29 x 43 in. Private collection.

Plaiting° a dark red love-knot into her long black hair.

And dark in the dark old inn yard a stable wicket° creaked

20 Where Tim the ostler° listened. His face was white and peaked.°
His eyes were hollows of madness, his hair like mouldy hay,
But he loved the landlord's daughter,
        The landlord's red-lipped daughter.
Dumb as a dog he listened, and he heard the robber say—

25 "One kiss, my bonny° sweetheart, I'm after a prize tonight,
But I shall be back with the yellow gold before the morning light;
Yet, if they press me sharply, and harry° me through the day,
Then look for me by moonlight,
        Watch for me by moonlight,

---

18 Bess is braiding *(plaiting)* a red ribbon into her hair.

19 A *wicket* is a small door or gate; this one leads into the stable.

20 As the *ostler* (a shorter form of hostler), it's Tim's job to take care of the horses at the inn. A *peaked* face looks pale and sickly.

25 *Bonny* (a Scottish word) means "good-looking, fine, or admirable."

27 To *harry* is to trouble, bother, or worry.

A Wet Winter's Evening, 1880. John Atkinson Grimshaw.
View the Art What does this painting tell you about the setting of this poem?

30   I'll come to thee by moonlight, though hell should bar
      the way."

      He rose upright in the stirrups. He scarce could reach
        her hand,
      But she loosened her hair in the casement.° His face
        burnt like a brand
      As the black cascade of perfume came tumbling over
        his breast;
      And he kissed its waves in the moonlight,
35   (O, sweet black waves in the moonlight!)
      Then he tugged at his rein in the moonlight, and
        galloped away to the west.

PART 2

      He did not come in the dawning. He did not come
        at noon;

---

32 The *casement* is the window frame, and the *brand* is a burning torch.

Summarize Think about the most important events of Part 1. What does the highwayman promise Bess?

And out of the tawny° sunset, before the rise of
    the moon,
When the road was a gypsy's ribbon, looping the
    purple moor,
40 A red coat troop° came marching—
        Marching—marching—
King George's men came marching, up to the old
    inn door.

They said no word to the landlord. They drank his
    ale instead,
But they gagged his daughter, and bound her, to the
    foot of her narrow bed.
45 Two of them knelt at her casement, with muskets at
    their side!
There was death at every window;
        And hell at one dark window;
For Bess could see, through her casement, the road
    that he would ride.

They had tied her up to attention, with many a
    sniggering jest.°
50 They had bound a musket beside her, with the
    muzzle beneath her breast!
"Now, keep good watch!" and they kissed her. She
    heard the doomed man say—
Look for me by moonlight;
        Watch for me by moonlight;
I'll come to thee by moonlight, though hell should bar the way!

55 She twisted her hands behind her; but all the knots
    held good!
She writhed° her hands till her fingers were wet with
    sweat or blood!
They stretched and strained in the darkness, and the
    hours crawled by like years,

Narrative Poetry How does the plot take an unexpected turn when the soldiers are introduced?

Narrative Poetry How do details about the setting affect the mood of the poem?

---

38 *Tawny* is a brownish-gold color.

40 The *red coat troop* is a group of soldiers wearing bright red coats.

49 Bess is tied to a pole, arms at her sides in what a soldier would call "at attention," while the soldiers laugh disrespectfully *(many a sniggering jest)*.

56 *Writhed* means "twisted and turned."

Till, now, on the stroke of midnight,
      Cold, on the stroke of midnight,
60 The tip of one finger touched it! The trigger at last
    was hers!

The tip of one finger touched it. She strove no more
    for the rest.
Up, she stood up to attention, with the muzzle
    beneath her breast.
She would not risk their hearing; she would not
    strive again;
For the road lay bare in the moonlight;
65   Blank and bare in the moonlight;
And the blood of her veins, in the moonlight,
    throbbed to her love's refrain.°

Tlot-tlot; tlot-tlot! Had they heard it: The horsehoofs
    ringing clear;
Tlot-tlot, tlot-tlot, in the distance? Were they deaf that
    they did not hear?
Down the ribbon of moonlight, over the brow of
    the hill,
70 The highwayman came riding—
      Riding—riding—
The red-coats looked to their priming!° She stood up,
    straight and still!

Tlot-tlot, in the frosty silence! *Tlot-tlot,* in the echoing
    night!
Nearer he came and nearer. Her face was like a light.
75 Her eyes grew wide for a moment; she drew one last
    deep breath,
Then her finger moved in the moonlight,
      Her musket shattered the moonlight,
Shattered her breast in the moonlight and warned
    him—with her death.

He turned. He spurred to the westward; he did not
    know who stood

Summarize What happens in lines 50–74?

BQ **BIG Question**
How does Bess show that the highwayman can count on her?

---

66 In a song or poem, the ***refrain*** is a phrase or verse that is repeated regularly.

72 The soldiers are ***priming*** their weapons, or loading their muskets with ammunition.

80 Bowed, with her head o'er the musket, drenched with her own red blood!
    Not till the dawn he heard it, and his face grew grey to hear
    How Bess, the landlord's daughter,
              The landlord's black-eyed daughter,
    Had watched for her love in the moonlight, and died in the darkness there.

85 Back, he spurred like a madman, shrieking a curse to the sky,
    With the white road smoking behind him and his rapier brandished° high.
    Blood-red were his spurs in the golden noon, wine-red was his velvet coat;
    When they shot him down on the highway,
              Down like a dog on the highway,
90 And he lay in his blood on the highway, with a bunch of lace at his throat.

    And still of a winter's night, they say, when the wind is in the trees,
    When the moon is a ghostly galleon tossed upon cloudy seas,
    When the road is a ribbon of moonlight over the purple moor,
    A highwayman comes riding—
95   *Riding—riding—*
    A highwayman comes riding, up to the old inn door.

    Over the cobbles he clatters and clangs in the dark inn yard.
    He taps with his whip on the shutters, but all is locked and barred.
    He whistles a tune to the window, and who should be waiting there
100 *But the landlord's black-eyed daughter,*
              Bess, the landlord's daughter,
    Plaiting a dark red love-knot into her long black hair. ❧

Summarize Why did the highwayman die?

---

86 The highwayman waved his sword threateningly *(brandished).*

After You Read

Respond and Think Critically

1. What is the setting of this poem? Include details from the poem to support your answer. [Recall]

2. Describe the actions of the soldiers. How does their behavior make you feel about the highwayman and Bess? Explain. [Interpret]

3. Lines 19–24 describe Tim the ostler. What role does Tim play in the poem? How do the soldiers know to wait for the highwayman in Bess's room? Explain. [Analyze]

4. Why do you think the highwayman reacts the way he does when he finds out what has happened to Bess? What does his reaction reveal about him? Explain. [Infer]

5. How would the poem be different if it ended just before the final two stanzas? Support your answer. [Compare]

6. **BQ** **BIG Question** What do Bess's actions show about her feelings toward the highwayman? Do you think her actions are foolish, heroic, or both? Explain. [Evaluate]

Academic Vocabulary

Bess made a drastic decision because she did not think she had an **alternative** solution to save the highwayman. In the preceding sentence, *alternative* means "offering a choice." Think about Bess's decision. What alternative decisions could she have made? Then fill in the blank for this statement: As an alternative to taking her own life, Bess could have _____.

TIP

Comparing
When you compare two things, you look at how they are alike and how they are different. To help answer question 5, first reread the last two stanzas of the poem.

- Notice the similarities and differences between the feeling, or mood, of the first three stanzas and the last two stanzas.

- What important information do you learn in the last two stanzas?

- How does this information add to the mood of the poem?

- How would the poem be different if the last two stanzas were not there?

FOLDABLES Keep track of
Study Organizer your ideas about
the **BIG Question** in your
unit Foldable.

Literary Element Narrative Poetry

Standards Practice EL7R1e, ELA7R1h, EIA7RC2b

1. Which events in this poem did you find especially alarming or striking? Explain.

2. What details in the opening stanza help to create a mysterious mood? Explain.

3. Describe what happens to Bess. Explain why.

Review: Setting

Standards Practice EL7R1c

4. Which of the following is a detail that describes the setting?
   A "his eyes were hollows of madness"
   B "the landlord's black-eyed daughter"
   C "she twisted her hands behind her"
   D "the wind was a torrent of darkness"

Reading Strategy Summarize

5. Refer back to the graphic organizer that you filled out as you read the poem. Use it to help you write a one-paragraph summary of the poem.

💬 Speaking and Listening

Performance With a small group, plan a choral reading of "The Highwayman." Individual group members can take turns reading parts of the poem. Other parts can be read by a chorus of group members. Begin by planning how you will divide the parts. Then practice reading the poem before presenting it to the class.

Grammar Link

Main and Helping Verbs A verb can be more than one word. Verbs of two or more words are called verb phrases. For example:

> One-word verb: Her finger **moved** in the moonlight.

> Verb phrase: They **had tied** her up to attention.

The most important word in a verb phrase is the **main verb**. The other verbs in the phrase are **helping verbs**. These verbs help the main verb tell when an action or state of being occurs. For example:

> They **had tied** her up to attention.

The verb phrase "had tied" includes the main verb *tied* and the helping verb *had*. The helping verb *had* tells that the action "to tie" takes place in the past.

Helping verbs may help the main verb tell whether an action or state of being will occur in the future. For example:

> I'**ll come** to thee by moonlight.

In the verb phrase "will come" (*I'll* is a contraction of the words *I* and *will*), come is the main verb and *will* is the helping verb. The helping verb *will* shows that the action "to come" takes place in the future. When you analyze the parts of a verb phrase, mentally cross out such words as *never, always,* and *not.* These words are adverbs, not verbs.

Practice Use the summary you have written of "The Highwayman," or work with a partner to create a short summary of the poem. Underline the main verbs and circle the helping verbs in your summary.

Vocabulary Workshop

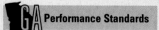 **Performance Standards**

For page 70

ELA7R2a Determine the meaning of unfamiliar words using context clues (e.g., contrast, cause and effect, etc.).

Context Clues

Connection to Literature

"The moon was a ghostly galleon tossed upon cloudy seas."

—Alfred Noyes, "The Highwayman"

Tip

Test-taking Tip To find context clues, look before and after the unfamiliar word for a synonym, a definition, an example, a restatement, or a contrast.

You can sometimes determine the meaning of an unfamiliar word by looking for **context clues,** or hints in nearby words and sentences. In the sentence above, *tossed upon the cloudy seas* is a context clue for the word *galleon,* which refers to a type of large sailing ship.

Here are various context clues you can use in "The Highwayman."

Type of Context Clue	Examples
Definition	The highwayman carried a <u>rapier</u>—*a long, lightweight sword*—at his side. Look for a definition. A *rapier* is a long, lightweight sword.
Example	The stable <u>wicket</u> creaked as *the wind blew it open and shut.* Look for an example of an action associated with the word. A *wicket* is a small door or gate.
Restatement	Tim's face was <u>peaked</u>. He looked *white and ill.* Look for the idea restated in different words. *Peaked* means "pale and sickly."
Contrast	Tim, *whose hair was "like mouldy hay,"* was no match for <u>bonny</u> Bess. Look for familiar text that contrasts with the thing or idea named by the unfamiliar word. *Bonny* means "good-looking or admirable."

TRY IT: For each sentence, identify the context clue and write a short definition of the underlined word.

1. The horse clattered over the <u>cobbles</u>, or paving stones.
2. The troops hunted highwaymen, burglars, and other <u>miscreants</u>.
3. The highwayman was wise to run from the gunshot but <u>imprudent</u> to try to fight the red coat troop.

LOG ON ▶ **Literature** Online

Vocabulary For more vocabulary practice, go to glencoe.com and enter the QuickPass code GL27534u1.

Part 2

Me, Myself, and I

Mirror Image, 1997. Lucile Montague. Pastel. Private Collection.

BQ BIG Question **Whom Can You Count On?**

What might the person in the picture *Mirror Image* think about his reflection? What image of yourself would you like to see reflected in a mirror?

The Good Samaritan

Connect to the Short Story

Think about a time when someone promised you something but did not give it to you. How did you feel? How did you react?

Partner Talk With a partner, talk about why it is important to keep promises. What happens when promises are broken?

Build Background

In "The Good Samaritan," a young person learns that adults sometimes break promises. The setting helps to lend truthfulness to the story.

- The story takes place in the southern part of Texas during the present day.
- The term "good Samaritan" comes from a Biblical story about a man who goes out of his way to help an injured stranger. A "good Samaritan" helps another person, even if he or she does not know or like that person.

Vocabulary

supervision (soo´ pər vizh´ ən) *n.* the act of watching or overseeing others (p. 76). *The teachers at the daycare provide supervision for the youngsters.*

standstill (stand´ stil) *n.* a stop in motion or progress (p. 78). *When it rained, our work in the garden came to a standstill.*

disrespect (dis´ ri spekt´) *n.* a lack of proper courtesy (p. 78). *The angry sports fan showed the referee disrespect by shouting at him.*

ritual (rich´ oo əl) *n.* a set routine (p. 80). *Drinking a cup of tea before going to sleep is part of Amy's bedtime ritual.*

Meet René Saldaña, Jr.

"Man, if I pick up a great book, I can't stop. I've got to finish it."
—René Saldaña, Jr.

Texas Writer René Saldaña, Jr., grew up in Nuevo Peñitas, a suburb in south Texas that he sometimes uses as a setting for his stories. Saldaña has taught middle and high school and now teaches aspiring teachers at Texas Tech University. He lives in Lubbock, Texas, with his wife, their two sons, and one cat.

Literary Works Saldaña has written short stories and novels for young adults, including *The Jumping Tree.*

René Saldaña, Jr., was born in 1968.

 Literature Online

Author Search For more about René Saldaña, Jr., go to glencoe.com and enter QuickPass code GL27534u1.

Set Purposes for Reading

BQ ▸ BIG Question

As you read the story, ask yourself, who can the main character, Rey, count on to be kind and admirable? Who in Rey's life is not so admirable? Why?

Literary Element ▸ Plot

A story's **plot** includes all the events that happen in the story. A plot is usually organized around **conflict,** or a struggle between opposing forces.

- The plot of a story begins with the **exposition.** The exposition introduces the characters, setting, and conflict.

- The **rising action** adds complications to the conflict. It includes all the events that lead to the climax.

- The **climax** is the point of the greatest interest or suspense in a story.

- The **falling action** is all of the events that happen after the climax.

- The **resolution** is the conclusion, or ending, of the story.

Understanding plot is important because it helps you determine the meaning of key events in a story. As you read, notice how the events lead up to the story's climax.

Reading Strategy ▸ Visualize

When you **visualize,** you create images, or pictures, in your mind as you read. You use the author's descriptions and details to vividly imagine characters, settings, and plot events. Visualizing is one of the best ways to understand and remember information in a short story.

Try these steps to visualize as you read.

- Pay attention to the story's sensory details, or the details that appeal to your sense of sight, sound, smell, touch, or taste.

- Try to imagine the scene as if it were taking place in a movie.

Use a graphic organizer like the one below to keep track of story details. Then, use the details to visualize the scene and draw a picture of it.

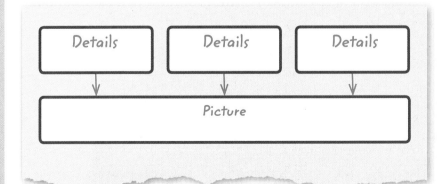

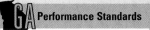

GA Performance Standards

For pages 72–83

ELA7R1e For literary texts, identify events that advance the plot and determine how each event explains past or present action(s) or foreshadows future action(s).

> **TRY IT**
>
> **Visualize** Think of something you can describe easily—for example, a pet or a family member. List descriptive details and then use those details to draw a picture of your subject.

The Good Samaritan

René Saldaña, Jr.

Diving Board, 2004. Lincoln Seligman. Acrylic. Private Collection.

know he's in there, I thought. I saw the curtains of his bedroom move, only a little, yes, but they moved.

Yesterday Orlie told me, "Come over tomorrow afternoon. We'll hang out by the pool."

I rang the doorbell again. Then I knocked.

The door creaked open. The afternoon light crept into the dark living room inch by slow inch. Mrs. Sánchez, Orlie's mom, stuck her head through the narrow opening, her body hidden behind the door. "Hi, Rey, how can I help you?"

"Ah, Mrs. Sánchez, is Orlando here?" I tried looking past her but only saw a few pictures hanging on the wall. One of the Sánchez family all dressed up fancy and smiling, standing in front of a gray marble background.

"No, he's not. He went with his father to Mission."

"Oh, because Orlando said he would be here, and told me to come over."

"They won't be back until later tonight," she said. "You can come by tomorrow and see if he's here. You know how it is in the summer. He and his dad are always doing work here and there. Come back tomorrow, but call first."

"It's just that he said I could come by and swim in your pool. Dijo,[1] 'Tomorrow, come over. I'll be here. We'll go swimming.'"

"I'm sorry he told you that, but without him or my husband here, you won't be able to use the pool," me dijo Mrs. Sánchez.

"Okay," I said.

"Maybe tomorrow?"

"Yeah, maybe."

But there was no maybe about it. I wouldn't be coming back. Because I knew that Orlando was in the house, he just didn't want to hang out. Bien codo con su pool.[2] Plain stingy. And tricky. This guy invited me and a few others over all summer to help his dad with some yard work because Mr. Sánchez told us, "If you help clean up the

Visualize Use the details here to imagine the door opening. What does this tell you about how Mrs. Sánchez feels about speaking to Rey?

BQ **BIG Question**
Do you think Rey can count on Orlando? Explain your answer.

---

1 *Dijo* (dē′ hō) is Spanish for "he said." *Me dijo* means "said to me."

2 *Bien* (bē en′) *codo* (kō′ dō) *con* (kōn) *su* (soo) Rey is saying in Spanish that Orlando doesn't like to share the pool with others.

yard, you boys can use the pool any time you want so long as one of us is here." And we cleaned up his yard. On that hot day the water that smelled of chlorine looked delicious to me. And after a hard day's work cleaning his yard, I so looked forward to taking a dip. I'd even worn my trunks under my work clothes. Then Mr. Sánchez said, "Come by tomorrow. I don't want you fellas to track all this dirt into the pool."

"We can go home and shower and be back," said Hernando.

"No, mejor que regresen mañana.[3] I'll be here tomorrow and we can swim. After lunch, okay. For sure we'll do it tomorrow," said Mr. Sánchez.

The following day he was there, but he was headed out right after lunch and he didn't feel safe leaving us behind without **supervision.** "If one of you drowns, your parents will be angry at me and . . ." He didn't say it, but he didn't need to. One of our parents could sue him. And he needed that like I needed another F in my Geometry I class! Or, we figured out later, he could have just said, "I used you saps to do my dirty work. And I lied about the pool, suckers!"

I don't know why we hadn't learned our lesson. Twice before he had gypped us this way of our time and effort. Always dangling the carrot in front of our eyes, then snatching it away at the last second.

One of those times he promised us soft drinks and snacks if we helped clean up a yard across the street from his house. It wasn't his yard to worry about, but I guess he just didn't like to see the weeds growing as tall as dogs. What if he had company? What would they think? And he was angling[4] for a position on the school board. How could a politico[5] live in such filth!

Visualize What sensory details help you visualize the pool?

Plot What conflict has developed in this story?

---

3 *Mejor* (me hōr′) *que* (ke) *regresen* (re gre′sen) *mañana* (män yä′nä) "It's better if you return tomorrow."

4 *Angling* means "trying to get."

5 A *politico* is a politician.

Vocabulary

supervision (so͞o′ pər vĭzh′ ən) *n.* the act of watching or overseeing others

Basketball. Kelly Brooks. Watercolor on paper. Private Collection.

Well, we did get a soft drink and chips, only it was one two-liter bottle of Coke and one bag of chips for close to ten of us. We had no cups, and the older, stronger boys got dibs[6] on most of the eats. "I didn't know there'd be so many of you," he said. "Well, share. And thanks. You all are good, strong boys."

The next time was real hard labor. He said, "Help me dig these holes here, then we can put up some basketball rims. Once the cement dries on the court itself, you all can come over and play anytime since it's kind of your court too. That is, if you help me dig the holes."

And we did. We dug and dug and dug for close to six hours straight until we got done, passing on the shovel from one of us to the next. But we got it done. We had our court. Mr. Sánchez kept his word. He reminded us we could come over to play anytime, and we took special care not to dunk and grab hold of the rim. Even the shortest kid could practically dunk it because the baskets were so low. But we'd seen the rims all bent down at the different yards at school. And we didn't want that for *our* court.

One day, we wanted to play a little three on three. After knocking on the different doors several times and getting no answer, we figured the Sánchez family had gone out. We decided that it'd be okay to play. We weren't going to do anything wrong. The court was far enough from the house that we couldn't possibly break a window. And Mr. Sánchez had said we could come over any time we wanted. It was *our* court, after all. Those were his words exactly.

A little later in the afternoon, Mr. Sánchez drove up in his truck, honking and honking at us. "Here they come. Maybe Orlando and Marty can play with us," someone said.

Visualize How do you picture this scene, based on the description?

---

6 Got **dibs** means "claimed the right to do or have something before anyone else."

Pues,[7] it was not to be. The truck had just come to a **standstill** when Mr. Sánchez shot out of the driver's side. He ran up to us, waving his hands in the air like a crazy man, first saying, then screaming, "What are you guys doing here? You all can't be here when I'm not here."

"But you told us we could come over anytime. And we knocked and knocked, and we were being very careful."

"It doesn't matter. You all shouldn't be here when I'm not home. What if you had broken something?" he said.

"But we didn't," I said.

"But if you had, then who would have been responsible for paying to replace it? I'm sure every one of you would have denied breaking anything."

"Este vato!"[8] said Hernando.

"Vato? Is that what you called me? I'm no street punk, no hoodlum. I'll have you know, I've worked my whole life, and I won't be called a vato. It's Mr. Sánchez. Got that? And you boys know what—from now on, you are not allowed to come here whether I'm home or not! You all messed it up for yourselves. You've shown me so much **disrespect** today you don't deserve to play on my court. It was a privilege and not a right, and you messed it up. Now leave!"

Hernando, who was fuming,[9] said, "Orale, guys, let's go." He took the ball from one of the smaller boys and began to run toward the nearest basket. He slowed down the closer he came to the basket and leapt in the air. I'd never seen him jump with such grace. He floated from the foul line, his long hair like wings, all the way to the basket. He grabbed the ball in both his hands and let go of it at the last moment. Instead of dunking the ball, he let it

Plot The conflict in this story is becoming more complicated. What part of the plot is this?

---

7 **Pues** (pwes) means "well."

8 The word **vato** (vä´tō) is Mexican-Spanish slang. It is used by young people most often when speaking to or about each other. It means "dude." **Este vato** means "this dude."

9 He was angry, or **fuming.**

Vocabulary

standstill (stand´stil) *n.* a stop in motion or progress

disrespect (dis´ri spekt´) *n.* a lack of proper courtesy

shoot up to the sky; then he wrapped his fingers around the rim and pulled down as hard as he could, hanging on for a few seconds. Then the rest of us walked after him, dejected.[10] He hadn't bent the rim even a millimeter. Eventually Orlie talked us into going back when his dad wasn't home. His baby brother, Marty, was small and slow, and Orlie wanted some competition on the court.

Today was it for me, though. I made up my mind never to go back to the Sánchezes'. I walked to the little store for a soda. That and a grape popsicle would cool me down. I sat on the bench outside, finished off the drink, returned the bottle for my nickel refund, and headed for home.

As soon as I walked through our front door, my mother said, "Mi'jo,[11] you need to go pick up your brother at summer school. He missed the bus."

"Again? He probably missed it on purpose, 'Amá.[12] He's always walking over to Leo's Grocery to talk to his little girlfriends, then he calls when he needs a ride." I turned toward the bedroom.

"Come back here," she said. So I turned and took a seat at the table. "Have you forgotten the times we had to go pick you up? Your brother always went with us, no matter what time it was."

"Yeah, but I was doing school stuff. Football, band. He's in summer school just piddling his time away!"

She looked at me as she brushed sweat away from her face with the back of her hand and said, "Just go pick him up, and hurry home. On the way back, stop at Circle Seven and buy some tortillas. There's money on the table."

I shook my head in disgust. Here I was, already a senior, having to be my baby brother's chauffeur.

I'd driven halfway to Leo's Grocery when I saw Mr. Sánchez's truck up ahead by the side of the road. I could just make him out sitting under the shade of his truck. Every time he heard a car coming his way, he'd

---

10 A **dejected** person feels sad or depressed.

11 **Mi'jo** (mē'hō) is a contraction of the Spanish translation of "my son."

12 **'Amá** (ä mä') is a shortened form of "Mama."

raise his head slightly, try to catch the driver's attention by staring at him, then he'd hang his head again when the car didn't stop.

I slowed down as I approached. Could he tell it was me driving? When he looked up at my car, I could swear he almost smiled, thinking he had been saved. He had been leaning his head between his bent knees, and I could tell he was tired; his white shirt stuck to him because of all the sweat. His sock on one leg was bunched up at his ankle like a carnation. He had the whitest legs I'd ever seen on a Mexican. Whiter than even my dad's. I kept on looking straight; that is, I made like I was looking ahead, not a care in the world, but out of the corner of my eye I saw that he had a flat tire, that he had gotten two of the **lug nuts** off but hadn't gotten to the others, that the crowbar lay half on his other foot and half on the ground beside him, that his hair was matted by sweat to his forehead.

I knew that look. I'd probably looked just like that digging those holes for *our* basketball court, cleaning up his yard and the one across the street from his house. I wondered if he could use a cold two-liter Coke right about now! If he was dreaming of taking a dip in his pool!

I drove on. No way was I going to help him out again! Let him do his own dirty work for once. He could stay out there and melt in this heat for all I cared. And besides, someone else will stop, I thought. Someone who doesn't know him like I do.

And I knew that when Mr. Sánchez got home, he'd stop at my house on his walk around the barrio.[13] My dad would be watering the plants, his evening **ritual** to relax from a hard day at work, and Mr. Sánchez would mention in passing that I had probably not seen him by the side of the road so I hadn't stopped to help him out; "Kids today," he would say to my dad, "not a care in the world, their heads up in the clouds somewhere." My dad would call me out and ask me to tell him and Mr. Sánchez why I

Visualize What details show how Mr. Sánchez feels?

Plot Rey has to make a decision. What part of the plot does this lead to?

Visual Vocabulary

A **lug nut** is a piece of metal with a threaded hole in the middle that goes on the end of a bolt to hold it in place.

---

13 A *barrio* (bä′ rē ō) is a neighborhood where Spanish-speaking people live.

Vocabulary

ritual (rich′ oo əl) *n.* a set routine

Lilo, 2004. Lincoln Seligman. Acrylic on canvas. Private Collection.

View the Art In what way does this painting remind you of the Sánchezes' pool?

hadn't helped out a neighbor when he needed it most. I'd say, to both of them, "That was you? I thought you and Orlie were in Mission taking care of some business, so it never occurred to me to stop to help a neighbor. Geez, I'm so sorry." Or I could say, "You know, I was in such a hurry to pick up my brother in La Joya[14] that I didn't even notice you by the side of the road."

I'd be off the hook. Anyways, why should I be the one to extend a helping hand when he's done every one of us in the barrio wrong in one way or another! He deserves to sweat a little. A taste of his own bad medicine. Maybe he'll learn a lesson.

---

14 *La Joya* (lä hoi´ ä) is a town in southern Texas.

But I remembered the look in his eyes as I drove past him. That same tired look my father had when he'd get home from work and he didn't have the strength to take off his boots. My father always looked like he'd been working for centuries without any rest. He'd sit there in front of the television on his favorite green vinyl sofa chair and stare at whatever was on TV. He'd sit there for an hour before he could move, before he could eat his supper and take his shower, that same look on his face Mr. Sánchez had just now.

What if this were my dad stranded[15] on the side of the road? I'd want someone to stop for him.

"My one good deed for today," I told myself. "And I'm doing it for my dad really, not for Mr. Sánchez."

I made a U-turn, drove back to where he was still sitting, turned around again, and pulled up behind him.

"I thought that was you, Rey," he said. He wiped at his forehead with his shirtsleeve. "And when you drove past, I thought you hadn't seen me. Thank goodness you stopped. I've been here for close to forty-five minutes and nobody's stopped to help. Thank goodness you did. I just can't get the tire off."

Thank my father, I thought. If it weren't for my father, you'd still be out here.

I had that tire changed in no time. All the while Mr. Sánchez stood behind me and a bit to my left saying, "Yes, thank God you came by. Boy, it's hot out here. You're a good boy, Rey. You'll make a good man. How about some help there?"

"No, I've got it," I answered. "I'm almost done."

"Oyes,[16] Rey, what if you come over tomorrow night to my house? I'm having a little barbecue for some important people here in town. You should come over. We're even going to do some swimming. What do you say?"

I tightened the last of the nuts, replaced the jack, the flat tire, and the crowbar in the bed of his truck, looked at him, and said, "Thanks. But I'll be playing football with the vatos." 🐾

Visualize How do you picture Rey's father based on this description?

Plot What makes this the climax of the story?

BQ BIG Question
How does Rey prove that he is a person others can count on?

---

15 **Stranded** means "left somewhere and not able to leave."
16 **Oyes** means "listen."

After You Read

Respond and Think Critically

1. Describe two events that affect the way Rey feels about Mr. Sánchez. Explain what you learn about their relationship. **[Analyze]**

2. How does Rey react when he sees Mr. Sánchez by the side of the road? Explain. **[Recall]**

3. How does Rey feel about his father? Explain. **[Infer]**

4. **Literary Element** Plot Reread the last two paragraphs of the story. Is this a good resolution? Explain. **[Evaluate]**

5. **Reading Strategy** Visualize Review the graphic organizer you created as you read. How does Mr. Sánchez react when he finds the boys playing basketball? Draw a picture of the scene. **[Interpret]**

6. **BQ** **BIG Question** What lesson does Rey learn about whom he can and cannot trust? Explain. **[Conclude]**

Vocabulary Practice

Match each boldfaced vocabulary word with a word from the right column that has the same meaning. Two of the words in the right column will not have matches. Then write a sentence using each vocabulary word in a sentence or draw or find a picture that represents the word.

1. **supervision**   a. habit
2. **standstill**   b. appreciation
3. **disrespect**   c. halt
4. **ritual**   d. rudeness
                            e. direction
                            f. privilege

Example: supervision

Sentence: The new employees needed more supervision than the more experienced workers.

Writing

Write a Journal Entry Think of a time when you were a good samaritan and helped someone with a problem. What was the problem? How did you help? Write a short narrative about the problem and what you did.

TIP

Analyzing
To answer question 1, look for major story events that involve both Rey and Mr. Sánchez.

- What does Mr. Sánchez ask Rey and his friends to do?
- How does Mr. Sánchez treat Rey and his friends?
- Does Mr. Sánchez keep his promises? What promises does Mr. Sánchez break?

 FOLDABLES Study Organizer Keep track of your ideas about the **BIG Question** in your unit Foldable.

 **Performance Standards**

For pages 84–85

ELA7R1b For literary texts, interpret a character's traits, emotions, or motivations and give supporting evidence from a text.

Genre Focus:
Short Fiction

Fiction is writing about invented people, places, or events. **Short fiction** focuses on a small number of events or on just one event. You can usually read a work of short fiction in a single sitting. Most works of short fiction contain the same elements as do longer works of fiction, such as novels. These elements include setting, characters, plot, point of view, and theme.

Short stories about realistic events are works of short fiction. Folktales, fairy tales, legends, myths, fables, and tall tales are also examples of short fiction.

Literary Elements

Setting is the time and place of the action in a work of fiction. Setting includes the customs, values, and beliefs of a place or time.

Characters are the actors in a fictional work. They can be people, animals, robots, or whatever the author chooses. The main character is called the **protagonist.**

Characterization refers to the methods the author uses to develop the personality of a character. In **direct characterization,** the author makes direct statements about a character's personality. In **indirect characterization,** the author reveals a character's personality through the character's words and actions and through what other characters think and say about the character.

Plot is the sequence of events in a fictional work. Plot is centered around **conflict**—a struggle between people, ideas, or forces.

Point of view is the vantage point from which a story is told. The person telling the story is the narrator. In **first-person point of view,** the narrator is a character in the story. In **third-person point of view,** the narrator is someone outside the story.

Theme is the main message of a story. A theme may be stated directly. However, many stories have an **implied** theme, suggested by what the characters learn or by what their experiences illustrate.

Dialogue is the written conversation between characters in a story. Dialogue brings characters to life by revealing their personalities and showing what they are thinking and feeling.

> ### TRY IT
> Using a diagram or chart like the ones on the next page, track the plot or the methods of characterization you find in a short story in this unit.

To better understand literary elements in fictional writing and how authors use them, look at the examples in the plot diagram and characterization chart below.

Stages in Plot Development for *The Wise Old Woman*

Climax is the point of greatest interest or suspense in the story.

The farmer takes his mother to the mountains but then changes his mind. He hides her in a small room in their house.

A neighboring ruler threatens to conquer the village unless the villagers complete a series of challenges. The farmer's mother secretly offers solutions to the challenges.

The lord of the village says that old people must be banished from the village and live in the mountains until they die. The farmer and other villagers disagree but are afraid of being punished.

The farmer confesses that he has been hiding his mother and admits it was she who solved the challenges.

A young farmer and his mother live in a village of Japan long ago.

The lord of the village admits he was wrong and decrees that older people be treated with respect and dignity.

Rising action develops the conflicts, or problems, in the story.

Falling action shows what happens after the climax.

Exposition introduces a story's setting, characters, and situation.

Resolution gives the story's final outcome.

Characterization Chart for Antonio Cruz from *Amigo Brothers*

Detail from the Story	Character Trait It Reveals	Direct or Indirect Characterization
The narrator says that "Antonio's lean form and long reach made him the better boxer."	talented	direct (narrator's statement)
Antonio says, "Yeah. We both know that in the ring the better man wins. Friend or no friend, brother or no . . ."	fair	indirect (character's words)
A gnawing doubt crept in. He cut negative thinking real quick by doing some speedy fancy dance steps, bobbing and weaving like mercury.	nervous	indirect (character's actions)

Literature Online

Literature and Reading For more selections in this genre, go to glencoe.com and enter Quickpass code GL27534u1.

Before You Read

The Lark and Her Children
and The Travelers and the Bear

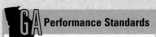
GA Performance Standards

For pages 86–89

ELA7R1g/ii For literary texts, explain and analyze the effects of figurative language.

Connect to the Fables

Think about how it feels to really need help with something. What are some times in life when you rely on others?

Quickwrite Freewrite for a few minutes about situations in which you have counted on others for help. What have you learned from those situations?

Build Background

Folktales and fables often contain proverbs. Proverbs are sayings that offer advice or state a well-known truth. Proverbs are usually short and easy to remember, and they often contain vivid images. Here are some proverbs that you may already know:

- "The early bird catches the worm."
- "Birds of a feather flock together."
- "Every cloud has a silver lining."

Set Purposes for Reading

BQ BIG Question

As you read, pay attention to the problems that the characters face and how they deal with them.

Literary Element Fable

A **fable** is a short, simple tale that teaches a lesson about human nature. The characters are often animals that speak, think, and act like people. The moral, or lesson, of the story is usually stated directly.

Understanding fables is important because such tales can teach values or give advice. As you read, think about the purpose and characteristics of each fable and what it teaches you.

Meet the Authors

Aesop

Author or Legend? Aesop is traditionally credited as the author of many ancient Greek fables. However, the fables may have been invented by different people. They were first written down in the fourth century B.C.

Jerry Pinkney

Author and Illustrator
Jerry Pinkney is an award-winning illustrator and reteller of folktales.

LOG ON ▶ **Literature** Online

Author Search For more about Aesop and Jerry Pinkney, go to glencoe.com and enter QuickPass code GL27534u1.

The Lark & Her Children

Aesop's Fables
Retold by Jerry Pinkney

A **lark** made her nest in a field of young wheat. By the time her eggs hatched, the wheat had grown straight and tall. All summer long the wheat ripened and grew golden while the young birds grew in size and strength.

The fledglings[1] were nearly ready to leave the nest when they heard the farmer talking to his sons. "The wheat's ripened at last," he said. "We'll call our friends and neighbors in to help us harvest it."

The little birds were frightened that their nest might be destroyed, and when their mother returned to the nest that night, they told her what they'd overheard. "Never fear, my children," the lark replied. "We still have some time left. Practice your flying and make sure your wings are strong."

A few days later the young larks once again heard the farmer talking. "That wheat must be harvested at once," he said. "We can't wait any longer for help from our friends. Tomorrow we'll set to work ourselves."

When her children told the lark what the farmer had said, she answered, "Then it's time for us to be gone. For once a man is ready to do his own work, there will be no more delay."

If you want something done, do it yourself.

Fable What characteristic of a fable is this?

---

1 *Fledglings* are young birds.

The Travelers and the Bear

Aesop's Fables
Retold by Jerry Pinkney

From *Aesop's Fables* ©2000 by Jerry Pinkney. Used with permission of Chronicle Books, LLC, San Francisco. Visit ChronicleBooks.com.

Two men were traveling through the forest together on a lonely trail. Soon they heard a sound up ahead as if heavy feet were trampling through the underbrush.

"It could be a bear!" one whispered with alarm, and quickly as he could, he scrambled up a tall tree. He had barely reached the first branch when a huge brown bear thrust aside the bushes and stepped out onto the path.

Hugging the trunk with both arms, the first traveler refused to lend a hand[1] to his terrified companion, who threw himself on the ground and prepared for death.

The bear lowered its great head and sniffed at the man, ruffling his hair with its nose. Then, to the amazement of both men, the fierce beast walked away.

The first traveler slid down from his tree. "Why, it almost looked as if the bear whispered something in your ear," he marveled.

"It did," said the second traveler. "It told me to choose a better companion for my next journey."

Misfortune is the true test of friendship.

---

1 *To lend a hand* means "to help."

BQ **BIG Question**
Can the second traveler count on the first traveler? Why or why not?

After You Read

Respond and Think Critically

1. In "The Lark and Her Children," why are the young birds frightened? Explain. [Recall]

2. In "The Lark and Her Children," why does the farmer decide that the wheat must be harvested at once? Explain. [Infer]

3. Do you agree or disagree with the lesson of "The Lark and Her Children"? Support your answer with good reasons. [Evaluate]

4. Do you think that the bear in "The Travelers and the Bear" actually spoke to the second traveler? Why or why not? [Conclude]

5. **Literary Element** Fable Which fable do you think is more effective in teaching its lesson? Explain. [Compare]

6. **BQ** BIG Question What does "The Travelers and the Bear" teach readers about friendship? Explain. [Conclude]

Academic Vocabulary

In "The Travelers and the Bear," the first traveler probably believes he is **justified** in not helping his companion. In the preceding sentence, *justified* means having a sufficient or logical reason for doing something. Do you think the first traveler is justified in not helping his friend? Why or why not? Would you have helped him?

Writing

Write a Scene The settings of fables are usually rural villages. Many fables do not include a description of these settings. What do you think these villages are like? Write a scene in which you describe the setting for one of these fables. Use sensory details in your description, appealing to all five senses if possible.

TIP

Evaluating
To answer question 3, you must consider the details of the story as well as your own ideas, opinions, and experiences.

- Start by reviewing the details of the story. Can the farmer count on his friends and neighbors? Identify the moral of the story.

- Think about what you know from experience. Can others always be relied on?

- Decide whether your experience supports or contradicts the moral of the story.

FOLDABLES Keep track of
Study Organizer your ideas about
the **BIG Question** in your unit Foldable.

 Literature Online

Selection Resources
For Selection Quizzes, eFlashcards, and Reading-Writing Connection activities, go to glencoe.com and enter QuickPass code GL27534u1.

Before You Read

The Force of Luck

Connect to the Folktale

Think about a time when you won a game, a contest, or a prize. Was your success the result of hard work, or was it luck?

Partner Talk With a partner, talk about whether success comes from a person's efforts or from luck. Can a person have control over his or her fate?

Build Background

Folktales are stories that have been passed down orally from one generation to another by storytellers. Almost every culture has its own folktales. These tales help reinforce and preserve a culture's values and traditions. "The Force of Luck" is part of the oral tradition of the Hispanic people who lived in the American Southwest. This story shares common elements with other folktales:

- The story is about ordinary people.
- The story takes place in a small village sometime in the past.
- The story features three main events.

Vocabulary

prosperous (pros´ pər əs) *adj.* having wealth or good fortune; successful (p. 92). *The prosperous actor lived in a mansion high in the hills.*

provisions (prə vizh´ ənz) *n.* food or supplies (p. 94). *The backpackers carried enough provisions for two weeks in the wilderness.*

novelty (nov´ əl tē) *n.* something new and unusual (p. 97). *For people living in hot climates, snow is a novelty.*

benefactors (ben´ ə fak´ tərz) *n.* people who help, especially by giving money or gifts (p. 100). *With support from several benefactors, the library was able to buy new computers.*

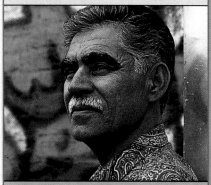

Meet Rudolfo A. Anaya

Southwestern Writer The land and culture of his native New Mexico have inspired Rudolfo A. Anaya since he was a child. Anaya was born in Pastura, a village on a vast plain covered with small farming communities. He has written that "the most important elements of my childhood are the people of those villages and the wide open plains."

Literary Works In his writing, Anaya draws on those childhood memories and on the Mexican myths and legends of his ancestors. Anaya is the author of short stories, novels, and plays.

Rudolfo A. Anaya was born in 1937.

 Literature Online

Author Search For more about Rudolfo A. Anaya, go to glencoe.com and enter QuickPass code GL27534u1.

Set Purposes for Reading

BQ ▶ BIG Question

As you read, ask yourself, what does this folktale suggest about luck and about relying on oneself?

Literary Element Character

A **character** is a person in a literary work. If a character is an animal, it displays human traits. A **main character** is the most important character in a work. A **minor character** is part of the story but is not the focus of the action. **Flat** characters reveal only one personality trait. **Round** characters show varied, and sometimes contradictory, traits.

As you read, pay attention to what the characters think about the events in the story. Notice what they say and how they act. Look for changes in the main character.

Reading Skill Analyze Plot

When you **analyze,** you look at the separate parts of something to understand the whole. When you analyze **plot,** you look at how the parts of the plot work together as a whole. Recall that a plot has five main parts: **exposition, rising action, climax, falling action,** and **resolution.**

To analyze plot, answer these questions:

- Who are the characters, and what is the conflict in the story?
- How do events in the story combine to advance the plot?
- What part of the story is most interesting or suspenseful?
- What happens at the end of the story? How was the reader prepared for the ending by what came before?

As you read, fill in a graphic organizer like the one below.

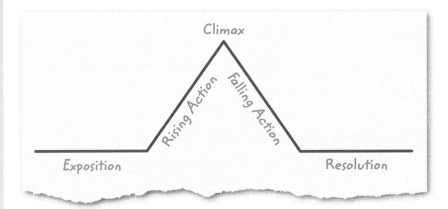

Performance Standards

For pages 90–103

ELA7R1f For literary texts, analyze characterization (dynamic and static) in prose and plays.

TRY IT

Analyze Every story has a plot—including the stories in movies, books, or television programs. Analyze the plot of your favorite movie, book, or television program. With a partner, discuss which events make up the story's rising action, climax, and resolution.

THE FORCE OF LUCK

Retold by Rudolfo A. Anaya

O nce two wealthy friends got into a heated argument. One said that it was money which made a man **prosperous,** and the other maintained that it wasn't money, but luck, which made the man. They argued for some time and finally decided that if only they could find an honorable man then perhaps they could prove their respective points of view.[1]

One day while they were passing through a small village they came upon a miller who was grinding corn and wheat. They paused to ask the man how he ran his business. The miller replied that he worked for a master and that he earned only four bits a day, and with that he had to support a family of five.

The friends were surprised. "Do you mean to tell us you can maintain a family of five on only fifteen dollars a month?" one asked.

"I live modestly to make ends meet," the humble miller replied.

The two friends privately agreed that if they put this man to a test perhaps they could resolve their argument.

"I am going to make you an offer," one of them said to the miller. "I will give you two hundred dollars and you may do whatever you want with the money."

---

1 *Prove their respective points of view* means that each man wanted to prove his opinion was the correct one.

Vocabulary

prosperous (pros′ pər əs) *adj.* having wealth or good fortune; successful

Farmers (Agricultores), 1935. Antonia Gattorna. Gouache and ink on paper laid down on board, 17 1/2 x 19 1/2 in. Private Collection.

Character What does the miller's statement tell you about his character?

"But why would you give me this money when you've just met me?" the miller asked.

"Well, my good man, my friend and I have a long-standing argument. He contends that it is luck which elevates a man to high position, and I say it is money. By giving you this money perhaps we can settle our argument. Here, take it, and do with it what you want!"

So the poor miller took the money and spent the rest of the day thinking about the strange meeting which had presented him with more money than he had ever seen. What could he possibly do with all this money? Be that as it may, he had the money in his pocket and he could do with it whatever he wanted.

When the day's work was done, the miller decided the first thing he would do would be to buy food for his family. He took out ten dollars and wrapped the rest of the money in a cloth and put the bundle in his bag. Then he went to the market and bought supplies and a good piece of meat to take home.

Analyze Plot What conflict does the miller face?

La Molendera 1, 1924. Diego Rivera. *Encaustica sobre tela,* 90 x 117 cm. Museo de Arte Moderno, Busque de Chapultepec, Mexico.

On the way home he was attacked by a **hawk** that had smelled the meat which the miller carried. The miller fought off the bird but in the struggle he lost the bundle of money. Before the miller knew what was happening the hawk grabbed the bag and flew away with it. When he realized what had happened he fell into deep thought.

"Ah," he moaned, "wouldn't it have been better to let that hungry bird have the meat! I could have bought a lot more meat with the money he took. Alas, now I'm in the same poverty as before! And worse, because now those two men will say I am a thief! I should have thought carefully and bought nothing. Yes, I should have gone straight home and this wouldn't have happened!"

So he gathered what was left of his **provisions** and continued home, and when he arrived he told his family the entire story.

When he was finished telling his story his wife said, "It has been our lot² to be poor, but have faith in God and maybe someday our luck will change."

The next day the miller got up and went to work as usual. He wondered what the two men would say about his story. But since he had never been a man of money he soon forgot the entire matter.

Three months after he had lost the money to the hawk, it happened that the two wealthy men returned to the village. As soon as they saw the miller they approached him to ask if his luck had changed. When the miller saw them he felt ashamed and afraid that they would think that he had squandered³ the money on worthless things. But he decided to tell them the truth and as soon as they had greeted each other he told his story. The men believed him. In fact, the one who insisted that it was money and not luck which made a man prosper took out another two hundred dollars and gave it to the miller.

2 Here, *lot* means "fate" or "final outcome."

3 *Squandered* means "spent" or "used in a reckless or wasteful manner."

Vocabulary

provisions (prə vizh′ ənz) *n.* food or supplies

Visual Vocabulary

A **hawk** is a bird of prey.

Character Describe the miller's wife.

Analyze Plot In what way does the man's action advance the plot? What do you think will happen to the money?

"Let's try again," he said, "and let's see what happens this time."

The miller didn't know what to think. "Kind sir, maybe it would be better if you put this money in the hands of another man," he said.

"No," the man insisted, "I want to give it to you because you are an honest man, and if we are going to settle our argument you have to take the money!"

The miller thanked them and promised to do his best. Then as soon as the two men left he began to think what to do with the money so that it wouldn't disappear as it had the first time. The thing to do was to take the money straight home. He took out ten dollars, wrapped the rest in a cloth, and headed home.

When he arrived his wife wasn't at home. At first he didn't know what to do with the money. He went to the pantry where he had stored a large **earthenware** jar filled with bran. That was as safe a place as any to hide the money, he thought, so he emptied out the grain and put the bundle of money at the bottom of the jar, then covered it up with the grain. Satisfied that the money was safe he returned to work.

That afternoon when he arrived home from work he was greeted by his wife.

"Look, my husband, today I bought some good clay with which to whitewash the entire house."

"And how did you buy the clay if we don't have any money?" he asked.

"Well, the man who was selling the clay was willing to trade for jewelry, money, or anything of value," she said. "The only thing we had of value was the jar full of bran, so I traded it for the clay. Isn't it wonderful, I think we have enough clay to whitewash these two rooms!"

The man groaned and pulled his hair.

"Oh, you crazy woman! What have you done? We're ruined again!"

"But why?" she asked, unable to understand his anguish.

"Today I met the same two friends who gave me the two hundred dollars three months ago," he explained. "And after I told them how I lost the money they gave me

Character What did the miller learn from his last experience with the money?

Visual Vocabulary

Earthenware is made from clay that is heated until it is hard.

another two hundred. And I, to make sure the money was safe, came home and hid it inside the jar of bran—the same jar you have traded for dirt! Now we're as poor as we were before! And what am I going to tell the two men? They'll think I'm a liar and a thief for sure!"

"Let them think what they want," his wife said calmly. "We will only have in our lives what the good Lord wants us to have. It is our lot to be poor until God wills it otherwise."

So the miller was consoled and the next day he went to work as usual. Time came and went, and one day the two wealthy friends returned to ask the miller how he had done with the second two hundred dollars. When the poor miller saw them he was afraid they would accuse him of being a liar and a spendthrift.[4] But he decided to be truthful and as soon as they had greeted each other he told them what had happened to the money.

"That is why poor men remain honest," the man who had given him the money said. "Because they don't have money they can't get into trouble. But I find your stories hard to believe. I think you gambled and lost the money. That's why you're telling us these wild stories."

"Either way," he continued, "I still believe that it is money and not luck which makes a man prosper."

"Well, you certainly didn't prove your point by giving the money to this poor miller," his friend reminded him. "Good evening, you luckless man," he said to the miller.

"Thank you, friends," the miller said.

"Oh, by the way, here is a worthless piece of lead I've been carrying around. Maybe you can use it for something," said the man who believed in luck. Then the two men left, still debating their points of view on life.

Since the lead was practically worthless, the miller thought nothing of it and put it in his jacket pocket. He forgot all about it until he arrived home. When he threw his jacket on a chair he heard a thump and he remembered the piece of lead. He took it out of the pocket and threw it

Analyze Plot In what way might the lead affect the events in the story?

---

4 A **spendthrift** is someone who spends money generously or wastefully.

under the table. Later that night after the family had eaten and gone to bed, they heard a knock at the door.

"Who is it? What do you want?" the miller asked.

"It's me, your neighbor," a voice answered. The miller recognized the fisherman's wife. "My husband sent me to ask you if you have any lead you can spare. He is going fishing tomorrow and he needs the lead to weight down the nets."

The miller remembered the lead he had thrown under the table. He got up, found it, and gave it to the woman.

"Thank you very much, neighbor," the woman said. "I promise you the first fish my husband catches will be yours."

"Think nothing of it," the miller said and returned to bed. The next day he got up and went to work without thinking any more of the incident. But in the afternoon when he returned home he found his wife cooking a big fish for dinner.

"Since when are we so well off we can afford fish for supper?" he asked his wife.

"Don't you remember that our neighbor promised us the first fish her husband caught?" his wife reminded him. "Well this was the fish he caught the first time he threw his net. So it's ours, and it's a beauty. But you should have been here when I gutted him! I found a large piece of glass in his stomach!"

"And what did you do with it?"

"Oh, I gave it to the children to play with," she shrugged.

When the miller saw the piece of glass he noticed it shone so brightly it appeared to illuminate the room, but because he knew nothing about jewels he didn't realize its value and left it to the children. But the bright glass was such a **novelty** that the children were soon fighting over it and raising a terrible fuss.

Now it so happened that the miller and his wife had other neighbors who were jewelers. The following morning when the miller had gone to work the jeweler's

Analyze Plot What are some clues that the glass may prove important to the plot?

novelty (nov′ əl tē) n. something new and unusual

wife visited the miller's wife to complain about all the noise her children had made.

"We couldn't get any sleep last night," she moaned.

"I know, and I'm sorry, but you know how it is with a large family," the miller's wife explained. "Yesterday we found a beautiful piece of glass and I gave it to my youngest one to play with and when the others tried to take it from him he raised a storm."

The jeweler's wife took interest. "Won't you show me that piece of glass?" she asked.

"But of course. Here it is."

"Ah, yes, it's a pretty piece of glass. Where did you find it?"

"Our neighbor gave us a fish yesterday and when I was cleaning it I found the glass in its stomach."

"Why don't you let me take it home for just a moment. You see, I have one just like it and I want to compare them."

"Yes, why not? Take it," answered the miller's wife.

So the jeweler's wife ran off with the glass to show it to her husband. When the jeweler saw the glass he instantly knew it was one of the finest diamonds he had ever seen.

"It's a diamond!" he exclaimed.

"I thought so," his wife nodded eagerly. "What shall we do?"

"Go tell the neighbor we'll give her fifty dollars for it, but don't tell her it's a diamond!"

"No, no," his wife chuckled, "of course not." She ran to her neighbor's house. "Ah yes, we have one exactly like this," she told the miller's wife. "My husband is willing to buy it for fifty dollars—only so we can have a pair, you understand."

"I can't sell it," the miller's wife answered. "You will have to wait until my husband returns from work."

That evening when the miller came home from work his wife told him about the offer the jeweler had made for the piece of glass.

"But why would they offer fifty dollars for a worthless piece of glass?" the miller wondered aloud. Before his wife could answer they were interrupted by the jeweler's wife.

Character What does the jeweler's wife's statement tell you about her character?

Analyze Plot Why might this event be part of the story's climax?

"What do you say, neighbor, will you take fifty dollars for the glass?" she asked.

"No, that's not enough," the miller said cautiously. "Offer more."

"I'll give you fifty thousand!" the jeweler's wife blurted out.

"A little bit more," the miller replied.

"Impossible!" the jeweler's wife cried, "I can't offer any more without consulting my husband." She ran off to tell her husband how the bartering[5] was going, and he told her he was prepared to pay a hundred thousand dollars to acquire the diamond.

He handed her seventy-five thousand dollars and said, "Take this and tell him that tomorrow, as soon as I open my shop, he'll have the rest."

When the miller heard the offer and saw the money he couldn't believe his eyes. He imagined the jeweler's wife was jesting[6] with him, but it was a true offer and he received the hundred thousand dollars for the diamond. The miller had never seen so much money, but he still didn't quite trust the jeweler.

"I don't know about this money," he confided to his wife. "Maybe the jeweler plans to accuse us of robbing him and thus get it back."

"Oh no," his wife assured him, "the money is ours. We sold the diamond fair and square—we didn't rob anyone."

"I think I'll still go to work tomorrow," the miller said. "Who knows, something might happen and the money will disappear, then we would be without money and work. Then how would we live?"

So he went to work the next day, and all day he thought about how he could use the money. When he returned home that afternoon his wife asked him what he had decided to do with their new fortune.

"I think I will start my own mill," he answered, "like the one I operate for my master. Once I set up my business we'll see how our luck changes."

BQ BIG Question
Whom does the miller count on?

---

5 **Bartering** is trading goods for other goods without using money.

6 **Jesting** means speaking or acting in a playful manner.

The next day he set about buying everything he needed to establish his mill and to build a new home. Soon he had everything going.

Six months had passed, more or less, since he had seen the two men who had given him the four hundred dollars and the piece of lead. He was eager to see them again and to tell them how the piece of lead had changed his luck and made him wealthy.

Time passed and the miller prospered. His business grew and he even built a summer cottage where he could take his family on vacation. He had many employees who worked for him. One day while he was at his store he saw his two **benefactors** riding by. He rushed out into the street to greet them and ask them to come in. He was overjoyed to see them, and he was happy to see that they admired his store.

"Tell us the truth," the man who had given him the four hundred dollars said. "You used that money to set up this business."

The miller swore he hadn't, and he told them how he had given the piece of lead to his neighbor and how the fisherman had in return given him a fish with a very large diamond in its stomach. And he told them how he had sold the diamond.

"And that's how I acquired this business and many other things I want to show you," he said. "But it's time to eat. Let's eat first then I'll show you everything I have now."

The men agreed, but one of them still doubted the miller's story. So they ate and then the miller had three horses saddled and they rode out to see his summer home. The cabin was on the other side of the river where the mountains were cool and beautiful. When they arrived the men admired the place very much. It was such a peaceful place that they rode all afternoon through the forest. During their ride they came upon a tall pine tree.

Analyze Plot How can you tell that the plot has now reached the falling action?

Character Why would the man not believe the miller?

Vocabulary

benefactors (ben´ə fak´tərz) n. people who help, especially by giving money or gifts

Eagle (Aguila), (detail). Diego Rivera. Overdoor mural, fresco. Secretaria de Educacíon Pública, Mexico City.

"What is that on top of the tree?" one of them asked.

"That's the nest of a hawk," the miller replied.

"I have never seen one; I would like to take a closer look at it!"

"Of course," the miller said, and he ordered a servant to climb the tree and bring down the nest so his friend could see how it was built. When the hawk's nest was on the ground they examined it carefully.

They noticed that there was a cloth bag at the bottom of the nest. When the miller saw the bag he immediately knew that it was the very same bag he had lost to the hawk which fought him for the piece of meat years ago.

"You won't believe me, friends, but this is the very same bag in which I put the first two hundred dollars you gave me," he told them.

"If it's the same bag," the man who had doubted him said, "then the money you said the hawk took should be there."

"No doubt about that," the miller said. "Let's see what we find."

The three of them examined the old, weatherbeaten bag. Although it was full of holes and crumbling, when they tore it apart they found the money intact.[7] The two men remembered what the miller had told them and they agreed he was an honest and honorable man. Still,

---

7 Something that is ***intact*** is undamaged and whole.

the man who had given him the money wasn't satisfied. He wondered what had really happened to the second two hundred he had given the miller.

They spent the rest of the day riding in the mountains and returned very late to the house.

As he unsaddled their horses, the servant in charge of grooming and feeding the horses suddenly realized that he had no grain for them. He ran to the barn and checked, but there was no grain for the hungry horses. So he ran to the neighbor's granary and there he was able to buy a large clay jar of bran. He carried the jar home and emptied the bran into a bucket to wet it before he fed it to the horses. When he got to the bottom of the jar he noticed a large lump which turned out to be a rag-covered package. He examined it and felt something inside. He immediately went to give it to his master who had been eating dinner.

"Master," he said, "look at this package which I found in an earthenware jar of grain which I just bought from our neighbor!"

The three men carefully unraveled the cloth and found the other one hundred and ninety dollars which the miller had told them he had lost. That is how the miller proved to his friends that he was truly an honest man.

And they had to decide for themselves whether it had been luck or money which had made the miller a wealthy man!

Analyze Plot How does the man's doubt provide a clue to what will happen in the story's resolution?

Character How do you think the miller feels about finding the money?

After You Read

Respond and Think Critically

1. What are the two wealthy men trying to prove? Explain. [Recall]

2. Explain how the miller loses his first gift. [Summarize]

3. What values do you think are promoted by this folktale? Explain. [Infer]

4. **Literary Element** Character Is the miller a realistic character? Is he a round or flat character? Use details from the story to support your answer. [Evaluate]

5. **Reading Skill** Analyze Plot Review the plot diagram you created as you read. List at least two events that make up the story's rising action. Then provide at least two events that make up the story's falling action. [Analyze]

6. **BQ** BIG Question Think about events and details from the folktale. Whom or what does the miller count on? [Conclude]

Vocabulary Practice

On a separate sheet of paper, write the vocabulary word that correctly completes each sentence. If none of the words fits the sentence, write "none."

prosperous   novelty   provisions   benefactors

1. We filled our cupboards with the necessary _____ to prepare for the coming storm.

2. My neighbor _____ reality television shows.

3. The animal shelter's _____ gave money, purchased supplies, and helped find homes for pets.

4. Amy was determined to be _____, so she worked hard and saved her earnings.

5. Within a few days, Juan's new unicycle was no longer a _____.

Writing

Write a Summary As you learned on page 59, writing a summary involves retelling the main ideas and most important details. Use your plot diagram and review the story to recall key events in "The Force of Luck." Then write a brief summary of the folktale.

TIP

Inferring
When you infer, you combine clues and details from the text with your own background knowledge. Think about what details and events in the story suggest about the best way to live.

- What kind of person is the miller?

- What does he do with the gifts of money? How does he act after the money is lost?

- What happens as a result of the miller giving the lead to the fisherman's wife? What lesson about life is the folktale suggesting?

FOLDABLES Study Organizer Keep track of your ideas about the **BIG Question** in your unit Foldable.

Literature Online

Selection Resources
For Selection Quizzes, eFlashcards, and Reading-Writing Connection activities, go to glencoe.com and enter QuickPass code GL27534u1.

Before You Read

Rosa

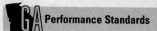 Performance Standards

For pages 104–106

ELA7R1c For literary texts, relate a literary work to information about its setting or historical moment.

Connect to the Poem

Think about a time when you faced a great challenge. How did you act? How did you feel?

Quickwrite Freewrite for a few minutes about a time you faced a challenge with courage. How did you stay calm and composed?

Build Background

From the late 1800s into the 1960s, a system of laws and practices known as segregation kept African Americans separate from white people in the American South.

- In Montgomery, Alabama, African American passengers had to ride in the back of public buses. They also had to give up their seats if white passengers wanted them.

- Rosa Parks was an African American woman who lived in Montgomery, Alabama. On December 1, 1955, she was arrested for refusing to give up her seat on a bus to a white passenger.

- In protest, African Americans in Montgomery stopped riding the buses. In 1956, the United States Supreme Court ended segregation on the buses.

Set Purposes for Reading

BQ BIG Question

As you read, notice the descriptions of Rosa. Ask yourself, whom does Rosa count on for help?

Literary Element Characterization

A character is a person in a literary work. **Characterization** is the method an author uses to develop the personality of a character. In **direct characterization,** the narrator or speaker—the voice of the poem—makes direct statements about a character's personality. In **indirect characterization,** the author reveals a character's personality through the character's words and actions and through what other characters think and say about the character.

As you read, ask yourself, what does the speaker tell me about Rosa Parks? How does the speaker describe Rosa?

Meet Rita Dove

"I see poetry as the root of all writing."

—Rita Dove

Poet Laureate Rita Dove had the special honor of serving two terms as Poet Laureate of the United States. She is best known for her poetry, but she has also written short stories, a novel, several essays, and a play. "Rosa" appeared in a book of poetry published in 1986. Rita Dove was born in 1952.

 Literature Online

Author Search For more about Rita Dove, go to glencoe.com and enter QuickPass code GL27534u1.

Rosa

Rita Dove

Civil Rights Activist, 1983. Marshall D. Rumbaugh. Painted limewood, height: 33 in. National Portrait Gallery, Washington, DC. Gift of Barry Bingham.

How she sat there,
the time right inside a place
so wrong it was ready.

That trim name with
5   its dream of a bench
to rest on. Her sensible coat.

Doing nothing was the doing:
the clean flame of her gaze
carved by a camera flash.

10   How she stood up
when they bent down to retrieve
her purse.° That courtesy.

---

12   When Rosa Parks was arrested, a police officer picked up her purse and carried it to the police car for her.

Characterization What do the details in lines 4–6 tell you about Rosa Parks?

BQ **BIG Question**
What did Rosa Parks teach others about standing up for oneself?

After You Read

Respond and Think Critically

1. In the poem, where is Rosa Parks? [Recall]

2. Restate the first stanza in your own words. [Paraphrase]

3. What does the speaker suggest by pointing out Rosa's "courtesy" in the fourth stanza? [Infer]

4. Think about the way Rosa appears in this poem. What do you find most impressive about her? Explain. [Connect]

5. **Literary Element** Characterization Is the description of Rosa an example of direct or indirect characterization? Is it both? Support your answer with details from the poem. [Analyze]

6. **BQ** BIG Question In this poem, how do Rosa's actions show that she's a person others can count on? Explain. [Analyze]

Spelling Link

Formation of Compound Words A **compound word** is made by joining two words to make a new word. Compound words can be spelled closed (as in *birthday*), hyphenated (as in *worn-out*), or open (as in *high school*). Keep the original spelling of both words, no matter how the words begin or end. If you aren't sure about the spelling of a compound word, check a dictionary.

Examples

surf + board = surfboard   heavy + duty = heavy-duty
count + down = countdown   living + room = living room

Practice On a sheet of paper, combine the words below to make as many compound words as you can. Share your answers with a partner.

home	down	room	wagon	wind
work	band	up	run	fall

 Writing

Write a Journal Entry Rosa Parks's actions helped to put an end to the unfair system of segregation. Think about a time that you, or someone you know, stood up for what was right or fair. What were you fighting for? What happened when you stood up? Tell the story in a journal entry. Use methods of direct and indirect characterization to describe the people you write about.

TIP

Inferring
To answer question 3, you have to use your knowledge and clues from the poem to make a good guess. Here are some tips to help you make an inference.

- Consider what you know about Rosa Parks. What happened to her when she refused to give up her seat?

- Read the last stanza carefully, looking for clues. What does Parks do in these lines? What else happens?

- Combine the clues you found with what you already know. Why do you think the speaker mentions Parks's "courtesy"?

FOLDABLES Keep track of
Study Organizer your ideas about
the **BIG Question** in your
unit Foldable.

 Literature Online

Selection Resources
For Selection Quizzes, eFlashcards, and Reading-Writing Connection activities, go to glencoe.com and enter QuickPass code GL27534u1.

GA Performance Standards

For pages 107–110

ELA7R1c For literary texts, relate a literary work to information about its setting or historical moment.

Social Perspective

on "Rosa" by Rita Dove

from
Rosa Parks: My Story

by Rosa Parks with Jim Haskins

Coretta Scott King Award Medal

Set a Purpose for Reading

Read this autobiographical excerpt to learn about the event that inspired the poem "Rosa."

Build Background

During the 1950s, many states in the South still enforced laws that supported racial segregation. The incident described in this excerpt took place in 1955 and sparked a boycott of the Montgomery, Alabama, buses.

Reading Skill Analyze Social Context

To analyze the social context of a literary work, gather background information about the social issues of the time. This selection gives background for the poem "Rosa." Use a graphic organizer to take notes on the social context.

"Rosa"	Social Context
Doing nothing was the doing	Rosa Parks gained attention by not giving up her seat.

When I got off from work that evening of December 1, I went to Court Square as usual to catch the Cleveland Avenue bus home. I didn't look to see who was driving when I got on, and by the time I recognized him I had already paid my fare. It was the same driver who had put me off the bus back in 1943, twelve years earlier. He was still tall and heavy, with red, rough-looking skin. And he was still mean-looking. I didn't know if he had been on that route before—they switched the drivers around sometimes. I do know that most of the time if I saw him on a bus, I wouldn't get on it.

I saw a vacant[1] seat in the middle section of the bus and took it. I didn't

---

1 *Vacant* means "empty." A vacant seat is a seat with nobody in it.

even question why there was a vacant seat even though there were quite a few people standing in the back. If I had thought about it at all, I would probably have figured maybe someone saw me get on and did not take the seat but left it vacant for me. There was a man sitting next to the window and two women across the aisle.

The next stop was the Empire Theater, and some whites got on. They filled up the white seats, and one man was left standing. The driver looked back and noticed the man standing. Then he looked back at us. He said, "Let me have those front seats," because they were the front seats of the black section. Didn't anybody

Before the December 21, 1956, Supreme Court ruling, African Americans in the South had to sit in the back seats on the bus.

View the Photo How does this photograph help you understand the times Rosa Parks tells about?

move. We just sat right where we were, the four of us. Then he spoke a second time: "Y'all better make it light on yourselves and let me have those seats."

The man in the window seat next to me stood up, and I moved to let him pass by me, and then I looked across the aisle and saw that the two women were also standing. I moved over to the window seat. I could not see how standing up was going to "make it light" for me. The more we gave in and complied,[2] the worse they treated us.

I thought back to the time when I used to sit up all night and didn't sleep, and my grandfather would have his gun right by the fireplace, or if he had his one-horse wagon going anywhere, he always had his gun in the back of the wagon. People always say that I didn't give up my seat because I was tired, but that isn't true. I was not tired physically, or no more tired than I usually was at the end of a working day. I was not old, although some people have an image of me as being old then. I was forty-two. No, the only tired I was, was tired of giving in.

The driver of the bus saw me still sitting there, and he asked was I going to stand up. I said, "No." He said, "Well, I'm going to have you arrested." Then I said, "You may do that." These were the only words we said to each

---

2 **Complied** means "went along with" or "did what was asked or ordered."

Rosa Parks was arrested again on February 22, 1956. She had dared to disobey another segregation law.

other. I didn't even know his name, which was James Blake, until we were in court together. He got out of the bus and stayed outside for a few minutes, waiting for the police.

As I sat there, I tried not to think about what might happen. I knew that anything was possible. I could be manhandled[3] or beaten. I could be arrested. People have asked me if it occurred to me then that I could be the test case the NAACP[4] had been looking for. I did not think about that at all. In fact if I had let myself think too deeply about what might happen

to me, I might have gotten off the bus, but I chose to remain.

Meanwhile there were people getting off the bus and asking for transfers, so that began to loosen up the crowd, especially in the back of the bus. Not everyone got off, but everybody was very quiet. What conversation there was, was in low tones; no one was talking out loud. It would have been quite interesting to have seen the whole bus empty out.

Or if the other three had stayed where they were, because if they'd had to arrest four of us instead of one, then that would have given me a little support. But it didn't matter. I never thought hard of them at all and never even bothered to criticize[5] them.

---

3 To **manhandle** someone is to treat that person roughly.

4 **NAACP** stands for National Association for the Advancement of Colored People. This group wanted to get rid of the laws that allowed unfair treatment of African Americans. The group hoped that if such laws were to be tested in a court case, the laws would then be made illegal.

5 To **criticize** is to point out what is bad about someone or something.

Eventually two policemen came. They got on the bus, and one of them asked me why I didn't stand up. I asked him, "Why do you all push us around?" He said to me, and I quote him exactly, "I don't know, but the law is the law and you're under arrest." One policeman picked up my purse, and the second one picked up my shopping bag and escorted me to the squad car. In the squad car they returned my personal belongings to me. They did not put their hands on me or force me into the car. After I was seated in the car, they went back to the driver and asked him if he wanted to swear out a warrant.[6] He answered that he would finish his route and then come straight back to swear out the warrant. I was only in custody,[7] not legally arrested, until the warrant was signed.

As they were driving me to the city desk, at City Hall, near Court Street, one of them asked me again. "Why didn't you stand up when the driver spoke to you?" I did not answer. I remained silent all the way to City Hall.

Rosa Parks sits in the front of a bus in Montgomery, Alabama, after the Supreme Court ruled segregation illegal on the city bus system on December 21, 1956. The man sitting behind Parks is Nicholas C. Chriss, a reporter for United Press International in Atlanta, Georgia.

6 A *warrant* is a document, or piece of paper, that gives a police officer the right to do something, such as arrest a person.

7 To be *in custody* is to be held by the police.

Respond and Think Critically

1. Write a brief summary of the main events in this excerpt before you answer the following questions. State the main events in your own words and in a logical order. **[Summarize]**

2. What did the bus driver mean when he said, "Y'all better make it light on yourselves and let me have those seats"? **[Interpret]**

3. What does Parks suggest was the reason that she did not obey the bus driver's order? **[Infer]**

4. **Text-to-Text** How do the following lines from Rita Dove's poem "Rosa" express the importance of Parks's experience: "the time right inside a place / so wrong it was ready"? **[Connect]**

5. **Reading Skill Analyze Social Context** Why was Parks's refusal to give up her seat such an important action in the 1950s? Provide details to support your answer.

6. **BQ BIG Question** Based on what you learned about Rosa Parks in this excerpt, how do you think she would answer the Big Question?

Part 3

Extraordinary Individuals

Chinese Doctor, 1998. Chen Lian Xing. Watercolor. Read Lantern Folk Art, Mukashi Collection.

BQ **BIG Question** **Whom Can You Count On?**

Why might the medical workers in the picture *Chinese Doctor* be considered remarkable people? What extraordinary individuals do you know?

Seventh Grade

Connect to the Short Story

Think about your first day of school at the beginning of a new school year. How do you feel on that day?

Quickwrite Freewrite for a few minutes about your experiences on the first day of school. What thoughts go through your mind? Do you think your experiences are similar to, or different from, other people's experiences?

Build Background

"Seventh Grade" is about Victor, a Mexican American boy growing up in Fresno, California.

- Fresno is located near the center of the state of California.

- Fresno has a large Mexican American community. Many of Gary Soto's short stories contain characters and settings that reflect Soto's own Mexican American community in Fresno. However, Soto has said that the experiences portrayed in his stories are universal, understandable to people of all backgrounds.

Vocabulary

ferocity (fə ros′ə tē) *n.* a wild fierceness (p. 115).
The injured dog snarled and growled with ferocity when anyone tried to approach it.

conviction (kən vik′shən) *n.* a firmness of belief or opinion (p. 116). *The candidates for mayor spoke with great conviction about their plans to improve the town.*

campus (kam′pəs) *n.* the land and buildings of a school (p. 117). *The library was at the north end of the campus.*

Meet Gary Soto

"Writing is my one talent. There are a lot of people who never discover what their talent is. . . . I am very lucky to have found mine."

—Gary Soto

A Meaningful Journey Gary Soto's experiences growing up in a Spanish-speaking neighborhood inspire much of his work. Like his parents and grandparents, Soto labored for a time as a migrant farm worker picking fruit. His love of literature came later, when he went to college. His writing includes award-winning poetry, novels, and memoirs.

Gary Soto was born in 1952.

 Literature Online

Author Search For more about Gary Soto, go to glencoe.com and enter QuickPass code GL27534u1.

Set Purposes for Reading

BQ BIG Question

In this story, Victor benefits from some unexpected help. As you read, ask yourself, how do other people help us in unexpected ways?

GA Performance Standards

For pages 112–122

ELA7R1f For literary texts, analyze characterization (dynamic and static) in prose and plays.

Literary Element Description

Description is writing that conveys an impression of a setting, person, animal, object, or event. Description often includes **sensory details**, which help readers see, hear, feel, smell, and taste the scenes that the author describes. Sensory details help to create **imagery.** For instance, a writer might create a vivid image of a school playground by describing the noisy cries of students playing soccer.

As you read, use the descriptions in the story to visualize, or picture in your mind, the characters, setting, and events.

Reading Strategy Make Inferences About Characters

When you **make inferences,** you combine clues in the selection with your own knowledge to figure out what the author does not tell you directly. Making inferences helps you to deepen your understanding of characters and events.

To make inferences about a character, pay attention to

- what the character thinks, says, and does
- how the character looks
- what others say about the character
- how others react to the character

Then use these clues and your own knowledge to understand the character's personality and actions. You may find it helpful to use a graphic organizer like the one below.

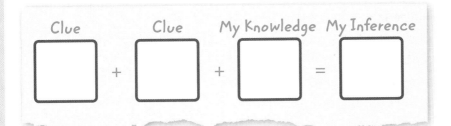

Clue + Clue + My Knowledge = My Inference

Seventh Grade

GARY SOTO

On the first day of school, Victor stood in line half an hour before he came to a wobbly card table. He was handed a packet of papers and a computer card on which he listed his one elective,[1] French. He already spoke Spanish and English, but he thought some day he might travel to France, where it was cool; not like Fresno, where summer days reached 110 degrees in the shade. There were rivers in France, and huge churches, and fair-skinned people everywhere, the way there were brown people all around Victor.

Besides, Teresa, a girl he had liked since they were in catechism[2] classes at Saint Theresa's, was taking French, too. With any luck they would be in the same class. Teresa is going to be my girl this year, he promised himself as he left the gym full of students in their new fall clothes. She was cute. And good at math, too, Victor thought as he walked down the hall to his homeroom. He ran into his friend, Michael Torres, by the water fountain that never turned off.

---

1 An *elective* is a class that a student chooses to take.

2 At *catechism* (kat′ə kiz′ əm) *classes,* students learn about the Roman Catholic religion.

They shook hands, *raza*-style,[3] and jerked their heads at one another in a *saludo de vato*.[4] "How come you're making a face?" asked Victor.

"I ain't making a face, *ese*. This *is* my face." Michael said his face had changed during the summer. He had read a GQ magazine that his older brother borrowed from the Book Mobile and noticed that the male models all had the same look on their faces. They would stand, one arm around a beautiful woman, and *scowl*. They would sit at a pool, their rippled stomachs dark with shadow, and *scowl*. They would sit at dinner tables, cool drinks in their hands, and *scowl*.

"I think it works," Michael said. He scowled and let his upper lip quiver. His teeth showed along with the **ferocity** of his soul. "Belinda Reyes walked by a while ago and looked at me," he said.

Victor didn't say anything, though he thought his friend looked pretty strange. They talked about recent movies, baseball, their parents, and the horrors of picking grapes in order to buy their fall clothes. Picking grapes was like living in Siberia,[5] except hot and more boring.

"What classes are you taking?" Michael said, scowling.

"French. How 'bout you?"

"Spanish. I ain't so good at it, even if I'm Mexican."

"I'm not either, but I'm better at it than math, that's for sure."

A tinny, three-beat bell propelled[6] students to their homerooms. The two friends socked each other in the arm and went their ways, Victor thinking, man, that's weird. Michael thinks making a face makes him handsome.

On the way to his homeroom, Victor tried a scowl. He felt foolish, until out of the corner of his eye he saw a girl

Description Which words or phrases in this paragraph help you visualize how the models look?

Make Inferences About Characters Why do you think Michael has changed his facial expression?

---

3 ***Raza-style*** (rä′ zä) refers to the way Mexican Americans or other Hispanic people do something.

4 ***Saludo de vato*** (sä lo͞o′ dō de vä′ tō) is a greeting.

5 ***Siberia*** is a very cold area in northern Asia.

6 ***Propelled*** means "pushed or moved forward by a force or *as if* by one."

Vocabulary

ferocity (fə ros′ ə tē) *n.* a wild fierceness

looking at him. Umm, he thought, maybe it does work. He scowled with greater **conviction**.

In homeroom, roll was taken, emergency cards were passed out, and they were given a bulletin to take home to their parents. The principal, Mr. Belton, spoke over the crackling loudspeaker, welcoming the students to a new year, new experiences, and new friendships. The students squirmed in their chairs and ignored him. They were anxious to go to first period. Victor sat calmly, thinking of Teresa, who sat two rows away, reading a paperback novel. This would be his lucky year. She was in his homeroom, and would probably be in his English and math classes. And, of course, French.

The bell rang for first period, and the students herded noisily through the door. Only Teresa lingered,[7] talking with the homeroom teacher.

"So you think I should talk to Mrs. Gaines?" she asked the teacher. "She would know about ballet?"

"She would be a good bet," the teacher said. Then added, "Or the gym teacher, Mrs. Garza."

Victor lingered, keeping his head down and staring at his desk. He wanted to leave when she did so he could bump into her and say something clever.

He watched her on the sly.[8] As she turned to leave, he stood up and hurried to the door, where he managed to catch her eye. She smiled and said, "Hi, Victor."

He smiled back and said, "Yeah, that's me." His brown face blushed. Why hadn't he said, "Hi, Teresa," or "How was your summer?" or something nice?

As Teresa walked down the hall, Victor walked the other way, looking back, admiring how gracefully she walked, one foot in front of the other. So much for being in the same class, he thought. As he trudged to English, he practiced scowling.

Description Which details in this paragraph appeal to a reader's senses?

Make Inferences About Characters What inferences might you make about Teresa based on what she says and does?

---

7 *Lingered* means "was slow to move or leave."

8 When you do something *on the sly,* you do it so that no one notices.

Vocabulary ....

conviction (kən vik′shən) *n.* a firmness of belief or opinion

In English they reviewed the parts of speech. Mr. Lucas, a portly man, waddled down the aisle, asking, "What is a noun?"

"A person, place, or thing," said the class in unison.[9]

"Yes, now somebody give me an example of a person— you, Victor Rodriguez."

"Teresa," Victor said automatically. Some of the girls giggled. They knew he had a crush on Teresa. He felt himself blushing again.

"Correct," Mr. Lucas said. "Now provide me with a place."

Mr. Lucas called on a freckled kid who answered, "Teresa's house with a kitchen full of big brothers."

After English, Victor had math, his weakest subject. He sat in the back by the window, hoping that he would not be called on. Victor understood most of the problems, but some of the stuff looked like the teacher made it up as she went along. It was confusing, like the inside of a watch.

After math he had a fifteen-minute break, then social studies, and, finally, lunch. He bought a tuna **casserole** with buttered rolls, some fruit cocktail, and milk. He sat with Michael, who practiced scowling between bites.

Girls walked by and looked at him.

"See what I mean, Vic?" Michael scowled. "They love it."

"Yeah, I guess so."

They ate slowly, Victor scanning the horizon[10] for a glimpse[11] of Teresa. He didn't see her. She must have brought lunch, he thought, and is eating outside. Victor scraped his plate and left Michael, who was busy scowling at a girl two tables away.

The small, triangle-shaped **campus** bustled with students talking about their new classes. Everyone was in a sunny mood. Victor hurried to the bag lunch area, where he sat down and opened his math book. He moved his lips

---

9 *In unison* means "all together."

10 *Scanning the horizon* is looking far ahead to find something in the distance.

11 When you look for a *glimpse* of someone, you try to get a quick look at him or her.

Vocabulary

campus (kam´pəs) *n.* the land and buildings of a school

as if he were reading, but his mind was somewhere else. He raised his eyes slowly and looked around. No Teresa.

He lowered his eyes, pretending to study, then looked slowly to the left. No Teresa. He turned a page in the book and stared at some math problems that scared him because he knew he would have to do them eventually.[12] He looked to the right. Still no sign of her. He stretched out lazily in an attempt to disguise his snooping.

Then he saw her. She was sitting with a girlfriend under a plum tree. Victor moved to a table near her and daydreamed about taking her to a movie. When the bell sounded, Teresa looked up, and their eyes met. She smiled sweetly and gathered her books. Her next class was French, same as Victor's.

They were among the last students to arrive in class, so all the good desks in the back had already been taken. Victor was forced to sit near the front, a few desks away from Teresa, while Mr. Bueller wrote French words on the chalkboard. The bell rang, and Mr. Bueller wiped his hands, turned to the class, and said, *"Bonjour."*[13]

"Bonjour," braved a few students.

Description How does the description of Victor's actions help you understand Victor's character?

---

12 *Eventually* means "in the end" or "finally."

13 *Bonjour* is French for "Good day" or "Hello."

"Bonjour," Victor whispered. He wondered if Teresa heard him.

Mr. Bueller said that if the students studied hard, at the end of the year they could go to France and be understood by the populace.

One kid raised his hand and asked, "What's 'populace'?"

"The people, the people of France."

Mr. Bueller asked if anyone knew French. Victor raised his hand, wanting to impress[14] Teresa. The teacher beamed and said, *"Très bien. Parlez-vous français?"*[15]

Victor didn't know what to say. The teacher wet his lips and asked something else in French. The room grew silent. Victor felt all eyes staring at him. He tried to bluff his way out by making noises that sounded French.

"La me vava me con le grandma," he said uncertainly.

Mr. Bueller, wrinkling his face in curiosity, asked him to speak up.

Great rosebushes of red bloomed on Victor's cheeks. A river of nervous sweat ran down his palms. He felt awful. Teresa sat a few desks away, no doubt thinking he was a fool. Without looking at Mr. Bueller, Victor mumbled, "Frenchie oh wewe gee in September."

Mr. Bueller asked Victor to repeat what he had said.

"Frenchie oh wewe gee in September," Victor repeated.

Mr. Bueller understood that the boy didn't know French and turned away. He walked to the blackboard and pointed to the words on the board with his steel-edged ruler.

"Le bateau," he sang.

"Le bateau," the students repeated.

"Le bateau est sur l'eau," he sang.

"Le bateau est sur l'eau."[16]

Victor was too weak from failure to join the class. He stared at the board and wished he had taken Spanish, not French. Better yet, he wished he could start his life over. He had never been so embarrassed. He bit his thumb until he tore off a sliver of skin.

Make Inferences About Characters Consider what you've learned about Victor. What can you infer about the real cause of his embarrassment?

---

14 If you *impress* someone, it means you have a strong effect on him or her.

15 *Très bien. Parlez-vous français?* means "Very well. Do you speak French?"

16 *Le bateau* is French for "the boat." *Le bateau est sur l'eau* means "The boat is on the water."

The bell sounded for fifth period, and Victor shot out of the room, avoiding the stares of the other kids, but had to return for his math book. He looked sheepishly[17] at the teacher, who was erasing the board, then widened his eyes in terror at Teresa who stood in front of him. "I didn't know you knew French," she said. "That was good."

Mr. Bueller looked at Victor, and Victor looked back. Oh please, don't say anything, Victor pleaded with his eyes. I'll wash your car, mow your lawn, walk your dog—anything! I'll be your best student, and I'll clean your erasers after school.

Mr. Bueller shuffled through the papers on his desk. He smiled and hummed as he sat down to work. He remembered his college years when he dated a girlfriend in borrowed cars. She thought he was rich because each time he picked her up he had a different car. It was fun until he had spent all his money on her and had to write home to his parents because he was broke.

Victor couldn't stand to look at Teresa. He was sweaty with shame. "Yeah, well, I picked up a few things from movies and books and stuff like that." They left the class together. Teresa asked him if he would help her with her French.

"Sure, anytime," Victor said.

"I won't be bothering you, will I?"

"Oh no, I like being bothered."

"*Bonjour*," Teresa said, leaving him outside her next class. She smiled and pushed wisps of hair from her face.

"Yeah, right, *bonjour*," Victor said. He turned and headed to his class. The rosebushes of shame on his face became bouquets of love. Teresa is a great girl, he thought. And Mr. Bueller is a good guy.

He raced to metal shop. After metal shop there was biology, and after biology a long sprint to the public library, where he checked out three French textbooks.

He was going to like seventh grade. 🔖

BQ **BIG Question**

How is Mr. Bueller someone Victor can count on?

Make Inferences About Characters Why do you think Victor checks out the French textbooks?

---

17 When you look *sheepishly* at someone, you show that you are shy and embarrassed.

After You Read

Respond and Think Critically

1. What promise does Victor make to himself about the school year? Why is Victor taking French? Explain. [Recall]

2. What happens during Victor's first French class? Support your answer with details from the story. [Summarize]

3. Why does Victor give the answer "Teresa" when his English teacher asks him for an example of a person? [Infer]

4. In what way might Mr. Bueller be similar to Victor? Explain. [Compare]

5. Do you think Victor is a believable character? Why or why not? [Evaluate]

6. **BQ** **BIG Question** Were you surprised that Victor could count on Mr. Bueller? Explain your answer. [Connect]

TIP

Evaluating
Here are some tips to help you evaluate whether Victor is a believable character:

- Think about Victor's words and actions and your own experiences.

- A believable character is one that is realistic, or one that reminds you of a real person. Does Victor seem as though he could be a student at your school? Why or why not?

FOLDABLES **Study Organizer** Keep track of your ideas about the **BIG Question** in your unit Foldable.

Connect to Math

Foreign Languages in U.S. Schools

In schools across the United States, students like Victor study a foreign language. The bar graph shows what percentage of students in the United States took foreign language classes in 2000 and which languages they studied.

On Your Own Answer the following questions on a separate sheet of paper.

1. What percentage of students studied a foreign language? What percentage studied a language other than Spanish?

2. Which foreign language was the most widely studied?

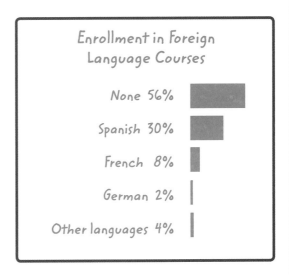

Enrollment in Foreign Language Courses

None 56%
Spanish 30%
French 8%
German 2%
Other languages 4%

Literary Element Description

1. What are three descriptions that the author provides to help you visualize this story?

2. How would "Seventh Grade" be different without descriptions of characters or setting? Use examples from the story to support your response.

Review: Character

As you learned on page 91, a **character** is a person in a literary work. Some characters are **flat**. Others are **round**. A flat character reveals only one personality trait. A character who shows varied and sometimes contradictory traits is called a round character.

Standards Practice ELA7R1f

3. Which character in the story is a round character?
   - A Michael
   - B Victor
   - C Belinda
   - D Mr. Lucas

Reading Strategy Make Inferences About Characters

Standards Practice ELA7R1b

4. Based on the story, you can infer that
   - A Michael has many girlfriends.
   - B Mr. Bueller speaks Spanish.
   - C Victor only eats tuna casserole.
   - D Teresa admires Victor.

Vocabulary Practice

On a separate sheet of paper, write the vocabulary word that correctly completes each sentence. If none of the words fits the sentence, write "none."

ferocity   conviction   campus

1. Kelsey spoke with great _____ about the need to protect the bird's habitat.

2. The weather changed suddenly, and the wind blew _____ through the trees.

3. Her _____ was heightened when she received her new bicycle.

4. The mother bear roared with _____ as she protected her cub from the hunters.

5. The map of the _____ shows where the library and the gym are located.

Academic Vocabulary

Victor **benefits** from Mr. Bueller's silence after French class. To become more familiar with the word *benefits,* fill out the graphic organizer below.

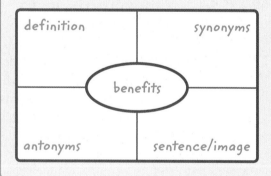

 Literature Online

Selection Resources For Selection Quizzes, eFlashcards, and Reading-Writing Connection activities, go to glencoe.com and enter QuickPass code GL27534u1.

Respond Through Writing

Autobiographical Narrative

Apply Description "Seventh Grade" describes Victor's experiences starting seventh grade. Write an autobiographical narrative about a recent experience you've had at school. Use description and imagery to describe the characters, setting, and events.

Understand the Task An autobiographical narrative is a story you tell about your own experiences. Using **description** and **sensory details,** or details that appeal to your reader's senses, will help your reader visualize your story. You'll tell your story using first-person point of view.

Prewrite Select one school experience that you remember well. Briefly describe the setting and characters. Use a graphic organizer similar to the one below to organize the events of the story. Be sure to put the events in the correct order. You may need to add more boxes.

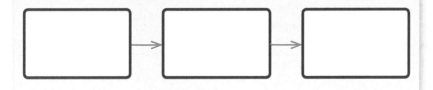

Draft Begin writing your autobiographical narrative, using your descriptions and graphic organizer as starting points. Be sure to use imagery to describe the setting, characters, and events. Include dialogue and descriptions of your characters' actions, gestures, and expressions. Make sure your narrative has a clear beginning, rising action, a climax, and a resolution.

Revise After you have written your first draft, read it to make sure that the events are in the right order. Rearrange parts as necessary so that your story is easy to follow. Check that your descriptions and imagery help bring the story to life. Add more details as needed.

Edit and Proofread Proofread your story, correcting any errors in spelling, grammar, and punctuation. Review the Grammar Tip in the side column for information on using quotation marks.

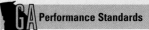 **Performance Standards**

For page 123

ELA7W2d Demonstrate competence in a variety of genres. Produce a narrative that includes sensory details and concrete language to develop plot, setting, and character.

> ## Grammar Tip

Quotation Marks
One way to make your autobiographical narrative more interesting is to add dialogue—the words that characters say. Use quotation marks to show a person's actual words. For example:

"Why were you late to school today?" Sherrie asked.

"I missed the bus," I told her.

Make sure that there are quotation marks before and after the character's words. Look at the dialogue in "Seventh Grade" to see more examples.

Before You Read

Thank You, M'am

Connect to the Short Story

Think about a time when someone you didn't know well had a positive influence on you. It might have been a real person, or even a character in a book or a movie.

Quickwrite Freewrite for a few minutes about the person who influenced you. Who was the person? How did that person influence you? How did that influence change your life?

Build Background

- This story was written during the 1950s. At that time, things cost less than they do today. For example, a comic book cost ten cents, and a good pair of shoes might have cost from five to ten dollars.

- Much of this story takes place in a rooming house, a house where people rent rooms in which to live. In many rooming houses, the renters share one living room and kitchen. In others, like the one Mrs. Jones lives in, tenants have their own small kitchen areas.

Vocabulary

whereupon (hwār′ə pôn) *conj.* at which time; after which (p. 128). *The man heard a loud noise, whereupon he dropped his grocery bag.*

mistrusted (mis trust′ed) *v.* regarded with suspicion or doubt (p. 130). *I mistrusted my ability to walk across the ice without slipping.*

Set Purposes for Reading

BQ BIG Question

As you read, ask yourself, how can extraordinary individuals persuade a person to change his or her ways?

Literary Element Characterization

Characterization includes all the methods that a writer uses to develop the personality of a character. Sometimes the narrator of a story tells you exactly what a character is like. This is called **direct characterization.** At other times, a character's personality is revealed through his or her words and actions and through what other characters think or say about him or her. This is called **indirect characterization.**

Characterization is important because it helps you get to know the characters—what they think, how they feel, and why they act the way they do. As you read, pay attention to what the narrator says about the characters. Ask yourself what a character's actions and words reveal about his or her personality.

Reading Skill Analyze Setting

When you **analyze setting,** you look closely at the setting to understand its significance to the story. Remember that setting is the time and place in which a story takes place.

Analyzing the setting will help you see how time and place affect the characters and events. Analyzing the setting will also help you understand the mood, or atmosphere, of the story.

To analyze setting, pay attention to details of the setting and how they affect the story. To track details of setting, you may find it helpful to use a web like the one below.

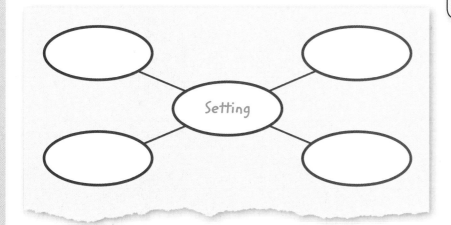

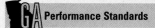

GA Performance Standards

For pages 124–133

ELA7R1f For literary texts, analyze characterization (dynamic and static) in prose and plays.

TRY IT

Analyze When you analyze something, you look at the separate parts to understand the whole. When you read instructions for how to put something together, you look at each step to understand how to assemble the whole object. Analyzing each step carefully helps you understand how the whole object fits together.

The City from Greenwich Village, 1922. John Sloan. Oil on Canvas, 26 x 33 3/4 in. National Gallery of Art, Washington, DC.

Thank You, M'am

Langston Hughes

She was a large woman with a large purse that had everything in it but hammer and nails. It had a long strap and she carried it slung[1] across her shoulder. It was about eleven o'clock at night, and she was walking alone, when a boy ran up behind her and tried to snatch her purse. The strap broke with the single tug the boy gave it from behind. But the boy's weight, and the weight of the purse combined caused him to lose his balance so, instead of taking off full blast as he had hoped, the boy fell on his back on the sidewalk, and his legs flew up. The large woman simply turned around and kicked him right square in his blue jeaned sitter. Then she reached down, picked the boy up by his shirt front, and shook him until his teeth rattled.

After that the woman said, "Pick up my pocketbook, boy, and give it here."

She still held him. But she bent down enough to permit him to stoop and pick up her purse. Then she said, "Now ain't you ashamed of yourself?"

Firmly gripped by his shirt front, the boy said, "Yes'm."

The woman said, "What did you want to do it for?"

The boy said, "I didn't aim to."

She said, "You a lie!"

By that time two or three people passed, stopped, turned to look, and some stood watching.

"If I turn you loose, will you run?" asked the woman.

"Yes'm," said the boy.

"Then I won't turn you loose," said the woman. She did not release him.

"I'm very sorry, lady, I'm sorry," whispered the boy.

"Um-hum! And your face is dirty. I got a great mind to wash your face for you. Ain't you got nobody home to tell you to wash your face?"

"No'm," said the boy.

"Then it will get washed this evening," said the large woman starting up the street, dragging the frightened boy behind her.

Analyze Setting When does this story take place? How might the time of day affect the action of the story?

Characterization What does this dialogue reveal about the two characters?

---

1 If something is *slung* across your shoulder, it is hung or thrown loosely over it.

He looked as if he were fourteen or fifteen, frail[2] and willow-wild,[3] in tennis shoes and blue jeans.

The woman said, "You ought to be my son. I would teach you right from wrong. Least I can do right now is to wash your face. Are you hungry?"

"No'm," said the being-dragged boy. "I just want you to turn me loose."

"Was I bothering you when I turned that corner?" asked the woman.

"No'm."

"But you put yourself in contact with me," said the woman. "If you think that that contact is not going to last awhile, you got another thought coming. When I get through with you, sir, you are going to remember Mrs. Luella Bates Washington Jones."

Sweat popped out on the boy's face and he began to struggle. Mrs. Jones stopped, jerked him around in front of her, put a **half nelson** about his neck, and continued to drag him up the street. When she got to her door, she dragged the boy inside, down a hall, and into a large kitchenette-furnished room at the rear of the house. She switched on the light and left the door open. The boy could hear other roomers laughing and talking in the large house. Some of their doors were open, too, so he knew he and the woman were not alone. The woman still had him by the neck in the middle of her room.

She said, "What is your name?"

"Roger," answered the boy.

"Then, Roger, you go to that sink and wash your face," said the woman, **whereupon** she turned him loose—at last. Roger looked at the door—looked at the woman—looked at the door—and went to the sink.

"Let the water run until it gets warm," she said. "Here's a clean towel."

---

2 If someone looks *frail*, he or she looks weak.

3 *Willow-wild* means looking wild like a willow tree. Willow trees have long, thin, drooping branches.

Vocabulary

whereupon (hwār′ə pôn) *conj.* at which time; after which

Jim, 1930. William H. Johnson. Oil on canvas, 21 5/8 x 18 1/4 in. Smithsonian American Art Museum, Washington, DC.

View the Art In what ways does the subject of this painting remind you of Roger?

"You gonna take me to jail?" asked the boy, bending over the sink.

"Not with that face, I would not take you nowhere," said the woman. "Here I am trying to get home to cook me a bite to eat and you snatch my pocketbook! Maybe you ain't been to your supper either, late as it be. Have you?"

"There's nobody home at my house," said the boy.

"Then we'll eat," said the woman. "I believe you're hungry—or been hungry—to try to snatch my pocketbook."

"I wanted a pair of blue suede shoes,"[4] said the boy.

"Well, you didn't have to snatch my pocketbook to get some suede shoes," said Mrs. Luella Bates Washington Jones. "You could of asked me."

"M'am?"

The water dripping from his face, the boy looked at her. There was a long pause. A very long pause. After he had dried his face and not knowing what else to do dried it again, the boy turned around, wondering what next. The door was open. He could make a dash for it down the hall. He could run, run, run, run, run!

---

4 **Blue suede shoes** are men's shoes made of soft leather. These shoes became popular in the late 1950s after Elvis Presley recorded a hit song called "Blue Suede Shoes."

The woman was sitting on the daybed.[5] After a while she said, "I were young once and I wanted things I could not get."

There was another long pause. The boy's mouth opened. Then he frowned, but not knowing he frowned.

The woman said, "Um-hum! You thought I was going to say but, didn't you? You thought I was going to say, but I didn't snatch people's pocketbooks. Well, I wasn't going to say that." Pause. Silence. "I have done things, too, which I would not tell you, son—neither tell God, if he didn't already know. So you set down while I fix us something to eat. You might run that comb through your hair so you will look presentable."

In another corner of the room behind a screen was a gas plate and an icebox.[6] Mrs. Jones got up and went behind the screen. The woman did not watch the boy to see if he was going to run now, nor did she watch her purse which she left behind her on the daybed. But the boy took care to sit on the far side of the room where he thought she could easily see him out of the corner of her eye, if she wanted to. He did not trust the woman not to trust him. And he did not want to be **mistrusted** now.

"Do you need somebody to go to the store," asked the boy, "maybe to get some milk or something?"

"Don't believe I do," said the woman, "unless you just want sweet milk yourself. I was going to make cocoa out of this canned milk I got here."

"That will be fine," said the boy.

She heated some lima beans and ham she had in the icebox, made the cocoa, and set the table. The woman did not ask the boy anything about where he lived, or his folks, or anything else that would embarrass him. Instead, as they ate, she told him about her job in a hotel beauty

Characterization Why do you think Mrs. Jones says this?

Analyze Setting Why does the boy choose to sit where Mrs. Jones can see him?

---

5 A **daybed** is a sofa that can be converted into a bed.

6 The **gas plate** is a small version of a stovetop, with burners fueled by gas. Before electricity, a block of ice cooled food inside a special box. Even today, some people use the word **icebox** to refer to a refrigerator.

Vocabulary . . . .

mistrusted (mis trust´ed) v. regarded with suspicion or doubt

shop that stayed open late, what the work was like, and how all kinds of women came in and out, blondes, red-heads, and Spanish. Then she cut him a half of her ten-cent cake.

"Eat some more, son," she said.

When they were finished eating she got up and said, "Now, here, take this ten dollars and buy yourself some blue suede shoes. And next time, do not make the mistake of latching onto my pocketbook nor nobody else's— because shoes come by devilish like that will burn your feet. I got to get my rest now. But I wish you would behave yourself, son, from here on in."

She led him down the hall to the front door and opened it. "Goodnight! Behave yourself, boy!" she said, looking out into the street.

The boy wanted to say something else other than, "Thank you, m'am," to Mrs. Luella Bates Washington Jones, but he couldn't do so as he turned at the barren stoop and looked back at the large woman in the door. He barely managed to say, "Thank you," before she shut the door. And he never saw her again. ❧

BQ › **BIG Question**
Think of all of Mrs. Jones's interactions with Roger. How does she show him that he can count on her?

Characterization What does Roger's inability to speak reveal about him?

Portrait of a Woman, 1932. John Wesley Hardrick. Oil on board, 30 x 24 in. Hampton University Museum, VA. Indianapolis Museum of Art in cooperation with Indiana University Press.
View the Art How does the author reveal Mrs. Jones's character? How does the painter reveal the character of his subject?

After You Read

Respond and Think Critically

1. In the first part of the story, what do you learn about Roger? Why does Roger try to steal Mrs. Jones's purse? [Infer]

2. What happens when Mrs. Jones brings Roger to her home? Explain. [Summarize]

3. What does Mrs. Jones communicate to Roger by leaving her door open? Explain. [Infer]

4. Why do you think Mrs. Jones tells Roger that she has done wrong things too? What does this add to the story? [Analyze]

5. Did you like or dislike the way this story ended? Did the ending surprise you? Explain. [Evaluate]

6. **BQ** **BIG Question** How does this story affect your thoughts about the Big Question, Whom can you count on? [Connect]

Vocabulary Practice

Choose the sentence that uses the vocabulary word correctly.

A. The girl yelled out in pain, **whereupon** the game was immediately brought to a halt.

B. The boy did a flip **whereupon** the grass was soft.

A. After missing four shots in a row, John **mistrusted** his ability to shoot free throws.

B. John **mistrusted** his basketball but later remembered leaving it in the garage.

Academic Vocabulary

Despite Roger's attempt to steal her purse, Mrs. Jones **assists** Roger by feeding him and giving him money for new shoes. Using context clues, try to figure out the meaning of the word *assists* in the sentence above. Check your guess in a dictionary.

TIP

Analyzing
To answer question 4, consider details in the story that describe Roger's behavior. Think about how you would feel in his place. How would Mrs. Jones's statement affect you?

- Examine Roger's behavior before Mrs. Jones tells him that she has done things she is not proud of. What is he tempted to do?

- How does Roger's behavior change after Mrs. Jones's statement?

 FOLDABLES **Study Organizer** Keep track of your ideas about the **BIG Question** in your unit Foldable.

 Literature Online

Selection Resources
For Selection Quizzes, eFlashcards, and Reading-Writing Connection activities, go to glencoe.com and enter QuickPass code GL27534u1.

Literary Element Characterization

1. Find a quotation and an action from the story that show characteristics of Roger's personality. Explain what they reveal.

2. Why doesn't Mrs. Jones ask Roger personal questions? What does this say about her character? Explain.

Review: Description

As you learned on page 113, authors use **description** to help readers visualize the characters, setting, and events of a story. **Imagery,** or language that appeals to the five senses, helps bring a story to life.

3. Think about this sentence from the selection: "Sweat popped out on the boy's face and he began to struggle." To which of the five senses does this description appeal? Is the decription effective? Explain.

Reading Skill Analyze Setting

Standards Practice ELA7R1e

4. What do you learn about Mrs. Jones from the time of day at which the story takes place?
   A. She works late.
   B. She shops during the day.
   C. She likes to go for walks.
   D. She often invites people to her home.

Grammar Link

Verb Tenses A verb is a word that shows action or a state of being. Verbs have different **tenses** to show when the action takes place.

Present tense shows actions and states of being that are happening now or happen regularly. For example:

> Mrs. Jones is a strong woman. (Mrs. Jones is strong right now.)

Past tense shows actions and states of being that are over and done. For example:

> Mrs. Jones was a strong woman. (Mrs. Jones was strong in the past.)

Future tense shows actions that are going to happen. For example:

> Mrs. Jones will be a strong woman. (Mrs. Jones isn't strong right now, but she's going to be.)

Practice Find sentences in "Thank You, M'am" that show the three tenses above. Write down each sentence, circle the verb or verbs, and list the verb tense. Then rewrite each sentence using a different verb tense.

Write with Style

Apply Imagery Write an opening paragraph like the first paragraph of "Thank You, M'am." Your paragraph should be about two characters. Include a variety of sentence types, as Hughes does in his paragraph. Use imagery to describe the characters' physical features, clothing, body language, and actions. Be sure to create imagery that helps your reader see, feel, smell, touch, taste, and hear your characters and the setting.

We Are All One

Connect to the Folktale

How much do you enjoy taking care of animals? If given the opportunity, would you provide food, shelter, or protection for an animal? for an insect? Why or why not?

Partner Talk With a partner, talk about the meaning of the expression "We are all one." Begin by deciding if you agree with these statements:

• What happens to one person affects everyone.

• Every person or thing is connected to every other person or thing; we're all part of one family.

Build Background

This folktale takes place in some legendary time in China. The Chinese people who came to live in the United States brought this folktale and others with them.

• Chinese people retold these tales to remind themselves of life at home and to show how to survive in a strange and often hostile land.

• The folktales were meant to teach children how a Chinese person should behave.

• During the Great Depression of the 1930s, the U.S. government created work projects to help the unemployed. Jon Lee was given the job of gathering and translating into English traditional stories from Chinese immigrants who were living in Oakland, California. "We Are All One" is a retelling of one of those stories.

Vocabulary

lacquer (lak′ ər) n. a liquid that is poured on wood or metal and dries to form a shiny coat (p. 137). *Lin's parents bought a black lacquer cabinet in Chinatown.*

omen (ō′ mən) n. a sign or an event thought to foretell good or bad fortune (p. 138). *Some people believe that finding a penny is a good omen.*

Meet Laurence Yep

"I see myself as someone who will always be on the border between two cultures. That works to my benefit as a writer because not quite fitting in helps me be a better observer."

— Laurence Yep

Both Insider and Outsider
Identity is an important issue in many of Laurence Yep's award-winning novels. He has explained, "In a sense I have no one culture to call my own since I exist . . . in several. However, in my writing I can create my own." Yep grew up as a Chinese American in an African American neighborhood in San Francisco. He attended school first in Chinatown, then in a white neighborhood.

Laurence Yep was born in 1948.

 Literature Online

Author Search For more about Laurence Yep, go to glencoe.com and enter QuickPass code GL27534u1.

Set Purposes for Reading

BQ BIG Question

As you read this story, pay attention to the extraordinary individuals and animals the old peddler counts on.

Literary Element | Theme

The **theme** of a literary work is its overall message about life or about human nature. Folktales across cultures contain similar themes. For example, "friendship is important" is a theme that is common to many folktales.

Discovering the theme of a story is important because it helps you to see a work's deeper meaning. A story's theme can teach you lessons about life. As you read, ask yourself: What is the author's main message? What is the author trying to tell me about life?

Reading Strategy | Interpret Plot Events

Plot is the sequence of events in a story. When you **interpret plot events,** you use your understanding of the world to decide what events in the plot mean. Do events in the plot resemble events in everyday life? Do they suggest a deeper meaning about life?

When you interpret something, you decide for yourself what it means to you. To interpret plot events, think about

- what you already know about human nature and about the world

- what the events in the story might mean

As you read, list plot events and their meaning in a graphic organizer like the one shown.

Plot Event	What This Event Might Mean

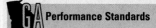

Performance Standards

For pages 134–143

ELA7R1d For literary texts, analyze recurring and similar themes across a variety of selections, distinguishing theme from topic.

TRY IT

Interpret Imagine that you are listening to your best friend talk about a soccer game. Your friend describes how the star player scored the winning goal. Think about how your friend's facial expression, tone of voice, and body language help you interpret whether your friend is pleased or disappointed with the results of the match.

We Are All One

Laurence Yep

Long ago there was a rich man with a disease in his eyes. For many years, the pain was so great that he could not sleep at night. He saw every doctor he could, but none of them could help him.

"What good is all my money?" he groaned. Finally, he became so desperate that he sent criers[1] through the city offering a reward to anyone who could cure him.

Now in that city lived an old candy peddler. He would walk around with his baskets of candy, but he was so kind-hearted that he gave away as much as he sold, so he was always poor.

When the old peddler heard the announcement, he remembered something his mother had said. She had once told him about a magical herb that was good for the eyes. So he packed up his baskets and went back to the single tiny room in which his family lived.

When he told his plan to his wife, she scolded him, "If you go off on this crazy hunt, how are we supposed to eat?"

Usually the peddler gave in to his wife, but this time he was stubborn. "There are two baskets of candy," he said. "I'll be back before they're gone."

Interpret Plot Events Is a mother's advice usually right or wrong? How does that help you know that the peddler will look for the magical herb?

---

1 Since few people could read in ancient times, the rich man had to employ ***criers,*** people who shouted out announcements or news, to make his offer known.

The next morning, as soon as the soldiers opened the gates, he was the first one to leave the city. He did not stop until he was deep inside the woods. As a boy, he had often wandered there. He had liked to pretend that the shadowy forest was a green sea and he was a fish slipping through the cool waters.

As he examined the ground, he noticed ants scurrying[2] about. On their backs were larvae[3] like white grains of rice. A rock had fallen into a stream, so the water now spilled into the ant's nest.

"We're all one," the kind-hearted peddler said. So he waded into the shallow stream and put the rock on the bank. Then with a sharp stick, he dug a shallow ditch that sent the rest of the water back into the stream.

Without another thought about his good deed, he began to search through the forest. He looked everywhere; but as the day went on, he grew sleepy. "Ho-hum. I got up too early. I'll take just a short nap," he decided, and lay down in the shade of an old tree, where he fell right asleep.

In his dreams, the old peddler found himself standing in the middle of a great city. Tall buildings rose high overhead. He couldn't see the sky even when he tilted back his head. An escort of soldiers marched up to him with a loud clatter of their black **lacquer** armor. "Our queen wishes to see you," the captain said.

The frightened peddler could only obey and let the fierce soldiers lead him into a shining palace. There, a woman with a high crown sat upon a tall throne. Trembling, the old peddler fell to his knees and touched his forehead against the floor.

But the queen ordered him to stand. "Like the great Emperor Yü of long ago, you tamed the great flood. We are all one now. You have only to ask, and I or any of my people will come to your aid."

Theme How is the expression "we are all one" a clue to the theme?

Theme Explain how the queen's speech reveals the theme of the folktale.

---

2 If an ant is **scurrying,** it is moving briskly or excitedly.

3 **Larvae** (lär′vē) is the plural of larva, which is the early, wormlike form of an insect. A caterpillar is the larva of a butterfly or moth.

Vocabulary
....

lacquer (lak′ ər) *n.* a liquid that is poured on wood or metal and dries to form a shiny coat

<u>View the Art</u> In what way do details of this picture help you better understand the story?

The old peddler cleared his throat. "I am looking for a certain herb. It will cure any disease of the eyes."

The queen shook her head regretfully.[4] "I have never heard of that herb. But you will surely find it if you keep looking for it."

And then the old peddler woke. Sitting up, he saw that in his wanderings he had come back to the ants' nest. It was there he had taken his nap. His dream city had been the ants' nest itself.

"This is a good **omen,**" he said to himself, and he began searching even harder. He was so determined to find the herb that he did not notice how time had passed. He was surprised when he saw how the light was fading. He looked all around then. There was no sight of his city—only strange hills. He realized then that he had searched so far he had gotten lost.

Night was coming fast and with it the cold. He rubbed his arms and hunted for shelter. In the twilight, he thought he could see the green tiles of a roof.

He stumbled through the growing darkness until he reached a ruined temple. Weeds grew through cracks in the stones and most of the roof itself had fallen in. Still, the ruins would provide some protection.

As he started inside, he saw a **centipede** with bright orange skin and red tufts of fur along its back. Yellow dots covered its sides like a dozen tiny eyes. It was also rushing

Visual Vocabulary

A **centipede** is a long, flat insect with many pairs of legs.

---

4 **Regretfully** means in a way that shows sorrow or disappointment.

Vocabulary

omen (ō′mən) *n.* a sign or an event thought to foretell good or bad fortune

into the temple as fast as it could, but there was a bird swooping down toward it.

The old peddler waved his arms and shouted, scaring the bird away. Then he put down his palm in front of the insect. "We are all one, you and I." The many feet tickled his skin as the centipede climbed onto his hand.

Inside the temple, he gathered dried leaves and found old sticks of wood and soon he had a fire going. The peddler even picked some fresh leaves for the centipede from a bush near the temple doorway. "I may have to go hungry, but you don't have to, friend."

Stretching out beside the fire, the old peddler pillowed his head on his arms. He was so tired that he soon fell asleep, but even in his sleep he dreamed he was still searching in the woods. Suddenly he thought he heard

Interpret Plot Events
The peddler protects the centipede. How might this act help the peddler later in the story?

Landscape, early 18th century. Yao Song. Private collection.

River Scene, 18th century. China. Free Library, Philadelphia, PA.

footsteps near his head. He woke instantly and looked
about, but he only saw the brightly colored centipede.

"Was it you, friend?" The old peddler chuckled and, lying
down, he closed his eyes again. "I must be getting nervous."

"We are one, you and I," a voice said faintly—as if from
a long distance. "If you go south, you will find a pine tree
with two trunks. By its roots, you will find a magic bead.

Theme How does the
centipede prove that
"we are all one"?

A cousin of mine spat on it years ago. Dissolve that bead in wine and tell the rich man to drink it if he wants to heal his eyes."

The old peddler trembled when he heard the voice, because he realized that the centipede was magical. He wanted to run from the temple, but he couldn't even get up. It was as if he were glued to the floor.

But then the old peddler reasoned with himself: If the centipede had wanted to hurt me, it could have long ago. Instead, it seems to want to help me.

So the old peddler stayed where he was, but he did not dare open his eyes. When the first sunlight fell through the roof, he raised one eyelid cautiously. There was no sign of the centipede. He sat up and looked around, but the magical centipede was gone.

He followed the centipede's instructions when he left the temple. Traveling south, he kept a sharp eye out for the pine tree with two trunks. He walked until late in the afternoon, but all he saw were normal pine trees.

Wearily he sat down and sighed. Even if he found the pine tree, he couldn't be sure that he would find the bead. Someone else might even have discovered it a long time ago.

But something made him look a little longer. Just when he was thinking about turning back, he saw the odd tree. Somehow his tired legs managed to carry him over to the tree, and he got down on his knees. But the ground was covered with pine needles and his old eyes were too weak. The old peddler could have wept with frustration,[5] and then he remembered the ants.

He began to call, "Ants, ants, we are all one."

Almost immediately, thousands of ants came boiling out of nowhere. Delighted, the old man held up his fingers. "I'm looking for a bead. It might be very tiny."

Then, careful not to crush any of his little helpers, the old man sat down to wait. In no time, the ants reappeared with a tiny bead. With trembling fingers, the old man took the bead from them and examined it. It was colored orange and looked as if it had yellow eyes on the sides.

---

5 **Frustration** means disappointment or irritation at being kept from doing or achieving something.

There was nothing very special about the bead, but the old peddler treated it like a fine jewel. Putting the bead into his pouch, the old peddler bowed his head. "I thank you and I thank your queen," the old man said. After the ants disappeared among the pine needles, he made his way out of the woods.

The next day, he reached the house of the rich man. However, he was so poor and ragged that the gatekeeper only laughed at him. "How could an old beggar like you help my master?"

The old peddler tried to argue. "Beggar or rich man, we are all one."

But it so happened that the rich man was passing by the gates. He went over to the old peddler. "I said anyone could see me. But it'll mean a stick across your back if you're wasting my time."

The old peddler took out the pouch. "Dissolve this bead in some wine and drink it down." Then, turning the pouch upside down, he shook the tiny bead onto his palm and handed it to the rich man.

The rich man immediately called for a cup of wine. Dropping the bead into the wine, he waited a moment and then drank it down. Instantly the pain vanished. Shortly after that, his eyes healed.

The rich man was so happy and grateful that he doubled the reward. And the kindly old peddler and his family lived comfortably for the rest of their lives.

Theme The gatekeeper and the peddler are different. How might this difference relate to the story's theme?

Theme What advice does this folktale offer?

After You Read

Respond and Think Critically

1. What is the peddler's first act of kindness toward another creature? Describe it. [Recall]

2. When the rich man sees the peddler at the gate, what does he say? What do the rich man's first words tell you about his personality? Explain. [Infer]

3. How does the story end? How do you think the peddler will act, now that his life has changed? Explain. [Analyze]

4. **Literary Element** Theme How does the title, "We Are All One," relate to the story's theme? Explain. [Analyze]

5. **Reading Strategy** Interpret Plot Events Review your chart of plot events. Which events do you think are most important to the story's theme? Explain. [Evaluate]

6. **BQ** BIG Question Who or what is the extraordinary individual in this story? Use details from the story to support your answer. [Interpret]

Vocabulary Practice

Respond to these questions.

1. Which item might be covered by **lacquer**—a shield or a dress?

2. What might be seen as a good **omen**—a star shooting across the sky or a dead flower in the grass?

Writing

Write a Blurb A blurb is a short piece of writing that praises and promotes something, such as a book or a movie. You often see a blurb on the cover of a book. What does "We Are All One" say about life? Write a blurb in which you answer this question. The story's title can help you answer the question.

TIP

Analyzing
Here are some tips to help you analyze how the story's title relates to its theme. Think about what the author shows you through the events, characters, and dialogue in the story.

- Think about when the title phrase is stated in the story.
- What do the characters do after saying the phrase?
- How do the characters' actions fit the theme and the phrase?

FOLDABLES Study Organizer Keep track of your ideas about the **BIG Question** in your unit Foldable.

LOG ON ▶ **Literature** Online

Selection Resources
For Selection Quizzes, eFlashcards, and Reading-Writing Connection activities, go to glencoe.com and enter QuickPass code GL27534u1.

GA Performance Standards

For pages 144–149

ELA7R1a For informational texts, analyze common textual features to obtain information.

Set a Purpose for Reading

Read to find out what workers are learning about managing and preserving forests.

Preview the Article

1. What does the **title** tell you about the article's topic? The **deck,** or subtitle, is just below the title. What details does it provide?

2. Scan the **subheads**. What will the writer describe in each part of the article?

Reading Skill

Determine the Main Idea and Supporting Details

To find the main idea of the article, look for important details. Then think about the one idea that all of the details are about. As you read, take notes about important details. Review your notes to determine the article's main idea.

TIME

Fireproofing the Forests

Logging doesn't work. Neither, in the long run, does fire fighting. As fires annually threaten western forests, the debate over a radical form of tree surgery heats up.

By J. MADELEINE NASH

On the outskirts of Flagstaff, Arizona, Wally Covington drives his pickup truck through a dense forest of ponderosa pines. At last he arrives at the spot where, in 1993, he and his co-workers took chain saws to hundreds of trees no bigger than telephone poles. They carted off the trunks and branches and then purposely set controlled fires to clear away the smaller trees. As a result, today this area is a beautiful woodland, partly shaded by the overhanging branches of 300-year-old trees. In the spaces between the trees, where the sun reaches, grasses and wildflowers thrive.

This is the way the ponderosa pine forests of the American Southwest used to look, says Covington, director of the Ecological Restoration Institute at Northern Arizona University. And it is the way they could look again if they were thinned, or the small trees were cut down to make room for the larger trees.

WATER BEARER: A scooper aircraft picks up lake water to drop on a fire in Glacier National Park in Montana.

View the Photograph Think about all the people and equipment needed to fight forest fires. How does this photo change the way you understand the jobs of firefighters?

decades. These uncontrollable fires have burned millions of acres of forests, killed numerous civilians[1] and firefighters, and burned thousands of homes.

So it is no surprise that these fires are fueling an intense debate. Should the U.S. Forest Service, to protect communities and restore healthy forests, approve tree thinning on a huge scale? If it does, what size trees ought to be thinned and in what sorts of forests? And if it does not, what are the options?

Some environmental groups fear that thinning might encourage logging, or the cutting down of large trees. They have taken the position that cutting down small trees is all right only in parts of the forests near areas where people live. Covington and others, however, believe that thinning, if done responsibly, is perhaps our last chance to restore health to many of our forests. But even Covington says that the science that supports thinning is still developing.

The Case for Thinning

For centuries fires have swept through the ponderosa pine forests of Arizona and New Mexico on average once or twice a decade, killing young trees but not larger trees. Scientists know this because these fires have left a series of healed-over burn scars in the trees'

But time is running out, he fears, because for more than a century these forests have not been managed correctly, and as a result, they—along with the communities around their edges—are threatened by uncontrollable fires.

Every year, it seems, the threat posed by fire looms larger. Some of the most intense wildfires in U.S. history have taken place in the last couple of

---

1   Here, *civilians* refers to anyone who is not a firefighter.

tissue beneath the bark. By dating the scars left in tree rings, Tom Swetnam of the University of Arizona and his co-workers reconstructed a fire history of southwestern forests that extends back to the 14th century. And the most striking discovery they made is that beginning in the late 1800s, there was a marked drop-off in the number of fires.

Why did the number of fires decrease at that time? Why do we have so many uncontrollable fires today? First, sheep, cattle, and other livestock were allowed to overgraze the grasses and other plants in the forests. Without these plants, ground fires were not able to spread and to burn litter, release nutrients,[2] and thin out saplings.[3] Then came decades of logging of large trees along with improved ways to fight fires. The makeup of the forest changed so that hundreds of small trees now crowd into acre-size plots,[4] where only a few dozen large trees used to thrive. The result is that millions of acres of southwestern forestland are packed

RING COUNTER: Tom Swetnam's pine has fire scars dating from 1583.

William F. Campbell/Getty Images

with enough wood to fuel wildfires of unequaled fury and destruction.

The situation has reached the point at which some experts are convinced that even controlled fires pose serious dangers to large, mature trees. More than 25 years ago, in fact, Covington and two Forest Service researchers experimented with the use of controlled fires in Coconino National Forest in Arizona, but they did not get the results they expected. The clumps of young trees the scientists hoped to kill survived, and the old-growth trees they hoped to save died.

Why? In the absence of fire for so long, too much fuel, in the form of dropped needles and branches, had collected at the bases of the largest trees. Yet not enough time had gone by to allow a similar buildup of fuel

---

2 **Nutrients** are substances that plants and animals get from food to stay alive and healthy.

3 **Saplings** are very young trees.

4 Small pieces of land are called **plots.**

beneath the smaller trees. As a consequence,[5] flames traveled quickly through the clumps of young trees but burned slowly for long periods of time at the feet of the giant trees, killing them.

For Covington the unexpected loss of so many old-growth trees was a wake-up call. Before setting fire loose in the pine forests of the Southwest again, he concluded that the forest had to be restored to its original structure. To learn what these forests looked like before human interference, Covington and his team studied old photos and read historic texts. They also looked at records kept by early foresters. In 1909 foresters had set up a series of experimental plots across the Southwest. Among these was an unlogged, eight-acre plot in Coconino National Forest[6] that was set aside as a long-term control. Covington made 1876 the reference year for this plot—it was the last year a fire had occurred there—and then reconstructed the way the forest had looked at the time. The difference between then and now, he found, was dramatic. In 1876 the plot supported just more than 20 trees an acre, compared with 1,250 some 120 years later!

This was the plot that Covington's team experimentally thinned in 1993 and 1994, taking care to preserve all

old-growth trees. The area now supports some 60 trees an acre, and as individual trees, they seem far healthier than before. For one thing, the outer coating of their needles has increased in toughness, which helps discourage plant-eating insects. For another, they are producing more resin,[7] which provides protection against damaging insects such as bark beetles. Best of all, thinning is no longer needed, as slow-burning controlled fires can now safely do the job.

The Value of Open Space
Many variables determine how a wildfire behaves, but among the most important are wind speed, topography,[8] air temperature, humidity,[9] and the amount of fuel. Forests with patches of open space have less fuel. But these types of forests have all but disappeared. At one time, the open spaces helped lessen the danger of horrific blazes. Today vast areas of forest have no open spaces but instead are packed with unburned kindling.[10]

Restoring these patches of open space is critical.[11] Unfortunately, there is no easy way to do this because the amount

---

5 *As a consequence* means "as a result."

6 *Coconino National Forest* is near Flagstaff, Arizona.

7 *Resin* is sap, or the sticky liquid made inside trees and other plants.

8 *Topography* refers to land features such as hills, valleys, and streams.

9 *Humidity* is a measurement of the moisture in the air.

10 *Kindling* refers to old, dry, fallen leaves, sticks, and branches that start on fire easily.

11 Here, *critical* means "extremely important."

BACK BURNER: In Arizona, a weary firefighter walks away from a blaze he has just set.

View the Photograph Why is it important that only trained firefighters set controlled burns?

of fuel varies widely from forest to forest. To many forest ecologists, dealing with fuel loads—whether by thinning, controlled burning, or a combination of the two—is the best strategy we have for making sure that the ponderosa pine forests survive into the future. And the good news, says Mark Finney, a researcher with the Forest Service's Fire Sciences Laboratory in Missoula, Montana, is that it probably won't be necessary to thin or control-burn every acre of forest at risk.

Most fuel-reduction measures have had fairly narrow goals, such as protecting valuable stands of trees. The logical[12] next step, as Finney sees it, is to use these measures across hundreds of thousands of acres. It is already clear, he notes, that controlled burns have the power to lessen the likelihood of large, destructive fires.

---

12 Something clear and reasonable is ***logical***.

Thayer Allyson Gowdy

Not All Forests Are Alike

Not all forests, however, are good candidates for thinning. Among the best examples are the lodgepole pine forests that grow at higher elevations across the mountains in the West. Lodgepole pines thrive in a cool, moist environment, which keeps fires at bay for long periods of time. So the lodgepoles grow densely together—so densely, in fact, that numerous smaller lodgepoles are shaded out and die from lack of light. These dead and dying trees, combined with lower-growing spruce and fir trees, provide a massive fuel load, which can lead to terrible blazes.

Yet attempting to thin lodgepole pine forests to prevent such fires would be foolish, say scientists, because these blazes serve important ecological functions. For instance, many lodgepole pines package their seeds in resin-sealed cones that can be opened only by intense heat. If the cones aren't opened, the seeds cannot take root and grow into saplings.

No one questions the value of thinning for fire control around homes and other structures. What is much harder to weigh is the balance of risks and benefits of thinning in terms of ecology. Great care needs to be taken so that thinning does not hurt the very forests it is supposed to heal.

Respond and Think Critically

1. Write a brief summary of this article before you answer the questions that follow. State the main ideas in your own words. How have the southwestern forests changed in the last 100 years? [Summarize]

2. Why do some people want to thin the forests? How would this affect tree growth in lodgepole pine forests? [Draw Conclusions]

3. For the last 100 years, foresters' policy has been to prevent forest fires. Do you think that this policy has helped or hurt the forests? Explain your response. [Evaluate]

4. **Text-to-Self** Would you rather live near a forest that has been thinned or near a forest whose trees have not been cut? Why? [Connect]

5. **Reading Skill** Determine Main Idea and Supporting Details Use the details you took notes about to determine the main idea of the article. What one idea are the details about? Explain.

6. **BQ** BIG Question In what ways are those who are studying forest management extraordinary? Why is their work important to us? Support your answer with details from the article.

Comparing Literature

The Rider and I'll Walk the Tightrope

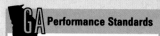
GA Performance Standards

For pages 150–153

ELA7R1d For literary texts, analyze recurring and similar themes across a variety of selections, distinguishing theme from topic.

BQ BIG Question

As you read these poems, think about how the speakers in the poems find strength to face life's challenges.

Literary Element Theme

You've learned that a **theme** is the message of a literary work, usually expressed as a general statement. Some works have a **stated theme,** which is expressed directly. Other works have an **implied theme,** which is revealed gradually through elements such as plot, character, setting, point of view, and symbol. As you read each poem, look for details that reveal the theme.

Reading Skill Compare and Contrast

You may not realize it, but you compare and contrast every day. When you compare, you look for similarities. When you contrast, you examine the differences. For example, you might compare and contrast two movies that you want to see. Both movies may star your favorite actor, but one movie may be scary and the other may be funny. When you think about the similarities and differences between the movies, you are comparing and contrasting them.

Comparing and contrasting the themes of two poems can help you to better understand them. On the following pages, you'll compare and contrast the themes of "The Rider" and "I'll Walk the Tightrope." As you read, look for details that give you clues about each poem's theme. Use a chart like the one below to record details from each poem. Then write down the themes.

	Details from the Poem	Theme of the Poem
"The Rider"		
"I'll Walk the Tightrope"		

Meet the Authors

Naomi Shihab Nye

Naomi Shihab Nye was born in 1952.

Margaret Danner

Margaret Danner was born in 1915.

 Literature Online

Author Search For more about Naomi Shihab Nye and Margaret Danner, go to glencoe.com and enter QuickPass code GL27534u1.

The Rider

Naomi Shihab Nye

A boy told me
if he rollerskated fast enough
his loneliness couldn't catch up to him.

the best reason I ever heard
5   for trying to be a champion.

What I wonder tonight
pedaling hard down King William Street
is if it translates to bicycles.

A victory! To leave your loneliness
10   panting behind you on some street corner
while you float free into a cloud of sudden azaleas,
luminous pink petals that have
    never felt loneliness,
no matter how slowly they fell.

Comparing Literature
What challenge does the speaker face?

I'll Walk the Tightrope

Margaret Danner

Fatima, 1994. Elizabeth Barakah Hodges. Acrylic, 23 x 18 in. Private Collection.

I'll walk the tightrope that's been stretched for me,
and though a wrinkled forehead, perplexed why,
will accompany me, I'll delicately
step along. For if I stop to sigh
5   at the earth-propped stride
of others, I will fall. I must balance high
without a parasol to tide°
a faltering step, without a net below,
without a balance stick to guide.

Comparing Literature What does the tightrope stand for?

Comparing Literature How does the speaker keep from falling?

---

7 A *parasol* is a small lightweight umbrella used as protection from the sun. Here, *tide* means "to aid or assist."

Comparing Literature

Now use the unit Big Question to compare and contrast "The Rider" and "I'll Walk the Tightrope." With a group of classmates, discuss questions such as,

- What motivates each speaker to face and overcome life's challenges?

- On whom or what does each speaker rely for strength?

- In what way does each speaker deal with his or her challenges?

Support each answer with evidence from the poems.

Literary Element Theme

Use the details you listed in your chart to think about the themes of "The Rider" and "I'll Walk the Tightrope." With a partner, answer the following questions.

1. What are the themes of "The Rider" and "I'll Walk the Tightrope"? How are the themes different? Discuss specific details from the poems that show these differences.

2. In what ways are the themes in both poems similar? For example, you might think about how the speakers' actions and emotions are similar.

Write to Compare

In one or two paragraphs, explain how the speakers in "The Rider" and "I'll Walk the Tightrope" face life's challenges. You might focus on these ideas as you write.

- Tell what challenges the speaker faces in each poem.

- Include details about whom the speakers count on.

- Explain how the speakers feel about overcoming their challenges.

- Explain how the similarities and differences in the themes affect your appreciation of the poems. Do you prefer one poem to the other? Why?

 Writing Tip

Signal Words As you write, use signal words such as *both, alike, similar, same* and *also* to show a comparison. Use *unlike, different, instead, in contrast,* and *however* to contrast items or ideas.

 Literature Online

Selection Resources
For Selection Quizzes, eFlashcards, and Reading-Writing Connection activities, go to glencoe.com and enter QuickPass code GL27534u1.

Performance Standards

For pages 154–159

ELA7W2c Demonstrate competence in a variety of genres. Produce a narrative that develops characters using standard methods of characterization.

Writing Workshop

Narrative

What challenges do people face in life? How can friends and family help? In this workshop, you will write a short story that will help you think about the Unit 1 Big Question: Whom Can You Count On?

Review the writing prompt, or assignment, below. Then read the Writing Plan. It will tell you what you will do to write your story.

Writing Assignment

A narrative tells a story. A fictional narrative is a story about imaginary people and events. Write a short story in which a character faces a challenge with the help of friends or family. The audience, or those reading your story, should be your classmates and teacher.

Prewrite

What different kinds of people do you count on? Look at the stories in this unit for examples, including "Seventh Grade" by Gary Soto.

Gather Ideas

Ask yourself the following questions and write down your answers:

- What are some conflicts, or challenges, that I or people I know have faced? How did people overcome these challenges, and who helped them? Which challenge might make a good story and why?

- Who are the main characters involved in the challenge? What do the characters look like? How do they act? What do they say?

- Where does the story take place? How does the setting relate to the conflict and the characters?

Choose a Point of View

Point of view is the relationship of the narrator, or storyteller, to the story. Point of view determines what the narrator is able to see and hear and therefore tell the reader. A story with **first-person point of view** is told by one of the characters, referred to as "I." The reader generally sees everything through that character's eyes. In a story with a **limited third-person point of view,** the narrator reveals the thoughts of only one character and refers to that character as "he" or "she." In a story with **omniscient point of view,** the narrator reveals the thoughts of several characters. If you choose first-person or third-person limited, you will also need to choose which character will be the focus of the story.

Writing Plan

- **Choose an appropriate narrator and point of view.**

- **Develop a plot that has an exposition (a beginning), rising action, a climax, falling action, and a resolution.**

- **Make the internal or external conflict the basis of the theme and all plot events.**

- **Add sensory details to describe setting and action.**

- **Use dialogue and description, including movement and expressions, to highlight similarities and differences among main and minor characters.**

Get Organized

Use your notes to make a plot diagram and a characterization chart.

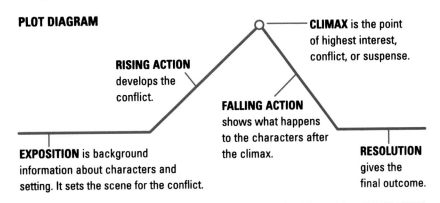

PLOT DIAGRAM

CLIMAX is the point of highest interest, conflict, or suspense.

RISING ACTION develops the conflict.

FALLING ACTION shows what happens to the characters after the climax.

EXPOSITION is background information about characters and setting. It sets the scene for the conflict.

RESOLUTION gives the final outcome.

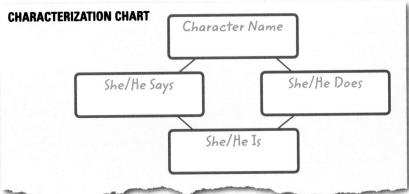

CHARACTERIZATION CHART

Character Name

She/He Says

She/He Does

She/He Is

Draft

Use the following tips to develop your draft.

Get It On Paper

- Begin your story with interesting dialogue, a detailed setting description, or an exciting action sequence.
- Tell the events from your plot diagram in the order in which they occur. For each event, freewrite what happens to the characters.
- Don't worry about paragraphs, spelling, or punctuation right now.
- When fifteen minutes are up, read what you've written. Write down more ideas as you think of them.

Develop Your Draft

1. Use the **point of view** and **narrator** you have chosen. Use *I* or *me* for first-person; *he, she, him,* or *her* for third-person and omniscient.

   Even though his mother didn't mind, Josh would still feel awful.

Literature Online

Writing and Research
For prewriting, drafting, and revising tools, go to glencoe.com and enter QuickPass code GL27534u1.

Drafting Tip

Time-Order Words Use words such as *after, before, finally, first, later, next, then, when,* and *while* to make the sequence of events clear.

2. Describe the events in the **plot** that lead up to and follow the **conflict.** Use words that tell readers what happened when.

> Suddenly, Evan exclaimed, "I can send an e-mail to remind you!"

3. Make every event in the plot part of the **internal** or **external conflict** upon which the theme of your story is based.

> He wanted to make her feel special, too, but no matter what, he always forgot.

4. Add **sensory details** to clearly describe the setting and events.

> Sitting in the shade of a big tree in Josh's backyard, Sarah and Evan thought about how to help Josh.

5. Use description and dialogue to develop the **main** and **minor characters.**

> "We have a big calendar in our kitchen," Sarah said, her serious face looking thoughtful.

TRY IT

Analyzing Cartoons
How is a messy room similar to a first draft? With a partner, decide what the cartoon suggests about organization.

Apply Good Writing Traits: Organization

Organization is the arrangement of events in a story. Good organization helps readers understand exactly what happens and how events are connected.

Read the sentence below from Gary Soto's story "Seventh Grade." Which words and phrases help you understand the sequence of events?

> On the first day of school, Victor stood in line half an hour before he came to a wobbly card table.

As you draft your story, use words and phrases that show how events are related. After you finish, read your draft and ask yourself whether any events are missing or out of place.

Analyze a Student Model

Every year Josh forgot his mom's birthday. Even though his mother didn't mind, Josh would still feel awful.

Josh's mother never forgot his birthday and always made him feel special on it. He wanted to make her feel special, too, but no matter what, he always forgot.

He could remember the capital of every state and all the stats of his favorite basketball player. Why couldn't he also remember such an important date?

This year, on his mom's birthday, Josh decided to make a plan, and he recruited his friends to help him.

"Next year," he explained, "I want to give a party for my mom to make up for all the years I've forgotten her birthday. Help me figure out how to remember it."

Sitting in the shade of a big tree in Josh's backyard, Sarah and Evan thought about how to help Josh.

"We have a big calendar in our kitchen," Sarah said, her serious face looking thoughtful. "If I write your mom's birthday on it, I'll see it every day that month."

Josh had tried calendars before, but after he wrote his mom's birthday down, he never looked at the calendar again. He hoped Sarah would have more luck.

Suddenly, Evan exclaimed, "I can send an e-mail to remind you!"

"But how will you remember to send the e-mail?" Josh groaned, leaning back against the tree trunk.

Evan said his e-mail let him send messages on a delayed schedule. He would have a reminder e-mail sent to Josh one month before his mom's birthday.

"With a month to spare," Josh said excitedly, "I'll have time to plan the perfect party."

"Just don't forget to check your e-mail," Evan teased him.

Point of View and Narrator

Use pronouns and character names to make it clear whether your narrator is a character in the story and what the point of view is.

Plot

Include time-order words and phrases that help readers understand the sequence of events.

Conflict

Explain clearly whether the conflict is external (between the main character and an outside force) or internal (within the main character).

Sensory Details

Give specific details that help readers see, hear, smell, taste, or feel the setting and the action.

Dialogue

Have characters speak in ways that tell readers about their personalities.

Word Choice Use a
dictionary or a thesaurus to
help you choose descriptive
and precise language.
Occasionally replace *said*
with words such as *joked,
exclaimed, replied,* or *teased.*

Revise

Now it's time to revise your draft so that your ideas really shine. Revising is what makes good writing great, and great writing takes work!

Peer Review Trade drafts with a partner. Use the chart below to review your partner's draft by answering the questions in the *What to do* column. Talk about your peer review after you have glanced at each other's drafts and written answers to the questions. Next, follow the suggestions in the *How to do it* column to revise your draft.

Revising Plan

What to do	How to do it	Example
Who is the narrator and what is the point of view?	Use pronouns such as *I* and *me* for the first-person point of view and *he, she, him,* and *her* for the third-person point of view and omniscient point of view.	Every year ~~I~~ ∧ Josh forgot ~~my~~ ∧his mom's birthday.
How does the plot rise to a climax and result in a resolution?	Write about events in the order they happen. Use words such as *before* or *tomorrow* to make the sequence clear. Add any events that are missing.	∧This year, on his mom's birthday, Josh decided to make a plan, and he recruited his friends to help him.
Is the conflict external or internal? Is it based in the theme, and is it part of each plot event?	Include events that help explain the conflict and theme. Delete events that are unnecessary or distracting.	He wanted to make her feel special, too, but no matter what, he always forgot. ~~Last year Sarah got Josh a new basketball for his birthday.~~
Which sensory details describe the setting and the action?	Choose specific and vivid words that help readers see, smell, taste, hear, and feel the setting and the action.	∧Sitting in the shade of a big tree in Josh's backyard, Sarah and Evan thought about how to help Josh.
Which dialogue shows the characters' personalities?	Have your characters speak words that show their character traits and how they think and feel.	~~"That works," he said.~~ ∧With a month to spare," Josh said excitedly, "I'll have time to plan the perfect party."

Edit and Proofread

For your final draft, read your narrative one sentence at a time. The **Editing and Proofreading Checklist** inside the back cover of this book may help you spot errors. Use the proofreading symbols to mark needed changes. Then make corrections.

Grammar Focus: Punctuation of Dialogue

Punctuate dialogue correctly to tell readers which characters are speaking and what they are saying. Below are examples of problems with the punctuation of dialogue and solutions from the Workshop Model.

Problem: It's not clear when the character starts and stops speaking.

With a month to spare, Josh said excitedly, I'll have time to plan the perfect party.

Solution: Place quotation marks before and after spoken words with the end punctuation mark (or a comma) inside the quotation marks.

"With a month to spare," Josh said excitedly, "I'll have time to plan the perfect party."

Problem: The speaker tag isn't clearly separated from the spoken words.

"Just don't forget to check your e-mail, Evan teased him."

Solution 1: Put a comma (or an end mark) and quotation marks at the end of the spoken words. Then add the speaker tag and a period.

"Just don't forget to check your e-mail," Evan teased him.

Solution 2: Begin with the speaker tag followed by a comma. Then enclose the spoken words and end punctuation in quotation marks.

Evan teased him, "Just don't forget to check your e-mail."

Present

It's almost time to share your writing with others. Write your narrative neatly in print or cursive on a separate sheet of paper. If you have access to a computer, type your narrative on the computer and check spelling. Save your document to a disk, and print it out.

Editing and Proofreading Tip

Quotation Marks When dialogue ends with an exclamation point or a question mark, this end mark goes inside the quotation marks and a period follows the speaker tag.

 Presenting Tip

Publishing Create an anthology of all the stories written by your classmates. Type the stories into a computer and then save them onto the same disk for storage.

 Literature Online

Writing and Research For editing and publishing tools, go to glencoe.com and enter QuickPass code GL27534u1.

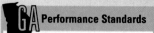

Performance Standards

For page 160

ELA7LSV2b When delivering and responding to presentations, organize information to achieve particular purposes and to appeal to the background and interests of the audience.

Speaking, Listening, and Viewing Workshop

Narrative Presentation

Activity

Connect to Your Writing Deliver an oral presentation of a narrative to your classmates. You might want to adapt the narrative you wrote for the Writing Workshop on pages 154–159. Remember that you focused on the Unit 1 Big Question: Whom Can You Count On?

Plan Your Presentation

Reread your story and highlight the sections you want to include in your presentation. Like your written narrative, your narrative presentation should have a plot with a beginning, a middle, and an end and should describe a specific setting. Be sure to include dialogue and descriptive details.

Rehearse Your Presentation

Practice your presentation several times. Try rehearsing in front of a mirror so that you can watch your movements and facial expressions. You may use note cards to remind you of the story's important events, but practice your narrative often enough that you won't lose eye contact with your audience.

Deliver Your Presentation

- Speak clearly and precisely.
- Adjust your speaking style to fit individual characters.
- Change the pace of your speaking to emphasize important moments throughout your story.
- Change the tone or volume of your voice to communicate emotions or build suspense.

Listening to Appreciate

As you listen, take notes on what you like about the story's delivery. Use these sentence frames to share your appreciation with the teller.

- I like the gesture/voice that you use for the character _____ because _____.
- The general mood or atmosphere of the story is _____. You cleverly create this mood by _____.
- I think the story's theme is _____. The story reminds me _____.

> **Presentation Checklist**

Answer the following questions to evaluate your presentation.

- ❏ Did you speak clearly and precisely and in styles that fit the characters?
- ❏ Did you change the pace of your speaking to fit the story's action?
- ❏ Did you vary the tone or volume of your voice to add interest to the story?
- ❏ Did you make eye contact with your audience?

 Literature Online

Speaking, Listening, and Viewing For project ideas, templates, and presentation tips, go to glencoe.com and enter QuickPass code GL27534u1.

Unit Challenge

Answer the Big Question

In Unit 1, you explored the Big Question through reading, writing, speaking, and listening. Now it's time for you to answer the Big Question by completing one of the Unit Challenges below.

WHOM Can You Count On?

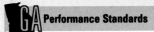

Performance Standards

For page 161

ELA7W2c Demonstrate competence in a variety of genres. Produce writing that creates an organizing structure appropriate to purpose, audience, and context.

Use the notes you took in your Unit 1 **Foldable** to complete your Unit Challenge.

Before you present your Unit Challenge, be sure to follow the steps below. Use this first plan if you choose to create a chart of obstacles you may face in the future and the people you can count on for help.

On Your Own Activity: Create a Chart

- ❏ Draw a chart. In the first column, list examples of obstacles you may face as you work toward your goals.
- ❏ In the second column, list ways to overcome the obstacles.
- ❏ In the third column, write down the names of people you can count on to help you.
- ❏ Keep this chart and add to it as you work toward your goals.

Use this second plan if you choose to write a handbook called "People You Can Count On." In the handbook, list and discuss people who can help teens overcome obstacles.

Group Activity: Write a Handbook

- ❏ List people in your community whom you can count on.
- ❏ Think about which people can help with which problems.
- ❏ Decide on headings for the handbook and divide the writing assignments among the members of your group.
- ❏ Share advice about possible changes to each other's work.
- ❏ Present your handbook to the class or send it to the school newspaper.

Independent Reading

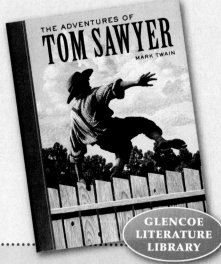

Fiction

To read more about the Big Question, choose one of these books from your school or local library.

The Adventures of Tom Sawyer

by Mark Twain

The Adventures of Tom Sawyer follows young Tom Sawyer and his friends through a series of mishaps, pranks, and narrow escapes, along the way revealing the humorous side of life. Set in the 1840s along the Mississippi River in Missouri, the book gives a view of pre–Civil War America and tells a timeless story of friendship and growing up.

The Chosen

by Chaim Potok

The story of two young Jewish men living in Brooklyn in the 1940s, *The Chosen* follows their lives and their relationships with their fathers and with each other. Despite their different backgrounds, the men form an enduring friendship and face tough issues of the times together.

Bridge to Terabithia

by Katherine Paterson

Two young classmates, Jess and Leslie, form a strong friendship as together they create an imaginary kingdom beyond a nearby creek. The events that follow forever change Jess's life.

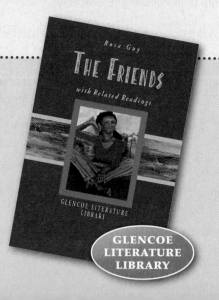

The Friends

by Rosa Guy

This coming-of-age novel deals with the relationship between two unlikely friends, Phyllisia Cathy and Edith Jackson. The novel details the bond the two girls forge as they deal with the pressures of family and friends.

Nonfiction

Anne Frank Remembered

by Miep Gies and Alison Leslie Gold

This memoir tells the story of Miep Gies, the woman who helped Anne Frank and her family hide from the Nazi forces in Amsterdam during World War II. The story shows the courage that Gies had despite great personal danger.

Stick Up for Yourself: Every Kid's Guide to Personal Power and Positive Self-Esteem

by Gershen Kaufman, Lev Raphael, and Pamela Espeland

This is a self-help guide to positive thinking, high self-esteem, and personal power. Read to learn how other kids handle life. The writing exercises in the book offer ways to connect to the text.

Harriet Tubman: Conductor on the Underground Railroad

by Ann Petry

This biography tells the exciting story of a woman who helped hundreds of enslaved people escape to freedom.

Write a Review

Write a review for your classmates of the book you read. Evaluate the author's craft as you explain what you found interesting, unusual, exciting, or even disappointing in the book. Explain why you would or would not recommend the book. Include specific examples and descriptive details to support your ideas.

Assessment

READING

Read the passage and answer the questions. Write your answers on a separate sheet of paper.

---

from **"The Old Demon"** by Pearl S. Buck

Old Mrs. Wang knew, of course, that there was a war. Everybody had known for a long time that there was a war going on and that Japanese were killing Chinese. But still it was not real and no more than hearsay since none of the Wangs had been killed. The Village of Three Mile Wangs on the flat banks of the Yellow River, which was old Mrs. Wang's clan village, had never seen a Japanese. This was how they came to be talking about Japanese at all.

It was evening and early summer, and after her supper Mrs. Wang had climbed the dike steps, as she did every day, to see how high the river had risen. She was much more afraid of the river than of the Japanese. She knew what the river would do. And one by one the villagers had followed her up the dike, and now they stood staring down at the <u>malicious</u> yellow water, curling along like a lot of snakes, and biting at the high dike banks.

"I never saw it as high as this so early," Mrs. Wang said. She sat down on a bamboo stool that her grandson, Little Pig, had brought for her, and spat into the water.

"It's worse than the Japanese, this old devil of a river," Little Pig said recklessly.

"Fool!" Mrs. Wang said quickly. "The river god will hear you. Talk about something else."

So they had gone on talking about the Japanese. . . . How, for instance, asked Wang, the baker, who was old Mrs. Wang's nephew twice removed, would they know the Japanese when they saw them?

Mrs. Wang at this point said positively, "You'll know them. I once saw a foreigner. He was taller than the eaves of my house and he had mud-colored hair and eyes the color of a fish's eyes. Anyone who does not look like us—that is a Japanese."

Then Little Pig spoke up in his disconcerting way. "You can't see them, Grandmother. They hide up in the sky in airplanes."

Mrs. Wang did not answer immediately. Once she would have said positively, "I shall not believe in an airplane until I see it." But so many things had been true which she had not believed—the Empress, for instance, whom she had not believed dead, was dead. The Republic, again, she had not believed in because she did not know what it was. She still did not know, but they had said for a long time there had been one. So now she merely stared quietly about the dike where they all sat around her. It was very pleasant and cool, and she felt nothing mattered if the river did not rise to flood.

"I don't believe in the Japanese," she said flatly.

They laughed at her a little, but no one spoke. Someone lit her pipe— it was Little Pig's wife, who was her favorite, and she smoked it.

"Sing, Little Pig!" someone called.

So Little Pig began to sing an old song in a high quavering voice, and old Mrs. Wang listened and forgot the Japanese. <u>The evening was beautiful, the sky so clear and still that the willows overhanging the dike were reflected even in the muddy water.</u> Everything was at peace. The thirty-odd houses which made up the village straggled along beneath them. Nothing could break this peace. After all, the Japanese were only human beings.

"I doubt those airplanes," she said mildly to Little Pig when he stopped singing.

But without answering her, he went on to another song.

Year in and year out she had spent the summer evenings like this on the dike. The first time she was seventeen and a bride, and her husband had shouted to her to come out of the house and up the dike, and she had come, blushing and twisting her hands together, to hide among the women while the men roared at her and made jokes about her.

All the same, they had liked her. "A pretty piece of meat in your bowl," they had said to her husband. "Feet a trifle big," he had answered deprecatingly. But she could see he was pleased, and so gradually her shyness went away.

1. In the village, Mrs. Wang is seen as a
   A. fool.
   B. wise woman.
   C. respected elder.
   D. feared community leader.

2. Which detail probably foreshadows events later in the story?
   A. "The Republic, again, she had not believed in because she did not know what it was."
   B. "Year in and year out she had spent summer evenings like this on the dike."
   C. "So Little Pig began to sing an old song in a high quavering voice"
   D. ". . . there was war going on and that Japanese were killing Chinese."

3. The story's physical and historical setting together create a sense of
   A. threat.
   B. mystery.
   C. romance.
   D. adventure.

4. In which of the following sentences does the narrator's description BEST develop the personality of Mrs. Wang?
   A. "I once saw a foreigner."
   B. They laughed at her a little, but no one spoke.
   C. "I don't believe in the Japanese," she said flatly.
   D. She was much more afraid of the river than of the Japanese.

5. What does the word *malicious* mean in this passage?
   A. still
   B. hateful
   C. flooding
   D. beautiful

6. What does Mrs. Wang fear most?
   A. war
   B. a flood
   C. airplanes
   D. the Japanese

7. Mrs. Wang became less confident in her beliefs as a result of
   A. meeting a foreigner.
   B. learning that the Empress was dead.
   C. hearing her husband's friends make jokes.
   D. seeing how high the river waters had risen.

8. What mood is created by the description in paragraph 13?
   A. peaceful
   B. threatening
   C. mysterious
   D. sad

9. Why does no one speak when Mrs. Wang says she doesn't believe in the Japanese?

   A. No one wants to talk about the war.

   B. Everyone hopes that Mrs. Wang is correct.

   C. The people don't want to argue with Mrs. Wang.

   D. The other villagers don't believe in the Japanese either.

10. Which of the following shows a way the river and the Japanese are alike in this passage?

    A. Both are familiar to the villagers.

    B. Both represent a danger to the village.

    C. Both are linked to ancient traditions.

    D. Both can either benefit or harm the village.

11. When the author says the water is "curling along like a lot of snakes," she is using

    A. a metaphor.

    B. personification.

    C. hyperbole.

    D. a simile.

12. In this passage, which of the following events is described out of chronological order?

    A. The villagers follow Mrs. Wang up the dike.

    B. Wang, the baker, asks what Japanese look like.

    C. Mrs. Wang's husband says her feet are a little too big.

    D. Mrs. Wang says that she doubts the existence of airplanes.

13. Which remark might Little Pig make to his wife if his grandmother could not hear him?

    A. "It's amazing how she's right about nearly everything."

    B. "One day I'm going to tell her exactly what I think of her."

    C. "She's got some strange ideas, but she's seen a lot of life."

    D. "She thinks she knows everything; in fact, she knows nothing."

14. Which sentence BEST describes the main theme of the passage?

    A. No one can avoid the effects of some world events.

    B. At one time, the Japanese and Chinese were at war.

    C. Sometimes newly married men and women are shy.

    D. People shouldn't worry too much about floods.

Literature Online

Standards Practice For more standards practice, go to glencoe.com and enter QuickPass code GL27534u1.

ENGLISH/LANGUAGE ARTS

Choose the best answer for each question. Write your answers on a separate sheet of paper.

1. Which verb form should be used to complete the sentence below?

   > History books tell us how people _____ in the past.

   A. live

   B. lived

   C. will live

   D. had been living

2. Which verb form should be used to complete the sentence below?

   > Of course, no one knows much about how people _____ in the future.

   A. live

   B. have lived

   C. are living

   D. will live

3. What is the BEST way to combine the three sentences below?

   > I think people will fly.
   > They will fly everywhere.
   > They will use personal airplanes to fly.

   A. People will fly everywhere and fly in personal airplanes, I think.

   B. I think people will use personal airplanes to fly everywhere.

   C. I think people in personal airplanes will fly in them and fly everywhere.

   D. I think people will fly, and they will fly everywhere, and they will use personal airplanes to fly.

4. What is the structure of the sentence below?

   > Although it has never been possible, people have always wanted to be able to travel through time.

   A. simple sentence

   B. compound sentence

   C. complex sentence

   D. compound-complex sentence

WRITING

Read your assigned topic in the box below. Use one piece of paper to jot down your ideas and organize your thoughts. Then neatly write your letter on another sheet of paper.

Persuasive Writing Topic

Writing Situation

Scientists have developed a time machine that can take people back to any point in human history. Your class has been selected to take the first day-long field trip in this incredible machine. Your teacher wants the class to help choose a destination.

Directions for Writing

Think of a time and place in human history you want to visit. Write a letter to your teacher to persuade her that your destination is the best choice. Provide reasons and vivid details about the destination to support your idea.

Writing Checklist

☐ Focus on a single topic.

☐ Organize your main points in a clear, logical order.

☐ Support your ideas or viewpoints with details and examples.

☐ Use precise, vivid words.

☐ Vary the length and structure of your sentences.

☐ Use clear transition words to connect ideas.

☐ Correct any errors in spelling, capitalization, punctuation, and usage.

WHY Do You Read?

THE BIG Question

> "Books took me, not so much to foreign lands and fanciful adventures, but to a place within myself that I have been exploring ever since."
>
> —WALTER DEAN MYERS

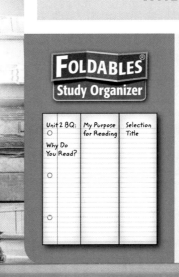

FOLDABLES
Study Organizer

Unit 2 BQ: Why Do You Read?	My Purpose for Reading	Selection Title
○		
○		
○		

Throughout Unit 2, you will read, write, and talk about the **BIG Question**— **"Why Do You Read?"** Use your Unit 2 **Foldable,** shown here, to keep track of your ideas as you read. Turn to the back of this book for instructions on making this **Foldable.**

WHY Do You Read?

How important is reading to everyday life? Think about it. You probably read many times throughout the day. Maybe you look at the newspaper to find out how a game went. Maybe you check television listings for the program you want to see. And sometimes you probably surf the Internet and connect with friends online.

As you read this unit, think about the reasons you read:

- For Fun
- For Information
- For Understanding

What You'll Read

When you want or need information, you can often find it in **informational text,** which is writing that includes facts and information without introducing personal opinion. Some types of informational text are how-to manuals, Web sites, and newspaper and magazine articles. The informational text and other selections in this unit will help you discover answers to the Big Question.

What You'll Write

As you explore the Big Question, you'll write notes in your Unit **Foldable.** Later, you'll use these notes to complete two writing assignments related to the Big Question.

1. **Write an Informational Document**
2. **Choose a Unit Challenge**
   - **On Your Own Activity: Make an Advertising Brochure**
   - **Group Activity: Create a TV Commercial**

What You'll Learn

Literary Elements

foreshadowing

alliteration

mood

metaphor and simile

author's purpose

text structure

diction

style

dialogue

conflict

text features

Reading Skills and Strategies

draw conclusions about characters

make predictions about plot

activate prior knowledge

question

skim and scan

monitor comprehension

evaluate characterization

analyze evidence

distinguish fact and opinion

Brer Rabbit & Brer Lion

Retold by Julius Lester

Dawn Raid, 1995. Christian Pierre. Acrylic on masonite, 20 x 30 in. Private collection. **View the Art** What does the painting tell you about the rabbit? How might the painting add to your understanding of the story?

Brer Rabbit was in the woods one afternoon when a great wind came up. It blew on the ground and it blew in the tops of the trees. It blew so hard that Brer Rabbit was afraid a tree might fall on him, and he started running.

He was trucking through the woods when he ran smack into Brer Lion. Now, don't come telling me ain't no lions in the United States. Ain't none here now. But back in yonder times, all the animals lived everywhere. The lions and tigers and elephants and foxes and what 'nall run around with each other like they was family. So that's how come wasn't unusual for Brer Rabbit to run up on Brer Lion like he done that day.

"What's your hurry, Brer Rabbit?"

"Run, Brer Lion! There's a hurricane coming."

Brer Lion got scared. "I'm too heavy to run, Brer Rabbit. What am I going to do?"

"Lay down, Brer Lion. Lay down! Get close to the ground!"

Brer Lion shook his head. "The wind might pick me up and blow me away."

"Hug a tree, Brer Lion! Hug a tree!"

"But what if the wind blows all day and into the night?"

"Let me tie you to the tree, Brer Lion. Let me tie you to the tree."

Brer Lion liked that idea. Brer Rabbit tied him to the tree and sat down next to it. After a while, Brer Lion got tired of hugging the tree.

"Brer Rabbit? I don't hear no hurricane."

Brer Rabbit listened. "Neither do I."

"Brer Rabbit? I don't hear no wind."

Brer Rabbit listened. "Neither do I."

BQ **BIG Question**

What is funny about a rabbit tying a lion to a tree?

"Brer Rabbit? Ain't a leaf moving in the trees."

Brer Rabbit looked up. "Sho' ain't."

"So untie me."

"I'm afraid to, Brer Lion."

Brer Lion began to roar. He roared so loud and so long, the foundations of the Earth started shaking. Least that's what it seemed like, and the other animals came from all over to see what was going on.

When they got close, Brer Rabbit jumped up and began strutting around the tied-up Brer Lion. When the animals saw what Brer Rabbit had done to Brer Lion, you'd better believe it was the forty-eleventh of Octorerarry before they messed with him again. 🔔

BQ **BIG Question**
What lesson is Brer Lion learning?

BQ **BIG Question**
Why might you read this folktale—for fun, for information, or for understanding?

Emma's Lion, 1994. Christian Pierre. Acrylic on masonite, 16 x 20 in. Private collection.

After You Read

Respond and Think Critically

1. Use your own words to describe the most important events in the story of Brer Rabbit and Brer Lion. [Summarize]

2. What personality traits does Brer Rabbit have that help him get the better of a much larger animal? Explain. [Analyze]

3. If you could add a moral, or lesson, to the end of "Brer Rabbit and Brer Lion," what would it be? Support your answer with details from the story. [Conclude]

4. Humor plays a large role in many folktales. Identify three details or aspects of this folktale that you found humorous. Which detail was funniest to you? [Identify]

Writing

Write a Summary Write a one-paragraph summary of the folktale. You may want to begin your summary with this topic sentence:

You would think that a lion would be smarter than a rabbit, but _____.

Remember that when you write a summary, you include the most important events and details in the story. You use your own words. Your summary should show that you understand the meaning of the story.

GA Performance Standards

ELA7W2g Demonstrate competence in a variety of genres. Produce writing that concludes with a detailed summary linked to the purpose of the composition.

Literature Online

Unit Resources For additional skills practice, go to glencoe.com and enter QuickPass code GL27534u2.

For Fun

Carnival Time in Willow Bend, 1987. Jane Wooster Scott. Oil on canvas.
Collection of Gregory Erwin.

BQ **BIG Question** **Why Do You Read?**

How does the painting *Carnival Time in Willow Bend* capture the idea of fun? What do
you read that brings fun into your life?

Before You Read

Charles

Connect to the Short Story

Have you ever heard the expression *read between the lines*?

Partner Talk With a partner, talk about the meaning of this expression. Give examples of moments when the expression might be used in conversation.

Build Background

Children entering school must learn to get along with one another, follow directions, and help with classroom activities. In preschool and kindergarten, children become accustomed to a school setting and learn to play together.

Vocabulary

deprived (di prīvd´) *v.* taken away, removed (p. 182). *Ryan was deprived of his snack because his little brother ate it.*

passionately (pash´ə nit lē) *adv.* enthusiastically, intensely (p. 183). *My father passionately cheers for his favorite baseball team.*

simultaneously (sī´məl tā´nē əs lē) *adv.* at the same time (p. 183). *Two runners reached the finish line simultaneously, so the judges were not certain who had won the race.*

maneuvered (mə nōō´vərd) *v.* guided with skill and design (p. 187). *He maneuvered the car carefully into the small parking space.*

lapses (laps´əs) *n.* interruptions, pauses (p. 187). *Our goalie is on guard for the whole game; he knows that any lapses can result in points for the other team.*

Meet Shirley Jackson

Full of Surprises Shirley Jackson's fiction is filled with strange twists and turns. In most of her novels and short stories, she explores the darker side of human nature. Some of her surprise endings shocked the readers of her day. However, she also wrote humorously about family life, as she does in "Charles."

Literary Works Jackson composed her stories while raising four children. Jackson wrote novels, plays, stories, and books for young people.

Shirley Jackson was born in 1919 and died in 1965.

 Literature Online

Author Search For more about Shirley Jackson, go to glencoe.com and enter QuickPass code GL27534u2.

Set Purposes for Reading

BQ BIG Question

As you read, ask yourself, which moments in this story strike me as humorous or funny? Why?

Literary Element Foreshadowing

Foreshadowing is an author's use of clues to prepare readers for events that will happen in a story. Authors use foreshadowing to build suspense and to maintain the readers' interest in a story.

Foreshadowing gives an alert reader hints about what to expect. In "Charles," Jackson uses the characters' actions and dialogue to hint at what will happen at the end. As you read, ask yourself what clues in the story foreshadow the ending. Before you finish the story, try to guess how it will end.

Reading Strategy Draw Conclusions About Characters

When you **draw conclusions about characters,** you use a number of pieces of information to make a general statement about a character or characters in a story.

Drawing conclusions about characters is important because it helps you understand why characters say and do certain things. It's a tool to help you see the larger picture of a story. To draw conclusions about characters, look for specific details about the characters. Then, make a general statement on the basis of these details. For example, a number of story details might lead you to conclude that one character is generous.

As you read "Charles," look for words and actions that help you draw conclusions about the characters. Use a chart like the one below to record details about the characters and the conclusions you draw from the details.

Character	Details About Character	Conclusion

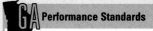

GA Performance Standards

For pages 178–189

ELA7R1e For literary texts, identify events that advance the plot and determine how each event explains past or present action(s) or foreshadows future action(s).

TRY IT

Draw Conclusions Think of a character from a television show or movie. Recall details about the character. How can those details be used to draw conclusions about the character and the outcome of the story? Remember that drawing a conclusion is like solving a mystery. You use clues to figure out something that the author does not explicitly tell you about the character.

Charles

Shirley Jackson

The day my son Laurie started kindergarten he renounced[1] corduroy overalls with bibs and began wearing blue jeans with a belt; I watched him go off the first morning with the older girl next door, seeing clearly that an era of my life was ended, my sweet-voiced nursery-school tot replaced by a long-trousered, swaggering[2] character who forgot to stop at the corner and wave good-bye to me.

He came home the same way, the front door slamming open, his cap on the floor, and the voice suddenly become raucous[3] shouting, "Isn't anybody here?"

Foreshadowing What do you learn about Laurie and his mother in this paragraph?

---

1 When Laurie **renounced** overalls, he rejected or gave them up.

2 **Swaggering** means "carrying oneself in a proud manner."

3 A **raucous** voice is loud and sounds rough.

At lunch he spoke insolently[4] to his father, spilled his baby sister's milk, and remarked that his teacher said we were not to take the name of the Lord in vain.

"How *was* school today?" I asked, elaborately casual.

"All right," he said.

"Did you learn anything?" his father asked.

Laurie regarded his father coldly. "I didn't learn nothing," he said.

"Anything," I said. "Didn't learn anything."

"The teacher spanked a boy, though," Laurie said, addressing his bread and butter. "For being fresh," he added, with his mouth full.

Draw Conclusions About Characters What ideas are you forming about Laurie?

"What did he do?" I asked. "Who was it?"

Laurie thought. "It was Charles," he said. "He was fresh. The teacher spanked him and made him stand in a corner. He was awfully fresh."

"What did he do?" I asked again, but Laurie slid off his chair, took a cookie, and left, while his father was still saying, "See here, young man."

The next day Laurie remarked at lunch, as soon as he sat down, "Well, Charles was bad again today." He grinned enormously and said, "Today Charles hit the teacher."

---

4 If someone is speaking *insolently*, he or she is talking in a boldly rude manner.

"Good heavens," I said, mindful of the Lord's name, "I suppose he got spanked again?"

"He sure did," Laurie said. "Look up," he said to his father.

"What?" his father said, looking up.

"Look down," Laurie said. "Look at my thumb. Gee, you're dumb." He began to laugh insanely.

"Why did Charles hit the teacher?" I asked quickly.

"Because she tried to make him color with red crayons," Laurie said. "Charles wanted to color with green crayons so he hit the teacher and she spanked him and said nobody play with Charles but everybody did."

The third day—it was Wednesday of the first week—Charles bounced a see-saw on to the head of a little girl and made her bleed, and the teacher made him stay inside all during recess. Thursday Charles had to stand in a corner during story-time because he kept pounding his feet on the floor. Friday Charles was **deprived** of blackboard privileges because he threw chalk.

On Saturday I remarked to my husband, "Do you think kindergarten is too unsettling for Laurie? All this toughness, and bad grammar, and this Charles boy sounds like such a bad influence."

"It'll be all right," my husband said reassuringly. "Bound to be people like Charles in the world. Might as well meet them now as later."

On Monday Laurie came home late, full of news. "Charles," he shouted as he came up the hill; I was waiting anxiously on the front steps. "Charles," Laurie yelled all the way up the hill, "Charles was bad again."

"Come right in," I said, as soon as he came close enough. "Lunch is waiting."

BQ BIG Question
What details in the story strike you as funny?

Draw Conclusions About Characters What conclusion can you draw about the mother's feelings about Laurie?

Foreshadowing How would you describe Laurie's behavior?

Vocabulary . . . .

deprived (di prīvd´) *v.* taken away, removed

"You know what Charles did?" he demanded, following me through the door. "Charles yelled so in school they sent a boy in from first grade to tell the teacher she had to make Charles keep quiet, and so Charles had to stay after school. And so all the children stayed to watch him."

"What did he do?" I asked.

"He just sat there," Laurie said, climbing into his chair at the table. "Hi, Pop, y'old dust mop."

"Charles had to stay after school today," I told my husband. "Everyone stayed with him."

"What does this Charles look like?" my husband asked Laurie. "What's his other name?"

"He's bigger than me," Laurie said. "And he doesn't have any galoshes and he doesn't ever wear a jacket."

Monday night was the first Parent-Teachers meeting, and only the fact that the baby had a cold kept me from going; I wanted **passionately** to meet Charles's mother. On Tuesday Laurie remarked suddenly, "Our teacher had a friend come to see her in school today."

"Charles's mother?" my husband and I asked **simultaneously.**

"Naaah," Laurie said scornfully. "It was a man who came and made us do exercises, we had to touch our toes. Look." He climbed down from his chair and squatted down and touched his toes. "Like this," he said. He got solemnly back into his chair and said, picking up his fork, "Charles didn't even *do* exercises."

"That's fine," I said heartily. "Didn't Charles want to do exercises?"

"Naaah," Laurie said. "Charles was so fresh to the teacher's friend he wasn't *let* do exercises."

"Fresh again?" I said.

Vocabulary

passionately (pash′ə nit lē) *adv.* enthusiastically, intensely

simultaneously (sī′ məl tā′ nē əs lē) *adv.* at the same time

"He kicked the teacher's friend," Laurie said. "The teacher's friend told Charles to touch his toes like I just did and Charles kicked him."

"What are they going to do about Charles, do you suppose?" Laurie's father asked him.

Laurie shrugged elaborately. "Throw him out of school, I guess," he said.

Wednesday and Thursday were routine; Charles yelled during story hour and hit a boy in the stomach and made him cry. On Friday Charles stayed after school again and so did all the other children.

With the third week of kindergarten Charles was an institution[5] in our family; the baby was being a Charles when she cried all afternoon; Laurie did a Charles when he filled his wagon full of mud and pulled it through the kitchen; even my husband, when he caught his elbow in the telephone cord and pulled telephone, ashtray, and a bowl of flowers off the table, said, after the first minute, "Looks like Charles."

During the third and fourth weeks it looked like a reformation[6] in Charles; Laurie reported grimly at lunch on Thursday of the third week, "Charles was so good today the teacher gave him an apple."

"What?" I said, and my husband added warily, "You mean Charles?"

"Charles," Laurie said. "He gave the crayons around and he picked up the books afterward and the teacher said he was her helper."

"What happened?" I asked incredulously.

"He was her helper, that's all," Laurie said, and shrugged.

"Can this be true, about Charles?" I asked my husband that night. "Can something like this happen?"

> **BQ** ▶ **BIG Question**
> What details in the description of the father's actions are amusing?

---

5 Here, *institution* means "a regular feature or tradition."

6 The *reformation* in Charles is a change for the better.

Playground. P. J. Crook. Acrylic on canvas, 116.8 x 132 cm. Private Collection.

View the Art How would you describe the mood of this painting? What elements contribute to the mood?

"Wait and see," my husband said cynically.[7] "When you've got a Charles to deal with, this may mean he's only plotting."[8]

He seemed to be wrong. For over a week Charles was the teacher's helper; each day he handed things out and he picked things up; no one had to stay after school.

---

7 When the father speaks ***cynically,*** he is reacting with doubt and disbelief.

8 ***Plotting*** means "planning with evil intent."

"The P.T.A. meeting's next week again," I told my husband one evening. "I'm going to find Charles's mother there."

"Ask her what happened to Charles," my husband said. "I'd like to know."

"I'd like to know myself," I said.

On Friday of that week things were back to normal. "You know what Charles did today?" Laurie demanded at the lunch table, in a voice slightly awed. "He told a little girl to say a word and she said it and the teacher washed her mouth out with soap and Charles laughed."

"What word?" his father asked unwisely, and Laurie said, "I'll have to whisper it to you, it's so bad." He got down off his chair and went around to his father. His father bent his head down and Laurie whispered joyfully. His father's eyes widened.

"Did Charles tell the little girl to say *that*?" he asked respectfully.

"She said it *twice*," Laurie said. "Charles told her to say it *twice*."

"What happened to Charles?" my husband asked.

"Nothing," Laurie said. "He was passing out the crayons."

Monday morning Charles abandoned the little girl and said the evil word himself three or four times, getting his mouth washed out with soap each time. He also threw chalk.

My husband came to the door with me that evening as I set out for the P.T.A. meeting. "Invite her over for a cup of tea after the meeting," he said. "I want to get a look at her."

"If only she's there," I said prayerfully.

"She'll be there," my husband said. "I don't see how they could hold a P.T.A. meeting without Charles's mother."

Foreshadowing Consider how happy Laurie is to repeat the word. What might this clue suggest about Laurie?

At the meeting I sat restlessly, scanning each comfortable matronly[9] face, trying to determine which one hid the secret of Charles. None of them looked to me haggard[10] enough. No one stood up in the meeting and apologized for the way her son had been acting. No one mentioned Charles.

After the meeting I identified and sought out Laurie's kindergarten teacher. She had a plate with a cup of tea and a piece of chocolate cake; I had a plate with a cup of tea and a piece of marshmallow cake. We **maneuvered** up to one another cautiously, and smiled.

"I've been so anxious to meet you," I said. "I'm Laurie's mother."

"We're all so interested in Laurie," she said.

"Well, he certainly likes kindergarten," I said. "He talks about it all the time."

"We had a little trouble adjusting, the first week or so," she said primly, "but now he's a fine little helper. With occasional **lapses,** of course."

"Laurie usually adjusts very quickly," I said. "I suppose this time it's Charles's influence."

"Charles?"

"Yes," I said, laughing, "you must have your hands full in that kindergarten, with Charles."

"Charles?" she said. "We don't have any Charles in the kindergarten." 🍃

Foreshadowing From this clue, how do you predict this story might end?

Draw Conclusions About Characters How does the teacher's remark change your view of Laurie?

---

9 A *matronly* face is a motherly, mature face.

10 A *haggard* person looks worn out as a result of grief, worry, illness—or dealing with a boy like Charles.

Vocabulary

maneuvered (mə nōō′ vərd) *v.* guided with skill and design

lapses (laps′ əs) *n.* interruptions, pauses

After You Read

Respond and Think Critically

1. How does Laurie change when he starts kindergarten? **[Recall]**

2. How does Laurie describe Charles's behavior? Include details from the story to support your answer. **[Recall]**

3. Compare Laurie's behavior at home with Charles's actions at school. How is their behavior similar? How is it different? **[Compare]**

4. What do you discover about Charles's identity? Why do you think Laurie tells stories about Charles at home? Explain. **[Infer]**

5. **BQ** BIG Question Which moments in "Charles" did you think were most humorous or entertaining? Why? **[Evaluate]**

Vocabulary Practice

On a separate sheet of paper, write the vocabulary word that correctly completes each sentence. If none of the words fits the sentence, write none.

simultaneously	maneuvered	lapses
deprived	passionately	

1. Mike and I think alike, so it was no surprise that we solved the mystery _____ .

2. Karen felt _____ that her work had been recognized at the awards assembly.

3. Today was very hot, so it was a bad day to be _____ of air conditioning.

4. Mai's eyes lit up as she spoke _____ about her favorite hobby.

5. I watched as he _____ the folded paper into the bottle.

6. My computer needs constant power, so any _____ in electricity could damage it.

Academic Vocabulary

Laurie had trouble with the **transition** between preschool and kindergarten. In the preceding sentence, *transition* refers to the move from one type of school to another. We all have transitions in life. List some transitions you've experienced. How did you feel about them at the time? How do you feel about them now?

TIP

Comparing
To answer question 3, think about Laurie's behavior at home and Charles's behavior at school.

- Start by reviewing details about each character. You may use your chart from page 179.

- Make a list of the similarities and differences between the boys. Use the list to help you organize your answer.

 Keep track of your ideas about the **BIG Question** in your unit Foldable.

 Literature Online

Selection Resources
For Selection Quizzes, eFlashcards, and Reading-Writing Connection activities, go to glencoe.com and enter QuickPass code GL27534u2.

Literary Element Foreshadowing

1. What clues throughout the story hint at the story's ending? Explain.

2. Do you think that the author included enough foreshadowing so that readers could guess the outcome of the story? Explain your answer.

Review: **Characterization**

As you learned on page 125, **characterization** includes the methods a writer uses to develop the personality of characters. In this story, Jackson primarily uses **indirect characterization.** She reveals Laurie's personality through Laurie's words and actions, as well as through his parents' reactions to him. In **direct characterization,** an author makes direct statements about a character's personality.

Standards Practice ELA7R1f

3. Which words best describe Laurie?
   A   honest and open
   B   clever and descriptive
   C   intelligent and well-behaved
   D   quiet and timid

Reading Strategy Draw Conclusions About Characters

Standards Practice ELA7R1f

4. Which word best suggests the mother's feelings at the end of the story?
   A   shocked
   B   proud
   C   joyful
   D   fearful

Grammar Link

Present Perfect Tense The **present perfect tense** of a verb names an action that happened at an indefinite time in the past. It also tells about an action that happened in the past and is still happening now. The present perfect tense consists of the helping verb *have* or *has* and the past participle of the main verb.

> Laurie's parents **have discussed** Charles's behavior in school several times.

Present Perfect Tense

Singular	Plural
I have discussed . . .	We have discussed . . .
You have discussed . . .	You have discussed . . .
He or she has discussed . . .	They have discussed . . .

Practice Using verbs in the present perfect tense, write three sentences about your experiences at school.

💬 Speaking and Listening

Literature Groups With a small group, discuss your own experience of adapting to school or kindergarten when you were young. Compare your experiences to Laurie's experiences in the story. Then, as a group, think of similarities and differences between group members' real-life experiences and Laurie's fictional experiences. Remember to build on the ideas of other speakers and to respect others' viewpoints.

Sarah Cynthia Sylvia Stout Would Not Take the Garbage Out

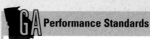
Performance Standards

For pages 190–193

ELA7R1g/i For literary texts, explain and analyze the effects of sound.

Connect to the Poem

You probably help out at home by doing household chores. Think about a time when you didn't complete a chore. What was the result?

List List chores that children often do around their homes. Which chores are you asked to do? How do you feel about doing them?

Build Background

This selection is a humorous poem about a girl who refuses to do a simple household chore.

- The poet uses exaggeration to show how the girl's stubborn refusal to do household chores affects those around her.

- Even humorous poems can teach a lesson, or moral. Many of Shel Silverstein's poems use humor to make meaningful comments about human nature or life.

Meet Shel Silverstein

Humorous Author Shel Silverstein wrote and illustrated books of children's poetry, but his quirky sense of humor appealed to adults as well. Besides writing and illustrating poetry and prose, Silverstein was a cartoonist and songwriter.

Silverstein was born in 1932 and died in 1999.

Set Purposes for Reading

BQ **BIG Question**

As you read this poem, ask yourself, why does the poet describe garbage in such detail? What effect is the poet aiming for?

Literary Element **Alliteration**

Alliteration is the repetition of consonant sounds, usually at the beginning of words or syllables. For example, Shel Silverstein uses alliteration in the following line: "*M*oldy *m*elons, dried-up *m*ustard." Authors use alliteration to add to the musical quality of their writing. Alliteration may also help authors emphasize certain points. In this poem, alliteration may help to emphasize the poem's humor. As you read the poem, look for lines that contain alliteration. Ask yourself, what effect is created by the alliteration?

 Literature Online

Author Search For more about Shel Silverstein, go to glencoe.com and enter QuickPass code GL27534u2.

Sarah Cynthia Sylvia Stout
Would Not Take the Garbage Out

Shel Silverstein

Sarah Cynthia Sylvia Stout
Would not take the garbage out!
She'd scour° the pots and scrape the pans,
Candy° the yams and spice the hams,
5 And though her daddy would scream and shout,
She simply would not take the garbage out.
And so it piled up to the ceilings:
Coffee grounds, potato peelings,
Brown bananas, rotten peas,
10 Chunks of sour cottage cheese.
It filled the can, it covered the floor,
It cracked the window and blocked the door
With bacon rinds and chicken bones,
Drippy ends of ice cream cones,
15 Prune pits, peach pits, orange peel,
Gloppy glumps of cold oatmeal,
Pizza crusts and withered greens,
Soggy beans and tangerines,
Crusts of black burned buttered toast,

Alliteration What does the alliteration in the title suggest about what type of poem this will be?

---

3 To *scour* a pot is to clean it by rubbing it vigorously.

4 *Candy* means "to preserve by cooking with sugar."

20   Gristly° bits of beefy roasts . . .
     The garbage rolled on down the hall,
     It raised the roof, it broke the wall . . .
     Greasy napkins, cookie crumbs,
     Globs of gooey bubblegum,
25   Cellophane from green baloney,
     Rubbery blubbery macaroni,
     Peanut butter, caked and dry,
     Curdled milk and crusts of pie,
     Moldy melons, dried up mustard,
30   Eggshells mixed with lemon custard,
     Cold french fries and rancid° meat,
     Yellow lumps of Cream of Wheat.
     At last the garbage reached so high
     That finally it touched the sky.
35   And all the neighbors moved away,
     And none of her friends would come to play.
     And finally Sarah Cynthia Stout said,
     "OK, I'll take the garbage out!"
     But then, of course, it was too late
40   The garbage reached across the state,
     From New York to the Golden Gate
     And there, in the garbage she did hate
     Poor Sarah met an awful fate,
     That I cannot right now relate
45   Because the hour is much too late.
     But children, remember Sarah Stout
     And always take the garbage out!

Alliteration How does alliteration affect the feeling of the poem?

BQ ▶ **BIG Question**
How does this line contribute to the poem's humor?

---

20 *Gristly* bits of meat are tough and hard to eat.

31 *Rancid* food is spoiled and has an unpleasant odor or taste.

After You Read

Respond and Think Critically

1. Who wants Sarah to take out the garbage? [Recall]

2. How do you know that Sarah is concerned that her friends no longer come over to play? Explain. [Infer]

3. Which lines contain exaggerated, or fantastic, descriptions, and which lines contain more realistic descriptions? Give three examples. [Compare]

4. At the end of the poem, Sarah meets an "awful fate." What do you think happens to her? [Conclude]

5. **Literary Element** Alliteration Write an example of alliteration from the poem. What effect is created by the alliteration? Is it humorous? Musical? Explain. [Analyze]

6. **BQ** BIG Question What makes this poem fun to read? Support your answer. [Evaluate]

Spelling Link

Adding suffixes to words with two or more syllables can cause spelling problems. Remember that when the last syllable of a word is accented, you should double the final consonant of the word if adding a suffix.

- commit + ed = committed

Do not double the final consonant of words if the

- suffix begins with a consonant (commit´+ ment = commitment)
- the accent is not on the last syllable (tra´vel + ed = traveled)
- accent moves when suffix is added (defer´+ ence = def´erence)
- word ends with two consonants (abrupt + ly = abruptly)

Practice On a sheet of paper, list these words and suffixes: refer + ence, salesman + ship, and desolate + ly. Combine each word and its suffix. Next to each word, explain why the final consonant was doubled or not doubled.

Writing

Write a Stanza A stanza is a group of lines forming a unit in a poem. Write a stanza of five to ten lines, describing a room in your school. Include at least three instances of alliteration in your stanza. To generate ideas, make a list describing details of your school. Use a dictionary and a thesaurus to help you create alliterative phrases.

TIP

Making Inferences
Remember that when you infer, you use information from the text to make a guess about what the author does not reveal directly.

- Recall that neither her father's shouting nor the huge mess makes Sarah take out the garbage.
- Reread lines 33–38.
- Ask yourself why Sarah finally agrees to take the garbage out.

FOLDABLES Study Organizer Keep track of your ideas about the BIG Question in your unit Foldable.

Literature Online

Selection Resources
For Selection Quizzes, eFlashcards, and Reading-Writing Connection activities, go to glencoe.com and enter QuickPass code GL27534u2.

Before You Read

After Twenty Years

Connect to the Short Story

Loyalty means being faithful. If you are loyal to a friend, you support him or her no matter what the situation. How important do you think loyalty is in a friendship?

Quickwrite Freewrite for a few minutes about whether or not you think a person should always expect loyalty from a friend. Support your opinion with examples.

Build Background

This story takes place in New York City in 1890. One of the main characters left New York around 1870 to go West to make his fortune.

- The first discovery of gold caused a gold rush in California, in 1848.
- In 1869 the railroad that joined the East and the West was completed. Many people in the United States moved from the East to the West to find new jobs.

Vocabulary

habitual (hə bich′ oo əl) *adj.* regular; usual; done out of habit (p. 196). *It was habitual for my father to lock the doors each night before going to bed.*

intricate (in′ tri kit) *adj.* complicated (p. 196). *The throne was covered with intricate carving.*

vicinity (vi sin′ ə tē) *n.* the area around a certain place (p. 196). *The number of bus stops increases in the vicinity of downtown.*

majority (mə jôr′ ə tē) *n.* the most of a group (p. 196). *The person with the majority of the votes will be class president.*

moderately (mod′ ər it lē) *adv.* to a limited degree (p. 200). *I'm moderately happy with my performance, though I wish I hadn't made any mistakes.*

Meet O. Henry

An Adventurous Life William Sydney Porter, who used the pen name O. Henry, led a varied but difficult life. He first worked in a drugstore in North Carolina and then as a sheepherder in Texas. He was also a bank teller, a fugitive in Honduras, a prisoner, a magazine editor, and a journalist before he began writing the stories that made him famous.

Surprise! Many of O. Henry's stories contain a surprise ending or an ironic twist. "The Gift of the Magi" is one of the most famous of his short stories with a twist. William Sydney Porter was born in 1862 and died in 1910.

Literature Online

Author Search For more about O. Henry, go to glencoe.com and enter QuickPass code GL27534u2.

Set Purposes for Reading

BQ BIG Question

Authors use various techniques, such as suspense, to maintain readers' interest. As you read this story, ask yourself, what details does the author include to keep me involved?

Literary Element Mood

Mood is the emotional quality or atmosphere of a literary work. Descriptive words, setting, dialogue, and characters' actions or gestures can all contribute to mood.

Mood is important because it affects a reader's feelings and expectations. As you read this story, pay attention to how O. Henry creates mood through dialogue and through descriptions of the characters and setting.

Reading Strategy Make Predictions About Plot

When you **make predictions,** you make guesses about what will happen next in a story. You base your predictions on the events and details you've read about so far, as well as on what you already know from your own experience.

Making predictions helps you become a more involved reader. It's okay if your predictions turn out to be incorrect. You predict to get involved in a story and to follow the story's twists.

To make predictions about plot,

- pay attention to descriptions of the characters and what the characters say and do.
- look for details about the time and place in which the story occurs.
- think about what you already know about the subject of the story, and guess what will happen next.

As you read this story, note details about setting, characters, and dialogue. Then, based on these details, write predictions about what will happen next. Use a chart like the one below.

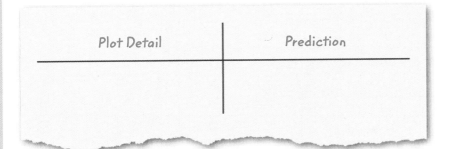

Plot Detail	Prediction

GA Performance Standards

For pages 194–201

ELA7R1h For literary texts, identify and analyze how an author's use of words creates tone and mood.

TRY IT

Make Predictions Imagine the following scene and make a prediction. Today is Carrie's first day at your school. You notice during math class that she seems friendly toward everyone, including you. Later at lunch, there is an empty seat next to you. Carrie makes eye contact with you and smiles as she walks toward your table. What do you predict will happen next?

Night Shadows, 1921. Edward Hopper. Etching, Whitney Museum of American Art, NY. Josephine N. Hopper bequest.

After Twenty Years

O. Henry

The policeman on the beat moved up the avenue impressively. The impressiveness was **habitual** and not for show, for spectators were few. The time was barely 10 o'clock at night, but chilly gusts of wind with a taste of rain in them had well nigh depeopled[1] the streets.

Trying doors as he went, twirling his club with many **intricate** and artful[2] movements, turning now and then to cast his watchful eye down the pacific thoroughfare,[3] the officer, with his stalwart[4] form and slight swagger, made a fine picture of a guardian of the peace. The **vicinity** was one that kept early hours. Now and then you might see the lights of a cigar store or of an all-night lunch counter; but the **majority** of the doors belonged to business places that had long since been closed.

Mood In what way do details about the setting help set the mood of the story?

---

1 The chilly winds make people stay indoors, leaving the streets *depeopled,* or without people.

2 The policeman twirls the club with an *artful,* or skillful, movement.

3 A *pacific thoroughfare* is a peaceful street.

4 *Stalwart* is another word for *strong.*

Vocabulary

habitual (hə bich′ oō əl) *adj.* regular; usual; done out of habit

intricate (in′ tri kit) *adj.* complicated

vicinity (vi sin′ə tē) *n.* the area around a certain place

majority (mə jôr′ə tē) *n.* the most of a group

When about midway of a certain block the policeman suddenly slowed his walk. In the doorway of a darkened hardware store a man leaned, with an unlighted cigar in his mouth. As the policeman walked up to him the man spoke up quickly.

"It's all right, officer," he said, reassuringly. "I'm just waiting for a friend. It's an appointment made twenty years ago. Sounds a little funny to you, doesn't it? Well, I'll explain if you'd like to make certain it's all straight. About that long ago there used to be a restaurant where this store stands—'Big Joe' Brady's restaurant."

"Until five years ago," said the policeman. "It was torn down then."

The man in the doorway struck a match and lit his cigar. The light showed a pale, square-jawed face with keen eyes, and a little white scar near his right eyebrow. His scarfpin was a large diamond, oddly set.

"Twenty years ago tonight," said the man, "I dined here at 'Big Joe' Brady's with Jimmy Wells, my best chum, and the finest chap[5] in the world. He and I were raised here in New York, just like two brothers, together. I was eighteen and Jimmy was twenty. The next morning I was to start for the West to make my fortune. You couldn't have dragged Jimmy out of New York; he thought it was the only place on earth. Well, we agreed that night that we would meet here again exactly twenty years from that date and time, no matter what our conditions might be or from what distance we might have to come. We figured that in twenty years each of us ought to have our destiny[6] worked out and our fortunes made, whatever they were going to be."

"It sounds pretty interesting," said the policeman. "Rather a long time between meets, though, it seems to me. Haven't you heard from your friend since you left?"

"Well, yes, for a time we corresponded,"[7] said the other. "But after a year or two we lost track of each other. You

Make Predictions About Plot Based on what you have read and what you already know, make a prediction about the meeting.

Make Predictions About Plot After learning more about the characters, does your prediction about what will happen in the story change?

---

5 A **chum** is a friend, and a **chap** is a man or boy.

6 **Destiny** is what the future holds for a person.

7 The two friends **corresponded**, or wrote letters to each other.

see, the West is a pretty big proposition,[8] and I kept hustling around over it pretty lively. But I know Jimmy will meet me here if he's alive, for he always was the truest, staunchest[9] old chap in the world. He'll never forget. I came a thousand miles to stand in this door tonight, and it's worth it if my old partner turns up."

The waiting man pulled out a handsome watch, the lids of it set with small diamonds.

"Three minutes to ten," he announced. "It was exactly ten o'clock when we parted here at the restaurant door."

"Did pretty well out West, didn't you?" asked the policeman.

"You bet! I hope Jimmy has done half as well. He was a kind of plodder,[10] though, good fellow as he was. I've had to compete with some of the sharpest wits going to get my pile. A man gets in a groove in New York. It takes the West to put a razor-edge on him."

The policeman twirled his club and took a step or two.

"I'll be on my way. Hope your friend comes around all right. Going to call time on him sharp?"[11]

"I should say not!" said the other. "I'll give him half an hour at least. If Jimmy is alive on earth he'll be here by that time. So long, officer."

"Good-night, sir," said the policeman, passing on along his beat, trying doors as he went.

There was now a fine, cold drizzle falling, and the wind had risen from its uncertain puffs into a steady blow. The few foot passengers astir in that quarter hurried dismally[12] and silently along with coat collars turned high and pocketed hands. And in the door of the hardware store the man who had come a thousand miles to fill an appointment, uncertain

Mood In what way do the man's words change the mood of the story?

---

8 In this sentence, **proposition** means "a challenging opportunity."

9 **Staunchest** means "most loyal and dependable."

10 A **plodder** is someone who moves slowly, but the meaning here is that Jimmy is not a quick thinker.

11 To **call time on him sharp** means "to expect him to arrive exactly on time."

12 **Dismally** means "in a sad or gloomy way."

Rainy Night, 1939. Charles Burchfield. Watercolor over pencil, 30 x 42 in. San Diego Art Museum, CA.

View the Art What does the scene pictured here have in common with the one O. Henry describes in this story?

almost to absurdity,[13] with the friend of his youth, smoked his cigar and waited.

About twenty minutes he waited, and then a tall man in a long overcoat, with collar turned up to his ears, hurried across from the opposite side of the street. He went directly to the waiting man.

"Is that you, Bob?" he asked, doubtfully.

"Is that you, Jimmy Wells?" cried the man in the door.

"Bless my heart!" exclaimed the new arrival, grasping both the other's hands with his own. "It's Bob, sure as fate.[14] I was certain I'd find you here if you were still in existence. Well, well, well!—twenty years is a long time. The old restaurant's gone, Bob; I wish it had lasted, so we could have had another dinner there. How has the West treated you, old man?"

"Bully;[15] it has given me everything I asked it for. You've changed lots, Jimmy. I never thought you were so tall by two or three inches."

"Oh, I grew a bit after I was twenty."

"Doing well in New York, Jimmy?"

Mood In what way does the arrival of the new character affect the mood of the story?

---

13 **Absurdity** is the state of being ridiculous.

14 **Fate** is your fortune, or what the future holds for you.

15 Here, **bully** is slang for "excellent" or "in the best way."

"**Moderately**. I have a position in one of the city departments. Come on, Bob; we'll go around to a place I know of, and have a good long talk about old times."

The two men started up the street, arm in arm. The man from the West, his egotism[16] enlarged by success, was beginning to outline the history of his career. The other, submerged in his overcoat, listened with interest.

At the corner stood a drug store, brilliant with electric lights. When they came into this glare each of them turned simultaneously to gaze upon the other's face.

The man from the West stopped suddenly and released his arm.

"You're not Jimmy Wells," he snapped. "Twenty years is a long time, but not long enough to change a man's nose from a Roman to a pug."[17]

"It sometimes changes a good man into a bad one," said the tall man. "You've been under arrest for ten minutes, 'Silky' Bob. Chicago thinks you may have dropped over our way and wires us she wants to have a chat with you. Going quietly, are you? That's sensible. Now, before we go on to the station here's a note I was asked to hand you. You may read it here at the window. It's from Patrolman Wells."

The man from the West unfolded the little piece of paper handed him. His hand was steady when he began to read, but it trembled a little by the time he had finished. The note was rather short.

> BOB: I was at the appointed place on time. When you struck the match to light your cigar I saw it was the face of the man wanted in Chicago. Somehow I couldn't do it myself, so I went around and got a plain clothes man[18] to do the job.
>
> Jimmy 🔊

Make Predictions About Plot Use the information from this sentence to predict what will happen next.

BQ BIG Question
What happens at the end of the story? Are you surprised?

---

16 A person's *egotism* is a great sense of self-importance.

17 A *Roman* nose is long and bold. A *pug* nose is short and thick.

18 Jimmy met Bob in his police uniform. A *plain clothes* man is a police officer who is working but not wearing his uniform.

Vocabulary
....

moderately (mod′ər it lē) *adv.* to a limited degree

After You Read

Respond and Think Critically

1. What promise did Bob make twenty years ago? [Recall]

2. What does Bob's physical reaction to the note tell you about his emotional state? Explain. [Interpret]

3. How has Jimmy been both more successful and less successful than Bob? [Compare]

4. **Literary Element** Mood How does the mood change over the course of the story? Support your answer with examples. [Analyze]

5. **Reading Strategy** Make Predictions About Plot Review the predictions you made as you read. Which predictions were true? What did predicting add to your experience of reading the story? Explain. [Evaluate]

6. **BQ** BIG Question O. Henry is widely considered a great and entertaining storyteller. Do you agree? Explain. [Evaluate]

Vocabulary

On a separate sheet of paper, write the vocabulary word that correctly completes each sentence. If none of the words fits the sentence, write "none."

habitual   vicinity   intricate   moderately   majority

1. A _____ of the people enjoyed the television show.

2. We discovered bear tracks near our tent, so we knew that wild animals were in the _____ of the campground.

3. The _____ designs on the book's pages amazed us.

4. Felipe was very shy, so we were _____ when he sang in front of the class.

5. Maria encouraged us to walk to school along a new route, instead of our _____ one.

6. The clothes were neither costly nor inexpensive; we considered them _____ priced.

Writing

Write a Letter Write a letter that Bob might have written to Jimmy. Tell Jimmy about the arrest and how Bob feels about what Jimmy did. Include a date, a salutation, a closing, and a signature.

TIP

Interpreting
The author has included an important detail that helps you understand how Bob feels when he reads the note.

- Find the part of the story in which Bob reads Jimmy's note.

- Reread the description of Bob's physical reaction to reading the note.

- Think about what this reaction reveals about Bob's emotions.

FOLDABLES Keep track of
Study Organizer your ideas about
the **BIG Question** in your
unit Foldable.

  Literature Online

Selection Resources
For Selection Quizzes, eFlashcards, and Reading-Writing Connection activities, go to glencoe.com and enter QuickPass code GL27534u2.

Slam, Dunk, & Hook

Connect to the Poem

What do you like about sports? Which games do you prefer, and why? Would you rather be playing a game or watching others play?

Write a Journal Entry Record your feelings about sports. Describe a game you enjoy and a game you dislike. Use a chart like the one below to organize your thoughts. Then, explain your feelings. Do you prefer to play sports or to watch them? Which do you value more—fierce competition between teams or intense loyalty among team members? Why?

I enjoy _____ because . . .	I dislike _____ because . . .

Build Background

Basketball was invented in 1891 by James Naismith, an instructor in physical education who lived in Springfield, Massachusetts. In need of an indoor game for the winter months, Naismith used a soccer ball and two peach baskets, one hung at each end of a gym. The rules Naismith made up for that game form the basis of today's game.

Meet Yusef Komunyakaa

"Students often have such a lofty idea of what a poem is, and I want them to realize that their own lives are where the poetry comes from."

—Yusef Komunyakaa

Poet and Educator The poet and educator Yusef Komunyakaa (ū´ sef kō mun yä´ kä) uses his Louisiana childhood and his time in Vietnam as an Army correspondent as resources for the material in his poetry. A winner of the Pulitzer Prize for Poetry in 1994, Komunyakaa writes poems on a wide variety of subjects, including jazz, racial prejudice, and war.

Yusef Komunyakaa was born in 1947.

 Literature Online

Author Search For more about Yusef Komunyakaa, go to glencoe.com and enter QuickPass code GL27534u2.

Set Purposes for Reading

BQ BIG Question

As you read, ask yourself, how does the structure and rhythm of this poem help to recreate the feel of an actual game of basketball?

 **Performance Standards**

For pages 202–207

ELA7R1g/ii For literary texts, explain and analyze the effects of figurative language.

Literary Element Metaphor and Simile

Figurative language is language that is used for descriptive effect, often to imply an idea indirectly. Expressions of figurative language are not literally true. They express a truth beyond the literal level. Two of the most common types of figurative language are **similes** and **metaphors.**

- A **simile** is an expression that uses *like* or *as* to compare two seemingly unlike things. The phrase "Elena runs like the wind" is a simile suggesting that Elena runs quickly.

- A **metaphor** is an expression that compares two seemingly unlike things. In contrast to similes, metaphors imply a comparison instead of stating it directly. Metaphors do not contain the words *like* or *as.* Take, for example, the sentence "Seth is a cheetah on the racetrack." Seth is not literally a cheetah. The author uses the metaphor to suggest that Seth runs quickly.

Similes and metaphors are great writing tools because they add colorful description with a minimum of words. Similes, metaphors, and other kinds of figurative language are especially prominent in poetry. As you read this poem, look for similes and metaphors. Ask yourself, what do the two objects of the comparison have in common? What new insight do I gain by thinking about the comparison?

Reading Strategy Visualize

When you **visualize,** you create pictures in your mind. For example, while reading nonfiction, you may picture the steps in a certain process or envision a place that the writer is describing. As you read fiction and poetry, you may picture what a character or setting looks like or imagine the actions that take place.

Visualizing is important because it makes a selection more vivid—it helps you "see" people, places, and things. If you visualize while you read, you will understand and remember the poem better.

As you read, imagine what the characters look like, and try to picture the setting. Pay attention to the details that the writer includes. Make sketches of what you "see" in your mind.

TRY IT

Visualize With a partner, pick a single sporting event. Then, working individually, list everything that comes to your mind as you picture the scene. After a few minutes of writing, stop and compare and contrast your list with your partner's. Which elements are similar and which are different?

Slam, Dunk, & Hook

Yusef Komunyakaa

Fast breaks. Lay ups. With Mercury's°
Insignia on our sneakers,
We outmaneuvered° the footwork
Of bad angels. Nothing but a hot
5   Swish of strings like silk
Ten feet out. In the roundhouse°

---

1   In ancient Roman mythology, **Mercury** was the swift messenger of the gods. He
was often portrayed wearing winged sandals.

3   If you **outmaneuvered** someone, you used clever movements to defeat that person.

6   **Roundhouse** is a slang term for sweeping movement—in this case, wide, swinging
arm movements.

Labyrinth° our bodies
Created, we could almost
Last forever, poised in midair
10 Like storybook sea monsters.
A high note hung there
A long second. Off
The rim. We'd corkscrew
Up & dunk balls that exploded
15 The skullcap of hope & good
Intention. Bug-eyed, lanky,
All hands & feet . . . sprung rhythm.
We were metaphysical° when girls
Cheered on the sidelines.
20 Tangled up in a falling,
Muscles were a bright motor
Double-flashing to the metal hoop
Nailed to our oak.
When Sonny Boy's mama died
25 He played nonstop all day, so hard
Our backboard splintered.
Glistening with sweat, we jibed°
& rolled the ball off our
Fingertips. Trouble
30 Was there slapping a blackjack°
Against an open palm.
Dribble, drive to the inside, feint,°
& glide like a sparrow hawk.
Lay ups. Fast breaks.
35 We had moves we didn't know
We had. Our bodies spun
On swivels of bone & faith,
Through a lyric slipknot
Of joy, & we knew we were
40 Beautiful & dangerous.

Figurative Language What figure of speech appears in these lines? What two things are being compared in line 21?

Visualize This simile compares a player to a sparrow hawk, a bird that flies at high speeds and changes directions quickly. How does this image help you visualize the player's movements?

BQ BIG Question
How might a thing be both beautiful and dangerous? What quality does this description suggest to you?

---

7 A *labyrinth* is a confusing, complicated arrangement.

18 Here, *metaphysical* means that the players seemed to go beyond the limits of the physical world.

27 To *jibe* is to be in harmony with one another.

30 A *blackjack* is a weighted, flexible, leather-covered weapon.

32 A *feint* is movement that is intended to "fake out" an opponent.

After You Read

Respond and Think Critically

1. Summarize the actions described in "Slam, Dunk, & Hook." [Summarize]

2. Why is "Slam, Dunk, & Hook" a good title for this poem? Explain your answer. [Analyze]

3. According to "Slam, Dunk, & Hook," team sports are dramatic, emotional, and exhilarating. Do you agree or disagree? Explain. [Evaluate]

4. What is Komunyakaa saying about the connection between friendship and basketball? Support your answer with details from the poem. [Interpret]

5. What overall message about team sports does "Slam, Dunk, & Hook" express? Explain. [Conclude]

6. **BQ** BIG Question Which sections of this poem did you find most powerful? Tell why you found the sections effective. [Evaluate]

 TIP

Summarizing

• To summarize a poem, write a sentence for every few thoughts or events described in the poem.

• Remember that the end of a line in poetry is not necessarily the end of a sentence or thought.

• In your own words, retell the main points of the poem in the order that they are presented.

FOLDABLES Keep track of
Study Organizer your ideas about
the **BIG Question** in your
unit Foldable.

Academic Vocabulary

Each member of a basketball team **contributes** to its success.

In the preceding sentence, *contributes* means "has a part in a group's effort." Think about a time when you contributed to a group's success. What did you contribute to the group? Explain.

 Literature Online

Selection Resources
For Selection Quizzes,
eFlashcards, and Reading-
Writing Connection activities,
go to glencoe.com and enter
QuickPass code GL27534u2.

Literary Element | Metaphor and Simile

Standards Practice ELA7R1g/ii

1. Read these lines from the poem.

   . . . we could almost
   Last forever, poised in midair
   Like storybook sea monsters.

   The author expresses his idea by including
   A   a metaphor to compare the players to a story book.
   B   a statement of fact about the players.
   C   a simile to compare the players to sea monsters.
   D   an honest statement about the game.

Review: Theme

As you learned on page 135, the **theme** of a work is its overall message about life or human nature.

Standards Practice ELA7W2a

2. Which sentence gives the best description of the theme of the poem?
   A   Athletes must struggle to acquire skills to play basketball.
   B   When girls are watching, the athletes play harder.
   C   Basketball helps players develop strength and grace.
   D   The life of an athlete is full of distractions and difficulties.

Reading Strategy | Visualize

3. Which images from "Slam, Dunk, & Hook" helped you visualize the action of the poem? To answer, refer to the sketches you created as you read.

4. Reread the first five lines of "Slam, Dunk, & Hook." Try to visualize the action that the poem describes. In your own words, write a few sentences explaining what is happening. Include vivid details from the poem.

Grammar Link

Past Perfect Tense The **past perfect tense** of a verb names an action that took place before another action or event in the past. The past perfect tense of a verb consists of the helping verb *had* and the past participle of the main verb. The past perfect tense is often used in sentences that contain a past tense verb in another part of the sentence.

We **had** just **arrived** when the play **began.**

The play **had been rewritten** several times before it **opened.**

Past Perfect Tense

Singular	Plural
I had started.	We had started.
You had started.	You had started.
He, she, or it had started.	They had started.

Practice Write three sentences about playing a sport, such as basketball, using verbs in the past perfect tense.

Write with Style

Apply Figurative Language You have been reading similes and metaphors; now try your hand at writing some. Write a short stanza or a few lines of a poem about a hobby or pastime that you or that some of your friends enjoy. Include at least one metaphor and one simile in your poem. Remember that a simile includes *like* or *as* and a metaphor makes a direct comparison.

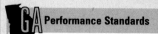 Performance Standards

For page 208

ELA7C1a Identify and write sentences correctly, avoiding fragments and run-ons, combining or revising sentences.

Grammar Workshop

Sentence Fragments

Yusef Komunyakaa uses complete sentences as well as sentence fragments in his poem "Slam, Dunk, & Hook." A complete sentence has both a subject and a predicate and expresses a complete thought. The subject tells what the sentence is about. The predicate tells what the subject does.

A high note hung there a long second.

In this complete sentence, *A high note* is the subject. The predicate is *hung there a long second.*

A sentence fragment does not express a complete thought. It may be missing a subject, a predicate, or both. In the examples below, notice how fragments can be made into complete sentences.

Problem 1 The fragment lacks a subject.

Nailed the hoop to our oak.

Solution Add a subject to form a complete sentence.

We nailed the hoop to our oak.

Problem 2 The fragment lacks a predicate.

Fast breaks.

Solution Add a predicate to form a complete sentence.

Fast breaks can catch your opponent off guard.

Problem 3 The fragment lacks a subject and a predicate.

Off the rim.

Solution Add a subject and a predicate to form a complete sentence.

The ball bounced off the rim.

TRY IT: Sentence Fragments

Rewrite these fragments into complete sentences by applying one of the solutions shown above.

1. Against an open palm.
2. Sonny Boy.
3. Cheered on the sidelines.

Tip

Watch out! You can use fragments when talking with friends or writing personal letters. Poets and other writers use fragments to produce a special effect. Use complete sentences, however, for school or business writing.

Tip

Helpful Hint To detect whether or not a thought is complete, ask yourself: Who or what is the sentence about? What is happening or being done?

 Literature Online

Grammar For more grammar practice, go to glencoe.com and enter QuickPass code GL27534u2.

Part 2

For Information

The Stargazers, 1995. Christian Pierre. Acrylic on canvas. Private Collection.

BQ BIG Question **Why Do You Read?**

How are the two people in the painting *The Stargazers* discovering information about the world? How do you find information about things that make you curious?

What Is a Knight?

Connect to the Article

Knights lived according to a strict set of rules. What rules do you follow each day at home and at school?

Quickwrite Write for a few minutes about knights you have seen in movies and read about in books. What do they look like? How do they behave?

Build Background

"What Is a Knight?" describes the characteristics of knights and the code of honor by which they lived in medieval Europe.

- Feudalism was a political system that created alliances, or bonds, between monarchs and nobles.

- Monarchs—kings and queens—gave nobles land in exchange for loyalty and military aid.

- Landholding nobles needed military groups to defend their lands. Nobles relied on knights and armies of peasants to defend their lands and fight for the royal army of the monarch.

Meet John Farman

Making History Fun
John Farman is the author of many entertaining history books for young people, including *The Short and Bloody History of Pirates*, *The Short and Bloody History of Spies*, and *The Shockingly Short History of Absolutely Everything*. "What Is a Knight?" comes from *The Short and Bloody History of Knights*, which was published in 2002.

 Literature Online

Author Search For more about John Farman, go to glencoe.com and enter QuickPass code GL27534u2.

Vocabulary

excess (ek´ses) *adj.* more than the usual amount (p. 212). *Kayla wiped the excess paint off her brush so that the paint wouldn't drip onto the floor.*

chivalry (shiv´əl rē) *n.* the customs of medieval knighthood (p. 213). *When the young man gave his bus seat to the woman who was standing, my grandmother remarked, "I guess chivalry still exists."*

suppresses (sə pres´es) *v.* puts down or stops (p. 214). *Mr. Sanchez suppresses the noise in his classroom without raising his voice.*

Set Purposes for Reading

BQ BIG Question

As you read, ask yourself, what were the roles and responsibilities of knights in medieval Europe?

Literary Element Author's Purpose

The **author's purpose** is the intention of the author. An author might write to entertain, to persuade, to describe, or to inform, or for a combination of these purposes.

Authors write about topics differently because of their own interests, experiences, and values. Once you understand the author's purpose, you can focus on what he or she wants you to "get" from the text.

As you read "What Is a Knight?" look for clues that tell you whether the author wants to entertain, persuade, or inform his readers.

Reading Strategy Activate Prior Knowledge

When you **activate prior knowledge,** you use information that you already know to better understand what you read. Remembering what you have learned, seen, or experienced can help you make sense of new information. It can also help you predict what a selection is about and what might happen next.

To activate prior knowledge before you read "What Is a Knight?" consider what you already know about

- a knight's responsibilities
- a knight's character and place in society
- the time period in which knights lived

The chart below can help you activate your prior knowledge. Use the points above as a guide and fill in the first column. Complete the second column by listing any questions that you would like to have answered. When you have finished reading, complete the third column.

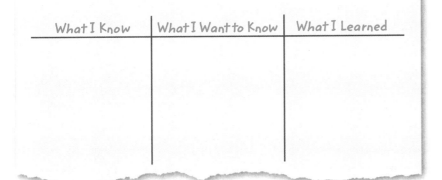

What I Know	What I Want to Know	What I Learned

GA Performance Standards

For pages 210–218

ELA7R1a For literary texts, distinguish between the concepts of theme in a literary work and the author's purpose in an expository text.

TRY IT

Activate Prior Knowledge
What stories do you know about knights from the Middle Ages? Were their lives easy or difficult? Discuss your ideas with a partner.

Teaching Knights to Joust, from 'Roman du Saint Graal,' 15th century. Vellum. Bibliotheque Municipale, Dijon, France.

What Is a Knight?

John Farman

Everyone thinks they know about knights: rich guys in flashy armor tearing around the countryside, killing **excess** dragons, rescuing damsels[1] trapped in towers, and knocking each other off of horses with long poles at special tournaments! I wanted to find out all the stuff we don't know. Like, where did knights buy their **armor**? How much did it cost? How easy was it to move, let alone fight, covered from head to foot in metal? What did they get paid fighting for the king? What did they eat? Where— and with whom—did they live? Were they really the brave, noble guys we are led to believe, or were some wimpy, cowardly, and dishonest? I'm going to try to tell you what knights were really like—warts and all—and what it was like to be one.

Author's Purpose After reading the title, what do you predict is Farman's purpose for writing?

Visual Vocabulary

Armor is covering worn to protect the body against weapons and injury.

---

1 **Damsels** are young unmarried women of noble birth.

Vocabulary

excess (ek´ses) adj. more than the usual amount

Career Knights

The first thing to remember is that knights were mercenaries (paid soldiers). They were paid, usually with large plots of land, to fight for their lord or king.

The second thing to remember is that they were supposed to conduct themselves according to a strict code of behavior. This was called **chivalry**.

Last and most important, the knights were part of a way of life, called the feudal system, that existed in Europe. Basically the feudal system helped a king obtain thousands of men for the wars he always fought. His barons and earls, in exchange for vast areas of land, pledged to provide armies on request. These barons and earls gave smaller parcels of their land to knights who, in return, promised to supply men (peasants) to do the fighting. In return for doing this, the knight assigned these peasants much smaller pieces of land to provide food for their families—and the knight's family.

How to Be a Knight

But who got to be a knight? For starters, before you get too excited, you had to be the son of a knight. Around the age of twelve, you went to another knight's house to learn how to knight—so to speak. The knight in question started you off as a page (young attendant) and then as a personal servant, called a squire. This duty involved grooming his horses, polishing his armor, and even serving him his breakfast, lunch, and dinner. In return he taught you how to ride horses and fight at the same time, as well as the code of chivalry as mentioned above.

Activate Prior Knowledge
Why wouldn't young men stay in their own homes and learn the skills of knighthood from their fathers?

Knight Time

Eventually, when the knight in charge of you decided you were ready, it was time for the big day. First you took a special bath in holy water and said prayers and stuff. Then you had to put on an outfit of white clothes and pray all

BQ **BIG Question**
What do you think you'll learn as you read "Knight Time"?

Vocabulary

chivalry (shiv´əl rē) *n.* the customs of medieval knighthood

night in front of your nice new armor as it sat on the altar. Just like Christmas, you weren't allowed to touch it until morning. After all of your relatives and friends had arrived at the church, you put on your armor while the priest blessed it and you. That done, another knight gave you a whack on the shoulder with the flat (hopefully) part of his sword and presto, you became a full-fledged knight.

Knights' Rules

The whole idea of how a knight should behave went under the general term of "chivalry." (Chivalry comes from *chevalerie*, the old French word for soldiers on horses.) Every knight was supposed to be bound by the rules of chivalry, which were as follows:

Author's Purpose Why do you think Farman uses a list to present information in this section?

1. A knight never tells lies.

2. He defends the Catholic Church (headed by the pope).

3. He defends the weak, **suppresses** the wicked, and honors God with noble acts (juggling? acrobatics?).

4. He is brave and loyal in defense of the knight who knighted him and that knight's lady.

5. Women (read "wealthy women") are held in high regard[2] (even though they had no legal rights or power).

6. The object in battle is always to capture the enemy, not to kill him.

7. Knights never fight during the pre-Easter period of Lent and even get a couple of days off at Christmas.

8. If a nobleman is captured, he has to be treated according to his rank.

2 *Regard* is a feeling of respect.

Vocabulary

suppresses (sə pres′es) *v.* puts down or stops

For Instance

In 1356 the Black Prince (Prince Edward of England) captured the king of France, John II, at Poitiers. The prince actually served the king at his own table and kept him in the most luxurious[3] prison that London, the capital of England, could offer.

How to Build a Feudal Army

First of all, knowing that he had to get an army together for a specific battle, a king first decided how many soldiers he needed (give or take a hundred). On the principle that you don't need a sledgehammer to crack a walnut, there was no point calling up 5,000 men to stop a brawl. After sizing up the battle, the king put the word out to all his earls and lords. They, in turn, supplied men in proportion to their quota[4] (which depended on how much land they'd received in the first place). Clear so far?

The earl then called on the knights to whom he had given land (fiefs) and told them how many men he needed. If there were enough soldiers available, many of these knights opted to pay scutage (tax that allowed them to buy their way out of fighting). With this kind of income, the king could buy the better services of professional soldiers! This was the beginning of armies as we know them today. (Earls, by the way, couldn't buy their way out of their own duty to fight—unless deemed too old, too young, too feeble, or too crazy.) If the battle or siege[5] went on for more than the free initial forty days, the king paid the knights and soldiers wages. Earls, naturally, were expected to do it for nothing.

The armies often found themselves in interesting situations. In the wars of 1294 between the English king Edward I and the Welsh rebels, the earl of Lancaster, who lorded over 263 knightly fiefs, turned up to fight for the king with only fifty men. The earl of Norfolk, who also had 263 fiefs, pitched in with only twenty-eight men, and

Activate Prior Knowledge
Why do you think some knights paid taxes to avoid fighting?

BQ BIG Question
Why do you think Farman includes this information?

---

3 A *luxurious* prison would be very comfortable, with fine furnishings.

4 A *quota* is a part or a share.

5 *Siege* is another word for *attack*.

the greatest baron of Devon, Hugh Courtney, with 92 fiefs, only managed twelve men—and so on. This wasn't a problem. The king received a lot of scutage money from those who preferred to pay up rather than go to war. The king could then distribute all the extra cash to the knights who'd showed up with their fair share of soldiers.

In the case of these Welsh wars, the campaign[6] continued well over the forty days, meaning that the king ran out of the old scutage money fairly quickly. This is where being able to jack up the taxation of the whole population becomes so convenient. Anyway, it all worked out just fine in the end (if you weren't Welsh). 🌿

---

6 Here, a *campaign* refers to a military operation.

Three Knights Leaving a Tournament, French School, 14th century. Vellum. Musée Condé, Chantilly, France. Ms 137/1687 f.144r

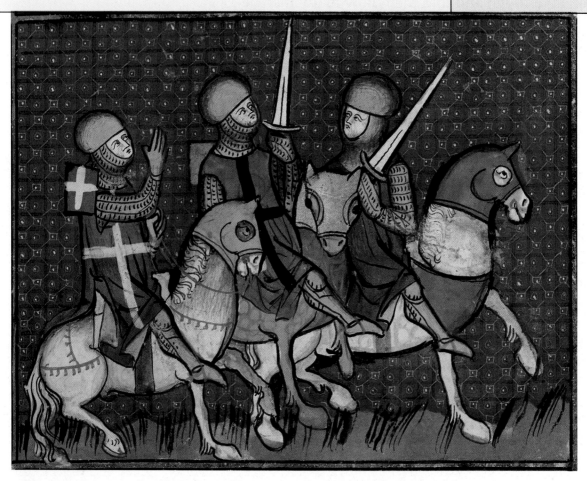

After You Read

Respond and Think Critically

1. How were young men chosen to train for knighthood? [Recall]

2. Use your own words to explain a knight's training. [Summarize]

3. Why do you think Farman provides the example of the Black Prince? [Analyze]

4. What comparison does Farman make between feudal armies and armies of today? [Compare]

5. Complete the chart that you began in the Before You Read section. Explain how well your prior knowledge helped you understand "What Is a Knight?" [Evaluate]

6. **BQ** BIG Question Which sections of "What Is a Knight?" did you find most interesting? Explain. [Evaluate]

Daily Life and Culture

Life in the Feudal Manor

In medieval Europe, most people lived on manors owned by lords or nobles. A manor included the lord's home, a chapel, a village, and surrounding farmland. Serfs, or peasants, were legally bound to the land, and they could not leave the manor. They provided labor, paid rents and taxes, and were subject to the lord's control.

A serf's labor included working the lord's land. The lord's land made up one-third to one-half of the cultivated land scattered throughout the manor. Serfs used the rest of the estate's land to grow food for themselves. Such tasks as building barns and digging ditches were part of labor.

Serfs usually worked about three days a week for their lords.

The serfs paid rent by giving the lords a share of every product they made or grew. Serfs also paid the lords for the use of the manor's common pasturelands, streams, ponds, and surrounding woodlands. It was the lord's duty to protect his serfs, giving them the safety they needed to grow crops.

Group Activity Discuss the following questions with a small group.

1. What contributions did serfs make to life on the feudal manor? Provide examples.

2. How did serfs benefit from living under a lord's control? Explain.

Literary Element | Author's Purpose

Standards Practice | ELA7RC2e

1. What is the author's main purpose for including the section "How to Build a Feudal Army"?
   A to entertain with exciting war stories
   B to inform about a knight's military role
   C to tell a story about a knight and an earl
   D to persuade readers that knights were strong and brave

Review: Description

As you learned on page 113, **description** is writing that creates an impression of a person, animal, object, event, or setting. Good descriptions help readers visualize what the author is describing.

2. Think about John Farman's question, "How easy was it to move, let alone fight, covered from head to foot in metal?" Explain how this description makes knights seem real to you.

3. To what senses does the following description appeal? "Another knight gave you a whack on the shoulder with the flat (hopefully) part of his sword and presto, you became a full-fledged knight."

Reading Strategy
Activate Prior Knowledge

4. Reread the opening paragraph of the article, in which the author relates his prior knowledge about knights. Which details are also part of your prior knowledge? What would you have added to the description?

5. Look again at the rules of chivalry. Which ones did you know before reading the selection? Which ones provided new information?

Vocabulary Practice

On a separate sheet of paper, write the vocabulary word that correctly completes each sentence. If none of the words fits the sentence, write "none."

excess   chivalry   suppresses

1. When Miko _____ her emotions, her cheeks turn red.

2. I thought _____ was an old tradition before I saw that gentleman's respectful behavior.

3. It is not necessary to _____ the students' grades.

4. Nina used the _____ fabric to make a small pillow.

5. We made several _____ decisions during the student council meeting.

Academic Vocabulary

The feudal system **benefited** barons, earls, and knights. To become more familiar with the word *benefited*, fill out the graphic organizer below.

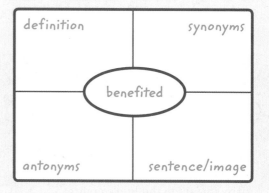

definition	synonyms
benefited	
antonyms	sentence/image

Respond Through Writing

For page 219

ELA7W2d Demonstrate competence in a variety of genres. Produce writing that develops the topic with supporting details.

Summary

Report Main Ideas and Events In "What Is a Knight?" Farman describes how young men became knights, the rules by which they lived, and their role in the feudal system. Write a summary of the article, reporting on its main ideas and important details.

Understand the Task When you **summarize** a selection, you use your own words to explain the **main idea** and most **important details.**

Prewrite Farman uses subheads to organize the article. These subheads can help you get started on your summary. Draw a six-column chart. Label each column with a subhead from the article. Then use your own words to list the most important ideas and details that appear under each subhead.

Career Knights	How to Be a Knight	Knight Time	Knights' Rules	For Instance	How to Build a Feudal Army

Draft Before you begin drafting, make an organizational plan. Remember that your paragraphs should include only the most important ideas and details. Then use a word processing program to create your draft. Include transition words and phrases such as *first of all, for example,* and *finally* to show connections among ideas.

Revise After you have written your first draft, read it to determine whether you have included only the main ideas and most important details. Make sure that you have not changed Farman's ideas or included your own opinions. If you have quoted directly from the article, make sure that you have used quotation marks. Rearrange, combine, or delete sentences as needed.

Edit and Proofread Proofread your paper, correcting any errors in spelling, grammar, and punctuation. Review the Grammar Tip in the side column for information on commas in a series.

> ## Grammar Tip

Commas in a Series
Use commas to separate items in a series.

Isaac brought the plates, cups, and silverware.

When listing three or more items, place a comma after each item except the last one. Notice that there is a comma before *and.* That comma is called a serial comma. Remember to use a serial comma whenever you are listing three or more items.

Performance Standards

For pages 220–221

ELA7R1c For informational texts, apply knowledge of common organizational structures and patterns.

Genre Focus:
Informational Text

Informational text is nonfiction writing that presents facts and information. It can tell you the latest news, how to make or do something, facts you need for schoolwork, or true stories about real people and places.

Newspaper and magazine articles, signs, schedules, how-to books, instruction manuals, and books on science and technology are some examples of informational text.

Text Elements

Text structure refers to the pattern writers use to organize their work. Understanding the text structure of a selection will help you locate and recall an author's ideas as well as understand the author's purpose. Some of the most common text structures involve **sequence,** the order in which thoughts are arranged.

Chronological order is a common form of sequencing. It shows the order in which events take place. History books, for example, usually present events in chronological order.

Spatial order tells you the order in which to look at objects. Spatial order is important in descriptive writing because it helps readers see an image the way an author does.

Order of importance refers to going from most to least important or the other way around. **Signal words** such as *principal, central,* and *important* point to the article's most significant ideas and information.

Cause-and-effect text structures show the relationship between outcomes (effects) and their causes. Cause-and-effect structures are used often in articles and books about science and history.

Compare-and-contrast text structures look at how two or more things are similar and how they are different.

Problem-and-solution text structures provide a way for writers to present a problem and offer a solution to it. Science books and articles often use this structure.

Text features can also help you find information quickly and efficiently. Recognizing and thinking about the following text features will help you understand informational text.

Graphics are images that help you understand information. They include photos, charts, graphs, and illustrations.

Titles, subheads, and boldfaced terms appear in larger or dark type to introduce text or grab a reader's attention.

Footnotes appear below the text and explain or reference something in it.

TRY IT

Using a diagram like either of those on the next page, identify the text elements of a work of informational text in this unit.

To better understand text elements in informational text and how writers use them to achieve their purposes, look at the examples in the diagrams below.

A cause-and-effect diagram can help you understand the series of events that take place in "The Story of an Eyewitness" and in other selections with a cause-and-effect text structure.

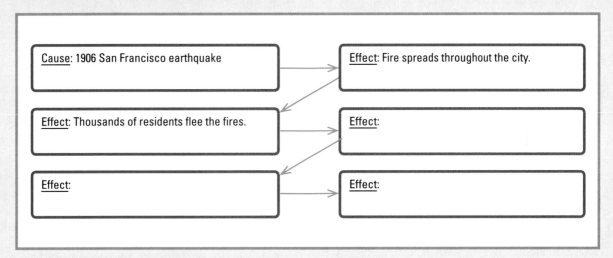

Cause: 1906 San Francisco earthquake → Effect: Fire spreads throughout the city.

Effect: Thousands of residents flee the fires. → Effect:

Effect: → Effect:

A Venn diagram can help you compare and contrast text elements between two selections, such as "One's Name Is Mud" and "Tending Sir Ernest's Legacy."

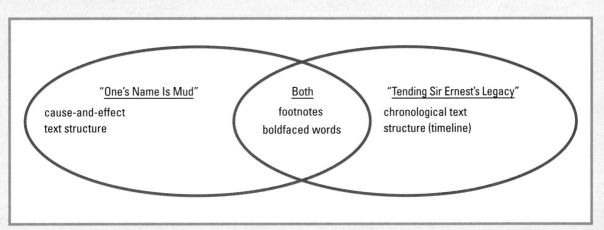

"One's Name Is Mud"
cause-and-effect
text structure

Both
footnotes
boldfaced words

"Tending Sir Ernest's Legacy"
chronological text
structure (timeline)

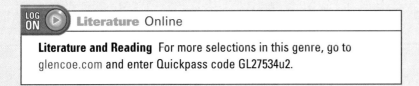

from *When Plague Strikes*

Connect to Nonfiction

What do you know about the living conditions of people in the Middle Ages? How did the living conditions affect people's health?

List Make a list of all the things you know about medicine from the Middle Ages. How did doctors treat ill people?

Build Background

In 1347, the bubonic plague, also known as the Black Death, spread through Europe. Its victims, whose skin blackened from internal bleeding, died within five days.

- The Black Death of the fourteenth century was not the only outbreak of the bubonic plague. Another outbreak occurred in A.D. 542, more than seven hundred years before the Black Death.

- Today, doctors know many ways to prevent the spread of germs. However, people of the fourteenth century did not understand where illnesses came from or how they spread.

Vocabulary

tolerate (tol′ə rāt′) *v.* to endure; put up with (p. 227). *My parents tolerate my room being slightly messy.*

devastated (dev′əs tā′tid) *v.* caused great pain, damage, or destruction; overwhelmed (p. 229). *The flood swept away the homes and devastated the entire town.*

discredited (dis kred′it′id) *v.* refused to accept as true or accurate; caused to be doubted or disbelieved (p. 234). *The medical team discredited the scientist's work after the scientist admitted he lied on his reports.*

implies (im plīz′) *v.* suggests without directly stating (p. 235). *Nora's silence implies she does not know the answer to the question.*

vulnerable (vul′nər ə bəl) *adj.* capable of being damaged or wounded; easily hurt (p. 236). *The baby bird was vulnerable to predators when it fell from the nest.*

Meet James Cross Giblin

"I try to write books that I would have enjoyed reading when I was the age of my readers."
—James Cross Giblin

Author of Nonfiction James Cross Giblin has written award-winning nonfiction books on subjects ranging from hieroglyphics to skyscrapers. He explains, "Nonfiction books . . . [give] me the opportunity to pursue my research interests, meet interesting and stimulating experts in various fields, and share my enthusiasm with a young audience." Giblin has been a writer all his life.

Literary Works Giblin is the author of more than 20 books for young people. *When Plague Strikes* was published in 1995.

James Cross Giblin was born in 1933.

LOG ON **Literature** Online

Author Search For more about James Cross Giblin, go to glencoe.com and enter QuickPass code GL27534u2.

Set Purposes for Reading

BQ BIG Question

As you read, ask yourself, what information about the plague interests you the most? Where could you research to learn more?

Literary Element Text Structure

Nonfiction authors use **text structure** to organize their ideas in a variety of ways, depending on their topic and purpose for writing. For example, an author may use **chronological order** to present events in time order. An author may also use **problem/solution** structure to examine how conflicts or problems are solved. **Cause-and-effect** structure explores the reasons for something and the results of events or actions. **Comparison-and-contrast** structure analyzes similarities and differences.

Identifying text structure helps you better locate an author's main ideas and understand his or her purpose for writing. Look for signal words and phrases to identify the structure of nonfiction writing.

As you read, ask yourself, how does the author organize ideas? How does the text structure reveal the purpose of the selection?

Reading Strategy Question

When you **question,** you ask yourself questions to make sure that you understand what you are reading. Questioning can improve your comprehension and help you focus on the most important information.

Sometimes it's difficult to remember or understand all the information the first time you read a sentence or a paragraph. There may be times when you need to ask yourself questions and reread to find the answers.

As you read, stop after every paragraph or two. Monitor your comprehension by asking yourself the following questions:

• What is the importance of the information?

• How is one event related to another event?

• Do I understand what I just read?

Keep track of your questions in a graphic organizer like the one below.

Passage from Text	Questions
	1.
	2.

Performance Standards

For pages 222–239

ELA7R1c For informational texts, apply knowledge of common organizational structures and patterns.

TRY IT

Question Imagine that you are listening to your science teacher describe a new animal just discovered in the rain forest. Although you find the animal fascinating, you don't understand all the terms your teacher uses to describe the animal. With a partner, discuss what questions you might ask your teacher to make sure you understand the teacher's description.

This engraving was meant to remind people that it was hopeless to try to escape death.

from When
PLAGUE
Strikes

James Cross Giblin

OUT OF THE EAST

Early in 1347, a mysterious disease attacked people living near the Black Sea in what is now southern Ukraine. Its victims suffered from headaches, felt weak and tired, and staggered when they tried to walk.

By the third day, the lymph nodes[1] in the sufferers' groins, or occasionally their armpits, began to swell. Soon they reached the size of hens' eggs. These swellings became known as buboes, from the Greek word for groin, *boubon*. They gave the disease its official name: the bubonic[2] plague.

The victim's heart beat wildly as it tried to pump blood through the swollen tissues. The nervous system started to collapse, causing dreadful pain and bizarre[3] movements of the arms and legs. Then, as death neared, the mouth gaped open and the skin blackened from internal bleeding. The end usually came on the fifth day.

Within weeks of the first reported cases, hundreds of people in the Black Sea region had sickened and died. Those who survived were terrified. They had no medicines with which to fight the disease. As it continued to spread, their fear changed to frustration, and then to anger. Someone—some outsider—must be responsible for bringing this calamity upon them.

The most likely candidates were the Italian traders who operated in the region. They bartered Italian goods for the silks and spices that came over the caravan routes from the Far East, then shipped the Eastern merchandise on to Italy. Although many of the traders had lived in the region for years, they were still thought of as being different. For one thing, they were Christians while most of the natives were Muslims.[4]

Deciding the Italians were to blame for the epidemic, the natives gathered an army and prepared to attack their trading post. The Italians fled to a fortress they had built

Text Structure How has the author organized the ideas in the first three paragraphs?

Question Why did people blame the Italian traders for the epidemic?

---

1 The *lymph nodes* are glands that filter out harmful substances.

2 *Buboes* (bū′bōz), *bubonic* (bū bon′ik)

3 *Bizarre* means "extremely strange."

4 *To barter* is to trade goods without using money. Traders traveled in groups, or *caravans*, along familiar roads for safety in deserts and dangerous regions. *Muslims* are people who follow Islam, the religion based on the teachings of Muhammad.

on the coast of the Black Sea. There the natives besieged[5] them until the dread disease broke out in the Muslim army.

The natives were forced to withdraw. But before they did—according to one account—they gave the Italians a taste of the agony their people had been suffering. They loaded **catapults** with the bodies of some of their dead soldiers and hurled them over the high walls into the fortress. By doing so, they hoped to infect the Italians with the plague.

As fast as the bodies landed, the Italians dumped them into the sea. However, they did not move quickly enough, for the disease had already taken hold among them. In a panic, the traders loaded three ships and set sail for their home port of Genoa in Italy. They made it only as far as Messina,[6] on the island of Sicily, before the rapid spread of the disease forced them to stop.

This account of what happened in southern Ukraine may or may not be true. But it is a fact that the bubonic plague—the Black Death—arrived in Sicily in October 1347, carried by the crew of a fleet from the east. All the sailors on the ships were dead or dying. In the words of a contemporary[7] historian, they had "sickness clinging to their very bones."

The harbormasters at the port of Messina ordered the sick sailors to remain on board, hoping in this way to prevent the disease from spreading to the town. They had no way of knowing that the actual carriers of the disease had already left the ships. Under cover of night, when no one could see them, they had scurried down the ropes that tied the ships to the dock and vanished into Messina.

The carriers were black rats and the fleas that lived in their hair. Driven by an unending search for food, the rats' ancestors had migrated slowly westward along the caravan routes. They had traveled in bolts of cloth and bales of hay, and the fleas had come with them.

Visual Vocabulary

Catapults (kat´ə pultz´) are war machines that were used like giant slingshots to hurl objects, such as large rocks.

Question What do you want to learn about the Black Death? What questions might guide you to find the answers?

---

5 The natives **besieged** the Italians by surrounding their fortress with armed forces.

6 **Genoa** (jen´ō ə), **Messina** (mə sē´nə)

7 **Contemporary** means "living or happening in the same period."

Although it was only an eighth of an inch long, the rat flea was a tough, adaptable[8] creature. It depended for nourishment on the blood of its host, which it obtained through a daggerlike snout that could pierce the rat's skin. And in its stomach the flea often carried thousands of the deadly bacteria that caused the bubonic plague.

The bacteria did no apparent harm to the flea, and a black rat could **tolerate** a moderate amount of them, too, without showing ill effects. But sometimes the flea contained so many bacteria that they invaded the rat's lungs or nervous system when the flea injected its snout. Then the rat died a swift and horrible death, and the flea had to find a new host.

Aiding the tiny flea in its search were its powerful legs, which could jump more than 150 times the creature's length. In most instances the flea landed on another black rat. Not always, though. If most of the rats in the vicinity were already dead or dying from the plague, the flea might leap to a human being instead. As soon as it had settled on the human's skin, the flea would begin to feed, and the whole process of infection would be repeated.

No doubt it was fleas, not Italian traders, that brought the bubonic plague to the Black Sea region, and other fleas that carried the disease on to Sicily. But no one at the time made the connection. To the people of the fourteenth century, the cause of the Black Death—which they called "the pestilence"[9]—was a complete and utter mystery.

When the first cases of the plague were reported in Messina, the authorities ordered the Italian fleet and all its sick crew members to leave the port at once. Their action came too late, however. Within days the disease had spread throughout the city and the surrounding countryside.

Text Structure How does the author organize the ideas that describe the process of infection?

---

8 **Adaptable** (ə dap′tə bəl) means "able to change to meet the needs of a certain situation."

9 **Pestilence** comes from a Latin word meaning "unhealthy" and refers to any highly infectious, widespread disease.

Vocabulary
. . . .

tolerate (tol′ə rāt′) v. to endure; put up with

Some of the plague's victims fled to the nearby town of Catania, where they were treated kindly at first. But when the citizens of Catania realized how deadly the disease was, they refused to have anything more to do with anyone from Messina or even to speak to them. As was to happen wherever the plague struck, fear for one's own life usually outweighed any concern a person might have felt for the life of another.

Question What caused the people of Catania to act as they did?

ON TO ITALY

From Sicily, trading ships loaded with infected flea-bearing rats carried the Black Death to ports on the mainland of Italy. Peddlers and other travelers helped spread it to inland cities such as Milan[10] and Florence.

Conditions in these medieval cities provided a splendid breeding ground for all types of vermin, including rats. There were no regular garbage collections, and refuse accumulated in piles in the streets. Rushes[11] from wet or marshy places, not rugs, covered the floors in most homes. After a meal, it was customary to throw bits of leftover food onto the rushes for the dog or cat to eat. Rats and mice often got their share, too.

Because the cities had no running water, even the wealthy seldom washed their heavy clothing, or their own bodies. As a result, both rich and poor were prime targets for lice and fleas and the diseases they carried—the most deadly being the bubonic plague.

Several Italian commentators noted an unusual number of dead rats in cities struck by the plague. It seems odd that no one linked this phenomenon[12] to the disease. Perhaps people were so used to being surrounded by vermin, dead and alive, that a few more didn't arouse that much concern. At any rate, the Italians sought other explanations for the terrible pestilence.

BQ **BIG Question**

Why did the author include this information about medieval cities?

---

10 *Milan* (mi lan′)

11 *Medieval* (mē′ dē ē′ vəl) refers to the Middle Ages, roughly A.D. 500–1450. *Vermin* are any insects or animals that are troublesome or harmful. *Refuse* (ref′ ūs) is another word for *garbage*. *Rushes* are reedy, grasslike plants.

12 Anything that is extremely unusual is a *phenomenon* (fə nom′ ə non′).

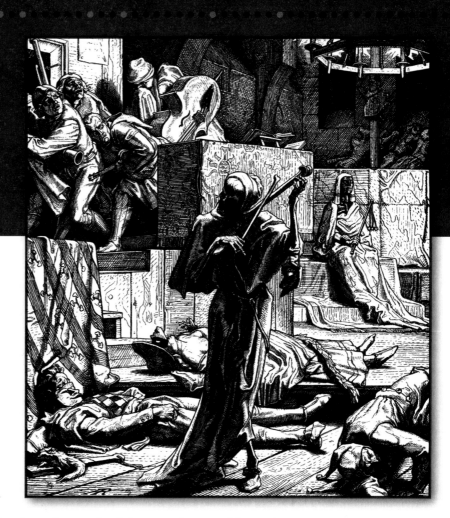

Grim Reaper, 1851. Wood engraving after Alfred Rethel.

View the Art How does this image illustrate people's beliefs about the plague?

Some scholars thought the plague had been triggered by a series of earthquakes that had **devastated** large areas of Europe and Asia between 1345 and 1347. They said the quakes had released poisonous fumes from the Earth's core, and some believed the Devil was behind it all.

Others claimed that climatic changes had brought warmer, damper weather and strong southerly winds that carried the disease north. They tried to predict its course by studying the colors of the sky at twilight and the shapes of cloud formations. Meanwhile, the death toll in both city and countryside continued to mount.

At Venice, one of Italy's major ports, the city's leaders decreed[13] that no one could leave an incoming ship for

---

13 To *decree* is to set forth an official rule, order, or decision.

Vocabulary

devastated (dev′ əs tā′ tid) *v.* caused great pain, damage, or destruction; overwhelmed

quaranta giorni—forty days—the length of time Christ was said to have suffered in the wilderness. From this decree comes the word *quarantine*,[14] which means any isolation or restriction on travel intended to keep a contagious disease from spreading. But the quarantine in Venice proved no more effective than the one imposed earlier at Messina. When the Black Death struck in December 1347, Venice had a population of about 130,000. Eighteen months later, only about 70,000 Venetians were still alive.

Other Italian cities tried harsher measures to halt the spread of the disease. As soon as the first cases were reported in Milan, the authorities sent the city militia[15] to wall up the houses where the victims lived. All those inside, whether sick or well, were cut off from their friends and neighbors and left to die.

The most complete account of the Black Death in Italy was given by the writer Giovanni Boccaccio,[16] who lived in the city of Florence. In the preface to his classic book *The Decameron,* Boccaccio wrote: "Some say that the plague descended upon the human race through the influence of the heavenly bodies, others that it was a punishment signifying God's righteous anger at our wicked way of life."

After describing the disease's symptoms, Boccaccio went on to say: "Against these maladies, it seemed that all the advice of physicians and all the power of medicine were profitless and futile.[17] Perhaps the nature of the illness was such that it allowed no remedy; or perhaps those people who were treating the illness, being ignorant of its causes, were not prescribing the appropriate cure."

One of the most alarming things about the bubonic plague was the way it struck. "It would rush upon its victims with the speed of a fire racing through dry or oily substances that happened to be placed within its reach," Boccaccio wrote. "Not only did it infect healthy persons

Text Structure What text structure does the author use to describe the attempts to stop the spread of the disease?

---

14 *Quarantine* (kwôr′ ən tēn′)

15 A military force made up of civilians who serve as soldiers during a time of emergency is called a *militia* (mi lish′ ə).

16 *Giovanni Boccaccio* (jō vä′ nē bō kä′ chē ō′)

17 *Futile* means "useless or not effective."

who conversed or had any dealings with the sick . . . but it also seemed to transfer the sickness to anyone touching the clothes or the other objects which had been handled or used by the victims."

Boccaccio reported seeing two pigs in the street, rooting through the ragged clothes of a poor man who had died of the plague. Within a short time, the pigs began to writhe and squirm as though they had been poisoned. Then they both dropped dead, falling on the same rags they had been pulling and tugging a few minutes earlier.

How did the people of Florence react to this mysterious and fatal disease? Some isolated themselves in their homes, according to Boccaccio. They ate lightly, saw no outsiders, and refused to receive reports of the dead or sick. Others adopted an attitude of "play today for we die tomorrow." They drank heavily, stayed out late, and roamed through the streets singing and dancing as if the Black Death were an enormous joke. Still others, if they were rich enough, abandoned their homes in the city and fled to villas[18] in the countryside. They hoped in this way to escape the disease—but often it followed them.

Whatever steps they took, the same percentage of people in each group seemed to fall ill. So many died that the bodies piled up in the streets. A new occupation came into being: that of loading the bodies on carts and carrying them away for burial in mass graves. "No more respect was accorded to dead people," Boccaccio wrote, "than would be shown toward dead goats."

The town of Siena, thirty miles south of Florence, suffered severe losses also. A man named Agnolo di Tura[19] offered a vivid account of what happened there:

"The mortality[20] in Siena began in May. It was a horrible thing, and I do not know where to begin to tell of the cruelty. . . . Members of a household brought their dead to a ditch as best they could, without a priest, without any divine services. Nor did the death bell sound. . . . And as

Text Structure What clues in this paragraph help you recognize the problem/solution structure?

---

18 A **villa** is a house, especially one in the country or at the seashore.

19 **Siena** (sē enʹə), **Agnolo di Tura** (ä nyōʹlō di tōōʹrə)

20 Here, **mortality** means simply "deaths" or "the dying."

A doctor of the 1700s wears a mask during an outbreak of plague in Venice. The beak of the mask probably contained fragrant herbs.

View the Art What kind of protection does the doctor think is provided by this type of mask?

soon as those ditches were filled, more were dug. I, Agnolo di Tura, buried my five children with my own hands. . . . And no bells tolled, and nobody wept no matter what his loss because almost everyone expected death. . . . And people said and believed, 'This is the end of the world.'"

Question Why do you think people thought it was the end of the world?

By the winter of 1348–49, a little more than a year after its first appearance in Sicily, the worst of the Black Death was over in Italy. No one knows exactly how many Italians died of the disease, because accurate medical records were not kept. Conservative[21] estimates put the loss at about a third of the population, but many scholars believe the death rate reached forty or fifty percent, especially in the cities.

In any case, it was the greatest loss of human life Italy had suffered in a comparable period of time—and a loss not equaled to the present day.

Meanwhile, the Black Death had swept on to France, entering that country via Marseilles and other southern ports. Before long it traveled inland and reached the city of Avignon,[22] where the Pope was then living.

Text Structure What type of organization does the author use to describe the plague's movement?

---

21 These estimates are cautious, or ***conservative,*** meaning that the numbers are likely to be too low rather than too high.

22 ***Marseilles*** (mär sā′), ***Avignon*** (ä vē nyōN′)

BETWEEN TWO RAGING FIRES

When the Black Death arrived in Avignon in the spring of 1348, this old walled city in southern France had been the home of the Pope and his College of Cardinals[23] for almost forty years. They had come there in 1309 to escape political unrest in Rome and had built a magnificent palace on the city's main square.

Pilgrims, priests, and diplomats crowded into Avignon from all over Europe to pay their respects to the Pope. Without meaning to, some of these visitors must have brought the pestilence with them. Between February and May, up to 400 people a day died of the plague in Avignon. When the graveyards were filled, the bodies of the dead had to be dumped into the Rhône River, which flowed through the heart of the city.

Many courageous priests ministered to the sick and dying even though they knew that they would probably become infected and die themselves. Meanwhile, Pope Clement VI decided it was his duty, as leader of the Roman Catholic Church on the Earth, to remain alive if at all possible. On the advice of his physician, he withdrew to his private rooms, saw nobody, and spent day and night between two fires that blazed on grates at opposite ends of his bedchamber.

What purpose were the fires supposed to serve? It was tied in with the theory of humors, which still dominated medical thought in the fourteenth century. This theory goes back to the Greek physician Hippocrates,[24] who lived from about 484 to 425 B.C. and is often called the "father of medicine."

Hippocrates examined sick persons carefully and honestly recorded the signs and symptoms of various diseases. But his knowledge of how the human body worked was extremely limited. He believed the body contained four basic liquids, which he called humors: blood, which came from the heart; phlegm, from the brain;

Question How might the visitors have brought the "pestilence" with them?

---

23 **College of Cardinals** is the group of high-ranking priests who act as advisers to the Pope. Here, *college* means "people who have the same purpose," not a school of higher learning.

24 **Hippocrates** (hi pok′ rə tēz)

yellow bile, from the liver; and black bile, from the spleen.[25]

If these humors were in balance, Hippocrates wrote, a person would enjoy good health. But if one of them became more important than the others, the person was likely to feel pain and fall victim to a disease. A physician's main job, therefore, was to try to restore and maintain a proper balance among the four humors.

Question What is the importance of this information about medical thought?

BLOOD AND BILE

Another Greek physician, Galen (A.D. 130–200), took the ideas of Hippocrates a step further. Galen stated that the four humors in the human body reflected the four elements that people believed were the basis of all life: earth, air, fire, and water. Blood was hot and moist, like the air in summer. Phlegm was cold and moist, like water. Yellow bile was hot and dry, like fire, and black bile was cold and dry, like earth. In other words, according to Galen, the human body was a smaller, contained version of the wider natural world.

Galen recommended certain treatments to keep the humors in balance. For example, if a patient was too hot, various foods were prescribed to make him or her cooler. If this treatment failed, the physician might perform bloodletting to reduce the amount of hot blood in the patient's system.

Text Structure How does the author organize the ideas in this paragraph?

Most of Galen's theories have been **discredited** in modern times, but for over a thousand years, until the sixteenth century, no physician thought of questioning them.

Most medieval physicians were actually scholar-priests. They spent their time analyzing the writings of Galen and Hippocrates and left the treatment of patients to surgeons and barber-surgeons.

Surgeons usually had some medical training in a university. They were regarded as skilled craftsmen,

---

25 Today, we know that **phlegm,** or mucus, is formed in the nose or throat, not the brain. **Bile** does not come from the liver, and the body uses it to aid digestion. The **spleen** filters blood and produces white blood cells. The **heart,** of course, pumps blood but does not produce it.

Vocabulary ....

discredited (dis kred′it′id) v. refused to accept as true or accurate; caused to be doubted or disbelieved

able to close wounds, set broken bones, and perform simple operations.

Most barber-surgeons were illiterate men whose only training came from serving as apprentices[26] to surgeons. As their name **implies,** they cut hair as well as setting simple fractures and bandaging wounds. Some say the traditional red-and-white-striped barber's pole comes from the time when barber-surgeons hung their bloody surgical rags in front of their shops to dry.

Two other groups of people played important roles in medieval medicine. Apothecaries[27] filled prescriptions and also prescribed herbs and drugs on their own. Nonprofessionals, many of them older women, provided medical care in rural areas where no surgeons or barber-surgeons were available. These nonprofessionals had no formal training and relied heavily on folk remedies that had been handed down from generation to generation in the countryside.

STRANGE TREATMENTS

This, then, was the medical scene when the Black Death raged through western Europe in the mid-fourteenth century. It helps to explain why physicians and surgeons were at such a loss to know what caused the epidemic, let alone how to treat it. It also answers the question of why the Pope's physician had him sit alone in his bedchamber between two raging fires.

Galen had written that diseases were transmitted[28] from person to person by miasmas,[29] poisonous vapors that arose from swamps and corrupted the air. The Pope's physician, who believed in Galen's theories, thought that

Question Who were the main caregivers in the "medical scene" at the time?

---

26 Someone who is *illiterate* is unable to read or write. *Apprentices* are beginners who learn their skills from experienced professionals.

27 *Apothecaries* (ə poth′ə ker′ēz) are druggists or pharmacists.

28 To *transmit* a thing is to send it, or cause it to pass, from one person or place to another.

29 *Miasma* (mī az′mə)

Vocabulary
....

implies (im plīz′) *v.* suggests without directly stating

hot air from the fires would combat any dangerous miasmas that got into the Pope's chamber and render[30] them harmless. (The Pope did survive, but it's doubtful whether the fires had anything to do with it except to make his chamber uncomfortable for rats and fleas.)

Other physicians and surgeons interpreted Galen's theories differently. Instead of fighting fire with fire, so to speak, they recommended fleeing from it. People were urged to leave warm, low, marshy places that were likely to produce miasmas and move to drier, cooler regions in the hills. If that was not possible, they were advised to stay indoors during the heat of the day, cover over any brightly lighted windows, and try to stay cool.

Hands and feet were to be washed regularly, but physicians warned against bathing the body because it opened the pores. This, they thought, made the body more **vulnerable** to attack by disease-bearing miasmas. Exercise was to be avoided for the same reason.

Sleep after eating and in the middle of the day was bad because the body was warmer then. And physicians cautioned their patients not to sleep on their backs at any time, because that made it easier for foul air to flow down their nostrils and get into their lungs.

To ward off[31] miasmas when one walked outside, physicians recommended carrying bouquets of sweet-smelling herbs and flowers and holding them up to the nose. Some say this practice was one of the inspirations for the old English nursery rhyme "Ring-a-ring o' roses." In the first published version it read as follows:

> Ring-a-ring o' roses,
>   A pocket full of posies,
> A-tishoo! A-tishoo!
>   We all fall down.

Question What advice did physicians and surgeons give to people?

---

30 To **render** a thing is to make or cause it to become.

31 The expression **ward off** means "to turn back; keep away."

Vocabulary ....

vulnerable (vul′nər ə bəl) *adj.* capable of being damaged or wounded; easily hurt

236   UNIT 2 Why Do You Read?

Those who link the rhyme to the plague think the ring o' roses was the rash that often signaled infection. The pocket full of posies referred to the flowers people carried to sweeten the air around them. A-tishoo! was the sound of sneezing, a common symptom of the disease, and "We all fall down" implied that all of its victims died.

Some prescribed treatments for the plague seem sensible or at least harmless: bed rest, drinking lots of liquids, and the application of salves made of herbs to the affected areas of the body. But other treatments hurt plague sufferers instead of helping them.

Surgeons who had studied Galen's theories believed that the Black Death interrupted the flow of the body's humors. Since the heart produced the most important of these liquids, blood, doctors thought one effective way to fight the plague and improve circulation was to bleed veins close to the heart.

The surgeons also thought that buboes, the swellings that characterized the disease, revealed where the body was being attacked, and they geared their treatment accordingly. If a buboe appeared in the region of the groin, for example, the surgeon drained blood from a vein leading to one of the organs in that area. By doing so, the surgeon meant to cool the body and help it fight the disease, but in fact bleeding only weakened the body's defenses.

ST. ROCH [32]

In the face of treatments like these, it's no wonder that people lost faith in their physicians and came to rely more and more on prayer. Many directed their prayers to St. Roch, who had died in 1327 and was the particular saint associated with the plague.

According to the legends told about him in France and Italy, Roch inherited great wealth as a young man. Like St. Francis, he gave it away to the poor and then went on a religious pilgrimage[33] to Italy. He was in Rome when an epidemic struck, but instead of fleeing, Roch stayed on to

BQ **BIG Question**

Why does the author provide information about the origin of the nursery rhyme?

---

32 **Roch** (rôk)

33 A **pilgrimage** is a long journey, especially to a holy place for a religious purpose.

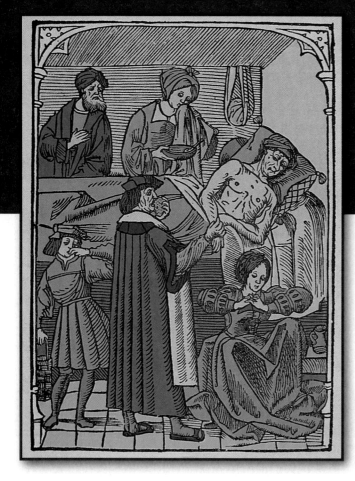

A doctor holding a vinegar-soaked sponge to his face treats a plague victim.

View the Art Why do you think the doctor holds the sponge to his face?

nurse the sick. Eventually, he caught the disease himself.

Roch left the city and went to the countryside, where he expected to die alone in the woods. But a dog carrying a loaf of bread in its mouth miraculously found him. Each day the dog reappeared with a fresh loaf, and Roch gradually recovered.

He got home to France safely, but his relatives failed to recognize him and had Roch arrested as an impostor. He died in jail, filling his cell with a mysterious white light. After Roch's story spread and he was made a saint, it was thought he would come to the aid of plague victims just as the dog had come to his aid in the Roman woods.

Even prayers to St. Roch did not halt the relentless march of the Black Death through France, however. At the peak of the plague, the death rate in Paris was reported to be 800 a day. By the time the epidemic had run its course in 1349, over 50,000 Parisians had died—half the city's population.

Question From the time that the plague arrived in Messina, Sicily, how long did it take to run its course?

After You Read

Respond and Think Critically

1. What were the symptoms of the Black Death? [Recall]

2. How would you have protected yourself from the plague, knowing only what the people of the day knew? Explain. [Connect]

3. In addition to causing death, what made the plague so frightening? Support your answer with details from the selection. [Interpret]

4. **Literary Element** Text Structure What text structures does the author use? How does the author's use of different text structures help to create a rounded picture of the plague? Explain. [Analyze]

5. **Reading Strategy** Question What questions did you ask as you read? How did asking questions affect your reading? [Analyze]

6. **BQ** BIG Question In your own words, explain what you learned about the Black Death, including how it was spread and how people tried to deal with the disease. [Summarize]

Vocabulary Practice

On a separate sheet of paper, write the vocabulary word that correctly completes each sentence. If none of the words fits the sentence, write "none."

tolerate   devastated   discredited   implies   vulnerable

1. I _____ the pain of bee stings by thinking funny thoughts.

2. Enrique raised his hand _____ to ask the teacher a question.

3. Many long-held theories about medicine have been _____ by recent studies.

4. The hurricane _____ the coastal region in just one night.

5. Our tour guide's _____ energy kept us going when we tired.

6. Ann made herself _____ by not wearing a bicycle helmet.

7. The footprint on the rug _____ that someone has been here.

Writing

Write a Journal Entry Imagine that you live in Europe in the fourteenth century. Write a journal entry describing how the plague has affected your town or city. Before you write, reread parts of the excerpt from *When Plague Strikes.* Take notes on the details you find most interesting. Use the notes to write your journal entry and describe your experience using chronological order.

TIP

Connecting
Remember that when you connect, you relate what you read to your own life.

- Reread the description of how people in the fourteenth century responded to the plague.

- Ask yourself questions such as these: *How would I have reacted? Would I have acted any differently?*

FOLDABLES Study Organizer Keep track of your ideas about the **BIG Question** in your unit Foldable.

LOG ON ▶ **Literature** Online

Selection Resources
For Selection Quizzes, eFlashcards, and Reading-Writing Connection activities, go to glencoe.com and enter QuickPass code GL27534u2.

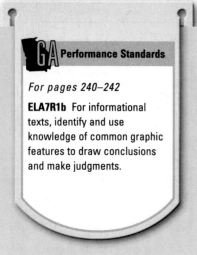
Set a Purpose for Reading

Read "Miracle Hands" to find out how Woosik Chung dealt with a childhood accident.

Preview the Article

1. Read the **title** and **deck**, or subtitle. Why might Woosik Chung's hands be called "miracle hands"?

2. What do the **photos** tell you about Chung's childhood and his life now?

Reading Skill

Identify Sequence

Sequence is the order in which events take place. The article begins when Chung is 28 and then goes back to a time when he was 3 years old. Throughout the article, Chung's age helps you identify the sequence of events.

As you read, create a time line to follow Chung's story.

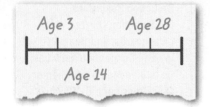

TIME

Miracle HANDS

Woosik Chung's hands were cut off when he was 3. Now he's becoming a surgeon.

By CHRISTINA CHEAKALOS and MATT BIRKBECK

When Woosik Chung was in his first year of medical school, a surgeon handed him a scalpel[1] to make a cut during a knee operation. "It was quite a rush," says Chung, 28. "At that moment, I understood that using my hands as a surgeon was an honor and a privilege."

In Chung's case, that moment was very close to a miracle. When he was 3 years old, both his hands were cut off in an accident. Then, in a risky operation, they were successfully reattached.

Chung's against-all-odds story started in 1978 as he played hide-and-seek with friends in a town in South Korea. Ducking behind a tractor, the curious little boy reached out to touch the moving fan of the tractor's engine. In a split second, the fan blades cut off both his hands at the wrists.

---

1 A **scalpel** is a small, sharp knife used in surgery.

"I hated that I had hurt myself," says Chung (near Seoul, South Korea after the accident).

Chung's horrified father saw the accident from his apartment window. He and his wife filled a bucket with ice and frantically ran to their screaming son. Both of his hands lay on the ground.

The boy's parents carried him to a hospital just blocks away. Since it was a national holiday, there weren't any doctors available who specialized in reattaching limbs. So Chung's father, John, an army surgeon, reattached Woosik's hands himself in a nine-hour operation. "I had never completed a surgery like that," says John. "But I was desperate.[2] I prayed and did my best."

His best, it turns out, was first-rate. It didn't seem that way, however, when the doctors removed Chung's casts two months later. The young boy couldn't move his hands. No one knew if Chung would ever regain the use of them.

2 Chung's father was *desperate,* or so needy as to be willing to try anything.

But a couple of years later, Chung was able to move his hands, eventually regaining full use of them. For that, Chung thanks his grandfather, a tae kwon do grand master who used this martial art as his grandson's physical therapy.[3] Chung says his grandfather taught him the discipline[4] he needed to practice several hours a day.

3 Like karate and judo, *tae kwon do* is a *martial art.* All three are forms of fighting and exercise. *Physical therapy* exercises help a person recover from an illness, an injury, or surgery.

4 *Discipline* means "control of behavior, especially self-control."

"My strength came from my grandfather teaching me tae kwon do," says Chung.

When Chung was 14, his family moved to the United States. After high school, he went to Yale University, where he earned a degree and was also a tae kwon do champ, ranking second in the U.S. He considered trying out for the 2000 Olympics but chose instead to study medicine. "When he told me," says his father, "I was very happy."

When he finishes his five-year program, Chung knows exactly what he wants to be: a hand surgeon. "The best way I can thank my dad," says Chung, "is to help others in similar situations."

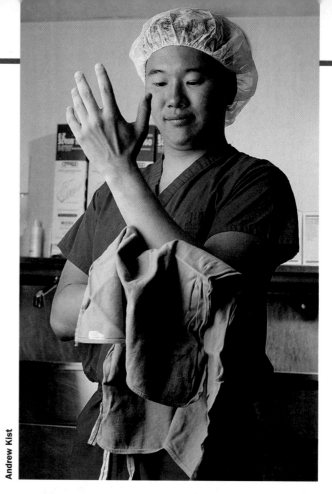

Andrew Kist

View the Photograph In what way does this photo relate to the title of the article?

Respond and Think Critically

1. Summarize the main events of Chung's life. State the main events in your own words and in a logical order. [Summarize]

2. Why do you think Chung chose medical school over the Olympics? [Analyze]

3. In what way was Chung's father as courageous as Chung? Explain. [Compare]

4. **Text-to-Self** What qualities does Chung possess that helped him overcome his injury? How might Chung's story inspire you or other readers? Explain. [Connect]

5. **Reading Skill** **Identify Sequence** How many years after his accident did Chung begin to regain the use of his hands? Review your time line to answer this question.

6. **BQ** **BIG Question** What did you learn from this article? What ideas and information in the article might prove helpful to you?

Before You Read

Functional Documents

Connect to the Functional Documents

Think about a time when you and your family or friends planned an outing.

Partner Talk With a partner, talk about how you and your family or friends prepared for your outing. What kind of information did you need to reach your destination on time?

Build Background

No matter where you live, you need to know your way around your community. That's why it is important to know how to read schedules, Web sites, maps, and other functional documents.

- **Schedules** often list the arrival and departure times of trains, buses, and other forms of transportation. Information in schedules is organized in vertical (up-and-down) columns and horizontal (left-to-right) rows. To find specific information on a schedule, you must look in the correct column and row.

- **Web pages** often contain important information about your community, including schedules and maps. **Maps** are representations of land and structures. Maps often use symbols and colors to represent different locations and structures.

Set a Purpose for Reading

Reading Strategy Skim and Scan

When you **skim** a document, you quickly look over a document to see what it's generally about. To skim effectively, follow these tips:

- Look for text features, such as subheads, captions, bold print, italics, and key words, to get a general idea of the content.

- Look for the pattern of organization, called the text structure. For example, if you find that a train schedule uses chronological order, it will be easier to locate the information you need.

When you **scan** a document, you quickly look over a document to find specific information or details. To scan effectively, follow these tips:

- Have a clear idea of what information you are seeking.

- Look only for key words that will guide you to the information you need.

Performance Standards

For pages 243–246

ELA7R1b For informational texts, identify and use knowledge of common graphic features to draw conclusions and make judgments.

Understand Schedules

Schedules help you locate information quickly. Think about when and why someone might use this schedule.

Train Schedule
#317 Oakwood - Greentown Line
Sunday

♿ Stations		AM	AM	AM	PM	PM	PM	PM
• Oakwood	LV:	7:05	9:05	10:05	2:05	5:05	7:05	10:05
• Rose Park		7:13	9:13	10:13	2:13	5:13	7:13	10:13
• Denfield		7:17	9:17	10:17	2:17	5:17	7:17	10:17
• Glenmoor		7:21	9:21	10:21	2:21	5:21	7:21	10:21
• River Grove		7:24	9:24	10:24	2:24	5:24	7:24	10:24
University Park		7:27	9:27	10:27	2:27	5:27	7:27	10:27
• Norwood		7:31	9:31	10:31	2:31	5:31	7:31	10:31
• Branston		7:35	9:35	10:35	2:35	5:35	7:35	10:35
• Fox Ridge		7:39	9:39	10:39	2:39	5:39	7:39	10:39
Lincoln Heights		7:42	9:42	10:42	2:42	5:42	7:42	10:42
• Lincoln		7:45	9:45	10:45	2:45	5:45	7:45	10:45
• Maple Crest		↓	9:47	10:47	↓	↓	↓	↓
• Evansville		↓	9:50	10:50	↓	↓	↓	↓
• Marion		7:50	9:54	10:54	2:50	5:50	7:50	10:50
Kingston		7:53	9:58	10:58	2:53	5:53	7:53	10:53
• Greentown	AR:	8:09	10:13	11:13	3:09	6:09	8:09	11:09

Oakwood · Rose Park · Denfield · Glenmoor · River Grove · University Park · Norwood · Branston · Fox Ridge · Lincoln Heights · Lincoln · Maple Crest · Evansville · Marion · Kingston · Greentown

Skim and Scan Skim the names of the train stations. Then scan to find out how many times the train stops at the Evansville station.

Understand Maps

You can use maps such as this online seating map to help you make plans for an event. How might the information on the "Seating Map for Basketball" section help you make plans for buying tickets to a basketball game?

Skim and Scan Suppose that you want to buy tickets for the circus. Is it possible to view a seating map for the circus? Scan the text features of the Web page, such as the headings and buttons, to find out.

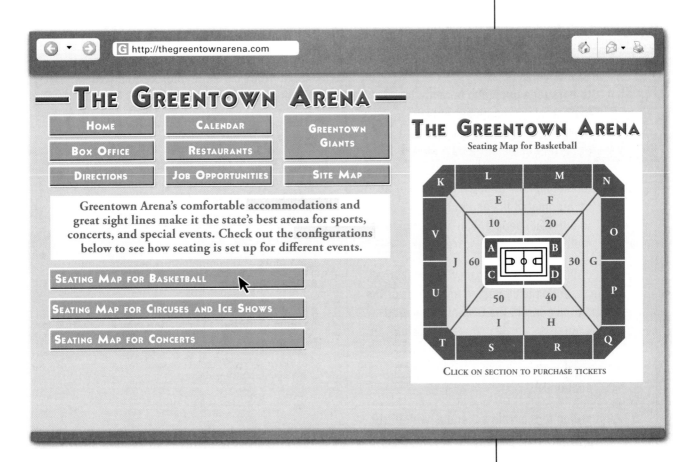

http://thegreentownarena.com

THE GREENTOWN ARENA

HOME	CALENDAR	GREENTOWN GIANTS
BOX OFFICE	RESTAURANTS	
DIRECTIONS	JOB OPPORTUNITIES	SITE MAP

Greentown Arena's comfortable **accommodations** and great sight lines make it the state's best arena for sports, concerts, and special events. Check out the **configurations** below to see how seating is set up for different events.

SEATING MAP FOR BASKETBALL

SEATING MAP FOR CIRCUSES AND ICE SHOWS

SEATING MAP FOR CONCERTS

THE GREENTOWN ARENA
Seating Map for Basketball

CLICK ON SECTION TO PURCHASE TICKETS

Vocabulary

accommodations (ə kom´ə da´shənz) *n.* places to stay or sleep, often where food is served

configurations (kən fig´yə rā´shənz) *n.* the arrangements of parts

Respond and Think Critically

Review the documents on pages 244–245. Then read each question below and select the best answer.

Standards Practice ELA7R1b

1. What is the main purpose of the train schedule?

   A to persuade people to take the train instead of driving an automobile

   B to inform people of the arrival and departure times of trains on the Oakwood-Greentown Line

   C to explain how to buy a train ticket at an automated ticket machine

   D to entertain people who like to solve math problems in their free time

2. According to the seating map for basketball, which section is closest to the center of the basketball court in the Greentown Arena?

   A section S

   B section K

   C section G

   D section B

3. According to the train schedule, which trip would take the least amount of time?

   A the trip from Glenmoor to Fox Ridge

   B the trip from River Grove to Lincoln

   C the trip from Norwood to Greentown

   D the trip from Oakwood to Denfield

4. Suppose you want to buy tickets to see a basketball game at the Greentown Arena. How might the seating map help you understand which section you would like to sit in? Explain.

5. Suppose you have tickets for a concert at the Greentown Arena. The concert begins at 8:30 P.M. Which train would you take from Fox Ridge in order to arrive in Greentown closest to 8:30 P.M.? Explain.

 Writing

Create a Map Imagine that there is a new student at your school who has moved into your neighborhood. Create a map of your school or your neighborhood to give to the new student. Your map should

- use colors and symbols to represent land and/or structures

- inform the student about the places that might be most important to someone who is new to the school or neighborhood

LOG ON ▶ **Literature** Online

Selection Resources For Selection Quizzes, eFlashcards, and Reading-Writing Connection activities, go to glencoe.com and enter QuickPass code GL27534u2.

Media Workshop

Media Elements

The front page of the *New York Times* states that the newspaper contains "All the news that's fit to print." However, in the present information age, more and more newspapers are producing online editions that feature graphics, animation, sound, and video. These Web editions take advantage of digital technology to keep people informed of the most up-to-date news.

Suppose you read two news articles about a flood in another state. The first article is in a local newspaper that is printed in black and white. The article contains no graphics, but the body of the article includes quotes from several flood victims who have lost everything.

The second article about the flood is on a news Web site. In addition to reading newly updated facts about the flood, you are able to watch a slideshow of color photographs, hear sound clips of victims describing their losses, and see a full-color interactive map that shows how much of the state is affected.

What effects would digital technology have on the journalists' ability to communicate information about the flood? How would features such as color, graphics, and sound affect your impressions and opinions? This chart will help you understand and think about how media makers use elements such as graphics and sound to affect viewers.

Element	What It Is	Example
Text and Content	**Text** is the words you see and hear. All the text together makes up **content**, or the information the story gives.	Flood victim: "Thankfully, we are able to stay with our relatives."
Graphics	**Graphics** are what you see in a story, such as color photographs, maps, or other images.	• Map of affected area • Color photographs of flood damage
Motion	**Motion** includes video footage.	• Video clip of citizens evacuating by car • Video clip of reporter interviewing a firefighter
Sound	**Sound** includes all audio, such as interviews and sound recordings.	• Audio clips of interviews with flood victims

GA Performance Standards

For page 247

ELA7LSV2a When responding to visual and oral texts and media, analyze the effect on the viewer of image, text, and sound in electronic journalism.

TRY IT

Analyze Media Elements Read a news article published on a reliable news Web site.

1. Summarize the news article in your own words.

2. Was the text effective in providing information? Why or why not?

3. Did the article include graphics or audio? How did the graphics or audio affect your opinions and impressions? How could graphics and audio have added to your understanding?

4. How did the production elements work together to make the article effective?

 Literature Online

Media Literacy For project ideas, templates, and media analysis guides, go to glencoe.com and enter QuickPass code GL27534u2.

The Story of an Eyewitness

Connect to the Article

Think about how people come together during times of need. During emergencies, such as natural disasters, how do people help each other?

Partner Talk With a partner, discuss your family's or school's emergency plans. For what emergencies has your family or school prepared?

Build Background

In "The Story of an Eyewitness," Jack London describes the devastating effects of an earthquake on the city of San Francisco, California, in 1906. London, who lived near San Francisco, was able to travel quickly to the city to give a firsthand report of the events.

- The earthquake started along the San Andreas Fault. The fault is a significant break in Earth's crust that runs from the northern end of the Gulf of California to the San Francisco area.

- As many as 3,000 people may have died as a result of the 1906 earthquake, and 225,000 were left homeless.

Vocabulary

wrought (rôt) *v.* worked; made; created (p. 250).
A solution was wrought by the village leaders.

residential (rez´ ə den´ shəl) *adj.* related to homes (p. 250).
Local homeowners objected to plans for a hotel in the town's residential area.

debris (də brē´) *n.* remains of something destroyed (p. 251).
The volunteers cleared the debris from the park after the windstorm.

disrupted (dis rupt´ ed) *v.* interrupted (p. 251).
A knock on the door disrupted our conversation.

hysteria (his ter´ē ə) *n.* overwhelming fear or emotion (p. 253). *The fire alarm caused hysteria in the auditorium.*

Meet Jack London

Life of Adventure Jack London lived a life as exciting as his adventure novels. Forced to earn a living at an early age, London made his way as a pirate, a sailor, and a coal shoveler before venturing into Alaska to search for gold. Finding none, he returned to California and began to write stories and novels based on his adventures. In 1906 a newspaper asked the author to write an account of a deadly earthquake in San Francisco.

Famous Works London's novels include *Call of the Wild* and *The Sea Wolf.*

Jack London was born in 1876 and died in 1916.

 Literature Online

Author Search For more about Jack London, go to glencoe.com and enter QuickPass code GL27534u2.

Set Purposes for Reading

BQ BIG Question

As you read, ask yourself, how do people react to natural disasters? What can I learn from this eyewitness report of an earthquake?

Literary Element | Diction

Diction refers to an author's choice and arrangement of words. Authors choose words carefully depending on their purpose for writing. In "The Story of an Eyewitness," London uses language that helps readers see, feel, and hear the settings and events that he observes. He wants readers to understand exactly what he is witnessing.

As you read, think about the words London chooses. Ask yourself, are the words appropriate and effective? Does the diction create vivid images in my mind? How might the diction be different if the events were described in a reference book?

Reading Strategy | Monitor Comprehension

When you **monitor comprehension,** you check to see how well you understand what you are reading. Understanding what you read is your most important task as a reader.

As you read, ask yourself questions about main ideas and events. When you can't answer a question, use one or more of these techniques: reread a section you did not understand, look up unfamiliar words, review photographs or illustrations, or reread footnotes to clarify information.

Use a chart like the one below to help monitor your comprehension. Begin by writing down what you already know about the San Francisco earthquake. Then write down what you would like to know. When you are finished reading, write down what you have learned. Reread, review, and clarify any information you don't understand.

What I Know	What I Want to Know	What I Learned

GA Performance Standards

For pages 248–261

ELA7R1h For literary texts, identify and analyze how an author's use of words creates tone and mood.

TRY IT

Monitor Comprehension When you read a difficult book or complicated instructions or study a foreign language, you should monitor your comprehension by slowing down when you read, going back to reread certain parts, and using a dictionary to look up unfamiliar words.

THE STORY OF
an Eyewitness

Jack London

The earthquake shook down in San Francisco hundreds of thousands of dollars' worth of walls and chimneys. But the conflagration¹ that followed burned up hundreds of millions of dollars' worth of property. There is no estimating within hundreds of millions the actual damage **wrought**. Not in history has a modern imperial city been so completely destroyed. San Francisco is gone. Nothing remains of it but memories and a fringe of dwelling houses on its outskirts. Its industrial section is wiped out. Its business section is wiped out. Its social and **residential** section is wiped out. The factories and warehouses, the great stores and newspaper strolling, the hotels and the palaces of the nabobs,² are all gone. Remains only the fringe of dwelling houses on the outskirts of what was once San Francisco.

Within an hour after the earthquake shock the smoke of San Francisco's burning was a lurid tower visible a hundred miles away. And for three days and nights this lurid tower swayed in the sky, reddening the sun, darkening the day, and filling the land with smoke.

On Wednesday morning at a quarter past five came the earthquake. A minute later the flames were leaping

Diction How does London's use of the words *wiped out* help you imagine the scene?

---

1 A **conflagration** is a very large, destructive fire.

2 **Nabobs** are well-known persons of great wealth.

Vocabulary . . . .

wrought (rôt) *v.* worked; made; created
residential (rez′ə den′shəl) *adj.* related to homes

The Valencia Hotel where 75 people were killed in the San Francisco earthquake of 1906.

upward. In a dozen different quarters south of Market Street, in the working-class ghetto, and in the factories, fires started. There was no opposing the flames. There was no organization, no communication. All the cunning adjustments of a twentieth century city had been smashed by the earthquake. The streets were humped into ridges and depressions, and piled with the **debris** of fallen walls. The steel rails were twisted into perpendicular and horizontal angles. The telephone and telegraph systems were **disrupted**. And the great water-mains had burst. All the shrewd contrivances and safeguards of man had been thrown out of gear by thirty seconds' twitching of the earth-crust.

Vocabulary

debris (də brē′) *n.* remains of something destroyed
disrupted (dis rupt′ed) *v.* interrupted

THE FIRE MADE ITS OWN DRAFT

By Wednesday afternoon, inside of twelve hours, half the heart of the city was gone. At that time I watched the vast conflagration from out on the bay. It was dead calm. Not a flicker of wind stirred. Yet from every side wind was pouring in upon the city. East, west, north, and south, strong winds were blowing upon the doomed city. The heated air rising made an enormous vacuum. Thus did the fire of itself build its own colossal[3] chimney through the atmosphere. Day and night this dead calm continued, and yet, near to the flames, the wind was often half a gale, so mighty was the vacuum.

Wednesday night saw the destruction of the very heart of the city. Dynamite was lavishly used, and many of San Francisco's proudest structures were crumbled by man himself into ruins, but there was no withstanding the onrush of the flames. Time and again successful stands were made by the fire-fighters, and every time the flames flanked around on either side or came up from the rear, and turned to defeat the hard-won victory. An enumeration[4] of the buildings destroyed would be a directory of San Francisco. An enumeration of the buildings undestroyed would be a line and several addresses. An enumeration of the deeds of heroism would stock a library and bankrupt the Carnegie medal fund.[5] An enumeration of the dead will never be made. All vestiges of them were destroyed by the flames. The number of the victims of the earthquake will never be known. South of Market Street, where the loss of life was particularly heavy, was the first to catch fire.

Remarkable as it may seem, Wednesday night while the whole city crashed and roared into ruin, was a quiet night. There were no crowds. There was no shouting

Monitor Comprehension
Why do you think dynamite was used to try to save the city?

---

3 Something *colossal* is immense or gigantic.

4 *Enumeration* is the act of naming, or listing, of items one by one.

5 The *Carnegie medal fund* was created in 1904 by American Andrew Carnegie (1835–1919) to honor persons who have performed heroic deeds.

Easy Street, San Francisco, 15 minutes after the fire began, during the 1906 earthquake.

and yelling. There was no **hysteria,** no disorder. I passed Wednesday night in the path of the advancing flames, and in all those terrible hours I saw not one woman who wept, not one man who was excited, not one person who was in the slightest degree panic stricken.

Before the flames, throughout the night, fled tens of thousands of homeless ones. Some were wrapped in blankets. Others carried bundles of bedding and dear household treasures. Sometimes a whole family was harnessed to a carriage or delivery wagon that was weighted down with their possessions. Baby buggies, toy wagons, and go-carts were used as trucks, while every other person was dragging a **trunk.** Yet everybody was gracious. The most perfect courtesy obtained. Never in all San Francisco's history, were her people so kind and courteous as on this night of terror.

A CARAVAN OF TRUNKS

All night these tens of thousands fled before the flames. Many of them, the poor people from the labor ghetto, had fled all day as well. They had left their homes burdened

Diction What does London's use of the word *harnessed* suggest about the people fleeing the fire?

Visual Vocabulary

A **trunk** is a large solid piece of luggage with a hinged lid that is used for transporting clothing and personal items.

Vocabulary

hysteria (his ter′ ē ə) *n.* overwhelming fear or emotion

with possessions. Now and again they lightened up, flinging out upon the street clothing and treasures they had dragged for miles.

They held on longest to their trunks, and over these trunks many a strong man broke his heart that night. The hills of San Francisco are steep, and up these hills, mile after mile, were the trunks dragged. Everywhere were trunks with across them lying their exhausted owners, men and women. Before the march of the flames were flung picket lines of soldiers. And a block at a time, as the flames advanced, these pickets retreated. One of their tasks was to keep the trunk-pullers moving. The exhausted creatures, stirred on by the menace of bayonets, would arise and struggle up the steep pavements, pausing from weakness every five or ten feet.

Often, after surmounting a heart-breaking hill, they would find another wall of flame advancing upon them at right angles and be compelled to change anew the line of their retreat. In the end, completely played out, after toiling for a dozen hours like giants, thousands of them were compelled to abandon their trunks. Here the shopkeepers and soft members of the middle class were at a disadvantage. But the working-men dug holes in vacant lots and backyards and buried their trunks.

THE DOOMED CITY

At nine o'clock Wednesday evening I walked down through the very heart of the city. I walked through miles and miles of magnificent buildings and towering skyscrapers. Here was no fire. All was in perfect order. The police patrolled the streets. Every building had its watchman at the door. And yet it was doomed, all of it. There was no water. The dynamite was giving out. And at right angles two different conflagrations were sweeping down upon it.

At one o'clock in the morning I walked down through the same section. Everything still stood intact. There was no fire. And yet there was a change. A rain of ashes was falling. The watchmen at the doors were gone. The police had been withdrawn. There were no firemen, no fire-engines, no men fighting with dynamite. The district had

Monitor Comprehension
What does London mean when he writes, "many a strong man broke his heart that night"?

Diction What effect do these short sentences create?

been absolutely abandoned. I stood at the corner of Kearney and Market, in the very innermost heart of San Francisco. Kearney Street was deserted. Half a dozen blocks away it was burning on both sides. The street was a wall of flame. And against this wall of flame, silhouetted sharply, were two United States cavalrymen sitting on their horses, calmly watching. That was all. Not another person was in sight. In the intact heart of the city, two troopers sat their horses and watched.

SPREAD OF THE CONFLAGRATION

Surrender was complete. There was no water. The sewers had long since been pumped dry. There was no dynamite. Another fire had broken out further uptown, and now from three sides conflagrations were sweeping down. The fourth side had been burned earlier in the day. In that direction stood the tottering walls of the Examiner Building, the burned-out Call Building,[6] the smoldering ruins of the Grand Hotel, and the gutted, devastated, dynamited Palace Hotel.

The following will illustrate the sweep of the flames and the inability of men to calculate their spread. At eight o'clock Wednesday evening I passed through Union Square.[7] It was packed with refugees. Thousands of them had gone to bed on the grass. Government tents had been set up, supper was being cooked, and the refugees were lining up for free meals.

At half past one in the morning three sides of Union Square were in flames. The fourth side, where stood the

A fire engine responds to the crisis following the San Francisco earthquake.

View the Photograph In what way is firefighting equipment different today?

---

6 The ***Examiner*** and the ***Call*** were San Francisco daily newspapers.

7 ***Union Square*** is a block in downtown San Francisco, which at the time of the fire was the location of the city's central hotel and shopping district.

The road outside the main post office in San Francisco, which has been ripped up by the force of an earthquake.

great St. Francis Hotel, was still holding out. An hour later, ignited from top and sides the St. Francis was flaming heavenward. Union Square, heaped high with mountains of trunks, was deserted. Troops, refugees, and all had retreated.

A FORTUNE FOR A HORSE!

It was at Union Square that I saw a man offering a thousand dollars for a team of horses. He was in charge of a truck piled high with trunks from some hotel. It had been hauled here into what was considered safety, and the horses had been taken out. The flames were on three sides of the Square and there were no horses.

Also, at this time, standing beside the truck, I urged a man to seek safety in flight. He was all but hemmed in by several conflagrations. He was an old man and he was on crutches. Said he: "Today is my birthday. Last night I was worth thirty thousand dollars. I bought some delicate fish and other things for my birthday dinner. I have had no dinner, and all I own are these crutches."

Monitor Comprehension
What does this description say about how San Francisco's citizens felt at the time?

I convinced him of his danger and started him limping on his way. An hour later, from a distance, I saw the truckload of trunks burning merrily in the middle of the street.

On Thursday morning at a quarter past five, just twenty-four hours after the earthquake, I sat on the steps of a small residence on Nob Hill. With me sat Japanese, Italians, Chinese, and negroes—a bit of the cosmopolitan flotsam[8] of the wreck of the city. All about were the palaces of the nabob pioneers of Forty-nine.[9] To the east and south at right angles, were advancing two mighty walls of flame.

I went inside with the owner of the house on the steps of which I sat. He was cool and cheerful and hospitable. "Yesterday morning," he said, "I was worth six hundred thousand dollars. This morning this house is all I have left. It will go in fifteen minutes." He pointed to a large cabinet. "That is my wife's collection of china. This rug upon which we stand is a present. It cost fifteen hundred dollars. Try that piano. Listen to its tone. There are few like it. There are no horses. The flames will be here in fifteen minutes."

Outside the old Mark Hopkins residence a palace was just catching fire. The troops were falling back and driving the refugees before them. From every side came the roaring of flames, the crashing of walls, and the detonations of dynamite.

THE DAWN OF THE SECOND DAY

I passed out of the house. Day was trying to dawn through the smoke-pall. A sickly light was creeping over the face of things. Once only the sun broke through the smoke-pall, blood-red, and showing a quarter its usual size. The smoke-pall itself, viewed from beneath, was a rose color that pulsed and fluttered with lavender shades.

Diction London chooses the words *sickly, creeping, face, smoke-pall,* and *blood-red* to describe the city. What image do his words create?

---

8 **Nob Hill** is a residential area of San Francisco with many mansions. Something that is **cosmopolitan** is composed of people, qualities, or elements from many different countries. Here, **flotsam** refers to homeless people who wander about from place to place.

9 The **pioneers of Forty-nine** are people who became wealthy during the California gold rush of 1849.

City buildings burning during the San Francisco fire in April 1906. Smoke billows out of several buildings, filling the sky.

View the Photograph In what ways does this photograph help illustrate London's descriptions?

Then it turned to mauve and yellow and dun.[10] There was no sun. And so dawned the second day on stricken San Francisco.

An hour later I was creeping past the shattered dome of the City Hall. Than it there was no better exhibit of the destructive force of the earthquake. Most of the stone had been shaken from the great dome, leaving standing the naked framework of steel. Market Street was piled high with the wreckage, and across the wreckage lay the overthrown pillars of the City Hall shattered into short crosswise sections.

This section of the city with the exception of the Mint[11] and the Post-Office, was already a waste of smoking ruins. Here and there through the smoke, creeping warily under the shadows of tottering walls, emerged occasional men and women. It was like the meeting of the handful of survivors after the day of the end of the world.

BEEVES SLAUGHTERED AND ROASTED

On Mission Street lay a dozen steers, in a neat row stretching across the street just as they had been struck down by the flying ruins of the earthquake. The fire had passed through afterward and roasted them. The human dead had been carried away before the fire came. At another place on Mission Street I saw a milk wagon. A

Monitor Comprehension
In what way does this description help you make sense of the word *beeves* in the subhead?

---

10 *Mauve* is a purplish-blue or rose color. *Dun* is a dull grayish-brown color.

11 The *Mint* is a building at which money is coined by the government.

steel telegraph pole had smashed down sheer through the driver's seat and crushed the front wheels. The milk cans lay scattered around.

All day Thursday and all Thursday night, all day Friday and Friday night, the flames still raged on.

Friday night saw the flames finally conquered, though not until Russian Hill and Telegraph Hill[12] had been swept and three-quarters of a mile of wharves and docks had been licked up.

THE LAST STAND

The great stand of the fire-fighters was made Thursday night on Van Ness Avenue. Had they failed here, the comparatively few remaining houses of the city would have been swept. Here were the magnificent residences of the second generation of San Francisco nabobs, and these, in a solid zone, were dynamited down across the path of the fire. Here and there the flames leaped the zone, but these fires were beaten out, principally by the use of wet blankets and rugs.

San Francisco, at the present time, is like the crater of a volcano, around which are camped tens of thousands of refugees. At the Presidio[13] alone are at least twenty thousand. All the surrounding cities and towns are jammed with the homeless ones, where they are being cared for by the relief committees. The refugees were carried free by the railroads to any point they wished to go, and it is estimated that over one hundred thousand people have left the peninsula on which San Francisco stood. The government has the situation in hand, and, thanks to the immediate relief given by the whole United States, there is not the slightest possibility of a famine. The bankers and business men have already set about making preparations to rebuild San Francisco. 🔖

BQ BIG Question
Why was it important for people to rebuild the city?

---

12 **Russian Hill** is an area in San Francisco where, at the time of the fire, many large houses were located. **Telegraph Hill** is an area in San Francisco that, at the time of the fire, was a popular residential neighborhood.

13 The **Presidio** is a San Francisco district at the northernmost tip of the city. It is the site of many military buildings.

After You Read

Respond and Think Critically

1. What two events occur Wednesday morning within minutes of each other? Explain. **[Identify]**

2. What is unusual about the behavior of the city's residents on Wednesday night? Explain. **[Recall]**

3. In what ways are "the cosmopolitan flotsam" and "the nabob pioneers" on Nob Hill different? What do they have in common? Support your answer with details from the article. **[Compare]**

4. In what way do London's word choice and writing style contribute to your understanding of the article? Explain. **[Analyze]**

5. Based on the ending of the selection, do you think San Francisco was successfully rebuilt? Support your conclusion. **[Conclude]**

6. **BQ** **BIG Question** How could the information in this article help people prepare for disasters? **[Connect]**

Vocabulary

Respond to these questions.

1. Who would be more likely to have **wrought** a ceramic vase—a potter or a cashier?

2. What would you expect to see in a **residential** area—mostly houses or businesses?

3. Where would you be more likely to find **debris**—in a library or at a construction site?

4. Which person would be more likely to have **disrupted** a movie—someone talking loudly or someone eating popcorn?

5. How would people experiencing **hysteria** behave—calmly or emotionally?

Academic Vocabulary

The 1906 earthquake in San Francisco **dramatically** changed the landscape of the city. In the preceding sentence, *dramatically* means "noticeably." *Dramatically* also has another meaning. For example: When the actress arrived on the scene, she was dressed **dramatically** in a long, rustling black gown with a velvet cape trailing from her shoulders. What do you think *dramatically* means in the preceding sentence? What is the difference between the two meanings?

TIP

Analyzing
To answer question 4, look for words and phrases in the article that caught your attention or made you react in a certain way.

- List words and phrases that London uses to describe the earthquake, fire, and overall crisis. What do his descriptions remind you of?

- How do London's descriptions of individuals during the crisis affect your understanding of the whole population of San Francisco during the crisis? Use specific examples.

 FOLDABLES Study Organizer Keep track of your ideas about the **BIG Question** in your unit Foldable.

 Literature Online

Selection Resources
For Selection Quizzes, eFlashcards, and Reading-Writing Connection activities, go to glencoe.com and enter QuickPass code GL27534u2.

Literary Element **Diction**

1. Look at the words *swept* and *licked up* in the third paragraph from the end of the article. How does the description change if you substitute the words *burned* and *destroyed?* Explain.

2. Choose a sentence in London's article and tell why a specific word in the sentence is an effective word choice. Support your answer.

Review: **Setting**

As you learned on page 39, **setting** is the time and place in which the events of a literary work occur. The setting often helps create an atmosphere, or mood. The setting of "The Story of an Eyewitness" is the city of San Francisco after the earthquake of 1906.

3. Why does London mention some buildings by name, such as the *Examiner* Building, the *Call* Building, and the St. Francis Hotel?

4. London says San Francisco after the fires is "like the crater of a volcano, around which are camped tens of thousands of refugees." What mood does this description create? Explain.

Reading Strategy **Monitor Comprehension**

Refer to the graphic organizer you made to answer the following questions.

5. How did the technological advancements of the early twentieth century hold up during the San Francisco earthquake and the fires of 1906? Give examples.

6. In the days immediately following the fires, what did San Francisco's bankers and business leaders do?

Grammar Link

Future tense shows actions that are going to happen. In the future tense, the word *will* is used with verbs.

Singular	Plural
I will go.	We will go.
You will go.	You will go.
He, she, or it will go.	They will go.

Consider this sentence:

The city council will vote on new safety measures at the next meeting.

The city council will vote in the future, so the writer uses the future tense *will vote.*

Practice Suppose you are the mayor of San Francisco at the time of the 1906 earthquake. Write three sentences that tell what you will do to rebuild the city. Use the future tense.

Write with Style

Apply Diction Write a paragraph describing an important event that you witnessed. Analyze London's word choice in the article and choose words that will create vivid pictures in your reader's mind. Use a word web to brainstorm descriptive words and phrases that will convey a strong image of the event.

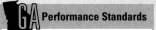 **Performance Standards**

For page 262

ELA7R2b Understand and acquire new vocabulary. Use knowledge of Greek, Latin, and Anglo-Saxon roots and affixes to determine the meaning of unfamiliar words.

Vocabulary Workshop

Word Parts

Connection to Literature

"An enumeration of the deeds of heroism would stock a library and bankrupt the Carnegie medal fund."

—Jack London, "The Story of an Eyewitness"

You can sometimes find clues to a word's meaning by looking at its parts. A **root** is a word part that is the base of many words. An **affix** is a part added at the beginning **(prefix)** or at the end **(suffix)** of a root that changes its meaning. For example, the root of *heroism* is *hero,* meaning "a brave person." The suffix *-ism* can mean "a characteristic behavior." Thus *heroism* means "the actions of a brave person."

Here are some other word parts from "The Story of an Eyewitness."

Word	Word Parts	Meanings
visible	*vis:* to see *-ible:* can be done	can be seen
telegraph	*tele-:* distant, far away *graph:* to write, written	a system for sending written messages across a distance
destruction	*de-:* opposite of, down *struct:* to build *-ion:* act, process	the act of tearing down or destroying

TRY IT: Use the chart above to help you answer each question.

1. If the prefix *in-* can mean "not" or "without," what does the word *invisible* mean?
2. If *scope* means "to see" or "an instrument for viewing or examining," what does the word *telescope* mean?
3. If the prefix *con-* means "together," what does the word *construction* mean?

 LOG ON **Literature** Online

Vocabulary For more vocabulary practice, go to glencoe.com and enter the QuickPass code GL27534u2.

Part 3

For Understanding

The Meal (The Bananas), 1891. Paul Gauguin. Oil on canvas, Musée d'Orsay, Paris.

BQ **BIG Question** **Why Do You Read?**

How might the people in the painting *The Meal (The Bananas)* learn to understand one another by sharing a dinner together? How does sharing your ideas about the books you read build understanding?

Before You Read

An Hour with Abuelo

Connect to the Short Story

Arturo, the narrator in this story, visits his grandfather in a nursing home. Think about a time you visited an elderly relative or friend.

Write a Journal Entry Write about the time you spent with your relative or friend. What did you talk about? How did you feel about the situation?

Build Background

This story is set in Brooklyn, New York, where Arturo's grandfather lives in a nursing home. The grandfather is from a small village in Puerto Rico, where he spent most of his life.

- Puerto Rico is an island about 1,000 miles southeast of Florida.

- Puerto Rico has its own government but is a commonwealth of the United States. Its people are United States citizens.

- Spanish is the main language in Puerto Rico.

Vocabulary

diploma (di plō′mə) *n.* a certificate indicating that a person has graduated from a school or a program (p. 270).
You need a college diploma for many careers today.

ignorant (ig′nər ənt) *adj.* without an education or knowledge (p. 270).
Reading the newspaper daily prevents a person from being ignorant about world affairs.

Meet Judith Ortiz Cofer

Mastering a New Language
English was not Judith Ortiz Cofer's first language. Born in Puerto Rico, she learned English only after her family moved to the United States. "It was a challenge," she said, "not only to learn English, but to master it enough to teach it and—the ultimate goal—to write poetry in it." Although she writes in English, Cofer's Puerto Rican heritage inspires most of her work.

Literary Works Cofer writes stories, poetry, and essays. "An Hour with Abuelo" comes from the book *An Island Like You: Stories of the Barrio.*

Judith Ortiz Cofer was born in 1952.

 Literature Online

Author Search For more about Judith Ortiz Cofer, go to glencoe.com and enter QuickPass code GL27534u2.

Set Purposes for Reading

BQ BIG Question

As you read, ask yourself, how might a grandfather from Puerto Rico and a grandson from the United States connect to each other?

Literary Element Style

Style is an author's personal way of using language through word choice, sentence length, sentence patterns, and much more. Style includes the narration of a story and the dialogue spoken by characters. The author of this story uses one style for Arturo's thoughts and another style for the grandfather's story.

Understanding an author's style is important because style helps reveal an author's purpose for writing. Style can also show how the author feels about his or her subject and audience.

As you read, ask yourself, what words does the author use to help me understand Arturo? What words does the author use to describe the grandfather? Notice how Cofer's choice of words, narration, and dialogue affects your understanding and appreciation of the story.

Reading Skill Recognize Author's Purpose

An **author's purpose** is his or her reason for writing. An author may write to tell a story, to explain, to persuade, to entertain, or to inform. In fact, an author may write one text for more than one purpose.

An author's purpose affects how he or she writes. Authors who write to explain or inform usually include facts and details. Authors who write to persuade include reasons that influence readers to agree with their arguments. Authors who write to entertain may describe funny or exciting situations. Authors who write to convey a message often explore a theme within a story. As you read, ask yourself why the author wrote this story. What was her purpose?

Use a graphic organizer like the one below to help you figure out the author's purpose. Note the differences between what Arturo and his grandfather say and think.

	Says	Thinks
Arturo		
Abuelo		

The author's reason for including these details was _____.

Performance Standards

For pages 264–274

ELA7R1h For literary texts, identify and analyze how an author's use of words creates tone and mood.

TRY IT

Recognize Author's Purpose
You recognize people's reasons for writing or speaking every day, even if you don't realize it. For example, your science teacher might describe how a caterpillar turns into a butterfly. What is your teacher's purpose for speaking? Suppose that your friend invites you to go to an amusement park. Why does your friend emphasize how much fun the trip will be?

an *hour with*
Abuelo

Judith Ortiz Cofer

Just one hour, *una hora*, is all I'm asking of you, son."
My grandfather is in a nursing home in Brooklyn, and
my mother wants me to spend some time with him, since
the doctors say that he doesn't have too long to go now. I
don't have much time left of my summer vacation, and
there's a stack of books next to my bed I've got to
read if I'm going to get into the AP English class I want.
I'm going stupid in some of my classes, and Mr. Williams,
the principal at Central, said that if I passed some reading
tests, he'd let me move up.

Besides, I hate the place, the old people's home,
especially the way it smells like industrial-strength[1]
ammonia and other stuff I won't mention, since it turns
my stomach. And really the abuelo[2] always has a lot of
relatives visiting him, so I've gotten out of going out

Style How does the
author's choice of words let
you know that a teenager is
telling this story?

---

1 Something ***industrial-strength*** is much stronger than normal.
2 The Spanish word for *grandfather* is ***abuelo*** (ä bweʹlō).

there except at Christmas, when a whole vanload of grandchildren are herded over there to give him gifts and a hug. We all make it quick and spend the rest of the time in the recreation area, where they play checkers and stuff with some of the old people's games, and I catch up on back issues of *Modern Maturity.* I'm not picky, I'll read almost anything.

Anyway, after my mother nags me for about a week, I let her drive me to Golden Years. She drops me off in front. She wants me to go in alone and have a "good time" talking to Abuelo. I tell her to be back in one hour or I'll take the bus back to Paterson. She squeezes my hand and says, *"Gracias, hijo,"*[3] in a choked-up voice like I'm doing her a big favor.

I get depressed the minute I walk into the place. They line up the old people in wheelchairs in the hallway as if they were about to be raced to the finish line by orderlies who don't even look at them when they push them here and there. I walk fast to room 10, Abuelo's "suite." He is sitting up in his bed writing with a pencil in one of those old-fashioned black hardback notebooks. It has the outline of the island of Puerto Rico on it. I slide into the hard vinyl chair by his bed. He sort of smiles and the lines on his face get deeper, but he doesn't say anything. Since I'm supposed to talk to him, I say, "What are you doing, Abuelo, writing the story of your life?"

It's supposed to be a joke, but he answers, *"Sí,* how did you know, Arturo?"

His name is Arturo too. I was named after him. I don't really know my grandfather. His children, including my mother, came to New York and New Jersey (where I was born) and he stayed on the Island until my grandmother died. Then he got sick, and since nobody could leave their jobs to go take care of him, they brought him to this nursing home in Brooklyn. I see him a couple of times a year, but he's always surrounded by his sons and daughters. My mother tells me that Don Arturo had once

Recognize Author's Purpose Arturo's comment to his mother is sharp and funny. What does it tell you about the author's purpose?

Recognize Author's Purpose What does Abuelo's response tell you about the author's purpose?

---

3 *Gracias, hijo* (grä´sēäs ē´hō) is Spanish for "Thank you, son."

> "His name is Arturo too. I was named after him. I don't really know my grandfather."

From Brooklyn Heights, 1925. George Copeland Ault. Oil on canvas, 30 x 20 in. The Newark Museum, Newark, NJ.

been a teacher back in Puerto Rico, but had lost his job after the war. Then he became a farmer. She's always saying in a sad voice, "*Ay, bendito!* What a waste of a fine mind." Then she usually shrugs her shoulders and says, "*Así es la vida.*" That's the way life is. It sometimes makes me mad that the adults I know just accept whatever is thrown at them because "that's the way things are." Not for me. I go after what I want.

Anyway, Abuelo is looking at me like he was trying to see into my head, but he doesn't say anything. Since I like stories, I decide I may as well ask him if he'll read me what he wrote.

I look at my watch: I've already used up twenty minutes of the hour I promised my mother.

Abuelo starts talking in his slow way. He speaks what my mother calls book English. He taught himself from a dictionary, and his words sound stiff, like he's sounding them out in his head before he says them. With his children he speaks Spanish, and that funny book English with us grandchildren. I'm surprised that he's still so sharp, because his body is shrinking like a crumpled-up brown paper sack with some bones in it. But I can see from looking into his eyes that the light is still on in there.

"It is a short story, Arturo. The story of my life. It will not take very much time to read it."

"I have time, Abuelo." I'm a little embarrassed that he saw me looking at my watch.

"Yes, *hijo*. You have spoken the truth. *La verdad*. You have much time."

Abuelo reads: "'I loved words from the beginning of my life. In the *campo*[4] where I was born one of seven sons, there were few books. My mother read them to us over and over: the Bible, the stories of Spanish conquistadors[5] and of pirates that she had read as a child and brought with her from the city of Mayagüez;[6] that was before she

Style What do these statements tell you about Abuelo? How are his words different from Arturo's?

---

4 In Spanish, *campo* (cäm´pō) means "country."

5 Any of the Spanish conquerors of Mexico, Peru, or other parts of the Americas in the sixteenth century are called *conquistadors* (cōn kēs´tä dōrz).

6 *Mayagüez* (mä yä gwes´) is a port city in western Puerto Rico.

married my father, a coffee bean farmer; and she taught us words from the newspaper that a boy on a horse brought every week to her. She taught each of us how to write on a slate with chalks that she ordered by mail every year. We used those chalks until they were so small that you lost them between your fingers.

"'I always wanted to be a writer and a teacher. With my heart and my soul I knew that I wanted to be around books all of my life. And so against the wishes of my father, who wanted all his sons to help him on the land, she sent me to high school in Mayagüez. For four years I boarded with a couple she knew. I paid my rent in labor, and I ate vegetables I grew myself. I wore my clothes until they were thin as parchment. But I graduated at the top of my class! My whole family came to see me that day. My mother brought me a beautiful *guayabera,* a white shirt made of the finest cotton and embroidered by her own hands. I was a happy young man.

"'In those days you could teach in a country school with a high school **diploma**. So I went back to my mountain village and got a job teaching all grades in a little classroom built by the parents of my students.

"'I had books sent to me by the government. I felt like a rich man although the pay was very small. I had books. All the books I wanted! I taught my students how to read poetry and plays, and how to write them. We made up songs and put on shows for the parents. It was a beautiful time for me.

"'Then the war came, and the American President said that all Puerto Rican men would be drafted. I wrote to our governor and explained that I was the only teacher in the mountain village. I told him that the children would go back to the fields and grow up **ignorant** if I could not teach them their letters. I said that I thought I was a better

Recognize Author's Purpose What message does Abuelo's story send to readers?

> **Vocabulary** ....
>
> **diploma** (di plō´mə) *n.* a certificate indicating that someone has graduated from a school or a program
>
> **ignorant** (ig´nər ənt) *adj.* without an education or knowledge

El Libro, 1997. Juan Lascano. Oil on canvas. Zurbaran Galeria, Buenos Aires, Argentina.

teacher than a soldier. The governor did not answer my letter. I went into the U.S. Army.

"'I told my sergeant that I could be a teacher in the army. I could teach all the farm boys their letters so that they could read the instructions on the ammunition boxes and not blow themselves up. The sergeant said I was too smart for my own good, and gave me a job cleaning latrines.[7] He said to me there is reading material for you there, scholar. Read the writing on the walls. I spent the war mopping floors and cleaning toilets.

"'When I came back to the Island, things had changed. You had to have a college degree to teach school, even the lower grades. My parents were sick, two of my brothers had been killed in the war, the others had stayed in Nueva York. I was the only one left to help the old people. I became a farmer. I married a good woman who gave me many good children. I taught them all how to read and write before they started school.'"

Abuelo then puts the notebook down on his lap and closes his eyes.

"*Así es la vida* is the title of my book," he says in a whisper, almost to himself. Maybe he's forgotten that I'm there.

For a long time he doesn't say anything else. I think that he's sleeping, but then I see that he's watching me through half-closed lids, maybe waiting for my opinion of his writing. I'm trying to think of something nice to say. I liked it and all, but not the title. And I think that he could've been a teacher if he had wanted to bad enough. Nobody is going to stop me from doing what I want with my life. I'm not going to let la vida get in my way. I want to discuss this with him, but the words are not coming

Recognize Author's Purpose Why did the author include this detail in the story?

Style What can you tell about Arturo from the way he narrates?

---

7 Another word for *toilets* is **latrines** (lə trēn′ z).

> ## "I'm about to ask him why he didn't keep fighting to make his dream come true,"

into my head in Spanish just yet. I'm about to ask him why he didn't keep fighting to make his dream come true, when an old lady in hot-pink running shoes sort of appears at the door.

She is wearing a pink jogging outfit too. The world's oldest marathoner,[8] I say to myself. She calls out to my grandfather in a flirty voice, "Yoo-hoo, Arturo, remember what day this is? It's poetry-reading day in the rec room! You promised us you'd read your new one today."

I see my abuelo perking up almost immediately. He points to his wheelchair, which is hanging like a huge metal bat in the open closet. He makes it obvious that he wants me to get it. I put it together, and with Mrs. Pink Running Shoes's help, we get him in it. Then he says in a strong deep voice I hardly recognize, "Arturo, get that notebook from the table, please."

I hand him another map-of-the-Island notebook—this one is red. On it in big letters it says, *POEMAS DE ARTURO.*

I start to push him toward the rec room, but he shakes his finger at me.

"Arturo, look at your watch now. I believe your time is over." He gives me a wicked smile.

Then with her pushing the wheelchair—maybe a little too fast—they roll down the hall. He is already reading from his notebook, and she's making bird noises. I look at my watch and the hour is up, to the minute. I can't help but think that my abuelo has been timing me. It cracks me up. I walk slowly down the hall toward the exit sign. I want my mother to have to wait a little. I don't want her to think that I'm in a hurry or anything. ﹏

Style What does Abuelo's "strong deep voice" tell you about how he's feeling?

BQ **BIG Question**
In what new way does Arturo understand Abuelo at the end of the story?

---

8 A *marathoner* is a person who runs a long-distance race.

After You Read

Respond and Think Critically

1. What reasons does Arturo give for not wanting to visit his grandfather, Abuelo, in the nursing home? [Recall]

2. What happens during Arturo's visit with Abuelo? Give details from the story to support your answer. [Summarize]

3. At the beginning of the story, why does Arturo believe that he doesn't have much in common with his grandfather? Explain. [Infer]

4. Why do you think Abuelo tells Arturo to look at his watch at the end of the story? What does this reveal about Abuelo? Explain. [Interpret]

5. In what way has Arturo's attitude changed by the end of the story? Explain. [Conclude]

6. **BQ** **BIG Question** Which part of his life story most helped you understand Abuelo? Explain. [Evaluate]

TIP

Making Inferences To answer question 3, you must closely read parts of Arturo's narration.

• Look for what Arturo says when he first starts to talk about his grandfather.

• Think about how the details make Abuelo seem different from Arturo.

• Based on the details, make an inference about why Arturo feels he has little in common with Abuelo.

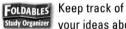 **FOLDABLES** **Study Organizer** Keep track of your ideas about the **BIG Question** in your unit Foldable.

View the Art

Village Life in Puerto Rico

This painting depicts a Puerto Rican village much like the one in which Arturo's grandfather grew up. What do you think life was like growing up in a village like this one?

Group Activity Discuss the following questions with classmates. Use evidence from "An Hour with Abuelo" to support your answers.

1. What does Abuelo's story tell readers about village life in Puerto Rico before World War II? Recall details about Abuelo's parents, childhood, and education.

2. What details in this painting reflect details in the story? Explain.

3. What does Abuelo call his book? Based on what you know about life in Puerto Rico, why do you think Abuelo chose that particular title? Explain.

El Sol Asombra, 1989. Rafael Ferrer. Oil on canvas, 60 x 72 in. Butler Institute of American Art, Youngstown, OH.

Literary Element Style

1. Describe Arturo's narration. What does it show you about his character?
2. Describe the writing style that the author uses when Abuelo tells his story. How is it different from Arturo's narration?

Review: Point of View

As you learned on page 9, **point of view** is the relationship of the narrator to the story. In **first-person point of view,** the narrator refers to himself or herself as "I." In this story, everything you learn is filtered through the eyes, ears, and thoughts of Arturo.

Using a graphic organizer like the one below, list examples of how the first-person point of view affects your knowledge of events, characters, and setting.

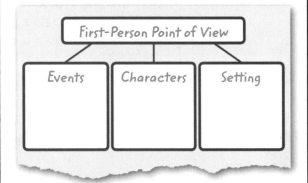

First-Person Point of View

Events | Characters | Setting

Reading Skill Recognize Author's Purpose

Standards Practice ELA7RC2e

3. Why did the author write this story?
   A to inform readers about family
   B to explain how to write a story
   C to entertain and to send a message
   D to persuade readers to visit Puerto Rico

Vocabulary Practice

On a separate sheet of paper, write the vocabulary word that correctly completes each sentence. If none of the words fits the sentence, write "none."

diploma

ignorant

1. He may appear to be knowledgeable about cars, but Thomas is actually quite _____ about mechanics.
2. When the principal handed me my _____, I knew that all my hard work had finally paid off.
3. Now that my father is retired, he wants to try writing a _____.
4. The more you read, the more _____ you will become.

Academic Vocabulary

When Abuelo came back to Puerto Rico after the war, he made a **commitment** to take care of his parents.

In the preceding sentence, *commitment* means "a promise" or "a pledge." Think about a time when you promised to do something important for someone. What did you promise to do? Why did you make this commitment?

LOG ON ▶ **Literature** Online

Selection Resources For Selection Quizzes, eFlashcards, and Reading-Writing Connection activities, go to glencoe.com and enter QuickPass code GL27534u2.

Respond Through Writing

Expository Essay

 Performance Standards

For page 275

ELA7W2c Demonstrate competence in a variety of genres. Produce a response to literature that organizes an interpretation around several clear ideas.

Interpret Theme In a short essay, interpret the theme of "An Hour with Abuelo" and explain how the story expresses this message.

Understand the Task The **theme** of a story is its message about life. In most stories, the author reveals the theme through plot, characters, setting, and point of view. When you **interpret** theme, you explain how these elements help express the story's message.

Prewrite Decide what you think is the story's theme. Then find details in the story that help reveal the theme. Think about how each story element helps you understand the theme.

Draft Before you begin drafting, make a plan. For example, you may decide to state the theme in your introduction. Then you may want to write about how certain story elements or details reveal the theme. After you determine your plan, write the story's theme in your own words. Use this sentence frame:

"An Hour with Abuelo" shows readers that _____.

Theme	Details	How Details Express the Theme
Sometimes people achieve their goals in unexpected ways.	• Abuelo gave up being a teacher. • He still taught his children how to read and write.	When life was hard, Abuelo found other ways to live out his dreams.

Word Bank

The following are some useful words that you might want to include in your essay. First check their meanings in a dictionary.

elder

generation

culture

goals

respect

Revise After you have written your draft, read it to make sure that each paragraph focuses on one topic. Add, remove, or rearrange sentences as necessary so that readers can identify the topic of each paragraph. Review the Word Bank in the side column for words you might want to use in your essay.

Edit and Proofread Proofread your paper, correcting any errors in spelling, grammar, and punctuation.

Before You Read

A Day's Wait

Connect to the Short Story

Think about a time when you were worried about something. Did you keep your worries to yourself, or did you share them with someone? If you decided to share your feelings, with whom did you share them? Do you think that you made the right decision? Explain your answer.

Graphic Organizer Create a word web like the one below about a time when you felt worried. In the center circle, list your reason for worrying. In the connecting circles, list your thoughts, feelings, and actions.

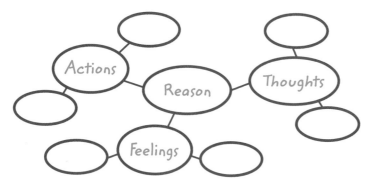

Build Background

In this story, a young boy has influenza, or the flu. For most people, the flu is not a serious illness. However, it can be quite serious for very young children and for older adults.

- The flu is contagious, which means it spreads from person to person usually through coughing and sneezing.

- Flu symptoms include headache, sore throat, and high fever.

- In the United States the Fahrenheit scale measures temperature. On this scale, water freezes at 32 degrees and boils at 212 degrees. The average human body temperature is 98.6 degrees.

- Many countries, including European countries, use the Celsius scale to measure temperature. On this scale, water freezes at 0 degrees and boils at 100 degrees. The average human body temperature is 37 degrees on the Celsius scale.

Meet Ernest Hemingway

"The writer's job is to tell the truth. . . . All you have to do is write one true sentence. Write the truest sentence that you know."

—Ernest Hemingway

A Direct Style A novelist and short-story writer, Ernest Hemingway became famous for his short, direct sentences. He credited his time as a news reporter, a career choice that trained him to say much in few words, for influencing his style as a storyteller. He was also known for his love of fishing, hunting, and bullfighting— interests that provided him with many story ideas. Hemingway wrote many classic works of fiction, including *The Old Man and the Sea* and *For Whom the Bell Tolls*. He was born in 1899 and died in 1961.

 Literature Online

Author Search For more about Ernest Hemingway, go to glencoe.com and enter QuickPass code GL27534u2.

Set Purposes for Reading

BQ BIG Question

As you read "A Day's Wait," ask yourself, why is communication important?

Literary Element Dialogue

Dialogue is conversation between characters in a literary work. It shows the exact words spoken by characters. In the short story "A Day's Wait," an example of dialogue is when the father asks his son, "What's the matter?" and the boy replies, "I've got a headache."

Dialogue is important because it helps bring characters to life. It helps readers understand what characters are thinking and feeling. It also moves the plot forward. To recognize dialogue in a short story, remember these tips:

- Dialogue may appear at the beginning, middle, or end of a sentence.
- The spoken words will be inside quotation marks. The part of the sentence that is not in quotation marks identifies the speaker.
- When the speaker changes, the new character's dialogue is shown on the next indented line.

As you read dialogue, ask yourself, who is speaking and what does the dialogue reveal about the speaker?

Reading Strategy Evaluate Characterization

Characterization refers to the methods an author uses to develop characters' personalities. **Direct characterization** is when an author tells you exactly what a character is like. **Indirect characterization** is when a character's personality is revealed through the character's words and actions and through what other characters think and say about the character.

When you evaluate characterization, you think critically about the details the author uses to reveal character. Evaluating characterization will help you deepen your appreciation of characters and of the author's technique. To evaluate characterization, ask yourself,

- How does the writer use direct and indirect characterization?
- What do I like and dislike about the characters?
- How believable are the characters' actions, thoughts, and feelings?

You may find it helpful to use a graphic organizer like the one below.

Character	Actions	Thoughts	Feelings	My Evaluation

GA Performance Standards

For pages 276–283

ELA7R1f For literary texts, analyze characterization (dynamic and static) in prose and plays.

TRY IT

Evaluate You evaluate books, music, and movies when you form an opinion about them. Think about your favorite book, song, or movie. What makes it your favorite? What do you look for in a good book, song, or movie?

A Day's Wait

Ernest Hemingway

He came into the room to shut the windows while we were still in bed and I saw he looked ill. He was shivering, his face was white, and he walked slowly as though it ached to move.

"What's the matter, Schatz?"[1]

"I've got a headache."

"You better go back to bed."

"No. I'm all right."

"You go to bed. I'll see you when I'm dressed."

But when I came downstairs he was dressed, sitting by the fire, looking a very sick and miserable boy of nine years. When I put my hand on his forehead I knew he had a fever.

"You go up to bed," I said, "you're sick."

"I'm all right," he said.

When the doctor came he took the boy's temperature.

"What is it?" I asked him.

"One hundred and two."

Downstairs, the doctor left three different medicines in different colored capsules with instructions for giving them. One was to bring down the fever, another a purgative, the third to overcome an acid condition. The germs of influenza can only exist in an acid condition, he

Evaluate Characterization What does the narrator's description say about the boy?

Dialogue Hemingway uses dialogue to set the plot in motion. Based on this dialogue, what do you think the story will be about?

---

1 **Schatz** (shäts) is a German term of affection meaning *dear* or *darling*.

explained. He seemed to know all about influenza and said there was nothing to worry about if the fever did not go above one hundred and four degrees. This was a light epidemic of flu and there was no danger if you avoided pneumonia.

Back in the room I wrote the boy's temperature down and made a note of the time to give the various capsules.

"Do you want me to read to you?"

"All right. If you want to," said the boy. His face was very white and there were dark areas under his eyes. He lay still in the bed and seemed very detached from what was going on.

I read aloud from Howard Pyle's *Book of Pirates;* but I could see he was not following what I was reading.

"How do you feel, Schatz?" I asked him.

"Just the same, so far," he said.

I sat at the foot of the bed and read to myself while I waited for it to be time to give another capsule. It would have been natural for him to go to sleep, but when I looked up he was looking at the foot of the bed, looking very strangely.

"Why don't you try to go to sleep? I'll wake you up for the medicine."

"I'd rather stay awake."

After a while he said to me, "You don't have to stay in here with me, Papa, if it bothers you."

"It doesn't bother me."

"No. I mean you don't have to stay if it's going to bother you."

I thought perhaps he was a little light-headed and after giving him the prescribed capsules at eleven o'clock I went out for a while. It was a bright, cold day, the ground covered with a sleet that had frozen so that it seemed as if all the bare trees, the bushes, the cut brush and all the grass and the bare ground had been varnished with ice. I took the young Irish setter for a little walk up the road and along a frozen creek, but it was difficult to stand or walk on the glassy surface and the red dog slipped and slithered and I fell twice, hard, once dropping my gun and having it slide away over the ice.

Dialogue What is the "it" the boy is talking about?

We flushed a **covey** of quail under a high clay bank with overhanging brush and I killed two as they went out of sight over the top of the bank. Some of the covey lit in trees but most of them scattered into brush piles and it was necessary to jump on the ice-coated mounds of brush several times before they would flush. Coming out while you were poised unsteadily on the icy, springy brush they made difficult shooting, and I killed two, missed five, and started back pleased to have found a covey close to the house and happy there were so many left to find on another day.

At the house they said the boy had refused to let anyone come into the room.

"You can't come in," he said. "You mustn't get what I have."

I went up to him and found him in exactly the position I had left him, white-faced, but with the tops of his cheeks flushed by the fever, staring still, as he had stared at the foot of the bed.

I took his temperature.

"What is it?"

"Something like a hundred," I said. It was one hundred and two and four tenths.

"It was a hundred and two," he said.

"Who said so?"

"The doctor."

"Your temperature is all right," I said. "It's nothing to worry about."

"I don't worry," he said, "but I can't keep from thinking."

"Don't think," I said. "Just take it easy."

"I'm taking it easy," he said and looked straight ahead. He was evidently holding tight on to himself about something.

"Take this with water."

"Do you think it will do any good?"

"Of course it will."

I sat down and opened the *Pirate* book and commenced to read, but I could see he was not following, so I stopped.

"About what time do you think I'm going to die?" he asked.

Evaluate Characterization
Compare the words the boy says with the narrator's description of his actions. What do you think the boy is feeling?

Hot Night, 1932. Robert Sargent Austin. Chalk on paper. Private Collection, ©DACS.
View the Art In what ways is the boy in the drawing similar to the boy in the story?

"What?"

"About how long will it be before I die?"

"You aren't going to die. What's the matter with you?"

"Oh, yes, I am. I heard him say a hundred and two."

"People don't die with a fever of one hundred and two. That's a silly way to talk."

"I know they do. At school in France the boys told me you can't live with forty-four degrees. I've got a hundred and two."

He had been waiting to die all day, ever since nine o'clock in the morning.

"You poor Schatz," I said. "Poor old Schatz. It's like miles and kilometers.² You aren't going to die. That's a different thermometer. On that thermometer thirty-seven is normal. On this kind it's ninety-eight."

"Are you sure?"

"Absolutely," I said. "It's like miles and kilometers. You know, like how many kilometers we make when we do seventy miles in the car?"

"Oh," he said.

But his gaze at the foot of the bed relaxed slowly. The hold over himself relaxed too, finally, and the next day it was very slack and he cried very easily at little things that were of no importance. ❧

Dialogue Which character says this? How do you know?

BQ **BIG Question**

Why was the boy afraid? What can you learn from the story?

---

2 A *kilometer* is a length of measurement in the metric system. One kilometer is equivalent to approximately .62 of a mile.

After You Read

Respond and Think Critically

1. What is the boy's illness? What is his temperature? [Recall]

2. The father notices his son's strange behavior. Why doesn't he try to find out what's bothering his son? Explain. [Infer]

3. Use your own words to retell why the boy is confused about the seriousness of his illness. [Summarize]

4. How do you think the boy feels when his father goes hunting? Explain. [Connect]

5. How can you tell that the boy has been under a great deal of pressure all day? Support your answer with details from the story. [Interpret]

6. **BQ** BIG Question Why does the boy hide his fear all day? Do you consider his behavior courageous or foolish? Explain. [Conclude]

Academic Vocabulary

The boy spent much of the day in **isolation** in his bedroom. In the preceding sentence, *isolation* means the condition of being alone. Think about how being alone made the boy feel. How did the boy's choice not to tell his father about his worries affect his feelings of isolation?

TIP

Making Inferences
To answer question 2, you must make an inference. When you make an inference, you use clues and details in the story and your own knowledge and understanding to learn something that the writer does not tell you directly.

- Review the father's conversation with the doctor. What does the father know about the boy's illness? How would this knowledge affect the father's actions?

- Look back at the father's interaction with his son. What clues in the story explain the father's reactions to his son's behavior?

 Keep track of your ideas about the **BIG Question** in your unit Foldable.

 Literature Online

Selection Resources
For Selection Quizzes, eFlashcards, and Reading-Writing Connection activities, go to glencoe.com and enter QuickPass code GL27534u2.

Literary Element Dialogue

1. Do you think the dialogue in this story is realistic and believable? Explain.

2. How would the story be different without dialogue? Would you have responded to the characters in the same way if they did not speak? Explain.

Review: Style

As you learned on page 265, style is an author's personal way of using language through word choice and sentence arrangement. Hemingway is known, and often praised, for his distinctive style, which frequently includes short, simple sentences and few details. In "A Day's Wait," Hemingway uses a variety of sentence types to make his writing interesting. In writing dialogue, Hemingway uses short, direct sentences that imitate natural speech, or the way that people really talk. Hemingway also uses longer, more complex sentence structures. Look back at the story to help you answer these questions.

3. Find an example of short, direct dialogue in the story. Does it imitate natural speech? Explain.

4. Find an example of a longer, more complex sentence in the story. Does it contain details? If so, what are they?

Reading Strategy Evaluate Characterization

Standards Practice ELA7R1f

5. Based on the story, how does the boy feel about being sick?
   A   He is afraid and worried.
   B   He is looking forward to getting better.
   C   He is angry with his father.
   D   He is happy being left alone.

Grammar Link

Irregular Verbs An **irregular verb** is a verb that varies in its past and past participle forms. *To become* is an irregular verb. You cannot add *-d* to form the past tense. You say "After the test, I became tired." The most irregular verb in the English language is *to be.*

The following are some examples of commonly used irregular verbs:

Present Tense	Past Tense	Past Participle
become	became	become
give	gave	given
ride	rode	ridden
take	took	taken

Practice Find a sentence in the story with an irregular verb. Write down the irregular verb and then write five sentences using the subjects *I, you, he/she/it, we,* and *they* and the past participle of the verb.

Write with Style

Apply Sentence Structure Write a paragraph about a character who is afraid of something he or she doesn't understand. Imitate Hemingway's writing style by varying your sentence structure. Use simple and compound sentences. Simple sentences have one main clause and no subordinate clauses. (The boy was afraid.) Compound sentences have two or more main clauses, usually joined by a comma and a coordinating conjunction. (The boy was afraid, and he cried.)

The Monkey Who Asked for Misery

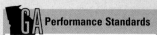

Performance Standards

For pages 284–288

ELA7R1e For literary texts, identify events that advance the plot.

Connect to the Folktale

In this folktale, the main character mistakes something bad for something good. Think about how someone might make that mistake. An example is wanting to do something that seems like fun but turns out to be dangerous or harmful.

Partner Talk With a partner, talk about how someone could mistake something bad for something good. What could happen as a result of this mistake?

Build Background

This folktale takes place in Haiti, a nation on the island of Hispaniola in the Caribbean Sea.

- A **folktale** is a traditional story that is passed down by word of mouth long before it is written. A folktale may change as each teller adds or varies details, but the basic story stays the same.

- Often folktales reinforce the traditions and values of the culture that preserves them. Folktales entertain and teach lessons.

- The characters in folktales may be animals, people with extraordinary powers, or ordinary people who have unusual experiences.

Set Purposes for Reading

BQ BIG Question

As you read, ask yourself what mistake Monkey makes and what lesson he learns. How might Monkey's story help readers?

Literary Element Conflict

Conflict is the central struggle between opposing forces in a story. Conflict is important in storytelling because it advances the plot. Characters have **external conflicts** when they struggle against some outside force, such as society. Characters have **internal conflicts** when they struggle against something inside themselves, such as their own emotions. As you read the folktale, ask yourself what conflicts Monkey faces and how the conflicts are resolved.

Meet Diane Wolkstein

International Storyteller
Diane Wolkstein has collected stories from Haiti, Israel, Egypt, Greece, and Turkey. She performs them at festivals, theaters, schools, and museums all over the world. She was born in 1942.

 Literature Online

Author Search For more about Diane Wolkstein, go to glencoe.com and enter QuickPass code GL27534u2.

The Monkey Who Asked for Misery

retold by Diane Wolkstein

Eight Huts in Haiti.
D. Roosevelt. Private
Collection.

onkey was sitting in a tree when a woman walked by on her way to market. Just as she passed, she tripped and the calabash[1] on her head fell off and broke. The sweet sugar-cane syrup in the calabash ran all over the ground.

"Good Lord, what Misery you have given me," she cried. "For three days I have been walking to market to sell this syrup and now I've lost it. Good Lord, Papa God, why did you give me such Misery?" But there was nothing to be done, so the woman continued on her way.

Monkey came down from the tree. What was this Misery Papa God had given the woman? He sniffed it. *Hmmm.* It

---

1 A **calabash** is a type of gourd, or large fruit. When hollowed out, they are often used as containers.

smelled good. He put one finger in and licked it. *Hmm.* He put in another finger. He put in his hand. And then one foot. And soon he was licking it up from the ground. *Th Th Th Th Th . . . Thh.* Then it was gone. But Monkey wanted more. He had not known Misery was so sweet. He decided to visit Papa God. He raced at top speed and found Papa God.

"Good morning, Papa God," said Monkey.

"Hello, Brother Monkey," said Papa God.

"I've come to see you, Papa God."

"Yes, Brother Monkey."

"Papa God—I want Misery."

"In the awful condition you're in, *you* want Misery?"

"Oh yes, Papa God, I need lots and lots and lots of Misery."

"Brother Monkey—"

"Papa God, I've already tasted Misery. I know how sweet it is."

"Well then, go over there. Do you see the three sacks? Take that one. No, not that one—*that* one. Yes. Put it on your back and walk until you come to a place where there are no trees. Then open it up. But remember, if you truly want lots of Misery, there must not be any trees in the place where you open it."

Monkey took the sack. He put it on his back. He thanked Papa God and left. He walked and walked and walked and walked and walked. He walked and walked and at last, he came to a place where there was not one tree to be seen. Monkey set the sack down. He looked in every direction. There was not one tree. He rubbed his stomach. He couldn't wait. He loosened the string of the sack and opened it up.

Rrrrrr. Rrrrr. Rrrrrrrr. Five huge dogs jumped out of the sack and began to chase Monkey. Monkey ran. The dogs followed close behind him. When Monkey had no breath left, a tree appeared. *One* tree. Monkey climbed that tree and the dogs barked and scratched, but they could not reach Monkey.

Papa God had sent the tree. Papa God sent the tree especially to Monkey.

Too much Misery at one time is not a good thing—even for Monkey. 🐾

Conflict What is Monkey's conflict? How is it both internal and external?

Conflict What type of conflict does Monkey now face?

BQ ▶ **BIG Question**
Why would someone retell this story?

After You Read

Respond and Think Critically

1. In your own words, tell what happens to the woman at the beginning of the story. [Summarize]

2. What clues in the story show that Monkey is an extraordinary animal? [Identify]

3. What mistake does Monkey make about "misery" at the beginning of the story? [Interpret]

4. What do this mistake and Monkey's other actions show about his character? [Analyze]

5. Why does Papa God decide to give Monkey the bag with dogs inside? [Infer]

6. **BQ** BIG Question How can you apply what you have learned from this folktale to your own life? Explain what you would do or not do. [Connect]

Academic Vocabulary

Monkey confused the sweet syrup with misery. **Consequently,** he wanted more of it.

In the preceding sentence, *consequently* means "as a result." Think about how Papa God's attitude toward Monkey changes when Monkey ignores his warnings about misery. What actions does Papa God take? Why does he do these things? Then fill in the blank in the following statement.

Papa God can't convince Monkey that misery is a bad thing. Consequently, Papa God decides to _____.

TIP

Summarizing
To answer question 1, remember that when you summarize, you retell events in your own words.

- Skim the beginning of the story to remind yourself of what happens to the woman.

- Using transitional words such as *first, next, then,* and *last,* retell what happens to the woman in your own words.

 Keep track of your ideas about the **BIG Question** in your unit Foldable.

 Literature Online

Selection Resources
For Selection Quizzes, eFlashcards, and Reading-Writing Connection activities, go to glencoe.com and enter QuickPass code GL27534u2.

Literary Element | Conflict

1. List three external conflicts characters have in this folktale.

2. Papa God wants to teach Monkey a lesson through conflict. Do you think it is fair of Papa God to give Monkey the bag of dogs when Monkey thinks he will be getting syrup? Explain.

Review: Theme

As you learned on page 135, the **theme** is the main idea or message of a story. Sometimes, the theme is stated in the story, but more often it is not. The theme may be shown through the actions of characters or in other ways. Folktales from different times and places often have similar themes or lessons. These themes are called **recurring,** or repeated, themes.

Because the theme of "The Monkey Who Asked for Misery" is not stated directly, the reader must determine what it is. Use the graphic organizer below to find clues in the folktale that help you identify the theme.

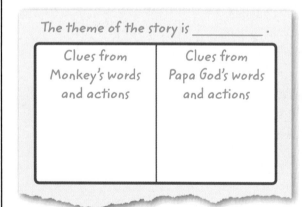

The theme of the story is _____.

Clues from Monkey's words and actions	Clues from Papa God's words and actions

Standards Practice ELA7R1d

3. The theme of the folktale is
   A   run fast when being chased by dogs.
   B   don't eat too many sweets.
   C   be careful when walking to the market.
   D   be careful what you desire.

Grammar Link

Infinitives An **infinitive** is a verb form that may function as a noun, an adjective, or an adverb. An infinitive is formed from the word *to* together with the base form of a verb.

> **To dance** well requires practice. (noun: subject of the sentence)

> My sister wants **to dance.** (noun: object of *wants*)

> Rafael had permission **to attend.** (adjective: describes what kind of permission)

> Angela left early **to meet** her sister at the airport. (adverb: answers the question *why?*)

How can you tell whether the word *to* is a preposition or part of an infinitive? If the word *to* comes immediately before a verb, it is part of the infinitive.

> Those young players want **to win.** (infinitive)

> The coach is pointing **to the pitcher.** (prepositional phrase)

Practice Write down three infinitives from the folktale. Tell whether they function as nouns, adjectives, or adverbs. Then, use an infinitive to write your own sentence about Monkey's experience.

Research and Report

Visual/Media Presentation Use the Internet or a library to research a culture's folktales. Select a folktale to read aloud to the class. Make a poster or an electronic presentation to display the folktale. Find art or photos in a book or on the Internet to illustrate the folktale. Include the name of the person who created the artwork and the name of the book or the Web site where the art appears.

Do Animals Lie?

Connect to the Magazine Article

Animals may deceive each other in order to survive, but do you think that they lie in the same way that people do?

Quickwrite Freewrite for a few minutes about why humans lie. Use your own knowledge to compare the way animals lie with the way that humans do.

Build Background

The magazine article "Do Animals Lie?" is about how animals survive by fooling other animals.

- Animals compete with one another for food and water. It may be necessary for animals to trick each other to get these necessities.

- Animals of the same kind compete with each other to produce offspring. Males may trick each other to be able to mate with females.

Vocabulary

survival (sər vī′ vəl) *n.* the continuation of life (p. 291). *The group worked for the survival of endangered species.*

predator (pred′ ə tər) *n.* an animal that kills and eats other animals (p. 292). *A spider is a predator that traps and eats flies and other insects.*

courtship (kôrt′ ship′) *n.* the act, process, and time period that leads up to mating between animals (p. 292). *During courtship, a male bird may display his colorful feathers to impress the female bird.*

parasites (par′ ə sīts′) *n.* plants or animals that live in or on other plants or animals and that get all they need from their hosts and provide nothing in return (p. 293). *Worms living inside the stomach of a dog are dangerous parasites that can make the dog sick.*

Meet Mary Batten

"I feel very lucky to be a science writer because I can follow my curiosity wherever my questions take me."

—Mary Batten

Nature Lover Mary Batten learned to love nature as a child playing in the woods and streams of rural Virginia. Today she writes books, television documentaries, and magazine articles about "anything and everything in the natural world," she says. Her topics include human behavior, ecology, animals, plants, health, disease, stars, and galaxies. She was born in 1937.

 Literature Online

Author Search For more about Mary Batten, go to glencoe.com and enter QuickPass code GL27534u2.

Set Purposes for Reading

BQ **BIG Question**

As you read, ask yourself, can we ever completely understand animal behavior?

Literary Element **Text Structure**

Text structure is the way a piece of writing is organized. Text structures in informational writing include **problem and solution, compare and contrast,** and **cause and effect.** The text structure of this article is **classification.** In classification, the writer creates groups on the basis of shared characteristics. In this article, each of the first four subheads groups together similar types of animals and describes behaviors of animals within each group. As you read, think about how the information in each subhead helps explain whether animals lie.

Reading Strategy **Analyze Evidence**

When you **analyze evidence,** you look at the writer's reasons, facts, examples, and details to see if they support the main idea of the writer's argument. Writers have to provide evidence from reliable sources to support their claims. A reliable source may be an expert on the subject, a reference book, or a reputable Web site. To analyze evidence, look at the writer's claims and ask yourself if she supports her claims with examples, facts, and reasons from reliable sources. Then decide if the writer's evidence is strong enough to persuade you to accept her claims.

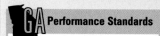

GA **Performance Standards**

For pages 289–296

ELA7R1c For informational texts, apply knowledge of common organizational structures and patterns.

> **TRY IT**
>
> **Analyze** Think of something you would like to change at your school. Now think of reasons, facts, and examples that support your idea to change something. Imagine that you are going to present your argument to the principal. Would your evidence be enough to persuade the principal to make the change?

Question: Do animals purposely lie as people do?

Writer's claim:

Evidence that animals do lie:	Do these examples show that animals purposely lie? Are there enough examples? Is the information from reliable sources?

My conclusion about the evidence:

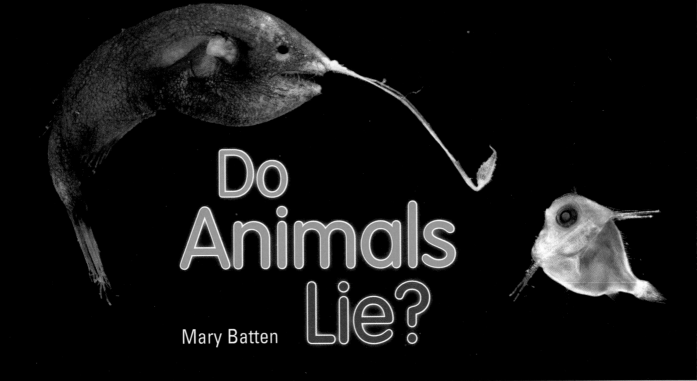

Do Animals Lie?

Mary Batten

It's no secret. Insects, birds, apes—all kinds of animals—cheat, bluff, and trick each other. Why? Because being deceptive[1] can give animals the edge on **survival.** It can help them escape their enemies, catch their prey, and even attract a mate.

PHONY FISH

An anglerfish is like a living lie. Dangling from a spine on the tip of its snout is a built-in fishing lure. Depending on the type of anglerfish, the fake bait may look like a worm, bunches of algae, or tiny shrimp—all tasty tidbits to a passing fish. When an angler is hungry, it simply casts its "rod" straight ahead and jiggles the false bait in front of its mouth. Pity the fish that is fooled and swims near. Snap! Rather than finding a meal, it ends up in the angler's stomach.

An anglerfish (left) tempts its prey with the tasty-looking fake bait on the tip of its snout.

Analyze Evidence What evidence does the writer provide to support her claim that the anglerfish is a "living lie"?

---

1 **Deceptive** behaviors are misleading actions, such as tricking or fooling someone or lying to someone.

Vocabulary

survival (sər vī′ vəl) *n.* the continuation of life

Although it's rather small, a comet fish doesn't need to flee when it is threatened by its enemies in the coral reef. Instead, it fools them by transforming its six-inch-long body into a copy of the six-inch-long head of a moray eel—a large, sharp-toothed **predator** that causes other reef animals to swim for their lives.

INSECT IMPOSTERS

Animals can usually tell males from females, but sometimes an individual isn't what he or she seems.[2] During **courtship**, a male scorpionfly must hunt and catch a tasty insect to present as a gift to a female. The insect gift must be just the right size, or a female will reject the male and fly away. When a courting male has caught an insect, he hangs from a leaf or twig and releases a special chemical perfume that signals females to come over and have a look. If a female likes the gift, she hangs in front of the male and lowers her wings to accept it. Then the male gives her the gift and mates with her while she eats it.

But sometimes a male scorpionfly is fooled. What looks like a female is really a male trickster that steals the gift and uses it to attract a female of his own. It might not seem fair, but it's a strategy that works. Deceitful male scorpionflies succeed in mating—and fathering babies—

The harmless comet fish (below) copies the dangerous looks of a moray eel (top).

Text Structure Why does the author group the anglerfish and comet fish together in this section of the article?

---

2 An *imposter* is a person who acts like something he or she is not.

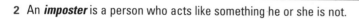

Vocabulary

predator (pred´ə tər) *n.* an animal that kills and eats other animals

courtship (kôrt´ship´) *n.* the act, process, and time period that leads up to mating between animals

more often than those that do their own hunting. The more babies an animal has, the more successful it is in passing its genes[3] on to future generations—the only kind of success that counts in evolution.

You've probably seen fireflies, or lightning bugs, flashing on a warm summer evening. Each species[4] of firefly has its own special flashing signal that males and females of that species use to tell each other when they are ready to mate. But the flashes of some female *Photuris* fireflies are deadly. These females can mimic, or imitate, the flashing signal that females of another group, named *Photinus*,[5] use to attract mates. When a *Photinus* male responds to the *Photuris's* false signal, he finds out too late that there is no mate waiting for him. The tricky *Photuris* female eats him instead.

But two can play the false flashing game, and sometimes the *Photuris* female is tricked. When she flashes her false signal, a sneaky *Photuris* male might approach her, mimicking the answering flashes of a *Photinus* male. The hungry *Photuris* female, expecting a *Photinus* male she can devour, instead finds herself greeting a male of her own species who is seeking a mate.

BLUFFING BIRDS

Brood **parasites,** a group of birds that includes cowbirds, cuckoos, and widow birds, have found a way to avoid much of the work of parenthood. They don't bother building nests. Instead, they sneak their eggs into other birds' nests and let them hatch the eggs. Some parasites are able to pull off this trick because their eggs mimic the size and color of the host birds' eggs. What happens when the sneaky parasite's egg hatches? The host birds usually

---

3 *Genes* are parts of the cells of all living things. They carry traits from parents to offspring.

4 A *species* is a group of living things that shares certain traits. Members of the same species are able to mate and have offspring.

5 *Photuris* and *Photinus* fireflies are two different species. They cannot mate and produce offspring.

Vocabulary

parasites (par′ə sīts′) *n.* plants or animals that live in or on other plants or animals and that get all they need from their hosts and provide nothing in return

feed the chick, mistaking it for one of their own.

Among birds called scrub jays, some are thieves. Scrub jays typically cache some of their food; that is, they bury bits of it to eat later. When food is scarce, they can always find a meal by returning to eat a stored snack. But sometimes when a scrub jay caches its food, it is watched by a thief. The thieving scrub jay waits until the coast is clear, then digs up the food and steals it!

Can you spot the cuckoo's egg in this nest belonging to another bird species?

That's pretty tricky. But scrub jays who do the work of caching have a trick of their own. Scientists have observed that they seem to know about the thieves and to be aware of when they're being watched by a bird that might be one. To outsmart the thieves, cautious scrub jays will come back in secret and rebury their food in a different spot.

Analyze Evidence Is reburying food to fool another bird an example of lying? Why or not?

CHEATING CHIMPS

Scientists who study monkeys and apes have reported a wide range of deceptive behaviors, particularly among chimpanzees. Chimps bluff, give warning calls when there is no predator in sight, do all sorts of sneaky things behind the troop leader's back, and try to outsmart each other.

In one example, a chimp named Yeroen, who had been the alpha, or top, male of a group of chimps at the Arnhem Zoo in the Netherlands, began limping badly after he was hurt in a fight with Nikkie, the new alpha male. But Yeroen only bothered to limp when he was within sight of Nikkie. As soon as he turned a corner or circled behind Nikkie, the limp mysteriously disappeared.

Puist, another chimp, had a different way of fooling rivals. After a fight, one chimpanzee will extend a hand, as if offering to shake and make up. When Puist was getting nowhere in a fight, she would sometimes stop, approach slowly, and extend her hand. When her opponent accepted her friendly gesture and did the same, Puist would grab the hand and launch another attack.

TRUE LIES?

Animals are deceptive, sure. But can any of them be said to purposely lie, like people do? Are their deceptions the result of deliberate choice—or just unthinking instinct?[6] In some cases, scientists aren't certain.

Fake fish bait and egg mimicry are deceits that evolved over many thousands of years through natural selection.[7] Traits such as these, which improve an animal's ability to survive and reproduce successfully, are passed on from parents to offspring, from one generation to another. Such deceptions are mere instinct. A baby cowbird doesn't decide to fool its host parents into feeding it. It just hatches from its egg and expects to be fed.

On the other hand, scientist Frans de Waal, the expert on primate[8] behavior who observed Yeroen and Puist, considers both their bluffs to be examples of calculated deception. Yeroen and Puist seemed able to imagine what another animal would do in a given situation, and acted accordingly. They behaved as if they were purposely fooling their foes—rather like human liars.

One thing seems clear—nature often favors the trickster. Perhaps even human tricksters. While we don't think of lying as a good thing, it's possible, say some scientists, that the efforts of early humans to trick and outsmart each other may have spurred the evolution of larger brains and greater intelligence, including the distinctly human ability to use language. Inventing clever tricks and lies requires brainpower. And so does the ability to see through them and seek the truth. Indeed, survival can depend on being smarter than the tricksters.

But purposely choosing not to lie—something only humans seem able to do—may be the smartest action of all. 🐾

---

6 **Instincts** are natural behavior patterns. Instincts are present at birth, not taught. Instinct causes living things to react without thinking to something in their environment.

7 **Natural selection** is a process that results in the survival of individuals and groups of plants and animals that are best suited for life in a particular environment.

8 **Primates** are a group of mammals that includes humans, apes, and monkeys.

Text Structure In what way is this section of the article different than the other sections?

BQ BIG Question
In what way do these statements affect your understanding of lying and human and animal behavior?

After You Read

Respond and Think Critically

1. How do female *Photuris* fireflies act as imposters? [Recall]

2. Have you ever had an experience with an animal in which the animal behaved deceptively? Describe your experience. Do you think the behavior was instinctive or on purpose? [Connect]

3. In your own words, explain why some scientists think that tricking and outsmarting may have helped humans develop greater intelligence. [Paraphrase]

4. **Literary Element** Text Structure Why do you think the author chose to use classification as the text structure for this article? [Analyze]

5. **Reading Strategy** Analyze Evidence How reliable is the evidence in this article? Use the graphic organizer you created to help you answer the question. [Evaluate]

6. **BQ** BIG Question How did reading this article change your understanding of animal behavior? Explain. [Evaluate]

Vocabulary Practice

Synonyms are words that have the same or nearly the same meaning. **Antonyms** are words that have opposite meanings. Identify whether each set of paired words are synonyms or antonyms. Then write a sentence using the first word of each pair or draw or find a picture that represents the word.

    survival and existence   courtship and dating
    predator and prey   parasites and hosts

Example:
survival and existence = synonyms

Sentence: The survival of our way of life depends on finding new sources of energy.

Writing

Write a Summary On page 219, you learned what a summary is. Write a summary of the article "Do Animals Lie?" Batten uses subheads to organize her article. These subheads can help you write a summary. Summarize the main idea and important details of each subhead. Use your own words, and be sure not to change Batten's ideas or to include your own opinion.

TIP

Evaluating
To answer question 6, think about what you learned about animal behaviors from the article. Then think about what you know to be true about animals from your own experience.

- What did you think about animal behavior before you read the article? What do you think after reading the article?

- Did any of the author's examples change your opinion about animal behavior? If so, which examples, and why?

FOLDABLES
Study Organizer Keep track of your ideas about the **BIG Question** in your unit Foldable.

 Literature Online

Selection Resources
For Selection Quizzes, eFlashcards, and Reading-Writing Connection activities, go to glencoe.com and enter QuickPass code GL27534u2.

One's Name Is Mud

Connect to the Essay

The English language has many expressions that refer to literary characters or people from history.

Graphic Organizer Create a chart like the one below. Use a dictionary or online sources to find the meanings of the underlined words in each sentence. Then write the meaning of each sentence.

Sentence	Meaning of words	Meaning of sentence
He added his <u>John Hancock</u> to the petition.		
She has the <u>Midas touch</u>.		

Meet Leonard Mann

Lover of Language Leonard Mann is a retired minister and the author of many books. "One's Name Is Mud" comes from his book titled *Green-Eyed Monsters & Good Samaritans*, which explores the possible origins of many common expressions. Leonard Mann lives in Lancaster, Ohio.

 Literature Online

Author Search For more about Leonard Mann, go to glencoe.com and enter QuickPass code GL27534u2.

Build Background

This essay discusses events surrounding the assassination of Abraham Lincoln.

- John Wilkes Booth shot President Lincoln as Lincoln was attending a play at Ford's Theater in Washington, D.C., in 1865.

- A man associated with Booth stabbed Lincoln's secretary of state, William Seward, that same night. Seward lived.

Vocabulary

conspirator (kən spir′ə tôr) *n.* a person who secretly plans with others to do something evil or illegal (p. 300).
He was a conspirator in the plan to dump trash into the river.

epithet (ep′ə thet′) *n.* a descriptive word or phrase used with or in place of a name (p. 300).
My friend Sally Gerhard is often laughing, so I use the epithet "Giggling Gerhard" when we are together.

integrity (in teg′rə tē) *n.* honesty; sincerity (p. 300).
George Washington showed his integrity by admitting to cutting down a cherry tree.

Set Purposes for Reading

BQ BIG Question

Read this essay to find out how a common phrase may have come into the English language.

Literary Element Diction

You've learned that **diction** refers to the author's choice and arrangement of words. Authors choose words carefully depending on their purpose for writing. Think about the word *bunny*. The exact meaning of *bunny* is "rabbit." That is its **denotation.** But many people think of a bunny as cute and cuddly. Those are **connotations** of the word *bunny*. An author may use the word *bunny* in order to create a certain feeling in the reader.

Diction, including denotation and connotation, is an important part of writing. Diction creates feelings and images for the reader and helps bring him or her into a selection.

As you read, notice the author's diction. How do certain words make you feel?

Reading Strategy Analyze Text Structure

In **cause-and-effect text structure,** the text is arranged to show the relationship between outcomes and their causes. A cause is a condition or event that makes something happen. What happens as the result of a cause is an effect. Cause-and-effect structures are used often in science, social science, and history books.

Cause and effect is important because it helps you understand the reasons for and the results of events or actions. Remember that one cause may have many effects.

As you read, ask yourself, why? What caused that to happen? Then, look for signal words, such as *because, so,* and *as a result*. You may find it helpful to use a graphic organizer like the one below. As you read, arrange ideas and events in the boxes and draw arrows to show how one idea or event flows into another.

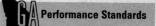

Performance Standards

For pages 297–301

ELA7R1c For informational texts, apply knowledge of common organizational structures and patterns.

> **TRY IT**
>
> With a partner, talk about a few experiences you've had that are examples of cause and effect. For example, *I wasn't happy with my grade on the math quiz, so I talked to my teacher after school*. Or, *Because my mother is working late this week, I am taking care of my younger brother.*

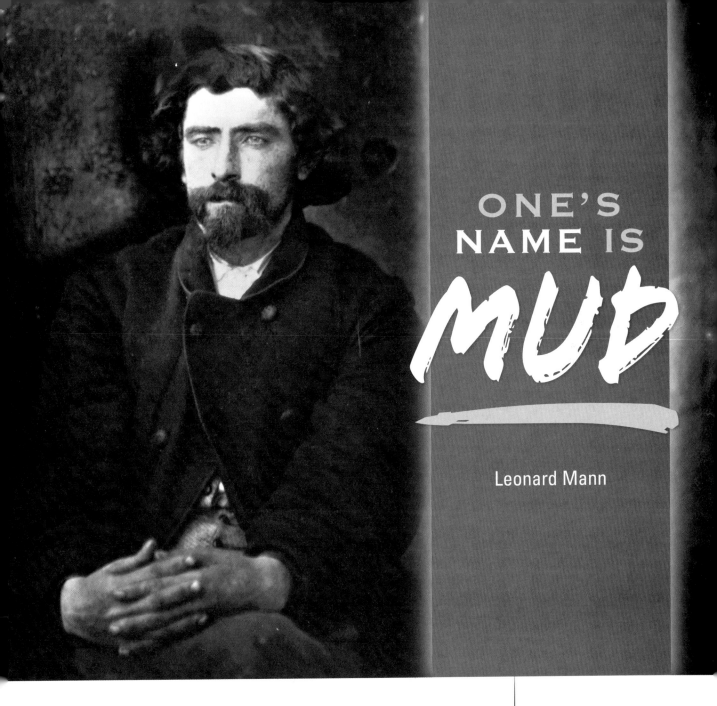

ONE'S NAME IS

MUD

Leonard Mann

After school, Johnny says to Marianne, "If I don't go straight home, my name will be mud." "My name will be mud if I go golfing today," says Joe, knowing he has promised to take his kids to the playground. The meaning is obvious: when in disfavor, *one's name is mud.* But why mud? Why not some other disagreeable thing?

BQ BIG Question

What do you think you'll read about in this selection?

The story begins just five days after the end of the Civil War, April 14, 1865. That evening, President Lincoln was seated in the balcony of Ford's Theater in Washington when John Wilkes Booth sneaked in and shot him. Leaping from the balcony, and breaking a leg in the leap, the assassin[1] managed to escape. At four o'clock the next morning he and a fellow **conspirator** were at the farmhouse door of Dr. Samuel Mudd near Bryantown, Maryland. Being a dedicated physician, the doctor set the stranger's broken leg, and later that day the two men rode away.

It was known within a few days that Dr. Mudd's patient had been Mr. Lincoln's assassin. Together with many others, Mudd was arrested and charged with involvement in the plot. Although no evidence was ever offered against him, in the hysteria[2] of the time, Dr. Mudd was found guilty, sentenced to life imprisonment, and incarcerated[3] at Fort Jefferson in the Gulf of Mexico. Feelings of hostility were so strong against him that his very name became an **epithet** denoting disfavor.

As time would tell, the popular attitude against the man was wholly unjustified. During an epidemic of yellow fever, the prisoner exhibited exceptional heroism. Because of this and other evidences of the man's innocence and **integrity**, he was granted a pardon by President Andrew Johnson in 1869. Tragically, though, in those first awful years the damage was done—the good doctor's name is still mud. ✍

Analyze Text Structure This event caused other events to happen. Find the effects in this paragraph.

Diction Why might an author choose to use *mud* instead of *wet earth*? What connotations does the word *mud* have?

---

1 An ***assassin*** is a person who murders an important person.

2 ***Hysteria*** is extremely emotional behavior or overwhelming fear.

3 ***Incarcerated*** means "put into jail."

Vocabulary

conspirator (kən spir′ə tôr) *n.* a person who secretly plans with others to do something evil or illegal

epithet (ep′ə thet′) *n.* a descriptive word or phrase used with or in place of a name

integrity (in teg′rə tē) *n.* honesty; sincerity

After You Read

Respond and Think Critically

1. What was President Lincoln doing when he was shot? **[Recall]**

2. Describe what happened to Booth from the time he shot President Lincoln until he and a fellow conspirator left Dr. Mudd's farmhouse. **[Summarize]**

3. Do you think that Dr. Mudd's punishment was fair? Explain. **[Evaluate]**

4. **Literary Element** Diction What is the author's attitude toward Dr. Mudd? Which words from the essay give you clues about the author's attitude? **[Analyze]**

5. **Reading Strategy** Analyze Text Structure Dr. Mudd's actions may have had an effect on the English language. In which paragraph do you find this effect? **[Analyze]**

6. **BQ** BIG Question What kind of information can you get from essays such as "One's Name Is Mud"? **[Interpret]**

Vocabulary Practice

Match each boldfaced vocabulary word with a word from the right column that has the same meaning. Two of the words in the right column will not have matches. Then write a sentence or draw or find a picture that represents each word.

1. conspirator   **a.** plotter
2. epithet   **b.** truthfulness
3. integrity   **c.** investigator
                        d. nickname
                        e. panic

Example:
dedicated

Sentence: The dedicated student rewrote his essay when he found incorrect information.

 Writing

Write a Letter Write a letter to Dr. Mudd. In the letter, explain whether you think he deserved to have the term "one's name is mud" associated with his name. Choose your words carefully and include words that have emotional connotations.

TIP

Evaluating
Question 3 asks for your opinion, as well as a reason for your answer. As you answer these types of questions, be sure to

• state your opinion clearly.

• support your opinion with information from the selection. Refer to specific facts, events, or people from the selection.

FOLDABLES Keep track of
Study Organizer your ideas about the **BIG Question** in your unit Foldable.

 Literature Online

Selection Resources For Selection Quizzes, eFlashcards, and Reading-Writing Connection activities, go to glencoe.com and enter QuickPass code GL27534u2.

Before You Read

Tending Sir Ernest's Legacy

Connect to the Web Site

Think of a time when you wanted to be the first to do something. How did it feel to push yourself to a goal? Who or what helped you with your challenge? What hurdles did you have to overcome?

Partner Talk With a partner, talk about a time when you set a goal and achieved it. Who or what helped you achieve your goal? How did you feel once you achieved it?

Build Background

"Tending Sir Ernest's Legacy" includes a timeline of Sir Ernest Shackleton's voyage across Antarctica and an interview with his granddaughter, Alexandra Shackleton.

- One of the seven continents, Antarctica is mostly covered by a large ice sheet.

- Lichens (a type of moss) and penguins thrive in Antarctica, despite the very cold temperatures.

- Travel to Antarctica was extremely difficult in Shackleton's time, the early part of the twentieth century. Today, icebreakers and aircraft make the journey easier.

- In the winter, temperatures in Antarctica range from -128.6°F to -76°F.

Vocabulary

legacy (leg′ə sē) *n.* anything received from an ancestor or a previous time (p. 305). *A love of music is the legacy my grandmother left me.*

pragmatic (prag mat′ik) *adj.* concerned with practical results (p. 309). *My pragmatic brother was able to quickly find a solution to our problem.*

futile (fū′til) *adj.* useless, hopeless, ineffective (p. 313). *Our attempts to find the contact lens in the swimming pool were futile.*

Meet Kelly Tyler-Lewis

PBS Producer Kelly Tyler-Lewis is a historian and a producer for the NOVA series on PBS. She first became interested in polar exploration when she saw a 1985 PBS program about the Antarctic expeditions of Robert Falcon Scott and Roald Amundsen. She began working for NOVA in 1989. She has worked on many television programs and films for NOVA, including *The Endurance: Shackleton's Epic Journey.*

 Literature Online

Author Search For more about Kelly Tyler-Lewis, go to glencoe.com and enter QuickPass code GL27534u2.

Set Purposes for Reading

BQ BIG Question

As you read, ask yourself, what would be exciting about being an explorer? What would be difficult?

Literary Element Text Features

Like books, magazine articles, and other forms of writing, Web sites have **text features** to help you find information quickly and easily. These text features include subheads, pictures, photographs, maps, illustrations, captions, charts, tables, and diagrams. Web sites, such as "Tending Sir Ernest's Legacy," often include a menu bar at the top of the page to help you navigate, or find your way around, the Web site and links that take you to other parts of the site or other sites.

Understanding text features will help you find information quickly. Make sure you look carefully at a Web site for links and other text features that can provide additional information.

As you read "Tending Sir Ernest's Legacy," notice how the information from the Web site is organized. In what ways do the text features help you find information?

Reading Skill Distinguish Fact and Opinion

A **fact** is a statement that can be proved to be true, such as "The sun sets in the west." An **opinion** is what a writer believes, based on his or her personal viewpoint. It cannot be proven. "The sunset was beautiful today" is an opinion. You, as a reader, can agree or disagree with an opinion.

When you read, you'll come across writers who try to convince you of their beliefs. When you **distinguish fact and opinion,** you tell when the writer is presenting a fact and when he or she is offering an opinion. Knowing the difference between facts and opinions will help you make up your own mind about the subject.

As you read, think about which parts of the timeline and interview are convincing. Are they facts or opinions? You can prove a fact by using references, such as books and reliable Web sites. If you can't prove a statement, then it is an opinion. Use a graphic organizer like the one below to help you distinguish fact and opinion as you read.

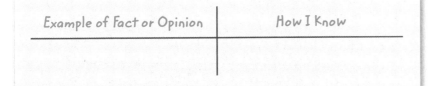

Example of Fact or Opinion	How I Know

GA Performance Standards

For pages 302–317

ELA7R1b For informational texts, identify and use knowledge of common graphic features to draw conclusions and make judgments.

TRY IT

Distinguish Fact and Opinion
A friend tells you about a movie he or she saw. How would you distinguish between the facts and opinions in your friend's story?

HOME   SEARCH   SITEMAP   FEEDBACK   BACK FORWARD

Tending Sir Ernest's Legacy:

An Interview with Alexandra Shackleton

by Kelly Tyler-Lewis for NOVA

EXPLORE ANTARCTIC ISLANDS | SITE MAP | RECOMMENDED BOOKS | E-MAIL US | FAQS

Sir Ernest could do far worse than have as his only granddaughter the Honorable Alexandra Shackleton. Life-president of the James Caird Society, which was founded to honor Shackleton and provide information about his expeditions, Ms. Shackleton looks after her grandfather's **legacy** about as well as the great man himself looked after his men.

Based in London, she has been instrumental in furthering Shackleton historical research, has contributed forewords to books on Antarctic exploration, and consulted for the Channel Four/First Sight Films television drama *Shackleton,* starring Kenneth Branagh. She has even had the honor to christen[1] three ships: the Royal Navy's Ice Patrol ship, *HMS Endurance;* the trawler *Lord Shackleton;* and, most recently, the British Antarctic Survey ship, *RRS Ernest Shackleton.*

In this intimate interview, hear insights about Sir Ernest's motivations and beliefs, strengths and imperfections, crushing disappointments and unparalleled achievements, as only a devoted granddaughter can have them.

NOVA: What was really pushing your grandfather to do this expedition to cross Antarctica?

Shackleton: Well, the Pole had been attained, so he had to abandon that dream. I think he considered it the last great Antarctic adventure—to cross the Antarctic from the Weddell Sea to the Ross Sea, a distance of about 1,800 miles. Of course, in those days it was felt that it should be done by somebody British. All of the nationalities felt that. The Germans felt that. The Americans felt that. The French felt that. And he considered he was pretty well fitted to do

Distinguish Fact and Opinion Is this statement a fact or an opinion? How do you know?

Text Features What text features tell you that this is an interview?

---

1   When you *christen* a ship, you give it a name in a ceremony.

Vocabulary
....

legacy (leg′ə sē) *n.* anything received from an ancestor or a previous time   Tending Sir Ernest's Legacy   **305**

it, having built up a reputation as a successful leader of the Nimrod Expedition [a 1907 attempt to reach the South Pole, of which he got within 100 miles before having to turn back].

NOVA: It was a pretty ambitious plan, given the stage of Antarctic exploration at that time. Was the monumental challenge part of the attraction?

Shackleton: It was ambitious, but I think he thought it was possible. He was a very practical person, and he would have never attempted anything that he thought could not be done. The main reason was that, above all, he had the lives of his men to consider.

NOVA: When your grandfather left England on the *Endurance*, the First World War[2] was about to start. What effect did that have on him?

Shackleton: Well, he offered his ship and men to Winston Churchill, who was Secretary of the Admiralty at the time. But he received a telegram back saying simply, "Proceed." So he felt it was perfectly honorable for him to proceed. He was then 40 years old, which would have been too old to fight, and he did lose two members of the expedition who were already in the army.

The thing one has to remember is that nobody thought the First World War would last more than a few months. It was a huge shock when they got back to South Georgia after their many, many adventures and found that the war was still raging.

NOVA: How do you think your grandfather felt at the moment when the *Endurance* was finally stuck in the ice,

BQ ▷ BIG Question
In what way do details in the interview affect your understanding of Shackleton?

Text Features Notice the links at the bottom of the Web page. What link would you click on if you wanted to find a list of books about Antarctic exploration?

2 The *First World War,* or World War I, lasted from 1914–1918.

and he realized he would never attain his goal of crossing Antarctica?

Shackleton: Well, when the ship got locked in the ice, it wasn't a sudden event, of course. The realization gradually dawned on them that the ship was not going to get out, that she was stuck—I think one of the crew members said "like an almond in toffee." Eventually, it became clear that she was being crushed by the ice and had no chance of rising above it. And my grandfather said to the captain, Frank Worsley, "the ship can't live in this, skipper." Then he started making plans for what could be done when the ship finally had to be abandoned. He was a great planner who was always working out what to do in every conceivable eventuality.

For several weeks the ship had been letting out terrible creaking and groaning noises like a human in agony, and then eventually my grandfather called out, "she's going boys," and they saw her disappear. He wrote in his diary, "I cannot write about it." He found it extremely distressing. Of course, it was the abandonment of his dream.

Yet he said to his men, quite calmly, "ship gone, stores gone, now we will go home." And he wrote in his diary, "a man must set himself to a new mark directly the old one goes." And what became his new mark was bringing every one of his 27 men home alive, from a part of the world where nobody knew they were. He knew there was no chance whatsoever of rescue. There were no communications. They might as well have been in space.

Distinguish Fact and Opinion Is this statement a fact or an opinion? Is it persuasive?

EXPLORE ANTARCTIC ISLANDS | SITE MAP | RECOMMENDED BOOKS | E-MAIL US | FAQS

HOME SEARCH SITEMAP FEEDBACK BACK FORWARD

NOVA: That was probably one of the toughest tests of his character, because he must have been bitterly disappointed.

Shackleton: Bitterly. Also, a ship is more to a sailor than just a floating home. It is a symbol. It's distressing for any captain, any leader of an expedition, to lose his ship.

NOVA: And yet he held himself together.

Shackleton: Indeed, and the men apparently felt reassured. After losing the ship, they felt rather adrift in every sense of the word, and yet he helped them to feel reassured. There was something to set themselves to do.

NOVA: What do you think was going through your grandfather's mind when they had to move onto the ice?

Shackleton: It was an awareness that there would almost certainly have to be a boat journey or several boat journeys. Each man was told he could bring two pounds weight of his own possessions. Leonard Hussey, who had a banjo, thought that he would have to leave it behind because it was too heavy, but my grandfather described it as a vital mental tonic. It proved to be that, though people got quite tired of his repertoire of six tunes.

My grandfather himself set an example. He threw out a handful of gold coins and his gold watch onto the snow, along with the Bible that Queen Alexandra had given him. He tore off the flyleaf[3] and put it in his pocket and threw the Bible onto the snow, but it was rescued by a sailor who thought it was very bad luck to throw a Bible away. Eventually both found their way to the Royal Geographical Society in London.

NOVA: How did you think he felt when he realized that his plan to travel over the ice was just not going to work?

EXPLORE ANTARCTIC ISLANDS | SITE MAP | RECOMMENDED BOOKS | E-MAIL US | FAQS

---

3 Here, a *flyleaf* is a specially printed page at the beginning of a book.

Shackleton: When that method didn't work, I think he simply switched to the next method. He was extremely **pragmatic,** and he always had many alternatives in his mind. Ernest Shackleton did not go in for soul-searching and self-recrimination. He would have called it a complete waste of valuable time.

NOVA: Now, on the journey to South Georgia aboard the *Caird,* how did your grandfather help the men cope with the horrendous conditions?

Shackleton: Well, he was well aware of the importance of a hot drink. Every man was fed every four hours, but if he noticed any member of the expedition failing slightly, he would order hot milk then and there, not just for him, but for everybody, so this man would not, as he put it, have doubts about himself. When he noticed one man suffering particularly from cold, he would rummage in the damp supplies and dig him out a pair of gloves.

NOVA: How do you think your grandfather felt when South Georgia appeared on the horizon?

Shackleton: When they saw South Georgia for the first time, and he realized that Worsley had accomplished his miracle of navigation, he felt huge relief, but sadly that was tempered instantly by the fact they could not land. There was a lee shore,[4] and they were very nearly driven onto the reefs and sunk. It took two days of agonies of thirst before they could actually land.

Distinguish Fact and Opinion How would you prove the statements in this paragraph?

EXPLORE ANTARCTIC ISLANDS | SITE MAP | RECOMMENDED BOOKS | E-MAIL US | FAQS

---

4 A *lee shore* is a shore toward which the wind is blowing. A lee shore can be dangerous to boats because they can be blown into the shore.

Vocabulary ....

pragmatic (prag mat´ik) *adj.* concerned with practical results

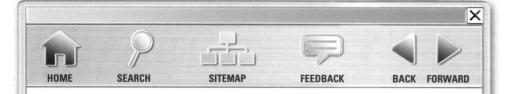

While they were struggling to land, Worsley said he felt this almost detached resentment that no one would ever know what they had accomplished. They would just be sunk as if they had been sunk at the beginning of the journey.

NOVA: Even today that journey is seen as nothing short of miraculous.

Shackleton: Yes. They had accomplished what many regard as the greatest small boat journey in the world, 800 miles across the stormiest seas in the world in a little boat not even 23 feet long—all the while encountering extremely harsh weather and suffering gales, privations[5] of thirst, hunger, and everything. It was a colossal achievement, and when they saw the black peaks of South Georgia, they felt huge relief and happiness.

NOVA: Was the *Endurance* expedition the greatest achievement of his life?

Shackleton: I think so, because against almost impossible odds he brought his 27 men home safely. The boat journey to South Georgia was an epic in itself, and climbing across the uncharted, unmapped island of South Georgia with no equipment was remarkable. To this day, no one has ever beaten his record of 30 miles in 36 hours.

Distinguish Fact and Opinion Is this statement a fact or an opinion? How can you tell?

EXPLORE ANTARCTIC ISLANDS | SITE MAP | RECOMMENDED BOOKS | E-MAIL US | FAQS

---

5 ***Privations*** are acts of taking away something, such as water or food.

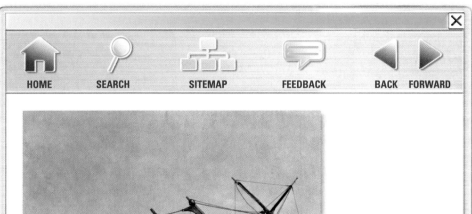

The *Endurance* in its final hours.

Text Features What additional information do the photo and caption provide?

Shackleton's Voyage of Endurance Timeline

When he left South Georgia Island on December 5, 1914, in his bid to be the first to cross the Antarctic continent, Ernest Shackleton had no idea that the next bit of land he touched (save for remote Elephant Island) would be that very same South Georgia—a year and a half later and after having not so much as set foot on the Antarctic continent. The story of what happened in between, outlined below, constitutes one of the most stupendous polar survival sagas of all time.

EXPLORE ANTARCTIC ISLANDS | SITE MAP | RECOMMENDED BOOKS | E-MAIL US | FAQS

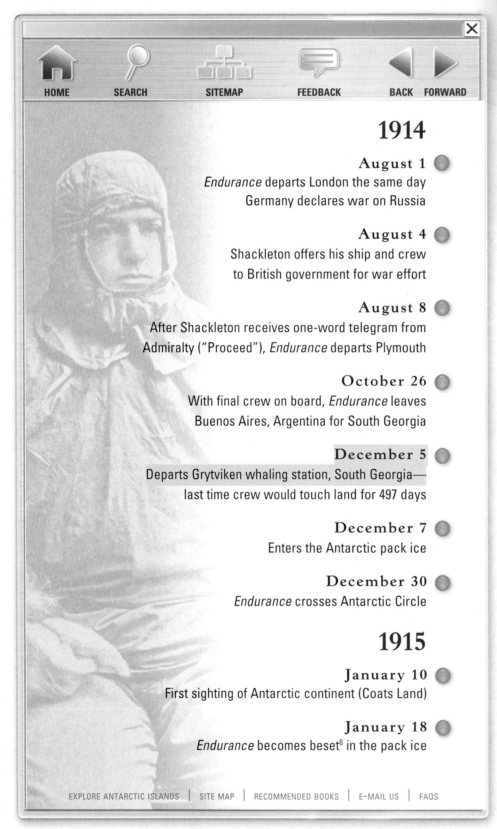

1914

August 1
Endurance departs London the same day
Germany declares war on Russia

August 4
Shackleton offers his ship and crew
to British government for war effort

August 8
After Shackleton receives one-word telegram from
Admiralty ("Proceed"), *Endurance* departs Plymouth

October 26
With final crew on board, *Endurance* leaves
Buenos Aires, Argentina for South Georgia

December 5
Departs Grytviken whaling station, South Georgia—
last time crew would touch land for 497 days

December 7
Enters the Antarctic pack ice

December 30
Endurance crosses Antarctic Circle

1915

January 10
First sighting of Antarctic continent (Coats Land)

January 18
Endurance becomes beset[6] in the pack ice

Text Features Which text features tell you this is a timeline?

EXPLORE ANTARCTIC ISLANDS | SITE MAP | RECOMMENDED BOOKS | E-MAIL US | FAQS

---

6 Here, **beset** means "surrounded" or "trapped."

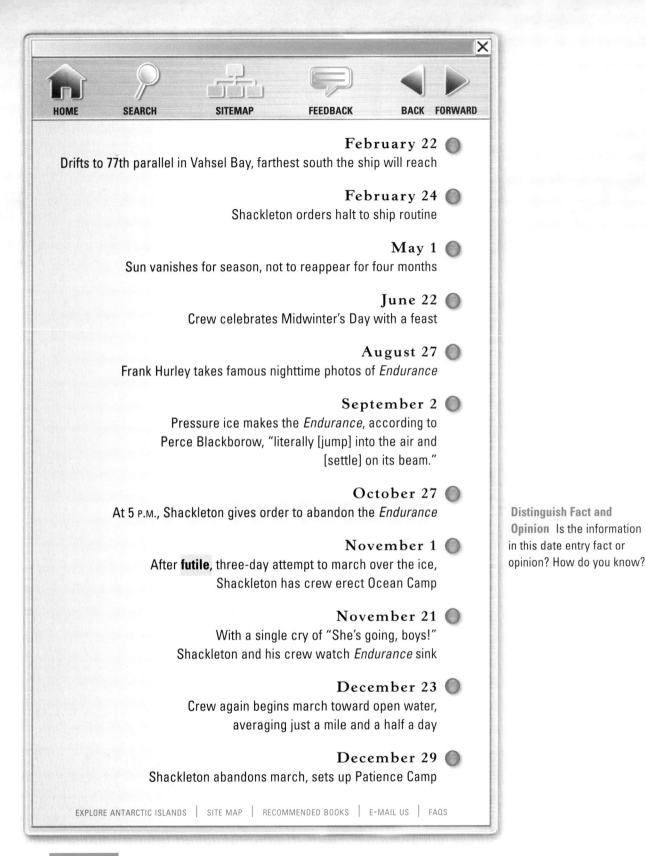

February 22

Drifts to 77th parallel in Vahsel Bay, farthest south the ship will reach

February 24

Shackleton orders halt to ship routine

May 1

Sun vanishes for season, not to reappear for four months

June 22

Crew celebrates Midwinter's Day with a feast

August 27

Frank Hurley takes famous nighttime photos of *Endurance*

September 2

Pressure ice makes the *Endurance*, according to Perce Blackborow, "literally [jump] into the air and [settle] on its beam."

October 27

At 5 P.M., Shackleton gives order to abandon the *Endurance*

November 1

After **futile**, three-day attempt to march over the ice, Shackleton has crew erect Ocean Camp

November 21

With a single cry of "She's going, boys!" Shackleton and his crew watch *Endurance* sink

December 23

Crew again begins march toward open water, averaging just a mile and a half a day

December 29

Shackleton abandons march, sets up Patience Camp

EXPLORE ANTARCTIC ISLANDS | SITE MAP | RECOMMENDED BOOKS | E-MAIL US | FAQS

Distinguish Fact and Opinion Is the information in this date entry fact or opinion? How do you know?

Vocabulary

futile (fū´til) *adj.* useless, hopeless, ineffective

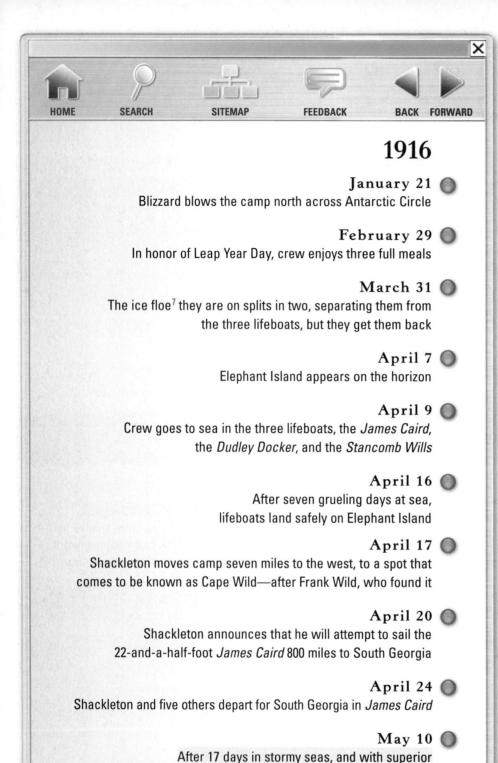

1916

January 21 ●
Blizzard blows the camp north across Antarctic Circle

February 29 ●
In honor of Leap Year Day, crew enjoys three full meals

March 31 ●
The ice floe[7] they are on splits in two, separating them from the three lifeboats, but they get them back

April 7 ●
Elephant Island appears on the horizon

April 9 ●
Crew goes to sea in the three lifeboats, the *James Caird*, the *Dudley Docker*, and the *Stancomb Wills*

April 16 ●
After seven grueling days at sea, lifeboats land safely on Elephant Island

April 17 ●
Shackleton moves camp seven miles to the west, to a spot that comes to be known as Cape Wild—after Frank Wild, who found it

April 20 ●
Shackleton announces that he will attempt to sail the 22-and-a-half-foot *James Caird* 800 miles to South Georgia

April 24 ●
Shackleton and five others depart for South Georgia in *James Caird*

May 10 ●
After 17 days in stormy seas, and with superior navigation by Frank Worsley, the *James Caird* miraculously arrives on the west coast of South Georgia

EXPLORE ANTARCTIC ISLANDS | SITE MAP | RECOMMENDED BOOKS | E-MAIL US | FAQS

Distinguish Fact and Opinion Which contains more opinions—the timeline or the interview?

---

7 An *ice floe* is a large sheet of ice floating on the surface of a body of water.

May 19

Shackleton, Worsley, and Crean set off to cross South Georgia's glacier-clad peaks to east-coast whaling stations

May 20

Having trekked without a break for 36 hours over glacier-clad mountains thousands of feet high, Shackleton, Worsley, and Crean arrive at Stromness whaling station

May 23

Shackleton, Worsley, and Crean depart on the English-owned Southern Sky to rescue men on Elephant Island, but are stopped by ice 100 miles short of the island

June 10

Uruguayan government loans the survey ship *Instituto de Pesca No 1*, which comes within sight of Elephant Island before pack ice turns it back

July 12

Chartered by the British Association, the schooner *Emma* sets out from Punta Arenas, but gets to within 100 miles of Elephant Island before storms and ice force it to return

August 25

Chilean authorities loan the *Yelcho*, a small steamer, which sets sail with Shackleton, Worsley, and Crean for Elephant Island

August 30

"I felt jolly near blubbing[8] for a bit & could not speak for several minutes," Wild wrote about seeing Shackleton arrive with the Yelcho, which rescued the party on this day, 22 months after they'd set out from South Georgia.

---

8 The phrase *I felt jolly near blubbing* is a British way of saying, "I felt really close to crying."

After You Read

Respond and Think Critically

1. What was the goal of Ernest Shackleton's expedition? Explain. [Recall]

2. How does Alexandra Shackleton feel about her grandfather? Use details from the interview to support your answer. [Infer]

3. How does the interviewer feel about Ernest Shackleton's expedition? Explain. [Infer]

4. Would you say that Shackleton's expedition was a success? Why or why not? [Analyze]

5. Do you think the interview shows an objective view of the expedition? Explain. [Evaluate]

6. **BQ** BIG Question Which details in the timeline and the interview helped you better understand the conditions in Antarctica and Shackleton's legacy? [Connect]

Vocabulary

Match each boldfaced vocabulary word with a word from the right column that has the same meaning. Two of the words in the right column will not have matches. Then write a sentence using each vocabulary word or draw or find a picture that represents the word.

1. **futile**   a. practical
2. **legacy**   b. hopeless
3. **pragmatic**   c. unsuspecting
                       d. myth
                       e. inheritance

Academic Vocabulary

Food was **distributed** to Shackleton's crew every four hours. In the preceding sentence, *distributed* means "handed out." Think about a time when you distributed something. To whom did you distribute the item or items?

TIP

Inferring
To answer question 2, you must think about details that are provided in the interview. You must also use your own knowledge of family relationships.

• Start by reviewing details in the story. What does Alexandra say about her grandfather? What opinions does she give?

• Consider what you know about family relationships. How might a family member who cares for another speak of him or her?

 Keep track of your ideas about the **BIG Question** in your unit Foldable.

 Literature Online

Selection Resources
For Selection Quizzes, eFlashcards, and Reading-Writing Connection activities, go to glencoe.com and enter QuickPass code GL27534u2.

Literary Element Text Features

1. What text features were used in the timeline and the interview? List examples.

2. How did these features add to your understanding of the subject? Explain.

Review: Author's Purpose

As you learned on page 211, the **author's purpose** is the intention of the author. For example, an author might write to explain, to tell a story, to persuade, to amuse, or to inform. An author may have more than one purpose for writing.

3. What do you think was the author's purpose for conducting and publishing the interview? Did the author have more than one purpose? Explain.

4. Which details in the interview reveal the author's purpose or purposes? For each of the purposes you identify, write down a sentence from the interview that supports it.

Reading Strategy Distinguish Fact and Opinion

5. Give two examples of facts provided in the interview. Then give two opinions. Were you easily able to distinguish the facts and opinions in the interview? Explain. To help you answer the question, refer to the graphic organizer you used as you read.

6. What did the opinions expressed add to your understanding of Shackleton and his legacy? Explain.

Grammar Link

Participles and Participial Phrases A **participle** is a verb form that can function as an adjective. **Present participles** are formed by adding *-ing* to a verb. For example:

> <u>crushing</u> disappointments
> a <u>floating</u> home

Past participles are formed by adding *-ed* to a verb. For example:

> <u>unparalleled</u> achievements
> an <u>abandoned</u> ship

Sometimes a participle that is used as an adjective is part of a phrase called a **participial phrase.** This is a group of words that include a participle and other words that complete its meaning. For example:

> <u>Trekking without a break for 36 hours,</u> Shackleton, Worsley, and Crean finally arrived at the whaling station.

The participial phrase, "Trekking without a break for 36 hours," modifies the nouns *Shackleton, Worsley,* and *Crean.*

Practice Write four sentences about events in the timeline or in the interview. The first two sentences should contain participles. The second two sentences should contain participial phrases.

Research and Report

Internet Connection Use the Internet to research other expeditions to dangerous, remote places. Find out who was involved, where they went, and what they did. Use only reliable Web sites and keep track of your sources. Check the validity of sources by examining several sources of information. Use word-processing software to create a report. Add maps and charts to your report, and share your report with the class.

GA Performance Standards

For pages 318–323

ELA7R1c For informational texts, apply knowledge of common organizational structures and patterns.

from Shipwreck at the Bottom of the World

by Jennifer Armstrong

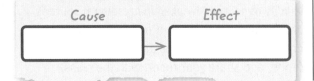

NCTE Orbis Pictus Award

Set a Purpose for Reading

Read to learn more historical facts about the journey of Sir Ernest Shackleton in the Antarctic.

Build Background

This selection focuses on the later part of Shackleton's expedition, when Shackleton and five of his men made a difficult journey by open boat to South Georgia Island, a mountainous island in the South Atlantic Ocean.

Reading Skill Identify Cause-and-Effect Relationships

To identify cause-and-effect relationships, look at how events are related to one another. A cause is an event or a condition that makes something happen. What happens as a result of a cause is an effect. As you read, take notes on cause-and-effect relationships using a graphic organizer like the one below.

Cause		Effect
	→	

The Boss

Imagine yourself in the most hostile place on earth. It's not the Sahara or the Gobi Desert. It's not the Arctic. The most hostile place on earth is the Antarctic, the location of the South Pole. When winter descends on the southern continent, the seas surrounding the land begin to freeze at the terrifying rate of two square miles every minute, until the frozen sea reaches an area of seven million square miles, about twice the size of the United States. Just imagine yourself stranded in such a place. In 1915, a British crew of 28 men *was* stranded there, with no ship and no way to contact the outside world. Fortunately they were led by Ernest Shackleton, a polar explorer famous for bringing his men home alive.

The crew was somewhat in awe of Ernest Shackleton, whom they all called Boss. Shackleton was a master at keeping his crew working together. Whenever he found two men who had quarreled and were not speaking to each other, he told them, "Stop and forget it," and made them shake hands.

Shipwreck: Stuck in the Ice

The last stop the expedition's ship, *Endurance,* made before taking on the challenge of the Antarctic was a whaling station on South Georgia Island. Soon after leaving the station on December 5, 1914, *Endurance* was caught in pack ice in the Weddell Sea and then frozen in place for the winter. All the crew could do was wait and hope that the drifting ice pack, which was slowly moving north, would carry them closer to land.

Toward the spring, great masses of ice pushed by the wind first toppled and then crushed the ship, forcing the men onto the ice. They tried to drag their three lifeboats toward land, but the boats weighed a ton each and enormous slabs of ice jutted out of the pack at all angles, blocking their way. Instead they made a camp and waited for the ice pack to break up. More than a year after *Endurance* first became stuck in the ice, the crew was able to row the lifeboats into the open ocean. At this point their lives depended on their making land at either Elephant or Clarence Island, the tiny islands at the tip of the Antarctic peninsula. If they missed the islands the nearest land was

South America, and they would almost certainly die at sea. After six horrific days in the lifeboats, they reached Elephant Island on April 16, 1916. But the island was barren and many of the men were near collapse. It was clear that somebody would have to try to reach the whaling station on South Georgia Island before winter set in.

Shipwreck: The Open Boat Journey

Shackleton handpicked five men for the relief party he would lead. The ship's carpenter refitted one of the lifeboats, the *James Caird,* for the journey. The men loaded it with bags of stone to keep it steady, boxes of food, a hand pump, a cook pot, a camp stove, two kegs of drinking water, and six reindeer-skin sleeping bags. As they shoved off, the 22 men left behind cheered and waved. "Good luck, Boss!" they shouted.

The living arrangements on board were uncomfortable and cramped. It was a tossup which was worse—being pounded up and down in the bow of the boat in a sorry excuse for sleep, or huddling in the cockpit as icy seas swept across thwarts and gunwales.[1] The men were dressed in wool, which got wet and stayed wet for the duration of the voyage. With temperatures below freezing, and no room to move around to get their blood stirred up, they were always cold. Miserably cold. Waves broke over the bows, where bucketfuls of

---

1 *Thwarts* are rowers' seats in a boat, and *gunwales* are the upper edges of a boat's sides.

On their seventh day at sea, the wind turned into a gale roaring up from the Pole; the temperature plummeted. The men began to fear that the sails would freeze up and cake with ice, becoming heavier and heavier until the boat toppled upside down. With the gale howling around their ears, they took down their sails.

Throughout the night, waves crashed over the *James Caird* and quickly turned to ice. At first the crew was relieved, since it meant the flimsy decking was sealed against further leaks. But when they awoke on the eighth day, they felt the clumsy, heavy motion of the boat beneath them and knew they were in trouble: 15 inches of ice encased the boat above the waterline, and she was rolling badly.

The ice had to come off. Taking turns, the men crawled on hands and knees over the deck, hacking away with an ax. "First you chopped a handhold, then a kneehold, and then chopped off ice hastily but carefully with an occasional sea washing over you," one of the men explained. Each man could stand only five minutes or so of this cold and perilous job at a time. Then it was the next man's turn.

By the time the gale ended, everything below was thoroughly soaked. The sleeping bags were so slimy and revolting that Shackleton had the two worst of them thrown overboard. Exposure was beginning to wear the men down. They were cold, frostbitten, and covered with salt-water blisters. Their legs were

Shackleton's ship *Endurance* stuck in polar ice.

water streamed through the flimsy decking. The bottom of the boat was constantly full of water, and the two men on watch who weren't steering were always bailing or pumping. The reindeer-skin sleeping bags were soaking wet all the time, and beginning to rot. Loose reindeer hair found its way into the men's nostrils and mouths as they breathed, into their water and food as they ate.

rubbed raw from the chafing of their wet pants, and they were exhausted from lack of sleep.

When someone looked particularly bad, the Boss ordered a round of hot milk for all hands. The one man he really wanted to get the hot drink into never realized that the break was for his benefit and so wasn't embarrassed, and all of the men were better off for having the warmth and nourishment.

The night after the gale ended, Shackleton was at the tiller, hunched against the cold. He glanced back toward the south and saw a line of white along the horizon. "It's clearing, boys!" he shouted. But when he looked again, he yelled, "For God's sake, hold on! It's got us!" Instead of a clearing sky, the white line to the south was the foaming crest of an enormous storm wave bearing down on them. When the wave struck, for a few moments the entire boat seemed to be submerged. Then for the next hour the men frantically pumped and bailed, laboring to keep the water from capsizing the *Caird*. They could hardly believe they had not foundered.[2]

On the twelfth day out from Elephant Island, they discovered that salt water had gotten into one of the two kegs of drinking water. Shackleton reduced the water ration to half a cup a day. The water had to be strained through gauze to remove the reindeer hair that had gotten into it—the hair had gotten into everything.

Ernest Shackleton, polar explorer.

View the Photograph How does this photo help you understand the physical hardships of Shackleton's journey?

On their fifteenth day out from Elephant Island they reached South Georgia Island, but it was obvious they were in for a storm. By noon the gale had blown up into hurricane force, lashing them with snow, rain, hail, and sleet. The howling winds were driving them straight toward the rocky coast.

Their only hope lay in trying to sail out of reach. The boat began clawing offshore, directly into the onrushing waves. Each wave now smashed into

---

2 If something *foundered,* it sank.

the *Caird* with such force that the bow planks opened and lines of water spurted in from every seam. All afternoon and into the night, the punishment continued.

Finally the hurricane began to decrease. With the storm over, the first watch crawled into the bows to try to catch some sleep. A meal was out of the question: the water was gone, and their mouths and tongues were so swollen with thirst that they could hardly swallow. When the sun rose, the men stared bleary-eyed at the coast of South Georgia. They had to land that day. Shackleton thought the weakest man among them would probably die if they didn't.

Shipwreck: The Rescue

They landed that evening, but they were on the wrong side of the island, the side opposite the whaling station. Afraid to take the battered boat to sea again, the three strongest men— Shackleton, Worsley, who was captain of *Endurance,* and second officer Crean—set out to cross the mountains that lay between them and the station. They stumbled into the station on May 19, 1916, 17 months after they had begun their expedition. They were so changed by their experience they were not recognized.

For the next four months Shackleton tried desperately to get a rescue ship to Elephant Island, where the men who had been left behind were

Shackleton's crew camped on ice, off ship

Shackleton and crew with lifeboat *James Caird*

huddled in a hut made of the remaining two lifeboats. Each time, the winter ice turned him back. Finally on August 30, more than four months after the *James Caird* had sailed away, the rescue ship arrived at the island. As soon as a boat lowered from the ship got within shouting distance, Shackleton called out, "Are all well?" "Yes!" someone shouted back. "We knew you'd come back," one of the men later told Shackleton, who said it was the highest compliment anyone ever paid him. ❧

Respond and Think Critically

1. Write a brief summary of the main events in this excerpt before you answer the following questions. For help on writing a summary, see page 219. [Summarize]

2. What does the nickname "Boss" reveal about how Shackleton's men felt about him? [Infer]

3. Why does one of the men on Elephant Island say, "We knew you'd come back," to Shackleton? [Interpret]

4. **Text-to-Text** How does this excerpt support the interviewer's statement in "Tending Sir Ernest's Legacy" that the journey was "nothing short of miraculous"? [Connect]

5. **Reading Skill** Identify Cause-and-Effect Relationships What caused Shackleton to choose a crew of five men to set out for South Georgia?

6. **BQ** BIG Question In what way does the excerpt add to your understanding of Shackleton and his men's experiences?

Comparing Literature

Aunty Misery and Strawberries

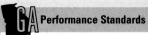
GA Performance Standards

For pages 324–331

ELA7R1d For literary texts, analyze recurring and similar themes across a variety of selections, distinguishing theme from topic.

BQ BIG Question

As you read "Aunty Misery" and "Strawberries," think about the important lessons that you can learn from the characters and events.

Literary Element Conflict

You've learned that **conflict** is the struggle between opposing forces in a story. An **external conflict** exists when a character struggles against an outside force, such as nature, fate, or another person. An **internal conflict** exists within the mind of a character who is torn between opposing feelings or goals.

A **recurring theme,** or repeated message, appears in different types of literature across cultures. In folktales and myths, conflicts are often meant to teach the reader a lesson. As you read "Aunty Misery" and "Strawberries," look for details that reveal each story's conflict and its theme.

Reading Skill Compare and Contrast

When you compare and contrast two things, you find out how they are alike and how they are different. You may not realize it, but you compare and contrast each time you shop. For example, when you shop for shoes, you look at several pairs before you buy a pair. One pair may be too tight; another may be the wrong color. By comparing and contrasting, you can choose the shoes that are right for you.

In this lesson, you will compare and contrast the conflicts in "Aunty Misery" and "Strawberries." As you read, ask yourself, what lesson does this conflict and its solution teach me about life? Use a comparison chart like the one below to record details about the conflicts and the themes.

	"Aunty Misery"	"Strawberries"
Conflicts		
Solutions		
Themes		

Meet the Authors

Judith Ortiz Cofer

Judith Ortiz Cofer came to New Jersey from Puerto Rico. She was born in 1952.

Gayle Ross

Gayle Ross shares traditional Cherokee tales. She was born in 1951.

 Literature Online

Author Search For more about Judith Ortiz Cofer and Gayle Ross, go to glencoe.com and enter QuickPass code GL27534u2.

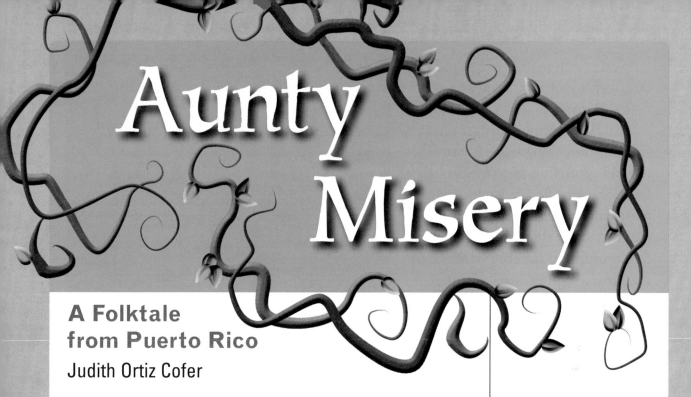

Aunty Misery

A Folktale from Puerto Rico

Judith Ortiz Cofer

This is a story about an old, a very old woman who lived alone in her little hut with no other company than a beautiful pear tree that grew at her door. She spent all her time taking care of this tree. The neighborhood children drove the old woman crazy by stealing her fruit. They would climb her tree, shake its delicate limbs, and run away with armloads of golden pears, yelling insults at *la Tia Miseria*,[1] Aunty Misery, as they called her.

One day, a traveler stopped at the old woman's hut and asked her for permission to spend the night under her roof. Aunty Misery saw that he had an honest face and bid the pilgrim come in. She fed him and made a bed for him in front of her hearth. In the morning the stranger told her that he would show his gratitude for her hospitality by granting her one wish.

"There is only one thing that I desire," said Aunty Misery.

"Ask, and it shall be yours," replied the stranger, who was a sorcerer in disguise.

"I wish that anyone who climbs up my pear tree should not be able to come back down until I permit it."

Comparing Literature

What is the conflict between Aunty Misery and the children? Begin writing in your comparison chart.

---

1 *La Tia Miseria* (lä tē´ə mē´ze rē´ə) means "Aunty Misery."

"Your wish is granted," said the stranger, touching the pear tree as he left Aunty Misery's house.

And so it happened that when the children came back to taunt[2] the old woman and to steal her fruit, she stood at her window watching them. Several of them shimmied up the trunk of the pear tree and immediately got stuck to it as if with glue. She let them cry and beg her for a long time before she gave the tree permission to let them go on the condition that they never again steal her fruit, or bother her.

Time passed and both Aunty Misery and her tree grew bent and gnarled[3] with age. One day another traveler stopped at her door. This one looked untrustworthy to her, so before letting him into her home the old woman asked him what he was doing in her village. He answered her in a voice that was dry and hoarse, as if he had swallowed a desert: "I am Death, and I have come to take you with me."

Thinking fast Aunty Misery said, "All right, but before I go I would like to pluck some pears from my beloved tree to remember how much pleasure it brought me in this life. But I am a very old woman and cannot climb to the tallest branches where the best fruit is. Will you be so kind as to do it for me?"

With a heavy sigh like wind through a tomb, Señor[4] Death climbed the pear tree. Immediately he became stuck to it as if with glue. And no matter how much he

Dona Rosita Morillo, 1944. Frida Kahlo. Oil on canvas mounted on masonite, 30 1/2 x 28 1/2 in. Fundacion Dolores Olmedo, Mexico City, D.F., Mexico.

View the Art In what ways does the subject of this painting remind you of Aunty Misery?

Comparing Literature

How does Aunty Misery trick Death?

---

2 To *taunt* means "to make fun of in a mean way."

3 Something that is *gnarled* is rough, twisted, and knotty, as a tree trunk or branches.

4 *Señor* (sen yôr´) is Spanish for "Mister."

cursed and threatened, Aunty Misery would not allow the tree to release Death.

Many years passed and there were no deaths in the world. The people who make their living from death began to protest loudly. The doctors claimed no one bothered to come in for examinations or treatments anymore, because they did not fear dying; the pharmacists' business suffered too because medicines are, like magic potions, bought to prevent or postpone the inevitable; priests and undertakers were unhappy with the situation also, for obvious reasons. There were also many old folks tired of life who wanted to pass on to the next world to rest from miseries of this one.

La Tia Miseria was blamed by these people for their troubles, of course. Not wishing to be unfair, the old woman made a deal with her prisoner, Death: if he promised not ever to come for her again, she would give him his freedom. He agreed. And that is why there are two things you can always count on running into in this world: Misery and Death: *La miseria y la muerte.*[5] 🦨

---

5 *Y la muerte* (ē lä mwer′tā) is Spanish for "and death."

Comparing Literature

Aunty Misery solves one of her own problems but causes problems for others. What are the consequences of her trick?

Still Life with Skull, 1895–1900. Paul Cezanne. Oil on canvas. ©The Barnes Foundation, Merion, PA.

Strawberries

Retold by Gayle Ross

*L*ong ago, in the very first days of the world, there lived the first man and the first woman. They lived together as husband and wife, and they loved one another dearly. But one day, they quarreled. Although neither later could remember what the quarrel was about, the pain grew stronger with every word that was spoken, until finally, in anger and in grief, the woman left their home and began walking away—to the east, toward the rising sun.

The man sat alone in his house. But as time went by, he grew lonelier and lonelier. The anger left him, and all that remained was a terrible grief and despair,[1] and he began to cry.

A spirit heard the man crying and took pity on him. The spirit said, "Man, why do you cry?"

The man said, "My wife has left me."

The spirit said, "Why did your woman leave?"

The man just hung his head and said nothing.

The spirit asked, "You quarreled with her?"

And the man nodded.

"Would you quarrel with her again?" asked the spirit.

The man said, "No." He wanted only to live with his wife as they had lived before—in peace, in happiness, and in love. "I have seen your woman," the spirit said. "She is walking to the east toward the rising sun."

---

1 *Despair* is the complete loss of hope or a feeling of desperation.

Comparing Literature

What conflict causes the woman to leave home? Continue to fill in your comparison chart.

Comparing Literature

What does the man realize after the anger leaves him?

The man followed his wife, but he could not overtake[2] her. Everyone knows an angry woman walks fast.

Finally, the spirit said, "I'll go ahead and see if I can make her slow her steps." So the spirit found the woman walking, her footsteps fast and angry and her gaze fixed[3] straight ahead. There was pain in her heart.

The spirit saw some huckleberry bushes growing along the trail, so with a wave of his hand, he made the bushes burst into bloom and ripen into fruit. But the woman's gaze remained fixed. She looked neither to the right nor to the left, and she didn't see the berries. Her footsteps didn't slow.

Again, the spirit waved his hand, and one by one, all of the berries growing along the trail burst into bloom and ripened into fruit. But still, the woman's gaze remained fixed. She saw nothing but her anger and pain, and her footsteps didn't slow.

And again, the spirit waved his hand, and, one by one, the trees of the forest—the peach, the pear, the apple, the wild cherry—burst into bloom and ripened into fruit. But still, the woman's eyes remained fixed, and even still, she saw nothing but her anger and pain. And her footsteps didn't slow.

Then finally, the spirit thought, "I will create an entirely new fruit—one that grows very, very close to the ground so the woman must forget her anger and bend her head for a moment." So the spirit waved his hand, and a thick green carpet began to grow along the trail. Then the carpet became starred with tiny white flowers, and each flower gradually ripened into a berry that was the color and shape of the human heart.

As the woman walked, she crushed the tiny berries, and the delicious aroma[4] came up through her nose. She stopped and looked down, and she saw the berries. She picked one and ate it, and she discovered its taste

Comparing Literature

Why do you think the woman doesn't see the huckleberries?

---

2 To **overtake** means "to catch up with" or "to reach and then pass."

3 A **fixed** gaze is steadily directed and unchanging.

4 An **aroma** is a smell or odor.

was as sweet as love itself. So she began walking slowly, picking berries as she went, and as she leaned down to pick a berry, she saw her husband coming behind her.

The anger had gone from her heart, and all that remained was the love she had always known. So she stopped for him, and together, they picked and ate the berries. Finally, they returned to their home, where they lived out their days in peace, happiness, and love.

And that's how the world's very first strawberries brought peace between men and women in the world and why to this day they are called the berries of love. 🍓

Comparing Literature

How do the berries help solve the conflict between the man and woman?

Strawberry Dance, 1983. G. Peter Jemison. Mixed media on handmade paper, 22 x 30 in. Private collection.

View the Art How does the mood of this artwork reflect the mood of the story's ending?

Comparing Literature

BQ BIG Question

Now use the unit Big Question to compare and contrast "Aunty Misery" and "Strawberries." With a group of classmates, discuss questions such as

- What is each story trying to teach readers about life and relationships?

- In what way are the life lessons in "Aunty Misery" and "Strawberries" similar to the life lessons in other folktales and myths that you've read?

- How can reading folktales and myths help people understand more about life?

Support each answer with evidence from the readings.

Literary Element Conflict

Use the details that you wrote in your comparison chart to think about conflict in "Aunty Misery" and "Strawberries." With a partner, answer the following questions.

1. In what ways are the conflicts in "Aunty Misery" and "Strawberries" different? Discuss specific details from the selections that show these differences.

2. In what ways are the conflicts in these selections similar? For example, you might think about how the conflicts affect the characters in each story.

Write to Compare

In one or two paragraphs, explain how the conflicts in "Aunty Misery" and "Strawberries" teach important messages about life. You might focus on these ideas as you write.

- Include details about how each conflict begins, whether each conflict is internal or external, and how each conflict is solved.

- Tell how each conflict and its resolution affects the theme of "Aunty Misery" and "Strawberries."

- Explain how the themes of the stories might help you deal with a conflict in your own life.

 Writing Tip

Connecting To think about how the themes might affect your own life, consider whether you might someday face conflicts similar to those faced by the characters. Think about how the themes relate to life, love, and happiness.

 Literature Online

Selection Resources
For Selection Quizzes, eFlashcards, and Reading-Writing Connection activities, go to glencoe.com and enter QuickPass code GL27534u2.

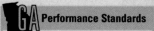 **Performance Standards**

For pages 332–337

ELA7W2a Demonstrate competence in a variety of genres. Produce technical writing that creates or follows an organizing structure appropriate to purpose, audience, and context.

 # Writing Workshop

Functional Document

Have you ever been to a historic site—a place that is significant for its association with a famous event or person? If so, perhaps you made use of a travel brochure to tell you about the place and how to get to it. In this workshop, you will write a travel brochure that will help you think about the Unit 2 Big Question: Why Do You Read?

Review the writing prompt, or assignment, below. Then read the Writing Plan. It will tell you what you will do to write your travel brochure.

Writing Assignment

A functional document gives readers useful facts, instructions, and other types of information for a specific purpose. Create a travel brochure about a specific historic site. Include a map with travel directions. The audience, or those reading your brochure, should be people who might want to visit the site.

Prewrite

What historic period interests you? Is there a historic site in your state that you would like to visit? Your brochure will tell people how to get to that site, so it will be important to provide clear travel directions and a map. The train schedule and stadium map in this unit are examples.

Gather Ideas

Make a list of specific historic periods that interest you. Then narrow down your list to one period. Research two or three historic sites from that period in reference books, in travel brochures or guides, or on the Internet. Take notes on interesting facts about the sites.

Choose a Place

Look over your notes and the information you have gathered and choose one of the historic sites for your travel brochure. Then work with a partner to explore your ideas.

Partner Talk With a partner, discuss details about the site you have chosen.

- List people, events, and artifacts that are especially interesting and briefly explain what makes them interesting.

- Work together to write a sentence that summarizes why you have chosen this place.

     _____ is an important historic site because _____.

Writing Plan

- **Make the purpose of the document clear to the audience.**

- **Present information in logical and effective organizational patterns.**

- **Include summaries of main ideas and supporting details to clarify information and interest the reader.**

- **Use visual aids, including images, to clarify and add to the information.**

- **Use text features to highlight and organize information.**

Get Organized

Use your notes to make two charts: a 5Ws-and-H chart about the site and a directions-and-map chart. Use the charts below as models.

5Ws-and-H Chart	
Who	people who occupied the site
What	type of site (e.g., battlefield) and its name
Where	location of the site
When	dates of historic period and events
Why	importance of the site
How	how the site was built or preserved

Directions-and-Map Chart—Castillo de San Marcos		
Details of Trip	Leg 1— Tallahassee, FL, to Jacksonville, FL	Leg 2— Jacksonville, FL, to Castillo de San Marcos
Starting Point	City Hall, Tallahassee	
Total Distance	156 miles	
Direction	East	
Highways	I-10	
Landmarks	Suwannee River	

Draft

Get It On Paper

- Review your notes and summary statement. Look at your charts.
- Your brochure should include one paragraph summarizing each of the main ideas and details from your 5Ws-and-H chart. Open with a statement to interest your audience in the site.
- Write your directions. Number the steps of each leg in order.
- Draw the directions on a sketch of a map.
- Don't worry about spelling, grammar, or punctuation right now.
- Read your completed draft. Add more information if you need to.

Develop Your Draft

1. In your introductory paragraph, make the **purpose** of your travel brochure clear to the **audience**.

> Take a step back in time at Castillo de San Marcos, the oldest fort in Florida.

Writing and Research
For prewriting, drafting, and revising tools, go to glencoe.com and enter QuickPass code GL27534u2.

Drafting Tip

Organization Present information in the most logical sequence for the topic. Depending on the site you choose, for example, *When* may come before *Who* or *Where*.

TRY IT

Analyzing Cartoons
Why might this computer program be especially useful for writing love letters? With a partner, discuss how this program is related to writing conventions.

"It's a special program for writing love letters. It corrects my spelling and grammar and automatically deletes anything I'll regret later."

2. Use three types of **organization.** In your introductory paragraph, organize facts by order of importance. In the directions, use chronological order. Organize your map in spatial order.

> 1. Start in Tallahassee, FL, and take U.S. 90 for 8 miles.
> 2. Go east on I-10 toward Lake City for 148 miles.

3. Include a **summary** of the main ideas and important details.

> Here you'll be an eyewitness to Florida history.

4. Be sure your **visual aids** match as well as clarify your directions.

> 7. Follow signs to SR A1A and Castillo de San Marcos National Monument.

5. Use **text features** such as headings, bold format, different fonts, and map symbols to organize and highlight information.

> How to Get There

Apply Good Writing Traits: Conventions

Conventions are the rules of language: grammar, usage, spelling, punctuation, capitalization, abbreviation, and paragraphing. Using them will make your directions and map easy to follow.

Read the excerpts below from a train schedule. Which conventions help you understand when and where the train stops?

Oakwood (LV):	7:05	9:05	10:05	2:05	5:05	7:05	10:05
Evansville:		9:50	10:50				
Greentown (AR):	8:09	10:13	11:13	3:09	6:09	8:09	11:09

As you draft your brochure, pay attention to the conventions of language. Fix any errors that would confuse your audience.

Analyze a Student Model

Step Back in Time

Take a step back in time at Castillo de San Marcos, the oldest fort in Florida. Here you'll be an eyewitness to Florida history. You'll see engraved Spanish cannons more than 300 years old and touch the walls of the first stone structure in North America. Adventure, science, and history await at Castillo de San Marcos.

What: Castillo de San Marcos National Monument

Why: Built by the Spanish to protect the city of St. Augustine from the British

When: Constructed 1672–1695; renovated 1738–1756

Who: Timucua, Guale, and Apalachee Indians along with Spanish, French, and British colonists

Where: In downtown St. Augustine, FL, southeast of Tallahassee, the state capital

How: Constructed of coquina, a soft limestone that, remarkably, stopped cannonballs

How to Get There

1. Start in Tallahassee, FL, and take U.S. 90 for 8 miles.
2. Go east on I-10 toward Lake City for 148 miles.
3. Head south onto I-295 toward St. Augustine. Go 20 miles.
4. Continue south on I-95 for another 20 miles.
5. Take SR 16 East. Go a little more than 5 miles.
6. Follow signs to SR A1A and Castillo de San Marcos National Monument.

Purpose and Audience
Address your audience appropriately and make your purpose clear from the beginning.

Organization
The information about the fort is presented in order of importance.

Supporting Details
Exact locations and directions help your audience follow the route.

Visual Aids
Make sure the map matches the written directions.

Text Features
Use map symbols to help your audience read the map.

Revising Tip

Technology Use the design features of your word-processing software to create graphics, adjust your margins, or experiment with various typefaces for headings.

Revise

Now it's time to revise your draft so that your ideas really shine. Revising is what makes good writing great, and great writing takes work!

Peer Review Trade drafts with a partner. Use the chart below to review your partner's brochure by answering the questions in the *What to do* column. Talk about your peer review after you have glanced at each other's brochures and written answers to the questions. Next, follow the suggestions in the *How to do it* column to revise your brochure.

Revising Plan

What to do	How to do it	Example
Is the purpose of the brochure clear?	Explain why people will want to visit the site.	Take a step back in time at Castillo de San Marcos, the oldest fort in Florida. ˄Adventure, science, and history await at Castillo de San Marcos.
Have you organized ideas effectively?	Present each type of information in the most logical order.	When: Constructed 1672–1695; renovated 1738–1756 Why: Built by the Spanish to protect the city of St. Augustine from the British
Will your audience be interested in the site?	Include specific details your audience would want to know.	Where: ˄In downtown St. Augustine, FL, ˄southeast of Tallahassee, the state capital.
Do map and directions agree?	Read your written directions while following your map.	3. Head ~~west~~ ˄south onto I-295 toward St. Augustine.
Have you included helpful text features?	Separate the parts of your brochure with headings.	˄How to Get There 1. Start in Tallahassee, FL, and take U.S. 90 for 8 miles.

Edit and Proofread

For your final draft, read your travel brochure one sentence at a time. Use the editing and proofreading checklist inside the back cover of this book. Then make corrections.

Grammar Focus: Capitalization

Be sure to capitalize proper nouns, or the names of specific persons, places, things, or ideas. Words that indicate particular sections of the country are proper nouns and should be capitalized. However, words that simply indicate direction are not proper nouns. Below are examples of problems with capitalization and solutions from the Workshop Model.

Problem: It's not clear whether a word is a proper noun or a common noun.

Here you'll be an eyewitness to florida history.

Solution: Capitalize the name of a specific state.

Here you'll be an eyewitness to Florida history.

Problem: A direction may be mistaken for a section of the country.

Go East on I-10 toward Lake City for 148 miles.

Solution: Use a lowercase letter for a direction.

Go east on I-10 toward Lake City for 148 miles.

Present

It's almost time to share your writing with others. Write your travel brochure neatly in print or cursive on a separate sheet of paper. You may want to fold your paper into a brochure format (a single sheet of paper folded into three columns). If you have access to a computer, type your brochure and directions on the computer and check spelling. Then add images, including your map, to your brochure. Save your document to a disk, and print it out to share with your classmates.

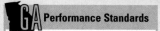
Speaking, Listening, and Viewing Workshop

Informative Presentation

Activity

Connect to Your Writing Deliver an informative presentation to your classmates. You might want to adapt the travel brochure you wrote for the Writing Workshop on pages 332–337. Remember that you focused on the Unit 2 Big Question: Why Do You Read?

Plan Your Presentation

Reread your travel brochure and highlight the sections you want to emphasize in your presentation. Like your written brochure, your informative presentation should be clear about the 5 Ws and H of the historic site.

Rehearse Your Presentation

Practice your presentation several times. Try rehearsing in front of a mirror so that you can watch your movements and facial expressions. Display enlarged images related to the site to refer to as you deliver your directions, or present them as a slide show. Practice your informative presentation often enough that you won't lose eye contact with your audience.

Deliver Your Presentation

○ Speak clearly and precisely.

○ Use visual aids to clarify your information.

○ Change the tone or volume of your voice to communicate emotions or add emphasis.

○ Change the pace of your speaking, slowing down to help clarify potentially confusing parts of the information about the historic site.

Listening to Learn

As you listen, take notes to make sure you understand the presentation. Use the following question frames to learn more about the information from the presenter. When you ask questions, remember to be respectful of the presenter's viewpoint.

○ I was confused about one part. Can you please review _____?

○ I was interested in _____. Can you tell me more about that?

○ I think the purpose of this historic site is _____. Is that correct?

▶ Presentation Checklist

Answer the following questions to evaluate your presentation.

❏ Did you speak clearly and precisely?

❏ Did you use visual aids to help clarify information?

❏ Did you vary the tone, pace, and volume of your voice to add interest to and clarify points in the presentation?

❏ Did you make eye contact with your audience?

Literature Online

Speaking, Listening, and Viewing For project ideas, templates, and presentation tips, go to glencoe.com and enter QuickPass code GL27534u2.

Unit Challenge

Answer the Big Question

In Unit 2, you explored the Big Question through reading, writing, speaking, and listening. Now it's time for you to answer the Big Question by completing one of the Unit Challenges below.

WHY Do You Read?

Performance Standards

For page 339

ELA7W2a Demonstrate competence in a variety of genres. Produce technical writing that creates or follows an organizing structure appropriate to purpose, audience, and context.

Use the notes you took in your Unit 2 **Foldable** to complete your Unit Challenge.

Before you present your Unit Challenge, be sure to follow the steps below. Use this first plan if you choose to make an advertising brochure that persuades people to read—especially those who have not yet discovered the benefits of reading.

On Your Own Activity: Make an Advertising Brochure

- ❏ Fold a sheet of paper into thirds to create six pages—three on one side of the paper and three on the other.
- ❏ In your brochure, list reasons why people should read.
- ❏ Cut pictures from magazines or newspapers that illustrate reasons why people read. Arrange and paste these into your brochure or draw your own pictures.

Use this second plan if you choose to create a TV commercial that sells the idea of reading.

Group Activity: Create a TV Commercial

- ❏ Brainstorm with your group a list of reasons to read.
- ❏ Choose five reasons you think your commercial can address. Think of examples to back up your reasons.
- ❏ Decide whether your commercial will be funny or serious.
- ❏ Write what the actors will do and say.
- ❏ Make sure your commercial is less than a minute long.
- ❏ Perform your commercial for the class. Use gestures and facial expressions that reflect the style of your commercial.

Independent Reading

Fiction

To read more about the Big Question, choose one of these books from your school or local library.

The Witch of Blackbird Pond

by Elizabeth George Speare

In Puritan New England in 1687, a high-spirited teenager befriends an old woman known as the Witch of Blackbird Pond and finds herself accused of witchcraft.

GLENCOE LITERATURE LIBRARY

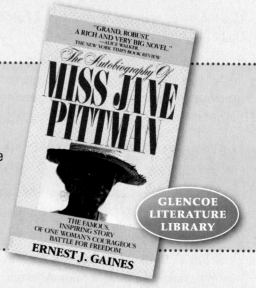

The Autobiography of Miss Jane Pittman

by Ernest J. Gaines

In this novel, 110-year-old Jane Pittman tells many stories of strength and courage. Born into slavery, she lives through the Civil War, Reconstruction, life on a Southern plantation, and the Civil Rights movement of the 1960s.

GLENCOE LITERATURE LIBRARY

A Wrinkle in Time

by Madeleine L'Engle

Meg Murry's father has mysteriously disappeared. Strangers from another planet bring upsetting news, sending Meg on a journey along with her brother Charles and her friend Calvin. The three set off to rescue a loved one from evil forces. Read this novel for fun, excitement, and suspense.

GLENCOE LITERATURE LIBRARY

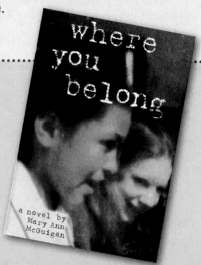

Where You Belong

by Mary Ann McGuigan

After thirteen-year-old Fiona, her mother, and three siblings are evicted from their home, Fiona sets out to discover where she belongs. Read the story to understand what Fiona experiences.

Nonfiction

Sea Otter Rescue: The Aftermath of an Oil Spill

by Roland Smith

When the oil tanker *Exxon Valdez* hit the rocks in Prince William Sound, Alaska, almost eleven million gallons of crude oil spilled into the water. The spilled oil damaged both sea and land and threatened wildlife. This book is a firsthand account of the animal rescue experts who helped save the lives of hundreds of sea otters.

Woodsong

by Gary Paulsen

This book explores the excitement of the famous Alaskan dogsled race, the Iditarod. Paulsen describes why he decided to work with a team of racing dogs and recounts his first dogsled race. He also describes the beauty of nature and the dangers it can present. Read to enjoy Paulsen's adventure and to learn about the Iditarod.

Things Change

by Troy Aikman

Former Dallas Cowboys quarterback Troy Aikman describes his life from childhood to three-time Super Bowl champ, showing how change can provide an opportunity for growth.

Keep a Reader Response Journal

Read one of these books, based on your own interest or a recommendation from a friend or classmate. As you read, write journal entries about what you find interesting, unexpected, or exciting. Be sure to support your responses with specific examples from the text.

Assessment

READING

Read the passages and answer the questions. Write your answers on a separate sheet of paper.

Violent Vesuvius

People who lived near Vesuvius in A.D. 79 thought of it as simply a very big hill. However, Vesuvius was really a sleeping volcano, silently and slowly building up pressure until it would one day explode.

On August 24, A.D. 79, after a series of small steam explosions made an opening at the top of the mountain, Vesuvius erupted. The blast shot pumice and ash toward the sky. After about half an hour, the pumice and ash rained down and began to blanket the city of Pompeii near the volcano. The sleeping giant had awakened, with a deafening roar.

What caused Vesuvius to erupt? The Earth's surface is made up of huge rock sheets called plates. When the plates move apart or hit one another, molten (melted, liquid) rock, called magma, from deep within the Earth is pushed to the surface by pressure from hot underground gases. The magma in Vesuvius was so hot and steam-filled that it turned to pumice. There was no <u>lava</u> in this eruption because the magma was too explosive and steam-filled to form lava.

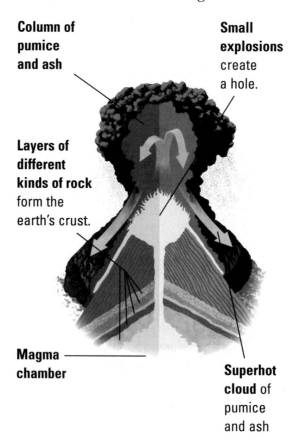

Column of pumice and ash

Small explosions create a hole.

Layers of different kinds of rock form the earth's crust.

Magma chamber

Superhot cloud of pumice and ash

1. What is the main idea of the first two paragraphs?

   A. Earth's surface is made up of huge plates.

   B. Ancient people were not prepared for Vesuvius's eruption.

   C. Many people lived near Vesuvius in A.D. 79.

   D. There was no lava in the eruption of Vesuvius.

2. The main cause of a volcanic eruption is

   A. the heating of underground gases.

   B. Earth's magma turning to pumice.

   C. a series of small steam explosions.

   D. the movement of Earth's plates.

3. Which of the following events occurred first?

   A. Vesuvius erupted.

   B. Magma turned into pumice.

   C. Ash rained down on Pompeii.

   D. Pressure in the Earth pushed magma to the surface.

4. What is the meaning of the word *lava* in this passage?

   A. huge rock sheets in the Earth

   B. liquid rock deep within the Earth

   C. molten rock that comes from a volcano

   D. pumice and ash that comes from a volcano

5. Which BEST describes the how the second paragraph is organized?

   A. It describes the cause and effects of the eruption.

   B. It presents all details of the eruption in chronological order.

   C. It arranges the details of the eruption in order of importance.

   D. It compares and contrasts what people thought about Vesuvius.

6. What information can the reader learn ONLY from the diagram with this passage?

   A. Magma lies inside the Earth.

   B. Pumice and ash shot into the sky.

   C. The Earth's crust is made up of several different kinds of rocks.

   D. A series of small explosions created an opening in the mountain.

7. What is the purpose of this passage?

   A. to demonstrate the importance of scientific research

   B. to point out how wrong people can be about volcanoes

   C. to persuade people to be prepared for sudden disasters

   D. to describe a famous eruption and explain what made it happen

 **Literature** Online

Standards Practice For more standards practice, go to glencoe.com and enter QuickPass code GL27534u2.

from **"The Stone"** by Lloyd Alexander

There was a cottager named Maibon, and one day he was driving down the road in his horse and cart when he saw an old man hobbling along, so frail and feeble he doubted the poor soul could go many more steps. Though Maibon offered to take him in the cart, the old man refused; and Maibon went his way home, shaking his head over such a pitiful sight, and said to his wife, Modrona:

"Ah, ah, what a sorry thing it is to have your <u>bones creaking and cracking</u>, and dim eyes, and dull wits. When I think this might come to me, too! A fine, strong-armed, sturdy-legged fellow like me? One day to go tottering, and have his teeth rattling in his head, and live on porridge, like a baby? There's no fate worse in all the world."

"There is," answered Modrona, "and that would be to have neither teeth nor porridge. Get on with you, Maibon, and stop borrowing trouble. Hoe your field or you'll have no crop to harvest, and no food for you, nor me, nor the little ones."

Sighing and grumbling, Maibon did as his wife <u>bade</u> him. Although the day was fair and cloudless, he took no pleasure in it. His ax-blade was notched, the wooden handle splintery; his saw had lost its edge; and his hoe, once shining new, had begun to rust. None of his tools, it seemed to him, cut or chopped or delved as well as they once had done.

"They're as worn out as that old codger I saw on the road," Maibon said to himself. He squinted up at the sky. "Even the sun isn't as bright as it used to be, and doesn't warm me half as well. It's gone threadbare as my cloak. And no wonder, for it's been there longer than I can remember. Come to think of it, the moon's been looking a little wilted around the edges, too.

"As for me," went on Maibon, in dismay, "I'm in even a worse state. My appetite's faded, especially after meals. Mornings, when I wake, I can hardly keep myself from yawning. And at night, when I go to bed, my eyes are so heavy I can't hold them open. If that's the way things are now, the older I grow, the worse it will be!"

8. What does the word *bade* mean in the passage?

   A. showed

   B. refused

   C. allowed

   D. commanded

9. Which BEST describes the mood of this passage?

   A. gloomy

   B. exciting

   C. peaceful

   D. suspenseful

10. The underlined phrase in the passage is an example of

    A. a simile.

    B. alliteration.

    C. a symbol.

    D. rhyme.

11. By responding to Maibon's complaints, Modrona shows herself to be

    A. cheerful.

    B. practical.

    C. intelligent.

    D. concerned.

12. Which event affects Maibon's day the MOST?

    A. His wife tells him to hoe his field.

    B. He works hard in his field.

    C. His realizes his tools are worn out.

    D. He sees a pitiful old man.

13. Which sentence below states a main theme of the selection?

    A. Husbands should not complain to their wives.

    B. A person's happiness mainly depends on his or her state of mind.

    C. A person cannot do good work without the right tools.

    D. A frail old man turns down a kind offer.

ENGLISH/LANGUAGE ARTS

Choose the best answer for each question. Write your answers on a separate sheet of paper.

1. Which sentence below contains a misspelled word?

   A. One day after recess the reel fire alarm sounded.

   B. We panicked and dashed down the hall.

   C. I had never before seen our principal so angry.

   D. It's not easy to leave the school safely in an emergency.

2. Which sentence below has an error in pronoun-antecedent agreement?

   A. Did all the students hear the alarm in their classrooms?

   B. Everyone pushed and shoved their fellow students.

   C. Tim and Jan said they had stayed calm.

   D. Did someone leave his or her backpack in the hall?

3. Which words should replace the word *get* in the last sentence below?

   > We had some problems with this emergency, but we practiced again today. Everyone knows what to do. We get it right next time.

   A. had got

   B. have gotten

   C. will get

   D. would have gotten

4. Which sentence below is a compound-complex sentence?

   A. Drills are important because emergencies do happen.

   B. Although it was raining, the alarm rang and everyone left class.

   C. Teachers chose student captains, and they made the drill orderly.

   D. The students are prepared for storms, floods, and fires.

WRITING

Read your assigned topic in the box below. Use one piece of paper to jot down your ideas and organize your thoughts. Then neatly write your article on another sheet of paper.

Expository Writing Topic

Writing Situation

Your school newspaper is trying to increase students' awareness of safety issues. You have been asked to write an article about an important safety device such as air bags, life vests, fire extinguishers, or anything similar.

Directions for Writing

Write a newspaper article that describes the safety device to your fellow students and explains why it is important. Include specific details that tell how it is used as well as why it should be used.

Writing Checklist

☐ Focus on a single topic.

☐ Organize your main points in a clear, logical order.

☐ Support your ideas or viewpoints with details and examples.

☐ Use precise, vivid words.

☐ Vary the length and structure of your sentences.

☐ Use clear transition words to connect ideas.

☐ Correct any errors in spelling, capitalization, punctuation, and usage.

WHAT Makes Life Good?

THE **BIG** Question

> " *There is no shortage of good days. It is good lives that are hard to come by.* "
>
> —ANNIE DILLARD

FOLDABLES®
Study Organizer

BQ Part 1 · BQ Part 2 · BQ Part 3

Throughout Unit 3, you will read, write, and talk about the **BIG** Question— **"What Makes Life Good?"** Use your Unit 3 **Foldable,** shown here, to keep track of your ideas as you read. Turn to the back of this book for instructions on making this **Foldable.**

WHAT Makes Life Good?

A friend's joke, a beautiful sunset, a kind word from a loved one—these are some things that make people smile. Think of your life. Whom do you enjoy being with? Where do you most enjoy going? What activities do you look forward to? How do these people, places, and activities affect your life?

As you read the selections in this unit, think about some of the things that make life good:

○ Appreciating Nature

○ Finding Humor and Delight

○ Love and Friendship

What You'll Read

In this unit, you will focus on reading **poetry.** Poems look different from stories and other kinds of literature because they are written in verse—that is, in lines instead of in continuous text. **Narrative poetry** tells a story. **Lyric poetry** tells about a speaker's thoughts and feelings. You will also read folktales, short stories, and other selections that will help you discover answers to the Big Question.

What You'll Write

As you explore the Big Question, you'll write notes in your Unit 3 **Foldable.** Later, you'll use these notes to complete two writing assignments related to the Big Question.

1. **Write an Expository Essay**

2. **Choose a Unit Challenge**

   ○ **On Your Own Activity: Make a Collage**

   ○ **Group Activity: Create a Character Study**

What You'll Learn

Literary Elements

line and stanza

imagery

free verse

style

repetition

tone

rhyme

alliteration

humor

rhythm and meter

metaphor and simile

symbol

motivation

Reading Skills and Strategies

interpret meaning

analyze style

analyze graphic stories

interpret imagery

connect to personal experience

draw conclusions about characters

The Pasture

Robert Frost

I'm going out to clean the pasture spring;
I'll only stop to rake the leaves away
(And wait to watch the water clear, I may):
I shan't be gone long.—You come too.

5 I'm going out to fetch the little calf
That's standing by the mother. It's so young,
It totters when she licks it with her tongue.
I shan't be gone long.—You come too.

Set a Purpose for Reading

Read "The Pasture" to find out what the speaker enjoys in life.

BQ **BIG Question**

How can you tell that the speaker appreciates nature?

Hay Meadows, 1938. Adolf Dehn. Watercolor on white wove paper, 14 1/4 x 21 3/8 in. Terra Foundation for American Art, Chicago, IL.

View the Art How does this painting help you better understand the poem?

After You Read

Respond and Think Critically

1. State in your own words the most important events in "The Pasture." [Summarize]

2. Why do you think Frost ends both stanzas with the same line? What effect does this have on the poem? Explain. [Interpret]

3. How does the speaker feel about his surroundings? Support your answer with details from the poem. [Infer]

4. After reading this poem, what do you think about common farm chores? Why might some people find them enjoyable to perform? [Evaluate]

Writing

Write a Summary To help reinforce your understanding of the poem, write a one-paragraph summary of it. First, find the chore or task described in each stanza. Then, look for important details about each chore or task, and use your own words to describe what the speaker plans to do. Your summary should also explain what you think is the meaning of the poem. You may want to begin your summary this way:

The speaker of "The Pasture" is going out to do two chores. The first is _____.

Performance Standards

For page 352

ELA7W2g Demonstrate competence in a variety of genres. Produce writing that concludes with a detailed summary linked to purpose.

Cow in Pasture, 1878. Winslow Homer. Watercolor and pencil on paper. Private collection.

LOG ON ▶ **Literature** Online

Unit Resources For additional skills practice, go to glencoe.com and enter QuickPass code GL27534u3.

Appreciating Nature

Sunrise by the Red Trees. Romy Ragan. Oil on canvas. Private Collection.

BQ BIG Question **What Makes Life Good?**

How does the painting *Sunrise by the Red Trees* celebrate the beauty of nature?
What scenes in nature do you appreciate?

Before You Read

From Blossoms

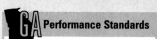

GA **Performance Standards**

For pages 354–357

ELA7R1g/iii For literary texts, explain and analyze the effects of graphics.

Connect to the Poem

Think about a moment in the summer when you were able to stop and appreciate the season's beauty.

Quickwrite Freewrite for a few minutes about this memorable moment. Use sensory details, details that appeal to the senses of hearing, sight, touch, taste, and smell.

Build Background

In the poem "From Blossoms," the speaker describes the experience of eating freshly picked peaches.

- The peaches are grown in an orchard. Orchards are areas of land used to grow groups of fruit or nut trees.

- Roadside stands are common in farming areas. At these stands, farmers sell their goods directly to the consumers. At most roadside stands, consumers can see the orchards and community where the fruit was grown.

Set Purposes for Reading

BQ **BIG Question**

As you read, ask yourself, how does the poet's choice of words show an appreciation for simple, natural pleasures?

Literary Element Line and Stanza

In poetry, a **line** is a series of words that appear as a single group. Often, lines are not complete sentences. They may have no end punctuation. A single thought may continue over the course of several lines. A **stanza** is a group of lines that form a unit in a poem. Stanzas are, in effect, the paragraphs of a poem.

Paying attention to the way a poem is divided into lines and stanzas is important. Recognizing the lines and stanzas will help you understand the poem's form, and often its meaning.

As you read, summarize or paraphrase each line and stanza. Clarify any parts that do not make sense.

Meet Li-Young Lee

"Each poem presents its own demands, its own requirements, and its own pleasures. Every encounter with the page is new. I proceed by unknowing."

—Li-Young Lee

Li-Young Lee was born in 1957 in Indonesia of Chinese parents. His family came to the United States in 1964. Lee currently lives in Chicago with his wife and children.

 Literature Online

Author Search For more about Li-Young Lee, go to glencoe.com and enter QuickPass code GL27534u3.

From Blossoms

Li-Young Lee

From blossoms comes
this brown paper bag of peaches
we bought from the boy
at the bend in the road where we turned toward
5 signs painted *Peaches.*

From laden boughs,° from hands,
from sweet fellowship in the bins,
comes nectar at the roadside, succulent°
peaches we devour, dusty skin and all,
10 comes the familiar dust of summer, dust we eat.

O, to take what we love inside,
to carry within us an orchard, to eat
not only the skin, but the shade,
not only the sugar, but the days, to hold
15 the fruit in our hands, adore it, then bite into
the round jubilance° of peach.

There are days we live
as if death were nowhere
in the background; from joy
20 to joy to joy, from wing to wing,
from blossom to blossom to
impossible blossom, to sweet impossible blossom.

Liberty on the Terrace, 1999.
Ann Patrick. Oil on board.
Private Collection.

Line and Stanza What idea does the poet introduce in the first stanza?

Line and Stanza How does the poet use these lines to build on the ideas from the first stanza?

BQ BIG Question
In these lines, what words convey the speaker's appreciation for nature?

---

6 The words *laden boughs* refer to tree limbs that are loaded with fruit.

8 *Succulent* means *juicy.*

16 *Jubilance* is a feeling of joy.

After You Read

Respond and Think Critically

1. What is the setting of this poem? That is, when and where do the events occur? Explain. [Recall]

2. What events or actions are described in the first two stanzas of the poem? Summarize the stanzas in your own words. [Summarize]

3. Why does the speaker "devour" the peaches, "dusty skin and all"? Explain. [Infer]

4. What does the speaker mean by saying that we "carry within us an orchard" when we eat a peach? Support your ideas with examples from the poem. [Interpret]

5. Why does the speaker say that there are days that we live "as if death were nowhere / in the background"? Explain. [Analyze]

6. **BIG Question** Think about how the speaker finds joy in the simple act of eating a peach. Describe a time when you stopped to appreciate something small or simple in nature. [Connect]

Academic Vocabulary

The speaker of the poem is a **consumer** of peaches. To become more familiar with the word *consumer,* fill out the graphic organizer below.

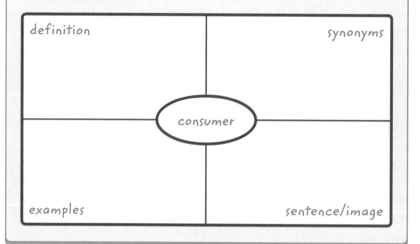

TIP

Inferring
To answer question 3, think about details relating to the speaker. Combine this information with your own experience to infer why the speaker "devours" the peach.

- Reread the second stanza. Find the words that the poet uses to describe the peaches.

- Think of a time that you were hungry, when food looked or smelled delicious to you. Describe the meal.

FOLDABLES Study Organizer Keep track of your ideas about the **BIG Question** in your unit Foldable.

 Literature Online

Selection Resources
For Selection Quizzes, eFlashcards, and Reading-Writing Connection activities, go to glencoe.com and enter QuickPass code GL27534u3.

Literary Element | Line and Stanza

1. In the first stanza, one sentence is divided into five separate lines. Why do you think the poet divided the sentence in this way? Do the line breaks affect the meaning or impact of the stanza? Explain.

2. Do the lines and stanzas in "From Blossoms" follow a regular pattern? Explain.

Review: Diction

As you learned on page 249, **diction** refers to an author's choice and arrangement of words. Diction can affect the feeling or tone of a poem. Reread the poem, paying attention to the poet's choice of words. Use a web like the one below to record especially vivid words and phrases.

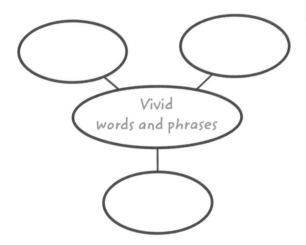

3. Choose two words or phrases you recorded in your web. What feelings did they appeal to? Why were they effective choices for this poem? Explain.

4. Which words are repeated in the last stanza? What effect does this repetition have?

Grammar Link

Nouns A word that names a person, a place, an object, or an idea is a **noun.** There are different kinds of nouns.

A **common noun** names a general, not a particular, type of person, place, thing, or idea. A common noun is not capitalized unless it begins a sentence. *Farmer, field, apple,* and *agriculture* are common nouns.

A **proper noun** names a particular person, place, or thing. Proper nouns are always capitalized. *Tina, Ohio River,* and *Zinnia Farm* are proper nouns

Concrete nouns name things that you can see or touch. *Clock* is a concrete noun. **Abstract nouns** name ideas, qualities, or characteristics. *Time* is an abstract noun.

Collective nouns name a group of people or things. *Flock, group, team,* and *family* are collective nouns.

Practice Write two sentences that describe what happens in "From Blossoms." Use at least one common, proper, concrete, abstract, and collective noun.

Research and Report

Visual/Media Presentation With a small group, prepare a presentation that includes images, music, and sound effects inspired by "From Blossoms." To begin, brainstorm a list of images, songs, and sound effects that fit the theme of the poem. Then, if possible, use presentation software to prepare your project. As you select images and music, recall what you learned about the ethical use of materials. Remember to attribute your sources appropriately. As a group, present your project to the class. Be prepared to explain why you chose your images and sounds.

Glory, Glory . . . , Birds Circling at Dusk, and *Bamboo Grove*

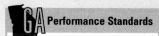

Performance Standards

For pages 358–361

ELA7R1g/ii For literary texts, explain and analyze the effects of figurative language.

Connect to the Haiku

Have you heard the expression "Less is more"? Do you agree with this expression? How would you describe a scene from nature, using as few words as possible?

List Think of a scene from nature. Make a list of words and short phrases that describe how the scene looks and how it makes you feel.

Build Background

Haiku is an ancient form of poetry from Japan.

- After World War II, haiku became popular around the world. It is still very popular in Japan.

- Traditionally, nature is the subject matter of haiku. However, modern writers have used this form to explore a wide variety of topics.

- A traditional haiku has three lines, with five syllables in the first and third lines and seven syllables in the middle line.

Set Purposes for Reading

BQ ▶ **BIG Question**

As you read these haiku, notice how each poet expresses his or her feelings about life and nature. What recurring themes or characteristics do the poems share? What makes them different?

Literary Element Imagery

Imagery is language that appeals to the senses and helps the reader see, hear, feel, smell, and taste the scenes described. Images help suggest emotions and establish mood, or atmosphere. As you read, look for examples of language that appeals to the five senses and ask yourself what emotions and moods the imagery creates.

LOG ON ▶ **Literature** Online

Author Search For more about Raymond R. Patterson, Ann Atwood, and Matsuo Bashō, go to glencoe.com and enter QuickPass code GL27534u3.

Meet the Authors

Matsuo Bashō

Matsuo Bashō was born into the samurai, or warrior class, in Japan and started writing poetry at the age of nine. He later taught poetry to many devoted students. Bashō was probably born in 1644; he died in 1694.

Haiku is a living art form. Many contemporary poets have experimented with the form, including **Raymond R. Patterson** and **Ann Atwood**. Patterson was born in 1929. He is a former director of Black Poets Reading. Atwood was influenced by nature throughout her life. She was born in 1913; she died in 1992.

Glory, Glory . . .

Haiku by
Raymond R. Patterson

Across Grandmother's knees
A kindly sun
Laid a yellow quilt.

Imagery What sensory details help you picture the scene in the poem? To what senses does this image appeal?

Birds Circling at Dusk

Haiku by Ann Atwood

Birds circling at dusk.
The first night of my journey—
yet how far from home!

Imagery What emotion does the image in this poem create?

Bamboo Grove

Haiku by Matsuo Bashō

Song of the cuckoo:
   in the grove of great bamboos,
     moonlight seeping through.

BQ BIG Question
How does the poet feel about nature? How can you tell?

After You Read

Respond and Think Critically

1. What are the settings of the three haiku? Describe them. [Identify]

2. In each haiku, what words or phrases provide clues to the time of day? [Identify]

3. In what ways are the three haiku similar and different? Explain. [Compare]

4. In your opinion, which poem makes the most effective use of the fewest words? Explain. [Evaluate]

5. **Literary Element** Imagery Describe the image in the first haiku. What feeling or mood does this image bring to mind? [Interpret]

6. **BQ** **BIG Question** Which poem best matches your own feelings about nature? Explain. [Connect]

TIP

Interpreting
To interpret the image in "Glory, Glory . . ." follow these steps:

- Reread the poem. Imagine how you would draw this scene.

- Think about the image that the sun's "yellow quilt" suggests.

- Consider how the image might express the speaker's feelings about Grandmother.

FOLDABLES **Study Organizer** Keep track of your ideas about the **BIG Question** in your unit Foldable.

Spelling Link

Spelling is related to sound. Spelling is also related to meaning. Notice that these words have similar meanings, even though some of their vowel sounds are different:

considerate ⟶ consideration

When you are unsure of a word's spelling, think about whether it is related to a word that you already know. Doing so may give you a clue to the correct spelling.

Practice The following word pairs have similar meanings. Write each word pair on a sheet of paper. Say each word aloud. Circle the vowel that sounds different in each word pair.

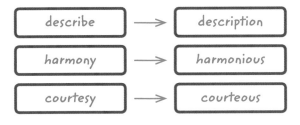

describe ⟶ description

harmony ⟶ harmonious

courtesy ⟶ courteous

 Writing

Write a Stanza Haiku consist of one stanza with three lines and traditionally have five syllables in the first and third lines and seven syllables in the middle line. Write a haiku on a subject related to nature. The list you made earlier may give you ideas for imagery.

 Literature Online

Selection Resources
For Selection Quizzes, eFlashcards, and Reading-Writing Connection activities, go to glencoe.com and enter QuickPass code GL27534u3.

Where Mountain Lion Lay Down with Deer

Connect to the Poem

Think about a special place outdoors. What makes this place special to you?

Graphic Organizer Create a graphic organizer like the one below. In the box in the center, briefly describe your special outdoor place. Write your answer to each question in the space provided.

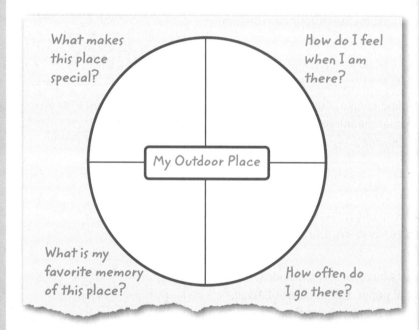

What makes this place special?

How do I feel when I am there?

My Outdoor Place

What is my favorite memory of this place?

How often do I go there?

Build Background

Leslie Marmon Silko is a Native American from the Laguna Pueblo tribe.

- The Laguna Pueblo reservation is in the west central part of New Mexico. This area is surrounded by cliffs, mesas (flat-topped hills), and canyons. A network of rivers supplies water to the region.

- Pueblo culture is closely tied to nature. Both living and nonliving things are believed to be powerful. Harmony with nature is central to Pueblo traditions.

- The Pueblo people's belief in the power of nature and in living in harmony with nature can be seen in "Where Mountain Lion Lay Down with Deer."

Meet Leslie Marmon Silko

"I see myself as a member of the global community. . . . When I write, I am writing to the world, not to the United States alone."

—Leslie Marmon Silko

Native American Heritage
Leslie Marmon Silko grew up on the Laguna Pueblo Indian Reservation in New Mexico, listening to tales told by her female relatives. These stories gave Silko a sense of identity and inspired her writing. Silko's own stories explore her Pueblo heritage and the conflict between traditional and modern ways.

Literary Works Silko has written novels, essays, and poetry collections, including *Voices Under One Sky.*

Leslie Marmon Silko was born in 1948.

 Literature Online

Author Search For more about Leslie Marmon Silko, go to glencoe.com and enter QuickPass code GL27534u3.

Set Purposes for Reading

BQ BIG Question

As you read, ask yourself, how can one's respect for nature show a connection to the past?

Literary Element Free Verse

Free verse is poetry that has no fixed pattern of rhyme, line length, stanza arrangement, or rhythm. Repetition and strong images are often used in free verse. The arrangement of lines and stanzas also adds to the poem's meaning.

Free verse enables poets to express their feelings and ideas in new and unique ways. Some poets use free verse to give their poems the natural, realistic rhythms of conversation. As you read, pay attention to the ways in which the word choice, imagery, and arrangement of lines help express the poem's meaning.

Reading Strategy Interpret Meaning

When you **interpret meaning,** you use your own understanding of the world to decide what the events or ideas in a literary work mean.

Interpreting meaning helps you understand the author's beliefs and feelings. It also helps you connect your own beliefs and feelings to the literary work. To interpret meaning, ask yourself:

- What is the author really trying to say here?
- In what way does the poem relate to my understanding of the world?
- What larger ideas might the poem be about?

Use a graphic organizer like the one below.

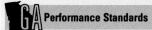

GA Performance Standards

For pages 362–367

ELA7R1g/iii For literary texts, explain and analyze the effects of graphics.

> ## TRY IT
>
> **Interpret Meaning** You interpret meaning every day. For example, think about a time when a friend was happy, angry, or upset. Could you tell how this person felt without even talking to him or her? What clues about his or her emotions did your friend give you?

Paraphrase the line or stanza.

_____

_____

What images does the poet use?

_____

_____

What feelings do you have when you read the line or stanza?

_____

_____

What deeper meaning does the line or stanza convey?

_____

_____

Looking Across the Grand Canyon, c.1910. Edward Henry Potthast. Oil on canvas. Phoenix Art Museum, AZ.

<u>*View the Art*</u> What feelings do you get when you look at this painting? How might the painting help you understand the meaning of the poem?

Where Mountain Lion Lay Down with Deer

— Leslie Marmon Silko —

I climb the black rock mountain
    stepping from day to day
               silently.
I smell the wind for my ancestors
5   pale blue leaves
        crushed wild mountain smell.
Returning
    up the gray stone cliff
    where I descended
10   a thousand years ago.
Returning to faded black stone
    where mountain lion lay down with deer.
It is better to stay up here
           watching wind's reflection
15   in tall yellow flowers.
The old ones who remember me are gone
        the old songs are all forgotten
and the story of my birth.
How I danced in snow-frost moonlight
20   distant stars to the end of the Earth
How I swam away
        in freezing mountain water
        narrow mossy canyon tumbling down
          out of the mountain
25   out of the deep canyon stone
      down
        the memory
            spilling out
            into the world.

BQ **BIG Question**
What does the speaker's silence suggest about her feelings toward nature?

Free Verse In what way does the line length and arrangement add to the poem's meaning?

Interpret Meaning Explain the feeling that the speaker is expressing in these lines.

After You Read

Respond and Think Critically

1. What is the setting of this poem? Include details from the poem in your answer. [Recall]

2. What does the title suggest about the setting of the poem? Explain. [Infer]

3. What does the line "stepping from day to day" tell you about the speaker and the setting? Explain. [Interpret]

4. Reread line 4. Why does the speaker mention her ancestors? Why, in your opinion, does the setting remind the speaker of the people who came before her? Explain. [Analyze]

5. Reread lines 14–15. What is the speaker describing? Explain. [Interpret]

6. BIG Question What image of nature from the poem appeals to you most? Explain. [Evaluate]

Academic Vocabulary

Leslie Marmon Silko's poem shows how important it is to **retain** our connections to nature and to our ancestors. Using context clues, try to figure out the meaning of the word *retain* in the sentence above. Check your guess in a dictionary.

TIP

Inferring
To answer question 2, think about what the poem says and use your own knowledge.

- Recall what you know about mountain lions and deer. Consider whether they would sleep side by side.

- Think about the Pueblo belief that everything in the natural world is powerful. Identify ways in which the poem reflects that belief.

FOLDABLES Study Organizer Keep track of your ideas about the **BIG Question** in your unit Foldable.

 Literature Online

Selection Resources
For Selection Quizzes, eFlashcards, and Reading-Writing Connection activities, go to glencoe.com and enter QuickPass code GL27534u3.

Literary Element Free Verse

1. Reread lines 7–11. What word does the poet repeat? What is the effect of this repetition? Decide if the repetition highlights a certain meaning or creates a musical effect within the poem. Explain your answer.

2. Reread lines 21–29. What action is described in these lines? Why do you think the poet arranged the lines in this way? Explain.

Review: Imagery

As you learned on page 358, **imagery** is language that uses sensory details to help the reader see, hear, feel, smell, and taste the scenes in the work.

3. Provide three examples of imagery in the poem that describe color. What effect does this imagery have? Explain.

4. Which details in lines 19–20 help create a vivid image of the scene? Explain.

5. Which details in lines 22–25 appeal to your sense of touch? Explain.

Reading Strategy Interpret Meaning

Standards Practice ▶ ELA7RC4a

6. The speaker's attitude toward her ancestors is best described as
   A hopeful.
   B humorous.
   C respectful.
   D fearless.

Grammar Link

Pronouns and Antecedents A **pronoun** is a word that takes the place of a noun, a group of words acting as a noun, or another pronoun. The word or group of words that a pronoun refers to is called its **antecedent.**

The woman recalled the memory of her ancestors.

In the sentence above, the pronoun is the word *her*. The word *woman* is the antecedent, or the word that the pronoun *her* refers to. When you use a pronoun, make sure that the pronoun refers clearly to its antecedent. If an antecedent is unclear, rewrite the sentence.

Unclear: *I touched a shell with my foot, and it broke.*

Clear: I touched a shell with my foot, and the shell broke.

Practice Write a sentence about Silko or the poem using a pronoun and an antecedent. Identify the pronoun and its antecedent in your sentence. For example,

Leslie Marmon Silko writes about her experiences as a Native American.

Her is the pronoun; *Leslie Marmon Silko* is the antecedent.

Write with Style

Apply Imagery Write a free-verse poem about an outdoor place you have visited. Your poem should be from five to ten lines long. Use the graphic organizer you made earlier to help you think about your place. Free verse does not follow a set pattern of lines, stanzas, or rhyme. In your poem, use imagery and repetition and vary the length and arrangement of lines.

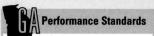
Performance Standards

For page 368

ELA7R2d Understand and acquire new vocabulary. Determine word meanings through the use of definition, example, restatement.

Vocabulary Workshop

Multiple-Meaning Words

Connection to Literature

"It is better to stay up here / watching wind's reflection / in tall yellow flowers."

—Leslie Marmon Silko, "Where Mountain Lion Lay Down with Deer"

Multiple-meaning words, such as *reflection,* have more than one definition, or **denotation.** In the line from Silko's poem, *reflection* means "a result or sign of something." *Reflection* can also mean "a mirror image" or "a serious thought."

In addition to their dictionary definitions, some words also express certain feelings or ideas, called **connotations.** Words can have different connotations—positive or negative—depending on how they are used.

Here are some other multiple-meaning words from "Where Mountain Lion Lay Down with Deer."

Word	Meanings	Examples
smell	an odor	The flowers have a pleasant *smell*.
	to use your nose to sense an odor	I can *smell* the leaves.
	to sense the presence of something	I *smell* victory.
pale	lacking intensity or depth of color	My shirt is *pale* green.
	lacking healthy color	When I was ill, my skin looked *pale*.
	feeble or weak	He made a *pale* attempt to speak.

TRY IT: Using the chart above, write the correct meaning of the underlined word. Then describe the word's connotation.

1. I <u>smell</u> my ancestors in the mountain wind.
2. The <u>pale</u> yellow leaves rustle in the wind.
3. The <u>smell</u> of crushed leaves filled the air.

Tip

Vocabulary Terms When you look up a multiple-meaning word in the dictionary, you'll see several related definitions within a single dictionary entry.

Test-taking Tip If you are not sure which meaning of a word is intended, look for context clues that define, restate, or give an example.

Literature Online

Vocabulary For more vocabulary practice, go to glencoe.com and enter the QuickPass code GL27534u3.

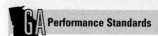

Performance Standards

For pages 369–372

ELA7R1g/ii For literary texts, explain and analyze the effects of figurative language.

Before You Read

Why the Waves Have Whitecaps

Connect to the Folktale

"Why the Waves Have Whitecaps" explains a natural event involving wind and water. Think of a powerful natural event, such as a thunderstorm, that you have experienced.

Quickwrite Freewrite for a few minutes about ways in which the natural world can seem human. Think about animals, plants, and landforms as well as such elements as wind, water, and storms.

Build Background

This folktale is written in dialect. Dialect is a form of language spoken by people of a certain region or group. Features of the dialect in this folktale include dropped vowel and consonant sounds (*'em* instead of *them*).

Folktales were passed down orally before being written down. Folklorists use dialect to capture a traditional culture's speech and story patterns.

Set Purposes for Reading

BQ **BIG Question**

As you read, ask yourself, how does the depiction of wind and water help me to understand nature?

Literary Element Style

Style is the way an author chooses and arranges words and sentences in a literary work. Style can reveal an author's purpose in writing and attitude toward the subject and audience. Diction, sentence structure, and use of imagery are some factors that make up an author's style. As you read, ask yourself, how does Hurston's style help me understand her purpose for writing?

Meet Zora Neale Hurston

Folklorist and Writer Zora Neale Hurston grew up in Eatonville, Florida, the country's first self-governed African American city. Sharing folktales was a common pastime in her close-knit community. She became interested in preserving African American folklore and began to collect tales in the rural South. Hurston is best known for her novel *Their Eyes Were Watching God.* She also published plays, stories, essays, and two collections of folklore. Zora Neale Hurston was born in 1891 and died in 1960.

Literature Online

Author Search For more about Zora Neale Hurston, go to glencoe.com and enter QuickPass code GL27534u3.

Waves, c.1917. Christopher Richard Wynne Nevinson. Oil on canvas. Private Collection.

Why the Waves Have Whitecaps

Zora Neale Hurston

De wind is a woman, and de water is a woman too. They useter[1] talk together a whole heap. Mrs. Wind useter go set down by de ocean and talk and patch and crochet.

They was jus' like all lady people. They loved to talk about their chillun, and brag on 'em.

Mrs. Water useter say, "Look at *my* chillun! Ah[2] got de biggest and de littlest in de world. All kinds of chillun. Every color in de world, and every shape!"

De wind lady bragged louder than de water woman:

"Oh, but Ah got mo' different chilluns than anybody in de world. They flies, they walks, they swims, they sings, they talks, they cries. They got all de colors from de sun. Lawd, my chillun sho is a pleasure. 'Tain't nobody got no babies like mine."

Mrs. Water got tired of hearin' 'bout Mrs. Wind's chillun so she got so she hated 'em.

One day a whole passle[3] of her chillun come to Mrs. Wind and says: "Mama, wese thirsty. Kin we go git us a cool drink of water?"

She says, "Yeah chillun. Run on over to Mrs. Water and hurry right back soon."

When them chillun went to squinch they thirst Mrs. Water grabbed 'em all and drowned 'em.

When her chillun didn't come home, de wind woman got worried. So she went on down to de water and ast for her babies.

"Good evenin' Mis' Water, you see my chillun today?"

De water woman tole her, "No-oo-oo."

Mrs. Wind knew her chillun had come down to Mrs. Water's house, so she passed over de ocean callin' her chillun, and every time she call de white feathers would come up on top of de water. And dat's how come we got white caps on waves. It's de feathers comin' up when de wind woman calls her lost babies.

When you see a storm on de water, it's de wind and de water fightin' over dem chillun. ❦

Style What are some examples of dialect in these sentences?

BQ ▶ **BIG Question**
How did the people who first told this folktale most likely feel about nature?

---

1 *Useter* means "used to."

2 *Ah* is dialect for *I*.

3 *Passle* means *parcel*. Here, it refers to a group of children.

After You Read

Respond and Think Critically

1. What human qualities does the author give to wind and water? Give details to support your answer. [Identify]

2. Why does Mrs. Water drown Mrs. Wind's children? [Recall]

3. According to the folktale, what causes whitecaps on water? Explain. [Summarize]

4. Recall the information you read about in Build Background. Why does the author use an African American dialect to tell this folktale? Explain. [Evaluate]

5. **Literary Element** Style Describe Zora Neale Hurston's style in this folktale. What are some examples of striking word choice and imagery in the folktale? How does Hurston's style contribute to the mood of the tale? Explain. [Analyze]

6. **BQ** BIG Question How does this folktale demonstrate appreciation for the force of nature? Explain. [Conclude]

Academic Vocabulary

In writing "Why the Waves Have Whitecaps," Zora Neale Hurston used dialect. She avoided **altering** the language of the original folktale. Use context clues to figure out the meaning of the word *altering* in the sentence above. Check your guess in a dictionary.

Writing

Write a Summary Writing a summary involves retelling the main idea and the most important details of a story in your own words. Recall the characters and key plot events of Hurston's "Why the Waves Have Whitecaps." Then write a brief summary of the folktale. Your summary should also explain what you think is the message or meaning of the folktale.

TIP

Analyzing
Here are some tips to help you analyze. Remember that when you analyze, you look at separate parts of a selection to understand the whole selection.

- Reread the folktale. Notice whether the author uses common, simple words or formal, detailed descriptions.

- Identify how the action takes place—through the narrator's description, through dialogue, or a combination of the two.

- Consider whether the use of dialect gives the folktale a formal or informal feel.

FOLDABLES Keep track of your ideas about the **BIG Question** in your unit Foldable.

Selection Resources
For Selection Quizzes, eFlashcards, and Reading-Writing Connection activities, go to glencoe.com and enter QuickPass code GL27534u3.

Part 2

Finding Humor and Delight

Serenade to Doris. Haydn Cornner. Oil on canvas. Private Collection, ©Portal Gallery Ltd.

BQ ⟩ **BIG Question** **What Makes Life Good?**

Why might some people laugh when they see the painting *Serenade to Doris*?
What situations make you respond with humor and delight?

373

from *An American Childhood*

Connect to the Memoir

Think back to when you were in elementary school. What is one of your favorite memories from that time in your life?

Quickwrite Freewrite for a few minutes about this memory. What happened? What makes the memory special?

Build Background

An American Childhood is set in Pittsburgh, Pennsylvania. Annie Dillard lived there in the 1940s and early 1950s. At that time, the city was at work on the "Pittsburgh Renaissance." People worked to clean up the city's environment, improve transportation, and renew the city's downtown.

- Pittsburgh is located at the point where the Monongahela and Allegheny rivers unite to form the Ohio River. Much of the city lies on hills surrounding this river junction.

- Pittsburgh has many distinct neighborhoods, 90 of which are officially recognized by the city.

- In 1950, more than 675,000 people lived in Pittsburgh. The population has declined since then.

Vocabulary

wholeheartedly (hōl´här´tid lē) *adv.* completely; sincerely (p. 377). *Keisha passes out flyers about recycling because she wholeheartedly believes that recycling is important.*

solitude (sol´ə tōōd´) *n.* the state of being alone or separate from others (p. 378). *He may have seemed lonely to others, but Tom enjoyed his solitude.*

embarked (em bärkd´) *v.* made a start (p. 378). *After preparing for several months, Catherine embarked on a challenging two-week hike.*

obscure (əb skyoor´) *adj.* not clearly seen; remote (p. 380). *After a long drive into the hills, we reached the obscure town.*

prolong (prə lông´) *v.* to lengthen in time (p. 381). *We decided to prolong our vacation by staying one more day.*

Meet Annie Dillard

"Writing a book is like rearing children—willpower has very little to do with it. . . . You do it out of love."

—Annie Dillard

Nature Writer Annie Dillard often writes about the beauty and violence of the natural world. She became interested in nature at an early age. As a girl, she collected rocks and insects and studied tiny organisms under a microscope. *"An American Childhood* is about the passion of childhood," Dillard says, "a child's vigor, and originality, and eagerness, and mastery, and joy."

Literary Works Dillard writes essays, poetry, fiction, and nonfiction. *An American Childhood* was published in 1987. Annie Dillard was born in 1945.

 Literature Online

Author Search For more about Annie Dillard, go to glencoe.com and enter QuickPass code GL27534u3.

Set Purposes for Reading

BQ ⟩ **BIG Question**

As you read, ask yourself, what makes this experience so delightful for the young Dillard? Why does she remember it vividly as an adult?

Literary Element Tone

Tone is the author's attitude toward the subject, ideas, theme, and characters or people in a text. The tone of a work may be witty or serious, sad or upbeat, scholarly or sarcastic, admiring or angry.

Tone is important because it affects how readers feel about what they are reading. You can identify the tone of a text by paying attention to word choice, sentence construction, the kinds of details the author uses, and the images the author creates.

A memoir, like an autobiography, shares an author's personal experiences. The tone of a memoir can reveal how the author feels about those experiences. As you read, ask yourself, does the author like the people she writes about, including her younger self? Is the tone happy or somber? Is it humorous, serious, or a bit of both?

Reading Skill Analyze Style

When you **analyze,** you look closely at separate parts of a text in order to better understand the entire text. **Style** is the way an author chooses and arranges words and sentences. An author's style often reveals his or her tone and purpose for writing.

To **analyze style,** pay attention to word choice, the use of imagery, sentence variety, and the degree of formality, or seriousness. As you read, think about how these separate elements work together to create an overall effect. Use a chart like the one below to keep track of the details that help create the author's style.

	Example or Description	How does this add to the author's style?
Word choice		
Use of imagery		
Sentence variety		
Degree of formality		

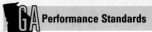

GA Performance Standards

For pages 374–383

ELA7R1h For literary texts, identify and analyze how an author's use of words creates tone and mood.

> **TRY IT**
>
> **Analyze** If you wanted to write an informal and humorous note to a friend, what words and phrases might you use? How would the note change if you decided to write in a serious, formal style? With a partner, talk about different ways that you could turn an informal, humorous note into a formal and serious note.

Campden Hill Square, 1996. Oil on canvas. Jeanne Maze. Private Collection.

from
An American Childhood

Annie Dillard

S ome boys taught me to play football. This was fine sport. You thought up a new strategy for every play and whispered it to the others. You went out for a pass, fooling everyone. Best, you got to throw yourself mightily at someone's running legs. Either you brought him down or you hit the ground flat out on your chin, with your arms empty before you. It was all or nothing. If you hesitated in fear, you would miss and get hurt: you would take a hard fall while the kid got away, or you would get kicked in the face while the kid got away. But if you flung yourself **wholeheartedly** at the back of his knees—if you gathered and joined body and soul and pointed them diving fearlessly—then you likely wouldn't get hurt, and you'd stop the ball. Your fate, and your team's score, depended on your concentration and courage. Nothing girls did could compare with it.

Boys welcomed me at baseball, too, for I had, through enthusiastic practice, what was weirdly known as a boy's arm. In winter, in the snow, there was neither baseball nor football, so the boys and I threw snowballs at passing cars. I got in trouble throwing snowballs, and have seldom been happier since.

On one weekday morning after Christmas, six inches of new snow had just fallen. We were standing up to our boot tops in snow on a front yard on trafficked Reynolds Street, waiting for cars. The cars traveled Reynolds Street slowly and evenly; they were targets all but wrapped in red ribbons, cream puffs.[1] We couldn't miss.

I was seven; the boys were eight, nine, and ten. The oldest two Fahey boys were there—Mikey and Peter— polite blond boys who lived near me on Lloyd Street, and who already had four brothers and sisters. My parents approved Mikey and Peter Fahey. Chickie McBride was there, a tough kid, and Billy Paul and Mackie Kean too,

Analyze Style Notice the sentence variety in the paragraph you just read. What impressions are you forming of the author's style?

BQ BIG Question
What activities did the narrator take delight in as a child?

1 ***Cream puff*** is slang for "an old, used car that is in good condition." It is also slang for a "weakling" or "pushover." By calling the cars ***cream puffs***, the narrator means that they were easy to hit with snowballs.

Vocabulary

wholeheartedly (hōl´ här´ tid lē) *adv.* completely; sincerely

from across Reynolds, where the boys grew up dark and furious, grew up skinny, knowing, and skilled. We had all drifted from our houses that morning looking for action, and had found it here on Reynolds Street.

It was cloudy but cold. The cars' tires laid behind them on the snowy street a complex trail of beige chunks like crenellated castle walls.[2] I had stepped on some earlier; they squeaked. We could have wished for more traffic. When a car came, we all popped it one. In the intervals between cars we reverted to the natural **solitude** of children.

I started making an iceball—a perfect iceball, from perfectly white snow, perfectly spherical, and squeezed perfectly translucent[3] so no snow remained all the way through. (The Fahey boys and I considered it unfair actually to throw an iceball at somebody, but it had been known to happen.)

I had just **embarked** on the iceball project when we heard tire chains come clanking from afar. A black Buick was moving toward us down the street. We all spread out, banged together some regular snowballs, took aim, and, when the Buick drew nigh,[4] fired.

A soft snowball hit the driver's windshield right before the driver's face. It made a smashed star with a hump in the middle.

Often, of course, we hit our target, but this time, the only time in all of life, the car pulled over and stopped. Its wide black door opened; a man got out of it, running. He didn't even close the car door.

He ran after us, and we ran away from him, up the snowy Reynolds sidewalk. At the corner, I looked back; incredibly, he was still after us. He was in city clothes: a suit and tie, street shoes. Any normal adult would have quit, having sprung us into flight and made his point. This

Analyze Style How does the repetition in this sentence show the author's attitude?

---

2 **Crenellated castle walls** have battlements, or notches, along the tops.

3 Light can shine through something that is **translucent**.

4 When the Buick **drew nigh**, it came close, or approached.

Vocabulary
....

solitude (sol′ə tōōd′) *n.* the state of being alone or separate from others

embarked (em bärkd′) *v.* made a start

Tideswell Berbyshire. Andrew Macara. Oil on canvas, 63.5 x 76.2 cm. Private Collection.

man was gaining on us. He was a thin man, all action. All of a sudden, we were running for our lives.

Wordless, we split up. We were on our turf; we could lose ourselves in the neighborhood backyards, everyone for himself. I paused and considered. Everyone had vanished except Mikey Fahey, who was just rounding the corner of a yellow brick house. Poor Mikey, I trailed him. The driver of the Buick sensibly picked the two of us to follow. The man apparently had all day.

He chased Mikey and me around the yellow house and up a backyard path we knew by heart: under a low tree, up a bank, through a hedge, down some snowy steps, and across the grocery store's delivery driveway. We smashed through a gap in another hedge, entered a scruffy backyard and ran around its back porch and tight between houses to Edgerton Avenue; we ran across Edgerton to an alley and up our own sliding woodpile to the Halls' front yard; he kept coming. We ran up Lloyd Street and wound through mazy backyards toward the steep hilltop at Willard and Lang.

Tone What does Dillard's tone reveal about her feelings toward the chase?

Analyze Style In this paragraph, how does the author's style capture the excitement of the chase?

He chased us silently, block after block. He chased us silently over picket fences, through thorny hedges, between houses, around garbage cans, and across streets. Every time I glanced back, choking for breath, I expected he would have quit. He must have been as breathless as we were. His jacket strained over his body. It was an immense discovery, pounding into my hot head with every sliding, joyous step, that this ordinary adult evidently knew what I thought only children who trained at football knew: that you have to fling yourself at what you're doing, you have to point yourself, forget yourself, aim, dive.

Mikey and I had nowhere to go, in our own neighborhood or out of it, but away from this man who was chasing us. He impelled us forward; we compelled him to follow our route. The air was cold; every breath tore my throat. We kept running, block after block; we kept improvising, backyard after backyard, running a frantic course and choosing it simultaneously,[5] failing always to find small places or hard places to slow him down, and discovering always, exhilarated, dismayed, that only bare speed could save us—for he would never give up, this man—and we were losing speed.

He chased us through the backyard **labyrinths** of ten blocks before he caught us by our jackets. He caught us and we all stopped.

We three stood staggering, half blinded, coughing, in an **obscure** hilltop backyard: a man in his twenties, a boy, a girl. He had released our jackets, our pursuer, our captor, our hero: he knew we weren't going anywhere. We all played by the rules. Mikey and I unzipped our jackets. I pulled off my sopping mittens. Our tracks multiplied in the backyard's new snow. We had been breaking new snow all morning. We didn't look at each other. I was cherishing my excitement. The man's lower pants legs were wet; his cuffs were full of snow, and there was a prow of snow beneath them on his shoes and socks. Some

Tone What is the tone of the memoir so far? What is Dillard's attitude toward the discovery she made that day?

Visual Vocabulary

A **labyrinth** is a set of winding, interconnected passages in which it is easy to get lost or lose one's way.

---

5 Events that happen *simultaneously* occur at the same time.

Vocabulary

obscure (əb skyoor′) *adj.* not clearly seen; remote

trees bordered the little flat backyard, some messy winter trees. There was no one around: a clearing in a grove, and we the only players.

It was a long time before he could speak. I had some difficulty at first recalling why we were there. My lips felt swollen; I couldn't see out of the sides of my eyes; I kept coughing.

"You stupid kids," he began perfunctorily.[6]

We listened perfunctorily indeed, if we listened at all, for the chewing out was redundant, a mere formality, and beside the point. The point was that he had chased us passionately without giving up, and so he had caught us. Now he came down to earth. I wanted the glory to last forever.

But how could the glory have lasted forever? We could have run through every backyard in North America until we got to Panama.[7] But when he trapped us at the lip of the Panama Canal what precisely could he have done to **prolong** the drama of the chase and cap its glory? I brooded about this for the next few years. He could only have fried Mikey Fahey and me in boiling oil, say, or dismembered us piecemeal, or staked us to anthills. None of which I really wanted, and none of which any adult was likely to do, even in the spirit of fun. He could only chew us out there in the Panamanian jungle, after months or years of exalting pursuit. He could only begin, "You stupid kids," and continue in his ordinary Pittsburgh accent with his normal righteous anger and the usual common sense.

If in that snowy backyard the driver of the black Buick had cut off our heads, Mikey's and mine, I would have died happy, for nothing has required so much of me since as being chased all over Pittsburgh in the middle of winter— running terrified, exhausted—by this sainted, skinny, furious red-headed man who wished to have a word with us. I don't know how he found his way back to his car. 🔥

Tone What is surprising about Dillard's tone as she remembers the chase?

BQ BIG Question
Why was Dillard happy about running from the driver? What made this a memorable moment for her?

---

6 Something done **perfunctorily** is done in a routine way, with little interest.

7 The Central American nation of **Panama** is known for the Panama Canal, which connects the Atlantic and Pacific oceans.

Vocabulary

prolong (prə lông′) v. to lengthen in time

After You Read

Respond and Think Critically

1. Using your own words, describe the main events of this episode from Annie Dillard's memoir of her childhood. [Summarize]

2. In what ways might the young Dillard have been different from other young people in her neighborhood? Explain. [Infer]

3. What do the events in this account tell you about Dillard's personality? Give details from the text to support your answer. [Analyze]

4. Describe the ending of the story. Do you feel that the ending was satisfying, considering what came before? Support your answer with details from the text. [Evaluate]

5. **BQ** BIG Question Dillard says that being chased delighted her because "nothing has required so much of me since." Think of a task or adventure that required much of you. Did it bring you the same delight? Explain. [Connect]

Vocabulary Practice

Choose the sentence that uses the vocabulary word correctly.

A. He did the chores **wholeheartedly,** without interest in finishing.
B. The actor threw himself **wholeheartedly** into learning the part.

A. The woman in the **obscure** hat asked me for directions.
B. Olivia may live in an **obscure** area, but she travels often.

A. Silas did not want to **prolong** the wait for another hour.
B. We have to **prolong** the entire distance to their house.

Academic Vocabulary

The driver's reaction was exciting to Dillard, in part, because it was **unpredictable.** To become more familiar with the word *unpredictable,* fill out the graphic organizer below.

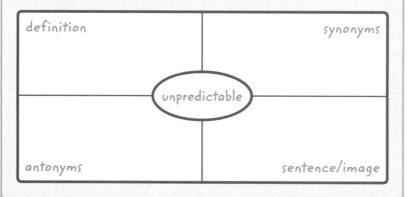

definition

synonyms

unpredictable

antonyms

sentence/image

TIP

Evaluating
Here are some tips to help you evaluate. Remember, when you evaluate, you make a judgment or form an opinion about something.

- Reread the description of the chase. Look for details that make the chase seem exciting. Also, look for places where Dillard explains how she feels about the chase.

- Think about the kind of ending that would be as exciting as the chase itself.

FOLDABLES Keep track of
Study Organizer your ideas about the **BIG Question** in your unit Foldable.

Literature Online

Selection Resources
For Selection Quizzes, eFlashcards, and Reading-Writing Connection activities, go to glencoe.com and enter QuickPass code GL27534u3.

Literary Element Tone

1. In your own words, how would you describe the overall tone of this memoir? Remember that the tone is the author's attitude toward the subject, theme, and characters or people described.

2. How does the author create the tone in this selection? Explain.

3. What effect do you think the author's tone has on readers? How does the tone make you feel about what happens in this memoir? Give details from the memoir to support your answer.

Review: Author's Purpose

As you learned on page 211, an author's purpose is his or her reason for writing. An author might write to entertain, to persuade, to describe, or to inform, or for a combination of these purposes.

4. Why do you think Annie Dillard chose to include the story of the snowball chase in her memoir?

5. What are some reasons that a person might write an autobiographical memoir?

Reading Skill Analyze Style

Standards Practice ELA7R1g/ii

6. Read this sentence from *An American Childhood.*

> We all spread out, banged together some regular snowballs, took aim, and, when the Buick drew nigh, fired.

The author expresses her style by

A describing a memorable event in her past.

B choosing words that paint a vivid image.

C describing a sequence of events.

D explaining the event in general terms.

Grammar Link

Indefinite Pronouns An **indefinite pronoun** is a pronoun that does not refer to a particular person, place, or thing.

> Does **anyone** enjoy making snowballs?
>
> Did **everybody** consider the man a hero, or did **nobody** but the author think so?
>
> **Nothing** is more exciting than a good chase.
>
> **Anything** would have been better than giving up.
>
> **Few** will have such an opportunity again, although **many** would like to.
>
> **Someone** drove up in a Buick.
>
> **Most** were perfectly formed, but **some** were irregular.
>
> **Others** stayed indoors.

Practice Look for three sentences in the excerpt from *An American Childhood* that include indefinite pronouns. Think about how the indefinite pronouns are used in each sentence. Then write three sentences of your own that contain the same indefinite pronouns.

Write with Style

Apply Tone Think of a memorable experience you had playing with your friends when you were younger. Write a paragraph describing the experience, using a tone that reflects how you felt at the time. To find the right tone and the words to describe it, use a graphic organizer like the one below. You may also use a thesaurus to find words that fit your tone.

How I Felt	Tone	Words to Use
I laughed and laughed.	Humorous	giggling, goofy, silly, hilarious

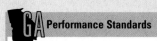

Performance Standards

For pages 384–387

ELA7R1b For informational texts, identify and use knowledge of common graphic features to draw conclusions and make judgments.

Set a Purpose for Reading

Read this article to learn how an everyday activity can improve a person's health.

Preview the Article

1. Read the **deck,** or subtitle. What does it suggest the article is about?

2. Scan the article to find the **subhead.** What point do you think the writers will make in the article's second part?

Reading Strategy

Evaluate Evidence

To evaluate evidence, first find the main idea. Next find the facts the writers use to support that idea. Then make a judgment about whether the evidence supports the writers' claims.

As you read, use a graphic organizer like the one below to keep track of the evidence.

Main idea: _____

Fact 1: _____

Fact 2: _____

TIME

The Giggle PRESCRIPTION

Laughter is the best medicine.

By TRACY EBERHART and ROBERT A. BARNETT

Go ahead, grin. Or better yet, laugh out loud. Laughter is an important part of a healthy life, according to Lee Berk, assistant professor of family medicine at the University of California. "Just thinking about a silly video you are going to watch can reduce feelings of tension, anger, and sadness," says Berk.

Berk and other researchers have done studies to confirm that laughing spells keep your body and mind healthy. In fact, Berk says, "Laughter is an instant vacation."

Laughing for a few seconds may give you the same workout as a minute of aerobic exercise by increasing the activity of the heart and stimulating

Arni Katz/Index Stock

circulation.[1] A good case of the giggles massages not only the heart but also the lungs, muscles, and digestive system. This increased physical activity, coupled with the feel-good mental benefits of having a good laugh, may have lifesaving effects.

According to studies done by doctors at the University of Maryland Medical Center in Baltimore, people with heart disease were 40% less likely to laugh in a variety of situations compared with people of the same age without heart disease. This may mean,

researchers say, that laughing can have something to do with helping to keep your heart healthy. Doctors are not sure exactly how laughter helps prevent heart disease, but they do know that mental stress causes physical changes that damage the lining of blood vessels, which can cause them to swell. At these sites of swelling, fat and cholesterol often build up, which can cause heart attacks. And because laughter can reduce mental stress, it may actually protect you against a heart attack!

---

1 **Stimulating circulation** means "encouraging the movement of blood through the body."

Laughing prevents disease and eases pain

Part of laughter's benefit is its positive effect on the immune system, which is the system that helps the body fight disease. Laughter helps your body stop the release of a hormone that weakens the immune system. Laughter also boosts your body's production of certain cells and proteins that fight infection and disease.

Hospitals and nursing facilities have learned to utilize[2] another of laughter's great benefits. Doctors have learned that, if a patient is in pain, a good laugh can help. Fits of laughter boost chemicals in the brain that control pain. Your ability to withstand pain is raised during laughter and for a short time after you laugh. For this reason, many hospitals use laughter programs, including clowns and other performing artists, as part of their patients' treatment.

But maybe kids already know that laughing makes them feel good. Studies show that young people laugh many more times a day than older people. Just try to keep your ability to laugh as you get older. And remember to be silly. It's good for you!

---

2 To *utilize* is to make use of.

For a long and healthful life, eat right, get plenty of sleep, and laugh as often as you can. Don't just wait for funny things to happen. Plan for humor in your life.

- Watch funny movies (with other people if possible). Laughing is contagious.
- Create a humor journal. Record some of the funny things that happen to you. When you talk about your day with family or friends, find the humorous moments in it.

- Observe young children. They do and say a lot of funny things.
- Collect funny cartoons. Post some around your room.
- Read joke books or funny stories.
- Visit a zoo and watch the monkeys.
- Spend time with people who have a good sense of humor.
- Play charades, using only funny titles.

Respond and Think Critically

1. Write a brief summary of the main ideas in this magazine article. For help on writing a summary, see page 219. [Summarize]

2. **Text-to-Self** Think about a time when laughing made you feel better. In what way did laughter help you? Explain. [Connect]

3. What does Professor Lee Berk mean when he says, "Laughter is an instant vacation"? Give details from the article to support your answer. [Interpret]

4. Doctors believe that laughter may help prevent heart attacks. Why do they believe this? [Analyze]

5. Reading Strategy Evaluate Evidence Use your graphic organizer to evaluate the evidence in the article. Does the evidence support the main idea? Is the evidence reliable? Do the writers show bias, or give opinions based on their personal preferences? Explain.

6. **BQ** BIG Question Based on the information in this article, what role do you think humor plays in life? Explain.

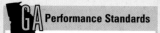

Performance Standards

For pages 388–389

ELA7R1g/i/ii/iii For literary texts, explain and analyze the effects of sound, figurative language, and graphics.

Genre Focus:
Poetry

Poetry is a kind of writing that uses not only words but also form, patterns of sound, imagery, and figurative language to convey its message. Any poem includes some or all of the elements described on these two pages.

Nursery rhymes, narrative poems, free verse, songs, and haiku are all examples of poetry.

Literary Elements

Structure refers to a poem's form, or appearance. Poems are divided into **lines.** A group of lines is called a **stanza.** Stanzas function like paragraphs in a story.

Imagery is created by the poet's use of words and phrases that appeal to the reader's senses of sight, sound, touch, taste, and smell.

Rhythm is a poem's pattern of stressed and unstressed syllables. A regular pattern— **meter**—creates a predictable rhythm. **Rhyme** is the repetition of the same or similar sounds, usually in the form of **end rhyme,** or stressed syllables at the ends of lines. **Internal rhyme** occurs within a line. A **rhyme scheme** is the pattern formed by a poem's end rhyme.

Sound devices are techniques that create a sense of rhythm or that emphasize particular sounds. Sound devices include **alliteration,** or the repetition of consonant sounds at the beginnings of words, such as *doubt* and *dare,* and **onomatopoeia,** or words or phrases that

imitate or suggest the sound they describe, such as *purr* and *bang.*

Figurative language is used by poets for descriptive effect. **Metaphors** and **similes** are examples of figurative language that compare unlike things. A metaphor describes one thing as if it were another. A simile uses *like* or *as* to compare things. A **symbol** is any object, person, place, or experience that means more than what it is. **Personification** refers to giving an animal, object, or idea human form or characteristics. **Idioms** are expressions that are particular to a region, a language, or a group of people.

TRY IT

Using a web like the one on the next page, identify the characteristics of a poem in this unit.

To better understand literary elements in poetry and how poets use them to create effects and express ideas, look at the examples in the web below.

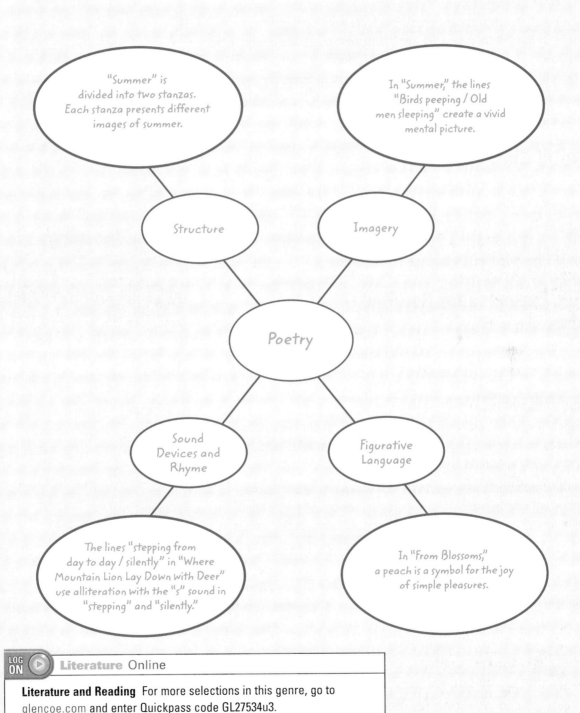

"Summer" is divided into two stanzas. Each stanza presents different images of summer.

In "Summer," the lines "Birds peeping / Old men sleeping" create a vivid mental picture.

Structure

Imagery

Poetry

Sound Devices and Rhyme

Figurative Language

The lines "stepping from day to day / silently" in "Where Mountain Lion Lay Down with Deer" use alliteration with the "s" sound in "stepping" and "silently."

In "From Blossoms," a peach is a symbol for the joy of simple pleasures.

LOG ON ▶ **Literature** Online

Literature and Reading For more selections in this genre, go to glencoe.com and enter Quickpass code GL27534u3.

Summer

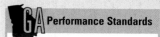

GA Performance Standards

For pages 390–392

ELA7R1g/i For literary texts, explain and analyze the effects of sound.

Connect to the Poem

The poem you are about to read describes hot summer days. Think about the things, large and small, that make summer special for you.

List Make a list of your favorite summer activities. In your list, use at least five vivid, descriptive words to show what makes the activities fun.

Build Background

In "Summer," Walter Dean Myers uses imagery to help readers understand and feel the speaker's summer experience. Imagery is language that helps readers see, hear, feel, smell, and taste the scenes described in a piece of writing. Imagery often helps create the mood, or atmosphere, of a poem.

Set Purposes for Reading

BQ BIG Question

As you read, ask yourself, what sights and sounds does the speaker associate with summer?

Literary Element Repetition

Repetition is the recurrence of sounds, words, phrases, lines, or stanzas in a speech or piece of writing. For example, in "Summer," some lines repeat the phrase "hot days."

Authors and poets use repetition to call readers' attention to important words and phrases. In poetry, repetition helps build rhythm, the pattern created by stressed and unstressed syllables. Repetition also helps create meaning and unity in a poem by tying together words and ideas.

As you read the poem, think about the effects of Myers's use of repetition. What sounds, words, phrases, and lines does he repeat?

Meet Walter Dean Myers

Writing for Self-Expression
As a boy, Walter Dean Myers had a speech difficulty that made it hard for people to understand him. A teacher encouraged him to express himself through writing. Today he is an award-winning author, recognized especially for his young-adult fiction. Myers has published dozens of books, including modern fairy tales, ghost stories, and poetry. "Summer" was published in 1993.

Walter Dean Myers was born in 1937.

Literature Online

Author Search For more about Walter Dean Myers, go to glencoe.com and enter QuickPass code GL27534u3.

Summer

Walter Dean Myers

Music Lesson #3, 2000.
Colin Bootman. Oil on board.
Private Collection.

I like hot days, hot days
Sweat is what you got days
Bugs buzzin from cousin to cousin
Juices dripping
5   Running and ripping
Catch the one you love days

Birds peeping
Old men sleeping
Lazy days, daisies lay
10 Beaming and dreaming
Of hot days, hot days,
Sweat is what you got days

Repetition What sounds
are repeated in these lines?
What feeling does the
repetition create?

BQ **BIG Question**
What makes life good for
the speaker?

After You Read

Respond and Think Critically

1. What objects and experiences does the speaker associate with summer? Explain. [Recall]

2. Why does the poet include the line "Bugs buzzin from cousin to cousin"? Explain what kind of event this suggests. [Interpret]

3. What mood does the line "Catch the one you love days" help to create? [Interpret]

4. How well do you think the poem captures the feeling of summer? Use details from the poem to support your answer. [Evaluate]

5. **Literary Element** Repetition The word *days* appears several times in the poem. What is the effect of this repetition? Explain. [Analyze]

6. **BQ** BIG Question The speaker describes the things he or she enjoys about summer. What would you add to the speaker's list? Explain. [Connect]

TIP

Interpreting
To answer question 2, you must use your own understanding of the world to decide what the ideas or details in a selection mean.

- Reread line 3 of the poem.

- Think about your experiences. Where are you likely to hear "bugs buzzin"? When do you get to spend time with two or more of your cousins or other relatives?

- Ask yourself, what does the speaker want me to picture when I read this line?

 Keep track of your ideas about the **BIG Question** in your unit Foldable.

Spelling Link

Unstressed Vowels Notice the **unstressed vowel sound** in the second syllable of *photograph.* In the dictionary, this sound is indicated by the schwa symbol (ə). To spell words with unstressed vowels, think of a related word in which the syllable containing the vowel sound is stressed. Then use the same letter to spell the word with the unstressed vowel.

Unknown Letter	Related Word	Correct Spelling
phot_graph	photography	photograph
inform_tive	information	informative

Practice On a sheet of paper, list the words *ridicule* and *observant.* Circle the unstressed vowel in each word. Next to each word, write a related word in which the vowel is stressed.

Writing

Write a Scene Which words remind you of the sights, sounds, tastes, and smells of summer? Write a description of something you do every summer. Make your scene vivid by repeating sounds, words, and phrases for emphasis. Check to see that your description is in a logical order, and use a thesaurus to find descriptive words that will appeal to your readers' senses.

 Literature Online

Selection Resources
For Selection Quizzes, eFlashcards, and Reading-Writing Connection activities, go to glencoe.com and enter QuickPass code GL27534u3.

Before You Read

Dreams

Connect to the Poem

This poem is about dreams. What dreams and goals do you have?

List Make a list of your dreams and goals. Next to each dream or goal, list actions you can take to achieve each one.

Build Background

Langston Hughes was a key figure of the Harlem Renaissance.

- The Harlem Renaissance was a cultural, intellectual, and artistic movement of the 1920s and early 1930s. The movement was centered in Harlem, a neighborhood in New York City.

- During this time, many African American writers and artists began to explore their own experiences, hopes, and dreams.

Set Purposes for Reading

BQ BIG Question

As you read, ask yourself, how can dreams and goals influence a person's life?

Literary Element Rhyme

Rhyme is the repetition of sounds at the ends of words that appear close to each other in a poem. *Gold/cold* and *trail/nail* are examples. **End rhyme** occurs at the ends of a poem's lines. **Internal rhyme** occurs within a line of poetry.

Poets use rhyme to emphasize words and ideas and to connect the lines of their poems. To find the **rhyme scheme**, or the pattern of rhyme formed by the end rhyme, mark each line according to the sound at the end. Mark the first line of a poem with an *a*. When you find another line that ends with the same sound, mark that line with an *a* also. Then mark the next end-of-the-line sound with a *b* and so on.

Mary had a little lamb	*a*
Its fleece was white as snow,	*b*
And everywhere that Mary went	*c*
The lamb was sure to go.	*b*

As you read, notice how Hughes uses rhyme and rhyme scheme.

GA **Performance Standards**

For pages 393–396

ELA7R1g/i For literary texts, explain and analyze the effects of sound.

Meet Langston Hughes

"The people I had grown up with . . . weren't people whose shoes were always shined, who had been to Harvard . . . But they seemed to me good people, too."

—Langston Hughes

The People's Poet Langston Hughes is known for poetry that depicts the lives of ordinary people struggling to earn a living. He was born in 1902 and died in 1967.

 Literature Online

Author Search For more about Langston Hughes, go to glencoe.com and enter QuickPass code GL27534u3.

Dreams

Langston Hughes

Langston Hughes (1902–1967), Poet, 1925. Winold Reiss. Pastel on artist board, 76.3 x 54.9 cm. Gift of W. Tjark Reiss in memory of his father, Winold Reiss. National Portrait Gallery, Washington, DC.

Hold fast to dreams
For if dreams die
Life is a broken-winged bird
That cannot fly.

5 Hold fast to dreams
For when dreams go
Life is a barren field
Frozen with snow.

Rhyme Which lines in this stanza have end rhyme? Why might the poet want to connect these lines?

BQ **BIG Question**
What connection do you see between cherishing dreams and enjoying life?

After You Read

Respond and Think Critically

1. In what way are dreams important in your life? Explain. [Connect]

2. In line 3, why does Hughes compare a life without dreams to a "broken-winged bird"? What is the point of the comparison? Explain. [Interpret]

3. Paraphrase, or restate, the lines of the poem's second stanza. Remember to use your own words. [Paraphrase]

4. Describe the image in the second stanza. According to the stanza, what is bad about a life without dreams? Compare the ideas in the second stanza with the ideas in the first stanza. How are the messages of the stanzas similar? How are they different? Explain. [Compare]

5. What advice does the speaker give readers in "Dreams"? Use details from the poem to support your answer. [Analyze]

6. **BQ** BIG Question What do you think this poem is saying about what is important in life? Explain. [Conclude]

Academic Vocabulary

In "Dreams," the speaker says that without the **capacity** to dream, people will lead empty lives.

In the sentence above, *capacity* means "ability." *Capacity* also has other meanings. Think about this sentence: Our classroom has a maximum *capacity* of fifty people. What do you think *capacity* means here? What is the difference between the two meanings?

TIP

Comparing
To answer question 4, you must identify details that make the two stanzas different. Then you must think about what the differences between the stanzas mean.

- Start by looking closely at both stanzas. Notice that the stanzas have details in common, such as the same first line. What details are different?

- The differences between the stanzas may seem small, but they are meaningful. What do the details tell you about the loss of dreams?

 FOLDABLES Keep track of
Study Organizer your ideas about the **BIG Question** in your unit Foldable.

 Literature Online

Selection Resources
For Selection Quizzes, eFlashcards, and Reading-Writing Connection activities, go to glencoe.com and enter QuickPass code GL27534u3.

Literary Element Rhyme

1. Using the letters *a, b, c, d,* and *e,* show the rhyme scheme of "Dreams."

2. The first stanza contains the rhyme *die/fly.* Why might Hughes have chosen to connect these two lines? Explain.

3. In the second stanza, *go* and *snow* rhyme. How does the poem connect letting dreams "go" with a field that is "frozen with snow"? Explain.

Review: Metaphor

As you learned on page 203, a **metaphor** is a figure of speech that compares seemingly unlike things. A metaphor describes one thing as if it were another without using connecting words such as *like* or *as.* Poets use metaphors to communicate deeper ideas and create vivid images.

Standards Practice **ELA7R1g/ii**

4. Which line from the poem contains a metaphor?
   A   Frozen with snow
   B   Life is a barren field
   C   For when dreams go
   D   Hold fast to dreams

Grammar Link

Subject Pronouns and Object Pronouns

A **pronoun** is a word used in place of a noun or a noun phrase. A pronoun used as a subject is a **subject pronoun**. A pronoun used as the object of a verb or a preposition is an **object pronoun**.

Subject Pronouns	Object Pronouns
Singular: I, you, he, she, it	Singular: me, you, her, him, it
Plural: we, you, they	Plural: us, you, them

When the subject or object names more than one person or thing, you may have to think about which pronoun to use. To determine which form of a pronoun to use, try isolating the pronoun.

Wrong: Mary, Phil, and him agreed.
Isolate the pronoun: Mary agreed; Phil agreed; he agreed.
Right: Mary, Phil, and he agreed.

Practice Rewrite each of the following sentences, using the correct pronoun.

1. My classmates and (I, me) read "Dreams," by Langston Hughes.

2. Our teacher asked Penelope and (I, me) to read the poem aloud.

Write with Style

Apply Sound Devices Review the rhyme scheme of "Dreams." Then write a stanza of your own, using the same rhyme scheme. Your stanza may explore the ideas in Langston Hughes's poem, or you may write about a different topic. Create your own metaphor and include it in your stanza.

Before You Read

Miracles

Connect to the Poem

The speaker in this poem talks about small events in life that he or she enjoys. List three small things you appreciate most about life.

Partner Talk With a partner, discuss commonplace things that you appreciate. How important are the little things in life?

Build Background

"Miracles" mentions Manhattan, an area of New York City. Walt Whitman spent much of his life in New York.

- Whitman was born in a small, rural village on Long Island, New York.

- Fascinated by the excitement of Manhattan, Whitman went to work in New York City when he was twenty-two years old.

- In New York City, Whitman worked as an editor, a printer, and a journalist. His poems and short stories appeared in many popular newspapers and magazines of the 1840s.

Set Purposes for Reading

BQ BIG Question

As you read the poem, ask yourself, what everyday activities and objects are important to the speaker? Why are they important?

Literary Elements Alliteration and Repetition

Alliteration is the repetition of consonant sounds, usually at the beginnings of words. An example of alliteration is the repetition of the *s* sound in the following lines from "Miracles":

> "Every square yard of the surface of the earth is spread
> with the same . . ."

In poetry and prose, **repetition** is the recurrence of sounds, words, phrases, lines, or stanzas. Alliteration is a type of repetition.

Alliteration and repetition affect the way a poem sounds when read aloud. Poets and authors use alliteration and repetition to help emphasize certain words and ideas.

As you read, look for examples of alliteration and repetition. Read the poem aloud to determine the effects of alliteration and repetition on your appreciation of the poem.

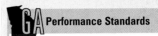

GA **Performance Standards**

For pages 397–399

ELA7R1g/i For literary texts, explain and analyze the effects of sound.

Meet Walt Whitman

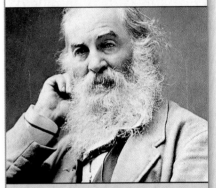

Free Thinker Walt Whitman was one of the earliest poets to express himself without using regular rhyme and rhythm. His free-flowing poetic style influenced many poets who came after him. Walt Whitman was born in 1819 and died in 1892.

 Literature Online

Author Search For more about Walt Whitman, go to glencoe.com and enter QuickPass code GL27534u3.

Miracles
Walt Whitman

Why, who makes much of a miracle?
As to me I know of nothing else but miracles,
Whether I walk the streets of Manhattan,
Or dart my sight over the roofs of houses toward
    the sky,
5 Or wade with naked feet along the beach just in the
    edge of the water,
Or stand under trees in the woods,
Or talk by day with any one I love . . .
Or sit at table at dinner with the rest,
Or look at strangers opposite me riding in the car.
10 Or watch honey-bees busy around the hive of a
    summer forenoon,°
Or animals feeding in the fields,
Or birds, or the wonderfulness of the sundown, or of
    stars shining so quiet and bright,
Or the exquisite° delicate thin curve of the new moon
    in spring;
These with the rest, one and all, are to me miracles,
15 The whole referring, yet each distinct and in
    its place.°
To me every hour of the light and dark is a miracle,
Every cubic inch of space is a miracle,
Every square yard of the surface of the earth is spread
    with the same,
Every foot of the interior swarms with the same.
20 To me the sea is a continual miracle,
The fishes that swim—the rocks—the motion of the
    waves—the ships with men in them,
What stranger miracles are there?

---

10 *Forenoon* is another word for *morning.*

13 Something that is *exquisite* has a rare beauty, charm, or perfection.

15 This line suggests that all of these small, separate miracles are involved in, or refer to, some greater miracle.

Alliteration and Repetition
What effect is created by the repetition of the word *or?*

BQ **BIG Question**
Which details in the poem suggest that the speaker delights in the goodness of life?

After You Read

Respond and Think Critically

1. What is your favorite detail or image in the poem? Explain. [Connect]

2. What are five of the objects or moments that the speaker calls "miracles"? [Recall]

3. In his descriptions of miracles, which of the five senses does Whitman appeal to? Give examples from the poem. [Interpret]

4. What do the miracles in the poem have in common? What attitude toward nature and human life does this poem convey? Explain. [Analyze]

5. **Literary Elements** Alliteration and Repetition What are some of the effects of the alliteration and repetition in this poem? Are these two elements used to create a particular musical sound? To reinforce certain ideas? Explain. [Analyze]

6. **BQ** BIG Question What is the theme, or overall message, of "Miracles"? Explain. [Interpret]

Spelling Link

Rule for *ie* and *ei* Think of the word *fields* in "Miracles." How do you know that the *i* comes before *e*? The following rhyme can help you remember the rule for spelling *ie* and *ei* words:

> Put *i* before *e*
> except after *c*
> or when sounding like a long *a*
> as in *neighbor* and *weigh*

There are some exceptions to this rule, including *either*, *height*, *neither*, *protein*, *seize*, and *weird*.

Practice Choose the correct spelling of each word.

1. achieve, acheive
2. viel, veil
3. relieve, releive
4. cieling, ceiling

 Writing

Write a Journal Entry What other miracles could Whitman have included in his poem? Write a journal entry that describes three objects or events you would add to Whitman's list. Explain why each is special to you and support your opinions with descriptions.

TIP

Analyzing
Here are some tips to help you analyze. Remember that when you analyze, you look at separate parts of a selection to understand the entire selection.

- Reread the poem, and notice the different types of events or things that the speaker considers miracles.

- Notice the general statements that the speaker makes about life and miracles.

- What do the examples of miracles and the speaker's statements about life say about his or her outlook on nature and life?

FOLDABLES Study Organizer Keep track of your ideas about the **BIG Question** in your unit Foldable.

Before You Read

The Tale of 'Kiko-Wiko

Connect to the Graphic Story

Think about a story you've written. How did you invent the characters? What were some of the traits of your characters? If your characters could talk, what would they tell you about the story?

Partner Talk With a partner, talk about a story you have both read. If the characters in the story could tell you their opinions about the story, what would they say? What would they think of the other characters and the story's events? What changes to the story's setting and plot would they suggest?

Build Background

The graphic story you are about to read is from a comic book series called *Akiko*.

- Akiko is a fourth-grade girl who goes on many exciting adventures.

- In the series, Akiko often travels to strange planets with her friends.

- The character Akiko is based on two famous characters from children's books: Dorothy from *The Wizard of Oz* and Alice from *Alice's Adventures in Wonderland*.

- The author began writing the Akiko stories when he lived in Japan. He picked a common Japanese name for his main character. 'Kiko is a nickname for Akiko.

Vocabulary

whimsical (hwim′zi kəl) *adj.* full of odd or lighthearted ideas (p. 402). *The whimsical story was about monsters and dragons.*

disruptions (dis rup′shənz) *n.* unwanted breaks or interruptions (p. 405). *It was difficult to concentrate on the game due to my little sister's constant disruptions.*

Meet Mark Crilley

Gifted Artist Mark Crilley began drawing at a young age. After college, he taught in Japan, where he invented the character Akiko. Since then, he has published more than fifty issues in the Akiko comic book series. He writes, "somewhere underneath all the silly drawings and slapstick humor lies a gentle reminder of the little fourth grader within us all."

 Literature Online

Author Search For more about Mark Crilley, go to glencoe.com and enter QuickPass code GL27534u3.

Set Purposes for Reading

BQ BIG Question

As you read, ask yourself, which parts of the story make me laugh? Which characters are funny? Why?

Literary Element Humor

In a literary work, **humor** is the quality that makes characters and their situations seem funny, amusing, or ridiculous. Humor often points out the **irony** of a situation—when the outcome of a situation is the opposite of what was expected.

Humor makes reading fun. Humorous characters and events help readers connect to and become more involved in what they are reading. As you read, ask yourself, which characters and events in the story make me smile or laugh?

Reading Skill Analyze Graphic Stories

Graphic stories are similar to comic strips, but the stories are usually longer. The purpose of many graphic stories is to entertain readers, but some also teach readers about history or current events.

When you **analyze graphic stories**, you pay attention to the special characteristics of graphic stories. For example, spoken words usually appear in dialogue balloons. A character's emotions or actions are often revealed in an illustration. Events take place in panels, or individual frames.

As you read "The Tale of 'Kiko-Wiko," notice how the illustrations and text work together to advance the story. Watch for elements that remind you of books, film, or television. Then compare the characteristics of the graphic story with the characteristics of traditional short stories. Use a graphic organizer like the one below.

Characteristics	Graphic Story	Traditional Story
story structure	panels or frames	paragraphs
illustrations		
dialogue		
narration		
plot		
character traits		

GA Performance Standards

For pages 400–409

ELA7R1g/iii For literary texts, explain and analyze the effects of graphics.

ELA7R1h Identify how an author creates tone.

TRY IT

Analyze With a partner, talk about comics that you have read in a newspaper or a comic book. What special features of comics help you understand their stories? Which comics are your favorites? Are they funny or serious? Do you like them more or less than traditional short stories?

Humor What is funny about the way 'Kiko speaks to the narrator?

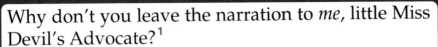

Why don't you leave the narration to *me*, little Miss Devil's Advocate?[1]

All right, all right.

You don't have to get snippy.

Thank you.

One day 'Kiko-Wiko was out for a walk when along came a monstrous ogre.[2]

GWAAAAAAR!!!

Hey there, ogre-man.

What's up?

Analyze Graphic Stories
What do the ogre's facial expression and dialogue show?

Hang on. She's not supposed to say that, is she?

No, she's not. I believe the line is, "Help, somebody help me."

Yeah, but he's not *scary* enough!

I mean, *look* at him. He's like something out of a *happy meal*...

Humor Who is talking here? What makes this conversation amusing?

---

1 A *devil's advocate* is someone who argues in favor of a less popular or less accepted idea.

2 An *ogre* (ō′ gər) is an imaginary monster in fairy tales.

Analyze Graphic Stories
How does the ogre feel?
How do you know this?

Humor What details in
this panel are especially
humorous?

Humor A person in what profession might say words like 'Kiko's? Why are the words funny when 'Kiko says them?

Analyze Graphic Stories
Describe 'Kiko's facial
expression as she looks at
the new ogre. What does it
tell you about her feelings?

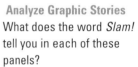

Analyze Graphic Stories
What does the word *Slam!* tell you in each of these panels?

BQ BIG Question
Where would you expect to see the words "The End"? Would this story be as enjoyable as a traditional story without pictures?

After You Read

Respond and Think Critically

1. According to 'Kiko-Wiko, what is wrong with the first ogre? [Recall]

2. What happens when the second ogre tries to scare 'Kiko-Wiko? Explain. [Summarize]

3. What is notable or interesting about the narrator in this graphic story? Explain. [Interpret]

4. Why does the narrator quit? Explain. [Infer]

5. How is 'Kiko-Wiko similar to and different from cartoon characters that you are familiar with? Support your answer with examples from the graphic story. [Compare]

6. **BQ** **BIG Question** Think about the way that reading or hearing a funny story can improve one's day. Why does laughter help make life good? Explain. [Connect]

TIP

Comparing
Here are some tips to help you compare.

- Think about the cartoon characters you are familiar with. Describe how they usually behave.

- Look back at the story for specific examples of how 'Kiko-Wiko acts.

- Ask yourself, how are 'Kiko-Wiko's actions and words like those of other cartoon characters? How are they different?

FOLDABLES **Study Organizer** Keep track of your ideas about the **BIG Question** in your unit Foldable.

Examine Media

The Gift of Laughter

"Mother Goose and Grimm" is a comic strip by Mike Peters. This strip originated in 1984 and is printed in more than 800 newspapers worldwide. It often focuses on fairy-tale themes. Read the strip below.

©2007 Grimmy, Inc. grimmy.com. Dist. by King Features Syndicate, Inc.

Group Activity Discuss the following questions with classmates.

1. On what does the "Mother Goose and Grimm" comic strip base its humor?

2. What do "The Tale of 'Kiko-Wiko" and the comic strip have in common?

3. Think of a comic strip that you read often. What do you like about it? Why do you think newspapers publish comic strips? Explain.

Literary Element **Humor**

1. Why is 'Kiko-Wiko's reaction to the first ogre humorous? Explain.

2. What other moments or aspects of the story do you consider amusing? Explain.

Review: **Characterization**

As you learned on page 104, **characterization** includes all the methods an author uses to develop the personality of characters. In "The Tale of 'Kiko-Wiko," the author uses **indirect characterization,** revealing the personality of a character through the character's words and actions and through what other characters think and say about him or her.

Standards Practice ELA7R1f

3. Which sentence best describes how 'Kiko-Wiko and the narrator deal with difficult situations?
   A   Each leaves when things are difficult.
   B   Each questions his or her own decisions.
   C   Each asks the other for help with difficulties.
   D   Both are determined to learn from others' mistakes.

Reading Skill **Analyze Graphic Stories**

4. What causes 'Kiko-Wiko to say that the narrator is unprofessional?

5. Look at the graphic organizer you filled in from page 401. What are the biggest differences between graphic stories and traditional stories? Explain, using details from "The Tale of 'Kiko-Wiko."

Vocabulary Practice

Respond to these questions.

1. What would you most likely describe as **whimsical**—a movie about a winter storm or a movie about a boy and his pet unicorn?

2. What would be most likely to cause **disruptions**—buying a new car or having unexpected house guests?

Academic Vocabulary

"The Tale of 'Kiko-Wiko" is the creative **concept** of Mark Crilley, who thought of the main character and her adventures. Using context clues, figure out the meaning of the word *concept* in the sentence above. Check your guess in a dictionary.

LOG ON ▶ **Literature** Online

Selection Resources For Selection Quizzes, eFlashcards, and Reading-Writing Connection activities, go to glencoe.com and enter QuickPass code GL27534u3.

Respond Through Writing

Review

 GA **Performance Standards**

For page 410

ELA7W2c Demonstrate competence in a variety of genres.

Convince an Audience "The Tale of 'Kiko-Wiko" is a graphic story that many readers find entertaining. Write a review in which you describe "The Tale of 'Kiko-Wiko." In your review, try to convince your audience of the benefits of reading graphic stories.

Understand the Task When you convince an audience, you present an opinion and try to persuade readers to think the same way you do. Writing a persuasive review requires you to focus your ideas, form clear opinions, and support your opinions with evidence and examples.

Prewrite Think of the benefits of reading graphic stories such as "The Tale of 'Kiko-Wiko." Make a web diagram like the one below. In the center oval, write Benefits of Reading Graphic Stories. Add several other ovals, labeling each with a benefit of reading graphic stories. In each oval, also list examples from "The Tale of 'Kiko-Wiko" that support the benefit.

Benefits
of Reading Graphic Stories

Draft Select the best ideas from your web diagram. Consider making each idea the focus of one paragraph. Draft the body paragraphs of the review. Think about any counterarguments that your readers might have and include details to support your ideas. Then draft the introduction and conclusion. This sentence frame might help you get started:

I like to read graphic novels because _____, _____, and _____.

Revise After you have drafted your review, read it to determine whether you have stated your opinions clearly and supported them adequately. You may want to place your strongest points at the beginning or the end of the essay. Add examples or other evidence to each paragraph to support your opinion, if necessary.

Edit and Proofread Proofread your review. Correct any errors in spelling, grammar, and punctuation.

Part 3
Love and Friendship

Development. Alberto Ruggieri.

BQ ▶ **BIG Question** **What Makes Life Good?**

What might the picture of a handshake show about the connection between two friends?
How can friendships with people you care about make your life good?

411

Before You Read

Annabel Lee

Connect to the Poem

Think about how you deal with difficult experiences in life. What activities help you through tough times?

Quickwrite Freewrite for a few minutes about how writing can help you deal with difficult experiences. How might expressing your feelings be a positive activity?

Build Background

Edgar Allan Poe lived a life as tragic as the lives he describes in some of his famous horror tales and poems. Like the speaker of "Annabel Lee," Poe experienced great loss in his life.

- Poe's mother, Elizabeth Arnold Poe, died of tuberculosis, a disease of the lungs, when he was only two years old. After her death, Poe and his sister, Rosalie, were separated and taken in by two different families.

- Poe's first love, Sarah Elmira Royster, became engaged to another man while Poe was a university student.

- In 1836 Poe married Virginia Clemm, pictured below. His love for her was the one shining light in his life. Many people believe that Poe wrote "Annabel Lee" after Virginia died of tuberculosis.

Meet Edgar Allan Poe

Love and Madness Death played a large part in Edgar Allan Poe's life, his fiction, and his poetry. Poe is best known for his detective stories (a form of fiction he helped originate) and tales of horror and madness. He wished, however, to be remembered for his poetry. "Annabel Lee," one of the poet's most popular romantic poems, was published two days after his early death.

Literary Works Poe's most famous works include his haunting poem, "The Raven," and two terrifying short stories, "The Tell-Tale Heart" and "The Pit and the Pendulum." The poem "Annabel Lee" was published in 1849.

Edgar Allan Poe was born in 1809 and died in 1849.

 Literature Online

Author Search For more about Edgar Allan Poe, go to glencoe.com and enter QuickPass code GL27534u3.

Set Purposes for Reading

BQ ▶ BIG Question

As you read, ask yourself, how is the speaker's life affected by his love for Annabel Lee?

GA Performance Standards

For pages 412–417

ELA7R1g/i For literary texts, explain and analyze the effects of sound.

ELA7R1g/ii Analyze the affects of figurative language.

Literary Elements ▸ Rhythm and Meter

Like songs, poems have rhythm. In poetry, **rhythm** is the pattern of beats made by stressed and unstressed syllables. Some poems have a predictable rhythm, called **meter.** To find the meter of a poem, try scanning, or reading the poem to find the pattern of stressed (´) and unstressed syllables (˘). Read this example from "Annabel Lee":

> ˘ ˘ ´ , ˘ ˘ ´ ˘ ˘ ´ ,
> It was many and many a year ago,

> ˘ ˘ ´ ˘ ˘ ´ ˘ ´ ,
> In a kingdom by the sea,

Rhythm and meter are important tools that poets use to convey meaning and mood and to add interest. Together, rhythm and meter may help to show how the speaker of a poem feels. The musical quality that these poetic devices create also makes a poem enjoyable to read. As you read, consider how the rhythm and meter of the poem create a musical effect and help you to understand the meaning of the poem.

Reading Strategy ▸ Interpret Imagery

In poetry, **imagery** consists of the "word pictures" that authors use to make their subjects more vivid. Images help readers visualize what is being described. They also often suggest emotions. Images appeal to one or more of the five senses: sight, hearing, touch, taste, or smell.

When you **interpret imagery,** you use your own knowledge and understanding to decide what feelings and ideas the images in a poem suggest. To interpret imagery in a poem, think about

- which of the five senses the image appeals to
- what the poet is really trying to say
- what your own knowledge and experience tell you
- what impression the words leave in your mind

As you read, fill in a chart like the one below.

Image	Senses Image Appeals To	What Image Suggests

> ### TRY IT
>
> **Interpret** Suppose your friend describes a new player on the basketball team as "a sleek cat gliding through the air." What do you know about cats and how they jump that helps you understand your friend's description of the player?

Annabel Lee

Edgar Allan Poe

It was many and many a year ago,
    In a kingdom by the sea,
That a maiden there lived whom you may know
    By the name of Annabel Lee;—

5 And this maiden she lived with no other thought
    Than to love and be loved by me.

She was a child and *I* was a child,
    In this kingdom by the sea,
But we loved with a love that was more than love—

10   I and my Annabel Lee—
With a love that the wingéd seraphs° of heaven
    Coveted° her and me.

And this was the reason that, long ago,
    In this kingdom by the sea,

15 A wind blew out of a cloud by night
    Chilling my Annabel Lee;
So that her high-born kinsmen came
    And bore her away from me,
To shut her up in a sepulchre°

20   In this kingdom by the sea.

The angels, not half so happy in Heaven,
    Went envying her and me:—

BQ BIG Question
What had once made the speaker happy?

Interpret Imagery To what senses does the image in lines 15 and 16 appeal?

11–12 ***Seraphs*** are high-ranking angels who are said to burn with love for God. Even these angels were jealous of *(coveted)* the love between the speaker and Annabel Lee.

19 A ***sepulchre*** (sep′ əl kər) is a tomb or burial place.

Lands End, Cornwall, 1888. William Trost Richards. Oil on canvas, 157.5 x 127 cm. Butler Institute of American Art, Youngtown, OH.

Yes! that was the reason (as all
    men know,
    In this kingdom by the sea)
25 That the wind came out of the
    cloud, chilling
    And killing my Annabel Lee.

But our love it was stronger
    by far than the love
    Of those who were older
    than we—
    Of many far wiser than we—
30 And neither the angels in
    Heaven above,
    Nor the demons down under
    the sea,
Can ever dissever° my soul
    from the soul
    Of the beautiful Annabel Lee:—

For the moon never beams without bringing me dreams
35   Of the beautiful Annabel Lee;
And the stars never rise but I see the bright eyes
    Of the beautiful Annabel Lee;
And so, all the night-tide, I lie down by the side
Of my darling, my darling, my life and my bride,
40   In her sepulchre there by the sea—
    In her tomb by the side of the sea.

Rhythm and Meter
What effect does the rhythm of these lines have on the poem?

---

32 To **dissever** is to separate or split apart.

Annabel Lee **415**

After You Read

Respond and Think Critically

1. What is the relationship between the speaker and Annabel Lee? What happened to Annabel Lee? Explain. **[Recall]**

2. What do you learn about the speaker of the poem? How did Annabel Lee feel about the speaker? Support your answer with details from the poem. **[Infer]**

3. According to the speaker, why did Annabel Lee experience the fate she did? Explain. **[Paraphrase]**

4. To be *idealized* means "to be made a model of perfection." Do you think that the speaker of the poem has idealized Annabel Lee? Explain. **[Interpret]**

5. How realistic does this poem seem to you? Can you imagine a real-life person experiencing the same thoughts and emotions as does the speaker? Explain. **[Evaluate]**

6. **BIG Question** How do you think the speaker of the poem would answer the Big Question? Do you agree with the speaker? Explain why or why not. **[Analyze]**

TIP

Evaluating
Use the questions below to help you answer question 5.

- How has the speaker reacted to the death of Annabel Lee?

- Which events in the poem seem realistic? Which events do not seem realistic?

- How do you react when you face a difficult experience? What helps you cope during hard times?

FOLDABLES Study Organizer Keep track of your ideas about the **BIG Question** in your unit Foldable.

View the Art

An Artist's Interpretation

Annabel Lee, c. 1890. James Abbott McNeill Whistler. 1890. Pastel on brown paper. Freer Gallery of Art, Washington, DC.

James Abbott McNeill Whistler created this pastel in 1890 to illustrate "Annabel Lee." Look carefully at the use of color and the setting. What mood does Whistler create?

Group Activity Discuss the following questions with classmates. Use evidence from "Annabel Lee" to support your answers.

1. How accurately does Whistler re-create the setting of the poem?

2. How accurately does Whistler re-create Annabel Lee? Consider her clothing and the amount of detail that you see.

3. How well does Whistler capture the mood of the poem? Explain.

Literary Elements Rhythm and Meter

1. How would you describe the rhythm of the poem? What does the rhythm add to the mood, or feeling, of the poem? Explain.

2. Reread stanzas 4 and 5. In stanza 5, what change do you notice in the rhythm and meter? Why do you think Poe introduced this change? Explain its effect.

Review: Rhyme

As you learned on page 393, **rhyme** is the repetition of sounds at the ends of words that appear close to each other in a poem. When poets use a pattern of rhyme formed by the end rhyme in a poem, they create a **rhyme scheme.** For example, notice the rhyming words in these lines from "Annabel Lee."

> It was many and many a year ago,
> > In a kingdom by the sea,
> That a maiden there lived whom you may know
> > By the name of Annabel Lee;—

The first four lines of stanza one have a rhyme scheme of *abab.*

3. What is the complete rhyme scheme of stanza one?

4. Which words rhyme in stanza two of the poem?

5. What does rhyme add to the poem's effect? Are there ideas that rhyme helps to emphasize? Explain.

Reading Strategy Interpret Imagery

6. List three images in "Annabel Lee." For each image, tell what sense or senses it appeals to. What feelings does each image suggest to you? Explain.

7. One possible theme, or message, of the poem is that love is powerful and everlasting. Identify three images that support this theme. Explain why you think the images suggest that love is powerful.

Academic Vocabulary

In "Annabel Lee," the speaker suffers the **ultimate** loss when Annabel Lee dies.

In the preceding sentence, *ultimate* means "greatest." It can also mean "last" or "final."

Read the following sentence: "The **ultimate** game of the day will decide the winner of the basketball championship for our school league." In what sense is *ultimate* used in this sentence? Explain.

Literature Online

Selection Resources For Selection Quizzes, eFlashcards, and Reading-Writing Connection activities, go to glencoe.com and enter QuickPass code GL27534u3.

Respond Through Writing

Expository Essay

Analyze Sound Devices In "Annabel Lee," Poe uses rhyme, alliteration, and repetition to show the speaker's thoughts about the death of his wife. In an expository essay, analyze these sound devices and explain their effect on the meaning of the poem.

Understand the Task **Rhyme** is the repetition of sounds at the ends of words that appear close to each other in a poem. Alliteration is the repetition of consonant sounds, usually at the beginnings of words or syllables. An example of alliteration is contained in the line, "It was <u>m</u>any and <u>m</u>any a year ago." Alliteration is a type of repetition. **Repetition** is the recurrence of sounds, words, phrases, lines, or stanzas. In your essay, identify examples of these **sound devices** and explain how they help reveal the message of the poem.

Prewrite Reread "Annabel Lee" to find examples of rhyme, alliteration, and repetition. Think about how these sound devices work together to create an overall effect. Keep track of your ideas in a chart like the one below.

	Example	Effect on Poem
Rhyme		
Alliteration		
Repetition		

Draft Before you begin your draft, decide how you will organize your essay. You may decide to write an introduction, a paragraph about each sound device and its effect, and then a conclusion. After you plan your organization, create a thesis statement. This sentence frame might help draft your thesis statement:

> Sound devices in "Annabel Lee" are used to create a feeling of _____.

Revise After you have written your first draft, read it to make sure that your ideas are in a logical order. Rearrange sentences or examples of sound devices as necessary.

Edit and Proofread Proofread your paper, correcting any errors in spelling, grammar, and punctuation. Review the Grammar Tip in the side column for information on hyphens in compound modifiers.

 GA Performance Standards

For page 418

ELA7W2f Demonstrate competence in a variety of genres. Produce writing that follows an organizational pattern appropriate to the type of composition.

> ### Grammar Tip
>
> **Hyphens**
> Use a hyphen to join a compound modifier that appears before a noun. For example:
>
> *Poe is known for his high-quality stories.*
>
> The hyphen shows that the words *high* and *quality* go together as a compound modifier.
>
> Be sure to hyphenate compound modifiers when they come before the word they describe but not when they come after. For example:
>
> **Before:** "Annabel Lee" is a well-written poem.
>
> **After:** "Annabel Lee" is a poem that is well written.

Before You Read

A Crush

Connect to the Short Story

Think about someone your age whom you wish you knew better. How could you let this person know that you want to get to know him or her?

List List ways you might quietly let someone know you'd like to get to know him or her better.

Build Background

W. Atlee Burpee & Co. is a mail-order seed company. A character in this story grows the following flowers from Burpee seeds.

- Zinnias have hairy stems and come in a variety of colors.
- Cornflowers have blue petals.
- Nasturtiums may be red, yellow, or orange.
- Marigolds may have yellow, orange, or red petals.
- Asters may be white, pink, yellow, purple, or blue.
- Four-o'clocks come in shades of white, yellow, pink, and red. Their name describes when their petals open: late afternoon.

Vocabulary

excess (ekʹses) *adj.* more than usual or necessary (p. 421). *After cleaning her closet, Tabitha donated her excess clothes to charity.*

speculation (spekʹyə lāʹshən) *n.* the act of forming an opinion or conclusion based on guesswork (p. 422). *Whether Mona or Trey would win the election for class president caused speculation among the students.*

improbable (im probʹə bəl) *adj.* not likely (p. 423). *If you leave now, it seems improbable that you'll miss the bus.*

illuminated (i lo͞oʹmə nāt id) *adj.* lit up (p. 424). *Illuminated by lights, the streets attracted late-night shoppers.*

discreetly (dis krētʹlē) *adv.* in a manner showing good judgment (p. 428). *Harry realized that he had walked in on a private discussion, so he discreetly walked away.*

Set Purposes for Reading

BQ ▶ BIG Question

As you read, ask yourself, how can kindness and affection help to make a person's life better?

Literary Element Symbol

A **symbol** is an object, a person, a place, or an experience that represents something else and means more than what it is. For example, a dove is a symbol of peace. A mountain may be a symbol of strength.

Authors use symbols to create deeper meaning and to emphasize themes in their works. Discovering the meaning of a symbol will help you gain a better understanding of a selection.

As you read "A Crush," look for words, images, and actions that may represent something else. Ask yourself, what do these things symbolize, and why are they important in this story?

Reading Strategy Draw Conclusions About Characters

When you **draw conclusions** as you read, you use pieces of information to make a general statement about characters, events, and ideas. You figure out more than what the author states directly.

Drawing conclusions about characters will help you understand the main idea or essential message of what you read. When you draw conclusions about characters, you can better understand why characters say and do certain things.

To draw conclusions about characters, look for details about the characters. Use these details to make general statements about the characters. As you read "A Crush," use the chart below to organize details about the characters. Then draw conclusions about the characters, their thoughts, and their actions.

Character Name	Details About the Character	What I Already Know	Conclusions I Can Draw About the Character

GA Performance Standards

For pages 419–432

ELA7R1g/ii For literary texts, explain and analyze the effects of figurative language.

> ### TRY IT
>
> **Draw Conclusions** Imagine that you saw a classmate pick up someone's papers from the floor, open the door for the teacher, and sit at lunch with a new student who has not yet made friends at school. What conclusion might you draw about this classmate?

A Crush

Cynthia Rylant

When the windows of Stan's Hardware started filling up with flowers, everyone in town knew something had happened. **Excess** flowers usually mean death, but since these were all real flowers bearing the aroma of nature instead of floral preservative,[1] and since they stood bunched in clear mason jars instead of impaled on styrofoam crosses, everyone knew nobody had died. So they all figured somebody had a crush and kept quiet.

Symbol What two events do flowers symbolize for the people in the town?

---

1 *Floral preservative* is a chemical that helps cut flowers stay fresh looking.

Vocabulary

excess (ek′ses) *adj.* more than usual or necessary

There wasn't really a Stan of Stan's Hardware. Dick Wilcox was the owner, and since he'd never liked his own name, he gave his store half the name of his childhood hero, Stan Laurel in the movies. Dick had been married for twenty-seven years. Once, his wife Helen had dropped a German chocolate cake on his head at a Lion's Club dance, so Dick and Helen were not likely candidates for the honest expression of the flowers in those clear mason jars lining the windows of Stan's Hardware, and **speculation** had to move on to Dolores.

Dolores was the assistant manager at Stan's and had worked there for twenty years, since high school. She knew the store like a mother knows her baby, so Dick—who had trouble keeping up with things like prices and new brands of drywall compound[2]—tried to keep himself busy in the back and give Dolores the run of the floor. This worked fine because the carpenters and plumbers and painters in town trusted Dolores and took her advice to heart. They also liked her tattoo.

Dolores was the only woman in town with a tattoo. On the days she went sleeveless, one could see it on the taut brown skin of her upper arm: "Howl at the Moon." The picture was of a baying coyote which must have been a dark gray in its early days but which had faded to the color of the spackling paste Dolores stocked in the third aisle. Nobody had gotten out of Dolores the true story behind the tattoo. Some of the men who came in liked to show off their own, and they'd roll up their sleeves or pull open their shirts, exhibiting bald eagles and rattlesnakes, and they'd try to coax out of Dolores the history of her coyote. All of the men had gotten their tattoos when they were in the service, drunk on weekend

---

2 **Drywall compound** and **spackling paste** (mentioned in the next paragraph) are used to prepare walls before painting.

Vocabulary

speculation (spek′yə lā′shən) *n.* the act of forming an opinion or conclusion based on guesswork

leave and full of the spitfire[3] of young soldiers. Dolores had never been in the service and she'd never seen weekend leave and there wasn't a tattoo parlor anywhere near. They couldn't figure why or where any half-sober woman would have a howling coyote ground into the soft skin of her upper arm. But Dolores wasn't telling.

That the flowers in Stan's front window had anything to do with Dolores seemed completely **improbable.** As far as anyone knew, Dolores had never been in love nor had anyone ever been in love with her. Some believed it was the tattoo, of course, or the fine dark hair coating Dolores's upper lip which kept suitors away. Some felt it was because Dolores was just more of a man than most of the men in town, and fellows couldn't figure out how to court someone who knew more about the carburetor of a car or the back side of a washing machine than they did. Others thought Dolores simply didn't want love. This was a popular theory among the women in town who sold Avon and Mary Kay cosmetics. Whenever one of them ran into the hardware for a package of light bulbs or some batteries, she would mentally pluck every one of the black hairs above Dolores's lip. Then she'd wash that grease out of Dolores's hair, give her a good blunt cut, dress her in a decent silk-blend blouse with a nice Liz Claiborne skirt from the Sports line, and, finally, tone down that swarthy, longshoreman[4] look of Dolores's with a concealing beige foundation, some frosted peach lipstick, and a good gray liner for the eyes.

Dolores simply didn't want love, the Avon lady would think as she walked back to her car carrying her little bag of batteries. If she did, she'd fix herself up.

The man who was in love with Dolores and who brought her zinnias and cornflowers and nasturtiums and

Draw Conclusions About Characters Notice the details in the description of Dolores. What conclusions are you forming about her?

---

3 When soldiers are off duty and allowed to go off base, they're on *leave*. When they're full of *spitfire*, they're quick-tempered and ready to fight.

4 A *swarthy longshoreman* is a dark or sunburned dockworker.

Vocabulary ·

improbable (im prob′ə bəl) *adj.* not likely

marigolds and asters and four-o'clocks in clear mason jars did not know any of this. He did not know that men showed Dolores their tattoos. He did not know that Dolores understood how to use and to sell a belt sander. He did not know that Dolores needed some concealing beige foundation so she could get someone to love her. The man who brought flowers to Dolores on Wednesdays when the hardware opened its doors at 7:00 A.M. didn't care who Dolores had ever been or what anyone had ever thought of her. He loved her and he wanted to bring her flowers.

Ernie had lived in this town all of his life and had never before met Dolores. He was thirty-three years old, and for thirty-one of those years he had lived at home with his mother in a small, dark house on the edge of town near Beckwith's Orchards. Ernie had been a beautiful baby, with a shock of shining black hair and large blue eyes and a round, wise face. But as he had grown, it had become clearer and clearer that though he was indeed a perfectly beautiful child, his mind had not developed with the same perfection. Ernie would not be able to speak in sentences until he was six years old. He would not be able to count the apples in a bowl until he was eight. By the time he was ten, he could sing a simple song. At age twelve, he understood what a joke was. And when he was twenty, something he saw on television made him cry.

Ernie's mother kept him in the house with her because it was easier, so Ernie knew nothing of the world except this house. They lived, the two of them, in tiny dark rooms always **illuminated** by the glow of a television set, Ernie's bags of Oreos and Nutter Butters littering the floor, his baseball cards scattered across the sofa, his heavy winter coat thrown over the arm of a chair so he could wear it whenever he wanted, and his box of Burpee seed packages sitting in the middle of the kitchen table.

These Ernie cherished. The seeds had been delivered to his home by mistake. One day a woman wearing a brown uniform had pulled up in a brown truck, walked quickly

Draw Conclusions About Characters From the details in the paragraph, what impressions are you forming of Ernie?

Vocabulary

illuminated (i lōō′mə nāt id) *adj.* lit up

424   UNIT 3 What Makes Life Good?

to the front porch of Ernie's house, set a box down, and with a couple of toots of her horn, driven off again. Ernie had watched her through the curtains, and when she was gone, had ventured[5] onto the porch and shyly, cautiously, picked up the box. His mother checked it when he carried it inside. The box didn't have their name on it but the brown truck was gone, so whatever was in the box was theirs to keep. Ernie pulled off the heavy tape, his fingers trembling, and found inside the box more little packages of seeds than he could count. He lifted them out, one by one, and examined the beautiful photographs of flowers on each. His mother was not interested, had returned to the television, but Ernie sat down at the kitchen table and quietly looked at each package for a long time, his fingers running across the slick paper and outlining the shapes of zinnias and cornflowers and nasturtiums and marigolds and asters and four-o'clocks, his eyes drawing up their colors.

Two months later Ernie's mother died. A neighbor found her at the mailbox beside the road. People from the county courthouse came out to get Ernie, and as they ushered him from the home he would never see again, he picked up the box of seed packages from his kitchen table and passed through the doorway.

Eventually Ernie was moved to a large white house near the main street of town. This house was called a group home, because in it lived a group of people who, like Ernie, could not live on their own. There were six of them. Each had his own room. When Ernie was shown the room that would be his, he put the box of Burpee seeds—which he had kept with him since his mother's death—on the little table beside the bed and then he sat down on the bed and cried.

Ernie cried every day for nearly a month. And then he stopped. He dried his tears and he learned how to bake refrigerator biscuits and how to dust mop and what to do if the indoor plants looked brown.

Ernie loved watering the indoor plants and it was this pleasure which finally drew him outside. One of the

Symbol What object or objects may be emerging as a symbol?

---

5 If you *ventured* somewhere, you went despite possible risk or danger.

young men who worked at the group home—a college student named Jack—grew a large garden in the back of the house. It was full of tomato vines and the large yellow blossoms of healthy squash. During his first summer at the house, Ernie would stand at the kitchen window, watching Jack and sometimes a resident of the home move among the vegetables. Ernie was curious, but too afraid to go into the garden.

Then one day when Ernie was watching through the window, he noticed that Jack was ripping open several slick little packages and emptying them into the ground. Ernie panicked and ran to his room. But the box of Burpee seeds was still there on his table, untouched. He grabbed it, slid it under his bed, then went back through the house and out into the garden as if he had done this every day of his life.

He stood beside Jack, watching him empty seed packages into the soft black soil, and as the packages were emptied, Ernie asked for them, holding out his hand, his eyes on the photographs of red radishes and purple eggplant. Jack handed the empty packages over with a smile and with that gesture became Ernie's first friend.

Jack tried to explain to Ernie that the seeds would grow into vegetables but Ernie could not believe this until he saw it come true. And when it did, he looked all the more intently[6] at the packages of zinnias and cornflowers and the rest hidden beneath his bed. He thought more deeply about them but he could not carry them to the garden. He could not let the garden have his seeds.

That was the first year in the large white house.

The second year, Ernie saw Dolores, and after that he thought of nothing else but her and of the photographs of flowers beneath his bed.

Jack had decided to take Ernie downtown for breakfast every Wednesday morning to ease him into the world outside that of the group home. They left very early, at 5:45 A.M., so there would be few people and almost no traffic to frighten Ernie and make him beg for his room. Jack and Ernie drove to the Big Boy restaurant which sat

Draw Conclusions About Characters Based on Jack's actions, what conclusion can you draw about him?

---

6 If you looked *intently* at an object, you looked at it in a firmly focused way.

Boulevard Diner, Worcester, MA, 1992. John Baeder. Oil on canvas, 30 1/4 x 48 1/4 in. O.K. Harris Works of Art, NY.

View the Art While Ernie was eating breakfast at the Big Boy restaurant, his life changed. Whose life might be changed at the diner in this painting?

across the street from Stan's Hardware. There they ate eggs and bacon and French toast among those whose work demanded rising before the sun: bus drivers, policemen, nurses, mill workers. Their first time in the Big Boy, Ernie was too nervous to eat. The second time, he could eat but he couldn't look up. The third time, he not only ate everything on his plate, but he lifted his head and he looked out the window of the Big Boy restaurant toward Stan's Hardware across the street. There he saw a dark-haired woman in jeans and a black T-shirt unlocking the front door of the building, and that was the moment Ernie started loving Dolores and thinking about giving up his seeds to the soft black soil of Jack's garden.

Love is such a mystery, and when it strikes the heart of one as mysterious as Ernie himself, it can hardly be spoken of. Ernie could not explain to Jack why he went directly to his room later that morning, pulled the box of

Draw Conclusions About Characters Why do you think Ernie is changing?

Burpee seeds from under his bed, then grabbed Jack's hand in the kitchen and walked with him to the garden where Ernie had come to believe things would grow. Ernie handed the packets of seeds one by one to Jack, who stood in silent admiration of the lovely photographs before asking Ernie several times, "Are you sure you want to plant these?" Ernie was sure. It didn't take him very long, and when the seeds all lay under the moist black earth, Ernie carried his empty packages inside the house and spent the rest of the day spreading them across his bed in different arrangements.

That was in June. For the next several Wednesdays at 7:00 A.M. Ernie watched every movement of the dark-haired woman behind the lighted windows of Stan's Hardware. Jack watched Ernie watch Dolores, and **discreetly** said nothing.

When Ernie's flowers began growing in July, Ernie spent most of his time in the garden. He would watch the garden for hours, as if he expected it suddenly to move or to impress him with a quick trick. The fragile green stems of

Symbol What do you think the flower packages symbolize to Ernie?

Draw Conclusions About Characters What can you conclude about Jack from his discreet action?

Vocabulary
....

discreetly (dis krēt′ lē) *adv.* in a manner showing good judgment

his flowers stood uncertainly in the soil, like baby colts on their first legs, but the young plants performed no magic for Ernie's eyes. They saved their shows for the middle of the night and next day surprised Ernie with tender small blooms in all the colors the photographs had promised.

The flowers grew fast and hardy,[7] and one early Wednesday morning when they looked as big and bright as their pictures on the empty packages, Ernie pulled a glass canning jar off a dusty shelf in the basement of his house. He washed the jar, half filled it with water, then carried it to the garden where he placed in it one of every kind of flower he had grown. He met Jack at the car and rode off to the Big Boy with the jar of flowers held tight between his small hands. Jack told him it was a beautiful bouquet.

When they reached the door of the Big Boy, Ernie stopped and pulled at Jack's arm, pointing to the building across the street. "OK," Jack said, and he led Ernie to the front door of Stan's Hardware. It was 6:00 A.M. and the building was still dark. Ernie set the clear mason jar full of flowers under the sign that read "Closed," then he smiled at Jack and followed him back across the street to get breakfast.

When Dolores arrived at seven and picked up the jar of zinnias and cornflowers and nasturtiums and marigolds and asters and four-o'clocks, Ernie and Jack were watching her from a booth in the Big Boy. Each had a wide smile on his face as Dolores put her nose to the flowers. Ernie giggled. They watched the lights of the hardware store come up and saw Dolores place the clear mason jar on the ledge of the front window. They drove home still smiling.

All the rest of that summer Ernie left a jar of flowers every Wednesday morning at the front door of Stan's Hardware. Neither Dick Wilcox nor Dolores could figure out why the flowers kept coming, and each of them assumed somebody had a crush on the other. But the flowers had an effect on them anyway. Dick started spending more time out on the floor making conversation with the customers, while Dolores stopped wearing T-shirts

7 **Hardy** means "strong and healthy."

to work and instead wore crisp white blouses with the sleeves rolled back off her wrists. Occasionally she put on a bracelet.

By summer's end Jack and Ernie had become very good friends, and when the flowers in the garden behind their house began to wither, and Ernie's face began to grow gray as he watched them, Jack brought home one bright day in late September a great long box. Ernie followed Jack as he carried it down to the basement and watched as Jack pulled a long glass tube from the box and attached this tube to the wall above a table. When Jack plugged in the tube's electric cord, a soft lavender light washed the room.

"Sunshine," said Jack.

Then he went back to his car for a smaller box. He carried this down to the basement where Ernie still stood staring at the strange light. Jack handed Ernie the small box, and when Ernie opened it he found more little packages of seeds than he could count, with new kinds of photographs on the slick paper.

"Violets," Jack said, pointing to one of them.

Then he and Ernie went outside to get some dirt. 🌺

Draw Conclusions About Characters Why do the flowers change the behavior of the people who work at Stan's Hardware?

BQ **BIG Question**

How do Jack's actions show that he cares about Ernie and wants to help Ernie live a more fulfilling life?

After You Read

Respond and Think Critically

1. Whom do Dolores and Dick Wilcox think the flowers are for? [Recall]

2. When you see flowers, what do they make you think of? Why? Explain. [Connect]

3. Why do you think the women in town judge Dolores the way they do? [Interpret]

4. Why does Ernie like his seed packages so much? Explain. [Infer]

5. What makes Jack a good caretaker and friend for Ernie? Support your answer with details from the story. [Evaluate]

6. **BQ** BIG Question How does Ernie's crush change his life and the lives of the other three characters in the story? Explain. [Analyze]

Vocabulary Practice

Match each boldfaced vocabulary word with a word from the right column that has the same meaning. Two of the words in the right column will not have matches. Then write an original sentence using each vocabulary word, or draw a picture that represents the word.

1. **excess**
2. **illuminated**
3. **discreetly**
4. **improbable**
5. **speculation**

a. cautiously
b. hastily
c. unlikely
d. extra
e. punctured
f. assumption
g. brightened

Example:

excess

Sentence: When we doubled the cake recipe, we used the excess batter to make cupcakes.

Academic Vocabulary

Born in 1954, Cynthia Rylant is a **contemporary** author who continues to fill her stories with characters that today's young people can relate to. Using context clues, try to figure out the meaning of the word *contemporary* in the preceding sentence. Check your guess in a dictionary.

TIP

Interpreting
To answer question 3, use details from the story and your own understanding of how people interact.

- Start by reviewing the description of Dolores. Then review the description of the other women. How is Dolores different from the other women?

- Think about what you know about people who are different from those around them. How do others often treat such people? Why?

 FOLDABLES Study Organizer Keep track of your ideas about the **BIG Question** in your unit Foldable.

 **Literature** Online

Selection Resources
For Selection Quizzes, eFlashcards, and Reading-Writing Connection activities, go to glencoe.com and enter QuickPass code GL27534u3.

Literary Element | Symbol

1. What does Dolores's tattoo symbolize to the people of the town? Explain.
2. In the story, what objects or events represent change for Ernie? Explain.

Review: **Mood**

As you learned on page 195, **mood** is the emotional quality or atmosphere of a story. Descriptive words, setting, dialogue, and characters' actions can all contribute to the mood of a story.

3. What, in your opinion, is the mood of the story? Use details from the story to support your answer.
4. Explain how dialogue and setting contributed to the mood of the story. Give specific examples in your answer.

Reading Strategy
Draw Conclusions About Characters

Standards Practice **ELA7R1f**

5. According to the story, how did Jack influence Ernie's life?
   - A He helped Ernie learn to garden and eased him into the outside world.
   - B He showed Ernie how to eat breakfast foods at the Big Boy restaurant.
   - C He persuaded Ernie to open his seed packages and plant the seeds.
   - D He taught Ernie how to talk to Dolores at the hardware store.

Grammar Link

Modifiers Two kinds of **modifiers,** or describing words, are adjectives and adverbs.

Adjectives are words that modify nouns and pronouns by answering these questions: Which one? What kind? How many?

I like <u>that</u> flower. (*Which one?* <u>that</u> flower)

I like <u>red</u> flowers. (*What kind?* <u>red</u> flowers)

I picked <u>two</u> flowers. (*How many?* <u>two</u> flowers)

Adverbs are words that modify verbs, adjectives, and other adverbs. Adverbs answer these questions: How? When? How often? Where? How much?

We ate breakfast <u>quickly</u>. (*How?* <u>quickly</u>)

I visited the garden <u>today</u>. (*When?* <u>today</u>)

We weed the garden <u>daily</u>. (*How often?* <u>daily</u>)

Plant the vegetables <u>here</u>. (*Where?* <u>here</u>)

It is <u>too</u> hot to work in the garden today. (*How much?* <u>too</u>)

Practice Find two adjectives and two adverbs in "A Crush." Then write two of your own sentences. One sentence should contain an adjective, and the other should contain an adverb.

💬 Speaking and Listening

Literature Groups There are some unanswered questions in this story: Why didn't Dick Wilcox or Dolores try to find out who sent the flowers? Why didn't someone from the restaurant see Ernie and Jack leaving the flowers? With a group, discuss possible responses to these questions. Use details from the story and your own experience to support your answers.

Before You Read

The Luckiest Time of All

Connect to the Short Story

Think of the first time you met a person who later became very important to you.

Quickwrite Freewrite for a few minutes about that first meeting with someone who would become important to you. How did you feel about the person then? Did you know he or she would become important in your life? How do you feel about that person now?

Build Background

In 1898 Ephraim Williams was the only African American circus owner in the United States. Williams employed 26 people and owned 100 Arabian horses. By 1910 Williams had founded the all-black circus called "Silas Green from New Orleans."

- The Silas Green show traveled throughout the South, performing one-night shows. It became one of the longest-lasting tent shows in U.S. circus history.

- Williams managed the show and performed tricks with his horses. Other acts included legendary blues singer Bessie Smith.

- The Silas Green show was popular with both black and white audiences and continued touring into the 1950s, even after Williams's death in the 1930s.

Set Purposes for Reading

BQ BIG Question

As you read, ask yourself, how does Mrs. Pickens show her love for her great-granddaughter Tee and for her husband? How does Tee show she loves her great-grandmother? What does Mrs. Pickens teach Tee about love?

Literary Element Motivation

Motivation is the reason why a character acts, feels, or thinks as he or she does. Understanding a character's motivation helps you understand the character more fully. To understand a character's motivation, ask why the characters talk, think, and act as they do.

Performance Standards

For pages 433–438

ELA7R1b For literary texts, interpret a character's traits, emotions, or motivations and give supporting evidence from a text.

Meet Lucille Clifton

Poet of Few Words Lucille Clifton is known as a poet who says much with few words. Her spare writing often depicts the lives of African American families and the courage needed to endure hardship. Clifton is the daughter of a steelworker and a laundress, who encouraged her ambitions and her love of the written word. Clifton is the author of many volumes of poetry and works of fiction for young people. She was born in 1936.

 Literature Online

Author Search For more about Lucille Clifton, go to glencoe.com and enter QuickPass code GL27534u3.

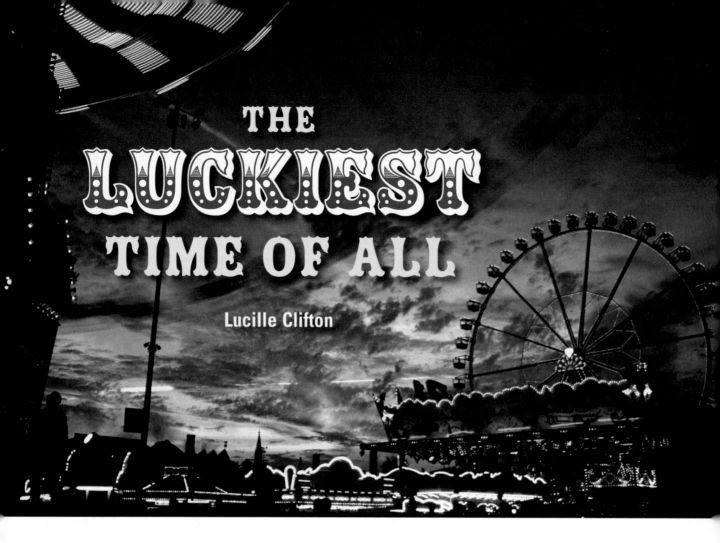

THE LUCKIEST TIME OF ALL

Lucille Clifton

Mrs. Elzie F. Pickens was rocking slowly on the porch one afternoon when her Great-granddaughter, Tee, brought her a big bunch of **dogwood blooms,** and that was the beginning of a story.

"Ahhh, now that dogwood reminds me of the day I met your Great-granddaddy, Mr. Pickens, Sweet Tee.

"It was just this time, spring of the year, and me and my best friend Ovella Wilson, who is now gone, was goin to join the Silas Greene. Usta be a kinda show went all through the South, called it the Silas Greene show. Somethin like the circus. Me and Ovella wanted to join that thing and see the world. Nothin wrong at home or nothin, we just wanted to travel and see new things and have high times. Didn't say nothin to nobody but one another. Just up and decided to do it.

Visual Vocabulary

Dogwood blooms are flowers, usually white or pink, from the dogwood tree or shrub.

"Well, this day we plaited our hair and put a dress and some things in a crokasack[1] and started out to the show. Spring day like this.

"We got there after a good little walk and it was the world, Baby, such music and wonders as we never had seen! They had everything there, or seemed like it.

"Me and Ovella thought we'd walk around for a while and see the show before goin to the office to sign up and join.

"While we was viewin it all we come up on this dancin dog. Cutest one thing in the world next to you, Sweet Tee, dippin and movin and head bowin to that music. Had a little ruffly skirt on itself and up on two back legs twistin and movin to the music. Dancin dancin dancin till people started throwin pennies out of they pockets.

"Me and Ovella was caught up too and laughin so. She took a penny out of her pocket and threw it to the ground where that dog was dancin, and I took two pennies and threw 'em both.

"The music was faster and faster and that dog was turnin and turnin. Ovella reached in her sack and threw out a little pin she had won from never being late at Sunday school. And me, laughin and all excited, reached in my bag and threw out my lucky stone!

"Well, I knew right off what I had done. Soon as it left my hand it seemed like I reached back out for it to take it back. But the stone was gone from my hand and Lord, it hit that dancin dog right on his nose!

"Well, he lit out after me, poor thing. He lit out after me and I flew! Round and round the Silas Greene we run, through every place me and Ovella had walked before, but now that dancin dog was a runnin dog and all the people was laughin at the new show, which was us!

"I felt myself slowin down after a while and I thought I would turn around a little bit to see how much gain that cute little dog was makin on me. When I did I got such a surprise! Right behind me was the dancin dog and right

Motivation Why do Elzie and Ovella throw their pennies?

---

1 **Crokasack** is a shortened form of "croker sack," a bag made of burlap or a similar rough material.

behind him was the finest fast runnin hero in the bottoms of Virginia.

"And that was Mr. Pickens when he was still a boy! He had a length of twine in his hand and he was twirlin it around in the air just like the cowboy at the Silas Greene and grinnin fit to bust.

"While I was watchin how the sun shined on him and made him look like an angel come to help a poor sinner girl, why, he twirled that twine one extra fancy twirl and looped it right around one hind leg of that dancin dog and brought him low.

"I stopped then and walked slow and shy to where he had picked up that poor dog to see if he was hurt, cradlin him and talkin to him soft and sweet. That showed me how kind and gentle he was, and when we walked back to the dancin dog's place in the show he let the dog loose and helped me to find my stone. I told him how shiny black it was and how it had the letter A scratched on one side. We searched and searched and at last he spied it!

"Ovella and me lost heart for shows then and we walked on home. And a good little way, the one who was gonna be your Great-granddaddy was walkin on behind. Seein us safe. Us walkin kind of slow. Him seein us safe. Yes." Mrs. Pickens' voice trailed off softly and Tee noticed she had a little smile on her face.

"Grandmama, that stone almost got you bit by a dog that time. It wasn't so lucky that time, was it?"

Tee's Great-grandmother shook her head and laughed out loud.

"That was the luckiest time of all, Tee Baby. It got me acquainted with Mr. Amos Pickens, and if that ain't luck, what could it be! Yes, it was luckier for me than for anybody, I think. Least mostly I think it."

Tee laughed with her Great-grandmother though she didn't exactly know why.

"I hope I have that kind of good stone luck one day," she said.

"Maybe you will someday," her Great-grandmother said.

And they rocked a little longer and smiled together. 🍂

Motivation Why is Mr. Pickens smiling and trying to catch the dog?

BQ **BIG Question**
How do Mrs. Pickens and her great-granddaughter show their love for each other?

After You Read

Respond and Think Critically

1. Why does Mrs. Pickens begin telling a story to her great-granddaughter? [Recall]

2. How does Elzie meet Mr. Pickens at the circus? Give details from the story. [Summarize]

3. Why does Mr. Pickens follow Elzie and Ovella home? Support your answer with details from the story. [Infer]

4. Mrs. Pickens smiles as she describes Mr. Pickens following her home. What does her smile say about her feelings about Mr. Pickens? Explain. [Interpret]

5. Why does Tee at first think the stone is unlucky? How does her great-grandmother feel about the stone? Explain. [Compare]

6. **BQ** ❯ BIG Question How do you show your affection for close friends and family members? How do your experiences help you understand the characters in the story? Explain. [Connect]

Academic Vocabulary

For Elzie and Ovella, the cute dancing dog was the **highlight** of the show. In the preceding sentence, *highlight* means something of special significance or interest. *Highlight* also has other meanings. For example: Jody's beautiful sculptures **highlight** her talent as an artist. What do you think *highlight* means in the preceding sentence? What is the difference between the two meanings?

TIP

Inferring
To answer question 3, think about Mr. Pickens actions in the story. Also, think about your own knowledge of people.

- Start by recalling what Mr. Pickens does in the story: are his actions kind, selfish, or mean?

- Think about how Mr. Pickens's actions might show his feelings toward Elzie.

FOLDABLES Keep track of
Study Organizer your ideas about the **BIG Question** in your unit Foldable.

 Literature Online

Selection Resources
For Selection Quizzes, eFlashcards, and Reading-Writing Connection activities, go to glencoe.com and enter QuickPass code GL27534u3.

Literary Element | Motivation

1. Why do Elzie and Ovella want to join the circus?

2. Why does Mrs. Perkins consider the time she almost got bitten by a dog to be "the luckiest time of all"?

Review: Dialogue

As you learned on page 277, **dialogue** is the conversation between characters in a story. Dialogue is shown by the use of quotation marks around the exact words of a character.

3. How does Mrs. Perkins show her feelings about her great-granddaughter through her dialogue? Explain your answer using details from the story.

4. Is the dialogue in the story realistic or unrealistic? Support your answer using details from the story.

5. Notice that the story is almost all dialogue. How would the story be different if it was written without any dialogue? Explain your answer.

Grammar Link

Comparative and Superlative Adjectives
The **comparative** form of an adjective is used to compare a person, place, or thing with another. To form the comparative of one-syllable words and many two-syllable words, add *-er* to the end.

Mrs. Pickens is <u>older</u> than Tee.

To form the comparative of adjectives of more than two syllables, use the word *more* or *less.*

Elzie is <u>more generous</u> than her friend.

The **superlative** form of an adjective compares a person, place, or thing with two or more persons, places, or things. To form the superlative of one-syllable words and many two-syllable words, add *-est* to the end. You may have to change the spelling of the root. Use a dictionary to check spelling.

Elzie was the <u>luckiest</u> girl at the show.

To form the superlative of adjectives of more than two syllables, use the word *most* or *least.*

Elzie was the <u>most excited</u> person watching the show.

Practice Write two sentences about the story, using a comparative adjective in the first sentence and a superlative adjective in the second sentence.

💬 Speaking and Listening

Oral Report Choose a work by Lucille Clifton and write an oral report with a summary of the work and a discussion of its theme, or main idea. Use examples from the work to support your ideas. As you present your report, maintain eye contact with your audience. Practice giving your report to a friend or family member before you present it to the class.

Comparing Literature

Superman and Me and *My First Memory (of Librarians)*

GA Performance Standards

For pages 439–447

ELA7R1c For literary texts, relate a literary work to information about its setting or historical moment.

ELA7R1d Analyze recurring themes.

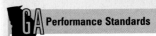

BQ BIG Question

As you read these paired selections, ask yourself, what do the narrator in "Superman and Me" and the speaker in "My First Memory (of Librarians)" have in common? What gives their lives joy and meaning?

Literary Element Setting

You've learned that **setting** is the time and place in which the events of a literary work take place. The setting often helps create the mood, or atmosphere, of a story. As you read the essay and the poem, notice details that describe when and where. Also look for ways in which the setting helps reveal the theme, or overall message, of each selection.

Reading Skill Compare and Contrast

When you compare, you look for similarities. When you contrast, you look for differences. Comparing and contrasting the settings of two selections can help you understand how setting gives meaning to a literary work.

On the following pages, you'll compare and contrast the settings of "Superman and Me" and "My First Memory (of Librarians)." Use a diagram like the one below to help compare and contrast the settings of the two selections. Record differences in the settings in the outer portions of each circle. Record how the settings are similar in the overlapping portion of the circles. Consider how the settings help reveal a similar theme across both selections.

"Superman and Me"   "My First Memory (of Librarians)"

Meet the Authors

Sherman Alexie

Sherman Alexie grew up in the state of Washington. He was born in 1966.

Nikki Giovanni

Nikki Giovanni is a poet, a professor, and a political activist. She was born in 1943.

 Literature Online

Author Search For more about Sherman Alexie and Nikki Giovanni, go to glencoe.com and enter QuickPass code GL27534u3.

Dove and Newspaper Hills. Kazu Nitta.

SUPERMAN and ME

Sherman Alexie

I learned to read with a *Superman* comic book. Simple enough, I suppose. I cannot recall which particular *Superman* comic book I read, nor can I remember which villain he fought in that issue. I cannot remember the plot, nor the means by which I obtained the comic book. What I can remember is this: I was three years old, a Spokane Indian boy living with his family on the Spokane Indian Reservation in eastern Washington state. We were poor by most standards, but one of my parents usually managed to find some minimum-wage job or another, which made us middle class by reservation standards. I had a brother and three sisters. We lived on a combination of irregular paychecks, hope, fear, and government-surplus food.

My father, who is one of the few Indians who went to Catholic school on purpose, was an avid[1] reader of westerns, spy thrillers, murder mysteries, gangster epics, basketball-player biographies, and anything else he could find. He bought his books by the pound at Dutch's Pawn Shop, Goodwill, Salvation Army, and Value Village. When he had extra money, he bought new novels at supermarkets, convenience stores, and hospital gift shops. Our house was filled with books. They were stacked in crazy piles in the bathroom, bedrooms, and living room. In a fit of unemployment-inspired creative energy, my father built a set of

Comparing Literature
Describe the setting of the narrator's childhood.

---

1 If you are an **avid** reader, you have a great enthusiasm for reading.

bookshelves and soon filled them with a random assortment of books about the Kennedy assassination, Watergate, the Vietnam War, and the entire twenty-three-book series of the Apache westerns.[2] My father loved books, and since I loved my father with an aching devotion, I decided to love books as well.

I can remember picking up my father's books before I could read. The words themselves were mostly foreign, but I still remember the exact moment when I first understood, with a sudden clarity, the purpose of a paragraph. I didn't have the vocabulary to say "paragraph," but I realized that a paragraph was a fence that held words. The words inside a paragraph worked together for a common purpose. They had some specific reason for being inside the same fence. This knowledge delighted me. I began to think of everything in terms of paragraphs. Our reservation was a small paragraph within the United States. My family's house was a paragraph, distinct from the other paragraphs of the LeBrets to the north, the Fords to our south, and the Tribal School to the west. Inside our house, each family member existed as a separate paragraph, but still had genetics and common experiences to link us. Now, using this logic, I can see my changed family as an essay of seven paragraphs: mother, father, older brother, the deceased[3] sister, my younger twin sisters, and our adopted little brother.

At the same time I was seeing the world in paragraphs, I also picked up that *Superman* comic book. Each panel, complete with picture, dialogue, and narrative, was a three-dimensional paragraph. In one panel, Superman breaks through a door. His suit is red,

Comparing Literature In what way does reading affect the narrator's view of his setting?

---

2 The ***Kennedy assassination*** refers to the death of U.S. President John F. Kennedy in 1963. During the administration of U.S. President Richard Nixon, a series of scandals called ***Watergate*** took place. During the ***Vietnam War*** (1954–1975), the United States helped South Vietnam fight North Vietnam. The ***Apache*** are a group of Native Americans.

3 ***Deceased*** is another word for *dead*.

blue, and yellow. The brown door shatters into many pieces. I look at the narrative above the picture. I cannot read the words, but I assume it tells me that Superman is breaking down the door. Aloud, I pretend to read the words and say "Superman is breaking down the door." Words, dialogue, also float out of Superman's mouth. Because he is breaking down the door, I assume he says, "I am breaking down the door." Once again, I pretend to read the words and say aloud, "I am breaking down the door." In this way, I learned to read.

This might be an interesting story all by itself. A little Indian boy teaches himself to read at an early age and advances quickly. He reads *Grapes of Wrath* in kindergarten when other children are struggling through Dick and Jane. If he'd been anything but an Indian boy living on the reservation, he might have been called a prodigy.[4] But he is an Indian boy living on the reservation, and is simply an oddity. He grows into a man who often speaks of his childhood in the third-person, as if it will somehow dull the pain and make him sound more modest about his talents.

A smart Indian is a dangerous person, widely feared and ridiculed by Indians and non-Indians alike. I fought with my classmates on a daily basis. They wanted me to stay quiet when the non-Indian teacher asked for answers, for volunteers, for help. We were Indian children who were expected to be stupid. Most lived up to those expectations inside the classroom, but subverted[5] them on the outside. They struggled with basic reading in school, but could remember how to sing a few dozen powwow songs. They were mono-syllabic in front of their non-Indian teachers, but could tell complicated stories and jokes at the dinner table. They submissively ducked their heads when confronted[6] by a

Comparing Literature Why does the narrator feel like an outsider in his setting?

---

4 A *prodigy* is a young person with exceptional talent.

5 If you *subverted* an idea, you went against it.

6 If you *confronted* someone, you met him or her face-to-face.

non-Indian adult, but would slug it out with the Indian bully who was ten years older. As Indian children, we were expected to fail in the non-Indian world. Those who failed were ceremonially accepted by other Indians and appropriately pitied by non-Indians.

I refused to fail. I was smart. I was arrogant.[7] I was lucky. I read books late into the night, until I could barely keep my eyes open. I read books at recess, then during lunch, and in the few minutes left after I had finished my classroom assignments. I read books in the car when my family traveled to powwows or basketball games. In shopping malls, I ran to the bookstores and read bits and pieces of as many books as I could. I read the books my father brought home from the pawnshops and secondhand stores. I read the books I borrowed from the library. I read the backs of cereal boxes. I read the newspaper. I read the bulletins posted on the walls of the school, the clinic, the tribal offices, the post office. I read junk mail. I read auto-repair manuals. I read magazines. I read anything that had words and paragraphs. I read with equal parts joy and desperation. I loved those books, but I also knew that love had only one purpose. I was trying to save my life.

Despite all the books I read, I am still surprised I became a writer. I was going to be a pediatrician.[8] These days, I write novels, short stories, and poems. I visit schools and teach creative writing to Indian kids. In all my years in the reservation school system, I was never taught how to write poetry, short stories, or novels. I was certainly never taught that Indians wrote poetry, short stories, and novels. Writing was something beyond Indians. I cannot recall a single time that a guest teacher visited the reservation. There must have been visiting teachers. Who were they? Where are they now? Do they

Comparing Literature In what way can books save someone's life?

---

7 An *arrogant* person is proud of himself or herself or feels that he or she is better than others.

8 A *pediatrician* is a doctor who specializes in the care of children.

exist? I visit the schools as often as possible. The Indian kids crowd the classroom. Many are writing their own poems, short stories, and novels. They have read my books. They have read many other books. They look at me with bright eyes and arrogant wonder. They are trying to save their lives. Then there are the sullen and already defeated Indian kids who sit in the back rows and ignore me with theatrical precision. The pages of their notebooks are empty. They carry neither pencil nor pen. They stare out the window. They refuse and resist. "Books," I say to them. "Books," I say. I throw my weight against their locked doors. The door holds. I am smart. I am arrogant. I am lucky. I am trying to save our lives. ✍

Comparing Literature How has the school setting changed since the narrator was a child? How has it stayed the same?

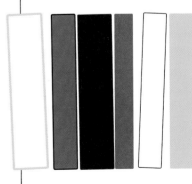

My First Memory (of Librarians)

Nikki Giovanni

This is my first memory:
A big room with heavy wooden tables that sat on
   a creaky wood floor
A line of green shades—bankers' lights—down
   the center
Heavy oak chairs that were too low or maybe I was
   simply too short
5   For me to sit in and read
So my first book was always big

In the foyer° up four steps a semi-circle desk
   presided
To the left side the card catalogue
On the right newspapers draped over what
   looked like a quilt rack
10 Magazines face out from the wall

The welcoming smile of my librarian
The anticipation in my heart
All those books—another world—just waiting
At my fingertips.

---

7 A *foyer* is a lobby or an entrance hall.

Comparing Literature What is the mood of the poem? In what ways do details in the setting affect the mood of the poem?

Comparing Literature

BQ BIG Question

Now use the unit Big Question to compare and contrast "Superman and Me" and "My First Memory (of Librarians)." With a group of classmates, discuss questions such as

- What do the narrator and the speaker both value in their lives? Why?

- How do the activities that they enjoy improve the quality of their lives?

Support each answer with evidence from the readings.

Literary Element Setting

Use the details you wrote in your diagram to think about the settings in "Superman and Me" and "My First Memory (of Librarians)." With a partner, answer the following questions.

1. In what ways are the settings different in "Superman and Me" and "My First Memory (of Librarians)"? Discuss specific details, feelings, and any other ways the two settings differ.

2. In what ways are the settings in both selections similar? For example, you might think about how the narrator and the speaker feel in the settings, what opportunities the settings offer, or other important ways you think that the settings are alike.

Write to Compare

In one or two paragraphs, explain how the settings contribute to the same general theme in "Superman and Me" and "My First Memory (of Librarians)." You might focus on these ideas as you write.

- Tell how the places described in the selections affect the narrator's and the speaker's views about themselves and their lives.

- Include details about the appearance of people, places, and things that influence the quality of the narrator's and the speaker's lives.

- Explain how similarities and differences in the setting, mood, and structure of each selection affect your responses to the two selections.

 Writing Tip

Transitional Words and Phrases As you write, use transitional words and phrases such as *then, as a result, therefore,* and *however* to connect the ideas in your paragraphs.

 Literature Online

Selection Resources
For Selection Quizzes, eFlashcards, and Reading-Writing Connection activities, go to glencoe.com and enter QuickPass code GL27534u3.

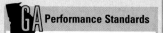 **Performance Standards**

For pages 448–453

ELA7W2c Produce a response to literature that organizes an interpretation around several clear ideas, premises, or images from the original work.

 # Writing Workshop

Response to Literature

Spending time with a loved one, making a friend smile, watching a beautiful sunset—these are all things that make people feel happy to be alive. What things bring joy into your life? In this workshop, you will write a response to literature that will help you think about the Unit 3 Big Question: What Makes Life Good?

Review the writing prompt, or assignment, below. Then read the Writing Plan. It will tell you what you will do to write your response to literature.

Writing Assignment

A response to literature is an expository essay in which you interpret aspects of a literary selection. Write an interpretation of how the Big Question "What Makes Life Good?" is addressed in one of the poems you have read in this unit. The audience, or those reading your essay, should be your classmates and teacher.

Prewrite

Which poem do you find most interesting in this unit? How does that poem address the Big Question?

Gather Ideas

Review the poems in the unit. As you reread them, take notes on how each poem addresses the Big Question. Write down any lines that address the Big Question especially well.

Choose a Poem

Choose one of the poems you have reviewed. To get started, talk about the poem with a partner.

Partner Talk With a partner, follow these steps:

1. Discuss the meaning of the poem. Use your own words to explain the main ideas of the poem to your partner.

2. With help from your partner, decide how the poem addresses the Big Question and write a thesis statement that explains your interpretation.

The poem _____ by _____ shows that _____ makes life good.

Writing Plan

- **Present the thesis, or main idea, of the essay in the introduction.**

- **Organize the essay around several clear, insightful ideas.**

- **Include evidence from the literary selection to support each idea and to show your understanding of the text.**

- **Use precise and vivid language to help readers understand your interpretation.**

- **Conclude by linking back to the thesis of the essay.**

 Prewriting Tip

Thesis Statement Remember that a thesis statement expresses the main idea of an essay. It makes a point that can be supported with examples, or evidence.

Get Organized

Create a web diagram of text evidence that supports your thesis.

Next, create an outline of your essay. Use your web to help you.

Thesis Statement: "From Blossoms" by Li-Young Lee shows that appreciating nature and enjoying special moments make life good.

I. Appreciating nature
    A. Title and line 1
    B. Line 6

II. Enjoying special moments
    A. Lines 13—14
    B. Lines 17—18

Draft

Get It On Paper

○ Review your notes, thesis statement, web, and outline.

○ Write several sentences connecting the poem to the Big Question.

○ For each body paragraph, write a topic sentence that explains how the text evidence addresses the Big Question.

○ End your essay by restating your thesis in a different way.

Develop Your Draft

1. State your **thesis** in your first paragraph. It should explain how the poem addresses the Big Question.

Lee shows that appreciating nature's gifts and enjoying life's special moments make it wonderful to be alive.

Writing and Research
For prewriting, drafting, and revising tools, go to glencoe.com and enter QuickPass code GL27534u3.

Transitions Use transitional phrases such as *in addition, on the other hand, later,* and *as a result* at the beginning of a paragraph to show how the ideas are related to those in the previous paragraph.

TRY IT

Analyzing Cartoons
Why might *old* and *lazy* not be the best words for the boy to use? With a partner, discuss how word choice affects people's reactions to your speaking and writing.

BOONDOCKS ©2003 Aaron McGruder. Reprinted with permission of UNIVERSAL PRESS SYNDICATE. All rights reserved.

2. **Organize** your body paragraphs around clear, insightful ideas. Begin each one with a sentence stating the main idea of the paragraph.

> Lee says that peaches are a gift from nature.

3. Include **evidence** that supports your ideas and that shows you understand the poem. Include line numbers with direct quotations.

> Those days are the special ones we never forget, "days we live / as if death were nowhere / in the background" (17–19).

4. Use **precise and vivid language** to interest readers.

> Every bite reminds us of where it came from and of how miraculous it is.

5. In your **conclusion**, restate your thesis in different words.

> In "From Blossoms," the simple act of eating a peach reminds the speaker of nature's gifts and of how important it is to savor special moments when they occur.

Apply Good Writing Traits: Word Choice

Use precise words that clearly express your images and ideas.

Read the sentences below from Annie Dillard's memoir, *An American Childhood*. How does Dillard's word choice help you "see" the image she describes?

> A soft snowball hit the driver's windshield right before the driver's face. It made a smashed star with a hump in the middle.

As you draft your response, choose lively verbs, specific nouns, and colorful adjectives and adverbs. Use a thesaurus for help.

Analyze a Student Model

Sometimes the simplest things bring people the most joy. In "From Blossoms" by Li-Young Lee, the speaker buys peaches from a roadside stand and eats them. However, this poem is about more than eating a delicious summer treat. Using this everyday experience, Lee shows that appreciating nature's gifts and enjoying life's special moments make it wonderful to be alive.

Lee says that peaches are a gift from nature. In the title of the poem and again in the first line, he reminds readers that fruit comes "from blossoms." He goes on to describe "the laden boughs" (6) of the trees that give people who buy the peaches "nectar at the roadside" (8). The peaches bring nature with them, he says, because as we eat them, we "carry within us an orchard" (12).

In addition, eating a peach is one of life's special moments, according to the poem. Biting into "the round jubilance of peach" (16) is a joyous experience. Every bite reminds us of where it came from and of how miraculous it is. We taste "not only the skin, but the shade, / not only the sugar, but the days" (13–14). The days the speaker is talking about refer to the time it takes for a peach to grow. They also refer to days like the one during which the poem's speaker stopped by the peach stand. Those days are the special ones we never forget, "days we live / as if death were nowhere / in the background" (17–19).

In "From Blossoms," the simple act of eating a peach reminds the speaker of nature's gifts and of how important it is to savor special moments when they occur.

Thesis

Notice how the writer states the thesis of the essay in the last sentence of the first paragraph.

Organization

Make sure that each paragraph provides details about one main idea that supports the thesis.

Examples from the Selection

To support the main idea, the writer has chosen a quotation from the poem, copied it exactly, and indicated which line it is from.

Vivid Language

The word *joyous* clearly expresses the speaker's delight in eating the peach.

Conclusion

End by reminding readers of your thesis.

Revise

Now it's time to revise your draft so your ideas really shine. Revising is what makes good writing great, and great writing takes work!

Peer Review Trade drafts with a partner. Use the chart below to review your partner's draft by answering the questions in the *What to do* column. Talk about your peer review after you have glanced at each other's drafts and written answers to the questions. Next, follow the suggestions in the *How to do it* column to revise your draft.

Revising Plan

What to do	How to do it	Example
Does your thesis clearly state how the poem addresses the Big Question?	Explain what the poem says about what makes life good.	Lee ~~writes about~~ ^shows that appreciating nature's gifts and enjoying life's special moments ^make it wonderful to be alive.
Is the body of your essay organized clearly?	Begin each paragraph with a main idea that supports your thesis.	^Lee says that peaches are a gift from nature. In the title of the poem....
Do you include examples from the text to support your ideas?	Choose lines from the poem that best support your main idea and cite them correctly.	^We taste "not only the skin, but the shade, / not only the sugar, but the days" (13–14).
Is your language precise and interesting?	Use precise words that clearly express your ideas.	Biting into "the round jubilance of peach" (16) is a ~~great~~ ^joyous experience.
Does your conclusion link back to your introduction?	Look back at your thesis and restate it in different words	^In "From Blossoms," the simple act of eating a peach reminds the speaker of nature's gifts and of how important it is to savor special moments when they occur.

Edit and Proofread

For your final draft, read your essay one sentence at a time. The Editing and Proofreading Checklist inside the back cover of this book may help you spot errors. Use the proofreading symbols to mark needed changes. Then make corrections.

Grammar Focus: Quotations from Poetry

Be sure to cite quotations from the poem correctly. Enclose the exact words from the poem in quotation marks followed by the line number in parentheses. If you quote more than one line at a time, use a forward slash (/) to show where the line breaks. Below are examples of problems with poetry quotations and solutions from the Workshop Model.

Problem: It's not clear which words are the writer's and which are from the poem.

He goes on to describe the laden boughs (6) of the trees that give people who buy the peaches nectar at the roadside (8).

Solution: Enclose the words from the poem in quotation marks.

He goes on to describe "the laden boughs" (6) of the trees that give people who buy the peaches "nectar at the roadside" (8).

Problem: Readers will not be able to find a quotation in the poem.

The peaches bring nature with them, he says, because as we eat them, we "carry within us an orchard."

Solution: Include the line number(s) of the quotation after the closing quotation marks but before the period.

The peaches bring nature with them, he says, because as we eat them, we "carry within us an orchard" (12).

Present

It's almost time to share your writing with others. Write your essay neatly in print or cursive on a separate sheet of paper. If you have access to a computer, type your essay on the computer and check spelling. Save your document to a disk, and print it out.

Grammar Tip

Quotations When quoting lines from a poem in your essay, double-check to make sure that you've copied the words exactly and cited the correct line number(s).

Presenting Tip

Publishing Include a copy of the poem you interpreted on a separate sheet of paper with your essay. Be sure to state the author and source of the poem.

Literature Online

Writing and Research For editing and publishing tools, go to glencoe.com and enter QuickPass code GL27534u3.

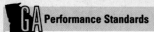
Performance Standards

For page 454

ELA7LSV2c When delivering and responding to presentations, show appropriate changes in delivery.

Speaking, Listening, and Viewing Workshop

Oral Response to Literature

Activity

Connect to Your Writing Deliver an oral response to literature to your classmates. You might want to adapt the response to literature that you wrote for the Writing Workshop on pages 448–453. Use supporting graphics and technology to strengthen your response. Remember that you focused on the Unit 3 Big Question: What Makes Life Good?

Plan Your Presentation

Reread your response to literature and highlight the sections you want to include in your presentation. Like your written response, your oral response should be organized around ideas—supported by details and examples—to help the audience understand your interpretation.

Rehearse Your Presentation

Practice your presentation several times. Try rehearsing in front of a mirror so that you can watch your movements and facial expressions. You may use note cards to remind you of your main points and text evidence, but practice your presentation often enough that you won't lose eye contact with your audience.

Deliver Your Presentation

○ Speak clearly and precisely.

○ Adjust your speaking style to help your audience distinguish between your ideas and quoted material from the text.

○ Change the tone, pace, and volume of your speaking to help emphasize important ideas in your interpretation.

○ Use gestures to direct the audience's attention to specific points.

Listening to Understand

As you listen, write questions you'd like to ask to elicit information. You can also use the following question frames to connect to and build on the speaker's ideas in a way that respects his or her viewpoints.

○ It seems to me that your attitude toward the subject of your interpretation is _____. Do others agree or disagree?

○ To summarize your interpretation: _____. Is that correct?

▶ Presentation Checklist

Answer the following questions to evaluate your presentation.

❏ Did you speak clearly and precisely—and in a style that distinguished your ideas from the literary text?

❏ Did you vary the tone, pace, and volume of your speaking to add emphasis?

❏ Did you use gestures to draw attention to specific points?

❏ Did you make eye contact with your audience?

Speaking, Listening, and Viewing For project ideas, templates, and presentation tips, go to glencoe.com and enter QuickPass code GL27534u3.

Unit Challenge

Answer the BIG Question

In Unit 3, you explored the Big Question through reading, writing, speaking, and listening. Now it's time for you to answer the Big Question by completing one of the Unit Challenges below.

WHAT Makes Life Good?

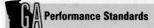

GA Performance Standards

For page 455

ELA7W1a Select a focus, an organizational structure, and a point of view based on purpose, genre expectations, audience, length, and format requirements.

Use the notes you took in your Unit 3 **Foldable** to complete your Unit Challenge.

Before you present your Unit Challenge, be sure to follow the steps below. Use this first plan if you choose to make a collage about what makes life good for you.

On Your Own Activity: Make a Collage

❏ Find and cut out pictures from old magazines or catalogs that show specific examples of what is important to you.

❏ Arrange and paste the images on a poster board.

❏ Present your collage to the class. Give facts about the images and offer descriptions about what they mean to you.

Use this second plan if you choose to create a character study. Your group should "interview" characters and speakers in this unit about what is important to them.

Group Activity: Create a Character Study

❏ Each group member tells how one character or speaker would answer *Who or what makes life good? Why?*

❏ Organize responses into these categories: **People, Feelings, Things,** and **Ideas and Goals.**

❏ Make a chart with a column for each category. Write the responses—and the character or speaker—in the columns.

❏ As a group, draw conclusions about what makes life good.

❏ Present the character study to the class.

Independent Reading

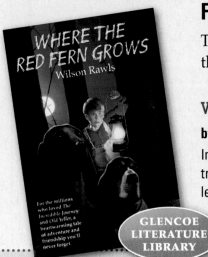

Fiction

To read more about the Big Question, choose one of these books from your school or local library.

Where the Red Fern Grows

by Wilson Rawls

In this well-loved classic, a young boy and the pair of hunting dogs he trains learn about hunting and life in the Oklahoma Ozarks. A tragedy leaves Billy grieving, but he learns important lessons about life.

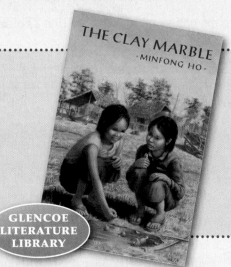

The Clay Marble

by Minfong Ho

In the 1970s, Dara, her mother, and her brother flee war-torn Cambodia, settling in a refugee camp on the Thailand border. When fighting erupts, Dara becomes separated from her loved ones and must use courage to reunite with her family.

The Summer of the Swans

by Betsy Byars

A fourteen-year-old girl wishes she had a normal and supportive family. She is tired of watching over her younger brother Charlie, who has a disability. When Charlie leaves the house at night to revisit the swans Sarah introduced him to earlier, he gets lost. As the neighbors search for Charlie, Sarah learns a little more about herself and her family.

Hoot

by Carl Hiaasen

When new restaurant construction threatens an owl community in a Florida town, local middle school kids use funny and interesting tactics to battle the adults and save the owls.

Nonfiction

My Life with the Chimpanzees

by Jane Goodall

The world's leading authority on chimpanzees describes her thirty years of living with and studying the chimpanzees of Tanzania. Read to learn about the challenges of balancing human progress with wildlife.

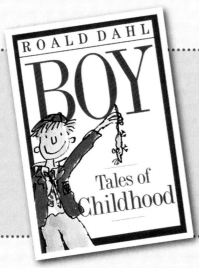

Boy: Tales of Childhood

by Roald Dahl

The popular novelist shares funny and sometimes sad stories of his childhood. Included are descriptions of his misadventures in boarding school and tales of his summer vacations on a remote island in Norway.

Escape: The Story of the Great Houdini

by Sid Fleischman

This biography of the great magician is filled with insider information about Houdini's work and life. His life story is just as magical and astonishing as his famous acts.

 Keep a Reader Response Journal

Read one of these books, based on your own interest or a recommendation from a friend or classmate. As you read, record frequent journal entries about what you found interesting, unexpected, challenging, or exciting in the book. Be sure to support your responses with specific examples from the text.

Assessment

READING

Read the poems and answer the questions. Write your answers on a separate sheet of paper.

"Ankylosaurus"[1] by Jack Prelutsky

Clankity Clankity Clankity Clank!
Ankylosaurus was built like a tank,
its hide was a fortress as sturdy as steel,
it tended to be an inedible meal.
5   It was armored in front, it was armored behind,
there wasn't a thing on its minuscule mind,
it waddled about on its four stubby legs,
nibbling on plants with a mouthful of pegs.
Ankylosaurus was best left alone,
10   its tail was a cudgel[2] of gristle and bone.
Clankity Clankity Clankity Clank!
Ankylosaurus was built like a tank.

[1]**ankylosaurus:** a type of dinosaur
[2]**cudgel:** a short, thick club used as a weapon

---

1. What makes the first line in this poem an example of onomatopoeia?

    A. The same sound is repeated.

    B. The initial consonants are repeated.

    C. The words imitate the sound of what they describe.

    D. It has a regular pattern of stressed and unstressed syllables.

2. Which line in the poem contains a metaphor?

    A. line 2

    B. line 3

    C. line 6

    D. line 8

"XXXVIII" by A. E. Housman

Oh stay at home, my lad, and plough
The land and not the sea,
And leave the soldiers at their <u>drill</u>
And all about the idle hill
Shepherd your sheep with me.

Oh stay with company and mirth[1]
And daylight and the air;
Too full already is the grave
Of fellows that were good and brave
And died because they were.

[1]**mirth:** laughing gladness

3. What is the rhyme scheme of the first stanza of this poem?

   A. *abcca*

   B. *ababc*

   C. *abbcc*

   D. *abccb*

4. In which line below are the stressed syllables correctly underlined?

   A. And <u>daylight</u> <u>and</u> the <u>air</u>

   B. And day<u>light</u> and <u>the</u> air

   C. And <u>daylight</u> and <u>the</u> air

   D. <u>And</u> daylight <u>and</u> the air

5. What is the meaning of the word *drill* in this poem?

   A. a sharp tool

   B. a mental exercise

   C. a marching exercise

   D. anything that is normally required

6. What is the MAIN reason the speaker wants the listener to stay at home?

   A. The speaker needs his help with the sheep.

   B. The speaker wants him to remain safe and happy.

   C. The speaker fears that no work will get done if he leaves.

   D. The speaker knows he would do badly at another way of life.

"Afternoon on a Hill" by Edna St. Vincent Millay

I will be the gladdest thing
Under the sun!
I will touch a hundred flowers
And not pick one.

5   I will look at cliffs and clouds
With quiet eyes,
Watch the wind bow down the grass,
And the grass rise.
And when the lights begin to show
10   Up from the town,
I will mark which must be mine,
And then start down.

7. Which phrase from this poem contains assonance?

   A. "hundred flowers"

   B. "cliffs and clouds"

   C. "with quiet eyes"

   D. "watch the wind"

8. Which line from this poem contains alliteration?

   A. line 1

   B. line 3

   C. line 9

   D. line 11

9. Which BEST describes the tone of this poem?

   A. excitement

   B. gentle regret

   C. peaceful joy

   D. determination

LOG ON **Literature** Online

Standards Practice For more standards practice,
go to glencoe.com and enter QuickPass code GL27534u3.

 **Standards Practice**

"Hope Is the Thing with Feathers" by Emily Dickinson

Hope is the thing with feathers
That perches in the soul,
And sings the tune without the words,
And never stops at all,

And sweetest in the gale is heard;
And <u>sore</u> must be the storm
That could abash[1] the little bird
That kept so many warm.

I've heard it in the chillest land,
And on the strangest sea;
Yet, never, in extremity,
It asked a crumb of me.

[1]**abash:** to make ashamed or embarrassed

---

10. What type of figurative language is used in the title of this poem?
    A. idiom
    B. simile
    C. metaphor
    D. personification

11. This poem compares hope to
    A. a bird.
    B. a tune.
    C. a storm.
    D. the soul.

12. What does the word *sore* mean in this poem?
    A. painful
    B. tender
    C. annoyed
    D. very great

13. Which sentence below states a main theme of this poem?
    A. People shouldn't hang onto false hope.
    B. Hope comforts people in even the worst situations.
    C. Birds sing their sweetest songs during storms.
    D. Sailors on the sea need hope more than anyone.

ENGLISH/LANGUAGE ARTS

Choose the best answer for each question. Write the answer on a separate sheet of paper.

1. Which word or words BEST fill in the blank in the sentence below?

   > Joel and Maria told Mrs. Lopez that anyone could write a poem _____ than an essay.

   A. easier   C. more easily

   B. more easier   D. most easily

2. How should the punctuation be corrected in the sentence below?

   > The students were enthusiastic about the poetry writing contest most had written poems before for Ms. Langford's English class.

   A. Add a semicolon after *enthusiastic.*

   B. Add a semicolon after *contest.*

   C. Add a semicolon after *poems.*

   D. Add a semicolon after *before.*

3. Which sentence below is written correctly?

   A. All the students read they're own poems.

   B. All the students red their own poems.

   C. All the students read there own poems.

   D. All the students read their own poems.

4. Which sentence below has correct pronoun-antecedent agreement?

   A. Everyone did their homework at Jen's house.

   B. Either Rick or Jim should bring his computer.

   C. Did anyone forget their umbrella?

   D. All of them brought his or her own music.

5. In which sentence below does the verb agree with the indefinite pronoun?

   A. Is everybody happy now?

   B. Are anyone at home?

   C. Do everything fit in the suitcase?

   D. Have each person packed?

6. How should the capitalization be corrected in the sentence below?

   > On her trip east, Dr. Sanchez visited Washington, D.C., hiked in the Appalachian Mountains, and rode a boat down the Potomac river.

   A. Use a capital *E* in *east.*

   B. Use small letters *d* and *c* in *D.C.*

   C. Use a small letter *m* in *Mountains.*

   D. Use a capital *R* in *river.*

WRITING

Read your assigned topic in the box below. Use one piece of paper to jot down your ideas and organize your thoughts. Then neatly write your letter on another sheet of paper.

Persuasive Writing Topic

Writing Situation

A local newspaper has published a letter to the editor urging schools to stop teaching poetry. The writer believes that reading poetry is a waste of students' time. Your principal has asked students to write their own letters to the editor that take the opposite view.

Directions for Writing

Write a letter to the editor to persuade readers that it can be worthwhile for students to spend time on poetry. Include details from poems you have read as examples to support your view.

Writing Checklist

- ☐ Focus on a single topic.
- ☐ Organize your main points in a clear, logical order.
- ☐ Support your ideas or viewpoints with details and examples.
- ☐ Use precise, vivid words.
- ☐ Vary the length and structure of your sentences.
- ☐ Use clear transition words to connect ideas.
- ☐ Correct any errors in spelling, capitalization, punctuation, and usage.

WHAT Influences You?

THE BIG Question

> " *If we're going to solve the problems of the world, we have to learn how to talk to one another.* "
>
> —RITA DOVE

FOLDABLES®
Study Organizer

Unit 4: Big Question
What Influences You?

Reading Selection
Title_____

Throughout Unit 4, you will read, write, and talk about the **BIG Question**— **"What Influences You?"** Use your Unit 4 **Foldable,** shown here, to keep track of your ideas as you read. Turn to the back of this book for instructions on making this **Foldable.**

WHAT Influences You?

Look around you. You see magazines, newspapers, posters, books, television shows, Web sites, and advertisements every day. Many of the things you read, see, or hear try to persuade you to buy something or take some action.

Think about two things that influence you:

- Life Experiences
- Persuasive Ideas

What You'll Read

In this unit, you'll read essays, or short works of nonfiction focused on a single topic. An essay can be formal or informal.

- **Formal essays** are serious and impersonal. **Informal essays** entertain as they inform.
- **Descriptive essays** describe a person, place, or thing. **Narrative essays** relate true stories.
- Many of the essays in this unit are **persuasive essays** that promote an opinion.

You'll also read short stories, poems, and an autobiography that may help you discover answers to the Big Question.

What You'll Write

As you explore the Big Question, you'll write notes in your Unit Foldable. Later, you'll use these notes to complete two writing assignments related to the Big Question.

1. **Write a Persuasive Essay**
2. **Choose a Unit Challenge**
   - **On Your Own Activity: Write a Poem or a Song**
   - **Group Activity: Make a Poster**

What You'll Learn

Literary Elements

conflict

resolution

thesis

anecdote

imagery

characterization

style

argument

allusion

author's perspective

tone

personification

Reading Skills and Strategies

make predictions about plot

analyze text structure

analyze theme

visualize

distinguish fact and opinion

recognize bias

evaluate argument

All Together Now
Barbara Jordan

On August 6, 1965, President Lyndon B. Johnson celebrated signing the Voting Rights Act into law with a group including (from left) Ralph Abernathy; Dr. Martin Luther King Jr.; and Clarence Marshall.

Set a Purpose for Reading

Read "All Together Now" to see how Barbara Jordan tries to influence others to create a tolerant society.

When I look at race relations today I can see that some positive changes have come about. But much remains to be done, and the answer does not lie in more legislation. We *have* the legislation we need; we have the laws. Frankly, I don't believe that the task of bringing us all together can be accomplished by government. What we need now is soul force—the efforts of people working on a small scale to build a truly tolerant, harmonious[1] society. And parents can do a great deal to create that tolerant society.

We all know that race relations in America have had a very rocky history. Think about the 1960s when Dr. Martin Luther King, Jr., was in his heyday and there were marches and protests against segregation and discrimination. The movement culminated[2] in 1963 with the March on Washington.

---

1 A **harmonious** society is one in which people are friendly and get along well together.

2 **Culminated** means "reached the highest point."

Following that event, race relations reached an all-time peak. President Lyndon B. Johnson pushed through the Civil Rights Act of 1964, which remains the fundamental piece of civil rights legislation in this century. The Voting Rights Act of 1965 ensured that everyone in our country could vote. At last, black people and white people seemed ready to live together in peace.

But that is not what happened. By the 1990's the good feelings had diminished. Today the nation seems to be suffering from compassion[3] fatigue, and issues such as race relations and civil rights have never regained momentum.[4]

Those issues, however, remain crucial. As our society becomes more diverse, people of all races and backgrounds will have to learn to live together. If we don't think this is important, all we have to do is look at the situation in Bosnia[5] today.

How do we create a harmonious society out of so many kinds of people? The key is tolerance— the one value that is indispensable[6] in creating community.

If we are concerned about community, if it is important to us that people not feel excluded, then we have to do something. Each of us can decide to have one friend of a different race or background in our mix of friends. If we do this, we'll be working together to push things forward.

One thing is clear to me: We, as human beings, must be willing to accept people who are different from ourselves. I must be willing to accept people who don't look as I do and don't talk as I do. It is crucial that I am open to their feelings, their inner reality.

BQ BIG Question

What events helped to influence Barbara Jordan's vision of a tolerant society?

Following the enactment of the 1965 Voting Rights Act, African Americans in Alabama wait in line to vote.

BQ BIG Question

Reread this paragraph. What steps does Jordan recommend people take to help build a cooperative society?

---

3 **Compassion** is sorrow for the suffering or trouble of another.

4 **Momentum** is a strength or force that keeps growing.

5 In the early 1990s, civil war erupted in Bosnia (boz'nē ə) between the Serbs and Croats. After a few months of fighting, the Serbs controlled most of the area. They attacked Sarajevo with the intent of killing all non-Serbs, a process known as *ethnic cleansing*.

6 **Indispensable** means "absolutely necessary."

What can parents do? We can put our faith in young people as a positive force. I have yet to find a racist baby. Babies come into the world as blank as slates and, with their beautiful innocence, see others not as different but as enjoyable companions. Children learn ideas and attitudes from the adults who nurture them. I absolutely believe that children do not adopt prejudices unless they absorb them from their parents or teachers.

The best way to get this country faithful to the American dream of tolerance and equality is to start small. Parents can actively encourage their children to be in the company of people who are of other racial and ethnic backgrounds. If a child thinks, "Well, that person's color is not the same as mine, but she must be okay because she likes to play with the same things I like to play with," that child will grow up with a broader view of humanity.

I am an incurable optimist.[7] For the rest of the time that I have left on this planet I want to bring people together. You might think of this as a labor of love. Now, I know that love means different things to different people. But what *I* mean is this: I care about you because you are a fellow human being and I find it okay in my mind, in my heart, to simply say to you, I love you. And maybe that would encourage you to love me in return.

It is possible for all of us to work on this—at home, in our schools, at our jobs. It is possible to work on human relationships in every area of our lives. 🐾

View the Photograph

Study the photo and think about how you can help create a harmonious society in your own school and neighborhood.

BQ ▸ **BIG Question**

What details does Jordan use to make a convincing case for community?

---

7 An *incurable optimist* is a person who will not change his or her positive outlook on life.

After You Read

Respond and Think Critically

1. Barbara Jordan begins her essay by asserting that good legislation is not enough to create a truly tolerant society. What else is needed, according to Jordan? [Recall]

2. What does Jordan mean when she says that the United States has "compassion fatigue"? Explain. [Interpret]

3. In what way is the United States a more harmonious society today than it was in the early 1960s? Use details from the essay to support your answer. [Compare]

4. According to Jordan, how can ordinary people affect the state of society? Explain. [Conclude]

5. Jordan's purpose in writing this essay was to persuade. Do you think that Jordan used convincing examples to back up her ideas? Explain. [Evaluate]

Writing

Write a Summary Write a one-paragraph summary of Barbara Jordan's essay. You may want to begin your summary with this topic sentence:

In her essay, "All Together Now," Barbara Jordan argues that _____.

Remember that when you summarize, you restate the author's main idea using your own words. Be sure to include the most important ideas from Jordan's speech and to put that information in a logical order. Your summary should show that you understand the essay's underlying meaning.

For page 470

ELA7W2g Produce writing that concludes with a detailed summary linked to the purpose of the composition.

 Literature Online

Unit Resources For additional skills practice, go to glencoe.com and enter QuickPass code GL27534u4.

Part 1

Life Experiences

Literature Walk, Central Park VII, 2001. Bill Jacklin. Oil on canvas. Private Collection.

BQ ❯ **BIG Question What Influences You?**

In the painting *Literature Walk,* a lone figure wanders through a city park. How would you describe the overall mood or feeling of this experience? What everyday life experiences influence you?

Before You Read

The Scholarship Jacket

Connect to the Short Story

Think about an award you have earned or would like to earn.

Partner Talk With a partner, talk about the award and about how a person might go about winning it. Discuss the experience of competing for awards. What is it like?

Build Background

This story takes place in recent time in a small town in Texas.

- A valedictorian is the student who has achieved the highest grades in a graduating class during all his or her years at school. This person is usually given the honor of giving the farewell address at the graduation ceremony.

- The word *valedictorian* comes from the Latin word *valedicere,* which means "to say farewell."

Vocabulary

eavesdrop (ēvz′drop′) *v.* to listen secretly to a private conversation (p. 475). *Janet tried to eavesdrop to find out more about the surprise party.*

coincidence (kō in′si dəns) *n.* a situation in which two or more events that seem related accidentally occur at the same time (p. 476). *It was a lucky coincidence that we both won tickets for the same show.*

policy (pol′ə sē) *n.* a guideline for actions or decisions (p. 476). *Mr. Trent's homework policy clearly states when makeup work is due.*

withdrawn (with drôn′) *adj.* shy, quiet, or unsociable (p. 478). *Sitting alone, Deon seemed unusually withdrawn at the dance.*

vile (vīl) *adj.* very bad; unpleasant; foul (p. 479). *A vile odor came from the lunch bag they found in the closet.*

Meet Marta Salinas

Short Story Writer Marta Salinas is the author of many short stories. Her short story "The Scholarship Jacket" was first published in *Cuentos Chicanos: A Short Story Anthology.* "Cuentos Chicanos" means "stories by Americans of Mexican descent." Her work has also appeared in the *Los Angeles Herald Examiner* and in *California Living* magazine.

Travel Writer, Too Salinas has also written and collaborated on several tourist guides for Argentina and Buenos Aires. Most of her guides are written in Spanish.

 Literature Online

Author Search For more about Marta Salinas, go to glencoe.com and enter QuickPass code GL27534u4.

Set Purposes for Reading

BQ BIG Question

As you read this story, ask yourself, what influences the main character as she deals with an unfair situation?

Literary Element Conflict and Resolution

Conflict is the central struggle between opposing forces in a story. An **external conflict** exists when a character struggles against some outside force, such as another person, nature, society, or fate. An **internal conflict** exists within the mind of a character who is torn between opposing feelings or goals. The **resolution** is the part of the plot that presents the final outcome of the story. At that time, the plot's conflicts are resolved and the story ends.

Conflict is important in storytelling because it advances the plot. Most plots are built around one or more conflicts. As you read, ask yourself, what conflicts are the characters facing? How might these conflicts be resolved?

Reading Strategy Make Predictions About Plot

When you **make predictions,** you guess what will happen next. To predict what will happen next in a story, think about the events and details you've read about so far. Consider, too, what you know about the subject of the story or about real life. Then make a guess about what may happen next in the **plot,** or sequence of events. After you've made a prediction, read on to see whether you guessed correctly.

Making predictions is important because it helps you closely follow the events in a story. Predicting helps you stay involved in a story and makes reading more interesting.

As you read "The Scholarship Jacket," predict what will happen next. Use a chart like the one below to record your predictions.

Plot Detail	My Prediction	What Happens

GA Performance Standards

For pages 472–481

ELA7R1e For literary texts, identify events that advance the plot and determine how each event explains past or present action(s) or foreshadows future action(s).

TRY IT

Make Predictions Imagine that you are walking to the lunch table where your friends are sitting. Before they notice you, you hear the word "balloons." As you get closer, they stop talking. Before your friend closes her notebook, you see a list beginning with the word "invitations." As you sit down, you remember that your birthday is next week. Predict what will happen next week.

THE SCHOLARSHIP JACKET

Marta Salinas

The small Texas school that I attended carried out a tradition every year during the eighth grade graduation; a beautiful gold and green jacket, the school colors, was awarded to the class valedictorian, the student who had maintained the highest grades for eight years. The scholarship jacket had a big gold S on the left front side and the winner's name was written in gold letters on the pocket.

My oldest sister Rosie had won the jacket a few years back and I fully expected to win also. I was fourteen and in the eighth grade. I had been a straight A student since the first grade, and the last year I had looked forward to owning that jacket. My father was a farm laborer who couldn't earn enough money to feed eight children, so when I was six I was given to my grandparents to raise. We couldn't participate in sports at school because there were registration fees, uniform costs, and trips out of town; so even though we were quite agile and athletic, there would never be a sports school jacket for us. This one, the scholarship jacket, was our only chance.

In May, close to graduation, spring fever struck, and no one paid any attention in class; instead we stared out the windows and at each other, wanting to speed up the last few weeks of school. I despaired every time I looked in the mirror. Pencil thin, not a curve anywhere, I was called "Beanpole" and "String Bean" and I knew that's what I looked like.

Conflict and Resolution
What struggle does the narrator's family face?

Make Predictions About Plot Predict if the scholarship jacket will cause a conflict. What details influence your prediction?

A flat chest, no hips, and a brain, that's what I had. That really isn't much for a fourteen-year-old to work with, I thought, as I absentmindedly wandered from my history class to the gym. Another hour of sweating in basketball and displaying my toothpick legs was coming up. Then I remembered my P.E. shorts were still in a bag under my desk where I'd forgotten them. I had to walk all the way back and get them. Coach Thompson was a real bear if anyone wasn't dressed for P.E. She had said I was a good forward and once she even tried to talk Grandma into letting me join the team. Grandma, of course, said no.

I was almost back at my classroom's door when I heard angry voices and arguing. I stopped. I didn't mean to **eavesdrop;** I just hesitated, not knowing what to do. I needed those shorts and I was going to be late, but I didn't want to interrupt an argument between my teachers. I recognized the voices: Mr. Schmidt, my history teacher, and Mr. Boone, my math teacher. They seemed to be arguing about me. I couldn't believe it. I still remember the shock that rooted me flat against the wall as if I were trying to blend in with the graffiti written there.

"I refuse to do it! I don't care who her father is, her grades don't even begin to compare to Martha's. I won't lie or falsify records. Martha[1] has a straight A plus average and you know it." That was Mr. Schmidt and he sounded very angry. Mr. Boone's voice sounded calm and quiet.

"Look, Joann's father is not only on the Board, he owns the only store in town; we could say it was a close tie and—"

The pounding in my ears drowned out the rest of the words, only a word here and there filtered through. " . . . Martha is Mexican. . . . resign. . . . won't do it. . . ." Mr. Schmidt came rushing out, and luckily for me went down the opposite way toward the auditorium, so he didn't see me. Shaking, I waited a few minutes and then went in and grabbed my bag and fled from the room.

Make Predictions About Plot How does the conversation Marta overhears affect your prediction about whether she will receive the jacket?

---

1 The main character is called "Martha" at school and "Marta" at home. Martha is an English version of the main character's Spanish name.

Vocabulary
....

eavesdrop (ēvz′drop′) v. to listen secretly to a private conversation

Mr. Boone looked up when I came in but didn't say anything. To this day I don't remember if I got in trouble in P.E. for being late or how I made it through the rest of the afternoon. I went home very sad and cried into my pillow that night so grandmother wouldn't hear me. It seemed a cruel **coincidence** that I had overheard that conversation.

The next day when the principal called me into his office, I knew what it would be about. He looked uncomfortable and unhappy. I decided I wasn't going to make it any easier for him so I looked him straight in the eye. He looked away and fidgeted with the papers on his desk.

"Martha," he said, "there's been a change in **policy** this year regarding the scholarship jacket. As you know, it has always been free." He cleared his throat and continued. "This year the Board decided to charge fifteen dollars— which still won't cover the complete cost of the jacket."

I stared at him in shock and a small sound of dismay[2] escaped my throat. I hadn't expected this. He still avoided looking in my eyes.

"So if you are unable to pay the fifteen dollars for the jacket, it will be given to the next one in line."

Standing with all the dignity I could muster,[3] I said, "I'll speak to my grandfather about it, sir, and let you know tomorrow." I cried on the walk home from the bus stop. The dirt road was a quarter of a mile from the highway, so by the time I got home, my eyes were red and puffy.

"Where's Grandpa?" I asked Grandma, looking down at the floor so she wouldn't ask me why I'd been crying. She was sewing on a quilt and didn't look up.

"I think he's out back working in the bean field."

I went outside and looked out at the fields. There he was. I could see him walking between the rows, his body bent over the little plants, hoe in hand. I walked slowly out to him,

Conflict and Resolution
What conflict does Marta face? Is it an internal or external conflict?

---

2 **Dismay** is a feeling of alarm or uneasiness.

3 To **muster** dignity is to gather or collect it.

trying to think how I could best ask him for the money. There was a cool breeze blowing and a sweet smell of **mesquite** in the air, but I didn't appreciate it. I kicked at a dirt clod. I wanted that jacket so much. It was more than just being a valedictorian and giving a little thank you speech for the jacket on graduation night. It represented eight years of hard work and expectation. I knew I had to be honest with Grandpa; it was my only chance. He saw me and looked up.

He waited for me to speak. I cleared my throat nervously and clasped my hands behind my back so he wouldn't see them shaking. "Grandpa, I have a big favor to ask you," I said in Spanish, the only language he knew. He still waited silently. I tried again. "Grandpa, this year the principal said the scholarship jacket is not going to be free. It's going to cost fifteen dollars and I have to take the money in tomorrow, otherwise it'll be given to someone else." The last words came out in an eager rush. Grandpa straightened up tiredly and leaned his chin on the hoe handle. He looked out over the field that was filled with the tiny green bean plants. I waited, desperately hoping he'd say I could have the money.

He turned to me and asked quietly, "What does a scholarship jacket mean?"

I answered quickly; maybe there was a chance. "It means you've earned it by having the highest grades for eight years and that's why they're giving it to you." Too late I realized the significance of my words. Grandpa knew that I understood it was not a matter of money. It wasn't that. He went back to hoeing the weeds that sprang up between the delicate little bean plants. It was a time consuming job; sometimes the small shoots were right next to each other. Finally he spoke again.

"Then if you pay for it, Marta, it's not a scholarship jacket, is it? Tell your principal I will not pay the fifteen dollars."

I walked back to the house and locked myself in the bathroom for a long time. I was angry with grandfather even though I knew he was right, and I was angry with the Board, whoever they were. Why did they have to change the rules just when it was my turn to win the jacket?

Visual Vocabulary

Mesquite (mes kēt′) is a small thorny tree. Its pleasant-smelling wood is a favored barbeque fuel in the Southwest.

Make Predictions About Plot How do you think Grandpa's decision will affect the rest of the events in the story?

New Mexico Peon, 1942. Ernest L.
Blumenschein. Oil on canvas,
40 x 25 in. Gerald Peters Gallery,
Sante Fe, NM.

View the Art Does the person in the
painting remind you of anyone in the
story? Explain.

It was a very sad and **withdrawn** girl who dragged into the principal's office the next day. This time he did look me in the eyes.

"What did your grandfather say?"

I sat very straight in my chair. "He said to tell you he won't pay the fifteen dollars."

The principal muttered something I couldn't understand under his breath, and walked over to the window. He stood looking out at something outside. He looked bigger than usual when he stood up; he was a tall gaunt[4] man with gray hair, and I watched the back of his head while I waited for him to speak.

"Why?" he finally asked. "Your grandfather has the money. Doesn't he own a small bean farm?"

I looked at him, forcing my eyes to stay dry. "He said if I had to pay for it, then it wouldn't be a scholarship jacket," I said and stood up to leave. "I guess you'll just have to give it to Joann." I hadn't meant to say that; it had just slipped out. I was almost to the door when he stopped me.

"Martha—wait."

I turned and looked at him, waiting. What did he want now? I could feel my heart pounding. Something bitter

4 A *gaunt* person is thin and bony.

and **vile** tasting was coming up in my mouth; I was afraid I was going to be sick. I didn't need any sympathy speeches. He sighed loudly and went back to his big desk. He looked at me, biting his lip, as if thinking.

"Okay. We'll make an exception in your case. I'll tell the Board, you'll get your jacket."

I could hardly believe it. I spoke in a trembling rush. "Oh, thank you sir!" Suddenly I felt great. I didn't know about adrenalin[5] in those days, but I knew something was pumping through me, making me feel as tall as the sky. I wanted to yell, jump, run the mile, do something. I ran out so I could cry in the hall where there was no one to see me. At the end of the day, Mr. Schmidt winked at me and said, "I hear you're getting a scholarship jacket this year."

His face looked as happy and innocent as a baby's, but I knew better. Without answering I gave him a quick hug and ran to the bus. I cried on the walk home again, but this time because I was so happy. I couldn't wait to tell Grandpa and ran straight to the field. I joined him in the row where he was working and without saying anything I crouched down and started pulling up the weeds with my hands. Grandpa worked alongside me for a few minutes, but he didn't ask what had happened. After I had a little pile of weeds between the rows, I stood up and faced him.

"The principal said he's making an exception for me, Grandpa, and I'm getting the jacket after all. That's after I told him what you said."

Grandpa didn't say anything, he just gave me a pat on the shoulder and a smile. He pulled out the crumpled red handkerchief that he always carried in his back pocket and wiped the sweat off his forehead.

"Better go see if your grandmother needs any help with supper."

I gave him a big grin. He didn't fool me. I skipped and ran back to the house whistling some silly tune. 🐾

Conflict and Resolution
How is Marta's conflict resolved?

BQ **BIG Question**
How do you think this experience influences Marta's view of her grandfather?

---

5 A chemical released into the blood in times of stress or excitement, **adrenalin** (ə dren′ əl in) increases the body's energy.

Vocabulary
....

vile (vīl) *adj.* very bad; unpleasant; foul

After You Read

Respond and Think Critically

1. What is the scholarship jacket? [Recall]

2. Why is the jacket so important to Marta? Explain. [Interpret]

3. Why are Mr. Schmidt and Mr. Boone arguing? Why might Mr. Schmidt have sounded so angry? Include details from the story in your answer. [Infer]

4. Why do you think the original policy regarding the scholarship jacket was changed? Explain. [Infer]

5. What does Grandpa mean when he says, "Then if you pay for it, Marta, it's not a scholarship jacket, is it?" Explain. [Interpret]

6. **BQ** **BIG Question** What might Marta's experience teach other people? Explain. [Analyze]

Vocabulary Practice

On a separate sheet of paper, write the vocabulary word that correctly completes each sentence. If none of the words fits the sentence, write "none."

| coincidence | eavesdrop | vile |
| withdrawn | policy | |

1. With my ear up to the wall, I could _____ on the discussion.

2. The cough medicine had a _____ taste that I hated.

3. The store's _____ on refunds was cash back for all items with a receipt.

4. My sister smiled and was _____ with the gift I made her.

5. We never _____ that the contest would be easy.

6. It was a _____ that I saw my cousin twice in one day.

7. On Jack's first day at his new school, he was quiet and _____.

Academic Vocabulary

Grandpa helps Marta **clarify** her thoughts about whether she should have to pay for the scholarship jacket. In the preceding sentence, *clarify* means "to clear up confusion." *Clarify* also has other meanings. Read this sentence: The muddy water will **clarify** when the dirt sinks to the bottom of the bucket. What does *clarify* mean here? What is the difference between the two meanings?

TIP

Inferring
To answer this question, use details from the story and your own experience. To remember the original policy, reread the original requirements for winning the jacket as explained at the beginning of the story.

- Reread the argument between Marta's teachers.

- Use information from the argument to piece together a reason for the policy change. Think about what the principal tells Marta when he calls her into his office.

- Not all of the information is included in the story. You will have to use clues that the author gives you.

 FOLDABLES **Study Organizer** Keep track of your ideas about the **BIG Question** in your unit Foldable.

 Literature Online

Selection Resources
For Selection Quizzes, eFlashcards, and Reading-Writing Connection activities, go to glencoe.com and enter QuickPass code GL27534u4.

Literary Element Conflict and Resolution

1. Reread the description of the principal's behavior during his conversations with Marta. What details show that the principal is facing an internal conflict? Explain.

2. What happens at the resolution of "The Scholarship Jacket"? What problem is solved? How do the characters feel? Explain.

Review: Symbol

As you learned on page 420, a **symbol** is an object, a person, a place, or an experience that stands for something else. For example, a soaring bird may represent freedom.

3. What does the scholarship jacket symbolize to Marta? Use details from the story to support your answer.

4. What might the bean plants in Grandpa's fields symbolize to him? Explain.

Reading Strategy Make Predictions About Plot

Standards Practice **GA** ELA71Re

5. Based on the story, which prediction accurately describes how Marta will try to solve problems in the future?
   A She will listen in on other people's conversations.
   B She will easily accept things that she dislikes.
   C She will ask for her grandfather's advice.
   D She will complain to her friends about her problems.

Grammar Link

Comparative and Superlative Adverbs

A comparative adverb compares two actions. A superlative adverb compares more than two actions. Most short adverbs add *-er* to form the comparative and *-est* to form the superlative.

> He spoke *louder* than Marta.

> He spoke the *loudest* of them all.

Long adverbs, and a few short adverbs, add *more* to form the comparative and *most* to form the superlative.

> Marta rode the bus *more often* than Ricky did.

> Of all the students, Marta rode the bus *most often*.

The words *less* and *least* are added to adverbs to form the negative comparative or negative superlative.

> She spoke less quickly to him.

> She spoke least quickly to Grandpa.

Some adverbs have irregular comparative and superlative forms.

Adverb	Comparative	Superlative
well	better	best
badly	worse	worst
little	less	least

Practice Find two sentences in the story with adverbs. Write the comparative and superlative forms of the adverbs. Then write new sentences with the adverb forms that you created.

Write with Style

Apply Figurative Language Imagine that you are writing a graduation speech. Think of a symbol that represents your graduation. Describe how the symbol represents the accomplishments of your class.

A Mason-Dixon Memory

Connect to the Narrative Essay

What would you do if a friend experienced discrimination? How would you act to defend your friend's rights?

Quickwrite Freewrite for a few minutes about how you think you would react in such a situation.

Build Background

In this essay, the Mason-Dixon line is described as "a kind of invisible border between the North and the South."

- Originally, the Mason-Dixon line was the boundary between Maryland and Pennsylvania.

- From 1765 to 1768, Charles Mason and Jeremiah Dixon surveyed the 233-mile-long invisible line to settle a land dispute between the Penn family of Pennsylvania and the Calvert family of Maryland.

- By 1820 the Mason-Dixon line had become the dividing line between the slave states of the South and the free states of the North.

Meet Clifton Davis

Multitalented Artist Clifton Davis is an actor, singer, and songwriter. His song "Never Can Say Goodbye" sold two million records. He has acted in several movies, Broadway plays, and TV shows. Davis told his "Mason-Dixon Memory" story to Mel White, who wrote it in Davis's voice.

Clifton Davis was born in 1945.

 Literature Online

Author Search For more about Clifton Davis, go to glencoe.com and enter QuickPass code GL27534u4.

Vocabulary

civic (siv´ik) *adj.* having to do with a city or citizenship (p. 484). *Our civic leaders are working to strengthen the city's schools.*

predominantly (pri dom´ə nənt´ lē) *adv.* mainly, mostly (p. 484). *Although the guests were predominantly adults, some children also attended the party.*

provoked (prə vōkd´) *v.* having brought out some action or emotion (p. 485). *The appearance of the ice cream truck provoked shouts of excitement from the children.*

forfeit (fôr´fit) *v.* to lose or lose the right to something (p. 485). *You will forfeit any prize you win if you don't follow the rules.*

facility (fə sil´ə tē) *n.* something, such as a building, built to serve a particular purpose (p. 490). *Many town residents were happy to see construction start on the new medical facility.*

Set Purposes for Reading

BQ BIG Question

As you read the essay, pay attention to the experiences of young people who would not accept racial discrimination. Ask yourself, how did their actions influence those around them?

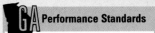
Performance Standards

For pages 482–493

ELA7R1a For literary texts, distinguish between the concepts of theme in a literary work and the author's purpose in an expository text.

Literary Element Thesis

The main idea of an essay is called the **thesis.** The **thesis statement** is usually a single sentence that tells the main idea. However, in a narrative essay that tells a story from the author's life, the thesis often is not stated directly. Instead, it is implied with suggestions and hints.

Recognizing the thesis or main idea is often the most important part of understanding an essay. The main idea is what the author most wants to show, prove, or explain. In narrative essays, authors frequently use vivid details and examples to make their main ideas clear. As you read, look for suggestions and hints that point to the author's thesis.

Reading Skill Analyze Text Structure

Analyzing text structure means looking closely at the pattern the author uses to present events and ideas. Narrative essays usually tell short, true stories from the author's life. Some narrative essays use a text structure called a frame story. The frame is the outer story, which usually precedes and then follows the inner, more important story. It is like a picture frame that holds a photograph.

Analyzing text structure is important because it helps you better understand the author's main idea and purpose. To analyze text structure, pay attention to

- where the frame and inner stories begin and end and what they have in common

- how the inner story reinforces the main idea of the frame story

As you read, keep track of the characters, events, and ideas in the inner and frame stories. Also, keep track of what the stories have in common. Use a graphic organizer like the one below.

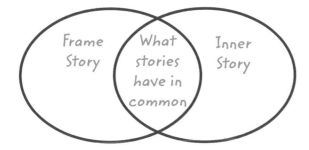

> ### TRY IT
>
> **Analyze** Have you ever been telling a story and become sidetracked by having to explain another story? How did the two stories relate to each other? How was this experience similar to reading a frame story?

A MASON-DIXON
MEMORY

Clifton Davis

Dondré Green glanced uneasily at the **civic** leaders and sports figures filling the hotel ballroom in Cleveland. They had come from across the nation to attend a fundraiser for the National Minority College Golf Scholarship Foundation. I was the banquet's featured entertainer. Dondré, an 18-year-old high school senior from Monroe, Louisiana, was the evening's honored guest.

"Nervous?" I asked the handsome young man in his starched white shirt and rented **tuxedo**.

"A little," he whispered, grinning.

One month earlier, Dondré had been just one more black student attending a **predominantly** white school.

Vocabulary

civic   (siv´ik) *adj.* having to do with a city or citizenship
predominantly   (pri dom´ə nənt´lē) *adv.* mainly, mostly

Although most of his friends and classmates were white, Dondré's race was never an issue. Then, on April 17, 1991, Dondré's black skin **provoked** an incident that made nationwide news.

"Ladies and gentlemen," the emcee[1] said, "our special guest Dondré Green."

As the audience stood applauding, Dondré walked to the microphone and began his story. "I love golf," he said quietly. "For the past two years, I've been a member of the St. Frederick High School golf team. And though I was the only black member, I've always felt at home playing at mostly white country clubs across Louisiana."

The audience leaned forward; even the waiters and bus boys stopped to listen. As I listened, a memory buried in my heart since childhood fought its way to life.

"Our team had driven from Monroe," Dondré continued. "When we arrived at the Caldwell Parish Country Club in Columbia, we walked to the putting green."

Dondré and his teammates were too absorbed to notice the conversation between a man and St. Frederick athletic director James Murphy. After disappearing into the clubhouse, Murphy returned to his players.

"I want to see the seniors," he said. "On the double!" His face seemed strained as he gathered the four students, including Dondré.

"I don't know how to tell you this," he said, "but the Caldwell Parish Country Club is reserved for whites only." Murphy paused and looked at Dondré. His teammates glanced at each other in disbelief.

"I want you seniors to decide what our response should be," Murphy continued. "If we leave, we **forfeit** this tournament. If we stay, Dondré can't play."

As I listened, my own childhood memory from 32 years ago broke free.

Thesis Given the clues in this paragraph, what may the author's thesis relate to?

Analyze Text Structure Who is the main character of the frame, or outer, story? What is the setting, or time and place of the story?

---

1 An *emcee* is the leader of a ceremony.

Vocabulary

provoked (prə vōkd´) *v.* having brought out some action or emotion

forfeit (fôr´fit) *v.* to lose or lose the right to something

In 1959 I was thirteen years old, a poor black kid living with my mother and stepfather in a small black ghetto on Long Island, New York. My mother worked nights in a hospital, and my stepfather drove a coal truck. Needless to say, our standard of living was somewhat short of the American dream.

Nevertheless, when my eighth-grade teacher announced a graduation trip to Washington, D.C., it never crossed my mind that I would be left behind. Besides a complete tour of the nation's capital, we would visit Glen Echo Amusement Park in Maryland. In my imagination, Glen Echo was Disneyland, Knott's Berry Farm, and Magic Mountain rolled into one.

My heart beating wildly, I raced home to deliver the mimeographed[2] letter describing the journey. But when my mother saw how much the trip cost, she just shook her head. We couldn't afford it.

After feeling sad for ten seconds, I decided to try to fund the trip myself. For the next eight weeks, I sold candy bars door-to-door, delivered newspapers, and mowed lawns. Three days before the deadline, I'd made just barely enough. I was going!

The day of the trip, trembling with excitement, I climbed onto the train. I was the only nonwhite in our section.

Our hotel was not far from the White House. My roommate was Frank Miller, the son of a businessman.

---

2 If a letter was *mimeographed*, many copies of the letter were made.

The White House

Leaning together out of our window and dropping water balloons on tourists quickly cemented our new friendship.

Every morning, almost a hundred of us loaded noisily onto our bus for another adventure. We sang our school fight song dozens of times—en route[3] to Arlington National Cemetery and even on an afternoon cruise down the Potomac River.

We visited the Lincoln Memorial twice, once in daylight, the second time at dusk. My classmates and I fell silent as we walked in the shadows of those thirty-six marble columns, one for every state in the Union that Lincoln labored to preserve. I stood next to Frank at the base of the nineteen-foot seated statue. Spotlights made the white Georgian marble seem to glow. Together, we read those famous words from Lincoln's speech at Gettysburg, remembering the most bloody battle in the War Between the States: " . . . we here highly resolve[4] that these dead shall not have died in vain — that this nation, under God, shall have a new birth of freedom . . ."

As Frank motioned me into place to take my picture, I took one last look at Lincoln's face. He seemed alive and so terribly sad.

The next morning, I understood a little better why he wasn't smiling. "Clifton," a chaperone said, "could I see you for a moment?"

The other guys at my table, especially Frank, turned pale. We had been joking about the previous night's direct waterballoon hit on a fat lady and her poodle. It was a stupid, dangerous act, but luckily nobody got hurt. We were celebrating our escape from punishment when the chaperone asked to see me.

"Clifton," she began, "do you know about the Mason-Dixon line?"

"No," I said, wondering what this had to do with drenching fat ladies.

"Before the Civil War," she explained, "the Mason-Dixon line was originally the boundary between Maryland and

---

3 **En route** means "on the way."

4 **Resolve** means "to make a firm decision."

Pennsylvania — the dividing line between the slave and free states." Having escaped one disaster, I could feel another brewing. I noticed that her eyes were damp and her hands were shaking.

"Today," she continued, "the Mason-Dixon line is a kind of invisible border between the North and the South. When you cross that invisible line out of Washington, D.C., into Maryland, things change."

There was an ominous[5] drift to this conversation, but I wasn't following it. Why did she look and sound so nervous?

"Glen Echo Amusement Park is in Maryland," she said at last, "and the management doesn't allow Negroes inside." She stared at me in silence.

I was still grinning and nodding when the meaning finally sank in.

"You mean I can't go to the park," I stuttered, "because I'm a Negro?"

She nodded slowly. "I'm sorry, Clifton," she said, taking my hand.

Thesis Recall the title of the story. How do you think the Mason-Dixon line will be important to the author's thesis?

"You'll have to stay in the hotel tonight. Why don't you and I watch a movie on television?"

I walked to the elevators feeling confusion, disbelief, anger, and a deep sadness. "What happened, Clifton?" Frank said when I got back to the room. "Did the fat lady tell on us?"

Without saying a word, I walked over to my bed, lay down, and began to cry. Frank was stunned into silence. Junior-high boys didn't cry, at least not in front of each other.

---

5 *Ominous* means "threatening."

It wasn't just missing the class adventure that made me feel so sad. For the first time in my life, I was learning what it felt like to be a "nigger." Of course there was discrimination in the North, but the color of my skin had never officially kept me out of a coffee shop, a church— or an amusement park.

"Clifton," Frank whispered, "what is the matter?"

"They won't let me go to Glen Echo Park tonight," I sobbed.

"Because of the water balloon?" he asked.

"No," I answered, "because I'm a Negro."

"Well, that's a relief!" Frank said, and then he laughed, obviously relieved to have escaped punishment for our caper with the balloons. "I thought it was serious!"

Wiping away the tears with my sleeve, I stared at him. "It *is* serious. They don't let Negroes into the park. I can't go with you!" I shouted. "That's pretty damn serious to me."

I was about to wipe the silly grin off Frank's face with a blow to his jaw when I heard him say, "Then I won't go either."

For an instant we just froze. Then Frank grinned. I will never forget that moment. Frank was just a kid. He wanted to go to that amusement park as much as I did, but there was something even more important than the class night out. Still, he didn't explain or expand.

The next thing I knew, the room was filled with kids listening to Frank. "They don't allow Negroes in the park," he said, "so I'm staying with Clifton."

"Me, too," a second boy said.

"Those jerks," a third muttered. "I'm with you, Clifton." My heart raced. Suddenly, I was not alone. A pint-size revolution had been born. The "water-balloon brigade,"[6] eleven white boys from Long Island, had made its decision: "We won't go." And as I sat on my bed in the center of it all, I felt grateful. But, above all, I was filled with pride.

BQ **BIG Question**
Reread the last two paragraphs. How does the experience of discrimination affect the narrator?

Thesis What is the "something" that is more important than going to the amusement park?

---

6 A *brigade* is a group of people organized for a specific purpose.

A Mason-Dixon Memory **489**

Dondré Green's story brought that childhood memory back to life. His golfing teammates, like my childhood friends, faced an important decision. If they stood by their friend it would cost them dearly. But when it came time to decide, no one hesitated.

"Let's get out of here," one of them whispered.

"They just turned and walked toward the van," Dondré told us. "They didn't debate it. And the younger players joined us without looking back."

Dondré was astounded by the response of his friends—and the people of Louisiana. The whole state was outraged and tried to make it right. The Louisiana House of Representatives proclaimed a Dondré Green Day and passed legislation permitting lawsuits for damages, attorneys' fees and court costs against any private **facility** that invites a team, then bars any member because of race.

As Dondré concluded, his eyes glistened with tears. "I love my coach and my teammates for sticking by me," he said. "It goes to show that there are always good people who will not give in to bigotry.[7] The kind of love they showed me that day will conquer hatred every time."

My friends, too, had shown that kind of love. As we sat in the hotel, a chaperone came in waving an envelope. "Boys!" he shouted. "I've just bought thirteen tickets to the Senators-Tigers game. Anybody want to go?"

The room erupted[8] in cheers. Not one of us had ever been to a professional baseball game in a real baseball park.

On the way to the stadium, we grew silent as our driver paused before the Lincoln Memorial. For one long moment, I stared through the marble pillars at Mr. Lincoln, bathed in that warm, yellow light. There was still no smile and no sign of hope in his sad and tired eyes.

---

7 **Bigotry** means "intolerance."

8 **Erupted** means "exploded or burst forth."

Vocabulary

facility (fə sil′ə tē) *n.* something, such as a building, built to serve a particular purpose

Analyze Text Structure
How do the inner and outer stories come together here?

BQ BIG Question
How did Dondré's experience influence his community?

The Lincoln Memorial in Washington, D.C., is a tribute to President Abraham Lincoln and a symbol of freedom and the sacrifices of the Civil War.

View the Photograph In what ways do images of monuments such as the Lincoln Memorial help you understand this essay better?

" . . . We here highly resolve . . . that this nation, under God, shall have a new birth of freedom . . ."

In his words and in his life, Lincoln made it clear, that freedom is not free. Every time the color of a person's skin keeps him out of an amusement park or off a country-club fairway, the war for freedom begins again. Sometimes the battle is fought with fists and guns, but more often the most effective weapon is a simple act of love and courage.

Whenever I hear those words from Lincoln's speech at Gettysburg, I remember my eleven white friends, and I feel hope once again. I like to imagine that when we paused that night at the foot of his great monument, Mr. Lincoln smiled at last.

As Dondré said, "The kind of love they showed me that day will conquer hatred every time."

Thesis Think back to the earlier description of the Lincoln statue. How does the description of a smiling Lincoln affect the author's thesis?

After You Read

Respond and Think Critically

1. What decision does Dondré's golf coach ask the team to make at the Caldwell Parish Country Club? [Recall]

2. In the essay, find the quotation from the Lincoln Memorial. In your own words, describe what Lincoln said he would do. [Paraphrase]

3. Think of the events described in the essay. Do you think the other boys would have defended Dondré or the narrator if they had not known them? Explain. [Conclude]

4. What does the Mason-Dixon line represent in this story? Explain. [Analyze]

5. Why were the settings of the frame and inner stories important to Dondré's and the narrator's experiences? Explain. [Evaluate]

6. **BQ** BIG Question What did the life experience of discrimination teach both the narrator and Dondré? Use evidence from the essay to support your answer. [Conclude]

Vocabulary Practice

Respond to these questions.

1. Which would you call a **civic** project—helping to clean up a park or painting your bedroom?

2. In which place would the people be **predominantly** children—an elementary school or an office building?

3. Which would your team rather **forfeit**—one point in a game or the whole game?

4. Which movie probably **provoked** laughter—a funny movie or a serious drama?

5. What would you describe as a sports **facility**—a collection of baseball cards or a building with athletic courts?

Academic Vocabulary

Davis's chaperone explained that Davis would be unable to go to the amusement park because the park's management **restricted** African Americans from entering. In the preceding sentence, *restricted* means "specifically excluded." Think about your own experiences. Have you ever been restricted from entering a place or taking part in an activity? Why? Was the restriction fair? Explain.

TIP

Paraphrasing
To answer question 2, use your own words to restate Lincoln's main ideas.

- Reread the quotation from Lincoln's Gettysburg Address included in the essay.

- Ask yourself, what is the main idea of the quotation?

- Check to make sure that you have used your own words and included the central points of the quotation.

FOLDABLES Study Organizer Keep track of your ideas about the **BIG Question** in your unit Foldable.

 Literature Online

Selection Resources
For Selection Quizzes, eFlashcards, and Reading-Writing Connection activities, go to glencoe.com and enter QuickPass code GL27534u4.

Literary Element Thesis

1. If the essay needed a new title, which of these would be BEST?
   A "A Forgotten Memory"
   B "How Love Conquers Hatred"
   C "A Special Baseball Game"
   D "The Speaker from Louisiana"

Review: Narrator and Point of View

As you learned on page 9, The person who tells a story is the **narrator.** When the narrator is a character in the story and uses first-person pronouns, the story uses **first-person point of view.** In a first-person narrative, all information about the story's characters and events comes from the narrator. A skillful reader must determine how the narrator's experience and opinions influence the telling of the story.

In a story with a **limited third-person point of view,** the narrator reveals the thoughts of only one character, but refers to that character as "he" or "she." In a story with an **omniscient point of view,** the narrator reveals the thoughts of several characters.

2. Who is the narrator of the frame story in "A Mason-Dixon Memory"? Who is the narrator of the inner story? Explain how the point of view from which the stories are told influences a reader's understanding of the stories' events.

Reading Skill Analyze Text Structure

3. How are Clifton Davis's and Dondré Green's stories similar? How are they different? To help you answer, use the graphic organizer you completed as you read the essay.

4. How would the essay change if the author did not use a frame story? Explain.

Grammar Link

Subjects and Predicates Every sentence has two parts: a subject and a predicate.

- The **complete subject** tells who or what a sentence is about.
- The **complete predicate** tells what the subject is doing, being, or has.

Dondré and his friends play golf.

Who plays golf? Dondré and his friends.

The complete subject is "Dondré and his friends."

What do Dondré and his friends do? They play golf.

The complete predicate is "play golf."

<u>Dondré and his friends play golf.</u>

Practice Underline the complete subjects in the following sentences from the selection once. Underline the complete predicates twice. Then write two of your own sentences. Underline the complete subjects once and the complete predicates twice.

Murphy paused and looked at Dondré.

Our hotel was not far from the White House.

I walked to the elevators feeling confusion, disbelief, anger, and a deep sadness.

💬 Speaking and Listening

Literature Groups In a group, talk about the discrimination that Dondré and Davis faced. How did this discrimination influence not only Dondré and Davis, but also those around them? How would you have reacted in Dondré's or Davis's place? Think about the experiences of people today. Discuss how they are similar to or different from the experiences described in the essay. Listen carefully to other speakers. Then ask questions that will help you to better understand their claims and conclusions.

Before You Read

Names/Nombres

Meet Julia Alvarez

"As a fiction writer, I find that the most exciting things happen . . . where two worlds collide or blend together."

—Julia Alvarez

Connect to the Autobiography

Have you ever stopped to think about your name? What does your name tell others about you?

Partner Talk With a partner, talk about what names mean to you. Does your own name seem to capture any of the real you?

Build Background

"Names/Nombres" is set in the early 1960s in New York City. Julia Alvarez was born in New York, but she lived in the Dominican Republic until the age of ten.

- The Dominican Republic is part of the West Indies, a group of islands that extends from Florida to Venezuela. The Dominican Republic is located on the island of Hispaniola.

- *Nombres* is Spanish for "names."

A Way of Making Sense

Asked where she finds the ideas for her richly detailed stories, Julia Alvarez says, "I think when I write, I write out of who I am and the questions I need to figure out. A lot of what I have worked through has to do with coming to this country and losing a homeland and a culture."

Literary Works Alvarez has written several novels, including *How the Garcia Girls Lost Their Accents, Yo!,* and *In the Time of the Butterflies.*

Julia Alvarez was born in 1950.

Vocabulary

ironically (ī ron′i klē) *adv.* in a way that is different from what would be expected (p. 497). *It rained every day except Friday; ironically, that's the only day I brought my umbrella.*

merge (murj) *v.* to join together so as to become one; unite (p. 499). *When the two classes merge, there won't be enough seats for everyone.*

inevitably (i nev′ə tə blē) *adv.* in a way that cannot be avoided or prevented (p. 499). *The car is designed so poorly that it will inevitably fail to sell.*

specified (spes′ə fīd′) *v.* explained or described in detail (p. 499). *At the box office, we specified that we wanted front-row seats.*

 Literature Online

Author Search For more about Julia Alvarez, go to glencoe.com and enter QuickPass code GL27534u4.

Set Purposes for Reading

BQ BIG Question

Julia Alvarez's names remind her of important life experiences. As you read, ask yourself, how do Alvarez's life experiences affect her?

Literary Element Anecdote

An **anecdote** is a brief, entertaining story based on a single interesting or humorous incident or event. Anecdotes are often biographical or autobiographical. Many anecdotes reveal some aspect of a person's character. For example, Julia Alvarez's anecdote about arriving in New York City shows that names are very important to her.

Anecdotes are effective because they "show" rather than "tell." Good authors help readers to picture events and actions through vivid anecdotes. Anecdotes also add action and humor.

As you read, look for anecdotes about Alvarez's life. Ask yourself, why did Alvarez include this anecdote? What does it reveal about her?

Reading Skill Analyze Theme

When you **analyze** something, you look at its individual parts to understand the whole. Analyzing can help you understand a work's **theme,** or the message about life that the author wants to convey.

Often an author implies, or hints at, the theme. When the theme is implied, analyzing the work's details will help you figure out the overall message. Analyzing will also help you notice **recurring themes,** or repeated themes, in two or more selections.

To analyze the theme of "Names/Nombres," think about the way the characters behave, the feelings that Alvarez expresses, and other details that hint at the overall message. Use a graphic organizer like the one below to list details that may hint at a theme.

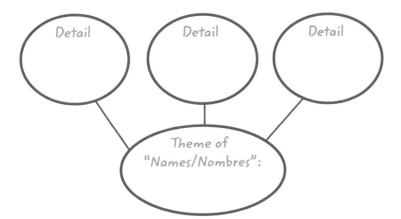

GA Performance Standards

For pages 494–503

ELA7R1d For literary texts, analyze recurring and similar themes across a variety of selections, distinguishing theme from topic.

TRY IT

Analyze Now that you've started thinking about theme, analyze the theme of one of your favorite movies. Think about how the characters and the scenes in the movie help express a message. What details about the characters and events are important? How do these details reveal the movie's theme?

NAMES / *Nombres*

JULIA ALVAREZ

Portrait of Virginia, 1929. Frida Kahlo. Fundacion Dolores Olmedo, Mexico City, D.F., Mexico.

*W*hen we arrived in New York City, our names changed almost immediately. At Immigration, the officer asked my father, *Mister Elbures,* if he had anything to declare. My father shook his head, "No," and we were waved through. I was too afraid we wouldn't be let in if I corrected the man's pronunciation, but I said our name to myself, opening my mouth wide for the organ blast of the *a,* trilling my tongue for the drumroll of the *r, All-vah-rrr-es!* How could anyone get *Elbures* out of that orchestra of sound?

At the hotel my mother was *Missus Alburest,* and I was *little girl,* as in, "Hey, little girl, stop riding the elevator up and down. It's *not* a toy!"

When we moved into our new apartment building, the super called my father *Mister Alberase,* and the neighbors who became mother's friends pronounced her name *Jew-lee-ah* instead of *Hoo-lee-ah.* I, her namesake, was known as *Hoo-lee-tah* at home. But at school, I was *Judy* or *Judith,* and once an English teacher mistook me for *Juliet.*

It took awhile to get used to my new names. I wondered if I shouldn't correct my teachers and new friends. But my mother argued that it didn't matter. "You know what your friend Shakespeare said, '*A rose by any other name would*

Anecdote Why do you think Alvarez begins with an anecdote?

Analyze Theme At this point, how does Alvarez feel about the name she is called by at home? How does she feel about her "new" names?

smell as sweet.'"[1] My family had gotten into the habit of calling any literary figure "my friend" because I had begun to write poems and stories in English class.

By the time I was in high school, I was a popular kid, and it showed in my name. Friends called me *Jules* or *Hey Jude,* and once a group of troublemaking friends my mother forbid me to hang out with called me *Alcatraz.*[2] I was *Hoo-lee-tah* only to Mami and Papi and uncles and aunts who came over to eat *sancocho*[3] on Sunday afternoons—old world folk whom I just as soon would go back to where they came from and leave me to pursue whatever mischief I wanted to in America. *JUDY ALCATRAZ:* the name on the Wanted Poster would read. Who would ever trace her to me?

My older sister had the hardest time getting an American name for herself because Mauricia did not translate into English. **Ironically,** although she had the most foreign-sounding name, she and I were the Americans in the family. We had been born in New York City when our parents had first tried immigration and then gone back "home," too homesick to stay. My mother often told the story of how she had almost changed my sister's name in the hospital.

After the delivery, Mami and some other new mothers were cooing over their new baby sons and daughters and exchanging names and weights and delivery stories. My

---

1 This line is from William Shakespeare's play *Romeo and Juliet.*

2 *Alcatraz* is an island in San Francisco Bay that once was the home of a very tough federal prison.

3 *Sancocho* (sän kō′chō) is a meat stew.

Vocabulary
....

ironically (ī ron′i klē) *adv.* in a way that is different from what would be expected

mother was embarrassed among the Sallys and Janes and Georges and Johns to reveal the rich, noisy name of *Mauricia*, so when her turn came to brag, she gave her baby's name as *Maureen*.

"Why'd ya give her an Irish name with so many pretty Spanish names to choose from?" one of the women asked her.

My mother blushed and admitted her baby's real name to the group. Her mother-in-law had recently died, she apologized, and her husband had insisted that the first daughter be named after his mother, *Mauran*. My mother thought it the ugliest name she had ever heard, and she talked my father into what she believed was an improvement, a combination of *Mauran* and her own mother's name *Felicia*.

"Her name is *Mao-ree-chee-ah*," my mother said to the group.

"Why that's a beautiful name," the new mothers cried. "*Moor-ee-sha, Moor-ee-sha*," they cooed into the pink blanket.

Moor-ee-sha it was when we returned to the States eleven years later. Sometimes, American tongues found even that mispronunciation tough to say and called her *Maria* or *Marsha* or *Maudy* from her nickname *Maury*. I pitied her. What an awful name to have to transport across borders!

My little sister, Ana, had the easiest time of all. She was plain *Anne*—that is, only her name was plain, for she turned out to be the pale, blond "American beauty" in the family. The only Hispanic-seeming thing about her was the affectionate nickname her boyfriends sometimes gave her, *Anita*, or as one goofy guy used to sing to her to the tune of the Chiquita Banana advertisement, *Anita Banana*.

Later, during her college years in the late '60s, there was a push to pronounce Third World[4] names correctly. I remember calling her long distance at her group house and a roommate answering.

"Can I speak to Ana?" I asked, pronouncing her name the American way.

"Ana?" The man's voice hesitated. "Oh! you mean *Ah-nah!*"

---

4 ***Third World*** refers to poorer, less developed countries, mainly in Latin America, Africa, and Asia.

Anecdote What does this anecdote reveal about Alvarez's mother and her experience of living in a new country?

BQ **BIG Question**
What influenced Alvarez to pronounce the name "Ana" in the American way?

The Musicans, 1979. Fernando Botero. Oil on canvas, 85 3/4 x 74 3/4 in. Private Collection.

View the Art How does this painting add to your understanding of the story?

Our first few years in the States, though, ethnicity[5] was not yet "in." Those were the blond, blue-eyed, bobby socks years of junior high and high school before the '60s ushered in peasant blouses, hoop earrings, **serapes.** My initial desire to be known by my correct Dominican name faded. I just wanted to be Judy and **merge** with the Sallys and Janes in my class. But **inevitably,** my accent and coloring gave me away. "So where are you from, Judy?"

"New York," I told my classmates. After all, I had been born blocks away at Columbia Presbyterian Hospital.

"I mean, *originally.*"

"From the Caribbean," I answered vaguely, for if I **specified,** no one was quite sure what continent our island was on.

---

5   ***Ethnicity*** is a word for certain things that a group of people shares, such as language, culture, history, race, and national origin. U.S. citizens come from many different ethnic backgrounds.

Vocabulary ....

merge   (murj) *v.* to join together so as to become one; unite

inevitably   (i nev′ə tə blē) *adv.* in a way that cannot be avoided or prevented

specified   (spes′ə fīd′) *v.* explained or described in detail

"Really? I've been to Bermuda. We went last April for spring vacation. I got the worst sunburn! So, are you from Portoriko?"[6]

"No," I shook my head. "From the Dominican Republic."

"Where's that?"

"South of Bermuda."

They were just being curious, I knew, but I burned with shame whenever they singled me out as a "foreigner," a rare, exotic friend.

"Say your name in Spanish, oh please say it!" I had made mouths drop one day by rattling off my full name, which according to Dominican custom, included my middle names, mother's and father's surnames for four generations back.

"Julia Altagracia Maria Teresa Alvarez Tavares Perello Espaillat Julia Pérez Rochet González," I pronounced it slowly, a name as chaotic with sounds as a Middle Eastern bazaar or market day in a South American village.

I suffered most whenever my extended family attended school occasions. For my graduation, they all came, the whole noisy, foreign-looking lot of old, fat aunts in their dark mourning dresses and hair nets, uncles with full, droopy mustaches and baby-blue or salmon-colored suits and white pointy shoes and fedora[7] hats, the many little cousins who snuck in without tickets. They sat in the first row in order to better understand the Americans' fast-spoken English. But how could they listen when they were constantly speaking among themselves in florid-sounding phrases, rococo[8] consonants, rich, rhyming vowels. Their loud voices carried . . .

How could I introduce them to my friends? These relatives had such complicated names and there were so

Analyze Theme Think about the Dominican custom of naming. How does it suggest the importance of family?

Anecdote What reservations does Alvarez express about introducing her relatives to friends?

---

6 **Bermuda** is an island group in the Atlantic Ocean, east of the United States. When Alvarez's classmates say **Portoriko**, they mean Puerto Rico.

7 A **fedora** is a soft felt hat with a curved brim and a crease along the top.

8 **Florid** and **rococo** both mean "very showy, highly decorated, or flowery."

many of them, and their relationships to myself were so convoluted. There was my Tía Josefina, who was not really an aunt but a much older cousin. And her daughter, Aída Margarita, who was adopted, *una hija de crianza.* My uncle of affection, Tío José, brought my *madrina* Tía Amelia and her *comadre* Tía Pilar.[9] My friends rarely had more than their nuclear family[10] to introduce.

After the commencement[11] ceremony my family waited outside in the parking lot while my friends and I signed yearbooks with nicknames which recalled our high school good times: "Beans" and "Pepperoni" and "Alcatraz." We hugged and cried and promised to keep in touch.

Our good-byes went on too long. I heard my father's voice calling out across the parking lot, *"Hoo-lee-tah! Vámonos!"*[12]

Back home, my *tíos* and *tías* and *primas,* Mami and Papi, and *mis hermanas* had a party for me with *sancocho* and a storebought *pudín,*[13] inscribed with *Happy Graduation, Julie.* There were many gifts—that was a plus to a large family! I got several wallets and a suitcase with my initials and a graduation charm from my godmother and money from my uncles. The biggest gift was a portable typewriter from my parents for writing my stories and poems.

Someday, the family predicted, my name would be well-known throughout the United States. I laughed to myself, wondering which one I would go by. 🖎

Analyze Theme Reread Alvarez's final comment. What is she suggesting about personal identity?

---

9 Something that is **convoluted** is twisted, coiled, and wound around. The rest of the paragraph identifies some of Alvarez's convoluted family relationships. **Tía** (tē′ə) and **Tío** (tē′ō) mean "Aunt" and "Uncle." **Una hija de crianza** (oō′ nə ē′hə dā krē än′zə) is an adopted daughter. **Madrina** (mə drē′nə) and **comadre** (kō mä′drā) both mean "godmother." Later, Alvarez mentions **primas** (prē′məs) and **hermanas** (ār män′əs), her female cousins and sisters.

10 Parents and their children make up what is called a **nuclear family.** An extended family includes other close relatives, such as grandparents, aunts, uncles, and cousins.

11 A **commencement** is a graduation ceremony.

12 **"Vámanos!"** (vä′ mə nōs) means "Let's go!"

13 A **pudín** (poō dēn′) is a pudding.

After You Read

Respond and Think Critically

1. How does your background affect your personal identity? How did Alvarez's background affect her? Explain. [Connect]

2. What happens almost immediately when the Alvarez family arrives in New York City? Explain. [Recall]

3. How does Alvarez feel about the pronunciation of her family's name at the immigration office? Use details to support your answer. [Infer]

4. How does Alvarez's attitude about blending in with her classmates change as she grows older? Explain. [Compare]

5. Is "Names/Nombres" an appropriate title for this autobiographical selection? Why or why not? [Evaluate]

6. **BQ** BIG Question How might Alvarez's experiences have influenced her to become a writer? Explain. [Conclude]

TIP

Evaluating
To answer question 5, you have to evaluate. Remember that when you evaluate, you make a judgment or form an opinion about something you have read.

- Scan through the selection and look for places where the author discusses names. In what way are names an important part of this autobiographical text?

- Does the selection's title reflect Alvarez's theme?

- The title is in English and in Spanish. Does it make sense for Alvarez to use both languages in the title?

 FOLDABLES Study Organizer Keep track of your ideas about the **BIG Question** in your unit Foldable.

You're the Critic

Julia Alvarez's Two Worlds

Read two passages of literary criticism about "Names/Nombres" below.

"With admirable candor and gentle touches of humor, she describes her struggles with cultural hybridism, historical and personal memory, the English language and the effects of all these on her literary career, which became for her an endless language lesson."

—Christina Cho

"Julia Alvarez is truly a citizen of two different worlds, and in her remarkable body of work, she does as much as any writer of her time to describe and define what divides those worlds, and what draws them together."

—Madison Smartt Bell

Group Activity Discuss the following questions with classmates.

1. Cho says that Alvarez uses "gentle touches of humor." What examples from the selection help illustrate this point?

2. Bell says Alvarez is "a citizen of two different worlds." How would you describe the two worlds?

Literary Element Anecdote

1. Briefly summarize what happens to Alvarez's mother when her daughter Mauricia is born.

2. Why do you think Alvarez includes this anecdote? What ideas does it help to get across? Explain.

3. Pick one other anecdote in Alvarez's narrative. What does it add to the story? Explain.

Review: Humor

As you learned on page 401, **humor** is what makes the characters and situations in a literary work seem amusing or funny. Authors use humor to express themes and to entertain readers.

4. Find an example of humor in "Names/Nombres." Then fill in a chart like the one below.

Situation	What makes it humorous?	Why does the author use humor?

Reading Strategy Analyze Theme

Standards Practice ELA7R1d

5. Which sentence gives the best description of the selection's theme about the connection between names and identities?

   A A person's name does not matter at all.

   B The names we use express our identities.

   C Be proud of your name and your heritage.

   D People cannot change their names or themselves.

Vocabulary Practice

Respond to these questions.

1. Which is something that happens **inevitably**—the sun coming up in the morning or a thunderstorm on a humid day?

2. If you **specified** what you wanted at the restaurant, what did you tell the server—that you wanted to order or that you wanted a Lemon-Lime Bonanza?

3. If you stayed up all night to study for a test, which situation would occur **ironically**—your falling asleep halfway through the test or your getting an A on it?

4. When would it be necessary to **merge** with a group of your classmates—when you are working on a team project with them or when you are all working on individual assignments?

Academic Vocabulary

Julia Alvarez writes that she found her full Dominican name embarrassing, despite the fact that it is **distinctive** and rich. In the preceding sentence, *distinctive* means "different from others." Think about a personal quality that makes you different from others and makes you proud. What is the quality, and what makes it *distinctive*?

Selection Resources For Selection Quizzes, eFlashcards, and Reading-Writing Connection activities, go to glencoe.com and enter QuickPass code GL27534u4.

Respond Through Writing

Research Report

Investigate Names In "Names/Nombres," Julia Alvarez writes about her different names. List any questions you have about names, such as: What do names mean? What names were popular in different eras? How do different cultures use names? Choose one topic that interests you and research it. In a short report, write what you learn.

Understand the Task Before you begin writing a research report, gather factual information from several different sources. Through your research, narrow your topic and draw your own conclusion about the topic. This conclusion will become the main idea, or thesis, of your report. You will have to back up your thesis with factual information.

Prewrite Begin by looking up the topic "names" in an encyclopedia or another general reference book. Use the information you read to guide your research. Then gather information from a variety of sources. The chart below shows some sources you might use.

almanacs	newspapers	DVDs
atlases	surveys	videos
encyclopedias	scholarly journals	CD-ROMs
magazines	Web sites	interviews

Draft Organize the information from your research in an outline. Write your thesis at the beginning of the outline. List the main ideas you want to cover. Below each idea, write the supporting details from your research. Keep track of where you found the information. Then write paragraphs that include the main ideas and supporting details.

Revise After you have finished your first draft, make sure that you have supported all your statements with facts from reliable sources. Make sure that you have documented your information correctly and include a list of sources you used. Refer to the Writing Handbook in the back of the book for help with documenting information. Read your report and make sure the paragraphs follow a logical order. Rearrange text as necessary so that your ideas are easy to follow.

Edit and Proofread Proofread your paper, correcting any errors in spelling, grammar, and punctuation. See the Word Bank in the side column for words you might use in your research report.

 Performance Standards

For page 504

ELA7W3a Use research and technology to support writing. Identify topics, ask and evaluate questions, and develop ideas leading to inquiry and research.

Word Bank

The following are some useful words you might want to include in your report. Check their meanings in a dictionary first to make sure you use them correctly.

ancestry

culture

ethnicity

heritage

surname

tradition

Before You Read

In a Neighborhood in Los Angeles

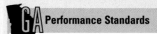
GA Performance Standards

For pages 505–508

ELA7R1g/ii For literary texts, explain and analyze the effects of figurative language.

Connect to the Poem

Think of a family member whom you love. What is special about this person?

List List the special qualities that you love about a family member. You could include the person's traits, as well as what makes this person unique.

Build Background

Francisco X. Alarcón came to Los Angeles from Mexico. "In a Neighborhood in Los Angeles" was originally written in Spanish.

- Spanish missionaries founded twenty-one missions in California between 1769 and 1823. One of the missions was located in what is now Los Angeles.

- When Mexico won its independence from Spain in 1821, California became part of Mexico. California did not become part of the United States until the mid-1800s.

Set Purposes for Reading

BQ BIG Question

As you read, notice how the speaker describes his grandmother. Ask yourself, why was his grandmother such a strong influence on him?

Literary Element Imagery

Imagery is language that creates vivid pictures and sensory impressions. Poets use words and phrases to create images that appeal to readers' senses. These words and phrases help readers see, hear, smell, touch, and taste the scenes described in the poem.

Imagery helps readers understand the poet's ideas clearly. It also makes poetry fun to read.

As you read, look for details that help you visualize the speaker and his grandmother.

LOG ON ▶ Literature Online

Author Search For more about Francisco X. Alarcón, go to glencoe.com and enter QuickPass code GL27534u4.

Meet Francisco X. Alarcón

Humble Beginnings Francisco X. Alarcón (al är kōn´) arrived in this country from Mexico with only five dollars in his pocket. He eventually earned three college degrees. As a poet, a professor, and a performer, Alarcón's mission is to bring his poetry to the widest possible audience.

Francisco X. Alarcón was born in 1954.

En un Barrio de Los Angeles

Francisco X. Alarcón

el español
lo aprendí
de mi abuela

mijito
5   no llores
me decía

en las mañanas
cuando salían
mis padres

10 a trabajar
en las canerías
de pescado

mi abuela
platicaba
15 con las sillas

les cantaba
canciones
antiguas

les bailaba
20 valses en
la cocina

cuando decía
niño barrigón
se reía

25 con mi abuela
aprendí
a contar nubes

In a Neighborhood in Los Angeles

Translated by Francisco Aragon

I learned
Spanish
from my grandma

mijito°
5   don't cry
she'd tell me

on the mornings
my parents
would leave

10 to work
at the fish
canneries

my grandma
would chat
15 with chairs

sing them
old
songs

dance
20 waltzes with them
in the kitchen

when she'd say
niño barrigón°
she'd laugh

25 with my grandma
I learned
to count clouds

Imagery What images do you see in lines 13 through 21?

---

4 *Mijito* (mē hē′tō) means "my little child."

23 The grandmother was teasing the speaker by calling him *niño barrigón* (nēn′yō bär′rē gōn′), which means "big-bellied boy."

a reconocer
en las macetas
30 la yerbabuena

mi abuela
llevaba lunas
en el vestido

la montaña
35 el desierto
el mar de México

en sus ojos
yo las veía
en sus trenzas

40 yo los tocaba
con su voz
yo los olía

un día
me dijeron:
45 se fue muy lejos

pero yo aún
la siento
conmigo

diciéndome
50 quedito al oído
mijito

to point out
in flowerpots
30 mint leaves

my grandma
wore moons
on her dress

Mexico's mountains
35 deserts
ocean

in her eyes
I'd see them
in her braids

40 I'd touch them
in her voice
smell them

one day
I was told:
45 she went far away

but still
I feel her
with me

whispering
50 in my ear
mijito

Imagery In lines 34–42, what details appeal to the reader's senses of sight, sound, smell, and touch?

BQ **BIG Question**
How can you tell that the grandmother left an enormous impression on the speaker?

After You Read

Respond and Think Critically

1. Why did the speaker spend time with his grandmother? [Recall]

2. What are some special memories of his grandmother that the speaker describes? Use details from the poem to support your answer. [Identify]

3. Did the speaker enjoy being with his grandmother? Explain. [Infer]

4. What message about human relationships does the poem express? [Conclude]

5. **Literary Element** Imagery What imagery do you think best shows how close the speaker was with his grandmother? Explain. [Evaluate]

6. **BQ** BIG Question How might the experiences the speaker had with his grandmother influence him? Use details from the poem to support your answer. [Conclude]

Spelling Link

Suffixes and the Silent *e* and Final *y* Many words end in silent *e*. Keep the silent *e* when adding a suffix that begins with a consonant. Drop the silent *e* when adding a suffix beginning with a vowel. When adding the suffix *-ly* to a word that ends in *-le,* drop the *le.*

wise + ly = wisely   gentle + ly = gently

skate + ing = skating   noise + y = noisy

When you add a suffix to words ending with a vowel + *y,* keep the *y.* For words ending with a consonant + *y,* change the *y* to *i* unless the suffix begins with *i.* To avoid having two *i*'s together, keep the *y.*

enjoy + ment = enjoyment   display + ed = displayed

merry + ment = merriment   worry + ing = worrying

Practice Combine each word with the suffix.

write + ing   delay + ed   final + ly   wary + ly

 Writing

Write a Scene Think about a close relationship you have with a relative or friend. Write a short scene about a conversation between the two of you that shows the importance of your relationship. Use imagery, sensory details, and dialogue to give a vivid description.

TIP

Inferring
To answer question 3, you must think about details in the poem as well as what you know about human relationships. Draw from your personal experience to fill in the gaps that the speaker leaves.

- Think about what the speaker and the grandmother mean to each other.

- Reread sections of the poem, looking for specific clues about their relationship.

- Construct your answer by stating your opinion first and then giving your reasons.

FOLDABLES Study Organizer Keep track of your ideas about the **Big Question** in your unit Foldable.

 Literature Online

Selection Resources
For Selection Quizzes, eFlashcards, and Reading-Writing Connection activities, go to glencoe.com and enter QuickPass code GL27534u4.

Vocabulary Workshop

Idioms

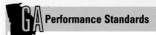
Performance Standards

For page 509

ELA7R2c Understand and acquire new vocabulary. Identify and explain idioms and analogies in prose and poetry.

Connection to Literature

"with my grandma / I learned / to count clouds"

—Francisco X. Alarcón, "In a Neighborhood in Los Angeles"

An **idiom** is a word or a phrase with a special meaning that is different from the ordinary meaning of the word or words. The speaker in Alarcón's poem says his grandma taught him "to count clouds." He might actually mean that she taught him how to count the number of clouds in the sky. It is more likely, however, that he means she taught him to daydream. Expressions such as "counting clouds" or "having your head in the clouds" are idioms that describe daydreaming.

There are two useful ways to figure out the meaning of an unfamiliar idiom. One is to think about what the ordinary meanings of the words suggest. The other is to look for context clues.

Here are some other popular idioms that incorporate the word *cloud*.

Idiom	Meaning
My mom's face will *cloud over* when she finds out my chores aren't done.	To *cloud over* is to become unhappy or worried.
I was *on cloud nine* when I got an A on the test.	To be *on cloud nine* is to be very happy.
Thanks to my sister's lie, we were all *under a cloud*.	To be *under a cloud* is to be suspected of something.

TRY IT: Write a short definition or phrase that could be substituted for each underlined idiom.

1. Grandma lives in Los Angeles, but Mexico is <u>close to her heart</u>.
2. Grandma and Francisco are buddies. They <u>stick together</u>.
3. Grandma sings to her grandson when he is <u>down in the dumps</u>.

> **Tip**
>
> **Vocabulary Terms** Idioms are words or phrases that have special meanings different from their literal meanings.
>
> **Test-taking Tip** To understand the meanings of idioms and other figures of speech, think about the ordinary meanings of the words. Then use context clues to help you figure out what the words mean in the current context.

 Literature Online

Vocabulary For more vocabulary practice, go to glencoe.com and enter the QuickPass code GL27534u4.

Before You Read

The War of the Wall

Connect to the Short Story

Think about the neighborhood around your home or school. Does any part of your neighborhood have a special meaning for you?

List Make a list of places in your neighborhood that you like or that are special to you. Think about why the places are special and how you would explain their importance to someone who does not live in your neighborhood.

Build Background

In this story, a woman puzzles the people of a neighborhood by painting a picture on the blank wall of a building. It is the same wall on which the narrator and a cousin had carved the name of a friend who had died in the Vietnam War.

- Painting murals, or large paintings on walls or ceilings, is a tradition that goes back to the earliest humans.

- Many public murals tell stories or show familiar scenes, activities, and characters from the surrounding community.

- About 58,000 Americans died serving in the Vietnam War, which lasted from 1965 to 1973.

Vocabulary

whiff (hwif) *n.* a quick puff or gust, especially of air, odor, or smoke (p. 513). *They noticed a whiff of fried chicken as they passed the restaurant.*

satchel (sach′əl) *n.* a carrying bag, often having a shoulder strap (p. 513). *She carried her school books in a blue satchel.*

aromas (ə rō′məz) *n.* pleasing smells or scents (p. 513). *As the pie baked, the aromas of cinnamon and apples filled the house.*

inscription (in skrip′shən) *n.* something written or carved on a surface as a lasting record (p. 520). *The inscription on the locket said "To my daughter."*

Meet Toni Cade Bambara

Civil Rights Activist Toni Cade Bambara was born in New York City. She lived, studied, and wrote in New York, France, and Italy. In addition to writing, Bambara was a civil rights activist who was especially interested in improving living conditions in U.S. cities. Her books include *Gorilla, My Love,* a short-story collection, and *The Salt Eaters,* a novel.

Toni Cade Bambara was born in 1939 and died in 1995.

 Literature Online

Author Search For more about Toni Cade Bambara, go to glencoe.com and enter QuickPass code GL27534u4.

Set Purposes for Reading

BQ BIG Question

As you read, ask yourself, how can art influence a community and its members?

Literary Element Characterization

Characterization includes all the methods that a writer uses to develop the personality of a character. Sometimes the narrator tells readers directly what a character is like. This is called **direct characterization**. Other times, readers learn about what a character is like through the character's words and actions and through what other characters say or think about the character. This is called **indirect characterization.**

Characterization is important because it makes characters seem real and believable. When you pay attention to details of characterization, you will deepen your understanding of the characters.

As you read, ask yourself, what does the narrator tell me about each character? How do each character's actions and words reveal his or her personality?

Reading Strategy Visualize

When you **visualize,** you create images, or pictures, in your mind. As you read, you use the author's descriptions and details to visualize the characters, setting, and events.

Visualizing helps you understand and enjoy what you read. It helps you "see" people, places, and things. Visualizing as you read also helps you remember the details of the story more clearly. To visualize as you read, focus on vivid details. Try to imagine the action of the story unfolding before you.

As you read, list vivid details. Then sketch what they help you "see" in your mind. Use a graphic organizer like the one below.

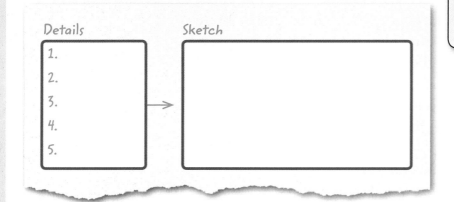

Details

1.
2.
3.
4.
5.

Sketch

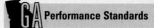

GA Performance Standards

For pages 510–523

ELA7R1b For literary texts, interpret a character's traits, emotions, or motivations and give supporting evidence from a text.

TRY IT

Visualize Think of a place that you know well. Describe this place to a partner using as many descriptive details as you can. Ask your partner to sketch the place from your description. Did your details allow your partner to correctly visualize and sketch the location? What other details could you have given to make the picture clearer? Then reverse roles, and try to visualize and sketch your partner's location.

THE WAR OF THE WALL

Toni Cade Bambara

Me and Lou had no time for courtesies.[1] We were late for school. So we just flat out told the painter lady to quit messing with the wall. It was our wall, and she had no right coming into our neighborhood painting on it. Stirring in the paint bucket and not even looking at us, she mumbled something about Mr. Eubanks, the barber, giving her permission. That had nothing to do with it as far as we were concerned. We've been pitching pennies against that wall since we were little kids. Old folks have been dragging their chairs out to sit in the shade of the wall for years. Big kids have been playing handball against the wall since so-called integration when the crazies 'cross town poured cement in our pool so we couldn't use it. I'd sprained my neck one time boosting my cousin Lou up to chisel Jimmy Lyons's name into the wall when we found out he was never coming home from the war in Vietnam to take us fishing.

Characterization What do you learn about the narrator and Lou in this paragraph? How is the information presented to you?

---

1 *Courtesies* are the words and actions of polite behavior.

"If you lean close," Lou said, leaning hipshot against her beat-up car, "you'll get a **whiff** of bubble gum and kids' sweat. And that'll tell you something—that this wall belongs to the kids of Taliaferro Street." I thought Lou sounded very convincing. But the painter lady paid us no mind. She just snapped the brim of her straw hat down and hauled her bucket up the ladder.

"You're not even from around here," I hollered up after her. The license plates on her old piece of car said "New York." Lou dragged me away because I was about to grab hold of that ladder and shake it. And then we'd really be late for school.

When we came from school, the wall was slick with white. The painter lady was running string across the wall and taping it here and there. Me and Lou leaned against the gumball machine outside the pool hall and watched. She had strings up and down and back and forth. Then she began chalking them with a hunk of blue chalk.

The Morris twins crossed the street, hanging back at the curb next to the beat-up car. The twin with the red ribbons was hugging a jug of cloudy lemonade. The one with yellow ribbons was holding a plate of dinner away from her dress. The painter lady began snapping the strings. The blue chalk dust measured off halves and quarters up and down and sideways too. Lou was about to say how hip it all was, but I dropped my book **satchel** on his toes to remind him we were at war.

Some good **aromas** were drifting our way from the plate leaking pot likker[2] onto the Morris girl's white socks. I could tell from where I stood that under the tinfoil was baked ham, collard greens, and candied yams. And knowing Mrs. Morris, who sometimes bakes for my mama's restaurant, a slab of buttered cornbread was

Visualize How does the author help you visualize the scene?

---

2 *Pot likker* (or "pot liquor") is the juices that come from collard greens and ham when they are cooked.

whiff (hwif) *n.* a quick puff or gust, especially of air, odor, or smoke

satchel (sach´əl) *n.* a carrying bag, often having a shoulder strap

aromas (ə rō´məz) *n.* pleasing smells or scents

probably up under there too, sopping up some of the pot likker. Me and Lou rolled our eyes, wishing somebody would send us some dinner. But the painter lady didn't even turn around. She was pulling the strings down and prying bits of tape loose.

Side Pocket came strolling out of the pool hall to see what Lou and me were studying so hard. He gave the painter lady the once-over, checking out her paint-spattered jeans, her chalky T-shirt, her floppy-brimmed straw hat. He hitched up his pants and glided over toward the painter lady, who kept right on with what she was doing.

"Whatcha got there, sweetheart?" he asked the twin with the plate.

"Suppah," she said all soft and countrylike.

"For her," the one with the jug added, jerking her chin toward the painter lady's back.

Still she didn't turn around. She was rearing back on her heels, her hands jammed into her back pockets, her face squinched up like the masterpiece she had in mind was taking shape on the wall by magic. We could have been gophers crawled up into a rotten hollow for all she cared. She didn't even say hello to anybody. Lou was muttering something about how great her concentration was. I butt him with my hip, and his elbow slid off the gum machine.

"Good evening," Side Pocket said in his best ain't-I-fine voice. But the painter lady was moving from the milk crate to the step stool to the ladder, moving up and down fast, scribbling all over the wall like a crazy person. We looked at Side Pocket. He looked at the twins. The twins looked at us. The painter lady was giving a show. It was like those old-timey music movies where the dancer taps on the tabletop and then starts jumping all over the furniture, kicking chairs over and not skipping a beat. She didn't even look where she was stepping. And for a minute there, hanging on the ladder to reach a far spot, she looked like she was going to tip right over.

"Ahh," Side Pocket cleared his throat and moved fast to catch the ladder. "These young ladies here have brought you some supper."

Characterization What do you learn about Side Pocket from the narrator's description of the sound of his voice?

Visualize To whom is the painter compared in this paragraph? How does this comparison help you visualize the scene?

"Ma'am?" The twins stepped forward. Finally the painter turned around, her eyes "full of sky," as my grandmama would say. Then she stepped down like she was in a trance.[3] She wiped her hands on her jeans as the Morris twins offered up the plate and the jug. She rolled back the tinfoil, then wagged her head as though something terrible was on the plate.

"Thank your mother very much," she said, sounding like her mouth was full of sky too. "I've brought my own dinner along." And then, without even excusing herself, she went back up the ladder, drawing on the wall in a wild way. Side Pocket whistled one of those oh-brother breathy whistles and went back into the pool hall. The Morris twins shifted their weight from one foot to the other, then crossed the street and went home. Lou had to drag me away, I was so mad. We couldn't wait to get to the firehouse to tell my daddy all about this rude woman who'd stolen our wall.

All the way back to the block to help my mama out at the restaurant, me and Lou kept asking my daddy for ways to run the painter lady out of town. But my daddy was busy talking about the trip to the country and telling Lou he could come too because Grandmama can always use an extra pair of hands on the farm.

Later that night, while me and Lou were in the back doing our chores, we found out that the painter lady was a liar. She came into the restaurant and leaned against the glass of the steam table, talking about how starved she was. I was scrubbing pots and Lou was chopping onions, but we could hear her through the service window. She was asking Mama was that a ham hock in the greens, and was that a neck bone in the pole beans, and were there any vegetables cooked without meat, especially pork.

"I don't care who your spiritual leader is," Mama said in that way of hers. "If you eat in the community, sistuh, you gonna eat pig by-and-by, one way or t'other."

Me and Lou were cracking up in the kitchen, and several customers at the counter were clearing their

Characterization How does the narrator feel about the painter?

---

3 To be in a ***trance*** means that someone is in a state of mind between sleeping and waking; the person is in a daze.

Hamburger Joint. Pam Ingalls.

throats, waiting for Mama to really fix her wagon[4] for not
speaking to the elders when she came in. The painter lady
took a stool at the counter and went right on with her
questions. Was there cheese in the baked macaroni, she
wanted to know? Were there eggs in the salad? Was it
honey or sugar in the iced tea? Mama was fixing Pop
Johnson's plate. And every time the painter lady asked a
fool question, Mama would dump another spoonful of rice
on the pile. She was tapping her foot and heating up in a
dangerous way. But Pop Johnson was happy as he could
be. Me and Lou peeked through the service window,
wondering what planet the painter lady came from. Who
ever heard of baked macaroni without cheese, or potato
salad without eggs?

4 To *fix her wagon* means "to put her in her place or show her who's boss."

"Do you have any bread made with unbleached flour?"[5] the painter lady asked Mama. There was a long pause, as though everybody in the restaurant was holding their breath, wondering if Mama would dump the next spoonful on the painter lady's head. She didn't. But when she set Pop Johnson's plate down, it came down with a bang.

When Mama finally took her order, the starving lady all of a sudden couldn't make up her mind whether she wanted a vegetable plate or fish and a salad. She finally settled on the broiled trout and a tossed salad. But just when Mama reached for a plate to serve her, the painter lady leaned over the counter with her finger all up in the air.

"Excuse me," she said. "One more thing." Mama was holding the plate like a Frisbee, tapping that foot, one hand on her hip. "Can I get raw beets in that tossed salad?"

"You will get," Mama said, leaning her face close to the painter lady's, "whatever Lou back there tossed. Now sit down." And the painter lady sat back down on her stool and shut right up.

Characterization What do you learn about Mama through her conversation with the painter?

All the way to the country, me and Lou tried to get Mama to open fire on the painter lady. But Mama said that seeing as how she was from the North, you couldn't expect her to have any manners. Then Mama said she was sorry she'd been so impatient with the woman because she seemed like a decent person and was simply trying to stick to a very strict diet. Me and Lou didn't want to hear that. Who did that lady think she was, coming into our neighborhood and taking over our wall?

"Wellllll," Mama drawled, pulling into the filling station so Daddy could take the wheel, "it's hard on an artist, ya know. They can't always get people to look at their work. So she's just doing her work in the open, that's all."

Me and Lou definitely did not want to hear that. Why couldn't she set up an **easel** downtown or draw on the sidewalk in her own neighborhood? Mama told us to quit fussing so much; she was tired and wanted to rest. She climbed into the back seat and dropped down into the warm hollow Daddy had made in the pillow.

Visual Vocabulary

An **easel** is a frame used to support an artist's canvas or paper while he or she works.

---

5 **Unbleached flour** does not have chemicals added to make it white.

All weekend long, me and Lou tried to scheme up ways to recapture our wall. Daddy and Mama said they were sick of hearing about it. Grandmama turned up the TV to drown us out. On the late news was a story about the New York subways. When a train came roaring into the station all covered from top to bottom, windows too, with writings and drawings done with spray paint, me and Lou slapped five. Mama said it was too bad kids in New York had nothing better to do than spray paint all over the trains. Daddy said that in the cities, even grown-ups wrote all over the trains and buildings too. Daddy called it "graffiti." Grandmama called it a shame.

We couldn't wait to get out of school on Monday. We couldn't find any black spray paint anywhere. But in a junky hardware store downtown we found a can of white epoxy paint, the kind you touch up old refrigerators with when they get splotchy and peely. We spent our whole allowance on it. And because it was too late to use our bus passes, we had to walk all the way home lugging our book satchels and gym shoes, and the bag with the epoxy.

When we reached the corner of Taliaferro and Fifth, it looked like a block party or something. Half the neighborhood was gathered on the sidewalk in front of the wall. I looked at Lou, he looked at me. We both looked at the bag with the epoxy and wondered how we were going to work our scheme. The painter lady's car was nowhere in sight. But there were too many people standing around to do anything. Side Pocket and his buddies were leaning on their cue sticks, hunching each other. Daddy was there with a lineman[6] he catches a ride with on Mondays. Mrs. Morris had her arms flung around the shoulders of the twins on either side of her. Mama was talking with some of her customers, many of them with napkins still at the throat. Mr. Eubanks came out of the barbershop, followed by a man in a striped poncho, half his face shaved, the other half full of foam.

BQ BIG Question

What do the narrator's and Lou's actions show about how important the wall is to them?

---

6 A worker who strings telephone lines is a *lineman.*

"She really did it, didn't she?" Mr. Eubanks huffed out his chest. Lots of folks answered right quick that she surely did when they saw the straight razor in his hand.

Mama beckoned[7] us over. And then we saw it. The wall. Reds, greens, figures outlined in black. Swirls of purple and orange. Storms of blues and yellows. It was something. I recognized some of the faces right off. There was Martin Luther King, Jr. And there was a man with glasses on and his mouth open like he was laying down a heavy rap. Daddy came up alongside and reminded us that that was Minister Malcolm X. The serious woman with a rifle I knew was Harriet Tubman because my grandmama has pictures of her all over the house. And I knew Mrs. Fannie Lou Hamer 'cause a signed photograph of her hangs in the restaurant next to the calendar.

Then I let my eyes follow what looked like a vine. It trailed past a man with a horn, a woman with a big white flower in her hair, a handsome dude in a tuxedo seated at a piano, and a man with a goatee holding a book. When I looked more closely, I realized that what had looked like flowers were really faces. One face with yellow petals looked just like Frieda Morris. One with red petals looked just like Hattie Morris. I could hardly believe my eyes.

"Notice," Side Pocket said, stepping close to the wall with his cue stick like a classroom pointer. "These are the flags of liberation," he said in a voice I'd never heard him use before. We all stepped closer while he pointed and spoke. "Red, black and green," he said, his pointer falling on the leaflike flags of the vine. "Our liberation[8] flag. And here Ghana, there Tanzania. Guinea-Bissau, Angola, Mozambique." Side Pocket sounded very tall, as though he'd been waiting all his life to give this lesson.

Mama tapped us on the shoulder and pointed to a high section of the wall. There was a fierce-looking man with his arms crossed against his chest guarding a bunch of children. His muscles bulged, and he looked a lot like my

Characterization Who is Mr. Eubanks talking about? What do his words and actions say about what he thinks of the person?

---

7 If you **beckoned** to someone, you called or signaled to him or her, usually with a wave or a nod.

8 **Liberation** is freedom achieved after a struggle. The names listed are of countries in Africa.

daddy. One kid was looking at a row of books. Lou hunched[9] me 'cause the kid looked like me. The one that looked like Lou was spinning a globe on the tip of his finger like a basketball. There were other kids there with microscopes and compasses. And the more I looked, the more it looked like the fierce man was not so much guarding the kids as defending their right to do what they were doing.

Then Lou gasped and dropped the paint bag and ran forward, running his hands over a rainbow. He had to tiptoe and stretch to do it, it was so high. I couldn't breathe either. The painter lady had found the chisel marks and had painted Jimmy Lyons's name in a rainbow.

"Read the **inscription,** honey," Mrs. Morris said, urging little Frieda forward. She didn't have to urge much. Frieda marched right up, bent down, and in a loud voice that made everybody quit oohing and ahhing and listen, she read,

> *To the People of Taliaferro Street*
> *I Dedicate This Wall of Respect*
> *Painted in Memory of My Cousin*
> *Jimmy Lyons* ❧

Visualize How does picturing the mural in your mind add to your understanding of the story?

BQ **BIG Question**

How does the narrator's reaction show the narrator's feelings about the wall?

View the Photograph How is the mural in the photo similar to or different than the mural you visualized as you read the story?

---

9 When Lou **hunched** the narrator, he nudged or bumped into the narrator on purpose.

Vocabulary . . . .

inscription (in skrip′shən) *n.* something written or carved on a surface as a lasting record

After You Read

Respond and Think Critically

1. What do the Morris twins bring to the artist? [Recall]

2. What happens when the painter tries to order food in the restaurant? Explain. [Summarize]

3. Do Lou's feelings about the painter change during the story? Use details from the story to support your answer. [Interpret]

4. What do you think the narrator feels after reading the inscription? Explain. [Infer]

5. What do you think of the way the painter behaves? Use details from the story to support your answer. [Evaluate]

6. **BQ** BIG Question Were the narrator and the painter influenced in the same way by the death of Jimmy Lyons in the Vietnam War? Explain. [Compare]

Vocabulary Practice

On a separate sheet of paper, write the vocabulary word that correctly completes each sentence. If none of the words fits the sentence, write "none."

whiff   satchel   aromas   inscription

1. Kelly filled her _____ with newspapers to deliver on her route.

2. Before he closed the door, we got a(n) _____ of the clean-smelling winter air.

3. Tonya made a(n) _____ of a horse and a cow with her new paints.

4. The _____ on the statue lists the names of local residents who fought in World War I.

5. I like the _____ colors of your painting in the hall.

6. On my birthday, the house was filled with the _____ of my favorite dishes.

Academic Vocabulary

The mural's spectacular color and figures show the artist's **creativity.** In the preceding sentence, *creativity* means "the ability to make something from skills and imagination." Think about something you like to do that involves skill and imagination. How do you show your own creativity?

TIP

Evaluating
When you evaluate something, you form an opinion or make a judgment about it. To answer question 5, think about the different examples of the painter's words and actions in the story, as well as the ways in which other characters react to her words and actions. Think about why the artist behaves as she does.

- Consider how the artist's actions and words are different from those of others in the neighborhood.

- Think of the artist's conversation with the Morris twins. She tells them she has her own dinner. What does this exchange tell you about the artist?

 Keep track of your ideas about the **BIG Question** in your unit Foldable.

 Literature Online

Selection Resources
For Selection Quizzes, eFlashcards, and Reading-Writing Connection activities, go to glencoe.com and enter QuickPass code GL27534u4.

Literary Element Characterization

1. Based on the narrator's description of the painting, in what way does the narrator change after viewing the painting? Explain.

Review: Motivation

As you learned on page 433, **motivation** is what makes characters act as they do. To understand a character's motivation, ask why the character speaks or acts as he or she does.

Standards Practice ⬛ ELA7R1b

2. Which detail from "The War of the Wall" best explains why the painter created the mural on the wall?
   A   The people of the neighborhood had damaged the wall.
   B   No one will look at the artist's other paintings.
   C   Many boys write on the wall with spray paint.
   D   The painter wants people to remember Jimmy Lyons.

Reading Strategy Visualize

3. What are some details the writer gives to help the reader visualize the characters in "The War of the Wall"? To help you answer, refer to the graphic organizer you created as you read.

4. List details that describe the mural that the artist paints on Taliaferro Street. Then sketch a picture of the mural.

Grammar Link

Compound Subjects and Predicates A **compound subject** is made up of two or more subjects that are joined by *and, or,* or *nor.* For example:

  Frieda, Hattie, and Side Pocket looked.

The subjects *Frieda, Hattie,* and *Side Pocket* are joined by *and.* The compound subject is "Frieda, Hattie, and Side Pocket."

  Neither Mama nor Daddy listened.

The subjects are *Mama* and *Daddy;* they are joined by *nor.* The compound subject is "Neither Mama nor Daddy."

A **compound predicate** is made up of two or more verbs that have the same subject and that are joined by *and, or,* or *nor.*

  The painter taped string and moved up.

The verbs *taped* and *moved* both go with the subject *painter.* The compound predicate is *taped and moved.*

  Side Pocket talks to the twins, watches the painter, and holds the ladder.

The verbs *talks, watches,* and *holds* go with the subject *Side Pocket.* The compound predicate is *talks, watches, and holds.*

Practice Look for two sentences in the story with compound subjects or predicates. Then write a sentence of your own that has a compound subject and a sentence that has a compound predicate.

Write with Style

Apply Imagery Use imagery, or description that appeals to the senses, to describe a piece of art that you like. The artwork may be in your classroom, at home, or in a book. While you write, think about or look at the artwork and describe as many details as you can. Make sure that your reader will be able to visualize the artwork just by reading your description.

Outdoor Art in America

— **Toni Cade Bambara**

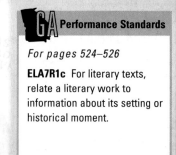

GA Performance Standards

For pages 524–526

ELA7R1c For literary texts, relate a literary work to information about its setting or historical moment.

Set a Purpose for Reading

Read to learn about the events that inspired Toni Cade Bambara's "The War of the Wall."

Build Background

Artists and activists use outdoor art, such as murals, to educate communities about their history and the social issues that affect them.

Reading Skill Analyze Cultural Context

To analyze the cultural context of a literary work, pay attention to details that reveal the values or beliefs of a group of people. Use this knowledge to understand the theme or message of a literary work. As you read, take notes about the cultural context using a chart like this one.

	1960s	1970s	1980s
What were artists' values?			
What were artists' goals?			

In the 1940s, the Rheingold Company started a contest. They would plaster posters of blondes and redheads all over buildings, buses, and highways asking the public to vote for the next Miss Rheingold. One day we found a huge metal grid in the vacant lot we used for play; the thing looked like a giant's easel. We knew it was not the playground equipment promised by the city's park and recreation division. A six-foot-square billboard of the new Miss Rheingold soon filled the grid. The city had decided to lease the lot to the company. Needless to say, I became a community organizer early.

During the 1960s, streets, parks, and other public spaces became the arena for millions of people determined to make democracy a reality for everyone in the country. Many of these determined people were activist artists of downpressed communities. They used their talents and skills to agitate[1] and educate for social change. These poets, singers, and others shared their training by moving from the privacy of their studios and working outdoors. There it was easier to mobilize neighborhoods around issues of discrimination and exploitation,[2] community and power.

A Chicago-based African-American artist collective called Afrocobra was instrumental in sparking an outdoor art movement throughout the country; it was most immediately experienced in the national black community. Walls of respect were done collectively, in keeping with the emphasis placed on community. The spirit of the outdoor art movement was arts-for-people's-sake. This idea challenged the arts-for-art's-sake notion that art is valuable only when it is done by one "special" individual and is housed in a big museum.

In the 1970s, youths who drew or painted on top of advertisements that cluttered their environment were called public artists by community people. The authorities called them criminals. To show that the city belonged, not just to corporations, but to young people too, these artists began practicing their craft in park tunnels, on bridges, and on trains. They risked arrest.

1 **Agitate** means "argue about or discuss a matter vigorously to arouse public interest and feeling."

2 **Exploitation** means "selfish or unfair use."

Mural in Boyle Heights, East Los Angeles, CA

View the Photograph How might this mural be a "wall of respect"? For whom does it show respect?

Detail of The Great Wall of Los Angeles, Los Angeles, CA commemorates early leaders of the civil rights movement including Rosa Parks, Los Angeles, CA.

There's an incredible work of collective outdoor art called "The Great Wall of Los Angeles." It was executed in the 1980s by more than one hundred people. Under the directorship of Mexican-American activist artist Judy Baca, the half-mile long mural depicts the history of California from the point of view of Native Americans and Mexican-Americans. Unlike the walls of the 1960s, it is not set in the neighborhood of the artists. Baca chose the wall of a flood channel in a very high-priced district of the San Fernando Valley. The artists were youths from working class neighborhoods of Los Angeles. Baca "sprang" many of them from juvenile detention centers where they'd been sentenced for art activity in tunnels, bridges, and trains. Warrior art I call it.

This warrior art, this rich heritage of outdoor art led me to write "The War of the Wall." I wondered how people in the neighborhood would react if a stranger started painting on a wall, *their* wall. What reasons might the artist have for painting? What might be the subject of her painting? What would people do if the artist wouldn't talk to them? From these questions came my story. ✌

Respond and Think Critically

1. Write a brief summary of the main events in this selection before you answer the following questions. For help on writing a summary, see page 219. [Summarize]

2. Why did artists of the 1960s move their art outdoors? Base your answer on Bambara's essay and any background knowledge you have of the 1960s. [Interpret]

3. In what ways were Bambara's feelings about the billboard contest different from her feelings about "The Great Wall of Los Angeles"? [Compare]

4. **Text-to-Text** In what ways did cultural events affect Bambara's purpose for writing "The War of the Wall"? How are the forms and purposes of "Outdoor Art in America" and "The War of the Wall" alike? How are they different? [Connect]

5. Reading Skill Analyze Cultural Context How has outdoor art changed from the time in "Outdoor Art in America" to today? Explain.

6. **BQ** BIG Question How did the billboard contest in the 1940s influence Bambara?

Performance Standards

For pages 527–529

ELA7R1a For informational texts, analyze common textual features to obtain information.

ELA7R1b Use knowledge of graphic features to draw conclusions.

Set a Purpose for Reading

Read to learn how a young Oprah Winfrey was influenced by an actor she saw on TV.

Preview the Article

1. What do the **title** and **deck,** or subtitle, tell you about the topic of the article?

2. What do the **photographs** tell you about the article?

Reading Skill

Distinguish Fact and Opinion

To decide whether you agree with a writer, you need to be able to distinguish, or tell the difference between, fact and opinion. A fact can be proved. An opinion is what someone believes or feels. As you read, make a chart of facts and opinions from the article.

Facts	Opinions

TIME

OPRAH WINFREY

Her influence has reached far and wide.

By SIDNEY POITIER

The future of a poor African American female born in Kosciusko, Mississippi, on January 29, 1954, was not promising. Oprah Gail Winfrey had enormous obstacles in front of her. She was born to unwed teenage parents and living in a segregated[1] society.

For the first six years of her life, Oprah was raised by her maternal[2] grandmother on a farm in rural Mississippi. Oprah's grandmother taught her how to read at an early age. The young girl developed a love for books that continues today. And by the age of 3, she was reciting speeches in church. Oprah often heard her grandmother tell others that Oprah was "gifted." Perhaps it was this feeling of being special

---

1 In a **segregated** society, people of different races or religions live separately.

2 Oprah's **maternal** grandmother was her mother's mother.

OPRAH WINFREY shares a moment with award-winning actor and film director and producer Sidney Poitier.

Dave Allocca/DMI/Time Life Pictures/Getty Images

Oprah was sitting on the linoleum floor of her mother's apartment watching television. She witnessed an event that connected to something deep inside of her. She saw me, a young African American actor, receive an Academy Award. Sharing in that moment and all it implied,[3] she later told me, caused her to say softly to herself, "If he can do that, I wonder what I could do?"

Life with her mother became worse, and as Oprah grew up, she repeatedly ran away and got in trouble. Her mother tried to place her in a home for troubled teens, but fortunately there were no openings. Oprah's father offered to take her into his home in Nashville, Tennessee. With strict rules and discipline, Oprah's father helped her turn her life around.

The journey of Oprah Winfrey had begun. For more than 20 years, Oprah's openness about her own life, compassion[4] for others, and vision for a better world have made her talk show enormously influential. Oprah inspires her viewers to effect[5] change in their lives and the lives of others. She is a perfect example of someone who has succeeded in spite of the disadvantages she has faced.

that helped Oprah get through the difficult years that she would later spend living with her mother.

Oprah moved in with her mother and half sister in Milwaukee, Wisconsin, when she was 6. She lived in a crowded two-bedroom apartment shared with family and friends. Oprah was lonely and unhappy. She suffered both physical and mental abuse from family members and friends of her family.

But even during those difficult years, seeds of hope were being planted. On April 13, 1964, 10-year-old

---

3 In this sentence, *implied* means "hinted" or "suggested."

4 A person shows *compassion* by showing concern or by helping others.

5 In this sentence, *effect* is a synonym for *make.*

Oprah's wide-ranging charity work with children and families in Africa and elsewhere, her popular book club and magazine, and her contributions to improving race relations—all speak to the human family, to touching hearts and leaving each one uplifted.

Besides being compassionate, Oprah is well-informed, dazzlingly curious, and as down-to-earth and loving as any human being I've ever known.

—from TIME, April 26, 2004

Oprah Winfrey waits onstage during the CFDA Fashion Awards on June 4, 2007, in New York City.

Respond and Think Critically

1. Write a brief summary of the main events included in this article before you answer the following questions. For help in writing a summary, see page 219. [Summarize]

2. What does the deck, also called a subtitle, tell you about the focus of this article? [Analyze]

3. Why do you think the writer wrote this article? Explain your answer. [Conclude]

4. **Text-to-Self** Has anyone ever influenced you in the way Sidney Poitier influenced Oprah Winfrey? Explain how that person has influenced you. [Connect]

5. Reading Skill Distinguish Fact and Opinion Does the writer provide enough evidence to support his claims, or opinions, about Oprah? Use the chart you completed as you read to support your answer.

6. **BQ** BIG Question How did Oprah Winfrey's early life experiences influence her actions as an adult? Explain your answer.

Before You Read

old age sticks

Performance Standards

For pages 530–532

ELA7R1g/iii For literary texts, explain and analyze the effects of graphics.

Connect to the Poem

Do most people take advice from people who are older than they are? Should they? Why or why not?

Partner Talk With a partner, discuss what older people can teach younger people. Also, discuss what younger people can teach their elders.

Build Background

Many free verse poems, such as "old age sticks," contain unusual line breaks and punctuation. These tips will help you strengthen your understanding of free verse poems.

- When reading a free verse poem, read it aloud, straight through to the end. Keep reading, even if you don't understand a word or phrase, or if the punctuation confuses you.

- Don't feel that you need to pause at the end of a line or stanza.

- Don't try to analyze the meaning of every line. Just think about your reactions to the whole poem.

- Read the poem again. Focus on the parts that confuse you.

- Finally, think about what the poem means to *you*. Reading a poem is a personal experience.

Set Purposes for Reading

BQ ▸ BIG Question

As you read, ask yourself, is youth aware of the reality of old age? Are we always aware of how others influence us?

Literary Element Style

Style includes the qualities that make a writer's work unlike the work of any other writer. Word choice, sentence variety, use of punctuation, and use of imagery are some factors that create style.

An author's style can reveal his or her purpose for writing. It can also show the author's attitude toward the subject and audience.

As you read, note some of the unusual choices that the poet made in writing this poem.

Meet E. E. Cummings

A master of free verse, Edward Estlin Cummings (who often wrote his name as e. e. cummings) was born in 1894 and died in 1962.

 Literature Online

Author Search For more about E. E. Cummings, go to glencoe.com and enter QuickPass code GL27534u4.

old age
sticks

E. E. Cummings

Old Man Walking in a Rye Field. Laurits Anderson Ring. Oil on canvas.

View the Art Study the painting carefully. How might it help you understand the poem better?

old age sticks
up Keep
Off
signs)&

5   youth yanks them
down(old
age
cries No

Tres)&(pas)
10 youth laughs
(sing
old age

scolds Forbid
den Stop
15 Must
n't Don't

&)youth goes
right on
gr
20 owing old

Style Note how the poet breaks up the word *trespass*. What does this tell you about his attitude?

BQ **BIG Question**
According to these lines, how do you think old age has influenced youth?

After You Read

Respond and Think Critically

1. What are the main images in this poem? Pick out the words and details that help you visualize the images. **[Recall]**

2. What signs does Cummings include in this poem? Explain what each one means. Why do you think he uses signs? **[Interpret]**

3. What is the special journey depicted in "old age sticks"? Who or what has changed by the end of the poem? **[Interpret]**

4. Think of a person you know who might enjoy reading this poem. Why would the poem appeal to this person? **[Connect]**

5. **Literary Element** Style What are two characteristics of E. E. Cummings's style, as shown in this poem? Explain. **[Analyze]**

6. **BQ** BIG Question What thoughts about youth do you think Cummings is communicating in this poem? Explain. **[Evaluate]**

Spelling Link

Addition of Prefixes

A **prefix** is a group of letters added to the beginning of a base word to change its meaning. Do not change the spelling of the base word when you add a prefix.

un- + done = undone   *mis-* + read = misread
il- + legible = illegible   *over-* + heat = overheat

Practice On a sheet of paper, match each prefix with a base word. Then tell how the addition of a prefix changed the word's meaning.

ir-	legal
il-	reach
un-	trust
over-	regular
mis-	locked

Example: *ir-* + regular = irregular   The meaning changed from "usual" to "not usual."

 Writing

Write a Journal Entry Write a journal entry about an older person, such as a relative or a neighbor, who has taught you something. In your entry, make a list of the things you learned and provide examples or anecdotes to show how the person taught you these things.

TIP

Visualizing
To answer question 1, you must picture the poet's ideas or descriptions in your mind. Visualizing is one of the best ways to understand a poem.

- Read how the poet describes a person, place, or thing.
- Ask yourself how the description is important.
- Think about what the image means.

FOLDABLES Study Organizer Keep track of your ideas about the **BIG Question** in your unit Foldable.

 Literature Online

Selection Resources
For Selection Quizzes, eFlashcards, and Reading-Writing Connection activities, go to glencoe.com and enter QuickPass code GL27534u4.

Part 2

Persuasive Ideas

Mondale-Hart-Jackson Presidential Debate, 1984. Franklin McMahon.

BQ BIG Question **What Influences You?**

In the picture of a TV presidential debate, three candidates present their viewpoints. What persuasive ideas do you imagine the candidates would use to influence voters? What persuasive ideas would influence a young person like you?

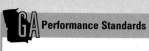
Performance Standards

For pages 534–535

ELA7R1d For informational texts, recognize and trace the development of the author's argument for and against an issue.

Genre Focus:
Essay

An **essay** is a short piece of nonfiction writing on a single topic. An essayist, or the author of an essay, usually has one or more purposes in mind: to give information about real people, places, and events; to entertain; or to persuade. In a **persuasive essay,** the author tries to convince readers to act or think in a certain way.

Literary Elements

Theme is the main point or message of an essay. The theme of an essay may be stated directly in a **thesis statement,** which is usually a single sentence that appears in the introduction.

Evidence and Support are used by writers to defend their thesis statements. Some types of evidence and support are examples, facts, and expert opinions.

Audience refers to the people the writer wishes to address in the essay. In order to make sure his or her message will be clear, the writer must think carefully about the ages, experience, and concerns of the audience. The writer also should anticipate objections the audience might raise and how he or she can best respond to them.

Argument is a specific type of persuasive writing in which a writer uses logic and evidence to influence a reader's ideas or actions.

Persuasive Techniques are used by writers to support their opinions or arguments. Writers must decide how best to appeal to their audience. While some appeals are straightforward, others reflect a "hidden agenda"—an attempt to manipulate the audience. An **appeal to logic or facts** targets a reader's sense of reason. Appeals to logic usually contain evidence demonstrating that a writer's argument is reasonable, or makes sense. The writer often presents statistics and reasoned thought to support his or her argument. An **appeal to emotion** stirs a reader's emotions, such as happiness or anger. Writers use certain words or images to inspire these strong emotions. An **appeal to ethics** addresses a reader's sense of right and wrong, or fairness. An **appeal to authority** includes quotations or information from an expert.

TRY IT

Using a chart like either of those on the next page, identify the main point of an essay in this unit and list the evidence supporting it.

To better understand literary elements in essays and how authors use them to persuade readers and achieve their purposes, look at the examples in the charts below.

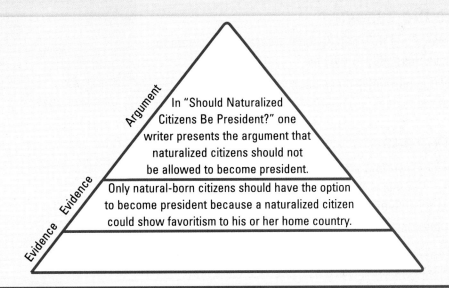

Argument

In "Should Naturalized Citizens Be President?" one writer presents the argument that naturalized citizens should not be allowed to become president.

Evidence Evidence

Only natural-born citizens should have the option to become president because a naturalized citizen could show favoritism to his or her home country.

Thesis
The thesis in "Toward a Rainbow Nation" is that people need to work together to change attitudes about race.

Support
1. At the narrator's school, people judge others according to their character. They do not judge people by their appearance.
2. The narrator explains that having different backgrounds makes her and her friends more powerful because they can teach each other new things.

Should Naturalized Citizens Be President?

Connect to the Essays

Most people believe that they can become whatever they want to be. Do you believe this? Why or why not?

Partner Talk With a partner, discuss what it means to be an American. What rights does an American citizen have?

Build Background

Many Americans believe that anyone can become president of the United States. But this is *not* true. The law says that only someone born in this country can become president.

- People born in the United States are natural-born citizens.

- Naturalized citizens are people who move here from other countries and gain the same rights as those who were born here.

- The basic laws of the United States are written in the Constitution, including the law that limits the office of the president to natural-born citizens.

Vocabulary

violates (vīʹə lāts´) *v.* treats without proper respect or breaks a law or regulation (p. 538). *Preventing people from voting violates their rights as citizens of the United States.*

ensure (en shoor´) *v.* to guarantee or make certain (p. 538). *Careful consideration of the pros and cons will help to ensure a wise decision.*

requirement (ri kwīr´mənt) *n.* something that is necessary; a demand or a condition (p. 539). *A presidential candidate must meet many requirements.*

assurance (ə shoor´əns) *n.* a guarantee or certainty (p. 539). *In order to become citizens, immigrants must make an assurance of loyalty to this country.*

crucial (krōō´shəl) *adj.* extremely important (p. 539). *Today's debate is crucial to the candidate's chance of winning the election.*

Meet the Authors

John Yinger

John Yinger is a professor at Syracuse University in New York. He has written several books on the effect of economic issues on racial and ethnic minorities. Yinger has served on the President's Council of Economic Advisers.

Matthew Spalding

Matthew Spalding is an expert on American political history, the Constitution, and religious liberty. A writer and editor, he also runs the Heritage Foundation's B. Kenneth Simon Center for American Studies.

 Literature Online

Author Search For more about John Yinger and Matthew Spalding, go to glencoe.com and enter QuickPass code GL27534u4.

Set Purposes for Reading

BQ BIG Question

As you read, ask yourself, which writer's argument more strongly influences the way I think about the issue?

Literary Element Argument

An **argument** is the reason or reasons a writer gives for his or her opinion. A writer may use different types of persuasive appeals to convince readers to agree with his or her opinion. A **logical appeal** uses evidence—facts, examples, and statistics—to persuade readers. An **emotional appeal** uses information or ideas to influence readers' feelings, or emotions. An **ethical appeal** addresses readers' views of right and wrong.

Understanding the kinds of appeals a writer uses will help you determine how well a writer supports his or her argument. As you read, ask yourself, what does each writer want me to believe? What appeals do they make? Do they support their claims with evidence?

Reading Skill Recognize Bias

Bias is favoritism toward or against something. When you **recognize bias** in a text, you are aware that the writer's opinion is influenced by his or her experiences or background. In other words, the writer favors an opinion based on personal preferences.

Bias influences the way in which a writer presents information. Recognizing bias will help you decide how strong a writer's argument is and whether you should agree with his or her opinion.

To recognize bias, pay attention to whether a writer

- treats both sides of the issue fairly
- has personal experience that may affect his or her opinions
- assumes ideas to be true without providing supporting evidence

As you read, look for bias in each writer's argument. Keep track of each argument by using a graphic organizer like the one below.

Main Idea:	
Writer's Personal Experience:	
Claim:	Supporting Evidence:
Claim:	Supporting Evidence:

GA Performance Standards

For pages 536–541

ELA7R1e For informational texts, identify evidence used to support an argument.

TRY IT

Recognize Bias People often believe that their favorite sports team is the best team. Do they believe this because their team plays the game better than other teams? Think about the personal experiences that might make a person favor a sports team. Explain why you, or someone you know, is the loyal fan of a certain team. Decide whether the reasons are based on facts, such as the team's win/loss record, or other reasons that may be based on personal preferences.

SHOULD
Naturalized Citizens BE President?

The Constitution says that only 'natural-born' citizens can be President. Should we change that?

YES My son, Jonah, came to the U.S. from Vietnam as a 4-month-old baby. When his second-grade class studied the presidency, he was told that he cannot run for President when he grows up, even if he wants to. According to the Constitution, only a "natural-born Citizen" can be President.

More than 12.8 million naturalized citizens, including 250,000 foreign-born adoptees like Jonah, are second-class citizens who cannot hold the highest office in the land.

The natural-born-citizen clause **violates** a central principle of American democracy: All citizens should have equal rights. When written, the Constitution embraced this principle but failed to protect the rights of women and of racial and ethnic minorities. The 14th, 15th, and 19th Amendments have been added to protect these groups. The next step is to remove the natural-born-citizen clause.

The Founding Fathers[1] included the . . . clause so no foreign prince could buy his way into the presidency. This concern is no longer relevant.[2] Some people say we still need this clause to **ensure** that the President is loyal to the country, but naturalized citizens are a very loyal group.

Moreover, the Constitution allows any natural-born citizen, loyal or not, to run for President and relies on voting rights and the judgment of the American people to keep disloyal people from being elected. These protections would work just as well if we let naturalized citizens run for President, too.

—JOHN YINGER, SYRACUSE UNIVERSITY

Recognize Bias How might Yinger's personal experience affect how he feels about this issue?

Argument Yinger lists other instances in which the Constitution was changed to protect a group of people. Which type of appeal does he use?

---

1 The *Founding Fathers* are the leaders who wrote the U.S. Constitution after the colonies won independence from Great Britain.

2 *Relevant* means "having a connection to something."

Vocabulary
....

violates (vī′ə lāts′) *v.* treats without proper respect or breaks a law or regulation

ensure (en shoor′) *v.* to guarantee or make certain

NO America has always been open to foreign-born immigrants becoming full and equal citizens—with one exception: Only a "natural-born Citizen" can become President. This **requirement** strikes a reasonable balance between our society's openness and the ongoing requirements of national security.

One of the legal conditions for becoming an American citizen is to be "attached to the principles of the Constitution of the United States." New citizens also must take an oath to renounce "all allegiance and fidelity"[3] to other nations. But in the case of the presidency we need even more **assurance** of that allegiance than an oath.

The presidency is unique: One person makes **crucial** decisions, many having to do with foreign policy and national security. With a single executive, there are no checks to override the possibility of foreign influence, or mitigate[4] any lingering favoritism for one's native homeland.

Unlike any other position or office, the attachment of the President must be absolute.[5] This comes most often from being born in—and educated and formed by—this country.

In general, constitutional amendments should be pursued only after careful consideration, when it is necessary to address a great national issue and when there is broad-based support among the American people. That is not the case here.

—MATTHEW SPALDING, THE HERITAGE FOUNDATION

---

3 To **take an oath** is to swear or promise to do something. To become a citizen, an immigrant must promise to give up (**renounce**) loyalty (**allegiance** and **fidelity**) to any other nation.

4 To make something less important is to **mitigate** it. Spalding is saying that there is danger in having a foreign-born president who may be too connected to his or her native land.

5 The writer is saying that the dedication (**attachment**) of the president must be complete and definite (**absolute**).

Arnold Schwarzenegger is a native of Austria. He became a U.S. citizen in 1983 and was elected governor of California in 2003. He cannot run for President unless the Constitution is changed.

Argument What emotional appeal is Spalding presenting?

BQ BIG Question

In Spalding's opinion, how might being born in a different country influence a person?

After You Read

Respond and Think Critically

1. Why can't Yinger's son run for president when he grows up? [Recall]

2. In what way has the Constitution been changed since it was written? Explain. [Identify]

3. What are the main arguments for and against allowing naturalized citizens to become president? [Summarize]

4. Yinger says that more than 12.8 million naturalized citizens cannot be president. Why does he include this fact? Explain. [Analyze]

5. Why do you think one of the legal conditions for becoming an American citizen is to be "attached," or dedicated, to the Constitution? Explain. [Infer]

6. **BQ** **BIG Question** Which argument do you think is more persuasive? Explain. [Evaluate]

TIP

Inferring
Remember that when you infer, you use clues in the text and your own knowledge to figure out what a writer does not explain directly.

• Recall what you know about the importance of obeying rules and laws.

• Consider what Spalding says about the "possibility of foreign influence."

FOLDABLES **Study Organizer** Keep track of your ideas about the **BIG Question** in your unit Foldable.

Just 10 years ago, Duom Deng, David Ayiik, and James Biar were refugees too. During Sudan's civil war, the three boys had seen their parents killed and their villages destroyed. Then they and thousands of other orphaned children walked 1,000 miles past to...

Examine Media

Political Advertisements

Since the mid-1800s, Americans have made items such as ribbons, plates, and buttons to show their support for presidential candidates. Wearing political buttons was once very popular. In the past, presidential buttons had the same function as do political T-shirts and bumper stickers today: they argue that voters should support a certain candidate, and they advertise what that candidate stands for.

On Your Own Read the buttons and answer the questions on a separate sheet of paper.

1. What message were the makers of the Lyndon B. Johnson (LBJ) button trying to send to voters? What are some appealing elements of the button?

2. What audience does the John F. Kennedy button attempt to convince? How is the small amount of space on the button used?

Literary Element Argument

1. Why did Yinger and Spalding write these essays?

   A   to explain how to change the Constitution

   B   to inform naturalized American citizens of citizens' rights

   C   to entertain people with stories of American history

   D   to persuade people to agree with their ideas about citizens' rights

Review: Style

As you learned on page 265, **style** is a writer's choice and arrangement of words and sentences. Style can help reveal a writer's attitude toward his or her topic or audience.

To identify style, pay attention to words or terms that the writer repeats. For example, Spalding repeats the term *national security* twice. The repetition of the term adds to Spalding's serious style and shows that he believes the topic is of great importance.

2. Yinger uses the word *loyal* twice in one sentence. What does the repetition of this word suggest about the writer's attitude toward the topic? Explain.

Reading Skill Recognize Bias

3. How would you describe Yinger's attitude toward naturalized citizens becoming president? In what way might his background affect his attitude toward the topic? Use examples from his essay to support your answer.

Vocabulary Practice

Respond to these questions.

1. Which most likely **violates** the city's litter laws—throwing an empty bottle into the street or throwing it into a garbage can?

2. Who could better **ensure** that a car will run well—an insurance salesperson or an auto mechanic?

3. Which would be a **requirement** for a driver's license—knowing how to park a car or needing a ride to school?

4. When would Greta have **assurance** that she passed the test—when she has completed the test or when her teacher has graded it?

5. What is **crucial** for a band to play well at a concert—well-trained musicians or a noisy audience?

Academic Vocabulary

John Yinger wants foreign-born citizens to have **access** to all the rights contained in the Constitution. In the preceding sentence, *access* means "the ability to obtain." Think about a right or benefit that you have as a member of a family, a team, or some other group. What did you do to gain access to that right or benefit?

Respond Through Writing

Persuasive Essay

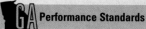 **GA Performance Standards**

For page 542

ELA7W2b Demonstrate competence in a variety of genres.

Argue a Position Two writers present their views on a topic in "Should Naturalized Citizens Be President?" In a persuasive essay, present your view about whether a student council president should have a vote on your county's school board.

Understand the Task When you argue a position, you "take sides" on an issue and try to persuade other people to believe as you do. To persuade readers, you must state your opinion clearly and confidently. Then you must support your opinion and claims with detailed evidence, such as facts and examples.

Prewrite Use a graphic organizer like the one below to help develop your main idea and the supporting evidence. Also, use the graphic organizer to predict what concerns your audience might have about your opinion and how you might respond to their counterarguments.

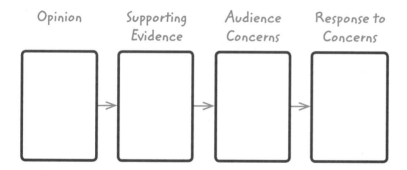

Draft Begin writing your persuasive essay. State your position clearly and explain each fact, reason, and example that supports it. Be sure to use persuasive techniques, such as repetition and persuasive appeals, to convince your audience of your opinion. This sentence frame might help you get started:

I believe that _____ because _____.

Revise After you have written your first draft, reread it to make sure it is well organized. Determine whether your paragraphs and ideas follow a logical order. Make sure that you support each of your claims with convincing evidence.

Edit and Proofread Proofread your paper, correcting any errors in spelling, grammar, and punctuation. See the Word Bank in the side column for words you might use in your persuasive essay.

> ### Word Bank
>
> The following are some useful words you might want to include in your persuasive essay. Check their meanings in a dictionary first to make sure you use them correctly.
>
> **conflict**
> **cooperation**
> **democracy**
> **implement**
> **partnership**
> **promote**
> **representation**

Before You Read

Functional Documents

GA Performance Standards

For pages 543–546

ELA7R1b For informational texts, identify and use knowledge of common graphic features to draw conclusions and make judgments.

Connect to the Functional Documents

Think about a time when you took part in a public meeting or event.

Partner Talk With a partner, discuss how you found out about the meeting or event. What information helped you make your decision to attend or told you what to do once you got there?

Build Background

Whether you are exploring new ideas or working hands-on with new technologies, knowing how to analyze informational signs and instructions is very important.

- **Signs** provide information about the purpose of an event as well as the necessary date, time, and location where the event will take place. Many signs also feature information meant to persuade readers to respond in a particular way.

- **Technical directions** provide detailed information about how to perform a process. The documents you are about to read include a sign advertising a voter-awareness meeting and technical instructions for using a voting machine.

Set a Purpose for Reading

Reading Skill Determine Main Ideas and Details

The **main idea** is the most important idea in a text. The examples, reasons, or ideas that further explain the main idea are called **supporting details.** Skilled readers analyze information on signs and in technical directions by locating the main idea and the details that support that idea. As you read, follow these tips:

- Quickly read through the sign's text looking for key words and concepts. Pay attention to heads and subheads.

- Look for the structure of the information. For example, in technical instructions, you might look for the order of the actions involved in the particular process.

Understand Signs

What kind of sign is this? Where might you see such a sign? Explain the organization's purpose for creating this sign.

VOTE *for* YOURSELF

invites YOU to attend a TOWN MEETING

WHO? **VOTE** *for* **YOURSELF** is a voter-awareness group designed to get individuals to think for themselves and vote in each and every election!

WHAT? We welcome one and all to join us for a free-flowing discussion of the issues that affect all our lives. VOTE FOR YOURSELF is hoping to inspire people to participate more fully in all future elections.

WHY? Elections are important! Yet surveys show that less than 45 percent of eligible voters turned out to vote in the last city election. We can do better! But first we have to understand the issues that affect our lives.

WHEN? Thursday, October 12, 7:00–9:00 P.M.

WHERE? Meade Auditorium, 717 Market Street, just 3 blocks west of Sterling Park

Join us and let your voice be heard! When the next election takes place, we need YOU to exercise your right and your civic duty to bring about positive changes in our community . . . and our world!

"The ignorance of one voter in a democracy impairs the security of all."—John F. Kennedy

Main Idea and Details
Notice the use of boldface type in the sign. Each boldface word along the left side of the sign introduces the main idea of the section. How do these text features help you understand the text?

Vocabulary

eligible (el′i jə bəl) *adj.* qualified to participate

Understand Technical Directions

The main idea of the technical directions is stated in the heading. What are the details that support the main idea?

VOTING MACHINE INSTRUCTIONS

Please read carefully.

Step One: Before You Vote

- Sign in at the polls.
- After you sign in, a voting official will give you a ballot card and a secrecy folder. The secrecy folder will allow you to return your ballot in privacy.
- Take your ballot card and secrecy folder to the voting booth. Do not begin voting until you are inside the voting booth.

Step Two: Marking Your Ballot

- Your voting booth contains a small voting machine. Place your ballot on top of the voting machine. The three holes on the left side of your ballot should fit over the vertical row of pegs on the machine.
- Use the punching implement to punch the oval next to the name of the candidate you select. For each office, select only one candidate.
- If you wish to vote for a person whose name is not on the ballot, write the name of your choice on the line below the list of candidates. Remember to punch the oval next to that line.
- Unmarked or improperly marked ballots will not be counted. If you make a mistake, return the spoiled ballot to a voting official and request a new one.

- After you have finished voting, remove your ballot and examine the back of it. Make sure you have completely punched through the ovals.
- Slide your ballot card in the secrecy folder.
- Return the ballot to the voting official at the OUT table.

Main Idea and Details
The document explains a step-by-step process. What process is being explained?

Vocabulary

polls (pōlz) *n.* places where votes are cast and recorded

ballot (bal´ət) *n.* a printed form used to cast a vote

After You Read

Respond and Think Critically

Review the documents on pages 544–545. Then read each question below and select the best answer.

Standards Practice ELA7RC2e

1. What is Vote for Yourself's main purpose for creating this sign?
   A to inform and persuade people to attend a meeting about voting issues
   B to inform and entertain people who don't usually vote
   C to explain voting and entertain people who vote
   D to explain voting and persuade people who do not vote

2. Which statement best expresses the beliefs of the group Vote for Yourself?
   A People should stay at home on Election Day.
   B People should write their own name on the ballot.
   C People should think independently and vote in every election.
   D People should not think for themselves.

3. How will you know if you have correctly placed your ballot on the machine?
   A A green light will go on.
   B You will be able to write in candidates.
   C The holes on the left of the ballot will fit over the pegs on the machine.
   D The holes on the left of the ballot will align with arrows on the machine.

4. Look at the Vote for Yourself sign. How do the subheadings *who, what, why, when,* and *where* aid the reader's understanding of the sign's message?

5. Suppose you want to vote for a candidate who is not listed on the ballot. What steps should you take to vote for the person? Explain.

 Writing

Create a Sign Make a sign that persuades classmates to attend an upcoming meeting at your school or in your community. Use felt-tip markers or poster paints to create an eye-catching sign. Your sign should

- appeal to people who share a common interest
- contain persuasive language about the event
- inform about the date, time, and place of the event

LOG ON ▶ **Literature** Online

Selection Resources For Selection Quizzes, eFlashcards, and Reading-Writing Connection activities, go to glencoe.com and enter QuickPass code GL27534u4.

Before You Read

Without Commercials

Performance Standards

For pages 547–552

ELA7R1g/ii For literary texts, explain and analyze the effects of figurative language.

Connect to the Poem

What makes a person truly beautiful? How do advertisements affect your ideas of beauty?

Partner Talk With a partner, discuss the variety of people you see in advertisements. Do ads reflect the many different types of people in the world?

Build Background

When Alice Walker was eight, one of her brothers accidentally shot her in the eye with a BB gun. Her blinded eye became covered with scar tissue. "I used to pray every night that I would wake up and somehow it would be gone. I couldn't look people in the eye because I thought I was ugly." This experience inspired Walker to write down her observations and feelings. Later, surgery repaired much of the scar tissue. The change helped improve her self-image.

Walker is considered a major American author. She is active in both the civil rights and women's rights movements. She helped reintroduce readers to the author Zora Neale Hurston, another important African American author.

Set Purposes for Reading

BQ **BIG Question**

Consider the many ways that people change their appearances. As you read, ask yourself, what influences people to make such changes?

Literary Element Allusion

An **allusion** is a reference in a literary work to a well-known character, place, or situation from another literary work, music, art, or history. When readers recognize an allusion in a literary work, it can enrich their understanding of the entire work. For example, if a character in a work is compared to Superman, readers might gain a greater appreciation for the good or strong qualities of the character.

As you read, look for allusions to well-known characters, places, situations, or stories.

Meet Alice Walker

A Literary Life From the time she was eight, Alice Walker kept a notebook of poetry. Many of her poems, short stories, and essays focus on the difficult lives of poor, heroic African American women. In 1983, Walker won the Pulitzer Prize for her novel *The Color Purple*. Alice Walker was born in 1944.

 Literature Online

Author Search For more about Alice Walker, go to glencoe.com and enter QuickPass code GL27534u4.

Listen,
stop tanning yourself
and talking about
fishbelly
5   white.
The color white
is not bad at all.
There are white mornings
that bring us days.
10 Or, if you must,
tan only because
it makes you happy
to be brown,
to be able to see
15 for a summer
the whole world's
darker
face
reflected
20 in your own.

Stop unfolding
your eyes.
Your eyes are
beautiful.
25 Sometimes
seeing you in the street
the fold zany°
and unexpected
I want to kiss
30 them
and usually
it is only
old
gorgeous
35 black people's eyes
I want
to kiss.

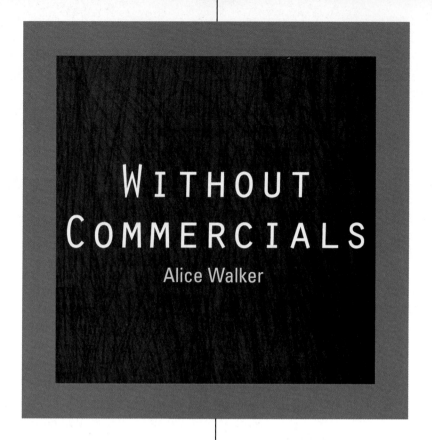

WITHOUT
COMMERCIALS
Alice Walker

BQ BIG Question

From these lines, what
do you infer about
the speaker's values
and beliefs?

27 Something *zany* is odd or crazy in a comical way.

Stop trimming
your nose.
40 When you
diminish°
your nose
your songs
become little
45 tinny, muted°
and snub.
Better you should
have a nose
impertinent°
50 as a flower,
sensitive
as a root;
wise, elegant,
serious and deep.
55 A nose that
sniffs
the essence°
of Earth. And knows
the message
60 of every
leaf.

Stop bleaching
your skin
and talking
65 about
so much black
is not beautiful
The color black
is not bad
70 at all.
There are black nights
that rock

Sunflower Time, 2003. Jim
Macbeth. Digital collage.

---

41 To **_diminish_** means "to make smaller in size."

45 In this context, **_muted_** means "muffled, softened, or less strong."

49 Something **_impertinent_** is improperly bold or rude.

57 Here, **_essence_** means "perfume."

us
in dreams.
75 Or, if you must,
bleach only
because it pleases you
to be brown,
to be able to see
80 for as long
as you can bear it
the whole world's
lighter face
reflected
85 in your own.

As for me,
I have learned
to worship
the sun
90 again.
To affirm°
the adventures
of hair.

For we are all
95 *splendid*
descendants
of Wilderness,
Eden:
needing only
100 to see
each other
without
commercials
to believe.

105 Copied skillfully
as Adam.

Original

as Eve.

BQ BIG Question
What attitude is the speaker expressing toward commercials?

Allusion To what story is the speaker referring?

---

91 To *affirm* is to state firmly and positively.

After You Read

Respond and Think Critically

1. Whom does the speaker address in the first stanza of the poem? Explain. [Recall]

2. What is the message or point of the first stanza? What message is expressed about people's differences? [Interpret]

3. What does the speaker suggest that people of every race have in common? Do you think Alice Walker shares these views? Explain how Walker's experiences may have helped to shape the ideas in the poem. [Conclude]

4. According to the poem, what effect do commercials have on people? Why is the poem called "Without Commercials"? [Analyze]

5. Choose your favorite example of imagery in the poem. Explain why it appeals to you. [Evaluate]

6. **BQ** BIG Question Why might people feel they should look like the people in commercials? If there were no commercials, do you think people would change their attitudes about how they look? Give reasons to support your opinion. [Connect]

Academic Vocabulary

Alice Walker's poem encourages readers to resist the temptation to change their appearances and to recognize the beauty in human **variations.**

In the preceding sentence, *variations* means "the extent to which something differs slightly from another thing." Alice Walker's poem discusses the variations within human appearances. Think about the different ideas and opinions you see and hear each day. How do these variations of opinions and ideas help you understand the world and see things in new ways?

TIP

Interpreting
Here are some tips to help you interpret. Remember that when you interpret, you apply your understanding of the world to decide what the ideas in a selection mean.

- Reread the Build Background section to find details that may have shaped Alice Walker's views on personal appearance.

- Summarize or paraphrase the speaker's attitude toward the popular opinion of beauty as expressed in the poem.

 FOLDABLES Study Organizer Keep track of your ideas about the **BIG Question** in your unit Foldable.

 Literature Online

Selection Resources
For Selection Quizzes, eFlashcards, and Reading-Writing Connection activities, go to glencoe.com and enter QuickPass code GL27534u4.

Literary Element | Allusion

An author or poet may use allusions to strengthen a particular description or idea.

1. In lines 66–67, the speaker makes an allusion to the saying, "Black is beautiful." Why do you think the speaker uses this allusion? Use examples from the poem to support your answer.

2. In lines 94–98, what does the speaker mean by saying "For we are all / *splendid* / descendants / of Wilderness, / Eden"? What allusion does the poet use? Explain.

Review: Simile

As you learned on page 203, a **simile** is a figure of speech that uses *like* or *as* to compare seemingly unlike things. Similes help create strong images and highlight distinct qualities in the things being described.

3. In lines 47–54, the poet uses similes to compare a nose to different things. To what does she compare a nose? Explain.

Grammar Link

Clauses A **clause** is a group of words that contains a subject and a predicate.

An **independent clause** expresses a complete thought and can stand alone as a sentence.

> Alice was playing.

A **dependent clause** cannot stand alone as a complete sentence.

> when she was blinded

Phrases A **phrase** is a group of words that acts in a sentence as a single part of speech but does not contain a subject and a predicate.

A **verb phrase** contains one or more helping verbs followed by a main verb.

> Her brother <u>had shot</u> her accidentally.

A **prepositional phrase** begins with a preposition and ends with a noun or a pronoun, which is called the object of the preposition.

> Her eye was covered <u>with scar tissue.</u>

Practice In the poem, find an independent clause and a dependent clause. Then, find a verb phrase and a prepositional phrase. Next, write a sentence about the poem that includes both kinds of clauses and phrases.

💬 Speaking and Listening

Literature Group With a small group, discuss the poem's main argument. Talk about the persuasive appeals included in the poem. In order to convince the reader, does the poem appeal to the reader's emotions? Does it use logic to convince the reader? Be sure to back up your ideas with details from the poem.

Toward a Rainbow Nation

Connect to the Essay

Think about your friends and classmates. Do you know people who come from cultures that are different from your own? Do your closest friends have the same background as you do?

List Imagine that you have the chance to meet a new student from a different culture and visit his or her home. Make a list of things you would like to know about the student's culture.

Build Background

In this essay, a teenage girl tells about her school, her friends, and her everyday life in South Africa.

- South Africa is a nation at the southern tip of the continent of Africa.

- From 1948 to 1994 a law called apartheid set limits on the lives of people of different races in South Africa. The word *apartheid* means "separateness."

- In 1994 apartheid officially ended in South Africa.

Vocabulary

obligation (ob´lə gā´shən) *n.* something a person must do because of laws or duty (p. 558).
Drivers have an obligation to obey stop signs.

optimistic (op´tə mis´tik) *adj.* believing that things will turn out for the best; hopeful (p. 558).
Amanda is optimistic that the weather will be warm and sunny for this weekend's picnic.

Meet Lavendhri Pillay

Young Author Lavendhri Pillay was born and raised in South Africa. She was only thirteen when she wrote this essay. At that time, South Africa was just starting to let students of different races attend the same schools.

Many People in One Land Pillay says that she loves living among people from many different backgrounds.

 Literature Online

Author Search For more about Lavendhri Pillay, go to glencoe.com and enter QuickPass code GL27534u4.

Set Purposes for Reading

BQ BIG Question

As you read, ask yourself, in what ways have Pillay's life experiences influenced her ideas about how people get along?

Literary Element Author's Perspective

Authors, as people, have backgrounds—where they're from, what they believe, what they like and dislike. The elements of an author's background help create the viewpoint from which he or she writes. This viewpoint is the **author's perspective.**

It is important to pay attention to the author's perspective because it can influence the author's opinions. When you identify perspective in an essay, you can better understand why the author feels the way he or she does.

As you read, note the details of the author's background that could influence her perspective. Ask yourself, what connections are there between the author's perspective and her opinions?

Reading Strategy Evaluate Argument

When you **evaluate an argument,** you make a judgment on how well an author is able to influence you. An effective argument should state a position clearly and have good reasons and examples that support it.

Evaluating an argument is important because it helps you think critically about an author's ideas. To evaluate an argument, look for some of the different appeals an author may use:

- a logical appeal with factual evidence, reasoned thought, and statistics

- an ethical appeal that addresses the reader's sense of right and wrong

- an emotional appeal that plays on feelings, such as fear or sympathy, to persuade the reader

As you read, identify Pillay's opinions and how she supports them. Then consider an opposing viewpoint for each opinion. Use a graphic organizer like the one below to evaluate Pillay's argument.

Pillay's Opinion	Her Support	Opposing Viewpoint

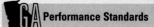
GA Performance Standards

For pages 553–560

ELA7R1d For informational texts, trace the development of the author's argument.

ELA7R1e Identify evidence used to support an argument.

TRY IT

Evaluate With a partner, choose a topic that you have different opinions about, such as a favorite food, a sport, or a hobby. Write a list of appeals and try to convince your partner to agree with you. Switch lists and decide how convincing your partner's appeals are. Is either of you persuaded to change your mind?

Rainbow Nation

Lavendhri Pillay

People ask me all the time, "What are you?" I say I'm South African. Then they say, "No-no-no, but what *are* you?" When I was small, I was always told that my great-grandfather came from India to pick sugarcane, but my family doesn't really have ties to India anymore. So I say, "I was born here, I've lived here my whole life, I don't know anything else, so I'm South African."

I've grown up different from a lot of other teenagers in South Africa because I've been subjected[1] to all different races and different kinds of people. I'm a really lucky person.

Since I was seven, I've gone to school at Sacred Heart, where everybody's completely mixed. We've got Coloured, black, British, Chinese, white, Indian, Afrikaans,[2] everybody. So from an early age I learned to accept these different people. In our school it's about what kind of reputation you make for yourself, what kind of person you are.

I've lived in Yeoville[3] most of my life with my mother, sister, and two brothers. It's a place where many cultures[4]

Author's Perspective
How does being South African influence the author's perspective?

---

1 Here, ***subjected*** means "exposed to."

2 Under the apartheid laws, a person of more than one race was called ***coloured.*** South Africa was once a British colony, and this is the British spelling. The ***Afrikaans*** are descendants of the Dutch settlers who moved to South Africa in the 1600s.

3 ***Yeoville*** (yō´vil) is a part of the city of Johannesburg where people of different races live in the same neighborhoods.

4 ***Cultures*** are groups of people who share a history or a way of life.

live. It's really nice living here because you get to find out about people and what their lives are like. You're not judging them; you can actually get to know what's going on with them. People in Yeoville don't care about what you look like; people are just themselves.

I have a really big group of friends, and within that group we have the whole country. But there's never been any weirdness between us at all. We aren't black, white, Indian, or Coloured; we're just us. We don't actually look at anybody's race; it's just, "Hey, you're my friend, you're a nice person, I like you."

We do regular teenage things together. We gossip a lot like normal girls, and on the weekends we sleep over at each other's houses and phone people and find out what they've been doing. We talk about music; we go to the movies; we swim.

Because we're mixed, we're more powerful; we get to learn from each other. If I were to be in a completely Indian community, it would always be the same things. But when I visit my friends' homes, I see differences in their settings, and all of our families deal with things totally differently. It's always a learning experience.

I've also been to Soweto and Eldorado Park [a Coloured township near Johannesburg] many times, and I've been able to see what other people are actually going through. It's good for me to see that I'm not the only person on earth and that not everybody lives like me. I've been able to grow up with everything I need. If I didn't see those places, I would think that everybody had normal houses and enough money to do what they wanted like I do. Then I think I'd be quite small-minded.

Evaluate Argument What kind of appeal does the author use here to support her argument?

Author's Perspective What perspective on her own life does the author gain from visiting Soweto and Eldorado Park?

A lot of our parents call my friends and me the rainbow nation. I think it makes them feel good to see us together; it's kind of like what everybody should be like racial-wise, how people should interact with each other, but don't. When our parents were small, they had apartheid, they didn't have the opportunity to mix, and I'm sure they envy us for having all of the new experiences that they never would have even dreamed of having when they were young.

But as a nation I don't think we can call ourselves the rainbow people yet. Most South Africans are still completely trapped in apartheid mentally. I've had a lot of experiences with racism, like at this restaurant when the people there wouldn't serve us because of our color. Everybody else got up and left when we came in, and then it took half an hour for the waiter to come serve us and then an hour to get our breakfast.

Evaluate Argument
What kind of appeal does the author use to support her claim that racism still exists?

Even though apartheid's not law anymore, it's still alive. People still divide themselves into these cliques:[5] black, Coloured, Indian, white. Like when my friends and I go to the mall, we notice that other people give us really weird looks. I think it's because we're so mixed, and others have been raised with this wall blocking them. They're like, Wow, what's wrong with that group? How can they be comfortable with each other?

I think it's good for people to see us, because it's showing them that you can have fun with another race; it's not abnormal. People need to see that aside from their cultural differences and their skin color, we all need the same basics: We all need to breathe, drink water, eat; we're all exactly the same. They should just look beyond what they've been taught, they should try and have an open mind about things. Most South Africans will probably find this very difficult, but it's definitely worth it.

If someone did come up to us and say she wanted to mix, we'd say, "All right, come join us!" If she was scared, I'd say, "I know it might be difficult because you haven't done it before, but all you have to do is think about what kind of people they are and not what they look like. Try

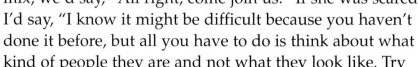

---

5 *Cliques* are groups of people who leave others out.

View the Photograph In what way does this photograph help you understand Pillay's perspective?

closing your eyes and talking to them, and then you'll get used to them and eventually you won't think about where they're from. You'll learn to appreciate people for who and what they are, to see past everything."

I think people my age should learn about apartheid because it is our past, it's our parents and our grandparents, it affects us. If we know the history of our country, we'll be able to know what was wrong about what people did, and not to do it again.

But at the same time, I think we should be making a future. We can't just get stuck in one place, always staying on the same subject. My generation was lucky enough to not have been part of the struggle against apartheid, to have been only young when elections happened; we've grown up in other times when race is no longer governed by law, no longer an **obligation.** That gives us the freedom to address anything. We need to learn how to move on, to look at other issues that affect us, to try and do better, more different things. Our generation is more open-minded than our parents', and this makes me **optimistic** about this country. Since it's up to us, I think we can change things. &

BQ **BIG Question**
Do you think the author could persuade a shy person to mix with a wide variety of people?

Vocabulary ....

obligation (ob′lə gā′shən) *n.* something a person must do because of laws or duty
optimistic (op′tə mis′tik) *adj.* believing that things will turn out for the best; hopeful

After You Read

Respond and Think Critically

1. How does the author feel about the diversity at her school? Explain. **[Recall]**

2. Why does the author's group of friends get along so well? Include details from the essay to support your answer. **[Analyze]**

3. Why do you think some people in South Africa still divide themselves into separate groups even though apartheid isn't the law? Support your answer with details from the essay. **[Interpret]**

4. Why does the author believe that having an open mind about race is "definitely worth it"? Explain. **[Infer]**

5. What effect does the author think apartheid has had on her generation? Explain. **[Analyze]**

6. **BQ** BIG Question What does the author want her generation to do to make South Africa a "rainbow nation"? **[Conclude]**

Vocabulary

Choose the sentence that uses the vocabulary word correctly.

A. While driving her mother's car, Anne thought it was her **obligation** to be careful and drive safely.

B. Anne received her **obligation** when she passed her driving test last week.

A. The coach is sure our football team will lose tomorrow because he is an **optimistic** person.

B. Because the coach is **optimistic,** he is telling everyone the football team will win the championship this year.

Academic Vocabulary

When the author writes that she calls herself South African, she describes part of her **identity**. In the preceding sentence, *identity* means "the personality of an individual." Think about your identity. What characteristics and experiences make up your identity?

TIP

Analyzing
When you analyze an essay, you look at separate parts of the essay in order to understand the whole.

- Reread details the author gives about her group of friends.

- Review positive and negative statements the author makes about South Africa's diversity, cliques, and her own experiences of friendship.

- Put together this information to decide why the author's group of friends gets along well.

 FOLDABLES Study Organizer Keep track of your ideas about the **BIG Question** in your unit Foldable.

 Literature Online

Selection Resources
For Selection Quizzes, eFlashcards, and Reading-Writing Connection activities, go to glencoe.com and enter QuickPass code GL27534u4.

Literary Element   Author's Perspective

1. Describe the author's experiences with different groups of people. How have her experiences affected her perspective on race in her country?

2. What is the author's perspective on whether apartheid still exists in South Africa? Explain.

Review: Author's Purpose

As you learned on page 211, an **author's purpose** is his or her intention in written work. An author's purpose may be to tell a story, to inform or explain, to entertain, or to persuade. An author may have more than one purpose in a piece of writing.

3. What do you think is the author's purpose in "Toward a Rainbow Nation"?

Reading Strategy   Evaluate Argument

4. The author believes that her generation should learn about apartheid. What reasons does the author provide to support her opinion? Explain.

5. Does the author support the argument that her generation needs to address issues in South Africa other than race? Explain, using details from your graphic organizer to support your answer.

Grammar Link

Main and Subordinate Clauses A **main clause** (also called an independent clause) has a subject and predicate and can stand alone as a sentence.

Pillay is a good writer

A **subordinate clause** (also known as a dependent clause) has a subject and a predicate but does not express a complete thought. A subordinate clause begins with a **subordinating conjunction**.

because she supports her ideas

Below are some common subordinating conjunctions.

after	since
although	though
because	until
before	when
if	where

Practice Look for two sentences in "Toward a Rainbow Nation" that contain main and subordinate clauses. Underline the main clause once and the subordinate clause twice. Then write two new sentences with main and subordinate clauses and subordinating conjunctions.

💬 Speaking and Listening

Speech Write a speech to persuade members of your school community to take action and bring students together. First, explain the problem, using examples to convince your listeners of the problem. Then give reasons why it is important to bring students together. Use an appeal to persuade your listeners to accomplish this goal. Finally, explain what actions students and staff can take to bring students together.

Before You Read

Heroes

Connect to the Essay

Think about people who are called heroes. What makes a person a hero?

Partner Talk With a partner, talk about the qualities a hero should have. Do all athletic champions deserve to be called heroes? Is there such a thing as an "everyday hero"?

Build Background

This essay first appeared as a newspaper column in 1981. It compares two athletic achievements, both of which occurred in the summer of 1981.

- The first event was when U.S. tennis player John McEnroe won the All-England Championships, a famous tennis tournament that takes place at Wimbledon, England, every summer.

- The young McEnroe had a reputation for behaving badly on the tennis court.

- The second event was when a group of people with disabilities successfully climbed to the top of Mount Rainier, a 14,000-foot mountain in Washington State.

- Although the group climbed Mount Rainier in summer, they braved falling ice and deep crevasses.

Vocabulary

summit (sum′it) *n.* the top, or highest point (p. 563). *From the ground, the campers could barely see the mountain's summit.*

punctuated (pungk′ chōō āt′ ed) *v.* emphasized (p. 564). *The tapping of her pencil punctuated the silence of the classroom.*

perspective (pər spek′ tiv) *n.* the ability to see things in their relative, or comparative, importance (p. 564). *The captain told the team to keep the loss in perspective and not worry too much about it.*

pageant (paj′ ənt) *n.* a show or exhibition (p. 564). *The pageant includes a talent competition.*

Meet Erma Bombeck

Talented Humorist Erma Bombeck was born in Dayton, Ohio. Her writing career began in junior high school, where she wrote newspaper columns. While attending college, Bombeck worked at a local newspaper and later wrote a humorous column about life as a newlywed. Bombeck used satire to share her views of suburban life. Her writings include newspaper columns, magazine articles, and books such as *At Wit's End* and *The Grass Is Always Greener Over the Septic Tank.*

Erma Bombeck was born in 1927 and died in 1996.

 Literature Online

Author Search For more about Erma Bombeck, go to glencoe.com and enter QuickPass code GL27534u4.

Set Purposes for Reading

Performance Standards

For pages 561–565

ELA7R1h For literary texts, identify and analyze how an author's use of words creates tone and mood.

BQ BIG Question

As you read, ask yourself, what makes the author's argument persuasive? What does the author think about what makes a hero?

Literary Element Tone

Tone is the author's attitude toward the subject, ideas, theme, and characters or people in a piece of writing. The tone of a written piece may be funny or serious, sad or upbeat, admiring or angry.

An author's tone can help readers figure out the author's perspective, or viewpoint. To identify the tone of a text, pay attention to word choice, sentence construction, the kinds of details the author includes, and the images the author creates.

As you read "Heroes," think about the author's tone. How does the author's tone persuade you to feel a certain way about heroes?

Reading Skill Analyze Text Structure

When you **analyze text structure,** you look at how a piece of writing is organized. A compare-and-contrast text structure shows the similarities and differences between people, things, and ideas. When authors use a compare-and-contrast structure, often they want to show how things that seem alike are different or how things that seem different are alike.

Analyzing a compare-and-contrast text structure can help you better understand an author's purpose for writing—the reason that he or she wants to share information with readers.

To analyze the compare-and-contrast text structure of "Heroes," pay attention to the similarities and differences between the two types of heroes that the author describes. Use a diagram like the one below to record ideas. Write the differences in the outer portions of the circles and the similarities in the overlapping portion of the circles.

TRY IT

Analyze Think about how you would try to convince a friend that your favorite song, book, or movie is better than your friend's favorite. Use comparisons and contrasts that support your argument that your favorite deserves top honors.

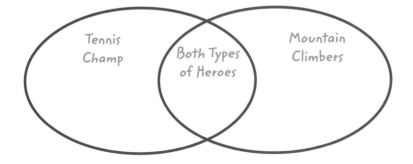

HEROES

Erma Bombeck

On the first Saturday of last month, a 22-year-old U.S. tennis player hoisted[1] a silver bowl over his head at Centre Court at Wimbledon.

The day before, five blind mountain climbers, a man with an artificial leg, an epileptic, and two deaf adventurers stood atop the snowcapped **summit** of Mount Rainier.

Analyze Text Structure
Why does Bombeck compare the accomplishments of McEnroe and the mountain climbers?

---

1 **Hoisted** is another word for *raised* or *lifted*.

Vocabulary

summit (sum′it) *n.* the top, or highest point

It was a noisy victory for the tennis player, who shared it with thousands of fans, some of whom had slept on the sidewalks outside the club for six nights waiting for tickets.

It was a quiet victory for the climbers, who led their own cheering, **punctuated** by a shout from one of them that echoed on the winds: "There's one for the epileptics!"

There was a lot of rhetoric[2] exchanged at Wimbledon regarding "bad calls."

At Mount Rainier they learned to live with life's bad calls a long time ago. The first man to reach the mountaintop tore up his artificial leg to get there.

Somehow, I see a parallel here that all Americans are going to have to come to grips with. In our search for heroes and heroines, we often lose our **perspective.**

We applaud beauty **pageant** winners; we ignore the woman without arms who paints pictures with a brush in her teeth. We extol[3] the courage of a man who will sail over 10 cars on a motorcycle; we give no thought (or parking place) to the man who threads his way through life in a world of darkness or silence.

The care and feeding of heroes is solely in the hands of the public. Not all winners are heroes. Not all people with disabilities are heroes. "Hero" is a term that should be awarded to those who, given a set of circumstances, will react with courage, dignity, decency, and compassion—people who make us feel better for having seen or touched them.

I think the crowds went to the wrong summit and cheered the wrong champion.

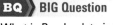 **Tone** Why does Bombeck use quotation marks when she refers to the "bad calls" at Wimbledon? How does her tone change when she refers to life's bad calls at Mount Rainier?

BQ BIG Question

What is Bombeck trying to persuade the public to do?

---

2 **Rhetoric** refers to skill in speaking. Bombeck is referring to how John McEnroe argued with the tennis judges about their calls.

3 When you **extol** someone, you praise that person highly.

Vocabulary

punctuated (pungk′ chōo āt′ ed) v. emphasized

perspective (pər spek′ tiv) n. the ability to see things in their relative, or comparative, importance

pageant (paj′ ənt) n. a show or exhibition

After You Read

Respond and Think Critically

1. Who is John McEnroe, and what is he known for? [Recall]

2. What event happened on Mount Rainier in 1981? Why was it significant? [Summarize]

3. Which of the two athletic achievements in the essay does Bombeck think is more worthy of praise? Explain. [Interpret]

4. **Literary Element** Tone What is the tone of the essay? Cite examples from the essay to support your answer. [Analyze]

5. **Reading Skill** Analyze Text Structure Look at the diagram you completed. Which contrast do you think best supports Bombeck's argument? Explain. [Compare]

6. **BQ** BIG Question Did the author persuade you that her ideas are correct? Explain. [Evaluate]

Vocabulary Practice

Respond to these questions.

1. What would you be more likely to see on a clear day at the **summit** of a mountain—a wide view or a limited view?

2. Which type of noise would have **punctuated** a construction site—a jackhammer or a whisper?

3. Who would have a better **perspective** on a situation—a person who is very emotional or a person who is calm and thoughtful?

4. Which would most likely take place in a **pageant**—a dance performance or a spelling test?

 Writing

Write a Letter Write a letter to a columnist at your local newspaper. Encourage the columnist to write an article about a hero in your community. Use a persuasive tone in your letter and include details that support why this person is a hero. Use some of the persuasive techniques you learned in this unit, such as repetition and emotional appeals. Try to convince the columnist that other people would enjoy reading about this person.

TIP

Evaluating
To answer question 6, you must evaluate the effectiveness of Bombeck's argument. Remember that when you evaluate, you make a judgment or form an opinion about a written work. Ask yourself these questions:

• Is Bombeck qualified to tell readers what makes a person a hero?

• Are Bombeck's ideas about heroes biased? Are they realistic?

• Does Bombeck present facts and opinions to support her ideas?

FOLDABLES Study Organizer Keep track of your ideas about the **BIG Question** in your unit Foldable.

 Literature Online

Selection Resources
For Selection Quizzes, eFlashcards, and Reading-Writing Connection activities, go to glencoe.com and enter QuickPass code GL27534u4.

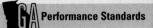
Performance Standards

For page 566

ELA7LSV2b When responding to visual and oral texts and media, identifies the techniques used to achieve the effects studied in each instance.

Media Workshop

Propaganda

Every day we are constantly exposed to persuasive ideas—no matter whether we are watching television, walking down the street, or talking to friends. Persuasive ideas come in many forms. For example, your favorite television program may be interrupted by a commercial with a message such as this:

"Oatsie O's cereal is crafted from wholesome whole grain and toasted to golden perfection. Oatsie O's aren't just good to taste—they're also good for your heart! Oatsie O's are medically proven to lower cholesterol in six weeks or less."

Words are powerful tools that carry information, but they can also affect you in other ways. Spreading ideas that help one cause or hurt another is called using **propaganda.** Advertisers use propaganda techniques to make their product more appealing than a competitor's product. Politicians often use propaganda to spread ideas that promote their party's cause as better than their opponent's cause.

The more you learn about the ways that words can sway you, the less likely you will be to accept everything people say as true.

This chart shows several strategies advertisers use to make their products seem appealing.

TRY IT

Analyze Propaganda With a partner, choose a television commercial you've both seen. Write a letter to the advertisers, giving feedback on the impact the commercial has had on you. Think about these questions as you draft your letter.

1. What is the purpose behind the commercial?

2. What is expressed through words, music, sound effects, and graphics?

3. What methods are used to persuade viewers?

4. What could you ask the advertisers to help you distinguish how propaganda is being used to influence your judgment?

Propaganda	What It Is	Example
Testimonial	Famous or well-known people "testify" about how good a product is.	"Gloria Glamour won't drive anything but the new Alada convertible."
Bandwagon	People are urged to follow the crowd.	"Everyone is talking about the new best-selling novel. Get your copy today!"
Glittering Generalities	Advertisers use positive-sounding words.	"Eat nothing but the healthiest! Oat Toasties build strong bones and strong minds."
Emotional Appeal	Ads contain words that appeal to emotions instead of to reasoning.	"To feel your best, you need to look your best. Wear Sharp Jeans."

LOG ON ▶ **Literature** Online

Media Literacy For project ideas, templates, and media analysis guides, go to glencoe.com and enter QuickPass code GL27534u4.

Before You Read

Primer Lesson

GA Performance Standards

For pages 567–569

ELA7R1g/ii For literary texts, explain and analyze the effects of figurative language.

Connect to the Poem

Think of a time when you said something in anger or frustration that you later regretted. What advice might you give to someone who is feeling angry or frustrated?

Quickwrite Freewrite for a few minutes about your experience. Describe the details of the situation and why you later regretted what you said.

Build Background

A *primer* is a small book that introduces and teaches a subject. The title of Carl Sandburg's poem, "Primer Lesson," suggests that readers might learn something by reading the poem.

- Instructional primers are used to teach people subjects or skills. For example, an instructional primer may teach elementary school children to read.

- Moral primers are used to teach people lessons about life. They teach readers the difference between right and wrong. For example, a children's story may act as a moral primer. It may teach its readers about sharing or kindness.

Set Purposes for Reading

BQ ⟩ BIG Question

As you read this poem, ask yourself, what is the speaker saying about the power of words?

Literary Element Personification

Personification is a figure of speech in which an animal, object, or idea is given human form or characteristics. "The impatient alarm clock shook me out of bed" is an example of personification. An object, the alarm clock, is described as though it were a person waking up another person.

Authors and poets use personification to make their writing more vivid and to describe things in a way that people can relate to.

As you read "Primer Lesson," look for examples of personification. Think about how the personification affects the poem's theme, or message.

Meet Carl Sandburg

Writer and Singer Carl Sandburg was born in Illinois and first saw the city of Chicago when he was 18 years old. Most of Sandburg's poems echo the poet's midwestern values. He also wrote stories and biographies, and he collected and sang folk music.

Carl Sandburg was born in 1878 and died in 1967.

LOG ON ▶ **Literature** Online

Author Search For more about Carl Sandburg, go to glencoe.com and enter QuickPass code GL27534u4.

Old Boots. Klaus Hackenberg.

PRIMER LESSON

Carl Sandburg

Look out how you use proud words.
When you let proud words go, it is
    not easy to call them back.
They wear long boots, hard boots; they
    walk off proud; they can't hear you
    calling—
Look out how you use proud words.

Personification What image of proud words does the poem create?

BQ > BIG Question
Why might the speaker want to warn readers about proud words?

After You Read

Respond and Think Critically

1. What does the speaker say might happen when you try to call back proud words? [Recall]

2. What does the speaker mean by "proud words"? Explain. [Interpret]

3. What might have influenced the speaker to give advice about using proud words? Explain. [Infer]

4. How valuable or helpful is the speaker's advice? Explain. [Evaluate]

5. **Literary Element** Personification How does the poem use personification to help convey the power of proud words? [Analyze]

6. **BQ** BIG Question How might this poem influence you in the future? Explain. [Connect]

Spelling Link

Doubling of the Final Consonant When you add a suffix to a word, you sometimes have to double the final consonant of the base word.

Double the final consonant of a word when

- the suffix begins with a vowel (*sit/sitting*)
- a word ends in one consonant preceded by only one vowel (*run/runner*)
- a word has only one syllable (*mop/mopping*)
- the accent is on a word's last syllable (*refer/referring*)

Do not double the final consonant when

- the suffix begins with a consonant (*use/useless*)
- the word ends in two consonants (*dress/dressed*)
- the accent is not on the last syllable (*travel/traveled*)
- the accent moves when the suffix is added (*defer/deference*)

Practice On a separate sheet of paper, list the words *skip, ask, infer, earn,* and *confess.* Add the suffixes *-ing* and *-ed* to each word. Use the spelling rules above to determine whether you need to double the final consonant.

Writing

Write a Blurb Write a posting for a Web site that contains Carl Sandburg's poetry. Explain what Sandburg means by "proud words." Also, tell why you think his poem does or does not express his message effectively. Use details from the poem to support your ideas.

TIP

Inferring
To answer question 3, you must use your own experience as well as clues in the poem.

- Think about instances in which you've used harsh words with someone. How did you feel after you said the harsh words?

- What does the speaker mean by "calling back" proud words? When have you tried to call back harsh words? Were you successful?

- Combine these pieces of information to answer the question.

FOLDABLES Study Organizer Keep track of your ideas about the **BIG Question** in your unit Foldable.

Literature Online

Selection Resources
For Selection Quizzes, eFlashcards, and Reading-Writing Connection activities, go to glencoe.com and enter QuickPass code GL27534u4.

Comparing Literature

Langston Terrace and *Home*

BQ > **BIG Question**

As you read these paired selections, ask yourself, what does *home* mean to the narrators of "Langston Terrace" and "Home"?

Literary Element Tone

Tone is the attitude of the author or narrator toward the subject, ideas, theme, or characters of a literary work. The tone of a literary work may be serious, humorous, somber, or even hopeful. The author's sentence construction and choice of words, details, and images help create the tone. As you read the essay and short story, pay attention to how tone helps support the theme, or main message, of each selection.

Reading Skill Compare and Contrast

Comparisons are similarities between items, while contrasts are differences. You might compare and contrast after-school activities, for example, to choose one that you like and that fits into your schedule.

Comparing and contrasting the tone of two literary selections can help you understand each selection's theme. On the following pages, you'll compare and contrast the tone of "Langston Terrace" and "Home." Use a chart like the one below to note similarities and differences between the two selections. As you read, write details from each selection that help you identify the tone. Explain how the tone of each selection supports its theme.

	Tone	Details Revealing Tone	How Details Support Theme
"Langston Terrace"			
"Home"			

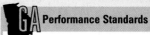

Performance Standards

For pages 570–579

ELA7R1d For literary texts, analyze recurring and similar themes across a variety of selections, distinguishing theme from topic.

Meet the Authors

Eloise Greenfield and Lessie Jones Little

Lessie Jones Little was born in 1906 and died in 1986. Her daughter, Eloise Greenfield, was born in 1929.

Gwendolyn Brooks

Gwendolyn Brooks was born in 1917 and died in 2000.

Literature Online

Author Search For more about Eloise Greenfield, Lessie Jones Little, and Gwendolyn Brooks, go to glencoe.com and enter QuickPass code GL27534u4.

Langston Terrace

Eloise Greenfield & Lessie Jones Little

I fell in love with Langston Terrace the very first time I saw it. Our family had been living in two rooms of a three-story house when Mama and Daddy saw the newspaper article telling of the plans to build it. It was going to be a low-rent housing project[1] in northeast Washington, and it would be named in honor of John Mercer Langston, the famous black lawyer, educator, and congressman.

Children at Play, 1947. Jacob Lawrence. Tempera on hardboard, 20 x 24 in. Georgia Museum of Art, Atlanta, GA.

Comparing Literature

In what way does the first sentence help set the tone of the essay? Add your thoughts to the chart.

---

1 A public ***housing project*** is homes built by the government for people who might not otherwise be able to afford to rent or buy homes.

So many people needed housing and wanted to live there, many more than there would be room for. They were all filling out applications,[2] hoping to be one of the 274 families chosen. My parents filled out one, too.

I didn't want to move. I knew our house was crowded—there were eleven of us, six adults and five children—but I didn't want to leave my friends, and I didn't want to go to a strange place and be the new person in a neighborhood and a school where most of the other children already knew each other. I was eight years old, and I had been to three schools. We had moved five times since we'd been in Washington, each time trying to get more space and a better place to live. But rent was high so we'd always lived in a house with relatives and friends, and shared the rent.

One of the people in our big household was Lillie, Daddy's cousin and Mama's best friend. She and her husband also applied for a place in the new project, and during the months that it was being built, Lillie and Mama would sometimes walk fifteen blocks just to stand and watch the workmen digging holes and laying bricks. They'd just stand there watching and wishing. And at home, that was all they could talk about. "When we get our new place . . ." "If we get our new place . . ."

Lillie got her good news first. I can still see her and Mama standing at the bottom of the hall steps, hugging and laughing and crying, happy for Lillie, then sitting on the steps, worrying and wishing again for Mama.

Finally, one evening, a woman came to the house with our good news, and Mama and Daddy went over and picked out the house they wanted. We moved on my ninth birthday. Wilbur, Gerald, and I went to school that morning from one house, and when Daddy came to pick us up, he took us home to another one. All the furniture had been moved while we were in school.

Comparing Literature

In what ways do Lillie and Mama's conversation and other details in this paragraph add to the tone of the essay?

---

2 **Applications** are forms used to make requests. People fill out applications for jobs, colleges, and apartment and house rentals.

Langston Terrace was a lovely birthday present. It was built on a hill, a group of tan brick houses and apartments with a playground as its center. The red mud surrounding the concrete walks had not yet been covered with black soil and grass seed, and the holes that would soon be homes for young trees were filled with rainwater. But it still looked beautiful to me.

We had a whole house all to ourselves. Upstairs and downstairs. Two bedrooms, and the living room would be my bedroom at night. Best of all, I wasn't the only new person. Everybody was new to this new little community, and by the time school opened in the fall, we had gotten used to each other and had made friends with other children in the neighborhood, too.

I guess most of the parents thought of the new place as an in-between place. They were glad to be there, but their dream was to save enough money to pay for a house that would be their own. Saving was hard, though, and slow, because each time somebody in a family got a raise on the job, it had to be reported to the manager of the project so that the rent could be raised, too. Most people stayed years longer than they had planned to, but they didn't let that stop them from enjoying life.

They formed a resident council to look into any neighborhood problems that might come up. They started a choral group and presented music and poetry programs on Sunday evenings in the social room or on the playground. On weekends, they played horseshoes and softball and other games. They had a reading club that met once a week at the Langston branch of the public library, after it opened in the basement of one of the apartment buildings.

The library was very close to my house. I could leave by my back door and be there in two minutes. The playground was right in front of my house, and after my sister Vedie was born and we moved a few doors down to a three-bedroom house, I could just look out of my bedroom window to see if any of my friends were out playing.

Comparing Literature

How do the details in this paragraph affect the tone of the essay?

There were so many games to play and things to do. We played hide-and-seek at the lamppost, paddle tennis and shuffleboard, dodge ball and jacks. We danced in fireplug showers, jumped rope to rhymes, played "Bouncy, Bouncy, Bally," swinging one leg over a bouncing ball, played baseball on a nearby field, had parties in the social room and bus trips to the beach. In the playroom, we played Ping-Pong and pool, learned to sew and embroider and crochet.

For us, Langston Terrace wasn't an in-between place. It was a growing place, a good growing-up place. Neighbors who cared, family and friends, and a lot of fun. Life was good. Not perfect, but good. We knew about problems, heard about them, saw them, lived through some hard ones ourselves, but our community wrapped itself around us, put itself between us and the hard knocks, to cushion the blows.

It's been many years since I moved away, but every once in a long while I go back, just to look at things and remember. The large stone animals that decorated the playground are still there. A walrus, a hippo, a frog, and two horses. They've started to crack now, but I remember when they first came to live with us. They were friends, to climb on or to lean against, or to gather around in the evening. You could sit on the frog's head and look way out over the city at the tall trees and rooftops.

Nowadays, whenever I run into old friends, mostly at a funeral, or maybe a wedding, after we've talked about how we've been and what we've been doing, and how old our children are, we always end up talking about our childtime in our old neighborhood. And somebody will say, "One of these days we ought to have a Langston reunion."[3] That's what we always called it, just "Langston," without the "Terrace." I guess because it sounded more homey. And that's what Langston was. It was home. ❧

Comparing Literature

How do the sentence constructions and other details in this paragraph affect the tone? How do they help express the essay's theme?

---

3 A *reunion* is a gathering of people who have been apart for a while.

Children Dancing, 1948. Robert Gwathmey. Oil on canvas, 32 x 40 in.
The Butler Institute of American Art, Youngstown, OH.

HOME

Gwendolyn
Brooks

What had been wanted was this always,
this always to last, the talking softly on
this porch, with the snake plant in the jardiniere
in the southwest corner, and the obstinate slip[1]
from Aunt Eppie's magnificent Michigan fern
at the left side of the friendly door. Mama,

---

1 A *jardinière* (järd´ən ēr´) is a decorative pot or plant stand.
Something that is *obstinate* is stubborn. A *slip* is a small part of a
plant that is used to grow a new plant.

Maud Martha and Helen rocked slowly in their rocking chairs, and looked at the late afternoon light on the lawn, and at the emphatic[2] iron of the fence and at the poplar tree. These things might soon be theirs no longer. Those shafts and pools of light, the tree, the graceful iron, might soon be viewed possessively by different eyes.

Papa was to have gone that noon, during his lunch hour, to the office of the Home Owners' Loan. If he had not succeeded in getting another extension, they would be leaving this house in which they had lived for more than fourteen years. There was little hope. The Home Owners' Loan was hard. They sat, making their plans.

"We'll be moving into a nice flat[3] somewhere," said Mama. "Somewhere on South Park, or Michigan, or in Washington Park Court." Those flats, as the girls and Mama knew well, were burdens on wages twice the size of Papa's. This was not mentioned now.

"They're much prettier than this old house," said Helen. "I have friends I'd just as soon not bring here. And I have other friends that wouldn't come down this far for anything, unless they were in a taxi."

Yesterday, Maud Martha would have attacked her. Tomorrow she might. Today she said nothing. She merely gazed at a little hopping robin in the tree, her tree, and tried to keep the fronts of her eyes dry.

"Well, I do know," said Mama, turning her hands over and over, "that I've been getting tireder and tireder of doing that firing. From October to April, there's firing to be done."

"But lately we've been helping, Harry and I," said Maud Martha. "And sometimes in March and April and in October, and even in November, we could build a little fire in the fireplace. Sometimes the weather was just right for that."

Comparing Literature

What is the tone of the first paragraph? Which elements help create the tone?

---

2 **Emphatic** means "strongly expressive" or "forceful."

3 **Flat** is another word for *apartment*.

She knew, from the way they looked at her, that this had been a mistake. They did not want to cry.

But she felt that the little line of white, somewhat ridged with smoked purple, and all that cream-shot saffron,[4] would never drift across any western sky except that in back of this house. The rain would drum with as sweet a dullness nowhere but here. The birds on South Park were mechanical birds, no better than the poor caught canaries in those "rich" women's sun parlors.

"It's just going to kill Papa!" burst out Maud Martha. "He loves this house! He lives for this house!"

Comparing Literature

What tone do the descriptions in this paragraph create?

Woman Holding Jug, 1932–1933. James A. Porter. Oil on canvas. Carl Van Vechten Gallery of Fine Art, Fisk University, Nashville, TN.

View the Art Which character from the story does the woman in this painting remind you of?

4 The orange-yellow color *(saffron)* is streaked or mixed *(shot)* with a cream color.

"He lives for us," said Helen. "It's us he loves. He wouldn't want the house, except for us."

"And he'll have us," added Mama, "wherever."

"You know," Helen sighed, "if you want to know the truth, this is a relief. If this hadn't come up, we would have gone on, just dragged on, hanging out here forever."

"It might," allowed Mama, "be an act of God. God may just have reached down, and picked up the reins."

"Yes," Maud Martha cracked in, "that's what you always say—that God knows best."

Her mother looked at her quickly, decided the statement was not suspect, looked away.

Helen saw Papa coming. "There's Papa," said Helen.

They could not tell a thing from the way Papa was walking. It was that same dear little staccato[5] walk, one shoulder down, then the other, then repeat, and repeat. They watched his progress. He passed the Kennedys', he passed the vacant lot, he passed Mrs. Blakemore's. They wanted to hurl themselves over the fence, into the street, and shake the truth out of his collar. He opened his gate—the gate—and still his stride[6] and face told them nothing.

"Hello," he said.

Mama got up and followed him through the front door. The girls knew better than to go in too.

Presently Mama's head emerged. Her eyes were lamps turned on.

"It's all right," she exclaimed. "He got it. It's all over. Everything is all right."

The door slammed shut. Mama's footsteps hurried away.

"I think," said Helen, rocking rapidly, "I think I'll give a party. I haven't given a party since I was eleven. I'd like some of my friends to just casually see that we're homeowners." 🐚

Comparing Literature

How does the tone help reveal the story's theme?

---

5 **Staccato** means "made of short, sharp sounds or movements."

6 Papa's **stride** is his way of walking.

Comparing Literature

Now use the unit Big Question to compare and contrast "Langston Terrace" and "Home." With a group of classmates, discuss questions such as

- What do you think *home* means to the narrator in the essay "Langston Terrace"?

- What do you think *home* means to the characters in the short story "Home"?

- How do the characters' experiences influence your ideas about what a home is?

Literary Element Tone

Use the details that you wrote in your chart to think about the tones of "Langston Terrace" and "Home." With a partner, answer the following questions.

1. In what ways are the tones of "Langston Terrace" and "Home" different? Discuss specific details that contribute to the differences.

2. In what ways are the tones of both selections similar? Consider the tone the authors create when they describe the different homes.

Write to Compare

In one or two paragraphs, explain how the tone of "Langston Terrace" and the tone of "Home" support the theme of each selection. You might focus on these ideas as you write.

- Tell how the narrator in "Langston Terrace" expresses feelings about the housing project as a whole, not just the family's house.

- Include details about how the characters in "Home" express their thoughts about the house. Explain why they talk about the problems with the house.

- Explain how the characters' situation in each selection affects the tone.

- Explain how the similarities and differences in tone help you understand what the authors mean by the word *home*.

 Writing Tip

Details Cite details from the selections to support the statements you make about tone. Choose vivid details so that your readers will easily recall them.

 Literature Online

Selection Resources
For Selection Quizzes, eFlashcards, and Reading-Writing Connection activities, go to glencoe.com and enter QuickPass code GL27534u4.

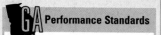 Performance Standards

For pages 580–585

ELA7W2c Produce a multi-paragraph persuasive essay that describes the points in support of the proposition, employing well-articulated, relevant evidence.

 # Writing Workshop

Persuasive Essay

What influences serve as positive models for our development? In this workshop, you will write a persuasive essay that will help you think about the Unit 4 Big Question: What Influences You?

Review the writing prompt, or assignment, below. Then read the Writing Plan. It will tell you what you will do to write your essay.

Writing Assignment

A persuasive essay usually argues for or against something and asks readers to believe something or to take action. Write an essay that contrasts two influences on society and persuades your readers to support one of them. The audience, or those reading your essay, should be your classmates and teacher.

Prewrite

Think about the influences of certain people or ideas presented in the selections in this unit. For example, in Erma Bombeck's persuasive essay "Heroes," whom does she say Americans admire as heroes?

Gather Ideas

Research several influences on society. What are two sides of each influence? Gather evidence for and against each side.

Choose a Topic

Choose an influence and write a sentence stating your position on it. Then create a Venn diagram to contrast two sides of the influence.

_____ is better for society than _____ because _____.

> ### ▶ Writing Plan
>
> - **Present a clear argument in the introduction.**
> - **Organize the evidence for the argument in the most persuasive order.**
> - **Address possible reader concerns and counterarguments.**
> - **Express strong feelings with precise and vivid language.**
> - **Conclude by summarizing the argument and asking readers to take action.**

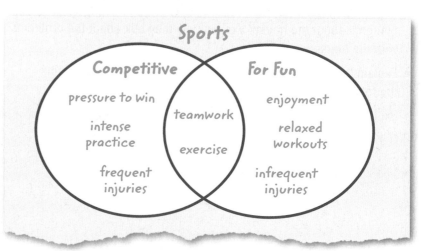

> **Prewriting Tip**
>
> Choose a topic you feel strongly about. You can argue most convincingly about something that is meaningful to you.

Get Organized

Your essay should include evidence that supports your position. As you organize your argument, consider the pros and cons of both sides and address possible counterarguments. You can present your points by side, discussing all the features of one side then all the features of the other; or by feature, comparing one feature on both sides then moving to the next feature. Then create an outline of your essay.

Thesis Statement: Playing a competitive sport is less beneficial than playing a sport for fun.

I. Healthful benefits
   A. Playing for fun
      1. Exercise without pressure to perform
   B. Playing competitively
      1. Two million sports-related injuries a year for kids
II. Social benefits

Draft

Use the following skills to develop the draft of your persuasive essay.

Get It On Paper

- Open with your position statement, or your argument.
- For each body paragraph, write a topic sentence that supports your argument. Add a sentence to support the topic sentence and a sentence to address a possible counterargument.
- End by summarizing your position and asking readers to take action.
- Don't worry about paragraphs, spelling, or grammar right now.
- Read what you've written. Include more information if you need to.

Develop Your Draft

1. State your **position** in your first paragraph. Make sure that your **argument** is clear.

The truth is, however, that playing a sport for fun is much better for young people than playing competitively.

Literature Online

Writing and Research
For prewriting, drafting, and revising tools, go to glencoe.com and enter QuickPass code GL27534u4.

Drafting Tip

An effective way to appeal to your readers is to think of rhetorical questions such as "Who should influence you?" or "Are you afraid of being influenced?" Then answer the questions in your argument.

TRY IT

Analyzing Cartoons
In what way is the girl in this cartoon *not* developing her own voice? With a partner, discuss what this cartoon suggests about writing in your own voice.

2. Organize your **evidence** either by side or by feature.

> Playing a sport, whether on an organized team or just with a group of kids, can be healthful.

3. Address **counterarguments** readers might have.

> Some people think that competitive sports also build character. I disagree, though.

4. Use **precise language** to make your argument clear and convincing.

> There's not much individual competition to be the "star."

5. In your conclusion, **summarize** your argument and include a **call to action** to your readers.

> Schools should start after-school programs that allow kids to play sports for fun without having to worry about medals, trophies, and championships.

Apply Good Writing Traits: Voice

Just as each person has a unique speaking voice, each author has a unique writing voice. A writer's word choice, sentence patterns, and tone create her voice and express her personality.

Read these sentences from Erma Bombeck's essay "Heroes." What can you tell about Bombeck from her writing voice?

> At Mount Rainier they learned to live with life's bad calls a long time ago.

> I think the crowds went to the wrong summit and cheered the wrong champion.

As you draft your essay, write sentences the way you'd say them. Read your writing aloud to be sure it sounds like you. Use a dictionary or thesaurus to help you modify your word choices.

Analyze a Student Model

Sports have a big influence on our lives. You can't open a newspaper, turn on the news, or surf the Internet without seeing coverage of some sport. Some people believe that kids benefit from playing a competitive sport. The truth is, however, that playing a sport for fun is much better for young people than playing competitively.

Playing a sport, whether on an organized team or just with a group of kids, can be healthful. It offers physical exercise in the fresh air. Kids who play a sport for fun can just enjoy exercising their bodies without the pressure to perform better than others. Playing competitive sports, on the other hand, also carries a risk of injury. According to one study, two million of the 7.2 million students who took part in high school sports in 2005–2006 suffered sports-related injuries. More of those injuries took place in competitions than in practice. Why? In competitions, kids worry more about winning than they do about being safe.

Playing sports for fun has social benefits as well. It builds character by giving kids a chance to practice teamwork and to follow rules without pressure. The emphasis is on working together so that everybody gets a chance to play and has fun. There's not much individual competition to be the "star." Some people think that competitive sports also build character. I disagree, though. Kids face a great deal of pressure to do well from coaches, parents, and teammates. If they let their team down, they're often harassed by other kids. This pressure can lead them to do anything to win, including cheating—and cheating certainly doesn't build character.

Playing sports is an important part of growing up in our culture. Participating for fun allows kids to develop important life skills while minimizing the risk of injury. Schools should start after-school programs that allow kids to play sports for fun without having to worry about medals, trophies, and championships. Let's leave competition to the professionals.

Argument in Introduction
State your position clearly in the first paragraph.

Evidence
Notice how this writer organizes evidence by feature, discussing the healthful aspects first of recreational sports and then of competitive sports.

Address Counterarguments
Anticipate counterarguments and explain why you don't support them.

Precise and Vivid Language
Choose strong, specific words, such as *harassed,* to express your position.

Conclusion
End by summarizing your argument and telling readers what they should believe or do.

Revising Tip

Vary your sentence structure to make your writing interesting. Using both short and long sentences will add rhythm to your essay. Start some sentences with participial phrases. To review participial phrases, turn to the Grammar Link on page 317.

Revise

Now it's time to revise your draft so your ideas really shine. Revising is what makes good writing great, and great writing takes work!

Peer Review Trade drafts with a partner. Use the chart below to review your partner's draft by answering the questions in the *What to do* column. Talk about your peer review after you have glanced at each other's drafts and written answers to the questions. Next, follow the suggestions in the *How to do it* column to revise your draft.

Revising Plan

What to do	How to do it	Example
Do readers understand the issue and your position on it from the beginning?	State your position on the issue clearly in the introduction.	~~Both competitive and recreational sports have benefits.~~ ʌThe truth is, however, that playing a sport for fun is much better for young people than playing competitively.
Is your evidence organized convincingly?	Present your points by side or by feature of the issue.	ʌPlaying sports for fun has social benefits as well. It builds character by giving kids a chance to practice teamwork and to follow rules without pressure.
Have you anticipated arguments against your position?	Address counterarguments with convincing facts and examples.	ʌThis pressure can lead them to do anything to win, including cheating.
Are any words confusing?	Replace general or inexact terms with specific and vivid nouns, verbs, and modifiers.	There's not much individual competition to be ~~good~~ ʌthe "star."
Does your conclusion summarize your position and ask readers to take action?	Restate your argument in different words and ask readers to take a specific stand or action.	ʌSchools should start after-school programs that allow kids to play sports for fun without having to worry about medals, trophies, and championships.

Edit and Proofread

For your final draft, read your essay one sentence at a time. The Editing and Proofreading Checklist inside the back cover of this book may help you spot errors. Use the proofreading symbols to mark needed changes. Then make corrections.

Grammar Focus: Parallelism

A good way to emphasize your points and make them memorable is to use parallel construction. To do this, state similar ideas in similar grammatical forms. Below are examples of a problem with parallel construction and possible solutions from the Workshop Model.

Problem: Similar ideas don't reinforce each other because they're stated in different forms.

Example A:

You can't open a newspaper, turn on the news, or surfing the Internet without seeing coverage of some sport.

Solution: State the similar ideas as phrases beginning with present-tense verbs.

You can't open a newspaper, turn on the news, or surf the Internet without seeing coverage of some sport.

Example B:

It builds character by giving kids a chance to practice teamwork. They also are following rules without pressure.

Solution: Combine the sentences, stating both objects as infinitives.

It builds character by giving kids a chance to practice teamwork and to follow rules without pressure.

Present

It's almost time to share your writing with others. Write your essay neatly in print or cursive on a separate sheet of paper. If you have access to a computer, type your essay on the computer and check spelling. Save your document to a disk, and print it out.

Grammar Tip

Parallelism is quite common in all types of writing—including the lyrics of many songs. Remember to use it whenever you can.

 ### Presenting Tip

Publishing To add weight to your argument, find a statistic from a well-respected source that supports your argument. Include it on the title page of your essay.

 Literature Online

Writing and Research For editing and publishing tools, go to glencoe.com and enter QuickPass code GL27534u4.

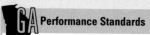
Speaking, Listening, and Viewing Workshop

Persuasive Speech

Activity

Connect to Your Writing Deliver a persuasive speech to your classmates. You might want to adapt the persuasive essay you wrote for the Writing Workshop on pages 580–585. Remember that you focused on the Unit 4 Big Question: What Influences You?

Plan Your Speech

Reread your persuasive essay and highlight the sections you want to include in your speech. Like your persuasive essay, your speech should present a clear, well-supported argument for your position on an issue affecting society and explain how the audience can act on it.

Rehearse Your Speech

Practice your speech several times. Try rehearsing in front of a mirror so that you can watch your movements and facial expressions. You may use note cards to remind you of your main points and persuasive evidence, but practice your speech often enough that you won't lose eye contact with your audience.

Deliver Your Speech

- Speak clearly and precisely.

- Adjust your speaking style to help your audience distinguish between your arguments and your counterarguments.

- Change the tone, pace, and volume of your speaking to emphasize important ideas in your speech.

- Use gestures and visual aids to direct the audience's attention to specific points and to clarify your argument.

Listening to Learn

As you listen, take notes to make sure you understand the speech. Use the following question frames to provide constructive feedback.

- I agree/disagree with your point about _____ because _____. Can you offer more evidence for your argument?

- I noticed you used the persuasive technique of _____. I thought that technique was/was not effective because _____.

- To summarize your speech: _____. Is that correct?

Speech Checklist

Answer the following questions to evaluate your presentation:

- ❑ Did you speak clearly and precisely—and with a style that distinguished your arguments from your counterarguments?

- ❑ Did you vary the tone, pace, and volume of your speaking to add emphasis?

- ❑ Did you use gestures and visual aids to draw attention to specific points?

- ❑ Did you make eye contact with your audience?

Unit Challenge

Answer the Big Question

In Unit 4, you explored the Big Question through reading, writing, speaking, and listening. Now it's time for you to answer the Big Question by completing one of the Unit Challenges below.

WHAT Influences You?

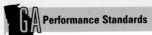

GA Performance Standards

For page 587

ELA7W2a Demonstrate competence in a variety of genres. Produce writing that engages the reader by establishing a context, creating a speaker's voice, and otherwise developing reader interest.

Use the notes you took in your Unit 4 **Foldable** to complete your Unit Challenge.

Before you present your Unit Challenge, be sure to complete the following steps. Use this first plan if you choose to write a poem or a song about someone who has had a positive influence on you.

On Your Own Activity: Write a Poem or a Song

- ❏ Think of a person who has had a positive influence on your life.
- ❏ List five to ten qualities that you admire in this person.
- ❏ Use your list to help you write a poem or a song that gives descriptions of what the person means to you.
- ❏ Use the characteristics of poetry, such as metaphor, simile, rhythm, and imagery, that you learned about on page 388.
- ❏ Present your poem or song to the class.

Use this second plan if you choose to make a poster showing whether or not you support the statement "Kids today watch too much TV."

Group Activity: Make a Poster

- ❏ Choose one group member to take notes on the discussion.
- ❏ Discuss the influence of television on you. Consider the influence of television on a young Oprah Winfrey.
- ❏ Decide as a group whether or not you support the statement "Kids today watch too much TV."
- ❏ Brainstorm words and phrases that support your argument.
- ❏ Decide which words and phrases could be illustrated.
- ❏ Organize your words, phrases, and images on the poster in a way that will appeal to the interests of the class.

Independent Reading

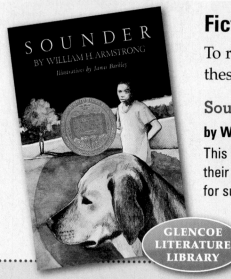

Fiction

To read more about the Big Question, choose one of these books from your school or local library.

Sounder

by William Armstrong

This prize-winning novel tells the story of a sharecropper family and their loyal hunting dog, Sounder. The book explores the family's struggle for survival—and the strength of their hope—in the rural south.

GLENCOE LITERATURE LIBRARY

The Slave Dancer

by Paula Fox

Jessie, a thirteen-year-old boy from New Orleans, is kidnapped by slave traders and taken to play music on a slave ship. Jessie witnesses the horrors of slavery and the slave trade firsthand.

GLENCOE LITERATURE LIBRARY

GLENCOE LITERATURE LIBRARY

Dragonwings

by Laurence Yep

In this award-winning novel, a small boy travels from China to San Francisco to live with the father he has never met. Together they endure hardships and sacrifice to make their special dream come true.

Father Figure

by Richard Peck

Since his parents' divorce, Jim has played substitute father to his younger brother. After their mother's death, the boys are sent to spend the summer with their long-absent father, and Jim's father-figure role is threatened.

Nonfiction

On the Way Home

by Laura Ingalls Wilder and Rose Wilder Lane

In her diary, the author of *Little House on the Prairie* describes her family's exciting 1894 journey from South Dakota to a new home in the Missouri Ozarks. Wilder's daughter adds her own memories of the trip.

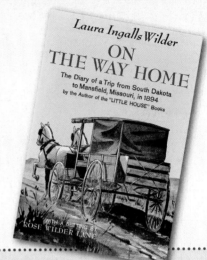

Finding Courage: History's Young Heroes and Their Amazing Deeds

by J. M. Bedell

This book profiles twenty-seven young people from around the globe who grew up to change the world through their determination and courage. Read to learn about such influential people as Louis Braille, the inventor of the Braille language, and Fa Mu-lan, the great Chinese warrior.

Vaqueros: America's First Cowmen

by Martin W. Sandler

The author looks at the history of vaqueros, or Hispanic cowmen, and their influence on cowboy folklore. The book retells legends of the vaqueros, including the deeds that showcased their courage, loyalty, and heroism.

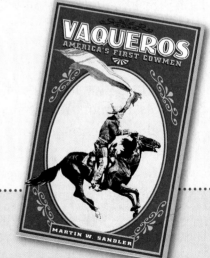

 Conduct Research

Use the Internet to research the author or topic of the book you read. Create an annotated list of works related to the author or topic that your classmates might like to read. Explain how each work relates to the book you read and include reasons why each work might be of interest to other readers your age.

Assessment

READING

Read the passages and answer the questions. Write your answers on a separate sheet of paper.

"A Glimpse of Home" by Kathryn Sullivan

I first saw the earth—the whole earth—from the shuttle *Challenger* in 1984. The view takes your breath away and fills you with childlike wonder. That's why every shuttle crew has to clean noseprints off their spacecraft's windows several times a day. An incredibly beautiful tapestry of blue and white, tan, black and green seems to glide beneath you at an elegant, stately pace. But you're actually going so fast that the entire map of the world spins before your eyes with each ninety-minute orbit. After just one or two laps, you feel, maybe for the first time, like a citizen of a planet.

All the colors and patterns you see seem powerful and yet somehow fragile. You see volcanoes spewing smoke, hurricanes roiling the oceans and even fine tendrils of Saharan dust reaching across the Atlantic. You also see the big, gray smudges of fields, paddies and pastures, and at night you marvel at the lights, like brilliant diamonds, that reveal a mosaic of cities, roads and coastlines—impressive signs of the hand of humanity.

Scientists tell us that our hand is heavy, that we are wiping out other species at an unprecedented rate and probably transforming our climate. Will the immense power of global systems withstand the impact of humanity? Or is it possible that our collective actions will change the nature of our planet enough to cripple its ability to support life?

I no longer believe that we can wait for all the scientific data needed to answer these questions conclusively. We must recognize immediately what it means to be citizens of this planet. It means accepting our obligation to be <u>stewards</u> of the earth's life-giving capacities. As homeowners, we wouldn't neglect or damage our houses until they weren't fit to live in. Why would we do that with our planet?

1. The author's argument in this essay is based mainly on
   A. repetition.
   B. appeals to authority.
   C. factual support for her views.
   D. emotional and ethical appeals.

2. Which sentence marks a major change in the author's tone?
   A. topic sentence of paragraph 1
   B. topic sentence of paragraph 2
   C. topic sentence of paragraph 3
   D. concluding sentence of the essay

3. In this essay, the author uses powerful imagery mainly to
   A. persuade readers to care for the earth.
   B. entertain readers with a poetic description.
   C. inform readers what occurs on a shuttle flight.
   D. provide a variety of views on the earth.

4. Which BEST describes how the author organizes the entire passage?
   A. The author compares and contrasts two points of view.
   B. The author narrates a story in chronological order.
   C. The author explains the sequence of steps in a process.
   D. The author describes a problem and discusses its solutions.

5. The BEST definition for the word *stewards* as it is used in this passage is
   A. "housekeeping servants."
   B. "respectful managers."
   C. "passenger attendants."
   D. "bookkeeping supervisors."

 Literature Online

Standards Practice For more standards practice, go to glencoe.com and enter QuickPass code GL27534u4.

from **"Rip Van Winkle"** by Washington Irving

Whoever has made a voyage up the Hudson must remember the Kaatskill Mountains. <u>They are a dismembered branch of the great Appalachian family, and are seen away to the west of the river, swelling up to a noble height, and lording it over the surrounding country</u>. . . . When the weather is fair and settled, they are clothed in blue and purple, and print their bold outlines on the clear evening sky; but sometimes, when the rest of the landscape is cloudless, they will gather a hood of gray vapors about their summits, which, in the last rays of the setting sun, will glow and light up like a crown of glory.

At the foot of these fairy mountains, the voyager may have descried the light smoke curling up from a village, whose shingled roofs gleam among the trees, just where the blue tints of the upland melt away into the fresh green of the nearer landscape. It is a little village, of great <u>antiquity</u>, having been founded by some of the Dutch colonists, in the early times of the province, just about the beginning of the government of the good Peter Stuyvesant[1] (may he rest in peace!) and there were some of the houses of the original settlers standing within a few years, built of small yellow bricks brought from Holland, having latticed windows and gable fronts, surmounted with weathercocks.

In that same village and in one of these very houses (which, to tell the precise truth, was sadly timeworn and weather-beaten), there lived many years since, while the country was yet a province of Great Britain, a simple good-natured fellow, of the name of Rip Van Winkle. He was a descendant of the Van Winkles who figured so gallantly in the chivalrous days of Peter Stuyvesant. He inherited, however, but little of the martial character of his ancestors. I have observed that he was a simple good-natured man; he was, moreover, a kind neighbor, and an obedient henpecked husband. Indeed, to the latter circumstance might be owing that meekness of spirit which gained him such universal popularity; for those men are most apt to be obsequious and conciliating abroad, who are under the discipline of shrews at home.

[1]**Peter Stuyvesant:** the last governor of the Dutch colony of New Netherland

6. Which word below BEST describes the tone created by the author through his vocabulary and sentence style?

A. formal

B. casual

C. humorous

D. sarcastic

7. The BEST description for Rip Van Winkle's wife is

A. sweet and gentle.

B. bossy and demanding.

C. generous and unselfish.

D. weak and dependent.

8. What does the word *antiquity* mean in this passage?

A. age

B. wealth

C. beauty

D. reputation

9. In this passage, Rip Van Winkle is characterized mainly through

A. his own thoughts.

B. his own actions.

C. the narrator's description.

D. the words of other characters.

10. What is the setting of the passage about Rip Van Winkle?

A. Holland in the present day

B. the United States in the 1990s

C. Great Britain in the 1700s

D. America during Colonial times

11. The description of the Kaatskill Mountains in the second sentence includes an example of

A. onomatopoeia.

B. simile.

C. personification.

D. characterization.

ENGLISH/LANGUAGE ARTS

Choose the best answer for each question. Write the answer on a separate sheet of paper.

1. Which word or words BEST fill in the blank in the sentence below?

   > I read all the time, and the books I read _____ are the ones about adventures in faraway places.

   A. frequentlier

   B. more frequently

   C. frequentliest

   D. most frequently

2. Which word BEST fills in the blank in the sentence below?

   > I like those books because reading them makes me feel as if I've been _____ away to another world.

   A. caried

   B. carried

   C. carryed

   D. carryied

3. Which word BEST fills in the blank in the sentence below?

   > I like those books because reading them makes me feel as if I've been _____ away to another world.

   A. amazing

   B. amazeing

   C. amazzing

   D. ammazing

4. Which sentence below is a compound sentence?

   A. Some people read folktales, and they enjoy them.

   B. I usually enjoy books about kids like me the most.

   C. Most of my friends and family members also read.

   D. Reading is fun because it requires imagination.

5. Which sentence below is a complex sentence?

   A. Jeri gave me a book, and I loved it.

   B. It was a very interesting mystery.

   C. I'll let you read it if you're interested.

   D. I often read mysteries and science fiction.

WRITING

*Read your assigned topic in the box below. Use one piece of paper to jot down
your ideas and organize your thoughts. Then neatly write your essay on another
sheet of paper.*

Persuasive Writing Topic

Writing Situation

The members of your book club are trying to decide on a book to read
for the next meeting. The book could be fiction, poetry, biography, history,
or any other genre that interests you.

Directions for Writing

Choose a book you think would be interesting and enjoyable. Write an
essay to convince your fellow members that they should read the book.
Include specific details about the book to support your position.

Writing Checklist

☐ Focus on a single topic.

☐ Organize your main points in a clear, logical order.

☐ Support your ideas or viewpoints with details and examples.

☐ Use precise, vivid words.

☐ Vary the length and structure of your sentences.

☐ Use clear transition words to connect ideas.

☐ Correct any errors in spelling, capitalization, punctuation, and usage.

HOW Can You Become Who You Want to Be**?**

Champion cyclist
Lance Armstrong

- Cancer survivor
- 7-time winner of
  the Tour de France
- Symbol of hope
  for many people

THE **BIG** Question

> *"Keep your eyes on the big picture. You don't have to win every stage of the tour to win at the end."*
>
> —LANCE ARMSTRONG

FOLDABLES®
Study Organizer

- short story
- journal
- biography
- legend
- poem
- BQ: How Can You Become Who You Want to Be?

Throughout Unit 5, you will read, write, and talk about the **BIG** Question— **"How Can You Become Who You Want to Be?"** Use your Unit 5 **Foldable,** shown here, to keep track of your ideas as you read. Turn to the back of this book for instructions on making this **Foldable.**

HOW Can You Become Who You Want to Be?

Whom do you admire? Why? How did that person become who he or she wanted to be? What goals will help you become the person *you* want to be?

Think about three ways that people achieve their life goals:

- Positive Actions
- Courage and Confidence
- People Who Lend a Hand

What You'll Read

Reading about people who have become who they wanted to be can help you explore this idea for yourself. In this unit, **biographies** and **autobiographies**—stories of real people's lives—are excellent sources of information and inspiration. You will also read short stories, poems, and other texts that can lead you to discover answers to the Big Question.

What You'll Write

As you explore the Big Question, you'll write notes in your Unit Foldable. Later, you'll use these notes to complete two writing assignments related to the Big Question.

1. **Write a Research Report**
2. **Choose a Unit Challenge**
   - **On Your Own Activity: Web Diagram**
   - **Group Activity: Letter of Advice**

What You'll Learn

Literary Elements

assonance and consonance
analogy
legend
author's purpose
setting
irony
symbol
voice
conflict
description
style
tone

Reading Skills and Strategies

draw conclusions about characters
make generalizations about characters
question
make predictions about plot
paraphrase
identify text structure
monitor comprehension
evaluate theme
interpret plot events

Tony Hawk

CHAIRMAN OF THE BOARD[1]

When Tony Hawk was nine years old, his brother, Steve, changed his life. Steve was twelve years older than Tony, and he loved surfing. The Hawks lived in San Diego, California, not far from the Pacific Ocean. Most mornings, Steve woke up early to surf before going to school. Because Steve loved surfing, he had tried out "sidewalk surfing." That's what early skateboarding was called. Steve had an old banana board in the garage. He took Tony to a nearby alley, showed him how to balance on the board, and gave him a push. Tony rolled and rolled until he ran into a fence. He couldn't figure out how to turn!

FALLING IN LOVE It was not love at first sight. Slowly, over the next year, though, Tony began skating more and more. One weekend, the mother of one of Tony's friends took the neighborhood kids to a skate park, in San Diego, called Oasis. Skaters whipped around riding the bowls, banks, pools, and other obstacles of the park. He loved it.

After that, Tony wanted to go every weekend. He nagged his parents to drive him there. If his brother or sisters were visiting, he made them take him. Soon he was asking for rides after school. He wanted to go every day.

Tony was competitive[2] with himself. That's what he

> **Set a Purpose for Reading**
>
> Read the excerpt from *Tony Hawk: Chairman of the Board* to learn how Tony became who he wanted to be.

---

1 The term ***chairman of the board*** usually means the chairman of the board of directors of a company. The author is playing with words here, referring to a different kind of board.

2 A ***competitive*** person likes to win and tries hard to do so.

liked about skateboarding: It wasn't a team sport. He didn't like letting his team down. With skateboarding, Tony could only let himself down—and he wasn't about to do that. That's why he would practice a single trick all day long.

FIRST CONTEST Tony was 11 when he competed in his first skateboard contest. There were more than 100 skaters in his age group! Tony was so nervous before the contest that he developed a stomachache. He didn't skate well and fell on easy tricks.

Tony had let himself down, and that was the worst feeling he had ever had. So, after that, Tony got serious about contests. He would skate the park before each competition. He drew a diagram of the pool (competitions were often held in swimming pools). Then he would map out where he would do his tricks and memorize his planned run.

Tony's strategy worked! He did a lot better. By the end of the year, he had won his age class. He also had become a member of the Oasis Skatepark team.

At 11, Tony also got his first sponsor, Dogtown Skateboards. Dogtown went out of business soon, but Tony quickly found another sponsor: Stacy Peralta, who owned part of Powell and Peralta, the hottest skateboard company at the time. Stacy named the Powell group of skaters The Bones Brigade.

TEENAGE PRO Tony's first big, out-of-town contest for Powell was in Jacksonville, Florida. He fell during his run and was so upset that he refused to talk to anybody afterward. But Stacy was a great coach, and with his help and hours of practice, Tony improved even more quickly than before. Before one local skating contest, in 1982, Stacy turned to Tony and asked him if he wanted to turn pro. Tony shrugged and said yes. He skated well and placed third against the best skaters in the world! He was 14.

CIRCUS SKATER Despite his early skateboarding success, Tony had a problem. He was too skinny to

BQ ▶ BIG Question
What positive actions has Tony taken?

BQ ▶ BIG Question
Besides Stacy Peralta, what other people have helped Tony so far?

do some of the harder aerial[3] tricks. He needed more weight to generate enough momentum[4] to fly above the ramp. But no matter how much food he ate, Tony couldn't put on weight. So he invented a different way to catch air. Instead of grabbing his board early, like all the other skaters, he ollied (did a no-hand aerial) into the air and then grabbed his board. That way he could use his legs more to launch himself off the lip of the ramp and do more tricks. The new style worked, but it looked a lot different from anybody else's style. Other pros made fun of Tony's skating. Some called him a "cheater" because of his technique.

Tony also invented a lot of tricks in which he would flip his board and then put it back under his feet. Today, every skater does flip tricks, but back then, skaters called him a "circus skater" for doing them.

By 1985, Oasis had closed down. Skateboarding had become less popular. But Tony kept skating with his friends, at Del Mar Skatepark, in San Diego. He kept inventing tricks, innovative[5] tricks. In a few years, all the skaters who had made fun of Tony were trying to learn from him!

CHAMPION OF THE WORLD After Tony turned pro, it took him awhile to get used to skating against older, more experienced skaters. He bobbed all over the contest results. Sometimes he would win, and sometimes he'd place 10th. When Tony skated poorly, it upset him, and he practiced harder. Soon he began winning a lot. He became the first pro skater to win three vert contests[6] in a row. In 1983, the National Skateboard Association was founded. It governed the world skateboard ranking. Tony was declared world champion. He was 15. 🛹

BQ **BIG Question**

How did Tony become the person he wanted to be?

---

3 An *aerial* (ār′ē əl) trick is done in the air.

4 *Momentum* is the force of a moving object. This force involves a combination of speed and weight, so Tony's skinniness made him unable to *generate*, or create, the momentum he needed.

5 *Innovative* tricks are new and creative.

6 In *vert contests* a skater flies into the air from a ramp (going "vertical") and lands back on the ramp.

After You Read

Respond and Think Critically

1. Use your own words to tell the most important events that describe Tony's journey from a "sidewalk surfer" to a skateboard champion. [Summarize]

2. In what way did Tony's brother Steve change Tony's life? [Interpret]

3. Why did other skateboarders make fun of Tony's skating or call him a "cheater"? [Analyze]

4. Does Tony deserve to be called the "chairman of the board"? Why or why not? [Evaluate]

Writing

Write a Summary Write a one-paragraph summary about the selection. You may want to begin your summary with this topic sentence:

This selection is about _____.

Notice that the selection is divided into parts with headings, such as First Contest and Teenage Pro. First write one sentence stating the main idea or event of the first paragraph. Then write a sentence about each part in chronological order. Your summary should also state the meaning of the selection in your own words.

Performance Standards

For page 602

ELA7W2b Produce a response to literature that demonstrates an understanding of the literary work.

 Literature Online

Unit Resources For additional skills practice, go to glencoe.com and enter QuickPass code GL27534u5.

Part 1

Positive Actions

Freedom March. Anna Belle Lee Washington. Oil on Canvas, 20 x 30 in. Private Collection.

BQ ⟩ **BIG Question How Can You Become Who You Want to Be?**

How are the people in the painting *Freedom March* taking positive actions? What positive actions would you like to take in your neighborhood to make it a better place?

Before You Read

If I Can Stop One Heart from Breaking and I Stepped from Plank to Plank

GA Performance Standards

For pages 604–607

ELA7R1g/i For literary texts, explain and analyze the effects of sound.

Connect to the Poems

Are you an outgoing person, or are you quiet and shy? Do you enjoy taking risks, or are you cautious and careful?

Partner Talk With a partner, discuss whether helping others can make one's life better. Can a shy person help others? How?

Build Background

During Emily Dickinson's lifetime, women were expected to get married, keep a comfortable home, and raise children.

- Dickinson chose to live differently from many women of her time. She never married and lived her entire life in her parents' home.

- Dickinson spent most of her time alone, writing poetry. She rarely traveled or visited others, but she maintained close relationships through writing letters to friends.

Set Purposes for Reading

BQ BIG Question

As you read, pay attention to what seems important to the speaker of each poem. Ask yourself, who does the speaker want to be? How does the speaker choose to live?

Literary Element Assonance and Consonance

Assonance is the repetition of vowel sounds, especially in a line of poetry. **Consonance** is the repetition of consonant sounds in stressed syllables. For example, in the sentence "Beautiful babies bounce," the three words repeat the consonant *b* sound.

Poets use assonance, consonance, and other sound devices to create pleasing combinations of sound and a sense of rhythm. Assonance and consonance are also used to emphasize particular words that are important to the poem's meaning. To find assonance and consonance in a poem, read the poem aloud and listen for repeated sounds. Notice how these sound combinations add to the musical quality of Dickinson's poems.

Meet Emily Dickinson

Private Poet Emily Dickinson was born in 1830. A shy woman, Dickinson seldom left her home in Amherst, Massachusetts. Her poetry, however, reveals a lively, sensitive, and original human being. Of the 1,775 poems she wrote, only seven were published during her lifetime, and none with her consent.

 Literature Online

Author Search For more about Emily Dickinson, go to glencoe.com and enter QuickPass code GL27534u5.

If I Can Stop One Heart from Breaking

Emily Dickinson

Mr. Robin. Fred Cuming. Oil on board. Private Collection, ©Manya Igel Fine Arts, London.

If I can stop one Heart from breaking
I shall not live in vain°
If I can ease one Life the Aching
Or cool one Pain

5 Or help one fainting Robin
Unto his Nest again
I shall not live in Vain.

---

2 To ***live in vain*** means "to have a life without purpose or value."

BQ > BIG Question
What positive actions does the speaker consider important?

Assonance and Consonance
Say the word *vain* aloud. In what other words in the poem is the vowel sound in *vain* repeated?

I Stepped from **Plank** to **Plank**

Emily Dickinson

I stepped from Plank to Plank
A slow and cautious way
The Stars about my Head I felt
About my Feet the Sea.

5 I knew not but the next
Would be my final inch –
This gave me that precarious Gait°
Some call Experience.

---

7 ***Precarious gait*** means "an uncertain or unsteady way of walking."

Assonance and Consonance
Read aloud the first stanza of the poem. What consonant sound is repeated?

After You Read

Respond and Think Critically

1. In "If I Can Stop One Heart from Breaking," whom does the speaker wish to help? [Recall]

2. What does the image of a fainting robin in "If I Can Stop One Heart from Breaking" suggest? [Interpret]

3. Why is it important for the speaker in "If I Can Stop One Heart from Breaking" to "not live in vain"? [Summarize]

4. In "I Stepped from Plank to Plank," why does the speaker step in a "cautious way"? [Infer]

5. Each poem teaches a lesson. Which lesson do you think is more valuable? Explain. [Evaluate]

6. **BQ** ❯ **BIG Question** What kind of person does the speaker of each poem choose to be? Explain. [Analyze]

Academic Vocabulary

In Emily Dickinson's time, many **restrictions** kept most women from doing things that men did. Women could not vote, many married women could not own property, and most women did not work outside the home. To become more familiar with the word *restrictions,* fill out the graphic organizer below.

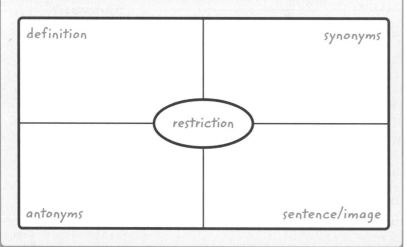

TIP

Inferring
To answer question 4, reread the first stanza of the poem "I Stepped from Plank to Plank." Ask yourself the following questions:

- On what is the speaker walking?

- Does this place seem to be safe and secure?

- What could happen if the speaker is not careful?

FOLDABLES Study Organizer Keep track of your ideas about the **BIG Question** in your unit Foldable.

LOG ON ▶ **Literature** Online

Selection Resources
For Selection Quizzes, eFlashcards, and Reading-Writing Connection activities, go to glencoe.com and enter QuickPass code GL27534u5.

Literary Element
Assonance and Consonance

1. Find one example of consonance and one example of assonance in the first stanza of "If I Can Stop One Heart from Breaking."

2. In "I Stepped from Plank to Plank," what vowel sound is repeated in the last line of the first stanza?

3. Why does Dickinson use assonance and consonance in her poetry? Use examples from the poems to support your answer.

Review: Theme

As you learned on page 135, the **theme** is the main message of a work of literature, usually expressed as a general statement about people or life. Some works have a stated theme, which is expressed directly. Other works have an implied theme, which is revealed through elements such as plot, character, setting, point of view, symbol, and irony.

Similar themes that occur again and again in different literary works are called **recurring themes.** Some recurring themes in literature are the value of friendship, the effects of loneliness or stubbornness, and the importance of love and forgiveness.

Standards Practice ELA7R1d

4. Which sentence best states the theme of "I Stepped from Plank to Plank"?
   A   Life is uncertain.
   B   Love is often temporary.
   C   Helping others gives meaning to one's life.
   D   It is important to face the future with feelings of hope.

Grammar Link

Commas in Introductory Clauses and Phrases   Adverb clauses and prepositional phrases that are used at the beginning of a sentence are called **introductory clauses** and **introductory phrases.** They "introduce" the rest of the sentence. Introductory adverb clauses are always followed by a comma.

If the poem is difficult, read it slowly.

If the clause appears at the end of the sentence, there is no comma. Use a comma after a long introductory phrase.

By using sound devices, Dickinson achieves a musical quality.

If the phrase appears at the end of the sentence, there is no comma. A comma is used after two or more introductory phrases, even if each one is short.

For fun in the evening, I write poetry.

Practice   Copy these sentences and add commas if needed.

1. As a poet of great skill Dickinson focused on familiar themes.

2. When she wrote letters to her friends she often included poems.

💬 Speaking and Listening

Speech   Give an informative speech about Emily Dickinson's role as a woman writer of the nineteenth century. Think about what you have learned about her life and the time in which she lived. Use the Internet or your school's media center to research these questions: What was expected of women during Dickinson's lifetime? How was Dickinson's life different than that of other women in her time? How does her poetry reflect her hopes? In your speech, include facts from Dickinson's life and examples from her poetry to support your main idea.

Before You Read

Hollywood and the Pits

Connect to the Short Story

Think about how you have changed during the past few years. Are there parts of your childhood self that you have left behind?

List Write a list of your interests and hobbies from a few years ago. Then add what your interests and hobbies are today. How has growing older affected your childhood interests?

Build Background

This story is set in 1968 in Los Angeles, California. In the middle of the city, close to the glamour of Hollywood, is an archaeological site filled with the skeletons of prehistoric creatures.

- The La Brea Tar Pits contain more than three million fossils from the last Ice Age, which occurred about 40,000 years ago. Fossils are hardened remains or prints of plants and animals.

- The pits were formed when sticky tar oozed up from inside the earth and created pools. Many prehistoric animals became stuck in the tar pits when they mistook them for pools of water and tried to drink from them.

Vocabulary

excavated (eks′kə vāt′əd) *adj.* uncovered or removed by digging; unearthed (p. 612). *Scientists cleaned the excavated fossils and shipped them to a museum.*

immobilized (i mō′bə līzd′) *v.* made unable to move; fixed in place (p. 612). *The cast immobilized Jonah's broken arm.*

painstaking (pānz′tā′king) *adj.* requiring close, careful labor or attention (p. 618). *Sewing the costumes for the school musical was painstaking work.*

predators (pred′ə tərz) *n.* animals that kill other animals for food (p. 618). *The nature show on television showed how predators find their prey.*

deception (di sep′shən) *n.* that which fools or misleads (p. 618). *A magician uses deception to trick an audience.*

Meet Cherylene Lee

From Stage to Science It is hard to imagine a successful stage, movie, and TV performer becoming a scientist, but that is just what Cherylene Lee did. Like the narrator in "Hollywood and the Pits," Lee was a child performer in her hometown of Los Angeles. After earning degrees in paleontology and geology, she began writing stories, poetry, and plays.

Literary Works Some of Lee's plays include *Wong Bow Rides Again* and *The Ballad of Doc Hay.* Her story "Hollywood and the Pits" appears in the collection *American Dragons: Twenty-five Asian American Voices,* edited by Laurence Yep and published in 1995.

Cherylene Lee was born in 1953.

 Literature Online

Author Search For more about Cherylene Lee, go to glencoe.com and enter QuickPass code GL27534u5.

Set Purposes for Reading

BQ BIG Question

As you read, think about the changes the narrator is experiencing. How does she respond to these changes?

Literary Element Analogy

An **analogy** is a comparison between two things, based on one or more elements that they share. In "Hollywood and the Pits," the author uses analogies to compare the narrator's experiences to the La Brea Tar Pits.

Authors often use analogies to explain something unknown in a familiar, concrete way. Analogies can help you better understand and visualize difficult or unfamiliar ideas. As you read, notice how the author adds sections about the La Brea Tar Pits to her story. Ask yourself, how is the information about the tar pits similar to the narrator's life?

Reading Strategy Draw Conclusions About Characters

When you **draw conclusions,** you use pieces of information to make a general statement about characters, events, or ideas. You use clues that the author gives you and your own knowledge and experience. Drawing conclusions can help you understand why characters act or think certain ways. To draw conclusions about a character:

- Notice details about the character, including his or her personality traits, actions, appearance, and feelings.

- Think about what these clues tell you that the author may not state directly. Use the clues to make a general statement about the character.

Use a graphic organizer like the one below to help you keep track of your thoughts about each character in the story.

Character:	Clues About the Character	What These Clues Mean
Personality Traits		
Actions		
Physical Descriptions		
Thoughts and Feelings		
	My Conclusions	

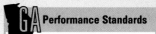

Performance Standards

For pages 608–623

ELA7R2c Understand and acquire new vocabulary. Identify and explain idioms and analogies in prose and poetry.

TRY IT

Draw Conclusions With a partner, think of a memorable character from a book, television show, or movie. What clues most help you understand this character? What can you conclude about the character from his or her thoughts and actions? Explain.

HOLLYWOOD AND THE PITS

Cherylene Lee

In 1968 when I was fifteen, the pit opened its secret to me. I breathed, ate, slept, dreamed about the La Brea[1] Tar Pits. I spent summer days working the archaeological dig[2] and in dreams saw the bones glistening, the broken pelvises, the skulls, the vertebrae looped like a woman's pearls hanging on an invisible cord. I welcomed those dreams. I wanted to know where the next skeleton was, identify it, record its position, discover whether it was whole or not. I wanted to know where to dig in the coarse, black, gooey sand. I lost myself there and found something else.

My mother thought something was wrong with me. Was it good for a teenager to be fascinated by death? Especially animal death in the Pleistocene?[3] Was it normal to be so obsessed[4] by a sticky brown hole in the ground in the center of Los Angeles? I don't know if it was normal or not, but it

---

1 **La Brea** (lə brā′ə)

2 An **archaeological** (är′ kē ə loj′ i kəl) **dig** is a place where objects such as ancient bones are dug up for study.

3 **Pleistocene** (plīs′ tə sēn′) is the name of the period that began about two million years ago, when glaciers covered much of North America and Europe.

4 **Obsessed** means "overly concentrated or focused on a single emotion or idea."

seemed perfectly logical to me. After all, I grew up in Hollywood, a place where dreams and nightmares can often take the same shape. What else would a child actor do? "Thank you very much, dear. We'll be letting you know."

I knew what that meant. It meant I would never hear from them again. I didn't get the job. I heard that phrase a lot that year.

I walked out of the plush office, leaving behind the casting director, producer, director, writer, and whoever else came to listen to my reading for a semiregular role on a family sit-com.[5] The carpet made no sound when I opened and shut the door.

I passed the other girls waiting in the reception room, each poring over her script. The mothers were waiting in a separate room, chattering about their daughters' latest commercials, interviews, callbacks, jobs. It sounded like every Oriental[6] kid in Hollywood was working except me.

My mother used to have a lot to say in those waiting rooms. Ever since I was three, when I started at the Meglin Kiddie Dance Studio, I was dubbed "The Chinese Shirley Temple"—always the one to be picked at auditions and interviews, always the one to get the speaking lines, always called "the one-shot kid," because I could do my scenes in one take—even tight close-ups. My mother would only talk about me behind my back because she didn't want me to hear her brag, but I knew that she was proud. In a way I was proud too, though I never dared admit it. I didn't want to be called a show-off. But I didn't exactly know what I did to be proud of either. I only knew that at fifteen I was now being passed over at all these interviews when before I would be chosen.

My mother looked at my face hopefully when I came into the room. I gave her a quick shake of the head. She looked bewildered.[7] I felt bad for my mother then. How could I explain it to her? I didn't understand it myself. We left saying polite good-byes to all the other mothers.

Draw Conclusions About Characters How do you think the narrator feels after leaving the office?

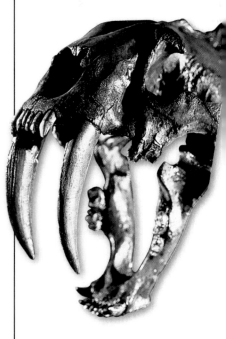

---

5 **Sit-com** is short for "situation comedy," the most common type of TV comedy series.

6 In the past, people of eastern Asia and their descendants were sometimes referred to as **Oriental**, which means "of the East."

7 Someone who is **bewildered** is very confused.

We didn't say anything until the studio parking lot, where we had to search for our old blue Chevy among rows and rows of parked cars baking in the Hollywood heat.

"How did it go? Did you read clearly? Did you tell them you're available?"

"I don't think they care if I'm available or not, Ma."

"Didn't you read well? Did you remember to look up so they could see your eyes? Did they ask you if you could play the piano? Did you tell them you could learn?"

The barrage[8] of questions stopped when we finally spotted our car. I didn't answer her. My mother asked about the piano because I lost out in an audition once to a Chinese girl who already knew how to play.

My mother took off the towel that shielded the steering wheel from the heat. "You're getting to be such a big girl," she said, starting the car in neutral. "But don't worry, there's always next time. You have what it takes. That's special." She put the car into forward and we drove through a parking lot that had an endless number of identical cars all facing the same direction. We drove back home in silence.

In the La Brea Tar Pits many of the **excavated** *bones belong to juvenile mammals. Thousands of years ago thirsty young animals in the area were drawn to watering holes, not knowing they were traps. Those inviting pools had false bottoms made of sticky tar, which* **immobilized** *its victims and preserved their bones when they died. Innocence trapped by ignorance. The tar pits record that well.*

I suppose a lot of my getting into show business in the first place was a matter of luck—being in the right place at the right time. My sister, seven years older than me, was a member of the Meglin Kiddie Dance Studio long before I started lessons. Once during the annual recital held at the Shrine Auditorium, she was spotted by a Hollywood agent

Draw Conclusions About Characters What impressions do you have so far of the narrator's mother?

Analogy In what way might the tar pits reflect the narrator's experience as a child actor?

---

8 A **barrage** is a heavy concentration or great outpouring, as of words.

excavated (eks′kə vāt′əd) *adj.* uncovered or removed by digging; unearthed

immobilized (i mō′bə līzd′) *v.* made unable to move; fixed in place

who handled only Oriental performers. The agent sent my sister out for a role in the CBS *Playhouse 90* television show *The Family Nobody Wanted*. The producer said she was too tall for the part. But true to my mother's training of always having a positive reply, my sister said to the producer, "But I have a younger sister . . ." which started my show-biz career at the tender age of three.

My sister and I were lucky. We enjoyed singing and dancing, we were natural hams, and our parents never discouraged us. In fact they were our biggest fans. My mother chauffeured us to all our dance lessons, lessons we begged to take. She drove us to interviews, took us to studios, went on location with us, drilled us on our lines, made sure we kept up our schoolwork and didn't sass back the tutors hired by studios to teach us for three hours a day. She never complained about being a stage mother. She said that we made her proud.

My father must have felt pride too, because he paid for a choreographer[9] to put together our sister act: "The World Famous Lee Sisters," fifteen minutes of song and dance,

Draw Conclusions About Characters Is the narrator's mother being helpful, or does she have other reasons for being involved in her daughters' show-business career?

---

9 A *choreographer* creates or directs dance movements.

As a child, Cherylene Lee performed with some of the great Hollywood entertainers. Here, she's seen with dancer Gene Kelly.

real vaudeville stuff. We joked about that a lot, "Yeah, the Lee Sisters— Ug-Lee and Home-Lee," but we definitely had a good time. So did our parents. Our father especially liked our getting booked into Las Vegas at the New Frontier Hotel on the Strip. He liked to gamble there, though he said the craps tables in that hotel were "cold," not like the casinos in downtown Las Vegas, where all the "hot" action took place.

In Las Vegas our sister act was part of a show called "Oriental Holiday." The show was about a Hollywood producer going to the Far East, finding undiscovered talent, and bringing it back to the U.S. We did two shows a night in the main showroom, one at eight and one at twelve, and on weekends a third show at two in the morning. It ran the entire summer often to standing-room-only audiences—a thousand people a show.

Our sister act worked because of the age and height difference. My sister then was fourteen and nearly five foot two; I was seven and very small for my age—people thought we were cute. We had song-and-dance routines to old tunes like "Ma, He's Making Eyes at Me," "Together," and "I'm Following You," and my father hired a writer to adapt the lyrics to "I Enjoy Being a Girl," which came out "We Enjoy Being Chinese." We also told corny jokes, but the Las Vegas audience seemed to enjoy it. Here we were, two kids, staying up late and jumping around, and getting paid besides. To me the applause sometimes sounded like static, sometimes like distant waves. It always amazed me when people applauded. The owner of the hotel liked us so much, he invited us back to perform in shows for three summers in a row. That was before I grew too tall and the sister act didn't seem so cute anymore.

Draw Conclusions About Characters How did the narrator feel about performing when she was younger?

Many of the skeletons in the tar pits are found incomplete—particularly the skeletons of the young, which have only soft cartilage connecting the bones. In life the soft tissue allows for growth, but in death it dissolves quickly. Thus the skeletons of young animals are more apt to be scattered, especially the vertebrae protecting the spinal cord. In the tar pits, the central ends of many vertebrae are found unconnected to any skeleton. Such bone fragments are shaped like valentines, disks that are slightly lobed—heart-shaped shields that have lost their connection to what they were meant to protect.

Analogy How do the scattered skeletons and bone fragments relate to what is happening in the narrator's life?

I never felt my mother pushed me to do something I didn't want to do. But I always knew if something I did pleased her. She was generous with her praise, and I was sensitive when she withheld it. I didn't like to disappoint her.

I took to performing easily, and since I had started out so young, making movies or doing shows didn't feel like anything special. It was part of my childhood—like going to the dentist one morning or going to school the next. I didn't wonder if I wanted a particular role or wanted to be in a show or how I would feel if I didn't get in. Until I was fifteen, it never occurred to me that one day I wouldn't get parts or that I might not "have what it takes."

When I was younger, I got a lot of roles because I was so small for my age. When I was nine years old, I could pass for five or six. I was really short. I was always teased about it when I was in elementary school, but I didn't mind because my height got me movie jobs. I could read and memorize lines that actual five-year-olds couldn't. My mother told people she made me sleep in a drawer so I wouldn't grow any bigger.

But when I turned fifteen, it was as if my body, which hadn't grown for so many years, suddenly made up for lost time. I grew five inches in seven months. My mother was amazed. Even I couldn't get used to it. I kept knocking into things, my clothes didn't fit right, I felt awkward and clumsy when I moved. Dumb things that I had gotten away with, like paying children's prices at the movies instead of junior admission, I couldn't do anymore. I wasn't a shrimp or a small fry any longer. I was suddenly normal.

Draw Conclusions About Characters How is the narrator adjusting to growing up?

Before that summer my mother had always claimed she wanted me to be normal. She didn't want me to become spoiled by the attention I received when I was working at the studios. I still had chores to do at home, went to public school when I wasn't working, was punished severely when I behaved badly. She didn't want me to feel I was different just because I was in the movies. When I was eight, I was interviewed by a reporter who wanted to know if I thought I had a big head.

"Sure," I said.

"No you don't," my mother interrupted, which was really unusual, because she generally never said anything. She wanted me to speak for myself.

I didn't understand the question. My sister had always made fun of my head. She said my body was too tiny for the weight—I looked like a walking Tootsie Pop. I thought the reporter was making the same observation.

"She better not get that way," my mother said fiercely. "She's not any different from anyone else. She's just lucky and small for her age."

The reporter turned to my mother, "Some parents push their children to act. The kids feel like they're used."

"I don't do that—I'm not that way," my mother told the reporter.

Draw Conclusions About Characters Based on what you've read, is the narrator's mother being truthful?

But when she was sitting silently in all those waiting rooms while I was being turned down for one job after another, I could almost feel her wanting to shout, "Use her. Use her. What is wrong with her? Doesn't she have it anymore?" I didn't know what I had had that I didn't seem to have anymore. My mother had told the reporter that I was like everyone else. But when my life was like everyone else's, why was she disappointed?

The churning action of the La Brea Tar Pits makes interpreting the record of past events extremely difficult. The usual order of deposition—the oldest on the bottom, the youngest on the top—loses all meaning when some of the oldest fossils can be brought to the surface by the movement of natural gas. One must look for an undisturbed spot, a place untouched by the action of underground springs or natural gas or human interference. Complete skeletons become important, because they indicate areas of least disturbance. But such spots of calm are rare. Whole blocks of the tar pit can become displaced, making false sequences of the past, skewing the interpretation[10] for what is the true order of nature.

Analogy How does the description of the displaced fossils compare to the narrator's feelings about her life?

That year before my sixteenth birthday, my mother seemed to spend a lot of time looking through my old scrapbooks, staring at all the eight-by-ten glossies of the shows that I had done. In the summer we visited with my grandmother often, since I wasn't working and had lots of free time. I would go out to the garden to read or sunbathe, but I could hear my mother and grandmother talking.

"She was so cute back then. She worked with Gene Kelly when she was five years old. She was so smart for her age. I don't know what's wrong with her."

"She's fifteen."

"She's too young to be an ingenue[11] and too old to be cute. The studios forget so quickly. By the time she's old enough to play an ingenue, they won't remember her."

"Does she have to work in the movies? Hand me the scissors."

Draw Conclusions About Characters What is the narrator's grandmother suggesting about the narrator's future?

My grandmother was making false eyelashes using the hair from her hairbrush. When she was young she had incredible hair. I saw an old photograph of her when it flowed beyond her waist like a cascading black waterfall. At seventy, her hair was still black as night, which made her few strands of silver look like shooting stars. But her hair had thinned greatly with age. It sometimes fell out in clumps. She wore it brushed back in a bun with a hairpiece for added fullness. My grandmother had always been proud of her hair, but once she started making false eyelashes from it, she wasn't proud of the way it looked anymore. She said she was proud of it now because it made her useful.

---

10 ***Skewing the interpretation*** is twisting it so that it is wrong or off the mark.

11 An ***ingenue*** (än´jə no͞o´) is an actress who plays innocent, inexperienced young women.

It was **painstaking** work—tying knots into strands of hair, then tying them together to form feathery little crescents. Her glamorous false eyelashes were much sought after. Theatrical make-up artists waited months for her work. But my grandmother said what she liked was that she was doing something, making a contribution, and besides it didn't cost her anything. No overhead. "Till I go bald," she often joked.

She tried to teach me her art that summer, but for some reason strands of my hair wouldn't stay tied in knots.

"Too springy," my grandmother said. "Your hair is still too young." And because I was frustrated[12] then, frustrated with everything about my life, she added, "You have to wait until your hair falls out, like mine. Something to look forward to, eh?" She had laughed and patted my hand.

My mother was going on and on about my lack of work, what might be wrong, that something she couldn't quite put her finger on. I heard my grandmother reply, but I didn't catch it all: "Movies are just make-believe, not real life. Like what I make with my hair that falls out—false. False eyelashes. Not meant to last."

*The remains in the La Brea Tar Pits are mostly of carnivorous animals. Very few herbivores are found—the ratio is five to one, a perversion of the natural food chain. The ratio is easy to explain. Thousands of years ago a thirsty animal sought a drink from the pools of water only to find itself trapped by the bottom, gooey with subterranean[13] oil. A shriek of agony from the trapped victim drew flesh-eating **predators**, which were then trapped themselves by the very same ooze which provided the bait. The cycle repeated itself countless times. The number of victims grew, lured by the image of easy food, the **deception** of*

> **Draw Conclusions About Characters** What is the grandmother trying to tell the narrator?

---

12 To be *frustrated* is to be kept from doing something or achieving some goal.

13 *Carnivorous* animals eat meat; *herbivores* eat mainly plants. The remains in the pits are a *perversion* because they give a false picture of reality. *Subterranean* means *underground*.

Vocabulary ....

painstaking (pānz′ tā′ king) *adj.* requiring close, careful labor or attention

predators (pred′ ə tərz) *n.* animals that kill other animals for food

deception (di sep′ shən) *n.* that which fools or misleads

an easy kill. The animals piled on top of one another. For over ten thousand years the promise of the place drew animals of all sorts, mostly predators and scavengers[14]*—dire wolves, panthers, coyotes, vultures—all hungry for their chance. Most were sucked down against their will in those watering holes destined to be called the La Brea Tar Pits in a place to be named the City of Angels, home of Hollywood movie stars.*

I spent a lot of time by myself that summer, wondering what it was that I didn't have anymore. Could I get it back? How could I if I didn't know what it was?

That's when I discovered the La Brea Tar Pits. Hidden behind the County Art Museum on trendy[15] Wilshire Boulevard, I found a job that didn't require me to be small or cute for my age. I didn't have to audition. No one said, "Thank you very much, we'll call you." Or if they did, they meant it. I volunteered my time one afternoon, and my fascination stuck—like tar on the bones of a **saber-toothed tiger.**

My mother didn't understand what had changed me. I didn't understand it myself. But I liked going to the La Brea Tar Pits. It meant I could get really messy and I was doing it with a purpose. I didn't feel awkward there. I could wear old stained pants. I could wear T-shirts with holes in them. I could wear disgustingly filthy sneakers and it was all perfectly justified. It wasn't a costume for a role in a film or a part in a TV sit-com. My mother didn't mind my dressing like that when she knew I was off to the pits. That was okay so long as I didn't track tar back into the house. I started going to the pits every day, and my mother wondered why. She couldn't believe I would rather be groveling[16] in tar than going on auditions or interviews.

While my mother wasn't proud of the La Brea Tar Pits (she didn't know or care what a fossil was), she didn't discourage me either. She drove me there, the same way she used to drive me to the studios.

---

14 A *scavenger* is an animal, such as a hyena or vulture, that feeds on dead, decaying animals.

15 *Trendy* describes what is currently popular. Wilshire Boulevard has many trendy shops, stores, and restaurants.

16 *Groveling* is lying or crawling facedown on the ground in a timid or fearful manner.

Analogy In what way might this description of the tar pits compare with Hollywood's movie industry?

A **saber-toothed tiger** was a predator in the cat family that had strong limbs, a muscular body, and a short tail.

"Wouldn't you rather be doing a show in Las Vegas than scrambling around in a pit?" she asked.

"I'm not in a show in Las Vegas, Ma. The Lee Sisters are retired." My older sister had married and was starting a family of her own.

"But if you could choose between . . . "

"There isn't a choice."

"You really like this tar-pit stuff, or are you just waiting until you can get real work in the movies?"

I didn't answer.

My mother sighed. "You could do it if you wanted, if you really wanted. You still have what it takes."

I didn't know about that. But then, I couldn't explain what drew me to the tar pits either. Maybe it was the bones, finding out what they were, which animal they belonged to, imagining how they got there, how they fell into the trap. I wondered about that a lot.

At the La Brea Tar Pits, everything dug out of the pit is saved— including the sticky sand that covered the bones through the ages. Each bucket of sand is washed, sieved, and examined for

Draw Conclusions About Characters Why do you think the narrator chooses the tar pits instead of show business?

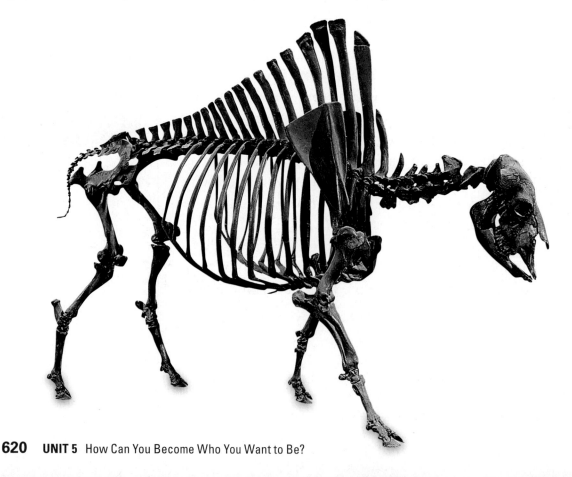

pollen grains, insect remains, any evidence of past life. Even the grain size is recorded—the percentage of silt to sand to gravel that reveals the history of deposition, erosion, and disturbance. No single fossil, no one observation, is significant enough to tell the entire story. All the evidence must be weighed before a semblance[17] of truth emerges.

The tar pits had its lessons. I was learning I had to work slowly, become observant, to concentrate. I learned about time in a way that I would never experience—not in hours, days, and months, but in thousands and thousands of years. I imagined what the past must have been like, envisioned Los Angeles as a sweeping basin, perhaps slightly colder and more humid, a time before people and studios arrived. The tar pits recorded a warming trend; the kinds of animals found there reflected the changing climate. The ones unadapted disappeared. No trace of their kind was found in the area. The ones adapted to warmer weather left a record of bones in the pit. Amid that collection of ancient skeletons, surrounded by evidence of death, I was finding a secret preserved over thousands and thousands of years. There was something cruel about natural selection and the survival of the fittest.[18] Even those successful individuals that "had what it took" for adaptation still wound up in the pits.

I never found out if I had what it took, not the way my mother meant. But I did adapt to the truth: I wasn't a Chinese Shirley Temple any longer, cute and short for my age. I had grown up. Maybe not on a Hollywood movie set, but in the La Brea Tar Pits. &

Life-size replicas of extinct mammals at the La Brea Tar Pits show visitors how the area's soft tar trapped Ice Age animals.

BQ **BIG Question**

Through her work in the tar pits, what is the narrator learning about herself?

---

17 A ***semblance*** of truth would be the slightest likeness of truth.

18 ***Natural selection and the survival of the fittest*** is the theory that plants and animals best suited to their environment tend to survive and pass on their characteristics to their offspring.

After You Read

Respond and Think Critically

1. What begins to happen to the narrator's show-business career after she turns fifteen? [Recall]

2. How did animals from thousands of years ago end up in the La Brea Tar Pits? [Summarize]

3. The narrator describes Hollywood as "a place where dreams and nightmares can often take the same shape." What does she mean? [Interpret]

4. How does the narrator feel about the change in her Hollywood career? Explain. [Analyze]

5. How does the narrator's relationship with her mother change throughout the story? [Analyze]

6. **BQ** BIG Question In what way is working in the tar pits a positive action for the narrator? [Evaluate]

TIP

Interpreting
Here are some tips to help you answer question 3.

- Recall what you know about Hollywood.

- Consider how the career of a Hollywood actor can change.

- Think about how Hollywood experiences might affect an actor's or performer's life.

 Keep track of your ideas about the **BIG Question** in your unit Foldable.

Connect to Science

Fossils in the La Brea Tar Pits

Scientists have collected more than one million bones from the La Brea Tar Pits. Fossils from hundreds of species of animals, plants, and other organisms have been excavated.

The fossils in the pits are well preserved partly because animal bones and other remains were buried so quickly. It took from a few weeks to two years for bones to be completely buried. Some bones have marks showing that they were exposed to changing temperatures, rodents, and erosion from water and wind.

Small items such as shells, tiny bones, insects, and plant remains are called *microfossils.* These tiny fossils can provide a great deal of information. For example, microfossils of wood, leaves, cones, and seeds indicate that the area's climate 40,000 years ago was not much different from that of the present day.

Group Activity Discuss the following questions with classmates.

1. Why are fossils from the tar pits so well preserved?

2. What natural events affected animal bones as they became fossils?

3. What can you learn from microfossils?

Literary Element | Analogy

1. Why is the story of the narrator's life interrupted from time to time with factual information about the tar pits?

2. Reread the description of the narrator's mother looking at old scrapbooks. Then reread the description of tar pits that appears just before the description of the scrapbooks. In what ways are the scrapbooks and the collections of fossils alike?

Review: Symbol

As you learned on page 420, a **symbol** is any object, person, place, or experience that stands for more than what it is. Authors use symbols in stories to add meaning and emphasize the theme, or a message about life that the author wants to express.

3. Recall the statement "Innocence trapped by ignorance" from the story. How does this phrase reflect Lee's use of symbolism in the story? Explain.

4. In what way might the grandmother's hair symbolize the narrator?

Reading Strategy
Draw Conclusions About Characters

Standards Practice **GA** ELA7R1b

5. Which statement accurately explains why the narrator enjoys working in the tar pits?
   A   Her mother encourages her to work there.
   B   The work is important and interesting.
   C   She can work with other people.
   D   She is able to use scientific tools.

Vocabulary Practice

Identify whether the words in each set have the same or the opposite meaning. Then write a sentence using each vocabulary word, or draw or find a picture that represents the word.

excavated and buried
immobilized and paralyzed
painstaking and uncomplicated
predators and hunters
deception and honesty

Example:
excavated and buried = opposite meaning

Sentence: Scientists collected hundreds of excavated animal bones and other fossils during the dig.

Academic Vocabulary

Many of the animals that were capable of **adaptation** still ended up in the tar pits. In the preceding sentence, *adaptation* means "the ability to change." Think about how you have changed in the last few years. What adaptations have you made?

Literature Online

Selection Resources For Selection Quizzes, eFlashcards, and Reading-Writing Connection activities, go to glencoe.com and enter QuickPass code GL27534u5.

Respond Through Writing

Expository Essay

Compare and Contrast Point of View In "Hollywood and the Pits," Cherylene Lee mixes styles of writing and points of view. In a short essay, compare and contrast the two points of view in the story. Your essay's audience, or readers, will be your teacher or classmates.

Understand the Task **Point of view** refers to the relationship of the narrator to the story. In this story, the narrator shares her experiences through first-person point of view. The story also has factual, third-person descriptions of the La Brea Tar Pits. When you **compare and contrast,** you examine similarities and differences.

Prewrite Using a chart like the one below, list the qualities of both types of writing found in Lee's story. Write about the similarities and differences in the style and tone in each point of view. Why did Lee choose these two approaches? How do they affect the story's theme?

The Narrator's Story	Tar Pit Descriptions
first-person point of view	third-person point of view
personal details	factual, scientific

Draft Before you begin drafting, make a plan. Consider organizing your essay so that you compare and contrast common elements. For example, one paragraph may compare and contrast the two points of view, and another paragraph may compare and contrast the two styles. Support your ideas and statements with evidence and details from the story.

Revise After you have written your draft, read it to determine whether the paragraphs follow a logical order. Be sure you have an introductory and a concluding paragraph. Rearrange text and add transitional sentences as necessary to make sure that your ideas are easy to follow. You may use a dictionary and a thesaurus to check your choice of words.

Edit and Proofread Proofread your paper, correcting any errors in spelling, grammar, and punctuation. Review the Grammar Tip in the side column for information on using dashes.

GA Performance Standards

For page 624

ELA7W1c Use traditional structures for conveying information.

▶ **Grammar Tip**

Dashes
Dashes are one way to show an interruption in a sentence. Writers may use this break in thought to define a term, provide an example, or add a comment. Dashes stand out, so they emphasize the information or point. For example:

The movie industry and the tar pits—two unrelated ideas—come together in "Hollywood and the Pits."

In typed papers, hit the hyphen key twice to make a dash. In handwritten papers, a dash is simply a longer hyphen.

Media Workshop

Media Ethics

The United States Constitution guarantees freedom of the press. Although free from most government regulations, print and broadcast journalists hold themselves to certain agreed-upon standards. When producing media, journalists must behave ethically. They must not engage in libel, slander, or plagiarism, and they must follow copyright laws.

Plagiarism, especially, is an unethical practice which should never be engaged in by journalists or by anyone else. Copyright laws and laws against plagiarism help protect a person's words and ideas. Journalists work hard to research, write, and produce their stories; copyright laws ensure that journalists are credited and paid for the reproduction of their work. There are legal consequences for plagiarism. There are also personal consequences. To avoid engaging in plagiarism, it's important to properly credit others for their ideas. For readers, it's important to remember that the ideas and facts presented in a work should be properly sourced and supported.

The chart below provides definitions of libel, slander, copyright violation, and plagiarism. When using sources, it is important to avoid any behavior resembling the behavior described in the examples.

Ethical Issue	What It Is	Example
Libel	false written or printed statement or image that harms a person's reputation	A reporter writes an article falsely accusing a presidential candidate of a crime.
Slander	verbal statement in front of a witness that harms the reputation of a third person	A radio newscaster states on the air that a celebrity has a disease that the celebrity does not have.
Copyright Violation	unauthorized publication, production, or sale of a written or visual work that legally belongs to someone else	A local television newscast uses a painting as part of its logo without the permission of the artist.
Plagiarism	act of representing another person's work as one's own	A reporter uses details and quotes from another reporter's article but takes credit for the work.

 Performance Standards

For page 625

ELA7LSV2b When responding to visual and oral texts and media, identify the techniques used to achieve the effects studied in each instance.

TRY IT

Analyze Media Ethics Suppose you need to create a public service announcement that encourages young people to vote. Write answers to the following ethics questions.

1. What must you do before you can quote a published poem in your announcement? Explain, using specific examples.

2. Can you use an idea you have seen in another public service announcement? Why or why not?

3. What facts and statistics must you include if you want to claim that some local leaders did not vote in the last few elections?

 Literature Online

Media Literacy For project ideas, templates, and media analysis guides, go to glencoe.com and enter QuickPass code GL27534u5.

Before You Read

Young Arthur

Connect to the Legend

Think about a time when a friend, relative, coach, or other person expected a great deal of you. What happened? How did you feel?

Graphic Organizer In a web like the one below, describe the feelings you have when much is expected of you.

"Great Expectations"

How I feel about expectations

How I feel about my potential

Build Background

Historians have not found evidence proving that a King Arthur existed. Still, stories about Arthur and his Knights of the Round Table have been told since the sixth century A.D. All together, these stories are known as the Arthurian legend.

- According to legend, after Arthur pulled the sword from the stone, he became king of England.
- King Arthur ruled from the castle Camelot.
- Famous books written about Arthur include Sir Thomas Malory's *Le Morte d'Arthur* (1485) and T. H. White's *The Once and Future King* (1958).

Vocabulary

melancholy (mel′ən kol′ē) *n.* sadness; depression (p. 629). *She was overwhelmed with melancholy after watching the sad movie.*

rebellion (ri bel′yən) *n.* uprising; organized resistance to government or another authority (p. 629). *The citizens planned a rebellion against their country's dictatorship.*

grievous (grē′vəs) *adj.* very serious (p. 630). *He fell from a ladder, but he avoided grievous injury.*

Meet Robert D. San Souci

"Books delighted and inspired me as a child—they continue to do so!"

—Robert D. San Souci

Bringing Folktales to Life
A picture book writer and a multiple award-winning author, Robert D. San Souci was born in San Francisco and continues to reside there today. Many of San Souci's books retell tales that bring to life the traditions of people and places around the world. His works include *Young Arthur, Cinderella Skeleton,* and *The Faithful Friend.*

San Souci was born in 1946.

 Literature Online

Author Search For more about Robert D. San Souci, go to glencoe.com and enter QuickPass code GL27534u5.

Set Purposes for Reading

BQ BIG Question

As you read, notice Arthur's positive actions. Ask yourself, how will Arthur's actions help him become the leader he is meant to be?

Literary Element Legend

A **legend** is a story that relates amazing events or accomplishments. The heroes in legends may be humans, animals, or even enchanted objects or forces of nature. Like folktales and myths, legends belong to the **oral tradition.** They are passed by word of mouth from one generation to the next. Some legendary human heroes actually lived, but over the years their reputations grew larger than life.

Legends often express the values of a culture. In "Young Arthur," for example, Arthur shows honor and courage. As you read, look for amazing events and larger-than-life characters. Ask yourself, what beliefs and values are important to the characters in the legend?

Reading Skill Make Generalizations About Characters

When you **make generalizations,** you form conclusions based on specific examples, ideas, or anecdotes in a text. When you make generalizations about characters, you use the details that the author gives you to form a general idea or conclusion about the characters.

Making generalizations can help you better understand characters and can also help you relate universal themes and ideas to a text. To make generalizations about characters,

- pay close attention to details about the characters
- think about what you already know about how people behave
- connect what the author tells you with what you already know

Then make a generalization about the characters. Use a graphic organizer like the one below to record your ideas.

What the Author Tells Me	What I Already Know	Generalization
Arthur is four years younger than his brother Kay. Arthur gets bruises and cuts at his lessons.		

Performance Standards

For pages 626–635

ELA7R1i For literary texts, identify and analyze similarities and differences in traditional literature from different cultures.

TRY IT

Make Generalizations Suppose that your friend and his younger brother were given a new video game system. Based on what you know about your friend and his brother, what generalization can you make about how well they will share the game?

Young Arthur

Court of Uther, c1470-c1480. Uther was the father of King Arthur. From "Premier volume des anchiennes et nouvelles croniques dangleterre". Roy 15 E IV. Folio No: 134 (detail). British Library, London.

Robert D. San Souci

King Uther[1] heard the baby's wail and leaped to his feet. There was a sharp rap at the chamber door, and a servant entered grinning happily. "You have a son," he told the king. Uther's joy knew no bounds. When he was ushered into Queen Igerna's[2] bedchamber, Uther looked lovingly at mother and son. "The boy's name shall be Arthur," he declared, "and he shall be a great king. For Merlin [the magician][3] has foretold that he will one day rule the greatest kingdom under heaven."

Legend In what way is Merlin's prediction characteristic of a legend?

---

1 In Arthurian legend, **Uther** Pendragon was an early king of Britain.

2 **Igerna** was Uther Pendragon's queen.

3 **Merlin** the magician is a major character in Arthurian legend. He usually appears as an elderly man who can see the future and who uses magic to guide and protect King Arthur.

But Uther's happiness did not last. His beloved queen died soon after Arthur's birth, and sadness sapped the king's spirit. He lost interest in ruling, and Merlin was unable to rouse him from his **melancholy.** "Unrest grows throughout the land," Merlin warned. "Your old foes are rising in **rebellion.** Give the babe into my keeping, for you have enemies even at court."

Anxious for his son's safety, Uther agreed. So Merlin, disguised as a beggar, took the infant Arthur to Sir Ector and his lady, who lived some distance from the court and all its dangers. He told them nothing about the child, save that his name was Arthur. The couple had recently lost their infant son and welcomed Arthur as their own. Soon rebellion divided the kingdom. Uther, reclaiming his old spirit, rallied[4] his knights and barons. With Merlin always beside him, he drove back his enemies.

But as Uther celebrated his victory in the town of Verulum, traitors poisoned the town's wells. The king and his loyal followers were stricken.[5] Merlin alone escaped. Though he tried his healing arts on Uther, he was forced to confess, "Sire, there is no remedy."

"Then," said the dying monarch, "I declare that my son shall be king of all this realm[6] after me. God's blessing and mine be upon him." With these words, Uther died.

When the rebels entered Verulum, only Merlin was alive.

"Tell us where Uther's son is hidden," they demanded, "so that we can slay him and end Uther's line."

Pippo Spano (1369–1426) from the Villa Carducci series of Famous Men and Women, c. 1450. Andrea del Castagno. Fresco.

---

4 **Reclaiming** means "getting back or recovering something that was lost." **Rallied** means "gathered together for action."

5 Here, **stricken** means "afflicted or overcome by disease or illness."

6 A **realm** is a kingdom.

Vocabulary
....

melancholy (mel′ən kol′ē) *n.* sadness; depression

rebellion (ri bel′yən) *n.* uprising; organized resistance to government or another authority

But Merlin vanished before their eyes.

Young Arthur was raised as a son in Sir Ector's house. He learned to read and write alongside his foster brother, Kay, who was four years older. By the time he was fifteen, Arthur was a tall, handsome, quick-witted lad. Though he had great strength, he also had a gentle manner.

Kay, who had recently been knighted,[7] decided to train Arthur in the knightly arts himself. But Kay was vain and jealous of the favor Arthur found with their father, so he was a harsh taskmaster. Arthur came away from his lessons in swordsmanship with many bruises and cuts. When he complained, Kay replied, "A knight must be thick-skinned and ready to bear even **grievous** wounds without flinching." Yet if Arthur so much as pricked his brother, Kay would bellow loudly for the physician.

Eventually Kay appointed Arthur his apprentice. This was an honor the younger boy would happily have forgone.[8] However, seeing that Sir Ector wished it so, Arthur sighed and agreed. But he felt in his heart that he already was a knight, though no lord had dubbed[9] him such.

Both Arthur and Kay knew it was vital to learn the arts of war. The kingdom was still at the mercy of upstart lords[10] who ruled by fire and sword.

The story of Uther's lost son, the true heir to the throne, would have been forgotten but for Merlin. One Christmas Eve, the long-absent magician reappeared and summoned the bishops, lords, and common folk to London's square. There he drove a **broadsword** halfway into a huge stone. Written on the blade in blazing gold letters were the words: "Whoso pulleth out the sword from this stone is born the rightful King of England."

---

7 A person who is **knighted** is given special status as a knight, or soldier, after a long period of training.

8 An **apprentice** is a person working under a skilled person to learn a trade, or in this case, how to be a knight. A person who has **forgone** something has willingly gone without it.

9 When someone is **dubbed** a knight, that person is formally given the title of knight.

10 **Upstart lords** are newly powerful and self-important.

Vocabulary ....

grievous (grē′vəs) *adj.* very serious

Make Generalizations About Characters How would you expect Arthur and Kay to get along?

Legend In what way is the sword in the stone unusual?

....

Visual Vocabulary

A **broadsword** is a sword with a broad, flat blade, used for cutting rather than thrusting.

....

In the days that followed, knights and barons, cowherds and bakers, an endless parade of would-be kings eagerly pulled at the sword. But none could loosen it, let alone draw it forth.

When they accused Merlin of trickery, he said, "The rightful king has not yet come. God will make him known at the proper time."

Now it happened that a great tournament was held in London. Among those who came were Sir Ector, Sir Kay, and young Arthur, who served Kay. So eager was the boy to see the jousts[11] that he forgot to pack Kay's sword. There was great upset when the mistake was discovered.

"Woe to you, boy," snarled Kay, "if your error costs me the victory I would otherwise win today!"

Even Sir Ector scolded Arthur and ordered, "Go back directly and fetch the missing sword."

Angry at his carelessness and impatient to see the contests, Arthur started homeward. Then he suddenly reined in his horse.

In the deserted city square was a massive stone with a sword plunged into its center. "Surely that sword is as good as the one left at home," he said. "I will borrow it. When Kay is finished, I will return it to this curious monument."

So saying, he dismounted,[12] scrambled up the stone, took the sword handle, and tugged. The sword did not move. Impatient to return to the tournament, he pulled again. This time, the sword slid easily out of the stone. In his haste, he did not notice the words upon the blade. Shoving the weapon into his belt, he remounted and raced to where Sir Kay waited his turn upon the field.

Merlin the Magician, c. 1352. Ms. Add. Meladius, 12228, fol. 202v.

BQ BIG Question

In what way might Arthur's actions affect his future?

---

11 *Jousts* were events at *tournaments,* or medieval sporting events, in which pairs of knights on horseback engaged in combat.

12 When Arthur *dismounted,* he got down from his horse.

The moment he saw the golden words upon the blade, Kay began to tremble with excitement. When Arthur asked what was amiss,[13] Kay shouted, "Go! Get away! You have caused enough trouble."

But Arthur was curious. So he followed as Kay ran to Sir Ector. "Look, Father!" cried Kay. "Here is the sword of the stone. Therefore, it is I who must be king of all this land!"

When Sir Ector and the others saw the sword and read the golden inscription,[14] they began to shout, "The sword from the stone! The king's sword!"

Hearing only this much, Arthur thought that he had stolen a king's weapon. As people hurried excitedly toward Kay, Arthur spurred his horse away, certain he had committed a great crime.

Looking back, he saw Kay and Sir Ector ride off, surrounded by the greatest lords of the realm. Were they taking Kay to trial? he wondered. Had he brought ruin upon Sir Ector's household?

"A true knight would not run away," he said to himself, "and I am a true knight in my heart." Fearful, but determined to do what was right, the boy wheeled his horse around.

The great square was now filled with people. Just how terrible a crime had he committed?

Upon the stone stood Kay, holding the sword. The crowd shouted each time he held the blade aloft. Then silence fell over the throng: Merlin had appeared at the edge of the square. People stood aside to let the magician approach the stone.

"Are you the one who pulled the sword from the stone?" Merlin asked.

"I am holding it, am I not?" Kay replied.

"The rightful king could pull it free a hundred times," said Merlin. "Slip the sword into the groove and pull it out again."

With a shrug, Kay reinserted the sword. But when he tried to jerk it free, it would not budge.

Make Generalizations About Characters Why do you think Kay tells Arthur to go away?

---

13 *Amiss* means "wrong."

14 An *inscription* is something written, carved, or engraved on a surface.

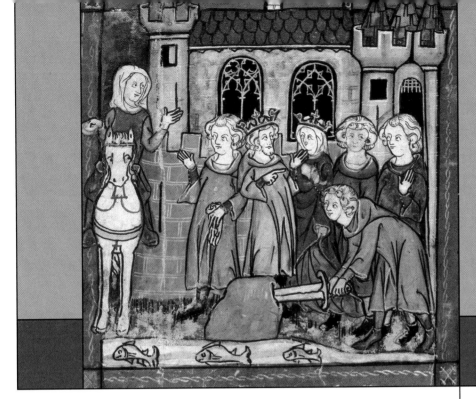

Arthur Pulling the Sword from the Stone. Shelfmark ID: Roy 14 E Folio No: 91 (detail)

Suddenly all eyes turned toward Arthur, who was pushing his way through the crowd, bellowing at the top of his lungs. "It wasn't Kay's fault! I brought him the sword!" Merlin peered closely at Arthur. Then he smiled and said, "Climb up and draw the sword from the stone." Uncertainly Arthur clambered up beside Kay. Grasping the pommel,[15] he easily pulled the sword out.

Then Merlin cried, "This is Arthur, son of Uther Pendragon, Britain's destined[16] king."

An astonished Sir Ector knelt to pay the boy homage,[17] followed by Kay and many others. But all around, there was growing confusion and dispute. Some cried, "It is the will of heaven! Long live the king!" while others cried, "It is Merlin's plot to put a beardless boy, a puppet, on the throne, and so rule the land."

[But] The cries of "Long Live King Arthur!" soon carried the day.

Make Generalizations About Characters From what you know about Arthur, why do you think he comes back to the square?

---

15 The *pommel* is the knob on the hilt, or handle, of a sword.

16 When a person's future is predetermined by known or unknown forces, that person is said to be *destined* to do or be something.

17 *Homage* is a showing of loyalty and respect.

After You Read

Respond and Think Critically

1. Who is Merlin? [Identify]

2. Use your own words to retell why Arthur is raised by Sir Ector. [Summarize]

3. Arthur believes that he is "a true knight in [his] heart." What does he mean by this? [Interpret]

4. Why is Arthur destined to be king? Use details from the story to explain your answer. [Infer]

5. What effect do Merlin's actions have on the plot? [Analyze]

6. **BQ** ❯ **BIG Question** It is Arthur's fate to be the king of England. In what ways do his actions help him become who he is meant to be? [Conclude]

Vocabulary Practice

On a separate sheet of paper, write the vocabulary word that correctly completes each sentence. If none of the words fits the sentence, write "none."

melancholy   rebellion   grievous

1. After the cruel king took away their lands and farms, the peasants were angry and started a _____.

2. After working so hard, I expected to be _____ for my efforts.

3. Some players on the team felt _____ after losing the big game.

4. When the computer programmer made a _____ mistake, the company's entire computer system crashed.

5. Her time is very _____, so do not waste it with foolish questions.

Academic Vocabulary ❯

When Merlin plunged the sword into the stone, no one could **anticipate** that Arthur would be the one to pull it out. In the preceding sentence, *anticipate* means "expect." *Anticipate* also has other meanings. For instance: Although Merlin was gifted at healing, he could not **anticipate** Uther's death. What do you think *anticipate* means in the preceding sentence? What is the difference between the two meanings?

TIP

Interpreting
To answer question 3, you must use your own understanding to determine what an idea in the story means. Here are some tips to help you interpret.

- The question asks about something Arthur tells himself. Scan the story and find the place in which Arthur says that he is a knight in his heart.

- Think about what you know about yourself and the world. What does it mean to know something in one's heart?

 Keep track of your ideas about the **BIG Question** in your unit Foldable.

 Literature Online

Selection Resources
For Selection Quizzes, eFlashcards, and Reading-Writing Connection activities, go to glencoe.com and enter QuickPass code GL27534u5.

Literary Element Legend

1. What elements in this story suggest that Arthur might have been a real person? What details suggest that he was not real? Explain.

2. How does this story illustrate the values of honor and courage? Use details to support your answer.

3. Why might people share this story from generation to generation?

Review: Motivation

As you learned on page 433, **motivation** is the reason that a character acts, feels, or thinks the way he or she does.

Standards Practice ELA7R1b

4. Based on the story, which sentence best explains why Merlin the magician drives the sword into the stone?
   A   He wants to help Sir Kay win the tournament.
   B   He intends to frighten people with his magic.
   C   He hopes to find out who is worthy of being king.
   D   He wants to prevent anyone except Arthur from becoming king.

Reading Skill
Make Generalizations About Characters

Standards Practice ELA7R1f

5. Which words best describe Arthur?
   A   bitter and vengeful
   B   bold and ambitious
   C   honorable and brave
   D   melancholy and lonely

Grammar Link

Subject-Verb Agreement Subject-verb agreement means choosing the verb form that matches, or agrees with, the subject.

If the subject is singular, the verb must also be singular. Most singular verbs end in -s.

   Kay <u>wants</u> to be king.

If the subject is plural, the verb must also be plural. Most plural verbs do not end in -s.

   Kay and Arthur <u>practice</u> fighting.

If the subject is *I* or *you,* most verbs do not end in -s.

   I <u>want</u> to read about King Arthur.

Practice Circle the subject and underline the verb. If the subject-verb agreement is incorrect, rewrite the sentence correctly.

1. Arthur gives Kay the sword.
2. The brothers loves their father.
3. You reads about medieval knights.

Research and Report

Internet Connection With a small group, use the Internet to research two legends from cultures other than that of England. Read the legends carefully. Ask yourself and your group members, what elements does this legend have in common with "Young Arthur"? Use a chart like the one below to keep track of the elements that the legends share.

Element	"Young Arthur"	Legend 1	Legend 2
brave, honorable hero	Arthur		

Medieval England

from Catherine, Called Birdy
by Karen Cushman

Newbery Medal

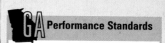
Performance Standards

For pages 636–639

ELA7R1c For literary texts, relate a literary work to information about its setting or historical moment.

Set a Purpose for Reading
Read this article to understand what life was like in thirteenth-century England.

Build Background
During the Middle Ages, people did not view themselves as free individuals who could choose their futures. One's place in society was passed down from generation to generation.

Reading Skill
Analyze Historical Context

To analyze the historical context of a text, gather background information about the time period to better understand the content and purpose of the text. As you read this article, think about how the information relates to the characters and events in "Young Arthur." Use a two-column chart like the one below to record your ideas.

"Young Arthur"	Historical Context
Uther rallied his knights and barons.	Barons and knights owed service to their landlords and king.

The England of 1290 is a foreign country. It would seem foreign even to people who have been to England or live there now. Things might look familiar—the same hills and sea and sky. People, young and old, short and tall, wear clothing we could identify and speak a language we might recognize. But their world is different from ours. The difference runs deeper than what they eat or where they bathe or who decides who marries whom. Medieval people live in a place we can never go, made up of what they value, how they think, and what they believe is true and important and possible.

The difference begins with how people saw themselves. Everyone had a particular place in a community, be it village, abbey, manor,[1] family, or

---

1 A *manor* was a parcel of land granted to a lord or nobleman.

guild.[2] Few people considered moving out of their place. Even people's names were linked to their place—Thomas Baker, William Steward, John At-Wood, Murgaw of Lithgow. Perkin, the goat boy who wants to be a scholar, is unusual.

Our ideas of individual identity, individual accomplishments and rights, individual effort and success did not exist. Family and community and guild and country were what mattered. No one was separate and independent, even the king.

This fixture of place was enforced by people's relationship to the land. When William, Duke of Normandy, conquered England in 1066, he decided that all the land belonged to him. He parceled out large estates to his supporters—barons and counts and dukes and great churchmen. They in turn rented smaller sections to abbots and knights, who let even smaller parcels to the farmers and millers and blacksmiths in the villages. Those on the bottom paid rent to those above, who paid it to the king, and everyone owed protection to those below them, making a great circle with everyone connected. The king was in cooperation with the lowest landholder, for the small bits of poor land in the farthest village could be traced back to the king, and the king owed patronage[3] and protection to all his people.

Some great noblemen held many manors with many villages scattered all across England. Some held but one knight's fee—that is, enough land to support one knight and his family, for which the knight owed service or the equivalent in money to his landlord. The villagers then rented parcels from the knight, in exchange for work or goods or money or all three.

Although great lords lived in castles and lesser lords in large manor houses, most English people in 1290 lived in villages, in small cottages lining the road from manor to church. A village might seem like a miniature to us, with perhaps thirty small cottages, tiny front yards full of vegetables and chickens, and the fields cut into strips so each tenant would have some good and some not-so-good land.

---

2 In the Middle Ages, a *guild* was a group of merchants or craftsmen.

3 *Patronage* is the support or assistance given by someone who is wealthy and influential.

Time in these villages moved slowly—not in a line from hour to hour, past to future, but again in a circle, marked by the passing of the seasons, the cycle of church festivals, and yearly village holidays. Daily life was marked by the rising and setting of the sun, for there were no watches or clocks, no gas lamps or electric lights, and candles were expensive and dangerous to use in a house of thatch and wood. Most people did not know what century it was, much less what year.

The future, then, to most medieval English meant not next week or next year or 1300, but the world to come, the afterlife, eternity, Heaven and Hell. Since the Church had a say in who went where in the next life, it had great authority in this one. The Church had power, lands, and riches. Church courts could condemn someone to death for heresy. Blasphemy[4] was not only a sin, but also a crime. Almost everyone loved God and worshipped Him in the same ways at the same times in the same kinds of places. The Church persecuted those who didn't. Everyone hoped the world to come would be better than this one.

Children, too, were part of the great circle of life, learning from their elders and passing that knowledge on to their own sons and daughters. Village children lived at home, learning at a young age to help about the cottage or fields, tending animals or those children younger than they. Children in town often were apprenticed to craftsmen or sent to be servants.

Noble children, both boys and girls, were sent to another noble home to be fostered. Once when a visitor from Italy asked why parents sent their children away, he was told, "Children learn better manners in other people's houses."

Boys served the lord of the manor while they trained to be knights. Girls went to a wealthy manor, where they attended the lady of the manor and learned music, sewing, household skills, and manners. They also learned doctoring, since the lady of the manor provided the only medical help most people got. Broken bones, bloody cuts, coughs, and even fatal diseases were treated by the lady with remedies she grew, picked, brewed, and bottled herself. Some herbal remedies were effective, such as the use of poppy flowers to ease pain. Some were not, as when a plant was used for ailments of the heart or liver because its leaf was shaped like a heart or a liver. There were no cures for most illnesses, no treatments for most diseases, no real alternatives to herbs, magic, and luck.

Girls were mostly trained for marriage. Marriage among the noble classes was not a matter of love but of economics. Marriages were arranged to increase land, gain allies, or pay back debts. Women were essentially

---

4 **Heresy** is a belief that differs from the accepted teachings of a religion. **Blasphemy** is words or actions that show a lack of respect for God or anything sacred.

property, used to further a family's alliances, wealth, or status.

When looked at from a safe, warm, well-fed perspective, the foreign country of medieval England might seem like a place of hard work, cruelty, and dirt. But the English of the Middle Ages also had a fondness for merriment, dancing, crude jokes, and boisterous games. Many households entertained themselves by the fire with riddles, roasted apples, and music. Villagers put aside their hard, tedious lives to dance around the Maypole,[5] jump the bonfires on Midsummer Night, and share Christmas dinner with their lord and lady.

Can we really understand medieval people well enough to write or read

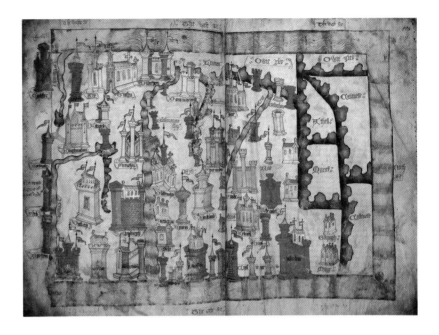

books about them? I think we can identify with those qualities that we share—the yearning for a full belly, the need to be warm and safe, the capacity for fear and joy, love for children, pleasure in a blue sky or a handsome pair of eyes. As for the rest, we'll have to imagine and pretend and make room in our hearts for all sorts of different people. 🍃

---

5 A *Maypole* is a pole decorated with flowers and ribbons, around which people dance on May Day.

Respond and Think Critically

1. Write a brief summary of the main ideas in this selection. For help on writing a summary, see page 219. [Summarize]

2. What is the author's purpose for explaining that the England of 1290 "would seem foreign even to people who have been to England or live there now"? Explain. [Interpret]

3. How did the land connect the people in England to the king? Explain. [Analyze]

4. **Text-to-Text** In what way was Young Arthur typical of a noble teenager of his day? Explain. [Connect]

5. Reading Skill Analyze Historical Context Explain how people in England in 1290 understood the idea of time. Support your answer with details from the selection.

6. **BQ** BIG Question Was it possible for people to become who they wanted to be in the Middle Ages? Or is it more possible in today's world? Explain.

from *The Autobiography of Malcolm X*

Connect to the Autobiography

Think about a book you read that changed the way you see the world. What was the book? When did you read it?

Partner Talk With a partner, talk about a book that opened a new world for you. How did the book change the way you see life?

Build Background

This excerpt from *The Autobiography of Malcolm X* describes a turning point in Malcolm X's life.

- Malcolm X was born Malcolm Little in Omaha, Nebraska.

- Malcolm's father, the Reverend Earl Little, died when Malcolm was six years old. Malcolm went to live with his older half-sister in Boston. There, he became involved in petty crimes. He was jailed for robbery from 1946 to 1952.

- While in prison, he converted to the Muslim religion and became a member of the Nation of Islam, changing his name to Malcolm X.

Vocabulary

circulation (sur´kyə lā´shən) *n.* the sharing of printed materials, such as books and newspapers, among readers (p. 645). *Nobody could check out the library book until it was put into circulation.*

emphasis (em´fə sis) *n.* special weight or importance (p. 646). *Most librarians place an emphasis on the importance of reading.*

rehabilitation (rē´hə bil´ə tā´shən) *n.* the act of restoring to good health or useful activity (p. 646). *Because she had been very ill, Tanya's rehabilitation took many months.*

maximum (mak´sə məm) *n.* greatest possible amount or number (p. 646). *Our team did so well that we won the maximum number of prizes allowed under the rules of the contest.*

Meet the Authors

Malcolm X

Dedicated to Civil Rights
Devoted to attaining civil rights for African Americans, Malcolm X was a leader who instilled racial pride in African Americans. Malcolm X was born in 1925 and died in 1965, the year *The Autobiography of Malcolm X* was published.

Alex Haley

A Successful Collaboration
Alex Haley became a writer while serving in the U.S. Coast Guard. Haley and Malcolm X worked together to compose *The Autobiography of Malcolm X.*

 Literature Online

Author Search For more about Malcolm X and Alex Haley, go to glencoe.com and enter QuickPass code GL27534u5.

Set Purposes for Reading

BQ BIG Question

As you read, ask yourself, why did Malcolm X work so hard to improve his ability to read and write? How did his positive actions help him become who he wanted to be?

Literary Element Author's Purpose

The **author's purpose** is the author's reason for writing. An author might write to entertain, to inform or explain, to persuade, or for a combination of these purposes. For example, an author might write an autobiography to share the story of his or her life. However, the author's purpose might also be to entertain readers with funny anecdotes or to persuade them to make changes in their own lives.

If you understand the author's intentions, you can better understand the text and form your own opinions about what you are reading. As you read, ask yourself, what ideas does the author express? What details does the author include? This will help you decide whether the author is trying to entertain, inform, explain, or persuade.

Reading Strategy Question

When you **question,** you ask yourself about what you are reading. You may ask questions about what you don't understand, or you may ask questions about whether certain information is important.

Asking questions will help you monitor your comprehension. When you ask questions, you can focus on specific ideas and reread for the information that you need to understand the text.

To generate questions, stop after every paragraph or two as you read. Ask yourself questions to make sure that you understand what you've read. Then reread to find the information that you need to answer the questions. Use a graphic organizer like the one below to keep track of your questions.

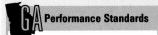

Performance Standards

For pages 640–647

ELA7RC2b Respond to a variety of texts.

ELA7RC2e Examine the author's purpose in writing.

TRY IT

Question Suppose that you are meeting a friend at a school play. You arrive late and the play has started. What questions do you ask your friend to help you understand what is going on?

Passage from Text	Questions
". . . to acquire some kind of a homemade education."	• What do the authors mean by "homemade"? • Who is going to teach him?
	•
	•

from
The Autobiography of
MALCOLM X

Malcolm X *with Alex Haley*

Malcolm X giving a speech in the early 1960s

It was because of my letters that I happened to stumble upon starting to acquire some kind of a homemade education. I became increasingly frustrated at not being able to express what I wanted to convey in letters that I wrote, especially those to Mr. Elijah Muhammad.[1] In the street, I had been the most articulate hustler[2] out there—I had commanded attention when I said something. But now, trying to write simple English, I not only wasn't articulate, I wasn't even functional. How would I sound writing in slang, the way I would *say* it, something such as, "Look, daddy, let me pull your coat about a cat,[3] Elijah Muhammad—"

Many who today hear me somewhere in person or on television, or those who read something I've said, will think I went to school far beyond the eighth grade. This impression is due entirely to my prison studies.

Question What questions might you ask yourself about the kind of impression Malcolm X is making on others?

---

1 ***Elijah Muhammad*** (i lī′ jə moo ham′ əd) (1897–1975) was the leader of the Black Muslim movement in the United States.

2 By calling himself an ***articulate hustler***, Malcolm X is saying that he had been a small-time criminal who could speak clearly and expressively.

3 To ***"pull your coat about a cat"*** is slang for "let me stop and tell you about a man."

It had really begun back in the Charlestown Prison, when Bimbi[4] first made me feel envy of his stock of knowledge. Bimbi had always taken charge of any conversations he was in, and I had tried to emulate[5] him. But every book I picked up had few sentences which didn't contain anywhere from one to nearly all of the words that might as well have been in Chinese. When I just skipped those words, of course, I really ended up with little idea of what the book said. So I had come to the Norfolk Prison Colony still going through only book-reading motions. Pretty soon, I would have quit even these motions, unless I had received the motivation that I did.

I saw that the best thing I could do was get hold of a dictionary—to study, to learn some words. I was lucky enough to reason also that I should try to improve my penmanship. It was sad. I couldn't even write in a straight line. It was both ideas together that moved me to request a dictionary along with some tablets and pencils from the Norfolk Prison Colony school.

I spent two days just riffling uncertainly through the dictionary's pages. I'd never realized so many words existed! I didn't know *which* words I needed to learn. Finally, just to start some kind of action, I began copying.

In my slow, painstaking, ragged handwriting, I copied into my tablet everything printed on that first page, down to the punctuation marks.

I believe it took me a day. Then, aloud, I read back, to myself, everything I'd written on the tablet. Over and over, aloud, to myself, I read my own handwriting.

I woke up the next morning, thinking about those words—immensely proud to realize that not only had I written so much at one time, but I'd written words that I never knew were in the world. Moreover, with a little effort, I also could remember what many of these words meant. I reviewed the words whose meanings I didn't remember. Funny thing, from the dictionary's first page right now, that *aardvark* springs to my mind. The

Author's Purpose Why do the authors write about Malcolm X's motivation to pursue learning?

Visual Vocabulary

An **aardvark** is a burrow-dwelling mammal that has a long, sticky tongue and powerful claws and feeds on ants and termites. It is native to southern and east-central Africa.

---

4 **Bimbi** is an inmate.

5 When you **emulate** someone, you try to become as good as or better than that person.

dictionary had a picture of it, a long-tailed, long-eared, burrowing African mammal, which lives off termites caught by sticking out its tongue as an anteater does for ants.

I was so fascinated that I went on—I copied the dictionary's next page. And the same experience came when I studied that. With every succeeding page, I also learned of people and places and events from history. Actually the dictionary is like a miniature encyclopedia. Finally the dictionary's A section had filled a whole tablet—and I went on into the B's. That was the way I started copying what eventually became the entire dictionary. It went a lot faster after so much practice helped me to pick up handwriting speed. Between what I wrote in my tablet, and writing letters, during the rest of my time in prison I would guess I wrote a million words.

I suppose it was inevitable that as my word base broadened, I could for the first time pick up a book and read and now begin to understand what the book was saying. Anyone who has read a great deal can imagine the new world that opened. Let me tell you something: from then until I left that prison, in every free moment I had, if I was not reading in the library, I was reading on my bunk. You couldn't have gotten me out of books with a wedge. Between Mr. Muhammad's teachings, my correspondence, my visitors—usually Ella and Reginald[6]—and my reading of books, months passed without my even thinking about being imprisoned. In fact, up to then, I never had been so truly free in my life.

The Norfolk Prison Colony's library was in the school building. A variety of classes was taught there by instructors who came from such places as Harvard and Boston universities. The weekly debates between inmate teams were also held in the school building. You would be astonished to know how worked up convict debaters and audiences would get over subjects like "Should Babies Be Fed Milk?"

Available on the prison library's shelves were books on just about every general subject. Much of the big private collection

Author's Purpose Why do the authors describe reading in such powerful, positive terms?

BQ **BIG Question**
How has reading changed Malcolm X's life?

---

6 *Ella* and *Reginald* are Malcolm X's sister and brother.

that Parkhurst[7] had willed to the prison was still in crates and boxes in the back of the library—thousands of old books. Some of them looked ancient: covers faded, old-time parchment-looking binding. Parkhurst, I've mentioned, seemed to have been principally interested in history and religion. He had the money and the special interest to have a lot of books that you wouldn't have in general **circulation.** Any college library would have been lucky to get that collection.

Malcolm X with his daughter

---

7 ***Parkhurst*** was a wealthy man who was interested in the education and training of prisoners.

Vocabulary

circulation (sur´ kyə lā´shən) *n.* the sharing of printed materials, such as books and newspapers, among readers

from The Autobiography of Malcolm X   **645**

As you can imagine, especially in a prison where there was heavy **emphasis** on **rehabilitation,** an inmate was smiled upon if he demonstrated an unusually intense interest in books. There was a sizable number of well-read inmates, especially the popular debaters. Some were said by many to be practically walking encyclopedias. They were almost celebrities. No university would ask any student to devour literature as I did when this new world opened to me, of being able to read and *understand*.

I read more in my room than in the library itself. An inmate who was known to read a lot could check out more than the permitted **maximum** number of books. I preferred reading in the total isolation of my own room.

When I had progressed to really serious reading, every night at about ten P.M. I would be outraged with the "lights out." It always seemed to catch me right in the middle of something engrossing.[8]

Fortunately, right outside my door was a corridor light that cast a glow into my room. The glow was enough to read by, once my eyes adjusted to it. So when "lights out" came, I would sit on the floor where I could continue reading in that glow.

At one-hour intervals the night guards paced past every room. Each time I heard the approaching foot-steps, I jumped into bed and feigned[9] sleep. And as soon as the guard passed, I got back out of bed onto the floor area of that light-glow, where I would read for another fifty-eight minutes—until the guard approached again. That went on until three or four every morning. Three or four hours of sleep a night was enough for me. Often in the years in the streets, I had slept less than that. ✒

Author's Purpose Why do the authors remind readers about Malcolm X's life on the streets?

---

8 Something *engrossing* grabs and holds a person's attention.

9 A person who *feigned* sleep was awake but tried to look as if he or she were asleep.

After You Read

Respond and Think Critically

1. What motivates Malcolm X to improve his reading and writing skills? [Recall]

2. What does Malcolm X mean when he says "it was inevitable" that he began to read and understand books? Explain. [Interpret]

3. What can you infer about prison life from Malcolm X's description of inmates getting "worked up" over a debate? [Infer]

4. **Literary Element** Author's Purpose Why did the authors write about Malcolm X's life? Give details to support your answer. [Analyze]

5. **Reading Strategy** Question Review your graphic organizer. What questions could you ask about the books that Malcolm X read at the Norfolk Prison Colony? [Connect]

6. **BQ** BIG Question Think about the work Malcolm X did to master reading. How important was this action in changing his life? Explain. [Evaluate]

Vocabulary Practice

On a separate sheet of paper, write the vocabulary word that correctly completes each sentence.

circulation   emphasis

rehabilitation   maximum

1. Tired of students arriving late, Mrs. Thomas placed great _____ on getting to the library on time.

2. After she injured her knee, Mia required many weeks of _____ .

3. You can't check out the book, because it was taken out of _____ .

4. What is the _____ amount of time I should spend on homework?

Writing

Write a Letter Imagine that you have a younger friend, relative, or neighbor who is having trouble reading and has lost interest in learning to do so. Write a letter to persuade your friend that it is important and worthwhile to learn to read. What can he or she gain from reading? Include examples and persuasive techniques to make your argument more convincing.

TIP

Inferring
To answer question 3, you have to use your knowledge and clues from what you read to make a good guess. Here are some tips to help you infer.

- Start by finding the details in the excerpt describing inmates getting "worked up" over a debate.

- Read the description carefully, looking for clues to help you guess. Ask yourself, what were the inmates debating? Why did they get so "worked up"?

- Consider why inmates would get excited about a debate. What is missing from the inmates' lives?

FOLDABLES Study Organizer Keep track of your ideas about the **BIG Question** in your unit Foldable.

 Literature Online

Selection Resources
For Selection Quizzes, eFlashcards, and Reading-Writing Connection activities, go to glencoe.com and enter QuickPass code GL27534u5.

Before You Read

New Directions

Connect to the Biography

Think about a time when you changed something in your life—at home, at school, or somewhere else. What happened when you tried a new direction?

Quickwrite Freewrite for a few minutes about the change you made. Why did you make the change? What does your decision say about you?

Build Background

"New Directions" is a biographical narrative about Maya Angelou's grandmother, Annie Johnson, and the changes Annie made at a specific time and place in her life.

- This biographical narrative is set in Stamps, Arkansas, in the early 1900s. During that time, African Americans did not yet have equal rights in many areas of the United States.

- Women's rights were also limited at that time. For example, women in the United States did not gain the right to vote until 1920.

- Although Maya Angelou spent some of her childhood with her mother in large cities, she was raised mainly by her grandmother in Stamps.

Vocabulary

disastrous (di zas′trəs) *adj.* awful, terrible (p. 650). *The party for my five-year-old niece was disastrous—half of the young guests cried the entire time.*

conceded (kən sēd′ed) *v.* admitted as true (p. 650). *Angela conceded that Mary was the better tennis player after Mary beat her three games in a row.*

balmy (bä′mē) *adj.* mild; soothing (p. 653). *Balmy spring days are his favorite time to work outdoors.*

Meet Maya Angelou

"There is a kind of strength . . . in black women. It's as if a steel rod runs right through the head down to the feet."

—Maya Angelou

A Person of Many Talents
Author, poet, playwright, editor, educator, professional stage and screen performer, and singer—each of these words describes Maya Angelou. Angelou's extraordinary career has taken her to many places around the world, including Egypt and Ghana. She read her poem "On the Pulse of Morning," commissioned by President Bill Clinton, at Clinton's 1993 inauguration. Angelou is the author of many books, including *I Know Why the Caged Bird Sings.*

Maya Angelou was born in 1928.

 Literature Online

Author Search For more about Maya Angelou, go to glencoe.com and enter QuickPass code GL27534u5.

Set Purposes for Reading

BQ ❯ BIG Question

At the beginning of this biographical narrative, Annie Johnson sets out on a new path. As you read, ask yourself, what obstacles does Annie face? In what ways do her positive actions help her achieve her goals?

Literary Element ❯ Setting

Setting is the time and place where the action occurs. "New Directions" has one general setting—Arkansas in the early 1900s. Within that larger setting, the story takes place in various specific places, such as the lumber mill.

It is important to pay attention to the setting. Details about the setting can help you visualize and better understand the time and place of the story. And sometimes the setting plays an important role in the story itself. As you read, ask yourself, how does the setting both set limitations and provide opportunities for Annie?

Reading Strategy ❯ Make Predictions About Plot

When you **make predictions about plot,** you guess what will happen next. To predict, think about what has happened so far and what you already know about the people or characters in a selection. Then guess what will happen next. As you read, check to see if your predictions were correct.

Predicting helps you look forward to events in the plot and pay attention to important details. When you predict, you get involved in what you read. To make predictions in "New Directions":

- Pay attention to the details in the narrative. What the author tells you about Annie might provide clues as to what she will do next.

- Remember that plot is organized around conflict. When Annie faces a problem, think about how she might solve it.

Use these clues to make predictions about plot. Use a graphic organizer like the one below.

What is Happening	My Prediction	What Actually Happens Next

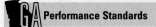

GA Performance Standards

For pages 648–654

ELA7R1c For literary texts, relate a literary work to information about its setting or historical moment.

TRY IT

Make Predictions You're getting ready to ride your bike to your friend's house, and you notice that your bike has a flat tire. Make a prediction about how the flat tire will affect the time at which you arrive at your friend's house. If you can't call to tell your friend what has happened, how do you predict your friend will react when you arrive?

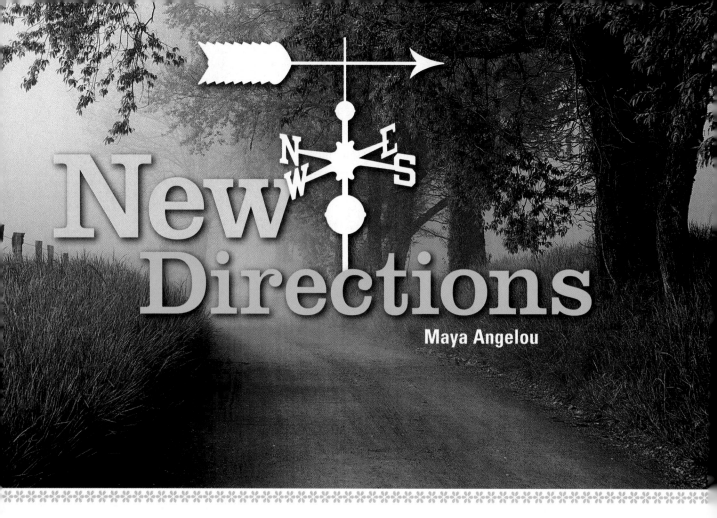

New Directions

Maya Angelou

In 1903 the late Mrs. Annie Johnson of Arkansas found herself with two toddling sons, very little money, a slight ability to read and add simple numbers. To this picture add a **disastrous** marriage and the burdensome[1] fact that Mrs. Johnson was a Negro.

When she told her husband, Mr. William Johnson, of her dissatisfaction with their marriage, he **conceded** that he too found it to be less than he expected, and had been secretly hoping to leave and study religion. He added that he thought God was calling him not only to preach but to do so in Enid, Oklahoma. He did not tell her that he knew a minister in Enid with whom he could study and who

Setting What do you know about the time and place in which Annie Johnson lived?

---

1 Something **burdensome** is hard to bear or troublesome.

Vocabulary

disastrous (di zas′trəs) *adj.* awful, terrible
conceded (kən sēd′ed) *v.* admitted as true

had a friendly, unmarried daughter. They parted amicably,[2] Annie keeping the one-room house and William taking most of the cash to carry himself to Oklahoma.

Annie, over six feet tall, big-boned, decided that she would not go to work as a domestic[3] and leave her "precious babes" to anyone else's care. There was no possibility of being hired at the town's cotton gin or lumber mill, but maybe there was a way to make the two factories work for her. In her words, "I looked up the road I was going and back the way I come, and since I wasn't satisfied, I decided to step off the road and cut me a new path." She told herself that she wasn't a fancy cook but that she could "mix groceries well enough to scare hungry away and from starving a man."

She made her plans meticulously[4] and in secret. One early evening to see if she was ready, she placed stones in two five-gallon pails and carried them three miles to the cotton gin. She rested a little, and then, discarding some rocks, she walked in the darkness to the saw mill five miles farther along the dirt road. On her way back to her little house and her babies, she dumped the remaining rocks along the path.

That same night she worked into the early hours boiling chicken and frying ham. She made dough and filled the rolled-out pastry with meat. At last she went to sleep.

2 When Annie and William **parted amicably**, they went their separate ways without feelings of anger or unfriendliness.

3 A **domestic** is a household servant.

4 When you perform a task **meticulously**, you do it very carefully.

Make Predictions About Plot Think about what options Annie has. What "new path" do you think she will take?

People picking cotton in Phillips County, Arkansas, in September 1938

The next morning she left her house carrying the meat pies, lard, an iron brazier,[5] and coals for a fire. Just before lunch she appeared in an empty lot behind the cotton gin. As the dinner noon bell rang, she dropped the savors[6] into boiling fat and the aroma rose and floated over to the workers who spilled out of the gin, covered with white lint, looking like specters.[7]

Most workers had brought their lunches of pinto beans and biscuits or crackers, onions and cans of sardines, but

---

5 A *brazier* is a metal container that holds burning coals for cooking food.

6 *Savors* are items that have a distinct taste, smell, or quality.

7 Another name for a ghost is a *specter.*

Setting Why are the time and place at which Annie sells her meat pies important to the success of her business?

The Crosset saw mill in Arkansas in the early twentieth century

View the Photograph Study the photo to see how the area developed around the mill. How might a setting like this have affected Annie Johnson's business?

they were tempted by the hot meat pies which Annie ladled out of the fat. She wrapped them in newspapers, which soaked up the grease, and offered them for sale at a nickel each. Although business was slow, those first days Annie was determined. She balanced her appearances between the two hours of activity.

So, on Monday if she offered hot fresh pies at the cotton gin and sold the remaining cooled-down pies at the lumber mill for three cents, then on Tuesday she went first to the lumber mill presenting fresh, just-cooked pies as the lumbermen covered in sawdust emerged from the mill.

For the next few years, on **balmy** spring days, blistering summer noons, and cold, wet, and wintry middays, Annie never disappointed her customers, who could count on seeing the tall, brown-skin woman bent over her brazier, carefully turning the meat pies. When she felt certain that the workers had become dependent on her, she built a stall between the two hives of industry and let the men run to her for their lunchtime provisions.

She had indeed stepped from the road which seemed to have been chosen for her and cut herself a brand-new path. In years that stall became a store where customers could buy cheese, meal, syrup, cookies, candy, writing tablets, pickles, canned goods, fresh fruit, soft drinks, coal, oil, and leather soles for worn-out shoes.

Each of us has the right and the responsibility to assess[8] the roads which lie ahead, and those over which we have traveled, and if the future road looms ominous[9] or unpromising, and the roads back uninviting, then we need to gather our resolve and, carrying only the necessary baggage, step off that road into another direction. If the new choice is also unpalatable,[10] without embarrassment, we must be ready to change that as well. 🔖

Make Predictions About Plot Think about what Annie has done so far. What do you predict will happen to her business?

BQ BIG Question

How do Annie's actions help her become the person she wants to be?

---

8 To *assess* something is to determine its meaning or importance.

9 Something *ominous* threatens harm or evil.

10 *Unpalatable* means *disagreeable* or *unacceptable.*

Vocabulary

balmy (bä′ mē) *adj.* mild; soothing

After You Read

Respond and Think Critically

1. Think about the traits that led Annie Johnson to success. What other traits do successful people you know have in common with Annie? [Connect]

2. What does the author mean by the statement, "Each of us has the right and the responsibility to assess the roads which lie ahead"? [Interpret]

3. Why does Annie carry pails of stones to the cotton gin and the saw mill? [Infer]

4. **Literary Element** Setting How does the setting affect the plot of this biographical narrative? Use details to support your answer. [Analyze]

5. **Reading Strategy** Make Predictions About Plot Refer to the predictions you made on the graphic organizer as you read. Were your predictions accurate? Explain. [Evaluate]

6. **BQ** BIG Question Do you agree with the author that "if the future road looms ominous," a person should "step off that road into another direction" by taking positive actions? Explain. [Conclude]

Vocabulary Practice

Identify whether the paired words in each set have a similar or different meaning. Then write a sentence using each vocabulary word, or draw or find a picture that represents the word.

> **disastrous** and fortunate
>
> **conceded** and denied
>
> **balmy** and chilly

Example:
conceded and denied = opposite meaning

Sentence: The candidate conceded defeat after it became obvious that his opponent had won the election.

Writing

Write a Summary Think about Annie Johnson's journey from an unhappy person with little money and little education to a successful store owner. Use your own words to retell the main events in Annie's story in the order in which they occurred.

TIP

Inferring
To answer question 3, use your own knowledge to figure out what the author does not state directly. Here are tips to help you infer.

- Look in the narrative for specific details about what Annie does after she returns from carrying the stones.

- Think about what Annie does at the cotton gin and the saw mill.

- Consider what carrying the stones would help Annie do.

FOLDABLES Study Organizer Keep track of your ideas about the **BIG Question** in your unit Foldable.

 Literature Online

Selection Resources
For Selection Quizzes, eFlashcards, and Reading-Writing Connection activities, go to glencoe.com and enter QuickPass code GL27534u5.

Part **2**

Courage and Confidence

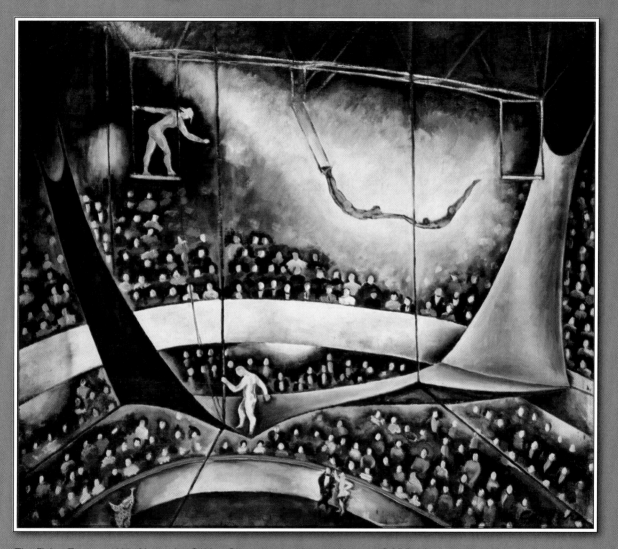

The Flying Trapeze, 1925. Alexander Calder. Oil on canvas. 91.4 x 106.7 cm. ©ARS, NY.

BQ ⟩ BIG Question **How Can You Become Who You Want to Be?**

In the painting *The Flying Trapeze,* the acrobats perform daring feats. Where do they find the courage and confidence to take such great risks? What performers do you admire for their courage and confidence?

Almost Ready

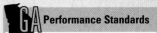

Performance Standards

For pages 656–658

ELA7R1g/ii For literary texts, explain and analyze the effects of figurative language.

Connect to the Poem

What is the real *you* like? Do you have your father's chin or your grandmother's sense of humor? Think about your physical characteristics and your personality traits. Are you satisfied with who you are today, or do you have plans to make changes in the future?

Quickwrite Freewrite for a few minutes about who you are today. Describe personality traits or accomplishments that make you proud.

PEANUTS reprinted by permission of United Feature Syndicate, Inc.

Set Purposes for Reading

BQ › BIG Question

As you read, ask yourself, what do I like about myself? How can I build self-confidence?

Literary Element | Irony

When something awful happens and you say "Oh, great!" you are being ironic. In literature, **verbal irony** exists when the author, or a character the author creates, says the opposite of what he or she really means. Similarly, **situational irony** exists when what actually happens in a situation is the opposite of what we expect. Irony can be humorous, as when someone says, "Nice weather" during a blizzard. It can also be used in a serious, or even a bitter, way. For example, you might mutter "Nice guy" after someone has done something rude. As you read "Almost Ready," look for examples of irony.

Meet Arnold Adoff

Award-Winning Writer
An award-winning poet, teacher, and lecturer, Arnold Adoff believes that "writing a poem is making music with words and space." His books include *Hard to Be Six* and *Slow Dance Heartbreak Blues*. Adoff was born in 1935.

 Literature Online

Author Search For more about Arnold Adoff, go to glencoe.com and enter QuickPass code GL27534u5.

Almost Ready

Arnold Adoff

I	as
am	this
going	cool
to	and
her	in-
birth-	control
day	young
party	dude:

as	as	as	as
soon	soon	soon	soon
as	as	as	as
I	I	I	I
find	find	find	find
my	my	my	my
new	hip	deep	right
shirt,	shoes,	voice,	mask.

Irony What details in the poem suggest that the speaker is not "in control"?

BQ BIG Question
How do you think the speaker can become who he wants to be?

After You Read

Respond and Think Critically

1. What images does the poem focus on? [Recall]

2. In what way does the arrangement of lines in the poem add to the poem's meaning? Explain. [Interpret]

3. What do the new shirt, hip shoes, and deep voice mean to the speaker? [Infer]

4. What does the title "Almost Ready" suggest about the inner conflict the speaker is feeling? [Analyze]

5. **Literary Element** Irony Why does the speaker feel he has to wear a mask to be cool? [Conclude]

6. **BQ** BIG Question "Almost Ready" suggests that young people often show an outside that looks "cool and in-control" even when they feel differently inside. Do you agree? Explain your answer. [Evaluate]

Spelling Link

Formation of Plurals The usual way to form plurals of a noun in English is to add *-s* or *-es* to the end of the word. Below are some other general rules for forming plurals:

- If the noun ends in *s, sh, ch, x,* or *z,* then add *-es.* (bus/buses, tax/taxes, buzz/buzzes)

- If the noun ends in a consonant + *y,* then change *y* to *i* and add *-es.* (candy/candies)

- If the noun ends in *lf,* then change the *f* to *v* and add *-es.* (calf/calves)

- If the noun ends in *fe,* then change the *f* to *v* and add *-s.* (wife/wives)

Practice On a sheet of paper, list these words: *kiss, life, self, sky, bully,* and *bunch.* Write the plural form of each word. Use the spelling rules as a guide.

Writing

Write a Blurb Have you ever read a blurb on the back cover of a book that made you want to read the book? Write an informative paragraph that could appear on the back of a book of Arnold Adoff's poetry. In the blurb, tell readers what the poem "Almost Ready" says about growing up and fitting in.

TIP

Interpreting
To answer question 2, think about how the arrangement of words on the page can be part of a poet's message.

- Look at the way the words of the poem are arranged. What might this tell you about the speaker?

- Does the arrangement of words remind you of anything? How does the arrangement connect to what the speaker is doing in the poem?

- Think about the main qualities of the speaker. How does the poem's form echo those qualities?

FOLDABLES Keep track of
Study Organizer your ideas about
the **BIG Question** in your
unit Foldable.

 Literature Online

Selection Resources
For Selection Quizzes, eFlashcards, and Reading-Writing Connection activities, go to glencoe.com and enter QuickPass code GL27534u5.

Vocabulary Workshop

Dictionary Skills

Connection to Literature

"The crowd shouted each time he held the blade aloft."

—Robert D. San Souci, *Young Arthur*

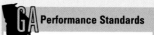
Performance Standards

For page 659

ELA7R2d Understand and acquire new vocabulary. Determine word meanings through the use of definition, example, restatement, or contrast.

If you didn't know the meaning of the word *aloft* or you wanted to use another word or phrase in its place, you could turn to a **dictionary** or a **thesaurus** for help. A dictionary provides the pronunciation, parts of speech, definitions, and sometimes the origin for words. A thesaurus lists synonyms, or words that have similar meanings. Both tools are available as books, on the Internet, and in word-processing programs.

Here are dictionary and thesaurus entries for the word *aloft*.

Word	Dictionary Entry	Thesaurus Entry
aloft	(ə lôft′) *adv.* **1** in or to a place far above the ground; high up. **2** far above the deck of a ship. [From the Old Norse phrase *ā lopt,* in the air.]	*adv.* **1** up in the air, far above the ground; toward the sky; in the celestial heights; overhead, above. **2** on the masts.

TRY IT: Use the dictionary and thesaurus entries above to help you answer these questions.

1. Which meaning of *aloft* is used in the following sentence? *The knight raised his sword aloft over and over again, and each time the crowd let out an excited cheer.*
2. Does the *a* in *aloft* sound like the *a* in *above* or in *wade*?
3. Which thesaurus entry would best replace *aloft* in the following sentence? *The pirate ship's flag flew proudly aloft.*

Tip

Vocabulary Terms Dictionary entries give the different meanings of a single word; thesaurus entries list different words that mean the same thing.

Test-taking Tip When you are preparing to take a test, use a dictionary to find the meanings of any unfamiliar words you encounter. In a notebook, make a list of these words and their meanings. Use a thesaurus to find one or two synonyms and antonyms for each word.

 Literature Online

Vocabulary For more vocabulary practice, go to glencoe.com and enter the QuickPass code GL27534u5.

Before You Read

Your World and *One*

Connect to the Poems

Think about a challenge that you face now or will face in the near future. Does it seem a bit scary or even overwhelming?

Graphic Organizer Create a chart like the one below to organize ideas that will help you face your current or future challenge. To fill in your graphic organizer, think about

• what you need to do in order to prepare for your challenge

• whom you can ask for help or advice

• which items or things may help you overcome your challenge

My Challenge:

Things to do	People who can help me	Materials that I'll need

Build Background

Both "Your World" and "One" are lyric poems. Lyric poems express thoughts or emotions about a subject.

• Like popular songs and commercials, lyric poetry is short and expresses strong personal feelings.

• Poets often place important words at the ends of the lines of lyric poetry. This placement helps poets emphasize certain feelings or ideas in the poem.

• The speaker in a lyric poem often tells about an event. As the speaker relates the experience, he or she comments on the feelings that the experience creates. Then the speaker usually describes the meaning of the event.

Meet the Authors

Georgia Douglas Johnson

An Inspiration Georgia Douglas Johnson was one of the first African American female poets to gain wide recognition. Georgia Douglas Johnson was born in 1877 and died in 1966.

James Berry

Caribbean Poet In his writings, Berry often conveys the importance of preserving the culture that defines the Caribbean. James Berry was born in Jamaica in 1924.

 Literature Online

Author Search For more about Georgia Douglas Johnson and James Berry, go to glencoe.com and enter QuickPass code GL27534u5.

Set Purposes for Reading

BQ ⟩ BIG Question

As you read, ask yourself, where do the speakers in these poems look for courage and confidence? What do they learn about themselves?

Literary Element Symbol

A **symbol** is any object, person, place, or experience that means more than what it is. For example, a dove may be a symbol of peace.

Writers use symbols in stories and poems to add meaning and to emphasize themes. Use these tips to help you identify symbols and understand their meaning.

- Look for repeated words, images, or actions. Ask yourself, what do they mean? Why are they important?
- Look for things or ideas that are important to the speakers or characters. Ask yourself, what do they care about? Why?

As you read, pay attention to how the poets use symbols to contribute to the meaning of the poems. Also, think about how the ideas in the poems are similar and different.

Reading Strategy Paraphrase

When you **paraphrase,** you retell something in your own words. If you read a sentence that you don't quite understand, for example, you might try paraphrasing it, or putting the sentence in your own words.

Paraphrasing while you read can help you monitor your comprehension, or check your understanding. Paraphrasing can also help you figure out the theme of a literary work.

As you read "Your World" and "One," read slowly and paraphrase lines or stanzas to better understand them. See if the lines or stanzas that you paraphrase help you determine the theme of each poem. Use a graphic organizer like the one below to record each poet's words and restate their ideas in your own words.

Line Number or Stanza	Paraphrase

Performance Standards

For pages 660–665

ELA7R1g/ii For literary texts, explain and analyze the effects of figurative language.

TRY IT

Paraphrase With a partner, read a short magazine or newspaper article. Then paraphrase a few sentences from the article. Take turns reading aloud what you have paraphrased. Make sure you restated the ideas in your own words and didn't copy the writer's words.

Your World

Georgia Douglas Johnson

The Ascent of Ethiopia, 1932. Lois Mailou Jones. Oil on canvas, 23 1/2 x 17 1/4 in. Milwaukee Art Museum. Purchase, African-American Aquisition Fund, matching funds from Suzanne and Richard Pieper, with additional funds from Arthur and Dorothy Nelle Sanders.

Your world is as big as you make it.
I know, for I used to abide°
In the narrowest nest in a corner,
My wings pressing close to my side.

5   But I sighted the distant horizon
Where the sky line encircled the sea
And I throbbed with a burning desire
To travel this immensity.°

I battered the cordons° around me
10   And cradled my wings on the breeze
Then soared to the uttermost reaches
With rapture,° with power, with ease!

---

2 Here, ***abide*** may mean either "dwell" or "remain."

8 Anything of great size or extent is an ***immensity.***

9 ***Cordons*** are barriers.

12 ***Rapture*** is the condition of being carried away by strong emotion, such as joy or love.

Symbol What might the distant horizon symbolize?

BQ **BIG Question**
What gives the speaker the courage to leave the "nest"?

ONE

James Berry

Sun Shower, 1995. Diana Ong. Computer graphic.

Only one of me
and nobody can get a second one
from a photocopy machine.

Nobody has the fingerprints I have.
5 Nobody can cry my tears, or laugh my laugh
or have my expectancy° when I wait.

But anybody can mimic° my dance with my dog.
Anybody can howl how I sing out of tune.
And mirrors can show me multiplied
10 many times, say, dressed up in red
or dressed up in grey.

Nobody can get into my clothes for me
or feel my fall for me, or do my running.
Nobody hears my music for me, either.

15 I am just this one.
Nobody else makes the words
I shape with sound, when I talk.

But anybody can act how I stutter in a rage.
Anybody can copy echoes I make.
20 And mirrors can show me multiplied
many times, say, dressed up in green
or dressed up in blue.

Paraphrase How would you paraphrase these two lines?

---

6 **Expectancy** is the feeling one has while looking forward to something.

7 To **mimic** is to copy or imitate.

After You Read

Respond and Think Critically

1. To what creature does the speaker of "Your World" compare himself or herself? [Recall]

2. How is the speaker of "Your World" different at the end of the poem? Support your answer with examples from the poem. [Analyze]

3. What advice might the speaker in "Your World" have for others who want to experience new things? [Conclude]

4. What is the theme of "One"? Explain. [Interpret]

5. Do you agree with the speaker of "One" about what is unique about a person and what is not? Explain. [Evaluate]

6. **BQ** BIG Question Select one of the poems, and explain how it may inspire a person to face life's challenges and set higher goals for himself or herself. [Analyze]

Academic Vocabulary

Georgia Douglas Johnson uses an **economy** of words to tell readers that they are responsible for meeting new challenges and expanding their worlds. In the preceding sentence, *economy* means "the efficient use of a resource." So, the sentence is stating that Johnson uses words efficiently, or without waste.

The word *economy* also has other meanings. For instance: The increase in new jobs is a sign that the nation's **economy** is growing. What do you think *economy* means in this second sentence? What is the difference between the two meanings?

TIP

Concluding
The speaker does not give direct advice to readers. Therefore, you must piece together clues to determine what the speaker might say to readers.

- Think about what the speaker says and does.
- Consider the way in which the speaker describes life in the "nest."
- Recall how the speaker feels about his or her choices.

 FOLDABLES Study Organizer Keep track of your ideas about the **BIG Question** in your unit Foldable.

 LOG ON **Literature** Online

Selection Resources
For Selection Quizzes, eFlashcards, and Reading-Writing Connection activities, go to glencoe.com and enter QuickPass code GL27534u5.

Literary Element Symbol

1. What do the speaker's wings symbolize in the first and third stanzas of "Your World"? Explain.

2. In "Your World," what does "battered the cordons" mean? How does the poet use this image as a symbol? Explain.

3. In the third and sixth stanzas of "One," the poet uses images of mirrors. What might mirrors symbolize in this poem? Explain.

Review: Alliteration

As you learned on page 190, **alliteration** is the repetition of consonant sounds, usually at the beginnings of words or syllables. Authors and poets use alliteration to emphasize certain words and ideas and to create a mood, or atmosphere. Read aloud the following sentence: "The brothers brazenly marched across the floor." When you hear the *br* sound twice in a row, your attention is drawn to the words *brothers* and *brazenly*. Think about the effect that the *br* sound creates.

4. Find an example of alliteration in "One." How does it contribute to the poem's mood, or atmosphere?

Reading Strategy Paraphrase

Standards Practice GA ELA7R1a

5. Which sentence best paraphrases the first stanza of "One"?

   A Because people are different, a photocopy machine can't copy them.

   B I can use a photocopy machine to make one copy of myself.

   C Because I am unique, a photocopy machine can't make a copy of me.

   D I am the only one who can use the photocopy machine to make copies.

Grammar Link

Agreement with Compounds A **compound subject** is two or more subjects joined by a conjunction. The verb form that agrees with a compound subject depends on the conjunction that joins the subjects.

- **Subjects joined by *and*:** When *and* joins subjects, use the plural verb form.

  The <u>poem and the story</u> <u>are</u> about challenges.
  (poem + story = they. Use *are*.)

- **Subjects joined by *or* or *nor*:** When *or* or *nor* joins subjects, the verb agrees with the subject that is closer to it.

  Stories or <u>poetry</u> <u>gives</u> you something to think about.
  (*Poetry* is closer to the verb. Poetry = *it*. Use *gives*.)

Practice Write the subject and the correct verb form for each sentence.

1. Neither Hana nor I (has, have) difficulty recognizing alliteration.

2. The poem's imagery and rhyme scheme (is, are) surprising.

3. When (does, do) you and your friends plan to read poetry by James Berry?

Write with Style

Apply Figurative Language "One" is an example of free verse, which is poetry that has no fixed pattern of meter, rhyme, line length, or stanza arrangement. Write a stanza of free verse and include one symbol for courage or confidence. Use techniques such as alliteration to emphasize important words and ideas. Arrange the lines of your stanza so that the symbol is introduced near the beginning and is repeated toward the end. Then review your stanza to make sure you've used vivid words. Use a thesaurus to find just the right words to express your ideas.

Before You Read

Four Skinny Trees and *Chanclas*

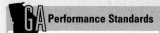
Performance Standards

For pages 666–671

ELA7R1g/ii For literary texts, explain and analyze the effects of figurative language.

Connect to the Vignette and Short Story

Think about a time when you felt awkward or embarrassed. How did you handle the situation?

Quickwrite Freewrite for a few minutes about a time when you overcame feelings of awkwardness or embarrassment.

Build Background

Author Sandra Cisneros is well known for her short stories and vignettes describing growing up as a Latina girl. A vignette is a short literary sketch that describes something or paints a picture in words. In the vignette "Four Skinny Trees," the narrator describes what she has in common with the trees outside her house.

The short story "Chanclas" takes place in a neighborhood where many Latinos live. *Chanclas* is a Spanish word meaning "old, worn-out shoes." Most of the action in the story takes place at a fiesta celebrating a baptism. A baptism is a formal ceremony that welcomes a new member, often a child, into the Christian church. A *fiesta*, or celebration, is often held after the ceremony.

Set Purposes for Reading

BQ ▶ BIG Question

As you read, ask yourself, how do the narrators draw courage and confidence from their surroundings and from other people?

Literary Element Voice

Voice is an author's distinctive **style,** or the way an author chooses and arranges words and sentences. An author's voice can reveal his or her purpose in writing and attitude toward his or her subject and audience. For example, Sandra Cisneros sometimes runs sentences together without punctuation. Her purpose is to quicken the pace of the story, build suspense, and make the words sound like spoken language.

As you read, ask yourself, how does Cisneros create a unique voice by choosing and arranging words and sentences? How does she use repetition and personification, a figure of speech in which an animal, object, or idea is given human form or characteristics? How does her voice appeal to my senses and emotions?

Meet Sandra Cisneros

A Distinctive Voice Sandra Cisneros's family was poor and moved frequently between the United States and Mexico, where her father's parents lived. Later, she wrote stories based on her early experiences of "third-floor flats, and fear of rats."

Cisneros was born in 1954.

 Literature Online

Author Search For more about Sandra Cisneros, go to glencoe.com and enter QuickPass code GL27534u5.

Four Skinny Trees

Sandra Cisneros

Trees, 1990. Gerrit Greve.

They are the only ones who understand me. I am the only one who understands them. Four skinny trees with skinny necks and pointy elbows like mine. Four who do not belong here but are here. Four raggedy excuses planted by the city. From our room we can hear them, but Nenny just sleeps and doesn't appreciate these things.

Their strength is secret. They send ferocious roots beneath the ground. They grow up and they grow down and grab the earth between their hairy toes and bite the sky with violent teeth and never quit their anger. This is how they keep.

Let one forget his reason for being, they'd all droop like **tulips** in a glass, each with their arms around the other. Keep, keep, keep, trees say when I sleep. They teach.

When I am too sad and too skinny to keep keeping, when I am a tiny thing against so many bricks, then it is I look at trees. When there is nothing left to look at on this street. Four who grew despite concrete. Four who reach and do not forget to reach. Four whose only reason is to be and be. 🐾

Visual Vocabulary

Tulips are bell-shaped flowers.

Voice What characteristics do you notice about the author's voice here?

Chanclas

Sandra Cisneros

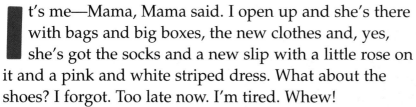

It's me—Mama, Mama said. I open up and she's there with bags and big boxes, the new clothes and, yes, she's got the socks and a new slip with a little rose on it and a pink and white striped dress. What about the shoes? I forgot. Too late now. I'm tired. Whew!

Six-thirty already and my little cousin's baptism is over. All day waiting, the door locked, don't open up for nobody, and I don't till Mama gets back and buys everything except the shoes.

Now Uncle Nacho is coming in his car, and we have to hurry and get to Precious Blood Church quick because that's where the baptism party is, in the basement rented for today for dancing and tamales and everyone's kids running all over the place.

Mama dances, laughs, dances. All of a sudden, Mama is sick. I fan her hot face with a paper plate. Too many tamales, but Uncle Nacho says too many this and tilts his thumb to his lips.

Everybody laughing except me, because I'm wearing the new dress, pink and white with stripes, and new underclothes and new socks and the old saddle shoes[1] I

Voice How does the sentence structure in this paragraph reflect the activity being described?

---

1 ***Saddle shoes*** tie with laces and rise to just below the ankle. What makes a saddle shoe distinctive is the band, or "saddle," of color across the middle that contrasts with the color of the rest of the shoe.

wear to school, brown and white, the kind I get every September because they last long and they do. My feet scuffed and round, and the heels all crooked that look dumb with this dress, so I just sit.

Meanwhile that boy who is my cousin by first communion[2] or something, asks me to dance and I can't. Just stuff my feet under the metal folding chair stamped Precious Blood and pick on a wad of brown gum that's stuck beneath the seat. I shake my head no. My feet growing bigger and bigger.

Then Uncle Nacho is pulling and pulling my arm and it doesn't matter how new the dress Mama bought is because my feet are ugly until my uncle who is a liar says, You are the prettiest girl here, will you dance, but I believe him, and yes, we are dancing, my Uncle Nacho and me, only I don't want to at first. My feet swell big and heavy like plungers, but I drag them across the linoleum floor straight center where Uncle wants to show off the new dance we learned. And Uncle spins me, and my skinny arms bend the way he taught me, and my mother watches, and my little cousins watch, and the boy who is my cousin by first communion watches, and everyone says, wow, who are those two who dance like in the movies, until I forget that I am wearing only ordinary shoes, brown and white, the kind my mother buys each year for school.

And all I hear is the clapping when the music stops. My uncle and me bow and he walks me back in my thick shoes to my mother who is proud to be my mother. All night the boy who is a man watches me dance. He watched me dance. 🍂

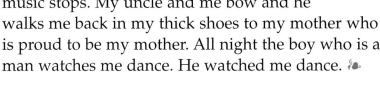

Voice Why might the author have chosen to break a grammar rule in this sentence?

BQ **BIG Question**
What gives the speaker the courage to dance?

---

2 In the Roman Catholic Church, children of a similar age often receive their first communion as a group. The speaker's *cousin by first communion* is someone who was in the same group when she received her first communion.

After You Read

Respond and Think Critically

1. In your own words, tell what happens in the first paragraph of "Four Skinny Trees." [Paraphrase]

2. What do you think makes the narrator of "Four Skinny Trees" strong? Support your answer with details from the story. [Interpret]

3. Why was the narrator in "Chanclas" waiting for her mother? Explain. [Recall]

4. Think about the importance the narrator of "Chanclas" places on her shoes. How does wearing the shoes affect the narrator's behavior? Explain. [Analyze]

5. Is "Chanclas" a fitting title for the story? Why or why not? Explain. [Evaluate]

6. **BQ** BIG Question How are the narrators of "Four Skinny Trees" and "Chanclas" similar? Where do the narrators find their courage and confidence? Use details to support your answer. [Evaluate]

Academic Vocabulary

You can tell that Uncle Nacho is a **significant** person in the speaker's family because he drives the family to the party and asks the narrator to dance. To become more familiar with the word *significant,* fill in the graphic organizer below.

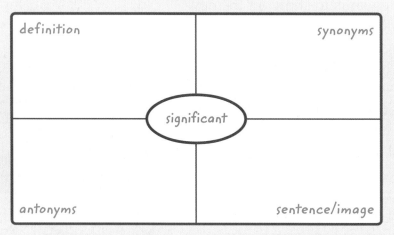

definition | synonyms

significant

antonyms | sentence/image

TIP

Evaluating
To answer question 6, you will need to think about the selections.

- Skim paragraphs two and four of "Four Skinny Trees" to see how the trees and the speaker are described. Explain the connection between the speaker and the trees. Consider how the trees influence the speaker.

- Think about how the narrator's emotions change from the beginning of "Chanclas" to the end of the story. Describe the change and what caused the speaker's feelings to change.

FOLDABLES
Study Organizer Keep track of your ideas about the **BIG Question** in your unit Foldable.

 LOG ON **Literature** Online

Selection Resources
For Selection Quizzes, eFlashcards, and Reading-Writing Connection activities, go to glencoe.com and enter QuickPass code GL27534u5.

Literary Element | Voice

1. Reread the last paragraph of "Four Skinny Trees." Why does Cisneros start each of the last three sentences in the same way?

2. Reread the paragraph in "Chanclas" in which the narrator describes her dance with Uncle Nacho. How does Cisneros's voice affect the mood, or atmosphere, of the story?

3. What makes Cisneros's voice unique in these two selections? Give examples from the text to support your answer. Use a graphic organizer like the one below to help you answer.

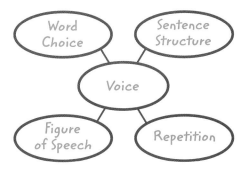

Review: Personification

As you learned on page 567, **personification** is a figure of speech in which an animal, object, or idea is given human form or characteristics. When an author uses personification, he or she also may use **metaphors** or **similes**. A simile uses the words *like* or *as* to compare unlike things. A metaphor makes a comparison without *like* or *as.*

4. What are some of the human characteristics that the speaker gives to the trees in "Four Skinny Trees"? How do these characteristics help the speaker?

5. How does the author use metaphor and simile in "Four Skinny Trees"? Support your answer with examples from the text.

Grammar Link

Agreement in Inverted Sentences Verbs and subjects in inverted sentences should agree. In an inverted sentence, all or part of the verb comes before the subject. There are two kinds of inverted sentences.

Questions To check the subject-verb agreement in questions, change the questions into statements.

Question: Where is my new shoes?
Statement: My new shoes is where.

The subject is *shoes. Shoes* is plural. So, the right verb form is *are,* not *is.*

Sentences that Begin with *Here* or *There* To find the subject of a sentence that begins with *here* or *there,* mentally remove the word from the sentence. Find the verb; then ask, "Who or what _____?"

There was many people at the party.

The verb is *was.* Ask yourself, "Who or what was?" *People* was. *People* is the subject. *People* is plural. The right verb is *were*, not *was.*

Grammar Practice Write three inverted sentences about either "Four Skinny Trees" or "Chanclas." Check the sentences for subject-verb agreement.

Write with Style

Apply Sound Devices Write a paragraph describing an object that represents you or an activity that you enjoy doing. Think carefully about how Cisneros creates a unique voice in her stories. Use repetition and figures of speech to emphasize important details and to show the way you feel about the object or the activity. Use a dictionary or thesaurus to help you choose words that have pleasing sounds. Read your paragraph aloud to a partner.

 **Performance Standards**

For pages 672–673

ELA7RC2b Respond to a variety of texts in multiple modes of discourse.

Genre Focus:
Biography and Autobiography

Biography and **autobiography** are nonfiction stories about the lives of real people. An autobiography is written by the person the story is about. A biography is written by someone other than the subject of the biography.

Biographical and autobiographical works can cover varying amounts of time, from a single experience to an entire lifetime. These works, which can be book-length or short, include travel journals, diary entries, eyewitness accounts, memoirs, and anecdotes.

Literary Elements

Narrator is the voice telling the story.

Point of view is the viewpoint from which the biography or autobiography is told. The story of a biography is told from the point of view of a writer who may or may not know the person who is the subject. However, the story of an autobiography is almost always told from the point of view of a writer who is describing his or her own life, using pronouns such as *I, me, we,* and *us.*

Style is the writer's choice and arrangement of words and sentences. Style can help express a writer's purpose for writing and reveal his or her attitude toward both subject and audience.

Setting is the time and place of a biography or an autobiography. In biography as well as autobiography, writers draw on actual events— such as political or social situations—that have happened in real places at real times. Setting might serve just as a background to the story, or it might be important to the events in it.

Plot is the sequence of events. Just like fiction, both biography and autobiography have a plot. The plot of a biography or an autobiography reveals a **conflict,** or central struggle. The plot's **resolution,** or final stage, reveals the outcome of the conflict.

Theme is the main idea or message about life that readers can learn from the biography or autobiography. A theme can be stated directly or implied. Writers describe events and details that convey the work's theme.

TRY IT

Using a chart like either of those on the next page, identify elements or analyze a character in a biography or an autobiography in this unit.

To better understand literary elements in biographies and autobiographies and how writers use them, look at the examples in the charts below.

Literary Elements Chart for *The Adventures of Marco Polo*

People	Setting
People in *The Adventures of Marco Polo* include Marco Polo, his father, and his uncle.	Part of this biography takes place in various locations—including Persia, Afghanistan, and the Pamir Mountains—on Polo's journey from Italy to China between 1271 and 1275.
Plot Conflict (problem)	**Plot Resolution (solution)**
Polo faces several conflicts on his journey to China, including an encounter with a tribe of people known as the Caraunas.	Polo arrives safely in China.

Characterization Chart for Zlata Filipović from *Zlata's Diary*

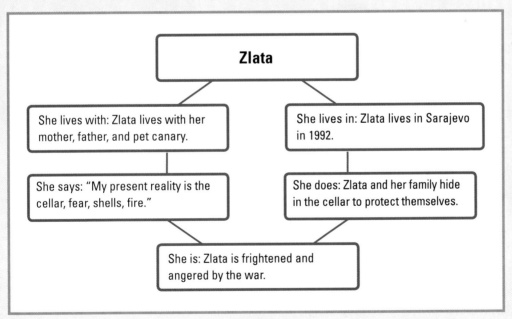

Zlata

She lives with: Zlata lives with her mother, father, and pet canary.

She lives in: Zlata lives in Sarajevo in 1992.

She says: "My present reality is the cellar, fear, shells, fire."

She does: Zlata and her family hide in the cellar to protect themselves.

She is: Zlata is frightened and angered by the war.

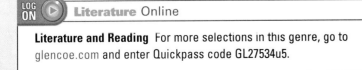

LOG ON ▶ **Literature** Online

Literature and Reading For more selections in this genre, go to glencoe.com and enter Quickpass code GL27534u5.

Before You Read

from *Zlata's Diary*

Connect to the Diary

How would it feel to watch your once peaceful community turn into a war zone?

List List words that describe how you might feel if you found yourself and your family in the middle of a war zone.

Build Background

In her diary, Zlata writes about Sarajevo, the capital of Bosnia. During the early 1990s, war broke out in Sarajevo over the decision to declare Bosnia's independence from the former country of Yugoslavia.

- Zlata began her diary before the war and continued it during the war. In 1993, she was airlifted to safety in Paris, and her diary was published.

- In Paris, Zlata began to live the ordinary life of a student again, studying at the International School.

- *Zlata's Diary* has been published in more than twenty languages. Zlata has traveled around the world with her parents, promoting peace and speaking on the behalf of children in war zones. She was awarded the "Special Child of Courage Award" by the Simon Wiesenthal Centre.

Vocabulary

cope (kōp) *v.* to deal with or try to overcome difficulties (p. 676). *Tim, who is afraid of insects, had to cope with his fears when we went camping.*

misery (miz′ ər ē) *n.* extreme unhappiness; despair (p. 678). *The flood caused misery for the families whose homes were destroyed.*

refugee (ref′ ū je′) *n.* a person who leaves his or her homeland because of danger or persecution and seeks safety in another place (p. 681). *The refugee fled from danger in her native country to safety on another continent.*

Meet Zlata Filipović

When Zlata Filipović started to write a diary, she was almost eleven years old. She lived with her parents in Sarajevo. Her life was very ordinary; she went to school, did her homework, and hung out with her friends. All that changed in 1992 when war broke out. For Zlata, "That was the day that time stood still." In her diary, she recorded the horrors of war that she and her friends and family experienced.

Zlata Filipović was born in 1980.

 Literature Online

Author Search For more about Zlata Filipović, go to glencoe.com and enter QuickPass code GL27534u5.

Set Purposes for Reading

BQ ▶ BIG Question

As you read, ask yourself, how have Zlata's experiences affected her life?

Literary Element ▮ Conflict

A **conflict** is a struggle between opposing forces. **External conflicts** occur between a person or a character and an outside force, such as another person, society, or nature. **Internal conflicts** occur within the mind of the person or the character when he or she is torn between opposing feelings or goals.

The events in most stories and many nonfiction selections revolve around conflict. As a reader, you can learn a lot about life by seeing how people and characters deal with conflicts. As you read, ask yourself, what conflicts does Zlata describe? How do Zlata and her family deal with these conflicts?

Reading Skill ▮ Identify Text Structure

When you **identify text structure,** you look at how a writer organizes his or her ideas. In a diary, a writer records thoughts and feelings on a regular basis. So, the main text structure of a diary is usually sequence of events, or chronological order. However, individual diary entries may reflect other types of text structures, such as spatial order, which describes or discusses things in the order they are arranged within a certain space.

Identifying text structure helps you locate and recall a writer's ideas and identify his or her purpose for writing. It also helps you understand how events in the text are related to past and future events. The structure of a diary allows you to understand what happened on a specific day or at a certain time. As you read *Zlata's Diary,* use a graphic organizer like the one below to keep track of the sequence of events. Also note the text structure of individual diary entries.

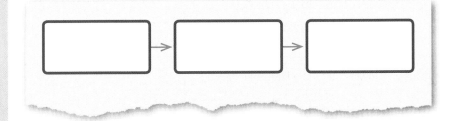

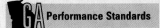

GA Performance Standards

For pages 674–683

ELA7R1e For literary texts, identify events that advance the plot and determine how each event explains past or present action(s) or foreshadows future action(s).

TRY IT

Identify For a day or more, write in a diary. Record the events that happen to you and around you in chronological order. Add your opinions and feelings about the events and the people involved in them. Remember that writing in a diary is a great way to think about your life and to record and understand your feelings.

from Zlata's Diary

Zlata Filipović

Saturday, May 2, 1992

Dear Mimmy,[1]

Today was truly, absolutely the worst day ever in Sarajevo. The shooting started around noon. Mommy and I moved into the hall. Daddy was in his office, under our apartment, at the time. We told him on the intercom to run quickly to the downstairs lobby where we'd meet him. We brought Cicko [Zlata's canary] with us. The gunfire was getting worse, and we couldn't get over the wall to the Bobars',[2] so we ran down to our own cellar.

The cellar is ugly, dark, smelly. Mommy, who's terrified of mice, had two fears to **cope** with. The three of us were in the same corner as the other day. We listened to the pounding shells,[3] the shooting, the thundering noise overhead. We even heard planes. At one moment I realized that this awful cellar was the only place that could save our lives. Suddenly, it started to look almost warm and nice. It was the only way we could defend ourselves against all this terrible shooting. We heard glass shattering in our street. Horrible. I put fingers in my ears to block out the terrible sounds. I was worried about Cicko. We had left him behind in the lobby. Would he catch cold there? Would something hit him? I was terribly hungry and thirsty. We had left our half-cooked lunch in the kitchen.

Identify Text Structure
What structure does Zlata use in this paragraph to organize her ideas?

---

1 Zlata decided on **Mimmy** as her diary's name, knowing that Anne Frank had called her diary Kitty.

2 The **Bobars** are close neighbors and family friends of the Filipovićs.

3 **Shells** are explosives fired from a gun or cannon.

Vocabulary

cope (kōp) v. to deal with or try to overcome difficulties

When the shooting died down a bit, Daddy ran over to our apartment and brought us back some sandwiches. He said he could smell something burning and that the phones weren't working. He brought our TV set down to the cellar. That's when we learned that the main post office (near us) was on fire and that they

View the Art How does this image of a young girl looking out of the bullet-shattered window of her Sarajevo home help you understand what it felt like to live in Bosnia during wartime?

had kidnapped our President. At around 8:00 we went back up to our apartment. Almost every window in our street was broken. Ours were all right, thank God. I saw the post office in flames. A terrible sight. The firefighters battled with the raging fire. Daddy took a few photos of the post office being devoured by the flames. He said they wouldn't come out because I had been fiddling with something on the camera. I was sorry. The whole apartment smelled of the burning fire. God, and I used to pass by there every day. It had just been done up. It was huge and beautiful, and now it was being swallowed up by the flames. It was disappearing. That's what this neighborhood of mine looks like, my Mimmy. I wonder what it's like in other parts of town? I heard on the radio that it was awful around the Eternal Flame. The place is knee-deep in glass. We're worried about Grandma and Granddad. They live there. Tomorrow, if we can go out, we'll see how they are. A terrible day. This has been the worst, most awful day in my eleven-year-old life. I hope it will be the only one. Mommy and Daddy are very edgy. I have to go to bed.

Ciao!⁴ *Zlata*

Conflict What conflict do Zlata and her family face? Is this conflict internal or external?

---

4 The Italian word *ciao* (chou) is an expression said when greeting or leaving other people; it means both *hello* and *goodbye*.

Sunday, May 3, 1992

Dear Mimmy,

Daddy managed to run across the bridge over the Miljacka and get to Grandma and Granddad. He came running back, all upset, sweating with fear and sadness. They're all right, thank God. Tito Street looks awful. The heavy shelling has destroyed shop windows, cars, apartments, the fronts and roofs of buildings. Luckily, not too many people were hurt because they managed to take shelter. Neda (Mommy's girlfriend) rushed over to see how we were and to tell us that they were OK and hadn't had any damage. But it was terrible.

We talked through the window with Auntie Bodia and Bojana just now. They were in the street yesterday when that heavy shooting broke out. They managed to get to Stela's cellar.

Zlata

Conflict In what ways is the war affecting the daily lives of the people in Zlata's neighborhood?

Tuesday, May 5, 1992

Dear Mimmy,

The shooting seems to be dying down. I guess they've caused enough **misery,** although I don't know why. It has something to do with politics.[5] I just hope the "kids"[6] come to some agreement. Oh, if only they would, so we could live and breathe as human beings again. The things that have happened here these past few days are terrible. I want it to stop forever. PEACE! PEACE!

BQ BIG Question
How is the war influencing Zlata's ideas about life?

---

5 **Politics** are the activities or affairs involved in running a government.

6 Zlata and her friends refer to the leaders on both sides of the war as the **kids.**

Vocabulary

misery (miz′ ər ē) *n.* extreme unhappiness; despair

I didn't tell you, Mimmy, that we've rearranged things in the apartment. My room and Mommy and Daddy's are too dangerous to be in. They face the hills, which is where they're shooting from. If only you knew how scared I am to go near the windows and into those rooms. So, we turned a safe corner of the sitting room into a "bedroom." We sleep on mattresses on the floor. It's strange and awful. But, it's safer that way. We've turned everything around for safety. We put Cicko in the kitchen. He's safe there, although once the shooting starts there's nowhere safe except the cellar. I suppose all this will stop and we'll all go back to our usual places.

Ciao! Zlata

Thursday, May 7, 1992

Dear Mimmy,

I was almost positive the war would stop, but today . . . Today a shell fell on the park in front of my house, the park where I used to play and sit with my girlfriends. A lot of people were hurt. From what I hear Jaca, Jaca's mother, Selma, Nina, our neighbor Dado and who knows how many other people who happened to be there were wounded. Dado, Jaca, and her mother have come home from the hospital, Selma lost a kidney but I don't know how she is, because she's still in the hospital AND NINA IS DEAD. A piece of shrapnel lodged[7] in her brain and she died. She was such a sweet, nice little girl. We went to kindergarten together, and we used to play together in the park. Is it possible I'll never see Nina again? Nina, an innocent eleven-year-old little girl— the victim of a stupid war. I feel sad. I cry and wonder why? She didn't do anything. A disgusting war has destroyed a young child's life. Nina, I'll always remember you as a wonderful little girl.

Love, Mimmy, Zlata

Children enjoy a playground in Bosnia in spring 1996. The war officially ended in September 1995.

Conflict What internal conflict is Zlata dealing with?

---

7 **Shrapnel** is a large shell loaded with metal fragments or pellets, which are also sometimes called *shrapnel*. The shell is meant to explode in the air over a target, spreading its contents across a wide area. Here, **lodged** means *stuck*.

Wednesday, May 13, 1992

Dear Mimmy,

Life goes on. The past is cruel, and that's exactly why we should forget it.

The present is cruel, too, and I can't forget it. There's no joking with war. My present reality is the cellar, fear, shells, fire.

Terrible shooting broke out the night before last. We were afraid that we might be hit by shrapnel or a bullet, so we ran over to the Bobars'. We spent all of that night, the next day, and the next night in the cellar and in Nedo's apartment. (Nedo is a **refugee** from Grbavica.[8] He left his parents and came here to his sister's empty apartment.) We saw terrible scenes on TV. The town in ruins, burning, people and children being killed. It's unbelievable.

The phones aren't working; we haven't been able to find out anything about Grandma and Granddad, Melica, how people in other parts of town are doing. On TV we saw the place where Mommy works, Vodoprivreda, all in flames. It's on the aggressor's[9] side of town (Grbavica). Mommy cried. She's depressed. All her years of work and effort up in flames. It's really horrible. All around Vodoprivreda there were cars burning, people dying, and nobody could help them. God, why is this happening?

I'M SO MAD I WANT TO SCREAM AND BREAK EVERYTHING!

Your Zlata

Conflict How does the destruction of Vodoprivreda affect Zlata's mother?

Identify Text Structure How does the text structure of this diary affect your understanding of the war?

---

8 **Grbavica** is a suburb of Sarajevo on the edge of a large area controlled by the Serb nationalists.

9 An **aggressor** is a person, group, or nation that causes a conflict or war.

Vocabulary

refugee (ref´ ū jē´) n. a person who leaves his or her homeland because of danger or persecution and seeks safety in another place

After You Read

Respond and Think Critically

1. Why are Zlata and her family worried about her grandparents? [Recall]

2. Why do you think Zlata and her friends call the leaders of the warring sides the "kids"? [Infer]

3. How does Zlata feel about her diary? [Analyze]

4. When talking about the post office, Zlata says, "It was huge and beautiful, and now it was being swallowed up by the flames. It was disappearing." How is Zlata's life like the burning post office? [Compare]

5. What are some of Zlata's qualities or characteristics? [Conclude]

6. **BQ** BIG Question How might overcoming a great hardship affect a person's future goals? What positive or negative effects might hardships have on a person? [Connect]

Vocabulary Practice

Choose the sentence that uses the vocabulary word correctly.

A. Eric, who is afraid of heights, had to **cope** with staying in a hotel room on the twentieth floor.

B. Eric, who likes heights, had to **cope** with staying in a hotel room on the twentieth floor.

A. The fire destroyed homes, bringing **misery** to many people.

B. The firefighters put out the fire and saved the homes, bringing **misery** to many people.

A. The **refugee** stayed in his home to escape war and persecution.

B. The **refugee** fled his country to escape war and persecution.

Academic Vocabulary

Zlata's sleeping area is **confined** to a small corner in the sitting room because her bedroom is no longer safe. To become more familiar with the word *confined,* fill out the graphic organizer below.

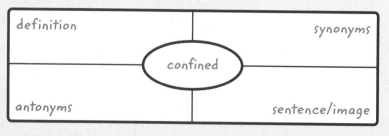

definition	synonyms
	confined
antonyms	sentence/image

TIP

Comparing
Remember that when you compare, you look at two things to see how they are similar or different. Start by thinking about what has happened to the post office building.

- Look for details in the diary entries that describe changes in Zlata's life.

- Note what Zlata used to do with her friends. Can she do these activities now?

- Combine your responses to the above statements and question to compare Zlata's life to the destruction of the post office.

FOLDABLES Study Organizer Keep track of your ideas about the **BIG Question** in your unit Foldable.

 Literature Online

Selection Resources
For Selection Quizzes, eFlashcards, and Reading-Writing Connection activities, go to glencoe.com and enter QuickPass code GL27534u5.

Literary Element Conflict

Standards Practice ELA7R1f

1. Which sentence gives the best description of how Zlata's father deals with living in a war zone?
   - A   He asks others for help.
   - B   He worries about himself first.
   - C   He relies on his wife and daughter.
   - D   He faces danger to take care of his family.

Review: Imagery

As you learned on page 358, **imagery** is language that helps the reader see, hear, feel, smell, and taste the scenes described in a selection. Writers use imagery to help readers visualize, or create a mental image, of people, place, and things.

2. To what senses do the descriptions in Zlata's first entry appeal?

3. What effect does Zlata create by writing that a neighborhood is "knee-deep in glass"?

Reading Skill Identify Text Structure

4. Why do you think Zlata chose to tell her story in the form of diary entries? Refer back to the graphic organizer you made as you read to help you answer the question.

5. What can you learn from Zlata's diary that you might not learn from a newspaper or magazine article about the same event? Explain.

Grammar Link

Making *To Be* Agree The verb *to be* has a variety of forms in the present and past tenses.

Present Tense Forms of *To Be*

Singular	Plural
I **am**	We **are**
You **are**	You **are**
He, she, it **is**	They **are**

Past Tense Forms of *To Be*

Singular	Plural
I **was**	We **were**
You **were**	You **were**
He, she, it **was**	They **were**

Always use the form of *to be* that agrees with the subject of the sentence. For example, which past tense form of *to be* is correct in the sentence below?

- Zlata's neighbors (was, were) hiding in the cellar.

  (The subject is *neighbors. Neighbors* is equal to *they.* The correct past-tense form to go with *they* is *were.*)

Practice Look for examples of the verb *to be* in *Zlata's Diary.* Decide whether Zlata has used the correct forms of the verb. Then write two of your own sentences that contain forms of the verb *to be.* In one sentence, use a present-tense form. In the other, use a past-tense form.

Speaking and Listening

Literature Groups In a group, discuss how *Zlata's Diary* answers the Big Question, "How Can You Become Who You Want to Be?" How do Zlata's experiences give her courage? How do her experiences affect her goals and her future? Use details from the text and from Build Background to help you answer these and any other questions you have about *Zlata's Diary.*

from *The Adventures of Marco Polo*

Connect to the Biography

Think of a time when you experienced something new. Did you go to a new place? Did you try a new activity?

Quickwrite Freewrite for a few minutes about what happened and how you felt during and after the experience.

Build Background

Marco Polo (1254–1324) was born in Venice, Italy. An adventurer and a merchant, Polo began his travels from Europe to Asia in 1271.

- Polo's father, Niccolò, and his uncle, Maffeo, started the family's tradition of trading in Asia. They built a positive relationship with Kublai Khan, the Mongol emperor of China.

- Polo, his father, and his uncle lived in China for about 20 years.

- In approximately 1292, Polo and his family left China to return to Venice. When they arrived home, their relatives and neighbors were shocked. They had thought that the Polos were dead.

- Polo was imprisoned shortly after his return to Venice. During his imprisonment, he met a writer named Rustichello. Polo dictated his adventures in Asia to Rustichello. The writings were published as *Il milione,* or "The Million."

Meet Russell Freedman

History Buff Russell Freedman grew up in San Francisco, California, in a literary household. His father worked in publishing, and famous authors were often guests at the Freedman house. As a student, Freedman enjoyed studying history and geography. He now writes history books and biographies for young readers. Freedman's books include biographies of Abraham Lincoln, Eleanor Roosevelt, and the Wright Brothers. *The Adventures of Marco Polo* was published in 2006. Russell Freedman was born in 1929.

 Literature Online

Author Search For more about Russell Freedman, go to glencoe.com and enter QuickPass code GL27534u5.

Vocabulary

desolate (des′ə lit) *adj.* lifeless or empty (p. 688). *The desolate area had no signs of life—neither animals nor plants.*

arid (ar′id) *adj.* extremely dry (p. 688). *Death Valley is an arid region of the United States.*

vegetation (vej′ə tā′shən) *n.* plant life (p. 689). *A rain forest has much vegetation.*

replenished (ri plenh′ishd) *v.* replaced something that has been used (p. 693). *We went to the grocery store and replenished the food in our cupboards.*

bartered (bär′tərd) *v.* traded without using money (p. 693). *At lunch, she bartered her granola bar for some chocolate milk.*

Set Purposes for Reading

BQ BIG Question

As you read, ask yourself, in what ways does Marco Polo show courage and confidence? How do these traits help him achieve his goals?

Literary Element Description

Description is writing that creates an impression, or a feeling, of a setting, a person, an animal, an object, or an event. Fiction and nonfiction authors use description so that readers can see, hear, taste, smell, and feel the scenes in a piece of writing.

Description is important because it helps readers visualize people, places, and actions. To identify description, look for details that appeal to the senses. As you read the biography, think about how the description helps you better understand the journey that Marco Polo took hundreds of years ago.

Reading Strategy Monitor Comprehension

When you **monitor comprehension,** you check to make sure that you understand what you're reading. For instance, you may come across an unfamiliar word. To monitor your comprehension, stop and ask yourself what the word means. If you don't know the meaning, check a dictionary or look for the meaning in a footnote.

As a reader, your most important task is understanding the material. To monitor comprehension as you read,

- ask yourself questions about the main ideas, people, and events
- reread any text you do not understand
- read footnotes to clarify unfamiliar terms, locations, or people
- use context clues to help you understand difficult words or ideas

As you read, keep track of any questions you have and try to answer them. Use a graphic organizer like the one below.

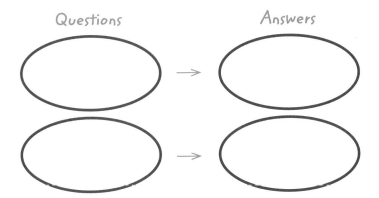

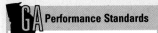
GA Performance Standards

For pages 684–697

ELA7R1g/ii For literary texts, explain and analyze the effects of figurative language.

TRY IT

Monitor Comprehension You probably already use strategies that help you monitor and improve your comprehension. If a friend tells you a story and uses a word you don't know, what do you do? If you are reading a set of instructions and don't understand a step of the process, what do you do?

Marco Polo (1254-1324) setting out with his uncles from Venice for Far East, 14th century. Manuscript. Ann Ronan Picture Library, London.

FROM **THE ADVENTURES OF**

Marco Polo
The Road to Cathay

Russell Freedman

The lands of what are now Turkey and Iran[1] were familiar territory to Italian merchants. But to Marco, who had never traveled far from Venice,[2] every mile brought new sights and experiences.

The Polos' caravan passed through busy cities where **minarets** soared above golden mosques[3] and merchants haggled in overflowing bazaars. In the countryside, they met wandering shepherds who carried their houses on horseback. "They live entirely off their flocks," wrote Marco, "and have clothing of animal skins and tents made of skins or felt."

Farther east, near the Caspian Sea,[4] Marco was astonished to see a fountain of oil gushing from the ground as though from a spring. "This oil is not good to eat [like olive oil]," he noted, "but is good for burning and is also used as an ointment to cure itches and scabs in men and camels. People come from long distances to fetch it, and in the surrounding country, no other oil is used in their lamps." Marco was probably the first European to describe a source of petroleum.

Riding past fortified castles and walled towns, creeping along twisting mountain roads, their caravan arrived at Tabriz, "a large and very noble city" in Persia,[5] and an important crossroads. From there, the Polos headed south, spending day after sweaty day in the saddle as they crossed a sun-baked plateau where "the wells and other watering places lie so far apart, you must travel long distances before your horses and pack mules have anything to drink." At length they reached the Persian Gulf[6] and the steamy port of Hormuz. "Traders come here by ship from all parts of India," wrote Marco, "bringing spices and drugs, precious stones and pearls, fabrics of silk and gold, elephants' tusks, and many other wares."

1 In medieval Europe, people referred to northern China as *Cathay. Turkey* and *Iran* are countries in Southwest Asia. They border each other.

2 *Venice* is a seaport and island city in Italy.

3 Followers of Islam (called Muslims) worship in buildings called *mosques.*

4 The *Caspian Sea* is a large body of water located between Europe and Asia.

5 If a castle is *fortified,* it is strengthened and protected against attacks. Modern-day Iran was once called *Persia.*

6 The *Persian Gulf* borders Iran to the south.

Minarets are towers found in most Islamic mosques.

Description What details in this paragraph help you understand how the shepherds live?

Monitor Comprehension What place is Marco Polo referring to when he says "here"? Why might traders from India go there?

At Hormuz, the Polos planned to find a ship that would take them to India. From there, they hoped, they could sail to the coast of China. But when they saw the poor condition of the vessels at Hormuz, they changed their plans: "Their ships are wretched affairs, and many of them get lost, because they are not fastened together with iron nails. Instead, the hulls are stitched together with twine made of coconut fibers. This makes it a risky business to sail in these ships. And you can take my word that many of them sink, because in the Indian Ocean,[7] the storms are often terrible."

They decided to backtrack and continue their journey by land. So the saddle-sore travelers rode north again as far as the city of Kerman,[8] then turned eastward toward the rising sun. All along, they had to watch for bandits who prowled the countryside, stalking caravans and hunting down stragglers. "Unless the merchants in the caravans are well-armed and equipped with bows, bandits will rob and slay them without mercy," Marco warned.

In eastern Persia, the Polos and their fellow travelers traded their horses for camels, which were better suited to make the long trip across the sand and stone desert that lay ahead—the Dasht-e-Lut, the Desert of Emptiness.[9] Camels and pack mules had to be loaded with goatskins filled with water and with enough food to last at least eight days. For long stretches during the desert crossing, "there are no towns or villages," wrote Marco. "It is all a **desolate** and **arid** waste. There are no animals at all, because they could find nothing to eat. A traveler has to carry with him all that he needs to eat or drink."

BQ ⟩ BIG Question

Given these dangers, why do you think Marco Polo decides to continue the journey over land?

---

7 The **Indian Ocean**, the world's third-largest ocean, stretches from east Africa to southeast Australia and from south Asia to Antarctica.

8 **Kerman** is a city in Iran.

9 **Dasht-e-Lut** is about 300 miles long and 200 miles wide. It is located in the central Iranian plateau.

Vocabulary ....

desolate (des′ə lit) *adj.* lifeless or empty

arid (ar′id) *adj.* extremely dry

Polo, Marco; Italian traveller of Asia; 1254-1324. Works: Le Livre des Merveilles du Monde (Travels of Marco Polo), 1298/99. Campsite of the herdsmen in Ciarcian (Charchan, eastern Turkistan) with cows, sheep, camels. Illumination. Paris, studio of the Boucicaut Master, c.1412. Ms.fr.2810, fol.21 v. Bibliothèque Nationale, Paris.

With no trace of **vegetation** in sight, they built glowing campfires of dry camel dung at night and ate their evening meal under the stars as the hobbled camels, grunting and grumbling, grazed nearby. In the confusion of the frosty dawn, after striking their tents, the drivers held the camels' necks to the ground while the baggage packs were being fastened to their backs, the great beasts struggling and groaning and roaring, the drivers kicking and cursing.

While making their way across this desert, the Polos' caravan was caught in a blinding sandstorm. Winds whipped and howled, kicking up clouds of sand and dust, turning the day as dark as night, making it impossible to see more than a few feet ahead. As sand swirled around the caravan, bandits galloped out of the darkness.

Marco had been told that the darkness was brought about by a spell conjured[10] up by the bandits, a robber

Description What details in this paragraph appeal to your senses?

---

10 *Conjured* means "caused by magic."

Vocabulary
....

vegetation (vej´ə tā´shən) *n.* plant life

Camel. China, Tang dynasty, 618-906 CE. Glazed pottery.

tribe known as the Caraunas: "When these robbers wish to raid and plunder, they cast a devilish spell, so that the day turns dark, and you can scarcely see your comrade riding beside you . . . when they have brought on the darkness, they ride side by side, sometimes thousands of them, and attack. Nothing they find in the open country, man, woman, or beast, can escape them. When they have taken captives who cannot pay a ransom, they kill the old folk, and the young men and women they lead away and sell as serfs[11] and slaves."

The Caraunas probably did not cast a spell, as Marco may have believed, but were shrewd enough to lie in wait and attack during a sandstorm. When they appeared without warning, the travelers and their camels scattered. The three Polos narrowly evaded capture, escaping to the safety of a village. But others in the caravan "were caught and sold, and some were put to death," according to Marco, who devotes only two sentences in his book to what must have been a terrifying experience.

Monitor Comprehension
Why does Marco Polo believe no one can escape the bandits?

11 **Serfs** are forced to work on land owned by someone else.

Moving on, the Polos passed from Persia into Afghanistan.[12] They were now following the southern branch of the Silk Road, the ancient caravan trail that linked the Chinese East to the Muslim West. As far back as the Roman Empire, long caravans of camels had traveled this perilous route, carrying great quantities of Chinese silk to the West, and returning East with cargoes of gold, gemstones, perfumes, **pomegranates,** and other precious goods, including music, knowledge, and novel[13] ideas.

Along the way they passed the ruins of Balkh, once one of the world's great cities, which had been sacked and ravaged a half-century earlier by the Mongol warriors of Genghis Khan.[14] "I can tell you that there used to be many fine palaces and mansions of marble, which can still be seen, but they are shattered now and in ruins," Marco reported. The desolate palaces were now dwelling places for ravens and screech owls which answered one another's cries, while in the empty halls the winds moaned.

As they approached the foothills of the Pamir Mountains in northern Afghanistan, Marco fell ill, from malaria perhaps. He recuperated,[15] he tells us, by going up into the mountains, "where the air is so pure and healthy, that when people who live below in the valleys and towns fall sick or come down with a fever, they lose no time in climbing into the mountains, where a few days' rest restores them to health."

When Marco recovered, the Polos went on their way. The trail, padded soft by centuries of camels, wound around precipitous[16] ledges through narrow, high-walled valleys and followed a rushing stream that led them higher and higher toward lofty snowcapped peaks. The pack mules scampered and clattered up jagged hillsides. The camels leaped from rock to rock, while the wind whistled across every ridge and whined through the canyons. They were now in the high Pamir, which the

Description What words in this paragraph help you visualize Balkh?

---

12 *Afghanistan* is a country to the east of Iran.

13 Here, *novel* means "new" or "different."

14 *Genghis Khan* was a ruler of the Mongol empire.

15 *Malaria* is a disease that is contracted by humans through mosquito bites. People with malaria experience fevers, chills, and sweating. If you *recuperated*, you recovered from an illness.

16 If a ledge is *precipitous,* it is very steep.

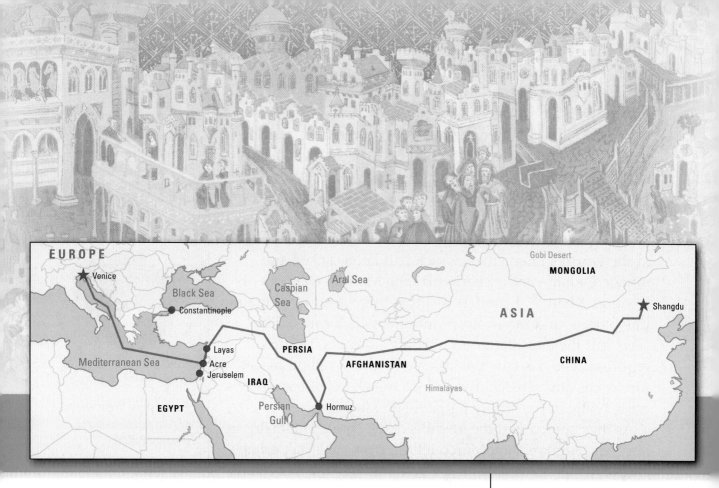

EUROPE
Venice
Black Sea
Constantinople
Mediterranean Sea
Layas
Acre
Jeruselem
EGYPT
IRAQ
Persian Gulf
Caspian Sea
Aral Sea
PERSIA
AFGHANISTAN
Hormuz
Himalayas
Gobi Desert
MONGOLIA
ASIA
CHINA
Shangdu

local people called the "Roof of the World." Ahead of them rose the towering mountains of the Hindu Kush,[17] "said to be the highest place in the world," wrote Marco.

On the other side lay the city of Kashgar in what is today China, a distance of 250 miles as the crow flies. But trudging along steep narrow trails with their animals and belongings, waiting out sudden blizzards, fording swollen rivers, making detours around avalanches, the Polos needed nearly two months to cross the mountains.

The trail they followed topped 15,000 feet. "No birds fly here because of the height and the cold," Marco reported. He noticed that "fire does not burn so brightly, nor give out as much heat as usual, and food does not cook as well." He believed that the weak flames were due to "this great cold." Actually, the flames were weak because of the oxygen-thin air at that altitude.

View the Art Trace Marco Polo's journey from Europe to Asia. What experiences did he have in the places where he stopped?

Monitor Comprehension
Use context clues in the paragraph to figure out the meaning of "as the crow flies."

---

17 The *Hindu Kush* is a mountain system that stretches from northern Pakistan into northeast Afghanistan. Its highest point is 25,236 feet.

On the other side of the mountains, the trail dropped down to a chilly and treeless plain. They moved on to the oasis city of Kashgar, an ancient trading center along the Silk Road with its fine gardens, orchards, and vineyards. There they **replenished** their supplies in open-air markets where merchants wearing silk turbans sold splendid rugs and **bartered** for horses.

Now they faced the most perilous part of their journey. They were about to cross the windswept Taklimakan Desert,[18] known as "the Sea of Death," and even today considered a forbidding place. As the local people in those days warned, "Go in and you won't come out." At the edge of the desert, which is roughly the size of modern Germany, was a town called Lop (present-day Charkhlik), where the Polos stopped for a week to refresh themselves and their animals and stock up on provisions.

They planned to cross at the desert's narrowest point, a trip that would take a month. Along the way they would find a few small oases, islands of trees and greenery fed by ancient irrigation channels that brought snow water from the distant Kunlun mountain range.[19] But as their camels plodded along, the oases became scarce, and the sand dunes rose mountain high.

Description What made crossing the Taklimakan Desert the most dangerous part of the journey?

"You must go for a day and a night before you find fresh water," Marco reported. "There are no birds or beasts because there is nothing for them to eat."

Though the desert seemed lifeless, the travelers heard weird lifelike sounds. "The truth is this," wrote Marco. "When travelers are on the move at night, and one of them happens to lag behind, or falls asleep, and loses touch with his companions, afterwards, when he wants to rejoin

---

18 The **Taklimakan Desert** is an area of about 125,000 square miles. It is located in northwest China.

19 The **Kunlun mountain range** is located in southern Central Asia. It extends from the Pamir Mountains.

replenished (ri plenh´ishd) *v.* replaced something that has been used

bartered (bär´tərd) *v.* traded without using money

them, he hears spirits talking to him as if they are his companions. Sometimes the spirits will call him by name, and make him stray from the path, so that he never finds it again. And in this way, many travelers have been lost and have perished. . . . Yes, and even by daylight travelers may hear these spirit voices, and often they hear the sounds of musical instruments, especially drums, and the clash of arms.[20]

"For this reason," Marco continued, "travelers make a point of staying very close together. They set up a sign pointing in the direction of the next day's travel before they go to sleep. And round the necks of their camels and pack animals they fasten little bells, so that by listening to the sound, they may prevent them from straying off the path."

Those ghostly voices can still be heard today in the Taklimakan. Modern travelers say that the sounds are produced by shifting sands, or by the moaning of winds blowing across the dunes. But some folks living there insist that the sounds come from the wailing of evil spirits.

As the Polos emerged safely from the dreaded desert, they were entering a world that few Europeans had seen. For the first time, Marco found himself among large numbers of Chinese, along with Mongols, Tibetans, Turks,[21] and others, peoples who spoke several languages and practiced different religions. Following the Silk Road, they met Buddhists, Muslims, and Christians, and saw monasteries, abbeys, and temples with golden statues of Buddha[22] and monks clad in saffron robes. They still had mountains and deserts to cross, but now they were deep in the realm of Kublai Khan,[23] and every step brought them closer to the legendary cities of the Chinese East.

Description In what way does this description help you imagine the desert?

---

20 Here, *arms* means "weapons."

21 *Mongols* are a group of people living throughout Central Asia. *Tibetans* are people from the country of Tibet. *Turks* are a group of people living in the country of Turkey and throughout Central Asia.

22 *Buddha* was the founder of the religion called Buddhism. *Buddhists* are people who follow Buddhism.

23 *Kublai Khan,* the grandson of Genghis Khan, was a Mongol emperor in China.

Caravan crossing the Silk Road. Detail of the map of Asia, from the Catalan Atlas. Spain, Majorca. 14th CE. Inv. 2° Kart. 13717.

When word of their approach reached the mighty ruler, he sent couriers[24] out to meet them and escort them to his summer capital at Shangdu (also known as Xanadu), which was still forty days' distant. Marco tells us that they arrived at Shangdu in the spring of 1275, three and a half years after they had set out from Venice. With their detours, they had traveled perhaps 8,000 miles before reaching their destination in China. And the Great Khan was waiting for them. 🐚

Monitor Comprehension
Who was the mighty ruler?

---

24 **Couriers** are messengers or people who guide travelers.

After You Read

Respond and Think Critically

1. What is the goal of Marco Polo's journey? [Recall]

2. Summarize what happens when the Polos arrive at Hormuz to sail to India. [Summarize]

3. Why might Marco Polo have included only two sentences in his book about the bandits' attack on his caravan? Explain. [Infer]

4. Why does the author include quotations from Marco Polo? Support your answer with details from the selection. [Analyze]

5. Do you think the Polos' decision at Hormuz was the right one? Explain. [Evaluate]

6. **BQ** **BIG Question** In what ways did Marco Polo show courage and confidence throughout his journey? How do you think Marco Polo might have answered the Big Question? Support your answers with details from the selection. [Analyze]

TIP

Evaluating
Here are some tips to help you evaluate. Remember that evaluating involves making a judgment about something.

- Reread the part of the biography that describes what happened at Hormuz.

- Think about the results of the decision the Polos made at Hormuz. What do you think might have happened if they had made a different decision?

 FOLDABLES Study Organizer Keep track of your ideas about the **BIG Question** in your unit Foldable.

Connect to Social Studies

Age of Exploration

The fifteenth and sixteenth centuries are often referred to as the Age of Exploration. During this time, explorers left Europe to sail the seas in search of new and faster trade routes. In the fifteenth and sixteenth centuries, Christopher Columbus, Sir Francis Drake, Vasco da Gama, Bartholomeu Dias, and Ferdinand Magellan all made important contributions to exploration. These explorers, however, were not the first to show interest in journeying to new and distant lands to seek trade and adventure.

During the tenth century, Erik the Red discovered Greenland. Later, his son, Leif Eriksson, is believed to have set foot in America. During the thirteenth century, Marco Polo was one of the first Europeans to cross Asia.

On Your Own Answer the following questions on a separate sheet of paper.

1. How might have explorers in the fifteenth and sixteenth centuries been inspired by earlier explorers?

2. What effect do you think the Age of Exploration had on the world?

Literary Element | Description

1. Which description from the biography do you think is most effective? Explain.

2. In what way does the author's use of description add to your understanding of Marco Polo's journey?

Review: Text Features

As you learned on page 303, **text features** are a part of many nonfiction texts. Text features include titles, subheads, decks, photographs, illustrations, captions, footnotes, and even bullets and boldfaced words. The excerpt from *The Adventures of Marco Polo* includes historical images from around the time period discussed in the selection. Read the captions to understand what the images show. Then review the map that accompanies the selection. Use the map to trace the journey described in the selection.

3. In your own words, describe one of the historical images that appears in the selection.

4. Refer to the map that shows Marco Polo's travels. Name three places shown on the map that are mentioned in the selection.

Reading Strategy | Monitor Comprehension

Use the graphic organizer you created to answer the following questions.

5. Which sections of the biography did you find difficult to understand? List two questions that you asked yourself. Then explain what you did to find answers to those questions.

6. List one question that a footnote helped you answer. In what way did the footnote help you better understand what you were reading?

Vocabulary Practice

Respond to these questions.

1. Which place would you describe as **desolate**—an empty school building or a playground full of children?

2. Which place would you describe as **arid**—a rain forest or a desert?

3. Which person **bartered**—a man who traded beads for a basket or a man who shared his crops with a neighbor?

4. Which one would need to be **replenished**—an empty refrigerator or a full gas tank?

5. Where would you most likely see **vegetation**—in a parking lot or in a park?

Academic Vocabulary

Marco Polo experiences a **conflict** when he must escape capture by the Caraunas. To become more familiar with the word *conflict*, fill out the graphic organizer below.

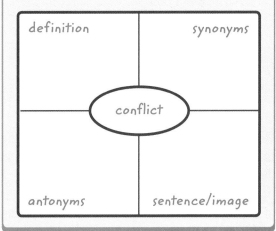

definition | synonyms

conflict

antonyms | sentence/image

Respond Through Writing

Short Story

Apply Description In the excerpt from *The Adventures of Marco Polo,* the author uses description to re-create Marco Polo's experiences. Write a short story about an adventure or exploration, using description to help your readers visualize what happens.

Understand the Task Remember that using **description** means including details that appeal to a reader's sense of sight, smell, taste, touch, and hearing. For example, you may use details that appeal to a reader's sense of hearing to introduce your story's setting.

Prewrite Imagine the setting of your story. Think of the major and minor characters that you want to include. Then select a point of view from which to write your story. For example, you may use first-person point of view *(I went on an adventure)* or third-person point of view *(**Paul Ramos** was a born explorer)*. Think of what will happen in the adventure you describe and construct the plot of your story. Use a plot diagram like the one below.

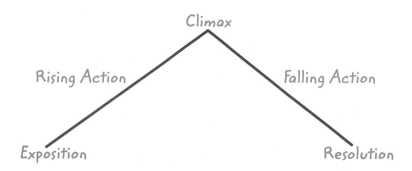

Draft To get started, freewrite about the setting and your characters. Use your plot diagram to help you write about the conflict that will move your plot forward. As you write, you may decide to change what happens in the story. Revisit your plot diagram to map out any changes in the plot. See the Word Bank in the side column for descriptive words you might use in your short story.

Revise After you've written your first draft, read it to make sure you've included effective descriptions. Add or delete descriptions as necessary so that your readers can visualize the setting, characters, and events. Include dialogue to make your characters seem real.

Edit and Proofread Proofread your short story, correcting any errors in spelling, grammar, and punctuation.

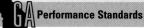 **Performance Standards**

For page 698

ELA7W2d Produce a narrative that includes sensory details and concrete language to develop plot and setting.

> ## Word Bank

The following are some useful words you might want to include in your short story. Check their meanings in a dictionary first to make sure you use them correctly.

brave
daring
exhilarating
exotic
extraordinary
imaginative
perilous
rare
strenuous
treacherous

Part 3

People Who Lend a Hand

Woman and Girl with Helping Hands. Todd Davidson.

BQ ▸ **BIG Question How Can You Become Who You Want to Be?**

What message do the images in the picture *Woman and Girl with Helping Hands* communicate to you? How can you realize your potential by lending a hand to help others?

Birthday Box and *To James*

Connect to the Short Story and the Poem

Think about a time you felt inspired to do your best. Were you giving your best effort because it was an activity you love doing? Or were you doing it for someone you love?

Quickwrite Freewrite for a few minutes about how it felt to do your best and how you feel about it now.

Build Background

Authors get ideas for their stories and poems in different ways.

- In 1995, an editor invited ten authors, including Jane Yolen, to write about a child who receives a beautiful, empty box as a birthday present. Each author's imagination was sparked by the same idea, yet each writer wrote a completely original piece of literature.

- Among Frank Horne's many accomplishments, he once coached a championship high school track team. The talent and efforts of a young runner inspired Frank Horne to write the poem "To James."

Vocabulary

stark (stärk) *adj.* plain; harsh, grim, or severe (p. 705). *The colorful costumes in the school play contrast with the stark set.*

festive (fes′tiv) *adj.* joyful; suitable for a celebration (p. 705). *We used decorations and flowers to make the house festive for the holiday.*

infinite (in′fə nit) *adj.* extremely great; having no limits or end (p. 706). *Small children seem to have an infinite amount of energy when they play.*

subtle (sut′əl) *adj.* characterized by cleverness; having a faint, delicate quality (p. 707). *Dad left a broom near the table as a subtle reminder that we should clean up after lunch.*

Meet the Authors

Jane Yolen

A Literary Life Jane Yolen wrote her first two books before she entered high school. Since that time, Yolen has written more than 250 books. "Birthday Box" was first published in 1995. Jane Yolen was born in 1939.

Frank Horne

An Accomplished Man Frank Horne's love of track began when he ran the quarter mile as a college student. He once told other African American poets, "Your task is definite, grand, and fine." Frank Horne was born in 1899.

 Literature Online

Author Search For more about Jane Yolen and Frank Horne, go to glencoe.com and enter QuickPass code GL27534u5.

Set Purposes for Reading

BQ BIG Question

As you read, ask yourself, how can an older person's wisdom and experience help a younger person become who he or she wants to be?

Literary Element Style

Style is the author's choice and arrangement of words and sentences. Authors sometimes repeat a series of words, phrases, or sentences that have a similar grammatical form. This technique, called parallelism, shows the relationship between ideas and emphasizes important thoughts.

Analyzing style can help you understand the meaning of a story or poem. As you read, ask yourself, how does the word choice and use of parallelism contribute to the meaning and purpose of each selection?

Reading Strategy Evaluate Theme

When you **evaluate,** you make a judgment or form an opinion about something that you read. When you evaluate theme, you form an opinion about the message that the author wants to convey.

Evaluating theme is important because it helps you form an opinion about what you're reading. It also helps you understand recurring themes, or themes that appear in more than one literary work. A short story and a poem can have a similar theme, even if they have different structures. To evaluate theme, think about the following questions:

- What message about life does the author want to convey?
- Do you agree with the author's message? Why or why not?

As you read, look for details that hint at the theme of each selection. Then use the details to analyze and evaluate each theme. In what ways are the themes of the selections similar? Use a graphic organizer like the one below.

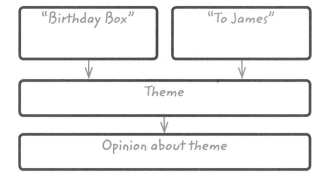

GA Performance Standards

For pages 700–711

ELA7R1d For literary texts, analyze recurring and similar themes across a variety of selections, distinguishing theme from topic.

TRY IT

Evaluate Imagine that the theme of a short story you just read is "Act first and think later." Discuss with a partner whether you think this statement is good advice for young people.

Birthday Box

Jane Yolen

Emerging Angel. John Bunker. Mixed Media.

I was ten years old when my mother died. Ten years old on that very day. Still she gave me a party of sorts. Sick as she was, Mama had seen to it, organizing it at the hospital. She made sure the doctors and nurses all brought me presents. We were good friends with them all by that time, because Mama had been in the hospital for so long.

The head nurse, V. Louise Higgins (I never did know what that *V* stood for), gave me a little box, which was sort of funny because she was the biggest of all the nurses there. I mean she was tremendous. And she was the only one who insisted on wearing all white. Mama had called her the great white shark when she was first admitted, only not to V. Louise's face. "All those needles," Mama had said. "Like teeth." But V. Louise was sweet, not sharklike at all, and she'd been so gentle with Mama.

I opened the little present first. It was a **fountain pen,** a real one, not a fake one like you get at Kmart.

"Now you can write beautiful stories, Katie," V. Louise said to me.

I didn't say that stories come out of your head, not out of a pen. That wouldn't have been polite, and Mama— even sick—was real big on politeness.

"Thanks, V. Louise," I said.

The Stardust Twins—which is what Mama called Patty and Tracey-Lynn because they reminded her of dancers in an old-fashioned ballroom—gave me a present together. It was a diary and had a picture of a little girl in pink, reading in a garden swing. A little young for me, a little too cute. I mean, I read Stephen King[1] and want to write like him. But as Mama always reminded me whenever Dad finally remembered to send me something, it was the

Visual Vocabulary

A **fountain pen** is a pen that has an ink cartridge that can be replaced. The cartridge automatically feeds a steady supply of ink to the writing point.

Style What details about V. Louise Higgins does the author repeat?

---

1 A very popular novelist, **Stephen King** writes tales of horror and the supernatural.

thought that counted, not the actual gift.

"It's great," I told them. "I'll write in it with my new pen." And I wrote my name on the first page just to show them I meant it.

They hugged me and winked at Mama. She tried to wink back but was just too tired and shut both her eyes instead.

Lily, who is from Jamaica, had baked me some sweet bread. Mary Margaret gave me a gold cross blessed by the pope, which I put on even though Mama and I weren't churchgoers. That was Dad's thing.

Then Dr. Dann, the intern[2] who was on days, and Dr. Pucci, the oncologist (which is the fancy name for a cancer doctor), gave me a big box filled to the top with little presents, each wrapped up individually. All things they knew I'd love—paperback books and writing paper and erasers with funny animal heads and colored paper clips and a rubber stamp that printed FROM KATIE'S DESK and other stuff. They must have raided a stationery store.

Style How does the author's use of humor help the reader understand Katie?

There was one box, though, they held out till the end. It was about the size of a large top hat. The paper was deep blue and covered with stars; not fake stars but real stars, I mean, like a map of the night sky. The ribbon was two shades of blue with silver threads running through. There was no name on the card.

"Who's it from?" I asked.

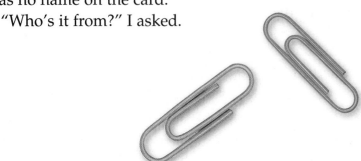

---

2 An *intern* is a recent medical school graduate who works under the supervision of experienced doctors.

None of the nurses answered, and the doctors both suddenly were studying the ceiling tiles with the kind of intensity they usually saved for X rays. No one spoke. In fact the only sound for the longest time was Mama's breathing machine going in and out and in and out. It was a harsh, horrible, insistent[3] sound, and usually I talked and talked to cover up the noise. But I was waiting for someone to tell me.

At last V. Louise said, "It's from your mama, Katie. She told us what she wanted. And where to get it."

I turned and looked at Mama then, and her eyes were open again. Funny, but sickness had made her even more beautiful than good health had. Her skin was like that old paper, the kind they used to write on with quill pens, and stretched out over her bones so she looked like a model. Her eyes, which had been a deep, brilliant blue, were now like the fall sky, bleached and softened. She was like a faded photograph of herself. She smiled a very small smile at me. I knew it was an effort.

"It's you," she mouthed. I read her lips. I had gotten real good at that. I thought she meant it was a present for me.

"Of course it is," I said cheerfully. I had gotten good at that, too, being cheerful when I didn't feel like it. "Of course it is."

I took the paper off the box carefully, not tearing it but folding it into a tidy packet. I twisted the ribbons around my hand and then put them on the pillow by her hand. It made the **stark** white hospital bed look almost **festive**.

Evaluate Theme Why is it important that Katie knows the box is a gift from her mother?

---

3 *Insistent* means "demanding attention or notice."

Vocabulary

stark (stärk) *adj.* plain; harsh, grim, or severe

festive (fes′ tiv) *adj.* joyful; suitable for a celebration

Under the wrapping, the box was beautiful itself. It was made of a heavy cardboard and covered with a linen material that had a pattern of cloud-filled skies.

I opened the box slowly and . . .

"It's empty," I said. "Is this a joke?" I turned to ask Mama, but she was gone. I mean, her body was there, but she wasn't. It was as if she was as empty as the box.

Dr. Pucci leaned over her and listened with a stethoscope,[4] then almost absently patted Mama's head. Then, with **infinite** care, V. Louise closed Mama's eyes, ran her hand across Mama's cheek, and turned off the breathing machine.

"Mama!" I cried. And to the nurses and doctors, I screamed, "Do something!" And because the room had suddenly become so silent, my voice echoed back at me. "Mama, do something."

I cried steadily for, I think, a week. Then I cried at night for a couple of months. And then for about a year I cried at anniversaries, like Mama's birthday or mine, at Thanksgiving, on Mother's Day. I stopped writing. I stopped reading except for school assignments. I was pretty mean to my half brothers and totally rotten to my stepmother and Dad. I felt empty and angry, and they all left me pretty much alone.

And then one night, right after my first birthday without Mama, I woke up remembering how she had said, "It's you." Not, "It's for you," just "It's you." Now Mama had been a high school English teacher and a writer herself. She'd had poems published in little magazines.

Style How does the parallelism in this paragraph emphasize Katie's feelings?

Evaluate Theme What message does Katie's mother want Katie to remember?

---

4 A **stethoscope** is an instrument used to listen to sounds made by the body's internal organs, especially the lungs and heart.

Vocabulary ....

infinite (in´fə nit) *adj.* extremely great; having no limits or end

She didn't use words carelessly. In the end she could hardly use any words at all. So—I asked myself in that dark room—why had she said, "It's you"? Why were they the very last words she had ever said to me, forced out with her last breath?

I turned on the bedside light and got out of bed. The room was full of shadows, not all of them real.

Pulling the desk chair over to my closet, I climbed up and felt along the top shelf, and against the back wall, there was the birthday box, just where I had thrown it the day I had moved in with my dad.

I pulled it down and opened it. It was as empty as the day I had put it away.

"It's you," I whispered to the box.

And then suddenly I knew.

Mama had meant *I* was the box, solid and sturdy, maybe even beautiful or at least interesting on the outside. But I had to fill up the box to make it all it could be. And I had to fill me up as well. She had guessed what might happen to me, had told me in a **subtle** way. In the two words she could manage.

I stopped crying and got some paper out of the desk drawer. I got out my fountain pen. I started writing, and I haven't stopped since. The first thing I wrote was about that birthday. I put it in the box, and pretty soon that box was overflowing with stories. And poems. And memories.

And so was I.

And so was I. 🖋

BQ **BIG Question**

In what way does the empty box encourage Katie to become a writer?

To James

Frank Horne

Do you remember
how you won
that last race . . . ?
how you flung your body
5   at the start . . .
how your spikes
ripped the cinders
in the stretch . . .
how you catapulted°
10   through the tape . . .
do you remember . . . ?
Don't you think
I lurched° with you
out of those starting holes . . . ?
15   Don't you think
my sinews° tightened

Style How does the repetition in lines 2–10 help you understand what's involved in winning a race?

---

9 To **catapult** is to leap or hurl oneself, as if from a giant slingshot.

13 To **lurch** is to move forward suddenly.

16 **Sinews,** or tendons, are cords of tissue that connect muscles to bones.

at those first
few strides . . .
and when you flew into the stretch
20 was not all my thrill
of a thousand races
in your blood . . . ?
At your final drive
through the finish line
25 did not my shout
tell of the
triumphant ecstasy°
of victory . . . ?

Live
30 as I have taught you
to run, Boy—
it's a short dash.
Dig your starting holes
deep and firm
35 lurch out of them
into the straightaway
with all the power
that is in you
look straight ahead
40 to the finish line
think only of the goal
run straight
run high
run hard
45 save nothing
and finish
with an ecstatic burst
that carries you
hurtling
50 through the tape
to victory . . .

Evaluate Theme What is the "goal" to which the speaker refers?

BQ **BIG Question**
What advice does the speaker give the runner for reaching his goals?

---

27 *Triumphant ecstasy* is a state of overwhelming joy or delight as a result of success or winning.

After You Read

Respond and Think Critically

1. How is Katie's mother able to buy Katie the birthday box? [Recall]

2. What is the relationship between the runner and the speaker in "To James"? [Identify]

3. Katie's mother plans a party even though she is ill. What can you infer about Katie's mother? Explain. [Infer]

4. How does the speaker in "To James" feel about the runner? How can you tell? Use examples from the poem to support your answer. [Interpret]

5. How does filling the box with her writing help Katie deal with her grief? Explain. [Analyze]

6. **BQ** **BIG Question** Both Katie and the runner have had individuals help them in life. How are these individuals similar? How are they different? Explain. [Compare]

TIP

Comparing
Here are some tips to help you compare the mother in the story and the speaker in the poem.

Think about

• the actions the mother and the speaker take and the ways they behave

• the advice they give

• how they are alike and different

FOLDABLES Study Organizer Keep track of your ideas about the **BIG Question** in your unit Foldable.

Vocabulary Practice

On a separate sheet of paper, write the vocabulary word that correctly completes each sentence. If none of the words fits the sentence, write "none."

| stark | festive | infinite | subtle |

1. The sky became _____ as the dark rain clouds blocked the sun.

2. When Mom looked at her watch, it was a _____ message for us to hurry.

3. Keisha put on a colorful dress because it made her feel _____ for the party.

4. The dog gazed at me with _____ eyes until I gave it a treat.

5. The painting added a touch of color to the _____ walls.

6. The number of stars in the sky seems _____ on a clear night.

Academic Vocabulary

The empty box that Katie receives from her mother **motivates** Katie to write stories and poems. In the preceding sentence, *motivates* means "causes something or someone to act." Think of an activity you like to do as much as Katie likes to write. What motivates you to do that activity?

 Literature Online

Selection Resources
For Selection Quizzes, eFlashcards, and Reading-Writing Connection activities, go to glencoe.com and enter QuickPass code GL27534u5.

Literary Element | Style

1. At the end of "Birthday Box," Katie says that her box "was overflowing with stories. And poems. And memories." How does the author's style help the reader understand the connection between Katie's writing and her memories? Explain.

2. Find an example in "To James" where the poet uses parallelism to emphasize the message of the speaker. What effect does it have? Explain.

Review: Metaphor

As you learned on page 203, a **metaphor** is a figure of speech that compares seemingly unlike things. In contrast to a simile, a metaphor implies a comparison without using the words *like* or *as*. An **extended metaphor** is an implied comparison that continues through a longer section of a piece of writing.

3. In line 32 of "To James," Frank Horne compares "it" to "a short dash." What two things does this metaphor compare?

4. What extended metaphor does Frank Horne use in "To James"? Explain.

Reading Strategy | Evaluate Theme

Standards Practice 🅖🅐 ELA7R1d

5. Read these sentences from "Birthday Box."

   But I had to fill up the box to make it all it could be. And I had to fill me up as well.

   Katie expresses the story's theme by
   A   understanding that Mama should have filled the box.
   B   realizing Mama's unusual gift was a form of good advice.
   C   making the box more important than her memories of Mama.
   D   worrying that she could not fill the box well enough.

Grammar Link

Subjects Separated from Verbs Subject-verb agreement can be challenging when a prepositional phrase separates the subject from its verb. When the subject and verb are not next to each other, you may wonder what the subject of the sentence is. For example, in the sentence below, is the subject *One* or *nurses*?

> One of the nurses (is, are) from Jamaica.

If you leave out the prepositional phrase, the subject becomes easier to find.

> One ~~of the nurses~~ (is, are) from Jamaica.

Once the prepositional phrase "of the nurses" is gone, you see that the subject is *one,* and the correct verb form is *is.*

Practice Choose the correct verb in the following sentences.

> Some members of the hospital staff (has, have) a birthday party.

> One of the gifts (surprise, surprises) Katie.

Then write two sentences of your own about the story or the poem in which the subject and the verb are separated by a prepositional phrase.

💬 Speaking and Listening

Performance With a small group, choose one person to read aloud "To James." The speaker should vary the tempo, volume, and pitch of his or her voice so that the poem comes alive for the listeners. The other members of the group should perform a pantomime to go with the reading. What movements imitate the runner's actions? How will your group emphasize the repetition in the poem? It may be helpful to write down the movements and lines, so that your group can practice the performance.

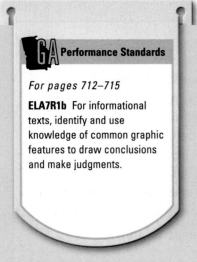

GA Performance Standards

For pages 712–715

ELA7R1b For informational texts, identify and use knowledge of common graphic features to draw conclusions and make judgments.

Set a Purpose for Reading

As you read, ask yourself, how do the boys from Sudan help others overcome hardships?

Preview the Article

1. What does the title, also called a **head** or **headline,** suggest the article is about?

2. What details do the **photographs** and **captions** provide?

Reading Strategy

Summarize

When you **summarize,** you put the main ideas and supporting details of a text into your own words. As you read, identify the most important ideas. Which details support these main ideas? Then write the information in a logical order.

Main Idea:

Detail 1
Detail 2
Detail 3

TIME

Message of HOPE

They became known as the Lost Boys of Sudan after fleeing the horrible civil war. Now three, who have done well in the United States, have returned to a refugee camp. Their goal is to help prepare others for fast food, phones, and life in America.

By ERICKA SÓUTER and DIETLIND LERNER

In a small, hot classroom in a crowded Kakuma, Kenya, refugee camp, a group of 20-year-olds sit at desks. They fire questions at three young men wearing shirts and ties. "What is the weather like in America?" asks one student. "Why are there murderers there?" asks another. "If obesity[1] is a problem, why are you skinny?" asks another. The men, who have photos of sports stars, roller coasters, and buses, answer with care. They also give some tips. "In America it is a very good thing to say thank you," says one. "When you get to America, everyone will ask if you are hungry," says another. "In our country it is insulting to ask that, so you say no. My advice to you is to say yes. We missed a lot of good food because of our culture!"

---

1 *Obesity* is the condition of being very overweight.

"I think a lot about how people here have too little," says Duom Deng (left, with James Biar, center, David Ayiik, and a group of Kenyan women who are neighbors to Kakuma's Sudanese refugees). "I want one day for the hunger to stop."

Just 10 years ago, Duom Deng, David Ayiik, and James Biar were refugees too. During Sudan's civil war, the three boys had seen their parents killed and their villages destroyed. Then they and thousands of other orphaned children walked 1,000 miles east to Ethiopia. Once there, they spent five years wandering between refugee camps. Eventually they settled in Kakuma. Aid workers called the thousands of male orphans the Lost Boys. (Girls also fled to the camps. For cultural reasons, they were placed with refugee foster[2] families.) "We made ourselves brothers," says Deng, who is in his mid-20s. "We learned by ourselves to be good to ourselves and to others."

That good sense stuck with Ayiik, Deng, and Biar when they came to the United States with 3,600 other Kakuma refugees. In less than five years, they changed from wide-eyed immigrants who had never seen a kitchen freezer to young men working their way through college in San Diego, California. Now they have returned to Kakuma—thanks to the help of the San Diego Rotary[3] Club. Their goal is to help the next group of U.S.-bound hopefuls prepare for their new home. "The desire to go back to the camp was straight from my heart," says Deng. "I wanted to see how the rest were doing. It was a big thought for me that I had left them."

Thousands of Kakuma's 86,000 refugees are Lost Boys. Most of them have applied for U.S. visas.[4] But until the visas are approved, the refugees live in mud huts, sleep on wooden slabs, and eat only grain and water. Most have never owned a book, which made the 1,000 donated dictionaries Deng, Ayiik, and Biar brought a hot item. Deng's digital camera was also a hit. Some of the kids had never seen their own image and collapsed in squeals of delight. Tulasi Sharma works at the camp. "It is so important for the students to see the Lost Boys," says Sharma. "To know that it is possible [to succeed] and to know that they have not been forgotten."

---

2 **Foster** means "sharing in family life even though not related by birth." The girls lived with refugee families, who looked after them.

3 The main goals of the **Rotary Club** are to help people in need and to build peace and understanding. It has "clubs" in many cities around the world, and members are called Rotarians.

4 A **visa** is an official document giving visitors permission to enter or leave a country.

The trip had an effect on the three from San Diego too. "I was really uncomfortable to see them that way," Deng says of his friends who live in poverty. "The food that they have is still not enough. They are not getting any vegetables or oils. The water gets cut off after just an hour. It is so sad to me."

The three have come a long way. In 1987 Deng's family, members of Sudan's Dinka tribe, had just settled down to dinner. Suddenly, Sudanese soldiers surrounded their tiny village. "We heard a cry from a neighbor," he recalls. "There were horses, guns, men everywhere." In the confusion, he was separated from his mother and father. But, like many parents, they had warned him that if the men with guns came, he should run east.

Louise Gubb

With the sounds of the village burning and people being shot, 6-year-old Deng ran with the other children. He was wearing a T-shirt and shorts—the only clothes he would have for the next two years. Deng and the other kids joined up with a larger group heading across the desert. "I remember eating leaves, I was so hungry and thirsty," he recalls. Hundreds died of hunger or were killed by lions and crocodiles, according to Ayiik. "I was very scared. I think I made it because I saw other kids like me and I tried to be strong like them," he says. "I couldn't give up."

Years later, the three arrived in the United States. They had only enough money to last for three months. Judy Bernstein is a volunteer who helped the young men get used to life in their new country. "They would put eggs and milk in the cupboard, not the refrigerator," she says. Lost Boys younger than 18 were placed in foster homes. The rest had to fend for[5] themselves. To get ready for job interviews, "they learned how to look someone in the eye, which is not part of the Dinka culture," explains Bernstein. Sharing, however, is part of their culture. When one Lost Boy got a job interview, he would bring three or four of his "brothers" so they might find work too.

---

5 The phrase *to fend for themselves* means "to take care of themselves without help from others."

Louise Gubb

"I was hoping all our friends would have the same chance," says Ayiik (left, with Biar, center, and Deng). "If they came to the U.S., they too could do better."

Many of them spent a lot of their early time in America exploring. They went to zoos and grocery stores. They tried fast food. And they learned to cook. "In Sudan only women cook," says Ayiik, who has grown very fond of burgers. "It was a hard thing to learn." Their first apartments were often in rough parts of town. Usually five guys shared two bedrooms. For the San Diego Lost Boys, the local Rotary Club became a place to go. Bernstein took Deng and Ayiik to the club to speak about their experiences. The young men formed their own group within the club. The Rotarians helped with English lessons and job training. Club member Stephen Brown helped them raise money to return to Kakuma. "Not only are they selfless and polite, but they present themselves with a dignity that's amazing, considering what they've gone through," he says. "They have big smiles and good senses of humor."

All three young men attend local colleges. Deng studies communication and general education. He also works at a graphic design company. Ayiik studies business accounting and works as a file clerk. Biar, the shyest of the three, studies education. "We passed a big disaster, and now we're having a good life and good experiences," says Deng. Eventually the men, who are all single, plan to return to Sudan. They want to help rebuild—and perhaps find wives. These days they seem neither boyish nor lost. As Simon Laur, a 24-year-old refugee in the Kakuma class, suggests, "Maybe we should call you the Found Boys."

Respond and Think Critically

1. Write a brief summary of the main events in this article before you answer the following questions. For help on writing a summary, see page 219. [Summarize]

2. **Text-to-Self** How might the story of the Lost Boys of Sudan help you face difficult challenges in your life? Explain. [Connect]

3. Why do you think the aid workers in the refugee camps call the boys from Sudan the "Lost Boys"? Explain. [Infer]

4. What does refugee Simon Laur mean when he says, "Maybe we should call you the Found Boys"? Explain. [Interpret]

5. **Reading Strategy** Summarize Does the deck, or subtitle, summarize the article well? Why or why not? Use the graphic organizer to help you explain your answer.

6. **BQ** BIG Question Without the help of the Rotary Club, could the boys have become who they wanted to be? Explain.

Before You Read

The Teacher Who Changed My Life

Connect to the Essay

Think about how it would feel to be a new student in a new school in a new country. Nearly everyone else speaks a language that you don't understand.

Quickwrite Freewrite about a time when you were a newcomer in a place where everyone else knew one another. How did you feel? How did other people treat you?

Build Background

In this personal essay, journalist Nicholas Gage describes coming to the United States in 1949 from Greece.

- Greece is in southern Europe on the Mediterranean Sea. In ancient times, it was the center of a very influential culture.

- Between 1940 and 1949, Greeks fought in two wars—World War II and a civil war. During this time, 600,000 Greeks were killed, including Nicholas Gage's mother.

- In the 1940s, many immigrants from war-torn countries such as Greece came to the United States. They hoped to find peace and opportunity for themselves and their families.

Vocabulary

ultimately (ul′tə mit lē) *adv.* in the end; finally (p. 719). *After much thinking, he ultimately decided to plant tomatoes instead of beans.*

tact (takt) *n.* the ability to handle people or situations without causing bad feelings (p. 722). *A person needs tact when trying to make new friends.*

ecstatic (ek stat′ik) *adj.* overwhelmed with joy or delight (p. 722). *My sister was ecstatic when she won the spelling bee.*

avidly (av′id lē) *adv.* eagerly; enthusiastically (p. 724). *When the new issue of my favorite magazine arrives, I avidly read every page.*

Meet Nicholas Gage

Searching for the Truth
When Nicholas Gage first came to the United States, he was nine years old and did not speak English. Thirty years later, when he left the United States for Greece, Gage was a top investigative reporter for *The New York Times*. He returned to Lia, the tiny remote village of his birth, to search for the people responsible for his mother's death.

Literary Works The best-selling book that Gage wrote about his search was named for his mother, *Eleni*. The autobiographical essay on the following pages is from Gage's memoir, *A Place for Us*, published in 1989.

Nicholas Gage was born in 1939.

 Literature Online

Author Search For more about Nicholas Gage, go to glencoe.com and enter QuickPass code GL27534u5.

Set Purposes for Reading

BQ BIG Question

As you read, think about how a young immigrant who did not know English grew up to become an award-winning American journalist. Who helped him along the way?

Literary Element Tone

The **tone** of a piece of writing expresses the author's purpose for writing and the author's feelings about his or her subject, ideas, or theme. An informal selection may have a light, humorous tone. Formal writing may have a serious tone. Some factors that contribute to tone are the author's choice of words, the kinds of details he or she includes, and the images he or she creates.

Tone helps shape the way readers feel about a selection's subjects and themes. Identifying the author's tone can help you better understand the author's purpose for writing.

As you read, think about the tone of the essay. How does the author feel about the events and people he describes?

Reading Strategy Interpret Plot Events

When you **interpret plot events,** you use your own understanding of the world to decide what the events or ideas in a selection mean. Interpreting is more than just understanding the facts or events as you read. It involves asking what the writer is really trying to say and then using your knowledge and experience to answer that question.

As you've learned, the sequence of events in a literary work is called the plot. Interpreting plot events can help you reach a deeper understanding of the selection and its main idea or message.

To interpret, ask yourself, what is the author really trying to say? What larger idea might these events be about? What do they mean? Use a graphic organizer like the one below to keep track of your ideas.

Plot Event	My Knowledge	Interpretation

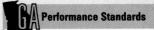

GA Performance Standards

For pages 716–727

ELA7R1h For literary texts, identify and analyze how an author's use of words creates tone and mood.

TRY IT

Interpret Think of a movie you know well. What is the main idea or theme of the movie? For example, it might be that true love overcomes all obstacles, good triumphs over evil, or that friendship is what matters most. Now think of a plot event in the movie. Why was that plot event included? How does the event show the theme of the movie? How would the theme be different if the plot event were changed?

The Teacher
Who Changed My Life

Nicholas Gage

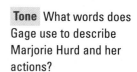

The person who set the course of my life in the new land I entered as a young war refugee—who, in fact, nearly dragged me onto the path that would bring all the blessings I've received in America—was a salty-tongued,[1] no-nonsense schoolteacher named Marjorie Hurd. When I entered her classroom in 1953, I had been to six schools in five years, starting in the Greek village where I was born in 1939.

When I stepped off a ship in New York Harbor on a gray March day in 1949, I was an undersized 9-year-old in short pants who had lost his mother and was coming to live with the father he didn't know. My mother, Eleni Gatzoyiannis, had been imprisoned, tortured, and shot by Communist guerrillas[2] for sending me and three of my four sisters to freedom. She died so that her children could go to their father in the United States.

The portly, bald, well-dressed man who met me and my sisters seemed a foreign, authoritarian[3] figure. I secretly resented him for not getting the whole family out of

---

1 A **salty-tongued** person speaks in a sharp, witty, and often sarcastic way.

2 **Guerillas** are members of small, organized forces. They're usually volunteers who are not soldiers in a regular army.

3 **Authoritarian** means "having or expecting complete obedience."

Greece early enough to save my mother. **Ultimately,** I would grow to love him and appreciate how he dealt with becoming a single parent at the age of 56, but at first our relationship was prickly,[4] full of hostility.

As Father drove us to our new home—a tenement in Worcester,[5] Mass.—and pointed out the huge brick building that would be our first school in America, I clutched my Greek notebooks from the refugee camp, hoping that my few years of schooling would impress my teachers in this cold, crowded country. They didn't. When my father led me and my 11-year-old sister to Greendale Elementary School, the grim-faced Yankee principal put the two of us in a class for the mentally retarded. There was no facility in those days for non-English-speaking children.

By the time I met Marjorie Hurd four years later, I had learned English, been placed in a normal, graded class and had even been chosen for the college preparatory track in the Worcester public school system. I was 13 years old when our father moved us yet again, and I entered Chandler Junior High shortly after the beginning of seventh grade. I found myself surrounded by richer, smarter and better-dressed classmates who looked askance[6] at my strange clothes and heavy accent. Shortly after I arrived, we were told to select a hobby to pursue during "club hour" on Fridays. The idea of hobbies and clubs made no sense to my immigrant ears, but I decided to follow the prettiest girl in my class—the blue-eyed daughter of the local Lutheran minister. She led me through the door marked "Newspaper Club" and into the presence of Miss Hurd, the newspaper adviser and English teacher who would become my mentor and my muse.[7]

Tone How do you think Gage felt about his new country?

---

4 Here, **prickly** means *difficult* or *troublesome.*

5 The founders of the city of **Worcester** brought its oddly pronounced name with them from England. It's pronounced as if it were spelled *Wooster,* with an *o* sound as in *wood.*

6 The expression **looked askance** means "looked with suspicion or disapproval."

7 A **mentor** is a wise and trusted counselor, and a **muse** is a source of artistic inspiration.

Vocabulary
....

ultimately (ul′tə mit lē) *adv.* in the end; finally

A formidable, solidly built woman with salt-and-pepper hair, a steely eye and a flat Boston accent, Miss Hurd had no patience with layabouts. "What are all you goof-offs doing here?" she bellowed at the would-be journalists. "This is the Newspaper Club! We're going to put out a *newspaper*. So if there's anybody in this room who doesn't like work, I suggest you go across to the Glee Club now, because you're going to work your tails off here!"

I was soon under Miss Hurd's spell. She did indeed teach us to put out a newspaper, skills I honed during my next 25 years as a journalist. Soon I asked the principal to transfer me to her English class as well. There, she drilled us on grammar until I finally began to understand the logic and structure of the English language. She assigned stories for us to read and discuss; not tales of heroes, like the Greek myths I knew, but stories of underdogs—poor people, even immigrants, who seemed ordinary until a crisis drove them to do something extraordinary. She also introduced us to the literary wealth[8] of Greece—giving me a new perspective on my war-ravaged, impoverished[9] homeland. I began to be proud of my origins.

One day, after discussing how writers should write about what they know, she assigned us to compose an essay from our own experience. Fixing me with a stern look, she added, "Nick, I want you to write about what happened to your family in Greece." I had been trying to put those painful memories behind me and left the assignment until the last moment. Then, on a warm spring afternoon, I sat in my room with a yellow pad and pencil and stared out the window at the buds on the trees. I wrote that the coming of spring always reminded me of the last time I said goodbye to my mother on a green and gold day in 1948.

Tone How does the author feel toward Miss Hurd?

BQ BIG Question
How has Miss Hurd helped the author so far?

---

8 Greece's *literary wealth*, dating from about 750 to 300 B.C., includes plays, poems, and other texts that greatly influenced the development of other cultures, such as those of Europe, Canada, and the United States.

9 *Impoverished* means "reduced to poverty" or "made very poor."

Nicholas Gage's third-grade class. Nicholas is in the back row, second from the left.

I kept writing, one line after another, telling how the Communist guerrillas occupied our village, took our home and food, how my mother started planning our escape when she learned that the children were to be sent to re-education camps behind the Iron Curtain[10] and how, at the last moment, she couldn't escape with us because the guerrillas sent her with a group of women to thresh wheat in a distant village. She promised she would try to get away on her own, she told me to be brave and hung a silver cross around my neck, and then she kissed me. I watched the line of women being led down into the ravine and up the other side, until they disappeared around the bend—my mother a tiny brown figure at the end who stopped for an instant to raise her hand in one last farewell.

---

10 During the years following World War II, the ***Iron Curtain*** was an imaginary barrier separating the former Soviet Union and its allies from the non-Communist world.

I wrote about our nighttime escape down the mountain, across the minefields, and into the lines of the Nationalist soldiers, who sent us to a refugee camp. It was there that we learned of our mother's execution. I felt very lucky to have come to America, I concluded, but every year, the coming of spring made me feel sad because it reminded me of the last time I saw my mother.

I handed in the essay, hoping never to see it again, but Miss Hurd had it published in the school paper. This mortified[11] me at first, until I saw that my classmates reacted with sympathy and **tact** to my family's story. Without telling me, Miss Hurd also submitted the essay to a contest sponsored by the Freedoms Foundation at Valley Forge, Pa., and it won a medal. The Worcester paper wrote about the award and quoted my essay at length. My father, by then a "five-and-dime-store chef," as the paper described him, was **ecstatic** with pride, and the Worcester Greek community celebrated the honor to one of its own.

For the first time I began to understand the power of the written word. A secret ambition took root in me. One day, I vowed, I would go back to Greece, find out the details of my mother's death and write about her life, so her grandchildren would know of her courage. Perhaps I would even track down the men who killed her and write of their crimes. Fulfilling that ambition would take me 30 years.

Meanwhile, I followed the literary path that Miss Hurd had so forcefully set me on. After junior high, I became the editor of my school paper at Classical High School and got a part-time job at the Worcester *Telegram and Gazette.* Although my father could only give me $50 and encouragement toward a college education, I managed to finance four years at Boston University with scholarships[12] and part-time jobs in journalism. During my last year of college, an article I wrote about a friend who had died in

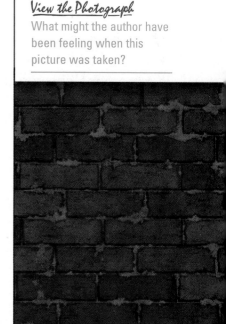

Young Nicholas poses with his sister and his father in 1950.

View the Photograph
What might the author have been feeling when this picture was taken?

---

11 *Mortified* means "greatly embarrassed."

12 A *scholarship* is money given to help a student continue his or her education.

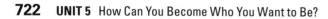
Vocabulary

tact (takt) *n.* the ability to handle people or situations without causing bad feelings

ecstatic (ek stat′ik) *adj.* overwhelmed with joy or delight

the Philippines—the first person to lose his life working for the Peace Corps[13]—led to my winning the Hearst Award for College Journalism. And the plaque was given to me in the White House by President John F. Kennedy.

For a refugee who had never seen a motorized vehicle or indoor plumbing until he was 9, this was an unimaginable honor. When the Worcester paper ran a picture of me standing next to President Kennedy, my father rushed out to buy a new suit in order to be properly dressed to receive the congratulations of the Worcester Greeks. He clipped out the photograph, had it laminated in plastic and carried it in his breast pocket for the rest of his life to show everyone he met. I found the much-worn photo in his pocket on the day he died 20 years later.

In our isolated Greek village, my mother had bribed a cousin to teach her to read, for girls were not supposed to attend school beyond a certain age. She had always dreamed of her children receiving an education. She couldn't be there when I graduated from Boston University, but the person who came with my father and shared our joy was my former teacher, Marjorie Hurd. We celebrated not only my bachelor's degree but also the scholarships that paid my way to Columbia's Graduate School[14] of Journalism. There, I met the woman who would eventually become my wife. At our wedding and at the baptisms of our three children, Marjorie Hurd was always there, dancing alongside the Greeks.

By then, she was Mrs. Rabidou, for she had married a widower when she was in her early 40s. That didn't distract her from her vocation[15] of introducing young minds to English literature, however. She taught for a total of 41 years and continually would make a "project" of

Interpret Plot Events How do you think Gage felt about fulfilling his mother's dream?

---

13 The **Peace Corps** is a U.S. program that sends volunteers to help people in developing countries improve their living conditions. It was begun by President John F. Kennedy in 1961.

14 After completing four years (usually) of study, college students receive an honor called a **bachelor's degree**. Some then go on to **graduate schools** for more advanced education and training.

15 One meaning of **vocation** is *occupation*. It can also refer to the particular work one feels called to do or is especially suited for.

some balky student in whom she spied a spark of potential.[16] Often these were students from the most troubled homes, yet she would alternately bully and charm each one with her own special brand of tough love until the spark caught fire. She retired in 1981 at the age of 62 but still **avidly** follows the lives and careers of former students while overseeing her adult stepchildren and driving her husband on camping trips to New Hampshire.

Miss Hurd was one of the first to call me on Dec. 10, 1987, when President Reagan, in his television address after the summit meeting with Gorbachev, told the nation that Eleni Gatzoyiannis' dying cry, "My children!" had helped inspire him to seek an arms agreement[17] "for all the children of the world."

"I can't imagine a better monument for your mother," Miss Hurd said with an uncharacteristic catch in her voice.

Although a bad hip makes it impossible for her to join in the Greek dancing, Marjorie Hurd Rabidou is still an honored and enthusiastic guest at all our family celebrations, including my 50th birthday picnic last summer, where the **shish kebab** was cooked on spits, clarinets and *bouzoukis* wailed, and costumed dancers led the guests in a serpentine[18] line around our colonial farmhouse, only 20 minutes from my first home in Worcester.

My sisters and I felt an aching void because my father was not there to lead the line, balancing a glass of wine on his head while he danced, the way he did at every celebration during his 92 years. But Miss Hurd was there, surveying the scene with quiet satisfaction. Although my parents are gone, her presence was a consolation, because I owe her so much.

Interpret Plot Events Why would this be an important moment for both Gage and Miss Hurd?

Visual Vocabulary

A **shish kebab** (shish′ kə bob′) is made with chunks of meat threaded on a long, thin skewer and broiled.

---

16 A *balky* student is one who tends to stop short and refuse to go on. A student with *potential* has qualities or abilities capable of being developed.

17 In 1987, **Mikhail Gorbachev** was the leader of the Soviet Union. An *arms agreement* is a treaty in which nations agree to put limits on certain weapons.

18 A *bouzouki* (boo zoo′kē) is a stringed instrument. A *serpentine* (sur′pən tēn′) line winds around, like a snake's body.

Vocabulary

avidly (av′id lē) *adv.* eagerly; enthusiastically

This is truly the land of opportunity, and I would have enjoyed its bounty even if I hadn't walked into Miss Hurd's classroom in 1953. But she was the one who directed my grief and pain into writing, and if it weren't for her I wouldn't have become an investigative reporter and foreign correspondent, recorded the story of my mother's life and death in *Eleni* and now my father's story in *A Place for Us*, which is also a testament to the country that took us in. She was the catalyst[19] that sent me into journalism and indirectly caused all the good things that came after. But Miss Hurd would probably deny this emphatically.

A few years ago, I answered the telephone and heard my former teacher's voice telling me, in that won't-take-no-for-an-answer tone of hers, that she had decided I was to write and deliver the eulogy[20] at her funeral. I agreed (she didn't leave me any choice), but that's one assignment I never want to do. I hope, Miss Hurd, that you'll accept this remembrance instead. 🍃

BQ BIG Question

How did Miss Hurd help Gage become the person he wanted to be?

---

19 Here, the ***testament*** is a statement of gratitude and respect. A ***catalyst*** is one who stirs to action.

20 At a funeral, the ***eulogy*** (ū′ lə jē) is a speech praising the person who has died.

The grown-up Nicholas and his former teacher, Majorie Hurd Rabidou, share a moment.

After You Read

Respond and Think Critically

1. What makes Gage decide to sign up for the Newspaper Club? [Recall]

2. How is Gage similar to and different from his classmates at Chandler Junior High? [Compare]

3. Gage refers to Miss Hurd as "my mentor and my muse." What does he mean? Why do you think Gage chose these words? [Interpret]

4. Why did Miss Hurd become such an important part of Gage's family life? [Analyze]

5. There are young people in this country today who are war refugees like Gage was. Do you think it is easier or harder for them to adjust to life in the United States than it was for Gage? Give reasons for your opinions. [Conclude]

6. **BQ** **BIG Question** Gage calls Miss Hurd "the teacher who changed my life." Have you ever had a teacher or mentor who changed your life? Explain. [Connect]

Vocabulary Practice

Identify whether each set of paired words has the same or the opposite meaning. Then use each vocabulary word in a sentence or draw or find a picture that represents the word.

1. **ultimately** and eventually
2. **tact** and insensitivity
3. **ecstatic** and miserable
4. **avidly** and excitedly

Academic Vocabulary

Nicholas Gage had to make **adjustments** when he started school in America. In the preceding sentence, *adjustments* means "adaptations or changes to meet new conditions." Think about a time when you've been faced with new conditions—perhaps in a new school, town, or neighborhood. What adjustments did you have to make?

TIP

Compare
To answer question 2, compare and contrast Gage with his classmates. Think about what you know about junior high school students.

- Ask yourself what all junior high school students have in common.

- Reread Gage's description of his classmates. What differences did he notice? What other differences might there have been?

 Keep track of your ideas about the **BIG Question** in your unit Foldable.

 Literature Online

Selection Resources
For Selection Quizzes, eFlashcards, and Reading-Writing Connection activities, go to glencoe.com and enter QuickPass code GL27534u5.

Literary Element Narrative Poetry

1. How does the tone change in different parts of the essay? Use details from the essay to support your answer.

2. What tone does Gage create when describing Miss Hurd? What does the tone reveal about the author's purpose for writing?

Review: Diction

As you learned on page 249, **diction** describes an author's use and arrangement of words. Authors will sometimes use **idioms,** or words or phrases that have a special meaning different from the ordinary meaning of the words. For example, to "put one's foot in one's mouth" is often used as an idiom. To determine the meaning of an idiom, think about what the ordinary meanings of the words suggest.

3. One example of an idiom in the selection is the expression that Miss Hurd uses with new members of the Newspaper Club: "you're going to work your tails off here." Determine the meaning of this idiom by looking at what the ordinary meanings of the words suggest.

Reading Strategy Interpret Plot Events

Standards Practice ELA7R1e

4. Which sentence gives the best description of how winning a writing contest affected the author when he was in junior high?
   A It made him want to join the Newspaper Club.
   B It helped him realize the power of writing.
   C It inspired him to become a teacher like Miss Hurd.
   D It taught him the importance of family and history.

Grammar Link

Indefinite pronouns do not refer to a particular person or thing. Certain indefinite pronouns are always singular, or equal to *he, she,* or *it.*

anybody	every	nobody
anyone	everybody	no one
anything	everyone	nothing
each	everything	somebody
either	neither	someone

Make the subject and verb agree in each sentence below. (Use the chart for help.)

Everybody (was, were) proud of Gage.

Everybody is singular, or equal to *he, she,* or *it.* So the correct verb form is *was.*

Each of the students (has, have) a copy of Gage's essay.

Omit the prepositional phrase to determine the correct verb.

Each of the students (has, have) a copy of Gage's essay.

Practice Write four sentences about Gage or Miss Hurd using singular indefinite pronouns as your sentence subjects. Underline the pronoun in each sentence and circle the verb. Use singular verbs with singular pronouns.

💬 Speaking and Listening

Oral Report Think about a person who has influenced you. Write an oral report about this person to share with the class. Describe how you know this person, what he or she is like, and how he or she has influenced you. Include examples and details that support your ideas and statements.

Comparing Literature

from *Barrio Boy* and *How I Learned English*

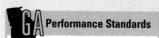
Performance Standards

For pages 728–737

ELA7R1i For literary texts, identify and analyze similarities and differences in traditional literature from different cultures.

BQ ▶ BIG Question

As you read these paired selections, think about how the main character in *Barrio Boy* and the speaker in "How I Learned English" try to become who they want to be.

Literary Element ▶ Setting

You've learned that **setting** is the time and place in which the events of a literary work take place. The setting often helps create the mood, or general feeling, of the story. As you read each selection, ask yourself, what details tell when and where the events take place? How does the setting help create the mood of the selection?

Reading Skill ▶ Compare and Contrast

When you compare, you look for similarities. When you contrast, you look for differences. When you compare and contrast two pieces of literature, you look at important parts, such as setting and theme, to see how those parts are alike or different. On the following pages, you'll compare and contrast the settings of the passage from *Barrio Boy* and the poem "How I Learned English." Use a comparison chart like the one below to record details about the setting. Then think about how the selections' different settings and structures might reveal similar themes.

Setting	*Barrio Boy*	"How I Learned English"
Time		
Place		
Mood		

Meet the Authors

Ernesto Galarza

A Mexican-American union leader and writer, Ernesto Galarza was born in 1905. He spent most of his life fighting for the rights of farm workers.

Ernesto Galarza died in 1984.

Gregory Djanikian

Gregory Djanikian was born in Egypt to Armenian parents in 1949. He moved to the United States as a young boy. He writes about life in the United States and problems in Armenia.

LOG ON ▶ Literature Online

Author Search For more about Ernesto Galarza and Gregory Djanikian, go to glencoe.com and enter QuickPass code GL27534u5.

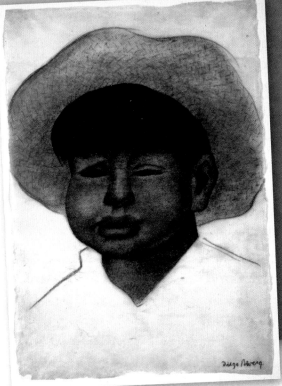

Cabeza de Nino, 1921–1929. Diego Rivera.

FROM BARRIO BOY

Ernesto Galarza

The two of us walked south on Fifth Street one morning to the corner of Q Street and turned right. Half of the block was occupied by the Lincoln School. It was a three-story wooden building, with two wings that gave it the shape of a double-T connected by a central hall. It was a new building, painted yellow, with a shingled roof that was not like the red tile of the school in Mazatlán.[1] I noticed other differences, none of them very reassuring.

We walked up the wide staircase hand in hand and through the door, which closed by itself. A mechanical contraption screwed to the top shut it behind us quietly.

Up to this point the adventure of enrolling me in the school had been carefully rehearsed. Mrs. Dodson had told us how to find it and we had circled it several times on our walks. Friends in the *barrio*[2] explained that

Comparing Literature

Galarza begins by describing the setting. List the details of the setting in your chart. Based on his description, how do you think he feels about this new place?

the director was called a principal, and that it was a lady and not a man. They assured us that there was always a person at the school who could speak Spanish.

Exactly as we had been told, there was a sign on the door in both Spanish and English: "Principal." We crossed the hall and entered the office of Miss Nettie Hopley.

Miss Hopley was at a roll-top desk[3] to one side, sitting in a swivel chair that moved on wheels. There was a sofa against the opposite wall, flanked by two windows and a door that opened on a small balcony. Chairs were set around a table and framed pictures hung on the walls of a man with long white hair and another with a sad face and a black beard.

The principal half turned in the swivel chair to look at us over the pinch glasses crossed on the ridge of her nose. To do this she had to duck her head slightly as if she were about to step through a low doorway.

What Miss Hopley said to us we did not know but we saw in her eyes a warm welcome and when she took off her glasses and straightened up she smiled wholeheartedly,[4] like Mrs. Dodson. We were, of course, saying nothing, only catching the friendliness of her voice and the sparkle in her eyes while she said words we did not understand. She signaled us to the table. Almost tiptoeing across the office, I maneuvered myself to keep my mother between me and the gringo[5] lady. In a matter of seconds I had to decide whether she was a possible friend or a menace.[6] We sat down.

Then Miss Hopley did a formidable[7] thing. She stood up. Had she been standing when we entered she would have seemed tall. But rising from her chair she soared. And what she carried up and up with her was a buxom superstructure, firm shoulders, a straight sharp nose, full cheeks slightly molded by a curved line along the

---

3 A **roll-top desk** is a writing desk with a slatted, movable top.

4 **Wholeheartedly** means "sincerely and enthusiastically."

5 A **gringo** lady is one who is white, North American, and not Hispanic.

6 **Menace** means "threat or danger."

7 **Formidable** means "causing fear because of size, strength, or power."

nostrils, thin lips that moved like steel springs, and a high forehead topped by hair gathered in a bun. Miss Hopley was not a giant in body but when she mobilized it to a standing position she seemed a match for giants. I decided I liked her.

She strode to a door in the far corner of the office, opened it and called a name. A boy of about ten years appeared in the doorway. He sat down at one end of the table. He was brown like us, a plump kid with shiny black hair combed straight back, neat, cool, and faintly obnoxious.[8]

Comparing Literature

In what ways does Ernesto's description of Miss Hopley show that he likes her?

Miss Hopley joined us with a large book and some papers in her hand. She, too, sat down and the questions and answers began by way of our interpreter. My name was Ernesto. My mother's name was Henriqueta. My birth certificate was in San Blas. Here was my last report card from the Escuela Municipal Numero 3 para Varones[9] of Mazatlán, and so forth. Miss Hopley put things down in the book and my mother signed a card.

As long as the questions continued, Doña[10] Henriqueta could stay and I was secure. Now that they were over, Miss Hopley saw her to the door, dismissed our interpreter and without further ado took me by the hand and strode down the hall to Miss Ryan's first grade.

This class photo was taken in the early 1900s, around the time Ernesto Galarza attended the Lincoln School. *View the Photograph* What can you learn about the school and the students from studying the photo?

---

8 *Obnoxious* means "annoying and disagreeable."

9 The mother's first name is *Henriqueta* (en´ ri kā´ tə). The writer was born in *San Blas,* a small city near Mazatlán. In Mazatlán, the writer attended a public school for boys, *Escuela Municipal para Varones* (es kwä´ lə mōō ni´ si päl´ pär´ ə vä rō´ nəs).

10 *Doña* (dōn´ yə) is a form of respectful address for a married woman, like the English words *lady* and *madam.*

Miss Ryan took me to a seat at the front of the room, into which I shrank—the better to survey her. She was, to skinny, somewhat runty me, of a withering height when she patrolled the class. And when I least expected it, there she was, crouching by my desk, her blond radiant face level with mine, her voice patiently maneuvering me over the awful idiocies of the English language.

During the next few weeks Miss Ryan overcame my fears of tall, energetic teachers as she bent over my desk to help me with a word in the pre-primer. Step by step, she loosened me and my classmates from the safe anchorage of the desks for recitations at the blackboard and consultations at her desk. Frequently she burst into happy announcements to the whole class. "Ito can read a sentence," and small Japanese Ito, squint-eyed and shy, slowly read aloud while the class listened in wonder: "Come, Skipper, come. Come and run." The Korean, Portuguese, Italian, and Polish first graders had similar moments of glory, no less shining than mine the day I conquered "butterfly," which I had been persistently[11] pronouncing in standard Spanish as boo-ter-flee. "Children," Miss Ryan called for attention.

---

11 Something that is done **persistently** is done repeatedly.

Comparing Literature

Based on his description, how do you think Ernesto feels about Miss Ryan?

The Shouldered Brown Butterfly (Penelope), 1992. Julie Virtue. Watercolor. Private Collection.

"Ernesto has learned how to pronounce *butterfly!*" And I proved it with a perfect imitation of Miss Ryan. From that celebrated success, I was soon able to match Ito's progress as a sentence reader with "Come, butterfly, come fly with me."

Like Ito and several other first graders who did not know English, I received private lessons from Miss Ryan in the closet, a narrow hall off the classroom with a door at each end. Next to one of these doors Miss Ryan placed a large chair for herself and a small one for me. Keeping an eye on the class through the open door she read with me about sheep in the meadow and a frightened chicken going to see the king, coaching me out of my phonetic[12] ruts in words like *pasture, bow-wow-wow, hay,* and *pretty,* which to my Mexican ear and eye had so many unnecessary sounds and letters. She made me watch her lips and then close my eyes as she repeated words I found hard to read. When we came to know each other better, I tried interrupting to tell Miss Ryan how we said it in Spanish. It didn't work. She only said "oh" and went on with *pasture, bow-wow-wow,* and *pretty.* It was as if in that closet we were both discovering together the secrets of the English language and grieving together over the tragedies of Bo-Peep. The main reason I was graduated with honors from the first grade was that I had fallen in love with Miss Ryan. Her radiant, no-nonsense character made us either afraid not to love her or love her so we would not be afraid, I am not sure which. It was not only that we sensed she was with it, but also that she was with us.

Like the first grade, the rest of the Lincoln School was a sampling of the lower part of town where many races made their home. My pals in the second grade were Kazushi, whose parents spoke only Japanese; Matti, a skinny Italian boy; and Manuel, a fat Portuguese who would never get into a fight but wrestled you to the ground and just sat on you. Our assortment of

12 **Phonetic** means "having to do with speech sounds."

nationalities included Koreans, Yugoslavs, Poles, Irish, and home-grown Americans.

Miss Hopley and her teachers never let us forget why we were at Lincoln: for those who were alien,[13] to become good Americans; for those who were so born, to accept the rest of us. Off the school grounds we traded the same insults we heard from our elders. On the playground we were sure to be marched up to the principal's office for calling someone a wop, a chink, a dago, or a greaser. The school was not so much a melting pot[14] as a griddle where Miss Hopley and her helpers warmed knowledge into us and roasted racial hatreds out of us.

At Lincoln, making us into Americans did not mean scrubbing away what made us originally foreign. The teachers called us as our parents did, or as close as they could pronounce our names in Spanish or Japanese. No one was ever scolded or punished for speaking in his native tongue on the playground. Matti told the class about his mother's down quilt, which she had made in Italy with the fine feathers of a thousand geese. Encarnación[15] acted out how boys learned to fish in the Philippines. I astounded the third grade with the story of my travels on a stagecoach, which nobody else in the class had seen except in the museum at Sutter's Fort. After a visit to the Crocker Art Gallery and its collection of heroic paintings of the golden age of California, someone showed a silk scroll with a Chinese painting. Miss Hopley herself had a way of expressing wonder over these matters before a class, her eyes wide open until they popped slightly. It was easy for me to feel that becoming a proud American, as she said we should, did not mean feeling ashamed of being a Mexican. 🍂

Comparing Literature

In what ways does this description help you understand the setting of Ernesto's school?

---

13 Here, **alien** refers to those who are foreign born.

14 **[wop . . . greaser]** These are all offensive names for people of various nationalities or lifestyles. Here, **melting pot** refers to the idea of a place where people of all races and cultures blend smoothly into a single society.

15 **Encarnación** (en kär nä sē ōn´) is a boy's name.

HOW I LEARNED

English

Gregory Djanikian

It was in an empty lot
Ringed by elms and fir and honeysuckle.°
Bill Corson was pitching in his buckskin jacket,
Chuck Keller, fat even as a boy, was on first,
5 His t-shirt riding up over his gut,

Ron O'Neill, Jim, Dennis, were talking it up
In the field, a blue sky above them
Tipped with cirrus.° And there I was,
Just off the plane and plopped in the middle
10 Of Williamsport, Pa. and a neighborhood game,

Unnatural and without any moves,
My notions° of baseball and America
Growing fuzzier each time I whiffed.°
So it was not possible that I,
15 Banished° to the outfield and daydreaming

Of water, or a hotel in the mountains,
Would suddenly find myself in the path
Of a ball stung by Joe Barone.
I watched it closing in
20 Clean and untouched, transfixed°

Comparing Literature

What details about the setting help you see the baseball game and understand who the speaker is? List them in your chart.

---

2 **Honeysuckle** is a bushy plant that has sweet-smelling flowers.

8 Here, **cirrus** means "high, thin clouds."

12 **Notions** are ideas, beliefs, or opinions.

13 In baseball, **whiffed** means "struck out, or swung and missed at the third strike to make an out."

15 **Banished** means "sent away."

20 **Transfixed** means "motionless, as from wonder or fear."

By its easy arc before it hit
My forehead with a thud.
I fell back,
Dazed, clutching my brow,
25 Groaning, "Oh my shin, oh my shin,"°

And everybody peeled away from me
And dropped from laughter, and there we were,
All of us writhing° on the ground for one reason
Or another.
30 Someone said "shin" again,

There was a wild stamping of hands on the
    ground,
A kicking of feet, and the fit
Of laughter overtook me too,
And that was important, as important
35 As Joe Barone asking me how I was

Through his tears, picking me up
And dusting me off with hands
    like swatters,°
And though my head felt heavy,
I played on till dusk
40 Missing flies and pop-ups and grounders

And calling out in desperation° things like
"Yours" and "take it," but doing all right,
Tugging at my cap in just the right way,
Crouching low, my feet set,
45 "Hum baby" sweetly on my lips.

Comparing Literature

What feeling do you get from the setting at this point in the poem?

---

25 When the ball hits the speaker in the **brow** (forehead) he calls it the wrong thing. The **shin** is the leg bone between the knee and the ankle.

28 **Writhing** is twisting, like a worm, as from pain, embarrassment, or laughter.

37 The speaker is comparing Joe's hands to fly **swatters,** the tools used to kill bugs.

41 **Desperation** is a feeling of hopelessness that causes a person to try anything.

Comparing Literature

BQ BIG Question

Now use the unit Big Question to compare and contrast *Barrio Boy* and "How I Learned English." With a group of classmates, discuss questions such as,

- What kind of person does each boy want to become?

- How does each boy try to become that person?

- Is each boy successful in becoming the person he wants to be? Explain.

Support each answer with evidence from the readings.

Literary Element Setting

Use the details you wrote in your chart to think about the settings in *Barrio Boy* and "How I Learned English." With a partner, answer the following questions.

1. In what ways are the settings different in *Barrio Boy* and "How I Learned English"? Discuss specific details, feelings, and any other ways the two settings differ.

2. In what ways are the settings in both pieces similar? For example, you might think about how Ernesto and the speaker first feel in the settings, how each adjusts to the setting, or other important ways you think that the settings are alike.

Write to Compare

In one or two paragraphs, explain how the settings reveal similar themes in *Barrio Boy* and "How I Learned English." You might focus on these ideas as you write.

- Tell how the place and time affect Ernesto's and the speaker's feelings about themselves and their lives.

- Include details from the selections about the appearance of people, places, and things that influence each boy's idea of who he wants to become.

- Explain how the similarities and differences in the structure of each selection affect your responses to the two selections.

 Writing Tip

Signal Words As you write, use signal words, such as *both, alike, similar, same,* and *also,* to show comparisons. Use *unlike, different, instead, in contrast,* and *however* to contrast items or ideas.

 Literature Online

Selection Resources
For Selection Quizzes, eFlashcards, and Reading-Writing Connection activities, go to glencoe.com and enter QuickPass code GL27534u5.

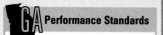

GA Performance Standards

For pages 738–745

ELA7W3a Use research and technology to support writing. Identify topics, ask and evaluate questions, and develop ideas leading to investigation and research.

Writing Workshop

Research Report

What positive actions have influenced famous people to become who they wanted to be? How can you take courage and confidence from their example for use in your own life? In this workshop, you will write a research report that will help you think about the Unit 5 Big Question: How Can You Become Who You Want to Be?

Review the writing prompt, or assignment, below. Then read the Writing Plan. It will tell you what you will do to write your research report.

Writing Assignment

In a research report, you investigate a topic or a subject and present information on it, drawing from a variety of reliable documented sources. Write a research report about a well-known historical or contemporary person that tells how that person's positive actions, courage, and confidence—as well as the positive actions of others— led that person to become who he or she wanted to be. The audience, or those reading your report, should be your classmates and teacher.

Prewrite

How did the people in the biographies and autobiographies in this unit become who they wanted to be? Think about the biography of Marco Polo, for example. What other famous historical or contemporary people might be good subjects for your report?

Gather Ideas

Make a list of famous people whom you want to learn more about. If you need help thinking of people, use these suggestions:

- Ask your family and friends whom they admire.
- Look through the selections in this unit.
- Check library books and Web sites.
- Brainstorm a list of people with a partner.

Choose a Subject

Choose a person from your list. Read about the person in a general reference book such as an encyclopedia. If you decide you are no longer interested in the person, choose another one from your list.

Write a sentence in which you name the subject of your research.

_____ is (was) a courageous person who has inspired others to do great things.

Writing Plan

- **Choose a subject and convey a clear and accurate perspective on him or her.**
- **Use multiple reliable sources to get information.**
- **Incorporate relevant facts and details as evidence to support the main idea of the report.**
- **Organize the report in a logical sequence, concluding with a summary of the main idea.**
- **Include in-text references and a list of works cited.**

Plan and Conduct Your Research

Focus your research on the person you have chosen. Ask specific questions about how the person's inner strength has helped others and about what exactly he or she did and when.

○ Consult multiple authoritative sources, such as magazines, journals, newspapers, Web sites, encyclopedias, and experts' opinions.

○ Take notes by recording this information in a research chart or database: item number, name of source, page number or Web address, publication details such as the copyright date, and the information itself. Indicate facts with the letter *F* and opinions with the letter *O*.

○ Consider summarizing a source's information in the chart. Remember that paraphrasing information is also helpful.

 Prewriting Tip

As you take notes, remember to put quotation marks around any information you take directly from a source. Make sure the quotation is accurate and correctly attributed.

Sample Source Entry

3 "King, Martin Luther, Jr." *Encyclopedia Britannica Online,* http://www.search.eb.com/eb/article-3915, (accessed October 29, 2007).
Summary: Martin Luther King Jr. was born on Jan. 15, 1929, in Atlanta, GA. [F] He came from a middle-class background rooted in faith. [F] His family seemed very loving. [O]

For more information about documenting sources, see the Media Workshop on page 625.

Evaluate Your Information

Gather information from a variety of sources. Primary sources are those written by people who actually experienced the event. Secondary sources are based on information gathered from primary and other sources.

Use only sources that you can trust. Secondary sources should be unbiased and should include supporting evidence. Ask yourself, "How important is this information to making my point?" and "Is the source reliable?" Make sure your sources are

authoritative, written by recognized experts on the topic;

accurate, can be verified with another print or online source;

reliable, published in trustworthy books, periodicals, or Web sites;

objective, associated with a person or an organization that is unbiased; and

up-to-date, based on the most current information.

Writing and Research
For prewriting, drafting, and revising tools, go to glencoe.com and enter QuickPass code GL27534u5.

Get Organized

Use your research to create an outline of your report. Include the source references from your research chart that you will use to support main ideas and supporting details.

I. Childhood influences
    A. People
        1. Playmates ("King," *Britannica Online*)
        2. Parents and grandparents ("King," *Britannica Online*)
II. Adult influences
    A. People
        1. Benjamin Mays (Bolden, 35)

Draft

Organize your information and add details to your writing. Use the following skills to develop your draft.

Get It On Paper

- Review your research information. Look at your outline.

- Begin with an interesting fact or quotation that draws your reader in. Connect it to a statement that makes your purpose clear.

- For each body paragraph in your outline, write a topic sentence that supports your main idea. Then add the information from your research that supports the topic sentence.

- End your report by summarizing the main idea.

- Don't worry about paragraphs, spelling, grammar, or punctuation right now.

- When you're finished, read what you've written. Include more information if you need to.

 Drafting Tip

Check off each time you use a piece of information from your chart or database. That way you will be sure to include all relevant information.

Develop Your Draft

1. Focus on the subject and convey a perspective on him or her. Begin with a fact or quotation that will interest your reader.

> When Martin Luther King Jr. was six, a white friend said he could no longer play with him because their schools were segregated ("King," *Britannica Online*).

2. Include information from multiple sources.

> King was born in Atlanta, GA, on January 15, 1929 ("Biography," *Nobel Prize Online*).

3. Support your ideas with details from your sources.

> Mays was an activist who had visited with Mohandas Gandhi in India (Bolden, 35).

4. Make sure that your organization is logical and that you have a summary conclusion.

> With the support of his family and teachers, he taught the world to love, not hate.

5. Include a list of sources.

> Works Cited
>
> "Biography: King, Martin Luther, Jr." *The Nobel Prize Online.* http://nobelprize.org (accessed October 29, 2007).

Analyzing Cartoons

Jeremy's thoughts show strong sentence fluency. They have rhythm and flow. If only his spoken words showed the same fluency!

© King Features Syndicate, Inc. Reprinted with special permission.

Apply Good Writing Traits:
Sentence Fluency

Sentences can be long or short, simple or complicated. When you talk with friends, you use a mixture of simple, compound, and complex sentences. Writers do the same thing.

Sentence fluency is the smooth flow of sentences varying in length and style. Writing that has strong sentence fluency sounds natural and is easy to read aloud. Sentence fluency includes many aspects of writing:

- word choice
- rhythm of words and sentences
- sentence beginnings
- sentence lengths
- sentence structures
- sentence fragments

The best way to check for sentence fluency is to read your writing aloud. You may want to read it several times, focusing on a different element of sentence fluency each time.

Read these quotations from the biography of Marco Polo. What can you tell about Marco Polo from the way he "speaks" on paper?

> It is all a desolate and arid waste.

> Their ships are wretched affairs, and many of them get lost, because they are not fastened together with iron nails.

> The air is so pure and healthy [in the mountains], that when people who live below in the valleys and towns fall sick or come down with a fever, they lose no time in climbing into the mountains, where a few days' rest restores them to health.

As you draft your research report, pay attention to the length of your sentences. Try reading your report aloud and ask yourself, "Is there a rhythm to my writing?"

Analyze a Student Model

When Martin Luther King Jr. was six, a white friend said he could no longer play with him because their schools were segregated ("King," *Britannica Online*).

That one incident may have had a profound effect on the future civil rights leader. King's positive actions, courage, and confidence inspired millions of people. His family and teachers helped him become who he wanted to be: an advocate for racial equality and peace.

King was born in Atlanta, GA, on January 15, 1929 ("Biography," *Nobel Prize Online*). His parents and grandparents were loving, deeply religious people. They tried to explain to him why they avoided taking elevators in City Hall and riding streetcars.

His family wasn't alone in developing the future leader. One of the most influential people in King's life was Benjamin Mays, a teacher and friend at Morehouse College. Mays was an activist who had visited with Mohandas Gandhi in India (Bolden, 35). After he graduated, King attended Crozer Theological Seminary, where he studied more about Gandhi.

Like Gandhi, Dr. Martin Luther King Jr. had the courage to stand against oppression. With the support of his family and teachers, he taught the world to love, not hate. In his own words, "Hate cannot drive out hate. Only love can do that" (Rappaport, 7).

Works Cited

"Biography: King, Martin Luther, Jr." *The Nobel Prize Online*. http://nobelprize.org (accessed October 29, 2007).

Bolden, Tonya. *M.L.K.: The Journey of a King*. New York: Harry N. Abrams, Inc., 2007.

"King, Martin Luther, Jr." *Encyclopedia Britannica Online*, http://www.search.eb.com/eb/article-3915, (accessed October 29, 2007).

Rappaport, Doreen. *Martin's Big Words: The Life of Dr. Martin Luther King, Jr.* New York: Hyperion Books, 2001.

Focus on the Subject
A brief story illustrating your point can be a powerful opener.

Include Information from Multiple Sources
Include information from more than one source.

Incorporate Relevant Support
Support your ideas with facts and details from your sources.

Organize Logically and Conclude with a Summary
Make sure that your report progresses in a logical way. Conclude with a restatement of your thesis.

List Sources
Be sure to include an accurate, correctly formatted bibliography or list of works cited.

Revise

Now it's time to revise your draft so your ideas really shine. Revising is what makes good writing great, and great writing takes work!

Peer Review Trade drafts with a partner. Use the chart below to review your partner's draft by answering the questions in the *What to do* column. Talk about your peer review after you have glanced at each other's drafts and written answers to the questions. Next, follow the suggestions in the *How to do it* column to revise your draft.

Revising Plan

What to do	How to do it	Example
Are the subject and perspective of your report clear to your audience?	Present your subject in the introduction.	When he ∧Martin Luther King Jr. was six, a white friend said he could no longer play with him because their schools were segregated.
Did you include information from multiple sources?	Use information from more than one source.	King was born in Atlanta, GA, on January 15, 1929 ("~~King, Britannica Online~~ ∧"Biography," Nobel Prize Online).
Are your major points supported by details from your sources?	Provide supporting details from your sources.	∧One of the most influential people in King's life was Benjamin Mays.
Does your report follow a logical order and include a conclusion?	Conclude with a restatement of your thesis.	∧With the support of his family and teachers, he taught the world to love, not hate.
Have you included a list of sources?	Create a final list of works cited.	∧Bolden, Tonya. M.L.K.: The Journey of a King. New York: Harry N. Abrams, Inc., 2007.

Revising Tip

Make sure you list the sources you used in your report. Even though you paraphrase or summarize the information from the source, you still must credit the source. For more on ethics, refer to the Media Workshop on page 625.

Edit and Proofread

For your final draft, read your report one sentence at a time. The Editing and Proofreading Checklist inside the back cover of this book may help you spot errors. Use the proofreading symbols to mark needed changes. Then make corrections.

Grammar Focus: Commas in Dates and Place Names

Be sure to place commas before and after the year when it is used with the month and the day. If only the month and the year are given, do not use a comma. Also, be sure to use commas before and after the name of a state or a country when it is used with the name of a city. Below is an example of a sentence with comma placement problems followed by the correct sentence from the Workshop Model.

Problem: The following sentence is missing commas.

King was born in Atlanta GA on January 15 1929.

Solution: Place commas after the city, state, and day.

King was born in Atlanta, GA, on January 15, 1929.

Using the Workshop Model as an example, be sure to correctly format the list of sources you used to prepare your report. Title your list *Works Cited.* (Use the term *Bibliography* if all your sources are printed media, such as books, magazines, or newspapers.)

Present

It's almost time to share your writing with others. Write your research report neatly in print or cursive on a separate sheet of paper. If you have access to a computer, type your research report on the computer and check spelling. Save your document to a disk, and print it out.

Grammar Tip

Commas Do not use a comma after a state if it is followed by a ZIP code.

 Presenting Tip

Visual Elements It is a good idea to include visual elements, such as photos or a timeline, to make your research report more interesting.

 Literature Online

Writing and Research For editing and publishing tools, go to glencoe.com and enter QuickPass code GL27534u5.

Performance Standards

For page 746

ELA7LSV2a When delivering and responding to presentations, give oral presentations or dramatic interpretations for various purposes.

Speaking, Listening, and Viewing Workshop

Oral Report

Activity

Connect to Your Writing Deliver an oral report to your classmates. You might want to adapt the research report you wrote for the Writing Workshop on pages 738–745. Remember that you focused on the Unit 5 Big Question: How Can You Become Who You Want to Be?

Plan Your Oral Report

Reread your research report and highlight the sections you want to include in your oral report. Like your research report, your oral report should present clear, well-researched information on a focused topic.

Rehearse Your Oral Report

Practice your oral report several times. Try rehearsing in front of a mirror so that you can watch your movements and facial expressions. You may use note cards to remind you of your main points and information, but practice your oral report often enough that you won't lose eye contact with your audience.

Deliver Your Oral Report

- Speak clearly and precisely.
- Adjust your speaking style to add interest to the information you present to your audience.
- Change the tone, pace, and volume of your speaking to help emphasize important information in your oral report.
- Use gestures and visual aids to direct the audience's attention to specific points, and cite sources for your information.

Listening to Learn

As you listen, take notes to make sure you understand the topic. Use the following sentence frames to learn more about the topic from the speaker and to provide feedback in a respectful way.

- The information about _____ seemed to come from personal bias rather than a source. Can you give the source of that information?
- Why did you choose to focus on this topic?
- To summarize the information in your oral report: _____. Is that correct?

► Oral Report Checklist

Answer the following questions to evaluate your oral report.

- ❏ Did you speak clearly and precisely—and in a style that helped add interest to information?
- ❏ Did you vary the tone, pace, and volume of your speaking to add emphasis?
- ❏ Did you use gestures and visual aids, and did you cite your sources?
- ❏ Did you make eye contact with your audience?

 Literature Online

Speaking, Listening, and Viewing For project ideas, templates, and media analysis guides, go to glencoe.com and enter QuickPass code GL27534u5.

Unit Challenge

Answer the Big Question

In Unit 5, you explored the Big Question through reading, writing, speaking, and listening. Now it's time for you to answer the Big Question by completing one of the Unit Challenges below.

HOW Can You Become Who You Want to Be?

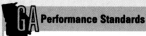

GA Performance Standards

For page 747

ELA7W2a Demonstrate competence in a variety of genres. Produce writing that engages the reader by establishing a context, creating a speaker's voice, and otherwise developing reader interest.

Use the notes you took in your Unit 5 **Foldable** to complete your Unit Challenge.

Before you present your Unit Challenge, be sure to complete the following steps. Use this first plan if you choose to create a web diagram showing who or what you want to become in life.

On Your Own Activity: Create a Web Diagram

- ❏ Draw a web diagram. In the center circle, write a clear and brief description of who or what you want to become.
- ❏ In any number of outer circles, write examples of what you'll need to do to become that person and skills that will help.
- ❏ Write a sentence or two beneath the web telling what you've learned about becoming who you want to be.

Use this second plan if you choose to write a letter giving someone advice that will help him or her become the person he or she wants to be.

Group Activity: Write a Letter of Advice

- ❏ Discuss the qualities a person needs to become who he or she wants to be. Pick one member to write two sentences on what the group decides are the most important qualities.
- ❏ Compose three sentences summarizing the steps someone must take to become who he or she wants to be.
- ❏ Use your sentences to create a letter that will be interesting to your classmates. Have each member sign the letter.
- ❏ Have one group member read the letter aloud to the class.

Independent Reading

Fiction

To read more about the Big Question, choose one of these books from your school or local library.

A Girl Named Disaster

by Nancy Farmer

When Nhamo, a Mozambican teenager, is faced with being forced into marriage, she flees in a stolen boat and finds herself alone in an uncharted lake. Nhamo must rely on herself as she faces the dangers of the African wilderness and learns what it means to be a young woman.

GLENCOE LITERATURE LIBRARY

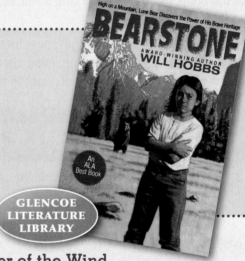

Bearstone

by Will Hobbs

A young, orphaned Native American boy, Cloyd Atcitty, is sent to live near the Colorado Rockies with an elderly rancher. Through life-changing experiences, Cloyd learns about himself, his cultural heritage, and the value of friendship and commitment.

GLENCOE LITERATURE LIBRARY

Shabanu: Daughter of the Wind

by Suzanne Fisher Staples

This book tells the story of Shabanu, a strong-willed and independent young woman who lives in a traditional nomadic culture of Pakistan. Shabanu sheds light on her life in the desert and her struggles with the rules and roles of women in her culture.

GLENCOE LITERATURE LIBRARY

Stargirl

by Jerry Spinelli

Mica Area High School is rocked by the appearance of a girl who is definitely not a part of the mainstream: Stargirl. In an environment of popularity and conformity, Stargirl tries to stay true to her unique self despite being rejected by her peers.

Nonfiction

The Code: The Five Secrets of Teen Success
by Mawi Asgedom

Mawi Asgedom came to the U.S. as a teenage refugee from Somalia, a nation that was in the middle of a civil war. In this book, Asgedom shares the secrets of success that he learned while overcoming life's many hardships.

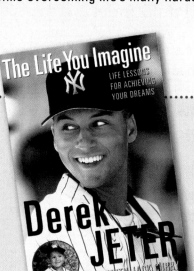

The Life You Imagine: Life Lessons for Achieving Your Dreams
by Derek Jeter with Jack Curry

Professional baseball player Derek Jeter tells about growing up in a multiracial family and chasing his dream of playing baseball in the big leagues. Read to find out how Jeter overcame life's obstacles to become an internationally known sports star.

Savion! My Life in Tap
by Savion Glover and Bruce Weber

Savion Glover is a master of tap dancing, wowing audiences across the nation with his fast feet and artistic style. In this book, Glover's rhythmic voice comes through the pages as he tells how mentors big and small helped him become a dancing sensation.

 Write an Interview

Write an interview directing questions to the author of the book you read. Create questions about important ideas, people, characters, or events in the book. Then use what you know about the author and the book to write possible answers that can be supported from your reading. With a partner, present your interview to the class.

Assessment

READING

Read the passage and answer the questions. Write your answers on a separate sheet of paper.

---

from **"The Day It Rained Cockroaches"** by Paul Zindel

The address of our new home was 123 Glen Street. We stopped in front, and for a few moments the house looked normal: brown shingles, pea-soup-green-painted sides, a tiny yellow porch, untrimmed hedges, and a rickety wood gate and fence. Across the street to the left was a slope with worn gravestones all over it. The best-preserved ones were at the top, peeking out of patches of poison oak.

The backyard of our house was an airport. I mean, the house had two acres of land of its own, but beyond the rear fence was a huge field consisting of a single dirt runway, lots of old propeller-driven Piper Cub-type planes, and a cluster of rusted hangars. This was the most underprivileged airport I'd ever seen, bordered on its west side by the Arthur Kill channel and on its south side by a Con Edison electric power plant with big black mountains of coal. The only great sight was a huge apple tree on the far left corner of our property. Its trunk was at least three feet wide. It had strong, thick branches rich with new, flapping leaves. It reached upward like a giant's hand grabbing for the sky.

"Isn't everything beautiful?" Mother beamed.

"Yes, Mom," I said.

Betty gave me a pinch for lying.

"I'll plant my own rose garden," Mother went on, fumbling for the key. "Lilies, tulips, violets!"

Mom opened the front door and we went inside. We were so excited, we ran through the echoing empty rooms, pulling up old, soiled shades to let the sunlight crash in. We ran upstairs and downstairs, all over the place like wild ponies. The only unpleasant thing, from my point of view, was that we weren't the only ones running around. There were a lot of cockroaches scurrying from our invading footfalls and the <u>shafts</u> of light.

"Yes, the house has a few roaches," Mother confessed. "We'll get rid of them in no time!"

"How?" Betty asked <u>raising an eyebrow</u>.

"I bought eight Gulf Insect Bombs!"

"Where are they?" I asked.

Mother dashed out to the car and came back with one of the suitcases. From it she spilled the bombs, which looked like big silver hand grenades.

"We just put one in each room and turn them on!" Mother explained.

She took one of the bombs, set it in the middle of the upstairs kitchen, and turned on its nozzle. A cloud of gas began to stream from it, and we hurried into other rooms to set off the other bombs.

"There!" Mother said. "Now we have to get out!"

"Get out?" I coughed.

"Yes. We must let the poison fill the house for four hours before we can come back in! Lucky for us there's a Lassie double feature playing at the Ritz!"

We hadn't been in the house ten minutes before we were driving off again!

I suppose you might as well know now that my mother really *loved* Lassie movies. The only thing she enjoyed more were movies in which romantic couples got killed at the end by tidal waves, volcanoes, or other natural disasters. Anyway, I was glad we were gassing the roaches, because they are the one insect I despise.

Tarantulas I like. Scorpions I can live with. But ever since I was three years old and my mother took me to a World's Fair, I have had nightmares about cockroaches. Most people remember an exciting water ride this fair had called the Shoot-the-Chutes, but emblazoned[1] on my brain is the display the fair featured of giant, live African cockroaches, which look like American cockroaches except they're six inches long, have furry legs, and can pinch flesh. In my nightmares about them, I'm usually lying on a bed in a dark room and I notice a bevy of giant cockroaches heading for me. I try to run away but find out that someone has secretly tied me down on the bed, and the African roaches start crawling up the sides of the sheets. They walk all over my body and then they head for my face. When they start trying to drink from my mouth is when I wake up screaming.

So after the movie I was actually looking forward to going back to the house and seeing all the dead cockroaches.

[1]**emblazoned:** permanently written

1. The mood created by the description of the setting in the first two paragraphs is mainly

   A. cheerful.

   B. dismal.

   C. frightening.

   D. violent.

2. In this passage, the narrator is characterized mainly by

   A. the actions of other characters.

   B. the words of other characters.

   C. his own thoughts.

   D. his words to others.

3. Which of the following describes the narrator's tone when he says, "This was the most underprivileged airport I'd ever seen"?

   A. cold anger

   B. deep longing

   C. bitter criticism

   D. gentle mockery

4. Why do the narrator and his sister run through the empty house?

   A. to frighten each other

   B. to explore the new house

   C. to escape the cockroaches

   D. to get away from their mother

5. Based on the events and the tone of the passage, it is likely the narrator

   A. never recovered from bad childhood experiences.

   B. was happy when he was young despite some difficulties.

   C. blames his mother for his unhappy childhood.

   D. is grateful for growing up wealthy and privileged.

6. Betty shows which of the following by *raising an eyebrow*?

   A. anger

   B. curiosity

   C. doubt

   D. amusement

7. Which sentence below describes a main theme of the passage?

   A. Cockroaches can be very dangerous.

   B. People must follow instructions carefully.

   C. Making friends in a new neighborhood can be hard.

   D. People often can find humor in difficult situations.

8. What does the word *shafts* mean in this passage?

   A. long handles or poles

   B. objects thrown like a spear

   C. beams shining through openings

   D. passages through the floors of a building

9. Why does the narrator despise cockroaches?

   A. They are filthy.

   B. They frighten him.

   C. They make scurrying noises.

   D. Killing them requires poison.

10. Which sentence below BEST describes the narrator's mother in this passage?

    A. She sees the bright side of difficult situations.

    B. She is completely impractical.

    C. She is afraid of ordinary things.

    D. She tends to worry about everything.

11. The sentence "It reached upward like a giant's hand grabbing for the sky" includes an example of

    A. onomatopoeia.

    B. a metaphor.

    C. alliteration.

    D. a simile.

12. The narrator tells about his experience at the World's Fair because he wants to

    A. reveal why the family moved to a new house.

    B. explain why he hates cockroaches.

    C. describe why his mother chose this house.

    D. tell why the airport is in such bad shape.

13. The mood of this passage could BEST be described as

    A. sad.

    B. serious.

    C. frightening.

    D. humorous.

14. The mood, tone, and events of the passage suggest that when the family returns from the movies

    A. the cockroaches will not be dead.

    B. the family will find dead cockroaches everywhere.

    C. the mother will move her family out of the house.

    D. the children will fight with their mother about the house.

 Literature Online

Standards Practice For more standards practice, go to glencoe.com and enter QuickPass code GL27534u5.

ENGLISH/LANGUAGE ARTS

Choose the best answer for each question. Write your answers on a separate sheet of paper.

1. What is the structure of the sentence below?

   > Spring has come, and everyone in our class is in a good mood.

   A. simple sentence

   B. compound sentence

   C. complex sentence

   D. compound-complex sentence

2. Which verb form should be used to complete the sentence below?

   > The trees next to the house on the corner _____ covered with blossoms.

   A. being

   B. be

   C. is

   D. are

3. Which word or words BEST fill in the blank in the sentence below?

   > Of all of our fruit trees, the cherry was the _____.

   A. splendider

   B. splendidest

   C. more splendid

   D. most splendid

4. Which verb form should be used to complete the sentence below?

   > There _____ not many things I liked more than cherry jam.

   A. was

   B. been

   C. were

   D. is

5. Which sentence below is written correctly?

   A. Although she turned ninety last year my great-grandmother has not slowed down.

   B. Although she turned ninety, last year my great-grandmother has not slowed down.

   C. Although she turned ninety last year, my great-grandmother has not slowed down.

   D. Although, she turned ninety last year, my great-grandmother has not slowed down.

WRITING

Read your assigned topic in the box below. Use one piece of paper to jot down your ideas and organize your thoughts. Then neatly write your essay on another sheet of paper.

Expository Writing Topic

Writing Situation

Your school is planning a project to help homeless people in your community. Your class has been discussing the people, things, and values that go into making a home.

Directions for Writing

Write an essay that explains to your classmates what you think people mean when they refer to "home." Include details about what makes a home feel like a home instead of just a building.

Writing Checklist

☐ Focus on a single topic.

☐ Organize your main points in a clear, logical order.

☐ Support your ideas or viewpoints with details and examples.

☐ Use precise, vivid words.

☐ Vary the length and structure of your sentences.

☐ Use clear transition words to connect ideas.

☐ Correct any errors in spelling, capitalization, punctuation, and usage.

WHY Share Stories?

THE BIG Question

> " *To be a person is to have a story to tell.* "
>
> —ISAK DINESEN

FOLDABLES®
Study Organizer

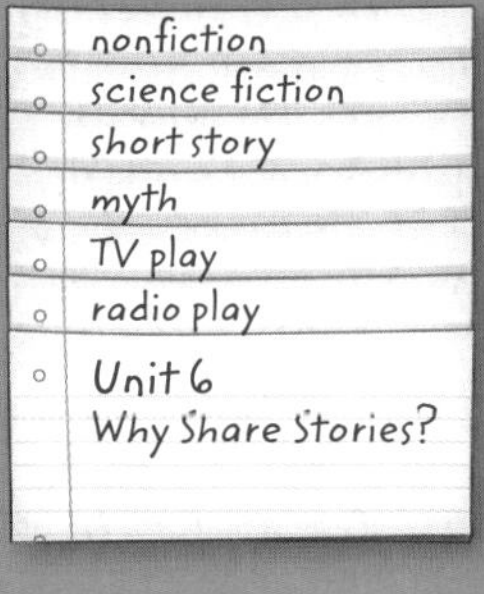

- nonfiction
- science fiction
- short story
- myth
- TV play
- radio play
- Unit 6
  Why Share Stories?

Throughout Unit 6, you will read, write, and talk about the **BIG Question**—"**Why Share Stories?**" Use your Unit 6 **Foldable,** shown here, to keep track of your ideas as you read. Turn to the back of this book for instructions on making this **Foldable.**

WHY Share Stories?

We share stories for many reasons. Sometimes we share them just for fun. We also share stories to keep the past alive and preserve our memories. Through storytelling, we can even share words of wisdom and comfort.

Think about these reasons that people share stories:

- Entertainment
- Messages and Lessons

What You'll Read

Drama, whether a stage play, a movie, or a TV show, brings literature to life. When you read a drama, you'll notice special features, such as stage directions and dialogue between characters. Just as you do when you read a short story, you must use your imagination to see the scenes and hear the actors. In addition to drama, in this unit you will read poems, short stories, and other texts that can help you discover answers to the Big Question.

What You'll Write

As you explore the Big Question, you'll write notes in your Unit Foldable. Later, you'll use these notes to complete two writing assignments related to the Big Question.

1. **Write an Expository Essay**
2. **Choose a Unit Challenge**
   - **On Your Own Activity: Multimedia List**
   - **Group Activity: Story Review**

What You'll Learn

Literary Elements

stage directions

teleplay

suspense

flashback

diction

description

Reading Skills and Strategies

analyze plot

monitor comprehension

analyze historical context

synthesize

interpret author's meaning

identify problems and solutions

Big Yellow TAXI

Joni Mitchell

They paved paradise
And put up a parking lot
With a pink hotel, a boutique
And a swinging hot spot
5 Don't it always seem to go
That you don't know what you've got
'Til it's gone
They paved paradise
And put up a parking lot

10 They took all the trees
And put them in a tree museum
And they charged the people
A dollar and a half just to see 'em
Don't it always seem to go,

Set a Purpose for Reading

Read "Big Yellow Taxi" to discover why people are concerned about our planet.

BQ BIG Question

What message does Mitchell share?

Gridlock, 2004. Patti Mollica. Acrylic. Collection of the artist.

View the Art Describe the setting of the painting. How might the painting help you better understand "Big Yellow Taxi"?

15 That you don't know what you've got
    'Til it's gone
    They paved paradise
    And put up a parking lot

    Hey farmer, farmer
20 Put away that DDT° now
    Give me spots on my apples
    But leave me the birds and the bees
    Please!
    Don't it always seem to go
25 That you don't know what you've got
    'Til it's gone
    They paved paradise
    And put up a parking lot

BQ **BIG Question**

How do you think Mitchell feels about the use of chemicals in farming?

---

20 ***DDT*** is a chemical that farmers used to kill insects. However, DDT also killed the birds that ate those insects. After it was found to be dangerous to humans, DDT was no longer allowed in the United States.

Late last night
30 I heard the screen door slam
And a big yellow taxi
Took away my old man
Don't it always seem to go
That you don't know what you've got
35 'Til it's gone
They paved paradise
And put up a parking lot

I said
Don't it always seem to go
40 That you don't know what you've got
'Til it's gone
They paved paradise
And put up a parking lot

They paved paradise
45 And put up a parking lot
They paved paradise
And put up a parking lot

BQ **BIG Question**

Why do you think Mitchell
wrote these song lyrics?

After You Read

Respond and Think Critically

1. Use your own words to tell the most important details in "Big Yellow Taxi." [Summarize]

2. What do the repeated lines tell you about the main idea? [Interpret]

3. Why would all the trees be put in a "tree museum"? [Infer]

4. What is Mitchell protesting? [Conclude]

 Writing

Write a Summary Write a one-paragraph summary of the song lyrics of "Big Yellow Taxi." Using your own words, state the main idea and include the most important details. Think about the message that Joni Mitchell is trying to convey. You may want to begin your paragraph with this topic sentence:

In "Big Yellow Taxi," Joni Mitchell writes about _____.

Then look for important details in each stanza, or group of lines.

 GA Performance Standards

For pages 758–762

ELA7W2b Produce a response to literature that demonstrates an understanding of the literary work.

 Literature Online

Unit Resources For additional skills practice, go to glencoe.com and enter QuickPass code GL27534u6.

Part 1

Entertainment

Carnival Series, 1998. George Merheb. Oil and acrylic on canvas. Private Collection.

BQ ❯ **BIG Question Why Share Stories?**

During the Middle Ages, court jesters in Europe entertained royal audiences with their stories. The picture of a carnival scene features the faces of jesters wearing silly hats. What stories do you imagine these jesters would tell? What entertaining stories have friends or family members told you?

GA **Performance Standards**

For pages 764–767

ELA7R1a For informational texts, analyze common textual features to obtain information.

Set a Purpose for Reading

Read "Ah, Wilderness!" to discover how one family lives without the sources of energy on which most people depend.

Preview the Article

1. What does the **title** suggest about the article's subject?

2. The last page of the article contains a **sidebar,** or a brief news story or graphic. What is its purpose?

Reading Strategy

Activate Prior Knowledge

When you activate prior knowledge, you use what you already know to understand new information. Think about what you already know about how energy is used in homes. Use a graphic organizer to record what you know.

Topic	What I Know
How electricity comes to my home	
Solar and wind power	

TIME

Ah, Wilderness!

Living in the middle of nowhere with solar panels and a few snowmobiles is not a choice many people would make. But the Bailis family did—and they've never looked back.

By AMANDA HINNANT

On this sunny day, the Bailis home has a breathtaking view of aspen forests and majestic, snowcapped mountains. The Bailises live on a mesa, a raised area of land with a flat top and steep cliffs on all sides, about twenty miles outside of Telluride, Colorado. Later, as twilight approaches, shadows outline the black trees and the San Juan Mountains.[1] Then, with surprising quickness, the sun sets, and the mesa plunges[2] into a deep, silent, solitary[3] darkness.

In contrast to the dark, hushed outdoors, the Bailis living room is bathed in light and positively hums with activity. Light from the fireplace, the center of

---

1 The **San Juan Mountains** in Colorado are some of the highest and most rugged mountains in the United States.

2 **Plunges** means "dips" or "moves downward suddenly."

3 Here, **solitary** is another word for *lonely.*

the family's house, casts a warm, buttery glow over Ray and Beth Bailis and their boys, Max, 8, and Finn, 3. Beth and Max are working at the computer while Ray and Finn are happily playing a board game.

Besides living in the middle of nowhere, the Bailis family lives "off the grid," which means that they generate[4] their own energy instead of relying on the area's power company. But being independent of the power company doesn't mean that it's the Dark Ages at the Bailis residence. Their home has all the modern conveniences that any 21st-century family could hope to have: microwave, Internet, washer and dryer, television. A big difference, however, is that the Bailises must plan the use of these appliances carefully. They know exactly how much or how little energy they can use. Running too many appliances at once will shut down the inverter,[5] which is roughly the same as blowing a fuse in your home.

For this family, rationing[6] energy has practically become second nature and is also a way to be closer to nature. Solar panels on the roof soak up the sun's energy, and a wind generator uses the wind to generate most of the house's power. For sunless days with

Thayer Allyson Gowdy

The Bailises' Colorado home in the San Juan Mountains generates its own power—day *and* night.

little wind, when neither solar panels nor a wind generator can do any good, there's a propane generator in the back.

Most of the time, Beth says, remote living makes you feel like you can do anything. And the Bailises know from experience that they can handle just about anything. When they moved into their house, it was heated by a woodstove that needed to be fed at 3 A.M., the propane generator didn't work very well, the roof didn't have any solar panels, and the old windows let the cold air leak in. Life in this remote spot was a lot like camping indoors. They burned lots and lots of candles and learned how to survive on very little energy without letting it affect them too much.

---

4 To **generate** energy is to produce or create energy.

5 An **inverter** is a device that converts electricity into a form that can be used in a home.

6 **Rationing** means "the controlled use of something."

Today snow is landing all around the house, swirling past the windows as if in a just-shaken snow globe. The snow determines how the Bailises dress as well as how they drive. Early on this snowy morning, the family members bundle into snow clothes. Each individual has two sets of gloves, goggles, and scarves (because one set is always wet). There aren't any snowplows rumbling by to clear the road so, from about November to May each year, the Bailis family must ride on snowmobiles from their house to their cars, parked 2½ miles away on the main road. Everything they carry, including briefcases, groceries, mail, and garbage, has to fit onto their snowmobiles or the sleds behind them. Beth and Ray commute to Telluride, where she is a landscape designer and he is in sales, and the boys make the trek[7] into town to go to school.

The chilly weather doesn't daunt[8] Max and Finn, who love the snow. "My boys are true polar bears," Beth says. When they are not busy with schoolwork or chores, they enjoy romping around outside. The boys may have inherited their love of the outdoors from their mother, who grew up on a large cattle ranch in Missouri and spent most of her childhood outside. "I was a child of nature," Beth says. "I would leave the house in the

Beth and Briar Rose, a neighbor's dog, go for a joyride in early winter.

Thayer Allyson Gowdy

morning and not come back until the afternoon. Fishing, walking the creek—I never felt afraid."

Beth hopes her boys will be connected with nature in the same way. Already she sees evidence of this connection dawning. She loves how Max, in all his self-portraits and family sketches, includes the mountain range behind their house. "He really has a sense of where he is from and who he is," she says. She expects that her boys' upbringing will help them feel unique,[9] the way she felt when she left the ranch and went to college. "It just gives them an identity," she explains.

---

7 A *trek* is a slow or difficult journey.

8 To *daunt* someone is to scare him or her.

9 A *unique* person is one of a kind, special because he or she is different from others.

Home Off the Range

The Bailises are just like any other American family—except . . .

- "Traffic" sounds they sometimes hear outside the house often come from a "bugling" herd of elk.

- Beth celebrates a sunny, windy day by running the vacuum cleaner and the dishwasher at the same time.

- The family snowmobiles have names: the Pig, Phazer, Wildcat, and Kitty Cat (the child-size one).

- They know the exact longitude and latitude of their house in case they have to be rescued by helicopter.

- The family is so accustomed to the 9,900-foot altitude that, when they visit Ray's sisters in California, they get giddy from the higher level of oxygen.

- Beth worries about mountain lions when the boys play out back.

The family gathers for an early Sunday dinner.

Thayer Allyson Gowdy

Respond and Think Critically

1. Write a brief summary of the main ideas in this article before you answer the following questions. For help on writing a summary, see page 219. [Summarize]

2. **Text-to-World** What could people such as the Bailises teach other people about the conservation of resources? [Connect]

3. In what way is Mrs. Bailis's life today similar to that of her childhood? [Compare]

4. How does the writer show that the Bailis family doesn't live as differently from other people as one might think? [Analyze]

5. **Reading Strategy** Activate Prior Knowledge Look at the chart you made about your prior knowledge. How did completing this chart help you as you read the article?

6. **BQ** BIG Question Why do you think the writer wanted to share the Bailis family's story?

Before You Read

The Miraculous Eclipse

Connect to the Play

Think about a time when someone told you an entertaining, but unbelievable, story. What made the story interesting?

Partner Talk With a partner, talk about incredible stories you have heard people tell. Why were they fun to hear?

Build Background

The Miraculous Eclipse is adapted from the novel *A Connecticut Yankee in King Arthur's Court,* by Mark Twain (1835–1910). Published in 1889, the book examines the legend of King Arthur through the eyes of a nineteenth-century American.

- In Twain's view, King Arthur's England is a brutal place. The sixth-century characters are foolish and superstitious.

- Twain uses the book to satirize, or attack in a witty way, the problems he saw in the United States in the 1880s, such as political corruption and high taxes.

Vocabulary

eclipse (i klips´) *n.* the partial or complete hiding from view of the sun or moon by another object in space (p. 776). *During the solar eclipse, the moon blocked the light from the sun.*

fanfare (fan´fār´) *n.* a short tune sounded by bugle, trumpets, or other brass instruments (p. 776). *A fanfare announced the entrance of the king and queen.*

barbarians (bär bār´ē əns) *n.* people from a culture that others see as uncivilized (p. 777). *The explorers mistakenly thought that the people on the island were barbarians.*

revenue (rev´ə nōō´) *n.* income; money taken in by a government or a business (p. 786). *The new salespeople helped increase the computer store's revenue.*

Meet Joellen Bland

Virginia Playwright Joellen Bland is an editorial assistant at the Marshall Foundation at Virginia Military Institute. She has been involved in all aspects of theatre, including directing, stage managing, costuming, and acting. She has also adapted many classic plays for young people.

Literary Works Bland's adaptations include *Nicholas Nickleby: A Play in Two Acts, Playing Scenes from Classic Literature: Short Dramatizations from the Best of World Literature,* and *Stage Plays from the Classics: One-Act Adaptations from Famous Short Stories, Novels, and Plays.*

 Literature Online

Author Search For more about Joellen Bland, go to glencoe.com and enter QuickPass code GL27534u6.

Set Purposes for Reading

BQ **BIG Question**

As you read, ask yourself, what makes Hank a good storyteller?

Literary Element **Stage Directions**

A play is a story intended to be performed by actors. The written form of a play is called a script. The script includes dialogue, or the words the actors speak, and stage directions. **Stage directions** are instructions that describe props, costumes, sounds, and lighting, as well as the appearance and actions of characters. Stage directions are often in italics and enclosed in brackets.

Stage directions are important because they give instructions to the actors and the people who help backstage during a play. When a play is read, stage directions help readers better visualize and understand characters and events. As you read, pay attention to how the stage directions affect your feelings toward the characters and events.

Reading Skill **Analyze Plot**

When you **analyze** as you read, you look at the different parts of a literary work in order to understand the work as a whole.

When you **analyze plot,** you try to understand how one event leads to another and advances the story. A plot is organized around a **conflict,** or central problem, which is introduced in the **exposition,** or the beginning of the story. The conflict builds with the **rising action** and reaches a high point at the story's **climax.** The climax is followed by **falling action,** and the **resolution** presents the final outcome.

To analyze the plot of *The Miraculous Eclipse,* ask yourself,

- What central conflict is introduced in the exposition?
- How do story events advance the plot?
- When does the plot reach its climax? How is the conflict resolved?

As you read, fill in a graphic organizer like the one below.

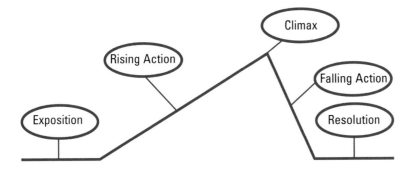

Performance Standards

For pages 768–789

ELA7R1e For literary texts, identify events that advance the plot and determine how each event explains past or present action(s) or foreshadows future action(s).

TRY IT

Analyze To practice analyzing plot, think about an episode of your favorite television show that you've seen recently. What was the main conflict in the episode? How did the events in the plot relate to the conflict? How was the conflict resolved?

The Miraculous Eclipse

Joellen Bland

Characters

OLD HANK MORGAN

BOY

HANK MORGAN,
A YOUNG MAN

CLARENCE, *PAGE*

SIR KAY, *KNIGHT OF
THE ROUND TABLE*

KING ARTHUR

MERLIN THE MAGICIAN

FOUR GUARDS

COURTIERS, *LORDS AND
LADIES*

KNIGHTS

SERVANTS

HERALD

SCENE 1

[*Time:* 1879.
Setting: A street in Hartford, Connecticut. A barrel stands center.
Before Rise: OLD HANK MORGAN *enters slowly right, followed by* BOY.]

BOY. Excuse me, Mr. Morgan.

OLD HANK. [*Stopping and turning.*] Yes?

BOY. Some of the boys have been telling me that . . . well, that you sure can tell a whale of a story!

OLD HANK. That's what they told you, is it? [*Fumbles in coat pockets, pulls out pipe.*] You're new in town, aren't you?

BOY. Yes, sir. The boys dared me to ask you to tell *your* version of the story of King Arthur and his knights of the Round Table.[1]

OLD HANK. They did, eh? Well, son, it just so happens I knew King Arthur well when I was a young man, so I can tell you anything you want to know about him.

BOY. [*Amazed.*] You knew King Arthur?

OLD HANK. [*Nodding.*] I knew all the folks at Camelot,[2] including that cagey old humbug, Merlin.[3]

BOY. [*In awe.*] You knew Merlin the Magician? But they all lived in the sixth century!

OLD HANK. [*Tamping his pipe.*] That's right. And if it weren't for Merlin, I might still be in the sixth century myself! [*Smiles.*] You don't believe me, do you?

BOY. Well, sir, if you've got some time, I'd like to hear your story. Then I'll tell you if I believe you.

BQ **BIG Question**
Why does the boy want Old Hank Morgan to share his story?

Analyze Plot What have you learned in the exposition of the play?

---

1 According to legend, ***King Arthur*** ruled England in the sixth century, bringing peace to the country. Arthur started an order of knights known as the ***Knights of the Round Table.***

2 King Arthur's castle was located at ***Camelot.***

3 Someone who is ***cagey*** is cautious, or wary of being tricked. A ***humbug*** is someone who tries to trick others.

OLD HANK. I've got all the time in the world. [*Sits on barrel and hunts through his pockets as he talks, finally coming up with tobacco pouch.* BOY *sits cross-legged on ground.*] You see, I was born and brought up right here in Hartford, Connecticut, so I am a Yankee[4] of the Yankees, and very practical.

BOY. That's what the boys said about you, Mr. Morgan.

OLD HANK. As a young man, I first went to work as a blacksmith. Then later I went over to the Colt Arms Factory and learned how to make guns, cannons, boilers, engines—all sorts of labor-saving machinery. If there wasn't a quick, new-fangled way to make a thing, I'd invent one. I became head supervisor and had a couple of thousand men under me.

BOY. [*Impressed.*] A couple of thousand? Whew!

OLD HANK. Some of them were pretty rough characters, too. [*Stands.*] Say, you just come on home with me and we'll sit on my front porch. It'll be more comfortable. [*Starts left.* BOY *follows, carrying barrel.*] I was a man full of fight when I was supervisor, but one day I met my match. A big fellow named Hercules[5] and I had a misunderstanding, and we went after each other with **crowbars.**

BOY. That must have been some fight!

OLD HANK. It was! Hercules knocked me down with a crusher to my head that made everything crack! My world just went out in total darkness, and when I came to, I wasn't at the arms factory any more. [OLD HANK *and* BOY *exit left. Lights dim to indicate shift of scene to a country road in England. Lights come up full again on* HANK MORGAN *as a young man. He holds his head in pain.*]

YOUNG HANK. Oh, my aching head! Hercules will pay for this, or my name isn't Hank Morgan! [*Looks around.*] Where am I? This doesn't look like any place I've seen around

4 A **Yankee** is a person from the northern United States or New England.
5 **Hercules** was a hero from Greek and Roman mythology known for great strength.

Visual Vocabulary
A **crowbar** is an iron or steel bar with a wedge-shaped end that is slightly bent. Crowbars are normally used to pry apart two objects.

Stage Directions What important information do these stage directions include?

Hartford. [SIR KAY, *wearing full armor, bounds in left with sworddrawn and takes threatening position in front of* HANK.]

SIR KAY. Will you joust, fair sir?

HANK. [*Staring rudely.*] Will I what?

SIR KAY. [*Waving sword.*] Will you fight with me to win land or lady or—

HANK. [*Interrupting.*] Now look here, who do you think you are, wearing that outlandish getup and swinging that dangerous weapon around? Get along back to the circus where you belong, or I'll report you!

SIR KAY. [*Holding swordpoint to* HANK'S *chest.*] My name is Sir Kay, and in the name of the King, I take you captive! You are now my property and must come with me at once!

HANK. [*Aside.*] If this fellow isn't part of a circus, he must be crazy. But I'd better play along with him, or he might get nasty with that sword. [*Raises his hands in surrender and turns back to* SIR KAY.] All right, Sir Kay, you've got me. Where to?

SIR KAY. This way! [*Starts off left, pushing* HANK *in front of him with sword.*]

HANK. Uh, by the way, Sir Kay, how far are we from Hartford?

SIR KAY. [*Puzzled.*] I have never heard of that place.

HANK. [*Stopping.*] Never heard of Hartford? [*Aside.*] I reckon he must be from out of state. [*Turns back to* SIR KAY.] Well, what town are we headed for? Bridgeport?

SIR KAY. [*Shaking his head.*] Camelot! [*Pushes* HANK *forward.*]

HANK. Camelot? There isn't any town by that name in Connecticut!

SIR KAY. You are not in Connecticut.

HANK. [*Stopping again.*] Well, where in the world am I?

SIR KAY. England! [HANK'S *mouth drops open in astonishment, as* SIR KAY *pushes him off left.*]

Analyze Plot What conflict does Young Hank face?

Stage Directions An *aside* is a comment heard by the audience but not by the other characters onstage. What does Hank's aside tell you about him?

[*Time:* England, in the year 528.
Setting: A courtyard in Camelot. At center is a throne on platform.
At Rise: COURTIERS, KNIGHTS, GUARDS and SERVANTS move busily
back and forth. SIR KAY and HANK enter left. At the sight of HANK,
all stop to stare and point at him.]

COURTIERS. [*Ad lib.*] Look there! Did you ever see anything like it? Look at his strange clothes! Be careful, don't get too close! [*Etc.*]

SIR KAY. [*Poking* HANK *with sword.*] I warn you, don't try to escape. [HANK *looks around, puzzled, as* CLARENCE *enters, smiling and looking* HANK *over from head to foot.*] My page,[6] Clarence [*Pointing to him.*], will keep you in charge until I come back for you. [*Exits right.*]

HANK. Page, did he say? Go on! A boy your size can't be much more than a paragraph!

CLARENCE. You have an unusual way of speaking, sir, but you are welcome! I hope you will find me to be your true friend.

HANK. Well, my boy, if you're really my friend, you can tell me where I am. That escapee from a circus who brought me here said this was England, but he's obviously not in his right mind.

CLARENCE. Nay, sir, my master, Sir Kay, spoke the truth. You are in England.

HANK. England. [*Shakes his head.*] Well, either *I'm* crazy or something just as awful has happened. Now tell me, honest and true, what is this place?

CLARENCE. Camelot, the court of King Arthur.

HANK. The King Arthur who had the Round Table?

CLARENCE. Is there any other, sir?

HANK. [*Hesitantly.*] And according to your notions, what year is it?

CLARENCE. The nineteenth of June, in the year five hundred twenty-eight.

HANK. [*Repeating words mechanically.*] Five twenty-eight? [*Turns away; in a daze.*] Five twenty-eight. [*Looks at*

---

6 A *page* is a boy who serves as a knight's assistant.

COURTIERS, *then at himself.*] I'm sure it was 1879 when I got up this morning. *I* look like 1879, but all these people look like . . . five twenty-eight. [*Pacing.*] Five twenty-eight . . . that was the year when a total **eclipse** of the sun occurred . . . on June 21st at three minutes past noon. Just two days from now. [*Suddenly.*] I've got an idea! If I can just keep hold of my senses for forty-eight hours, I'll know for certain if this boy is telling me the truth. [*Turns back to* CLARENCE.] Tell me, Clarence, who is this Sir Kay?

CLARENCE. A brave knight, sir, and foster brother to our liege[7] the King. You are his prisoner, and as soon as dinner is finished, he will exhibit you before the King and brag about capturing you. He'll exaggerate the facts a little, but it won't be safe to correct him. Then you'll be flung into a dungeon.

HANK. [*Horrified.*] Flung into a dungeon? What for?

CLARENCE. [*Casually.*] It is the custom. But never fear, I'll find a way to come and see you, and I'll help you get word to your friends who will come and ransom you.

HANK. Well, I'm much obliged to you, Clarence, but you see, all my friends won't even be born for more than thirteen hundred years. [***Fanfare*** *of trumpets is heard off right.*]

CLARENCE. King Arthur is coming now. [HERALD *enters right, holding trumpet, and walks center.*]

HERALD. His Royal Majesty, King Arthur! [KING ARTHUR *enters, followed by* MERLIN, *and attended by several* KNIGHTS. *He sits on throne center.* COURTIERS[8] *bow low and stand in groups at either side of throne.* SIR KAY *enters right, seizes* HANK *by arm and pushes him to his knees in front of* KING ARTHUR.]

---

7 In medieval times, people loyal to a king or lord referred to him as *liege.*

8 *Courtiers* attend to a king or queen at his or her court.

Vocabulary

eclipse (i klips′) *n.* the partial or complete hiding from view of the sun or moon by another object in space

fanfare (fan′fār′) *n.* a short tune sounded by bugle, trumpets, or other brass instruments

Analyze Plot What role do you think the eclipse will play in the plot?

Stage Directions What is the difference between Hank's and Clarence's reactions?

Visual Vocabulary

A **herald** is an official who carries important news and messages.

SIR KAY. [*Bowing low.*] My lord King, most noble knights and ladies of the realm! Behold this curious captive I have conquered!

KING ARTHUR. And where did you find this strange creature, Sir Kay?

SIR KAY. I came upon this horrible ogre, my liege, in a far land of **barbarians** called Connecticut. Everyone there wears the same ridiculous clothing that he does, but I warn you, do not touch him! His clothing is enchanted! [*COURTIERS gasp and step back.*] It is intended to secure him from harm, but I overpowered the enchantment through my strong will and great courage! I killed his thirteen attending knights in a three hours' battle and took him prisoner!

HANK. [*Starting to rise.*] Now, just a minute—

SIR KAY. [*Pushing HANK down.*] Behold this enchanted, man-devouring monster who tried to escape from me by leaping into the top of a tree at a single bound!

HANK. [*Starting up again.*] Now, look here, you're carrying this thing a little too far—

SIR KAY. [*Pushing him down roughly.*] Behold this menacing barbarian while you may, good people, for at noon on the twenty-first he shall die!

HANK. [*Jumping up.*] What? What have I done to deserve death? I haven't even been in this century more than half an hour!

SIR KAY. You have suffered defeat at my hands, and I decide if you live or die. You must die!

KING ARTHUR. Well done, Sir Kay. But if his clothing is enchanted, how do you propose to put him to death? [*COURTIERS murmur excitedly.*]

BQ **BIG Question**
Why do you think Sir Kay exaggerates his story?

Analyze Plot What main conflict is developing?

Vocabulary

barbarians (bär bär′ē əns) *n.* people from a culture that others see as uncivilized

SIR KAY. Surely Your Majesty's mighty magician, Merlin, can break the enchantment.

COURTIERS. [*Ad lib.*] Yes, yes! Merlin will know what to do! Try, Merlin! [*Etc.*]

MERLIN. Make way, please. [*He steps forward, makes several sweeping passes with his arms.* COURTIERS *fall back respectfully, and watch him intently.*] How can all of you be so dull? Has it not occurred to anyone here but me that the thing to do is to remove the enchanted clothing from this— [*In disgust.*] this creature, and thus make him helpless and harmless? Proceed.

HANK. [*Starting to back away.*] Now, hold on here. . . . Hey! [*FOUR GUARDS seize* HANK, *push him to floor, pull off his boots, stockings, overalls, sweater, etc., leaving him wearing only his suit of long underwear.*]

MERLIN. [*With a wicked laugh.*] Now he is powerless!

SIR KAY. To the dungeon with him!

KING ARTHUR. A cheer for Sir Kay, truly a brave knight of the Table Round! [*HANK is dragged out left by* GUARDS, *as* COURTIERS *cheer* SIR KAY. *Curtain.*]

SCENE 2

[*Setting: Dungeon cell. Pile of straw and low stool are center. May be played before curtain.*
At Rise: CLARENCE *sits on stool, watching* HANK, *who lies sleeping on straw.* HANK *stirs, stretches, his eyes still closed.*]

HANK. [*Not seeing* CLARENCE.] What an astonishing dream I've just had! King Arthur's Court! What nonsense! [*Yawns and stretches.*] I reckon the noon whistle will blow shortly, and then I'll go down to the factory and have it out with Hercules. [*Turns over, opens his eyes sleepily, sees* CLARENCE, *and sits up abruptly.*] What! Are you still here? Go away with the rest of the dream! Scat!

Stage Directions What do the stage directions reveal about Merlin?

Stage Directions How do the stage directions help you understand what is happening in this scene?

CLARENCE. [*Laughing.*] Dream? What dream? [*Stands up.*]

HANK. Why, the dream that I'm in the court of a king who never existed, and that I'm talking to you who are nothing but a work of my imagination!

CLARENCE. [*Sarcastically.*] Indeed! And is it a dream that you're going to be burned tomorrow?

HANK. Burned! [*Jumps up.*] I'm still in the dungeon! This dream is more serious than I thought. [*Pleading.*] Clarence, my boy, you're the only friend I've got. Help me think of a way to escape from this place.

CLARENCE. Escape? Why, the corridors are guarded by at least twenty men at arms. You cannot hope to escape. Besides . . . [*Hesitantly.*] . . . there are other obstacles more overpowering than men at arms.

HANK. What are they?

CLARENCE. [*Nervously.*] Oh, I dare not tell you!

HANK. But you must! Come, be brave! Speak out!

CLARENCE. [*Looking around fearfully, then speaking close to* HANK'S *ear.*] Merlin, that terrible and mighty magician, has woven wicked spells about this dungeon. No man can escape it and live! [*Nervously.*] There, I have told you. Now be merciful, and do not betray me, or I am lost!

HANK. [*Laughing.*] Merlin has cast a few spells, has he? That cheap old humbug? Bosh!

CLARENCE. [*Falling to his knees in terror.*] Oh, beware of what you say! These walls may crumble on us at any moment. Call back your awful words before it is too late!

HANK. [*Turning away; to himself.*] If everyone here is as afraid of Merlin's pretended magic as Clarence is, certainly a superior man like me with my nineteenth-century education ought to be shrewd enough to take advantage of this situation. [*Thinks a moment, then turns back to* CLARENCE.] Come on, Clarence, get up and pull yourself together. [*CLARENCE stands.*] Do you know why I laughed at Merlin?

Analyze Plot How do you think Hank might resolve his problem?

CLARENCE. [*Timidly.*] No, and I pray you won't do it again.

HANK. I laughed because I'm a magician myself.

CLARENCE. [*Recoiling.*[9]] You?

HANK. I've known Merlin for seven hundred years, and—

CLARENCE. Seven hundred years?

---

9 *Recoiling* means "pulling back in fear or disgust."

HANK. Don't interrupt! He has died and come alive again thirteen times. I knew him in Egypt three hundred years ago, and in India over five hundred years ago. He's always getting in my way everywhere I go, but his magic doesn't amount to shucks compared to mine. Now, look here, Clarence, I'll be your friend, and you must be mine.

CLARENCE. I *am* your friend, I assure you!

HANK. Good. Now, you get word to the King that I am the world's mightiest and grandest magician, and that if any harm comes to me I will quietly arrange a little calamity that will make the fur fly in these realms.

CLARENCE. [*Terrified.*] Yes, yes, at once! [*Backs off right, then turns and runs out.*]

HANK. That should get me off the hook pretty quick. [*Struts back and forth confidently for a moment, then suddenly stops.*] Ah! What a blunder I've made! I sent Clarence off to alarm the King with the threat of a calamity I haven't thought of yet! These sixth-century people are childish and superstitious. They believe in miracles. Suppose they want to see a sample of my powers? Suppose the King asks me to name my calamity? [*HANK sinks down onto stool, chin in hands, as lights fade out. In a moment, lights come up again. HANK remains on stool in same position.*] I've got to stall for time. I can't think of anything. [*Looks off right.*] Here's Clarence. I have to look confident. [*CLARENCE enters right, dejectedly.*] Well?

CLARENCE. I took your message to my liege the King, and he was very much afraid. He was ready to order your release, but Merlin was there and spoiled everything.

HANK. I might have known.

Stage Directions How does Clarence react to Hank's story?

Analyze Plot In what way do these lines add tension to the plot?

CLARENCE. He persuaded the King that you are crazy, and that your threat is nothing but foolishness because you have not named your calamity. Oh, my friend, be wise and name it, or you may still be doomed! [HANK, *deep in thought, frowns, then suddenly smiles.*]

HANK. Ah! I have it! Just in time, too. [*Turns to* CLARENCE *and draws himself up haughtily.*] How long have I been shut up in this miserable hole?

CLARENCE. Since yesterday evening.

HANK. Then today is the twentieth of June?

CLARENCE. Yes.

HANK. At what time tomorrow am I to be burned?

CLARENCE. [*Shuddering.*] At high noon.

HANK. Listen carefully. I will tell you what to say to the King. [*In deep, measured tones.*] Tell him that at high noon tomorrow I will smother the entire world in the dead blackness of midnight!

CLARENCE. [*Falling to his knees.*] Oh, have mercy!

HANK. [*Dramatically.*] I will blot out the sun, and it will never shine again! The fruits of the earth shall rot for lack of light, and the people of the earth shall famish and die to the last man! Go! Tell the King! [CLARENCE *staggers to his feet and backs off right, in terror.*]

HANK. [*Slapping his knee.*] Ha! The eclipse will be sure to save me, and make me the greatest man in the kingdom besides! Furthermore, I'll be the boss of the whole country within three months. After all, I have thirteen hundred years' head start on the best educated man in the kingdom! [*Sits down, smiling, then suddenly frowns.*] Hm-m, I hope my threat won't be too much for these simple people. Suppose they want to compromise? Then what do I do? [*Lights fade out for a moment to indicate brief passage of time, then come up again.* HANK *remains seated.*] Of course, if they want to compromise,

Analyze Plot How do you think King Arthur will respond to Hank's threat?

I'll listen, but I'll have to stand my ground and play my hand for all it's worth. [*1ST and 2ND GUARDS enter right.*]

1ST GUARD. Come! The stake is ready!

HANK. [*Terrified.*] The stake! [*GUARDS seize him.*] But . . . but . . . wait a minute! The execution is tomorrow!

2ND GUARD. The order has been changed and set forward a day. Come! [*GUARDS drag HANK, speechless, out right. Curtain.*]

SCENE 3

[*Setting: Courtyard in Camelot. There is a stake center, with bundles of wood stacked around it.*
At Rise: COURTIERS, CLARENCE, KING ARTHUR, *and* MERLIN *stand right and left, as* HANK *is dragged in right by* 1ST *and* 2ND GUARDS. CLARENCE *goes over to* HANK, *speaks to him quietly.*]

CLARENCE. [*To HANK.*] My friend, it was through *my* efforts that the change was made for the day of your execution.

HANK. *Your* efforts? [*GUARDS tie HANK to stake and pile wood around him.*]

CLARENCE. Yes, and hard work it was, too. When I named your calamity, the King and all his court were stricken with terror. Then I had an idea. I told them that your power would not reach its peak until tomorrow, and that if they would save the sun, they must kill you today while your magic is still working. In the frenzy of their fright, they swallowed my lie, and here you are!

HANK. [*Miserably.*] Clarence, how could you!

CLARENCE. [*Excitedly.*] You only need to make a *little* darkness, and the people will go mad with fear and set you free. They will take me for a featherheaded fool, and you will be made great! But I beg of you, spare our blessed sun, for me—your one true friend! [*Backs away into crowd.*]

HANK. [*Miserably.*] My one, true, featherheaded friend! You have ruined me!

MERLIN. [*Approaching* HANK, *waving his arms and sneering.*] You call yourself a magician? Then stop the devouring flames if you can! I defy you! [*Beckons to* GUARD, *who comes forward with torch.* HANK *throws up his arms in an attitude of despair, and suddenly lights begin to dim. All gasp and look up.*]

COURTIERS. [*Ad lib.*] Look! The sun is disappearing! It's getting dark, and it's only noon! [*Etc.*]

HANK. [*Looking up in surprise.*] The eclipse! It's starting! I don't know where it came from, or how it happened, but I'd better make the most of it, or I'm done for! [*Strikes grand attitude, pointing upward.*]

MERLIN. [*Frantically.*] Apply the torch!

KING ARTHUR. I forbid it! [MERLIN *snatches torch from* GUARD *and starts toward stake.*]

HANK. Stay where you are! If any man moves, even the King, I will blast him with thunder and lightning! [COURTIERS *step back.* MERLIN *hesitates, then hands torch to* GUARD, *and backs away.*]

KING ARTHUR. [*To* HANK.] Be merciful, fair sir. It was reported to us that your powers would not reach their full strength until tomorrow, but—

HANK. That report was a lie. My powers are at full strength *now!* [COURTIERS *crowd around* KING ARTHUR *frantically.*]

COURTIERS. [*Ad lib.*] Oh, save us! Give him whatever he wants! Do whatever he wants, only save the sun! [*Etc.*]

KING ARTHUR. Name your terms, reverend[10] sir, but banish this calamity!

HANK. [*Looking up.*] Well . . . I must have some time to consider.

KING ARTHUR. But it grows darker every moment!

---

10 Someone who is ***reverend*** is worthy of great respect.

COURTIERS. [*Ad lib.*] It's getting colder and colder! The night winds are blowing at noon! It's the end of the world! [*Etc.*]

HANK. Nevertheless, I must think! [*Looks up as lights continue to dim to almost complete darkness; to himself.*] What *is* this? How am I to tell whether this is the sixth century or not with this eclipse coming a day early? [*Pulls sleeve of 3RD GUARD.*] What day of the month is this?

3RD GUARD. [*Stepping back, terrified.*] The twenty-first, reverend sir.

HANK. The twenty-first! [*To himself.*] That featherheaded Clarence told me today was the twentieth! [*With sigh of relief.*] But his mistake about the date, and his good intentions in changing my day of execution, have saved me after all! I'm in King Arthur's court, all right, and there's only one course for me to take. [*Turns to KING.*] Sir King, whether or not I blot out the sun forever, or restore it, is up to you. You shall remain King and receive all the glories and honors that belong to you. But you must appoint me your perpetual minister,[11] and give me one percent of all increases in **revenue** I may create for the state.

KING ARTHUR. It shall be done! Away with his bonds! Do him homage,[12] all of you, for he is now at my right hand and clothed with power and authority! Now, sweep away this darkness and bring the light again.

[*GUARDS untie HANK.*]

HANK. [*To himself.*] I wish I knew how long this eclipse is supposed to last! [*To KING.*] Sir King, I may be clothed in power and authority in your eyes, but in my eyes, I am practically naked. I must have my clothes back.

Analyze Plot How has Clarence's confusion saved Hank and helped resolve the conflict?

---

11 A **minister** is a high government official.

12 To do **homage** is to pay special respect to someone or something.

Vocabulary
....

revenue (rev′ə noo′) *n.* income; money taken in by a government or a business

KING ARTHUR. They are not good enough. Bring him costly garments! Clothe him like a prince! [*KING claps his hands several times, and servants rush in with rich robe, plumed hat, jeweled sword, etc., and start to put them on HANK.*]

HANK. [*As he is being clothed.*] Let it be known that I shall be called The Boss, and all who do as I say and don't get in my way will be spared any further calamities. [*Turning.*] As for you, Merlin, beware! Your magic is weak, and I have knowledge of enchantments that can knock you out of commission forever!

MERLIN. [*Menacingly.*] You have not seen the last of me!

KING ARTHUR. Everything shall be as you say, Sir Boss, only bring back the sun!

CLARENCE. [*On his knees.*] For your one true friend's sake, bring back the sun!

HANK. [*To himself.*] I hope it's time. [*Solemnly lifts his arms and gazes upward.*] Let the enchantment dissolve and pass harmlessly away! [*Darkness continues. The people stir uneasily. HANK waves his arms in grand flourish. Still it remains dark. HANK makes more flourishes, and slowly lights begin to come up, gradually becoming brighter and brighter. COURTIERS shout for joy.*]

CLARENCE. Oh, thank you, Sir Boss! You have worked a wondrous miracle, but I beg of you, never do it again!

HANK. Don't worry, Clarence, I won't perform this particular miracle again. Come, my boy, I'll find some suitable quarters in the castle and set up a factory. You can be my assistant, and I'll show you how to make all kinds of other miracles. [*Starts off left with his arm around CLARENCE'S shoulders, then suddenly stops, scratching his head.*] A Connecticut Yankee in King Arthur's Court! You know, a situation like this has all kinds of possibilities! And if I ever get back to Hartford, what a story I'll have to tell! [*Exits left with CLARENCE as COURTIERS bow to him, and curtain falls.*] 🍂

Stage Directions What important information do the stage directions add to this scene?

BQ **BIG Question**
What is the most entertaining part of Old Hank's story?

After You Read

Respond and Think Critically

1. Why does the Boy ask Old Hank to tell him a story? **[Recall]**

2. In your own words, briefly retell how Hank got from Hartford, Connecticut, to King Arthur's court. **[Summarize]**

3. Based on the way Merlin reacts to Hank, what can you infer about Merlin's ability to perform magic? Explain. **[Infer]**

4. How does King Arthur's court react to the eclipse? What does their reaction suggest about the author's view of sixth-century England? Explain. **[Infer]**

5. At the end of the play, Hank says, "a situation like this has all kinds of possibilities." How do you think Hank will take advantage of his situation? Use details to support your answer. **[Conclude]**

6. **BQ** **BIG Question** Have you ever known a good storyteller? What qualities made this person's stories entertaining? **[Connect]**

Vocabulary Practice

On a separate sheet of paper, write the vocabulary word that correctly completes each sentence. If none of the words fits the sentence, write "none."

eclipse fanfare barbarians revenue

1. The _____ signaled that the prince was entering the room.

2. The stranded hikers waited for a _____ to rescue them.

3. We looked up into the sky to watch the lunar _____.

4. Most of the store's _____ came from selling sandwiches.

5. It was very _____ that we didn't get completely lost.

6. You shouldn't think of people as _____ just because they are from a different culture.

Academic Vocabulary

Hank escapes death by taking advantage of the **coincidence** that the eclipse begins just as he needs to prove his magical powers. In the preceding sentence, *coincidence* means "the occurrence of events that happen at the same time by accident." Think about a coincidence that has occurred in your life. How were you able to take advantage of the coincidence?

TIP

Inferring

To answer question 3, you have to use your own knowledge and clues from the play to make an educated guess. Here are some tips to help you make an inference.

- Read the parts of the play in which Merlin appears. Then think about the times when Merlin is called upon to do magic.

- Consider what you already know about the world and the way people act. Do people sometimes take advantage of other people's foolishness?

FOLDABLES Study Organizer Keep track of your ideas about the **BIG Question** in your unit Foldable.

 Literature Online

Selection Resources
For Selection Quizzes, eFlashcards, and Reading-Writing Connection activities, go to glencoe.com and enter QuickPass code GL27534u6.

Literary Element Stage Directions

1. How do the stage directions help you understand the main characters of the play? Explain.

2. Describe Camelot, based on the stage directions.

3. The plot of this play centers on an eclipse. How does the author use stage directions to present the eclipse? Explain.

Review: Setting

As you learned on page 39, **setting** is the time and place in which the events in a literary work occur. A story may occur in a single time and place. A story may also have more than one setting. The setting often helps create the mood, or atmosphere, of the story.

4. What are the settings in this play?

5. How do the settings contribute to the play's plot? Use details from the play to support your answer.

Reading Skill Analyze Plot

Standards Practice ELA7R1e

6. Which sentence gives the best description of how Hank deals with the difficult situations he faces?
   A. Hank uses magical powers that he discovers when he is in the sixth century.
   B. Hank picks fights with anyone who causes trouble for him.
   C. Hank relies on his speaking abilities to argue his way out of problems.
   D. Hank uses the advantages he has as a person from the nineteenth century.

Grammar Link

Parallelism Parts of a sentence joined by *and* or another coordinating conjunction (*for, nor, but, or, so, yet*) must be **parallel.** This means that these parts must all have the same grammatical form.

> Hank <u>followed</u> the road and <u>saw</u> the castle.

This sentence is parallel because the two parts joined by the coordinating conjunction *and* are both past-tense verbs: *followed* and *saw.*

> Hank likes <u>working</u> and <u>to tell</u> stories.

This sentence is not parallel. *Working* is a gerund, or a verb form ending in *-ing* that acts as a noun, and *to tell* is an infinitive. To make the sentence parallel, make both parts gerunds or both parts infinitives.

> Hank likes <u>working</u> and <u>telling</u> stories. (all gerunds)

> Hank likes <u>to work</u> and <u>to tell</u> stories. (all infinitives)

Practice Write two sentences of your own about Hank's adventure in King Arthur's court. In each sentence, include a coordinating conjunction. Make sure that all parts of the sentence are parallel.

🗩 Speaking and Listening

Performance With a small group, choose a part of the play to perform for your classmates. Choose the part that you think will entertain your audience the most. Decide who will play each character. Then rehearse your lines. Practice using speaking techniques, such as inflection, enunciation, and eye contact, to make your presentation more effective.

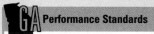
Performance Standards

For page 790

ELA7R2b Understand and acquire new vocabulary. Use knowledge of Greek, Latin, and Anglo-Saxon roots and affixes to determine the meaning of unfamiliar words.

Vocabulary Workshop

Word Origins

Connection to Literature

"Stay where you are! If any man moves, even the King, I will blast him with thunder and lightning!"

—Joellen Bland, *The Miraculous Eclipse*

Knowing a word's origins, or **etymology,** can help you use the word correctly. Many English words have Anglo-Saxon, Greek, or Latin origins. *Thunder,* for example, is rooted in the Anglo-Saxon, or Old English, word *thunor.* In Anglo-Saxon mythology, the god Thunor is similar to the Norse god of thunder, Thor. Other words or phrases—such as *Achilles' heel,* which means "a personal weakness"—come from Greek or Roman mythology.

Here are the roots of some other English words.

Word	Origin	English Meaning
herculean (hur´kyə lē´ən)	The root is *Hercules,* the name of a hero in Greek and Roman mythology.	requiring great strength (like that of Hercules) or effort
solar	The root *sol* is a Latin word that means "sun." Sol was the sun god in Roman mythology.	related to or produced by the sun
wondrous	The root *wondr* is from *wundor,* an Old English word that means "wonder."	amazing or wonderful

TRY IT: Using the chart above, write the answers to these questions.

1. What is a herculean task?
2. What is solar energy?
3. How would you define the word *wonderment*?

Part 2

Messages and Lessons

The Young, the Wise & the Rest Is History. Bella Easton. Oil on panel, 81 x 91.4 cm. Private Collection.

BQ BIG Question **Why Share Stories?**

In the painting, a woman wearing a kimono bows as she teaches the children. How do you think the children respond to the woman's lesson? What messages and lessons have you shared with younger listeners?

**Performance Standards**

For pages 792–793

ELA7R1b For informational texts, identify and use knowledge of common graphic features to draw conclusions and make judgments.

Genre Focus:
Drama

Dramas are stories that are meant to be performed by actors on a stage or in front of movie or television cameras. The script of a drama includes the words the actors speak as well as descriptions of the action and the scenery.

Stage plays, movies, and television shows are all forms of drama.

Literary Elements

Script refers to the printed version of a drama. The script for a movie is called a **screenplay,** and the script for a television show is called a **teleplay.**

Characters are the people or animals in a work of literature. In drama, the **cast of characters** is a list at the beginning of a drama that gives the characters' names and sometimes also briefly describes them.

Dialogue is the lines spoken by the characters. In a script, the words that a character speaks follow the name of that character.

Theme is the author's main message in a drama. To find clues to the theme, look at what the characters say, what they do, and what they value.

Stage directions are words, often in italics and enclosed within brackets, that describe the characters and the setting of the drama. Stage directions also tell actors how to move or speak. These directions may include notes concerning sets, props, sound effects, and lighting. For movies and television shows, stage directions may also contain details about camera placement and movement.

Acts and scenes divide most long dramas. A drama is divided first into smaller parts called acts. Acts are then divided into even smaller sections called scenes. Acts and scenes change to show a change in time or setting.

Plot is the series of events in a drama as well as in other forms of literature. A typical plot includes five stages. The **exposition** establishes the story's characters, setting, and situation. The **rising action** introduces the story's conflicts, or struggles. The **climax** is the point of greatest interest or suspense in a story. During the **falling action,** readers see the logical results of the climax. The **resolution** is the final stage of a plot. It reveals the outcome of the story.

> **TRY IT**
>
> Using a diagram or chart like the ones on the next page, track the plot development or analyze a character in a drama in this unit.

To better understand literary elements in drama and how authors use them, look at the examples in the plot diagram and characterization chart below.

Stages in Plot Development for *The Miraculous Eclipse*

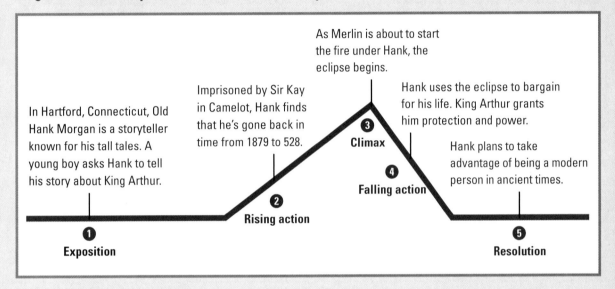

As Merlin is about to start the fire under Hank, the eclipse begins.

Hank uses the eclipse to bargain for his life. King Arthur grants him protection and power.

Imprisoned by Sir Kay in Camelot, Hank finds that he's gone back in time from 1879 to 528.

In Hartford, Connecticut, Old Hank Morgan is a storyteller known for his tall tales. A young boy asks Hank to tell his story about King Arthur.

Hank plans to take advantage of being a modern person in ancient times.

❸ Climax

❹ Falling action

❷ Rising action

❶ Exposition

❺ Resolution

Characterization Chart for Steve Brand from *The Monsters Are Due on Maple Street*

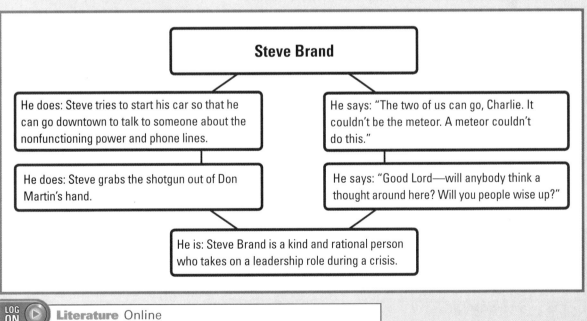

Steve Brand

He does: Steve tries to start his car so that he can go downtown to talk to someone about the nonfunctioning power and phone lines.

He says: "The two of us can go, Charlie. It couldn't be the meteor. A meteor couldn't do this."

He does: Steve grabs the shotgun out of Don Martin's hand.

He says: "Good Lord—will anybody think a thought around here? Will you people wise up?"

He is: Steve Brand is a kind and rational person who takes on a leadership role during a crisis.

Before You Read

The Monsters Are Due on Maple Street, Act I

Connect to the Teleplay

How would you and your neighbors react if the power in your neighborhood suddenly went out and cars wouldn't start? What could cause this to happen?

Partner Talk With a partner, talk about how you think your neighbors would react to a series of strange occurrences on your street.

Build Background

The teleplay "The Monsters Are Due on Maple Street" first aired on TV in 1960. The stage directions for a teleplay include terms that involve camera angles and movements. Knowing the most important terms can help you visualize the action.

- *Pan* means to turn the camera to follow or scan an object.
- *Cut* means to switch the camera from one scene to another.
- A *close-up* is a camera shot taken near a subject.
- A *long shot* is a camera shot taken far away from a subject.

Vocabulary

infinity (in fin′ə tē) *n.* an unlimited amount of time or space (p. 797). *Outer space seems like an infinity to us humans.*

reflective (ri flek′ tiv) *adj.* showing serious and careful thinking; thoughtful (p. 798). *Reading the poem, Laura seemed reflective.*

instill (in stil′) *v.* to put in gradually, little by little (p. 803). *Parents try to instill in their children the value of kindness.*

revelation (rev′ə lā′ shən) *n.* information that is new, especially surprising, or valuable (p. 806). *The revelation of his hidden talent astonished us.*

accusations (ak′yə zā′shəns) *n.* statements that suggest someone has done wrong (p. 807). *My brother's accusations that I took his backpack were false.*

Meet Rod Serling

"You are traveling through another dimension . . . next stop, the Twilight Zone!"
—Rod Serling

Through Another Dimension Rod Serling was one of the most popular writers in television broadcasting. "The Monsters Are Due on Maple Street" is from *The Twilight Zone,* a popular fantasy and science fiction television series. Serling once said, "The moment we clasp hands with our neighbor, we build the first span to bridge the gap between the young and the old."

Literary Works Between 1951 and 1955, Serling wrote more than 70 TV dramas. In the five seasons that *The Twilight Zone* was on television, from 1959 to 1964, he wrote approximately two-thirds of the show's 56 plays.

 Literature Online

Author Search For more about Rod Serling, go to glencoe.com and enter QuickPass code GL27534u6.

794   UNIT 6 Why Share Stories?

Set Purposes for Reading

BQ BIG Question

As you read, ask yourself, what lessons can I learn about human nature from this teleplay?

Literary Element Teleplay

A **teleplay** is a play written or adapted for television. Its format is similar to that of a stage play. Like a stage play, a teleplay is divided into **acts** and **scenes.** Stage directions meant for the actors and the studio crew appear in italic type and are enclosed in brackets. In stage directions, the author

- describes the characters, settings, and mood of the story
- expresses thoughts that help the cast and crew understand what they need to know
- tells the actors, camera operators, and other crew members what to do

As you read, pay attention to how the stage directions help you visualize characters and events.

Reading Strategy Monitor Comprehension

When you **monitor comprehension,** you check to make sure you understand what you read. Skillful readers ask questions about what they read and pay close attention to the characters, actions, and events to make sure they understand what is happening. To monitor your comprehension,

- summarize what you read by answering *who, what, where, when,* and *why*
- clarify what you don't understand by careful rereading
- question important ideas and story elements

Use a chart like the one below to help you understand any parts of the teleplay that may be confusing.

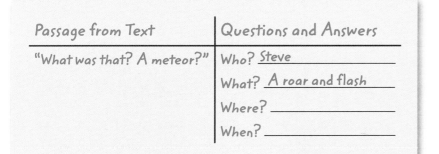

Passage from Text	Questions and Answers
"What was that? A meteor?"	Who? Steve
	What? A roar and flash
	Where? _____
	When? _____

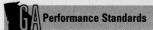
GA Performance Standards

For pages 794–811

ELA7RC2 Recognize and use the features of disciplinary texts (e.g., charts, graphs, photos, maps, highlighted vocabulary).

TRY IT

Monitor Comprehension
Imagine that your friend tells you that he has just received the most incredible gift. What questions would you ask him to find out more about the gift? How are you monitoring your comprehension when you ask your friend these questions?

the Monsters
are due on MAPLE STREET

Rod Serling

CHARACTERS

| Narrator | Figure One | Figure Two |

RESIDENTS OF MAPLE STREET

Steve Brand	Charlie's Wife	Woman
Mrs. Brand	Tommy	Man One
Don Martin	Sally, Tommy's mother	Man Two
Pete Van Horn	Les Goodman	
Charlie	Mrs. Goodman	

ACT 1

[*Fade in on a shot of the night sky. The various nebulae[1] and planet bodies stand out in sharp, sparkling relief, and the camera begins a slow pan across the Heavens.*]

NARRATOR'S VOICE. There is a fifth dimension beyond that which is known to man. It is a dimension as vast as space, and as timeless as **infinity.** It is the middle ground between light and shadow—between science and superstition. And it lies between the pit of man's fears and the summit of his knowledge. This is the dimension of imagination. It is an area which we call The Twilight Zone.

[*The camera has begun to pan down until it passes the horizon and is on a sign which reads "Maple Street." Pan down until we are shooting down at an angle toward the street below. It's a tree-lined, quiet residential American street, very typical of the small town. The houses have front porches on which people sit and swing on gliders, conversing across from house to house.* STEVE BRAND *polishes his car parked in front of his house. His neighbor,* DON MARTIN, *leans against the fender watching him. A Good Humor man rides a bicycle and is just in the process of stopping to sell some ice cream to a couple of kids. Two women gossip on the front lawn. Another man waters his lawn.*]

NARRATOR'S VOICE. Maple Street, U.S.A., late summer. A tree-lined little world of front porch **gliders,** hop scotch, the laughter of children, and the bell of an ice cream vendor.

[*There is a pause and the camera moves over to a shot of the Good Humor man and two small boys who are standing alongside, just buying ice cream.*]

NARRATOR'S VOICE. At the sound of the roar and the flash of light it will be precisely 6:43 P.M. on Maple Street.

---

1 The word *nebulae* (neb′yə lē′) refers to bright, cloudlike masses of dust and gases that are visible in the night sky.

Vocabulary

infinity (in fin′ə tē) *n.* an unlimited amount of time or space

Teleplay This text is in italics and is surrounded by brackets. What part of the teleplay is it?

Visual Vocabulary

Gliders are pieces of furniture that are often placed outside. They allow a smooth backward and forward movement.

[*At this moment one of the little boys,* TOMMY, *looks up to listen to a sound of a tremendous screeching roar from overhead. A flash of light plays on both their faces and then it moves down the street past lawns and porches and rooftops and then disappears.*
Various people leave their porches and stop what they're doing to stare up at the sky. STEVE BRAND, *the man who's been polishing his car, now stands there transfixed,[2] staring upwards. He looks at* DON MARTIN, *his neighbor from across the street.*]

STEVE. What was that? A meteor?

DON. [*Nods.*] That's what it looked like. I didn't hear any crash though, did you?

STEVE. [*Shakes his head.*] Nope. I didn't hear anything except a roar.

MRS. BRAND. [*From her porch.*] Steve? What was that?

STEVE. [*Raising his voice and looking toward porch.*] Guess it was a meteor, honey. Came awful close, didn't it?

MRS. BRAND. Too close for my money! Much too close.

[*The camera pans across the various porches to people who stand there watching and talking in low tones.*]

NARRATOR'S VOICE. Maple Street. Six-forty-four P.M. on a late September evening. [*A pause.*] Maple Street in the last calm and **reflective** moment . . . before the monsters came!

[*The camera slowly pans across the porches again. We see a man screwing a light bulb on a front porch, then getting down off the stool to flick the switch and finding that nothing happens.*
Another man is working on an electric power mower. He plugs in the plug, flicks on the switch of the power mower, off and on, with nothing happening.

Teleplay Why did the author include these detailed stage directions?

---

2 To be ***transfixed*** is to be made motionless, as from wonder or fear.

Vocabulary . . . .

reflective (ri flek´ tiv) *adj.* showing serious and careful thinking; thoughtful

Through the window of a front porch, we see a woman pushing her finger back and forth on the dial hook. Her voice is indistinct and distant, but intelligible and repetitive.]

WOMAN. Operator, operator, something's wrong on the phone, operator!

[*MRS. BRAND comes out on the porch and calls to STEVE.*]

MRS. BRAND. [*Calling.*] Steve, the power's off. I had the soup on the stove and the stove just stopped working.

WOMAN. Same thing over here. I can't get anybody on the phone either. The phone seems to be dead.

[*We look down on the street as we hear the voices creep up from below, small, mildly disturbed voices highlighting these kinds of phrases:*]

VOICES.
Electricity's off.
Phone won't work.
Can't get a thing on the radio.
My power mower won't move, won't work at all.
Radio's gone dead!

[*PETE VAN HORN, a tall, thin man, is seen standing in front of his house.*]

VAN HORN. I'll cut through the back yard . . . See if the power's still on on Floral Street. I'll be right back!

[*He walks past the side of his house and disappears into the back yard. The camera pans down slowly until we're looking at ten or eleven people standing around the street and overflowing to the curb and sidewalk. In the background is STEVE BRAND's car.*]

STEVE. Doesn't make sense. Why should the power go off all of a sudden, and the phone line?

DON. Maybe some sort of an electrical storm or something.

CHARLIE. That don't seem likely. Sky's just as blue as

Monitor Comprehension
What do the actions described in this stage direction suggest is happening on Maple Street?

Teleplay Why do you think these comments are spoken by "voices" rather than by individual characters?

Portrait of Orleans, 1950. Edward Hopper. Oil on canvas, 26 x 40 in.
Fine Arts Museum of San Francisco, CA.

View the Art Describe the setting of the painting. How is the setting similar to the setting of the teleplay?

anything. Not a cloud. No lightning. No thunder. No nothing. How could it be a storm?

WOMAN. I can't get a thing on the radio. Not even the portable.

[*The people again murmur softly in wonderment and question.*]

CHARLIE. Well, why don't you go downtown and check with the police, though they'll probably think we're crazy or something. A little power failure and right away we get all flustered³ and everything.

Monitor Comprehension
What has happened so far? Briefly summarize what has happened up to this point.

---

3 To be **flustered** is to be embarrassed, nervous, or confused.

STEVE. It isn't just the power failure, Charlie. If it was, we'd still be able to get a broadcast on the portable.

[*There's a murmur of reaction to this.* STEVE *looks from face to face and then over to his car.*]

STEVE. I'll run downtown. We'll get this all straightened out.

[*He walks over to the car, gets in it, turns the key. Looking through the open car door, we see the crowd watching him from the other side.* STEVE *starts the engine. It turns over sluggishly and then just stops dead. He tries it again and this time he can't get it to turn over. Then, very slowly and reflectively, he turns the key back to "off" and slowly gets out of the car.*
The people stare at STEVE. *He stands for a moment by the car, then walks toward the group.*]

STEVE. I don't understand it. It was working fine before . . .

DON. Out of gas?

STEVE. [*Shakes his head.*] I just had it filled up.

WOMAN. What's it mean?

CHARLIE. It's just as if . . . as if everything had stopped. [*Then he turns toward* STEVE.] We'd better walk downtown. [*Another murmur of assent*[4] *at this.*]

STEVE. The two of us can go, Charlie. [*He turns to look back at the car.*] It couldn't be the meteor. A meteor couldn't do *this*.

[*He and* CHARLIE *exchange a look, then they start to walk away from the group.*
We see TOMMY, *a serious-faced fourteen-year-old in spectacles who stands a few feet away from the group. He is halfway between them and the two men, who start to walk down the sidewalk.*]

TOMMY. Mr. Brand . . . you better not!

STEVE. Why not?

Teleplay What do these stage directions reveal that the dialogue doesn't tell you?

---

4 An expression of agreement is **assent**.

TOMMY. They don't want you to.

[*STEVE and* CHARLIE *exchange a grin, and* STEVE *looks back toward the boy.*]

STEVE. *Who* doesn't want us to?

TOMMY. [*Jerks his head in the general direction of the distant horizon.*] Them!

STEVE. Them?

CHARLIE. Who are them?

TOMMY. [*Very intently.*] Whoever was in that thing that came by overhead.

[*STEVE knits his brows for a moment, cocking his head questioningly. His voice is intense.*]

STEVE. What?

TOMMY. Whoever was in that thing that came over. I don't think they want us to leave here.

[*STEVE leaves* CHARLIE *and walks over to the boy. He kneels down in front of him. He forces his voice to remain gentle. He reaches out and holds the boy.*]

STEVE. What do you mean? What are you talking about?

TOMMY. They don't want us to leave. That's why they shut everything off.

STEVE. What makes you say that? Whatever gave you that idea?

WOMAN. [*From the crowd.*] Now isn't that the craziest thing you ever heard?

TOMMY. [*Persistently but a little intimidated[5] by the crowd.*] It's always that way, in every story I ever read about a ship landing from outer space.

Monitor Comprehension
Who is the "them" that Tommy refers to? What makes you think so?

---

5 An *intimidated* person feels frightened or threatened.

WOMAN. [*To the boy's mother,* SALLY, *who stands on the fringe of the crowd.*] From outer space, yet! Sally, you better get that boy of yours up to bed. He's been reading too many comic books or seeing too many movies or something.

SALLY. Tommy, come over here and stop that kind of talk.

STEVE. Go ahead, Tommy. We'll be right back. And you'll see. That wasn't any ship or anything like it. That was just a . . . a meteor or something. Likely as not— [*He turns to the group, now trying to weight his words with an optimism*[6] *he obviously doesn't feel but is desperately trying to* **instill** *in himself as well as the others.*] No doubt it did have something to do with all this power failure and the rest of it. Meteors can do some crazy things. Like sunspots.

DON. [*Picking up the cue.*] Sure. That's the kind of thing— like sunspots. They raise Cain[7] with radio reception all over the world. And this thing being so close—why, there's no telling the sort of stuff it can do. [*He wets his lips, smiles nervously.*] Go ahead, Charlie. You and Steve go into town and see if that isn't what's causing it all.

[STEVE *and* CHARLIE *again walk away from the group down the sidewalk. The people watch silently.*
TOMMY *stares at them, biting his lips, and finally calling out again.*]

TOMMY. Mr. Brand!

[*The two men stop again.* TOMMY *takes a step toward them.*]

TOMMY. Mr. Brand . . . please don't leave here.

[STEVE *and* CHARLIE *stop once again and turn toward the boy. There's a murmur in the crowd, a murmur of irritation and concern as if the boy were bringing up fears that shouldn't be*

Monitor Comprehension
Why doesn't Tommy want Steve and Charlie to go downtown? What do the adults think about Tommy's statements?

---

6 ***Optimism*** means "a hopeful or cheerful view of things."

7 The expression to ***raise Cain*** means "to cause trouble."

Vocabulary
....

instill (in stil´) *v.* to put in gradually, little by little

brought up; words which carried with them a strange kind of validity[8] that came without logic but nonetheless registered and had meaning and effect. Again we hear a murmur of reaction from the crowd.

TOMMY is partly frightened and partly defiant[9] as well.]

TOMMY. You might not even be able to get to town. It was that way in the story. Nobody could leave. Nobody except—

STEVE. Except who?

TOMMY. Except the people they'd sent down ahead of them. They looked just like humans. And it wasn't until the ship landed that—

[*The boy suddenly stops again, conscious of the parents staring at them and of the sudden hush of the crowd.*]

BQ **BIG Question**

Why is Tommy trying to explain what happened in the science fiction story?

---

8 Something that is true and supported by facts is valid and thus has ***validity***.

9 A ***defiant*** person shows bold resistance to authority or an opponent.

SALLY. [*In a whisper, sensing the antagonism*[10] *of the crowd.*] Tommy, please son . . . honey, don't talk that way—

MAN ONE. That kid shouldn't talk that way . . . and we shouldn't stand here listening to him. Why this is the craziest thing I ever heard of. The kid tells us a comic book plot and here we stand listening—

[*STEVE walks toward the camera, stops by the boy.*]

STEVE. Go ahead, Tommy. What kind of story was this? What about the people that they sent out ahead?

TOMMY. That was the way they prepared things for the landing. They sent four people. A mother and a father and two kids who looked just like humans . . . but they weren't.

[*There's another silence as* STEVE *looks toward the crowd and then toward* TOMMY. *He wears a tight grin.*]

STEVE. Well, I guess what we'd better do then is to run a check on the neighborhood and see which ones of us are really human.

[*There's laughter at this, but it's a laughter that comes from a desperate attempt to lighten the atmosphere. It's a release kind of laugh. The people look at one another in the middle of their laughter.*]

CHARLIE. There must be somethin' better to do than stand around makin' bum jokes about it. [*Rubs his jaw nervously.*] I wonder if Floral Street's got the same deal we got. [*He looks past the houses.*] Where is Pete Van Horn anyway? Didn't he get back yet?

[*Suddenly there's the sound of a car's engine starting to turn over. We look across the street toward the driveway of* LES GOODMAN's *house. He's at the wheel trying to start the car.*]

Teleplay Would you be able to visualize Steve and his actions without the stage directions?

Monitor Comprehension How do the neighbors feel about Tommy's story?

---

10 The ***antagonism*** of a crowd is the unfriendly feelings and behavior of the people.

SALLY. Can you get it started, Les?

[*He gets out of the car, shaking his head.*]

GOODMAN. No dice.

[*He walks toward the group. He stops suddenly as behind him, inexplicably[11] and with a noise that inserts itself into the silence, the car engine starts up all by itself.* GOODMAN *whirls around to stare toward it.*
The car idles roughly, smoke coming from the exhaust, the frame shaking gently.
GOODMAN's *eyes go wide, and he runs over to his car. The people stare toward the car.*]

MAN ONE. He got the car started somehow. He got his car started!

[*The camera pans along the faces of the people as they stare, somehow caught up by this* **revelation** *and somehow, illogically, wildly, frightened.*]

WOMAN. How come his car just up and started like that?

SALLY. All by itself. He wasn't anywheres near it. It started all by itself.

[*DON approaches the group, stops a few feet away to look toward* GOODMAN's *car and then back toward the group.*]

DON. And he never did come out to look at that thing that flew overhead. He wasn't even interested. [*He turns to the faces in the group, his face taut and serious.*] Why? Why didn't he come out with the rest of us to look?

CHARLIE. He always was an oddball. Him and his whole family. Real oddball.

Teleplay Why do you think the author chose to pan the faces of the people in the crowd?

---

11 Something that happens **inexplicably** (in´iks plik´ə blē) is impossible to understand or explain.

Vocabulary . . . .

revelation (rev´ə lā´shən) *n.* information that is new, especially surprising, or valuable

DON. What do you say we ask him?

[*The group suddenly starts toward the house. In this brief fraction of a moment they take the first step toward performing a **metamorphosis** that changes people from a group into a mob. They begin to head purposefully across the street toward the house at the end. STEVE stands in front of them. For a moment their fear almost turns their walk into a wild stampede, but STEVE's voice, loud, incisive,[12] and commanding, makes them stop.*]

STEVE. Wait a minute . . . wait a minute! Let's not be a mob!

[*The people stop as a group, seem to pause for a moment, and then much more quietly and slowly start to walk across the street. GOODMAN stands alone facing the people.*]

GOODMAN. I just don't understand it. I tried to start it and it wouldn't start. You saw me. All of you saw me.

[*And now, just as suddenly as the engine started, it stops and there's a long silence that is gradually intruded upon by the frightened murmuring of the people.*]

GOODMAN. I don't understand. I swear . . . I don't understand. What's happening?

DON. Maybe you better tell us. Nothing's working on this street. Nothing. No lights, no power, no radio. [*And then meaningfully.*] Nothing except one car—yours!

[*The people pick this up and now their murmuring becomes a loud chant filling the air with **accusations** and demands for action. Two of the men pass DON and head toward GOODMAN, who backs away, backing into his car and now at bay.*][13]

GOODMAN. Wait a minute now. You keep your distance—all of you.

---

12 Steve's *incisive* voice is sharp and forceful.

13 An animal that is ***at bay*** is cornered and must turn and face its pursuers.

Vocabulary

accusations (ak′yə zā′shəns) *n.* statements that suggest someone has done wrong

So I've got a car that starts by itself—well, that's a freak thing, I admit it. But does that make me some kind of a criminal or something? I don't know why the car works—it just does!

[*This stops the crowd momentarily and now* GOODMAN, *still backing away, goes toward his front porch. He goes up the steps and then stops to stand facing the mob.*
We see a long shot of STEVE *as he comes through the crowd.*]

STEVE. [*Quietly.*] We're all on a monster kick, Les. Seems that the general impression holds that maybe one family isn't what we think they are. Monsters from outer space or something. Different than us. Fifth columnists[14] from the vast beyond. [*He chuckles.*] You know anybody that might fit that description around here on Maple Street?

Monitor Comprehension
What is a "monster kick"? Why does Steve say that?

GOODMAN. What is this, a gag or something? This a practical joke or something?

[*We see a close-up of the porch light as it suddenly goes out. There's a murmur from the group.*]

GOODMAN. Now I suppose that's supposed to incriminate me! The light goes on and off. That really does it, doesn't it?

[*He looks around the faces of the people.*]

I just don't understand this— [*He wets his lips, looking from face to face.*] Look, you all know me. We've lived here five years. Right in this house. We're no different from any of the rest of you! We're no different at all. Really . . . this whole thing is just . . . just weird—

Teleplay How do the dialogue and stage directions combine to show Goodman's feelings?

WOMAN. Well, if that's the case, Les Goodman, explain why— [*She stops suddenly, clamping her mouth shut.*]

GOODMAN. [*Softly.*] Explain what?

STEVE. [*Interjecting.*] Look, let's forget this—

---

14 *Fifth columnists* are traitors.

CHARLIE. [*Overlapping him.*] Go ahead, let her talk. What about it? Explain what?

WOMAN. [*A little reluctantly.*] Well . . . sometimes I go to bed late at night. A couple of times . . . a couple of times I'd come out on the porch and I'd see Mr. Goodman here in the wee hours of the morning standing out in front of his house . . . looking up at the sky. [*She looks around the circle of faces.*] That's right, looking up at the sky as if . . . as if he were waiting for something. [*A pause.*] As if he were looking for something.

[*There's a murmur of reaction from the crowd again. We cut suddenly to a group shot. As GOODMAN starts toward them, they back away frightened.*]

GOODMAN. You know really . . . this is for laughs. You know what I'm guilty of? [*He laughs.*] I'm guilty of insomnia.[15] Now what's the penalty for insomnia? [*At this point the laugh, the humor, leaves his voice.*] Did you hear what I said? I said it was insomnia. [*A pause as he looks around, then shouts.*] I said it was insomnia! You fools. You scared, frightened rabbits, you. You're sick people, do you know that? You're sick people—all of you! And you don't even know what you're starting because let me tell you . . . let me tell you—this thing you're starting—that should frighten you. As God is my witness . . . you're letting something begin here that's a nightmare! 🐾

BQ **BIG Question**

Why does Les Goodman tell the crowd that they are sick and should be frightened of what they're starting?

---

15 *Insomnia* is restless sleep or the inability to fall asleep.

After You Read

Respond and Think Critically

1. What is the first sign of trouble on Maple Street? **[Recall]**

2. At the beginning of the teleplay, what is the mood on Maple Street? What causes the mood to change? Explain. **[Analyze]**

3. Why does the character known as "Woman" suspect Les Goodman of causing the trouble on the street? **[Summarize]**

4. What role do you think Tommy plays in this drama? **[Interpret]**

5. What kind of "nightmare" is Goodman talking about at the end of Act I? Explain. **[Interpret]**

6. **BQ** **BIG Question** What message do you think the author might be sending to the audience of this television show? Explain. **[Conclude]**

Vocabulary Practice

On a separate sheet of paper, write the vocabulary word that correctly completes each sentence. If none of the words fits the sentence, write "none."

infinity   reflective   instill   revelation   accusations

1. A _____ person is unlikely to make a quick decision.

2. The lawyer repeated the _____ that the man had lied.

3. I _____ my mother to take a class at the community college.

4. Teachers try to _____ good work habits in their students.

5. The mystery ended with an amazing _____.

6. The immensity of the universe seems to approach _____.

7. He received many _____ after his piano recital.

Academic Vocabulary

The people on Maple Street were too involved with the events on their street to have an **objective** view. To become familiar with the word *objective,* fill out the graphic organizer below.

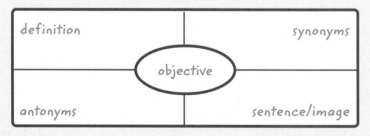

definition | synonyms

objective

antonyms | sentence/image

TIP

Interpreting
Answering question 5 requires you to interpret Goodman's last line in the act.

- Think about the word *nightmare.* Its dictionary definition, or denotation, says that a nightmare is a bad dream. Its connotation, or implied meaning, is that it is a bad situation. Which meaning do you think Goodman is using?

- Now think about what has happened so far in the teleplay. Think about how the people are behaving.

- Apply your knowledge of human nature to answer the question.

 FOLDABLES **Study Organizer** Keep track of your ideas about the **BIG Question** in your unit Foldable.

 **LOG ON** ▶ **Literature** Online

Selection Resources
For Selection Quizzes, eFlashcards, and Reading-Writing Connection activities, go to glencoe.com and enter QuickPass code GL27534u6.

1. Which part of the teleplay—the dialogue or the stage directions—has most helped you understand the characters so far? Why? Use details from the text to support your answer.

2. Why do you think the author, Rod Serling, ended Act I at this particular point? Explain.

Review: Mood

As you learned on page 195, **mood** is the emotional quality or atmosphere of a literary work. Writers choose details to create a mood or feeling that brings a scene to life. Descriptions, setting, dialogue, and characters' actions can all contribute to the mood of a piece of writing.

3. How does Tommy change the mood on Maple Street in "The Monsters Are Due on Maple Street"? Explain.

4. Describe the mood at the end of the first act of "The Monsters Are Due on Maple Street." Use details from the text to support your description.

Reading Strategy Monitor Comprehension

Standards Practice ᴳᴬ ELA7R1e

5. Which statement best expresses Tommy's explanation for the strange occurrences on Maple Street?
   A. They were caused by a meteor.
   B. They were set off by a power outage.
   C. They happened because of sun spots.
   D. They were caused by invaders from outer space.

Grammar Link

Agreement of Collective Nouns A **collective noun** names a group.

- audience
- faculty
- committee
- class

A collective noun is considered to be singular when it names a group that acts as a unit. A collective noun is considered to be plural when it refers to the members of a group acting as individuals.

- **Singular Collective:** The TV audience is wondering what will happen next. (Because the group is acting as one unit, the collective noun *audience* is singular.)

- **Plural Collective:** The committee do not agree on what caused the strange events. (The members of the committee are acting as individuals. Because the group is not acting as one unit, the collective noun *committee* is plural.)

Grammar Practice Write two sentences for each of the following nouns. Use each as a singular collective noun and then as a plural collective noun.

   crowd   group   family

Research and Report

Visual/Media Presentation Make a class presentation of the teleplay "The Monsters Are Due on Maple Street." Research to find out how to enhance the presentation with sound effects, props, and music. Make a list of the items you will need, and then use the Internet or other library resources to find them. Consider using a digital camera and video-editing software to film and edit your presentation. Make sure to credit the sources of any materials that were created by other people.

The Monsters Are Due on Maple Street, Act II

Connect to the Teleplay

Think about a time when someone you know was afraid. How did that person's behavior change?

Partner Talk With a partner, talk about why a person might behave differently in a group than when he or she is alone.

Build Background

This teleplay reflects the political situation in the United States during the 1950s and 1960s.

- After World War II, many people feared that the Soviet Union, a Communist country, might start a war against the United States.

- Because of the political climate, paranoia (an irrational fear or distrust) gripped many people. U.S. Senator Joseph McCarthy claimed that Communists were influencing Americans, including members of the movie industry and government officials.

- McCarthy's claims were investigated, and none was found to be true. Still, many wrongly accused people suffered because they had lost their jobs, marriages, and families.

Vocabulary

legitimate (li jit′ ə mit) *adj.* authentic or genuine (p. 816). *Experts determined that the vase was a fake and not a legitimate antique.*

warrant (wôr′ ənt) *n.* a written document giving permission to do a search or seize a person or property (p. 819). *The officer would not enter the house without a warrant from a judge.*

converging (kən′ vurj′ ing) *v.* coming together at a place or point (p. 822). *The fans were converging on the stadium for the big game.*

explicit (eks plis′ it) *adj.* clearly expressed or revealed (p. 825). *She told us exactly what to do; her directions were explicit.*

Set Purposes for Reading

BQ BIG Question

As you read, ask yourself, what message does this story send about how a group of people might react when they are afraid?

Literary Element Suspense

Suspense is the feeling of curiosity and uncertainty about what is going to happen next in a literary work. Authors can build suspense by raising questions in the reader's mind about the characters, by describing a mood that is threatening or mysterious, and by **foreshadowing,** or providing clues that prepare readers for events that will happen later.

The feeling of suspense that an author creates draws readers into the story. As you read the selection, look for events that advance the plot and determine whether they foreshadow future events.

Reading Strategy Analyze Historical Context

When you **analyze historical context,** you look at how the ideas and themes of a literary work reflect the historical period in which it was written. You look at features of the historical period, such as the political and cultural atmosphere, and you consider how these features might have influenced the author.

Analyzing historical context is important because it provides you with a background to better understand author's purpose and theme, or the message about life that the author wants to convey. To analyze historical context,

- research the historical period in which the teleplay was written using an encyclopedia or another reliable source

- think about how the setting, mood, and events of the teleplay relate to the historical period in which it was written

- think about how the historical period might have influenced the author's purpose for writing

Use a chart like the one below to help you analyze historical context.

"The Monsters Are Due on Maple Street"	What does it relate to in history?
Setting	
Mood	
Events	

GA Performance Standards

For pages 812–828

ELA7R1h For literary texts, identify and analyze how an author's use of words creates tone and mood.

TRY IT

Analyzing Suppose that your class is staging a play written during a historical period of peace and prosperity, or wealth. With a partner, discuss what the setting of the play would look like. What would the mood, or emotional quality, of the play be like?

---

the Monsters are due on **MAPLE STREET**

Rod Serling

ACT 2

[*We see a medium shot of the* GOODMAN *entry hall at night. On the side table rests an unlit candle.* MRS. GOODMAN *walks into the scene, a glass of milk in hand. She sets the milk down on the table, lights the candle with a match from a box on the table, picks up the glass of milk, and starts out of scene.* MRS. GOODMAN *comes through her porch door, glass of milk in hand. The entry hall, with table and lit candle, can be seen behind her.*

Outside, the camera slowly pans down the sidewalk, taking in little knots of people who stand around talking in low voices. At the end of each conversation they look toward LES GOODMAN'S *house. From the various houses we can see candlelight but no electricity, and there's an all-pervading quiet that blankets the whole area, disturbed only by the almost whispered voices of the people as they stand around. The camera pans over to one group where* CHARLIE *stands. He stares across at* GOODMAN'S *house.*

We see a long shot of the house. Two men stand across the street in almost sentry-like poses. Then we see a medium shot of a group of people.]

Room for Tourists, 1945. Edward Hopper. Oil on canvas, 30 1/4 x 42 1/8 in.
Yale University Art Gallery, New Haven, CT. Bequest of Stephen Carlton Clark.

View the Art What mood does the artist create in this painting? How is the mood similar to, or different from, the mood of the teleplay?

SALLY. [*A little timorously.*]¹ It just doesn't seem right, though, keeping watch on them. Why . . . he was right when he said he was one of our neighbors. Why, I've known Ethel Goodman ever since they moved in. We've been good friends—

---

1 *Timorously* (tim′ ər əs lē) means "lacking courage or self-confidence; timidly."

CHARLIE. That don't prove a thing. Any guy who'd spend his time lookin' up at the sky early in the morning—well, there's something wrong with that kind of person. There's something that ain't **legitimate.** Maybe under normal circumstances we could let it go by, but these aren't normal circumstances. Why, look at this street! Nothin' but candles. Why, it's like goin' back into the dark ages or somethin'!

> [STEVE *walks down the steps of his porch, walks down the street over to Les Goodman's house, and then stops at the foot of the steps.* GOODMAN *stands there, his wife behind him, very frightened.*]

GOODMAN. Just stay right where you are, Steve. We don't want any trouble, but this time if anybody sets foot on my porch, that's what they're going to get—trouble!

STEVE. Look, Les—

GOODMAN. I've already explained to you people. I don't sleep very well at night sometimes. I get up and I take a walk and I look up at the sky. I look at the stars!

MRS. GOODMAN. That's exactly what he does. Why this whole thing, it's . . . it's some kind of madness or something.

STEVE. [*Nods grimly.*] That's exactly what it is—some kind of madness.

CHARLIE'S VOICE. [*Shrill, from across the street.*] You best watch who you're seen with, Steve! Until we get this all straightened out, you ain't exactly above suspicion yourself.

STEVE. [*Whirling around toward him.*] Or you, Charlie. Or any of us, it seems. From age eight on up.

WOMAN. What I'd like to know is—what are we gonna do? Just stand around here all night?

Analyze Historical Context
How do Charlie's words relate to the historical context of the 1950s and 1960s?

Suspense What sort of incident might this line foreshadow?

Vocabulary
....

legitimate (li jit′ ə mit) *adj.* authentic or genuine

CHARLIE. There's nothin' else we can do! [*He turns back looking toward* STEVE *and* GOODMAN *again.*] One of 'em'll tip their hand. They got to.

STEVE. [*Raising his voice.*] There's something you can do, Charlie. You could go home and keep your mouth shut. You could quit strutting around like a self-appointed hanging judge and just climb into bed and forget it.

CHARLIE. You sound real anxious to have that happen, Steve. I think we better keep our eye on you too!

DON. [*As if he were taking the bit in his teeth, takes a hesitant step to the front.*] I think everything might as well come out now. [*He turns toward* STEVE.] Your wife's done plenty of talking, Steve, about how odd you are!

CHARLIE. [*Picking this up, his eyes widening.*] Go ahead, tell us what she's said.

[*We see a long shot of* STEVE *as he walks toward them from across the street.*]

STEVE. Go ahead, what's my wife said? Let's get it all out. Let's pick out every idiosyncrasy[2] of every single man, woman, and child on the street. And then we might as well set up some kind of kangaroo court.[3] How about a firing squad at dawn, Charlie, so we can get rid of all the suspects? Narrow them down. Make it easier for you.

DON. There's no need gettin' so upset, Steve. It's just that . . . well . . . Myra's talked about how there's been plenty of nights you spent hours down in your basement workin' on some kind of radio or something. Well, none of us have ever seen that radio—

Suspense How might the use of a long shot heighten the suspense of the teleplay at this point?

---

2 An *idiosyncrasy* (id′ ē ə sing′krə sē) is a personal way of acting; an odd mannerism.

3 A *kangaroo court* is an unofficial, irregular trial in which the verdict is often decided beforehand and fair legal procedures are ignored.

Stormy Midnight, 1995. Jane Wilson. Oil on linen, 18 x 18 in. Private Collection.

[*By this time* STEVE *has reached the group. He stands there defiantly close to them.*]

CHARLIE. Go ahead, Steve. What kind of "radio set" you workin' on? I never seen it. Neither has anyone else. Who you talk to on that radio set? And who talks to you?

STEVE. I'm surprised at you, Charlie. How come you're so dense all of a sudden? [*A pause.*] Who do I talk to? I talk to monsters from outer space. I talk to three-headed green men who fly over here in what look like meteors.

[STEVE'*s wife steps down from the porch, bites her lip, calls out.*]

MRS. BRAND. Steve! Steve, please. [*Then looking around, frightened, she walks toward the group.*] It's just a ham radio[4] set, that's all. I bought him a book on it myself. It's just a ham radio set. A lot of people have them. I can show it to you. It's right down in the basement.

STEVE. [*Whirls around toward her.*] Show them nothing! If they want to look inside our house—let them get a search **warrant.**

CHARLIE. Look, buddy, you can't afford to—

STEVE. [*Interrupting.*] Charlie, don't tell me what I can afford! And stop telling me who's dangerous and who isn't and who's safe and who's a menace. [*He turns to the group and shouts.*] And you're with him, too—all of you! You're standing here all set to crucify—all set to find a scapegoat[5]—all desperate to point some kind of a finger at a neighbor! Well now look, friends, the only thing that's gonna happen is that we'll eat each other up alive—

[*He stops abruptly as* CHARLIE *suddenly grabs his arm.*]

Analyze Historical Context
At the time that this teleplay was first aired on television, Communism was commonly called "the red menace." How would the use of this word affect the teleplay's first audience?

---

4 ***Ham radio,*** also known as amateur radio, is a hobby in which a person operates his or her own radio station, sending messages by voice or Morse code.

5 A ***scapegoat*** is someone who is made to take the blame and suffer for the mistakes or misfortunes of another person or a group.

Vocabulary

warrant (wôr′ənt) *n.* a written document giving permission to do a search or seize a person or property

CHARLIE. [*In a hushed voice.*] That's not the only thing that can happen to us.

[*Cut to a long shot looking down the street. A figure has suddenly materialized in the gloom and in the silence we can hear the clickety-clack of slow, measured footsteps on concrete as the figure walks slowly toward them. One of the women lets out a stifled cry. The young mother grabs her boy as do a couple of others.*]

TOMMY. [*Shouting, frightened.*] It's the monster! It's the monster!

[*Another woman lets out a wail and the people fall back in a group, staring toward the darkness and the approaching figure. We see a medium group shot of the people as they stand in the shadows watching.* DON MARTIN *joins them, carrying a shotgun. He holds it up.*]

DON. We may need this.

STEVE. A shotgun? [*He pulls it out of* DON'S *hand.*] Good Lord—will anybody think a thought around here? Will you people wise up? What good would a shotgun do against—

[*Now* CHARLIE *pulls the gun from* STEVE'S *hand.*]

CHARLIE. No more talk, Steve. You're going to talk us into a grave! You'd let whatever's out there walk right over us, wouldn't yuh? Well, some of us won't!

[*He swings the gun around to point it toward the sidewalk. The dark figure continues to walk toward them. The group stands there, fearful, apprehensive, mothers clutching children, men standing in front of wives.* CHARLIE *slowly raises the gun. As the figure gets closer and closer he suddenly pulls the trigger. The sound of it explodes in the stillness. There is a long angle shot looking down at the figure, who suddenly lets out a small cry, stumbles forward onto his knees and then falls forward on his face.* DON, CHARLIE, *and* STEVE *race forward over to him.* STEVE *is there first and turns the man over. Now the crowd gathers around them.*]

Suspense Which details of these stage directions increase the suspense in the teleplay?

BQ **BIG Question**
What message is the author sending about how people behave when they are fearful?

STEVE. [*Slowly looks up.*] It's Pete Van Horn.

DON. [*In a hushed voice.*] Pete Van Horn! He was just gonna go over to the next block to see if the power was on—

WOMAN. You killed him, Charlie. You shot him dead!

CHARLIE. [*Looks around at the circle of faces, his eyes frightened, his face contorted.*] But . . . but I didn't know who he was. I certainly didn't know who he was. He comes walkin' out of the darkness—how am I supposed to know who he was? [*He grabs* STEVE.] Steve—you know why I shot! How was I supposed to know he wasn't a monster or something? [*He grabs* DON *now.*] We're all scared of the same thing, I was just tryin' to . . . tryin' to protect my home, that's all! Look, all of you, that's all I was tryin' to do. [*He looks down wildly at the body.*] I didn't know it was somebody we knew! I didn't know—

[*There's a sudden hush and then an intake of breath. We see a medium shot of the living room window of* CHARLIE's *house. The window is not lit, but suddenly the house lights come on behind it.*]

WOMAN. [*In a very hushed voice.*] Charlie . . . Charlie . . . the lights just went on in your house. Why did the lights just go on?

DON. What about it, Charlie? How come you're the only one with lights now?

GOODMAN. That's what I'd like to know.

[*A pause as they all stare toward* CHARLIE.]

GOODMAN. You were so quick to kill, Charlie and you were so quick to tell us who we had to be careful of. Well, maybe you had to kill. Maybe Peter there was trying to tell us something. Maybe he'd found out something and came back to tell us who there was amongst us we should watch out for—

Analyze Historical Context
How does this statement reflect the mood, or atmosphere, of the 1950s?

[CHARLIE *backs away from the group, his eyes wide with fright.*]

CHARLIE. No . . . no . . . it's nothing of the sort! I don't know why the lights are on, I swear I don't. Somebody's pulling a gag or something.

[*He bumps against* STEVE, *who grabs him and whirls him around.*]

STEVE. A *gag*? A gag? Charlie, there's a dead man on the sidewalk and you killed him. Does this thing look like a gag to you?

[CHARLIE *breaks away and screams as he runs toward his house.*]

CHARLIE. No! No! Please!

[*A man breaks away from the crowd to chase* CHARLIE. *We see a long angle shot looking down as the man tackles* CHARLIE *and lands on top of him. The other people start to run toward them.* CHARLIE *is up on his feet, breaks away from the other man's grasp, lands a couple of desperate punches that push the man aside. Then he forces his way, fighting, through the crowd to once again break free, jumps up on his front porch. A rock thrown from the group smashes a window alongside of him, the broken glass flying past him. A couple of pieces cut him. He stands there perspiring, rumpled, blood running down from a cut on the cheek. His wife breaks away from the group to throw herself into his arms. He buries his face against her. We can see the crowd* **converging** *on the porch now.*]

VOICES.
It must have been him.
He's the one.
We got to get Charlie.

[*Another rock lands on the porch. Now* CHARLIE *pushes his wife behind him, facing the group.*]

Vocabulary ....

converging (kən´vurj´ing) *v.* coming together at a place or point

CHARLIE. Look, look I swear to you . . . it isn't me . . . but I do know who it is . . . I swear to you, I do know who it is. I know who the monster is here. I know who it is that doesn't belong. I swear to you I know.

GOODMAN. [*Shouting.*] What are you waiting for?

WOMAN. [*Shouting.*] Come on, Charlie, come on.

MAN ONE. [*Shouting.*] Who is it, Charlie, tell us!

DON. [*Pushing his way to the front of the crowd*] All right, Charlie, let's hear it!

[CHARLIE'*s eyes dart around wildly.*]

CHARLIE. It's . . . it's . . .

MAN TWO. [*Screaming.*] Go ahead, Charlie, tell us.

CHARLIE. It's . . . it's the kid. It's Tommy. He's the one.

[*There's a gasp from the crowd as we cut to a shot of* SALLY *holding her son* TOMMY. *The boy at first doesn't understand and then, realizing the eyes are all on him, buries his face against his mother.*]

SALLY. [*Backs away.*] That's crazy! That's crazy! He's a little boy.

WOMAN. But he knew! He was the only one who knew! He told us all about it. Well, how did he know? How could he have known?

[*The various people take this up and repeat the question aloud.*]

VOICES.
How could he know?
Who told him?
Make the kid answer.

DON. It was Charlie who killed old man Van Horn.

WOMAN. But it was the kid here who knew what was going to happen all the time. He was the one who knew!

[*We see a close-up of* STEVE.]

STEVE. Are you all gone crazy? [*Pause as he looks about.*] Stop.

[*A fist crashes at* STEVE's *face, staggering him back out of the frame of the picture.*
There are several close camera shots suggesting the coming of violence. A hand fires a rifle. A fist clenches. A hand grabs the hammer from VAN HORN's *body, etc. Meanwhile, we hear the following lines.*]

DON. Charlie has to be the one—Where's my rifle—

WOMAN. Les Goodman's the one. His car started! Let's wreck it.

MRS. GOODMAN. What about Steve's radio—He's the one that called them—

MR. GOODMAN. Smash the radio. Get me a hammer. Get me something.

STEVE. Stop—Stop—

CHARLIE. Where's that kid—Let's get him.

MAN ONE. Get Steve—Get Charlie—They're working together.

[*The crowd starts to converge around the mother, who grabs the child and starts to run with him. The crowd starts to follow, at first walking fast, and then running after him. We see a full shot of the street as suddenly* CHARLIE's *lights go off and the lights in another house go on. They stay on for a moment, then from across the street other lights go on and then off again.*]

MAN ONE. [*Shouting.*] It isn't the kid . . . it's Bob Weaver's house.

WOMAN. It isn't Bob Weaver's house, it's Don Martin's place.

Suspense What kinds of violent acts might these close-up stage directions foreshadow?

CHARLIE. I tell you it's the kid.

DON. It's Charlie. He's the one.

[*We move into a series of close-ups of various people as they shout, accuse, scream, interspersing[6] these shots with shots of houses as the lights go on and off, and then slowly in the middle of this nightmarish morass[7] of sight and sound the camera starts to pull away, until once again we've reached the opening shot looking at the Maple Street sign from high above. The camera continues to move away until we dissolve to a shot looking toward the metal side of a space craft, which sits shrouded in darkness. An open door throws out a beam of light from the illuminated interior.*
Two figures silhouetted against the bright lights appear. We get only a vague feeling of form, but nothing more **explicit** *than that.*]

FIGURE ONE. Understand the procedure now? Just stop a few of their machines and radios and telephones and lawn mowers . . . Throw them into darkness for a few hours, and then you just sit back and watch the pattern.

FIGURE TWO. And this pattern is always the same?

FIGURE ONE. With few variations. They pick the most dangerous enemy they can find . . . and it's themselves. And all we need do is sit back . . . and watch.

FIGURE TWO. Then I take it this place . . . this Maple Street . . . is not unique.

FIGURE ONE. [*Shaking his head.*] By no means. Their world is full of Maple Streets. And we'll go from one to the other and let them destroy themselves. One to the other . . . one to the other . . . one to the other—

BQ **BIG Question**
What message about humans does the author reveal through Figure One and Figure Two's dialogue?

Analyze Historical Context
How might this remark help reveal the theme of the teleplay?

---

6 **Interspersing** means "scattering or mixing in over brief periods."

7 A **morass** (mə ras′) is any difficult or confused condition or situation.

Vocabulary

explicit (eks plis′ it) *adj.* clearly expressed or revealed

[*Now the camera pans up for a shot of the starry sky and over this we hear the* NARRATOR'S VOICE.]

NARRATOR'S VOICE. The tools of conquest do not necessarily come with bombs and explosions and fallout.[8] There are weapons that are simply thoughts, attitudes, prejudices— to be found only in the minds of men. For the record, prejudices[9] can kill and suspicion can destroy and a thoughtless frightened search for a scapegoat has a fallout all its own for the children . . . and the children yet unborn. [*A pause.*] And the pity of it is . . . that these things cannot be confined to . . . The Twilight Zone!

---

8 **Fallout** is the radioactive dust particles that result from a nuclear explosion and that fall to Earth from the atmosphere.

9 **Prejudices** are unfavorable opinions or judgments formed unfairly.

After You Read

Respond and Think Critically

1. What does Charlie do when he thinks the figure walking down Maple Street is an enemy? [Recall]

2. What causes the people of Maple Street to act so angry and scared? Explain. [Summarize]

3. Based on your personal experience, how do you think the people of Maple Street might have solved their problems differently? Explain. [Connect]

4. How do the people on Maple Street change from the beginning of the teleplay to the end? Use details to support your answer. [Analyze]

5. Does Steve play a positive role in the play? Explain your answer. [Evaluate]

6. **BQ** **BIG Question** What message or lesson does the aliens' dialogue send? Explain. [Conclude]

TIP

Connecting
To answer question 3, find links between the teleplay and your own experiences.

• Think about a time you helped a friend or group of friends overcome fear or nervousness.

• Ask yourself, how was I able to help a friend or a group of friends overcome these fears? What strategy did I use? How did it help?

 FOLDABLES Study Organizer Keep track of your ideas about the **BIG Question** in your unit Foldable.

Just 10 years ago, Duom Deng, David Ayiik, and James Biar were refugees too. During Sudan's civil war, the three boys had seen their parents killed and their villages destroyed. Then they and thousands of other orphaned children walked 1,000 miles east to ...

Examine Media

Fear as a Selling Tool

In the 1950s, people feared that nuclear weapons might be used against Americans. Fear prompted many people to build bomb shelters. This ad ran in a popular magazine.

> **PROTECT**
> **YOUR LOVED ONES!**
> **Build a Small Atomic Shelter for Your Family & Valuable Possessions**
>
> *Write now for blueprints*
> **Complete set $7.50**
> **BLUEPRINTS FOR SURVIVAL**
> 35 West 53rd Street, NY

Group Activity Discuss the following questions with classmates. Use information from the teleplay and the advertisement to support your answers.

1. To what emotion does this advertisement appeal?

2. Would the advertisement have been effective in the 1950s? Why or why not?

3. What modern products are advertised using an emotional appeal similar to the appeal in this advertisement?

4. Are these modern advertisements effective? Why or why not?

Literary Element Suspense

Standards Practice ELA7R1h

1. Which line from the teleplay foreshadows the neighbors' behavior near the end of Act II?
   A. Let them get a search warrant.
   B. We'll eat each other up alive.
   C. I talk to monsters from outer space.
   D. Somebody's pulling a gag or something.

Review: Conflict

As you learned on page 675, **conflict** is the central struggle between opposing forces in a story or play. An **external conflict** exists when a character struggles against an outside force, such as another person. An **internal conflict** exists within the mind of a character who is torn between opposite feelings or goals. Serling uses an external conflict among the neighbors of Maple Street to tell his story.

Standards Practice ELA7R1e

2. Which sentence gives the best description of how the Maple Street residents react to the mysterious events occurring on their street?
   A. They cling to one another.
   B. They hide in their homes.
   C. They turn against one another.
   D. They unite against the aliens.

Reading Skill Analyze Historical Context

3. What evidence in the play shows that Serling meant to teach a lesson about the atmosphere of paranoia in the 1950s? Use both the graphic organizers that you completed to help you with your answer.

Vocabulary Practice

Respond to these questions.

1. What kinds of directions are **explicit**—detailed directions or vague directions?

2. Which is a **legitimate** need of a young adult—healthy food or video games?

3. Who would be more likely to need a **warrant**—a detective or a sales clerk?

4. Who would be more likely to be **converging** on a music hall—a jazz band or a swim team?

Academic Vocabulary

As the events grew more mysterious, Steve **perceived** that his once friendly neighbors were becoming hostile and suspicious. In the preceding sentence, *perceived* means noticed. Think about what words and actions Steve noticed about his neighbors, and then fill in the blank for this statement:

_____ was something that Steve perceived his neighbors doing.

 Literature Online

Selection Resources For Selection Quizzes, eFlashcards, and Reading-Writing Connection activities, go to glencoe.com and enter QuickPass code GL27534u6.

Respond Through Writing

Expository Essay

 Performance Standards

For page 829

ELA7W2f Produce writing that follows an organizational pattern appropriate to the type of composition.

Evaluate Plot In a short essay, evaluate how realistic the plot and characters of "The Monsters Are Due on Maple Street" are as shown through the teleplay's dialogue and stage directions. The audience of your essay will be your teacher or classmates.

Understand the Task The **plot** is the sequence of events in a literary work. **Characters** are the people in the literary work. **Dialogue** is the words spoken by actors. **Stage directions** contain information that helps actors know what to do. When characters, dialogue, and plot are realistic, they resemble people, spoken words, and events in real life. Think about the teleplay's dialogue and stage directions, and make a judgment about how realistic you think the plot and characters are.

Prewrite Make a plan for writing by recording events in the teleplay that you think are realistic or unrealistic. Use your plan to develop the main idea of your essay. Keep track of your ideas in a chart like the one below.

Event	What is realistic?	What is unrealistic?
Tommy gives his explanation for the power outage.	He is upset and worried.	He would suggest that space invaders caused the problem.

Draft Organize your information into a logical sequence. Plan an introductory paragraph, one paragraph about each of two or three important events, and a conclusion. After you design your plan, write a thesis statement. Consider using a sentence frame like this one:

The plot is/is not realistic in "The Monsters Are Due on Maple Street" because _____, _____, and _____.

Revise After writing your first draft, read it to be sure your paragraphs follow a logical order. Make sure that you support all statements with examples from the text. Then revise to improve organization. Use a dictionary or thesaurus to check word choice.

Edit and Proofread Proofread your paper, correcting any errors in spelling, grammar, and punctuation. Review the Grammar Tip in the side column for information on writing in the active voice.

Grammar Tip

Active Voice Verbs have two voices. The active voice shows that the subject does something or is something. The **passive voice** refers to the subject that is acted upon. The active voice is usually preferred in most writing. It produces stronger, less wordy sentences than the passive voice. Use the active voice whenever possible.

Active: *The neighbors chased Charlie.*

Passive: *Charlie was chased by the neighbors.*

The Bird Like No Other

Connect to the Short Story

Recall a time when someone acted in a way that you appreciate or respect. What did this person do? How did it affect you?

Quickwrite Freewrite for a few minutes about a person who has influenced you. What do you admire about this person?

Build Background

Dorothy West moved to Harlem in 1926. Harlem is a neighborhood in New York City. During the 1920s, it was the birthplace of an artistic movement known as the Harlem Renaissance.

- West began writing stories at age seven. She started two magazines that published writings by African Americans.

- In 1943, West moved to Martha's Vineyard, a small island off the coast of Massachusetts. She continued to write throughout her life.

- The story "The Bird Like No Other" comes from her book *The Richer, the Poorer.* It was published in 1995, a few years before West's death. By then, she was the last living member of the Harlem Renaissance.

Vocabulary

uncommitted (un′ kə mit′id) *adj.* not having or showing a particular opinion, view, or course of action (p. 835). *Aileen wasn't sure whom to vote for, so I knew she was uncommitted to either candidate.*

woe (wō) *n.* great sadness or suffering; great trouble or misfortune (p. 835). *The news report told of the destruction and woe caused by the wildfires.*

initiative (i nish′ə tiv) *n.* the action of taking the first step (p. 836). *Deondra took the initiative to start a recycling program at her school.*

soberly (sō′ bər lē) *adv.* very seriously (p. 838). *My parents soberly discussed whether we should move to a new neighborhood.*

Meet Dorothy West

"There is no life that does not contribute to history."
—Dorothy West

Just a "Kid" Dorothy West was just nineteen years old when she arrived in New York City. Other Harlem Renaissance writers knew her as "the Kid." Her writing career spanned eight decades.

Literary Works West's books include two novels—*The Living Is Easy* and *The Wedding*—and a collection of short stories and essays titled *The Richer, the Poorer.*

Dorothy West was born in 1907 and died in 1998.

 Literature Online

Author Search For more about Dorothy West, go to glencoe.com and enter QuickPass code GL27534u6.

Set Purposes for Reading

BQ BIG Question

As you read, ask yourself, what lesson does Colby learn from Aunt Emily?

Literary Element Flashback

A **flashback** is an interruption in a chronological story that describes a scene that happened at an earlier time. Flashbacks give readers background information that helps to explain the main events of the plot.

Authors use flashbacks to fill in details in a story. A flashback can show another side to a character or help explain the character's actions or feelings. In "The Bird Like No Other," a flashback helps explain the relationship between Colby and Aunt Emily.

As you read, notice when the author uses flashbacks. Ask yourself, what does each flashback explain? How does each flashback deepen my understanding of the characters?

Reading Strategy Synthesize

When you **synthesize,** you combine parts or pieces into something new. When you were younger, you probably played with toys that you could snap together or arrange in different ways. You could make a new creation each time, depending on how you fit the pieces together. When you read, you synthesize by combining ideas to create a new idea.

Synthesizing is important because it helps you move to a higher level of thinking. When you synthesize, you go beyond remembering what you learned from someone else—you reach a new understanding. To synthesize, ask yourself:

- What ideas or information have I learned from this selection?
- Do I understand something more than the main ideas here?
- Can I create something else from what I now know?

As you read, fill in a graphic organizer like the one below.

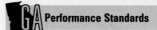

GA Performance Standards

For pages 830–839

ELA7R1e For literary texts, identify events that advance the plot and determine how each event explains past or present action(s) or foreshadows future action(s).

TRY IT

Synthesize With a partner, discuss a topic you've just studied or read about. What did you know about this topic before? What new information did you learn? How did you combine ideas—new information plus what you already knew—to arrive at a new understanding of the topic?

The *Bird* Like No Other

Dorothy West

Colby ran through the woods. He ran hard, as if he were putting his house and family behind him forever. The woods were not a dark forest of towering trees. They were just scrub oak and stunted pine with plenty of room for the sun to dapple[1] the road. The road, really a footpath worn by time, was so much a part of Colby's summers that at any point he knew how many trees to count before he reached the one with the hollow that caught the rain and gave the birds a drinking cup.

As the clearing came in sight with its cluster of cottages, Colby began to call Aunt Emily, the stridency[2] in his voice commanding her to shut out the sweeter sounds of summer.

Whatever Aunt Emily was doing, Colby knew, she would stop what she was doing. Wherever she was, she would start for the porch, so that by the time Colby pounded up the stairs, she would be sitting on her old porch glider, waiting for him to fling himself down beside her and cool his hot anger in her calm.

Aunt Emily was a courtesy aunt, a family friend of many years. When Colby's mother was a little girl, she played with Aunt Emily's little boy when they came on holiday from their separate cities. Then Aunt Emily lost her little boy in a winter accident on an icy street. When vacation time came again, it took all her courage to reopen her cottage. But she knew she must do it this saddest

Flashback What does this flashback tell you about Aunt Emily?

---

1 The sun would *dapple* the road by casting spots of light into the shadows.

2 To speak with *stridency* is to talk in a loud, harsh way.

24 Lakeber Avenue, 1986. Lucy
Rawlinson. Acrylic on board.
Private Collection.

summer of all if she was ever to learn to live in a world
that could not bend its tempo to the slow cadence[3] of grief.

Colby's sister made frequent visits with her dolls. She
brought the dolls that didn't cry or didn't wet because
they were always rewarded with a tea party for their good
behavior. She eased the summer's sorrow for Aunt Emily,
who felt an obligation to show this trusting child a
cheerful face and to take an interest in her eager talk.

---

3 **Tempo** means "pace" or "speed," and **cadence** means "rhythm" or "beat."

When I Was a Child, 1996. Dr. Samella Lewis. Oil on canvas, 39 3/4 x 30 in. Stella Jones Gallery, New Orleans, LA.

All the same, though Aunt Emily felt a bit ungrateful thinking it, a little girl dressing her dolls for a tea party is no substitute for a little boy playing cowboys and Indians at the top of his lungs.

Colby's family would have agreed with her. His mother adored him because he was her long-awaited son, five years younger than the youngest of his three sisters. His father was pleased and proud to have another male aboard.

But Colby couldn't see where he came first with anybody. As far as he was concerned he was always at the bottom of a heap of scrapping sisters. No matter how good he tried to be, his day most generally depended on how good his sisters decided to be. His rights were never mightier than their wrongs.

Aunt Emily had been Colby's sounding board[4] ever since the summer he was four. One day that summer, his mother

Flashback How can you tell that this is another flashback?

---

4 A *sounding board* is a person to whom one expresses opinions or ideas as a way of testing, or sounding, them out.

postponed a promised boat ride because his sisters had fought with each other all morning over whose turn it was to use the paint box that somebody had given them together. When they began to make each other cry, they were sent upstairs as punishment, and the outing was postponed.

Colby felt he was being punished for blows he hadn't struck and tears he hadn't caused. He had to tell somebody before he burst. Since he knew the way to Aunt Emily's, he went to tell her.

She took a look at his clouded-over face, plumped him down on her old porch glider, then went inside to telephone his mother that Colby wasn't lost, just decamped.[5] His mother told her what had happened, and Aunt Emily listened with **uncommitted** little clucks. She wasn't any Solomon[6] to decide if it was more important to punish the bad than to keep a promise to the good.

She could hear him banging back and forth on the glider, waiting in hot impatience to tell his tale of **woe.** The old glider screeched and groaned at his assault on its unoiled joints.

Standing inside her screen door, wincing in sympathy, Aunt Emily knew that neither she nor any nearby neighbor could take that tortured sound much longer. She tried to think of something to distract Colby's mind until he calmed down. A blue jay flew across her line of vision, a bird familiar to the landscape, but the unexciting sight bloomed into an idea.

Shutting the screen door soundlessly, approaching Colby on whispering feet, she put her finger to her lips and sat down beside him.

Synthesize What do you suppose Aunt Emily's idea is?

---

5 Here, **_decamped_** refers to having run away, quickly and secretly.

6 Famous for his great wisdom, **_Solomon_** was a king of Israel in the tenth century B.C.

uncommitted (un′kə mit′id) *adj.* not having or showing a particular opinion, view, or course of action

woe (wō) *n.* great sadness or suffering; great trouble or misfortune

As he stared at her round-eyed, his swinging suspended, she said softly, "Colby, before you came the most beautiful bird I ever saw was sitting on my hydrangea bush. He almost took my breath. I never saw a bird of so many colors. When you came running, he flew away. But if we don't talk or make any noise, he may come back."

After a moment of reflection, Colby's curiosity pulled out the plug in his sea of troubles, and he settled back.

That was the way this gentle fiction began. When Aunt Emily decided that the beautiful bird was gone for the day, Colby was wearing an agreeable face of a normal color. Taking the **initiative,** a shameless triumph over a small boy, Aunt Emily plunged into a story before Colby could get his mouth open to begin his own.

For the rest of that summer, and in the summers that followed, when Colby came glad or when Colby came only a little bit mad, the right to speak first was his automatically. But when Colby came breathing fire, by uncanny coincidence,[7] the bird like no other had just left the yard.

It was soon routine for Colby to seal his lips and settle down to wait.

Now he was eight, and on this angry morning when he flung himself up Aunt Emily's stairs, and flung himself down beside her on the poor old glider that responded as expected to a sudden shock, it was plainly a morning to search the sky for the bird like no other.

Before Aunt Emily could comb a fresh story out of her memory, Colby got a speech in ahead of her. He said in an excited whisper, "I see it, I see it. I see the bird you said was so beautiful. I guess he's every color in the world."

Jerking upright in stunned surprise, making the glider wearily protest, Aunt Emily asked in a shaken voice, "Where?"

"On that tree over there, see, over there."

Flashback What does this scene reveal about the characters?

Flashback How does the sequence of the story shift here?

---

7 In an ***uncanny coincidence,*** two events strangely happen at the same time.

Vocabulary ....

initiative (i nish′ ə tiv) *n.* the action of taking the first step

Full Moon Gossip, 1997. Gustavo Novoa. Acrylic on canvas, 36 x 36 in.
Wally Findlay Galleries, NY.

View the Art Which aspects of this painting are realistic? Which are imaginative?
Could any of these birds be "the bird like no other"? Explain your answer.

By a confluence[8] of golden sunlight and blue sky and
green leaves and shimmering summer air, a bird on a
swinging bough took on an astonishing beauty.

For a moment Aunt Emily couldn't believe her eyes. But
in another moment her eyes stopped playing tricks. And
suddenly she wanted to stop playing tricks, too.

"Colby, look again. That's a jay. There never was a bird
like the one I told you about. I made him up."

As if to give credence[9] to her confession, the bird on the
bough released itself from its brief enchantment and flew
away in the dress of a blue jay.

Colby spoke slowly. "Why did you make up a bird to
tell me about?"

Synthesize What leads
Colby to believe that this is
"the bird like no other"?

---

8 A *confluence* is a flowing together, or meeting, of two or more things.

9 Here, *credence* means "believability."

Bird in Flight, Bird Series II, 1981. Freshman Brown. Primacolors on paper.
Private collection.

Aunt Emily started to answer, but asked instead, "Don't you know why, Colby?"

"I think so," he said **soberly.**

"Will you tell me?"

"To make me sit still so I wouldn't say bad things about my family when I was mad. But you didn't want to make me sit still like a punishment. So you made me sit still like we were waiting to see something wonderful."

"I see the wonderful thing I've been waiting for. I see a little boy who's learned about family loyalty. It's as beautiful to look at as that bird."

Colby got up. He scuffed his sneakers. "Well, I guess I'll go home now. See you, Aunt Emily."

He bounded down the stairs and began to run home, running faster and faster. Aunt Emily's eyes filled with sentimental tears. He was trying to catch up with the kind of man he was going to be. He was rushing toward understanding. 🐦

BQ ▸ **BIG Question**

What valuable lessons does Colby learn?

Vocabulary ....

soberly (sō′ bər lē) *adv.* very seriously

After You Read

Respond and Think Critically

1. What usually causes Colby to run to Aunt Emily's cottage? [Recall]

2. Why does Aunt Emily welcome Colby's visits? [Interpret]

3. Why does Aunt Emily admit to Colby that she made up the story about the bird? Explain. [Infer]

4. **Literary Element** Flashback Summarize the events in the flashback that describes Colby's visit to Aunt Emily when he was four years old. [Summarize]

5. **Reading Strategy** Synthesize Consider this statement: "The key to writing flashbacks is that they must be integrated into the plot, while casting light on an issue or a character." Think about the flashbacks in the story. Then combine the statement above with what you learned in the story's flashbacks. What is the value of using flashbacks in writing? Explain. [Synthesize]

6. **BQ** BIG Question Is it appropriate for Aunt Emily to lie to Colby about the bird? Why or why not? [Evaluate]

Vocabulary Practice

Choose the best answer for each question.

1. Whom would you describe as **uncommitted**?
   A. a person with firm beliefs
   B. a person who changes his or her mind often

2. Who is more likely to experience **woe**?
   A. someone who has bad luck
   B. someone who has good luck

3. Whom would you describe as having **initiative**?
   A. a person who often needs to be reminded to do something
   B. a person who gets the job done without being asked

4. Which person is more likely to behave **soberly**?
   A. a news reporter
   B. a comedian

 Writing

Write a Journal Entry Recall a time when someone helped you deal with a problem. How did this person help you? What advice did he or she offer? Write a journal entry in which you describe and reflect on what happened.

TIP

Summarizing
Here are some tips to help you summarize. Remember that when you summarize, you retell the main ideas or events. To summarize the flashback, ask yourself:

- Why does Colby run to Aunt Emily's cottage?
- What happens when Colby arrives at Aunt Emily's?
- What does Aunt Emily tell Colby?
- How does Colby react?

FOLDABLES Study Organizer Keep track of your ideas about the **BIG Question** in your unit Foldable.

 Literature Online

Selection Resources
For Selection Quizzes, eFlashcards, and Reading-Writing Connection activities, go to glencoe.com and enter QuickPass code GL27534u6.

Before You Read

There Will Come Soft Rains

Connect to the Short Story

What would it be like to live in a house that does everything for you? The house would be powerful—maybe more powerful than you.

Partner Talk With a partner, talk about what it might be like to live in a world that is run by computers and robots. How would you feel if a computer decided what you could eat or wear?

Build Background

Ray Bradbury wrote "There Will Come Soft Rains" in 1951. At that time, people were still recovering from World War II. Many people were worried about nuclear war.

- Nuclear weapons are among the most powerful weapons. One atomic bomb can destroy an entire city.

- In the 1950s, people feared that a nuclear war would destroy everyone and everything on Earth. Bradbury and others wrote stories exploring what could happen as a result of such a war.

Vocabulary

shriveled (shriv´əld) *adj.* shrunken and wrinkled (p. 843). *After sitting in the sun for many days, the apples were dry and shriveled.*

charred (chärd) *adj.* burned (p. 843). *Only ash and charred wood remained in the fire pit after the flames went out.*

inconvenience (in´kən vēn´yəns) *n.* something that causes difficulty, discomfort, or bother (p. 844). *Road construction is an inconvenience because it causes traffic jams.*

frenzy (fren´zē) *n.* a state of wild, intense emotion or excitement (p. 845). *In a frenzy, the shoppers ran toward the store's sale section.*

whims (wimz) *n.* sudden or unexpected ideas (p. 847). *The new babysitter tried to satisfy the children's whims in order to maintain peace in the home.*

Meet Ray Bradbury

Storming the World with Words Ray Bradbury began writing as a boy. "My parents had given me a toy typewriter for Christmas," Bradbury wrote, "and I stormed it with words. Anytime I liked I could turn a faucet on each finger and let the miracles out, yes, into machines and onto paper where I might freeze and control them forever. I haven't stopped writing since."

Literary Works Bradbury's first book of short stories, *Dark Carnival,* was followed by *The Martian Chronicles.* His novels include *Fahrenheit 451; Dandelion Wine* and its sequel, *Farewell Summer;* and *Death Is a Lonely Business.* In 2007 the Pulitzer Prize board awarded Bradbury a special citation for his distinguished career.

Ray Bradbury was born in 1920.

 Literature Online

Author Search For more about Ray Bradbury, go to glencoe.com and enter QuickPass code GL27534u6.

Set Purposes for Reading

BQ BIG Question

Many people worry about what the future will bring. As you read, ask yourself, in what way is Bradbury warning readers about the future?

Literary Element Diction

Diction is an author's choice and arrangement of words. Words sometimes have a figurative, or implied, meaning as well as a literal, or actual, meaning. **Denotation** refers to the dictionary meaning of a word. **Connotation** refers to a word's implied or suggested meaning. For example, an author may use *house* in a description of the setting. However, if the author uses *mansion,* you recognize that the word implies wealth.

Paying attention to words' literal and implied meanings helps you understand the author's attitude, beliefs, and message. As you read the short story, notice Bradbury's use of figurative language, and look for words that have connotations. Ask yourself, what is Bradbury suggesting with the words he chooses?

Reading Strategy Interpret Author's Meaning

When you **interpret an author's meaning,** you use information from the text and your own understanding of the world to figure out the author's lesson or message. Examining plot, characters, and diction are ways to interpret an author's meaning. As you read, consider whether

- the author presents the characters positively or negatively
- the plot implies judgment by the author
- the characters and setting are symbolic of something else
- the diction, or word choice, reveals the author's attitude or meaning

As you read, think about why the author presents machines as characters. Use a graphic organizer like the one below.

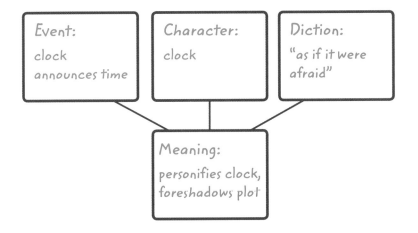

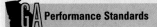

GA Performance Standards

For pages 840–852

ELA7R1g/ii For literary texts, explain and analyze the effects of figurative language.

TRY IT

Interpret Advertisements are everywhere—in magazines and on television, billboards, the radio, and the Internet. Ads are designed to grab your attention and convey a message quickly. Think of an ad that stands out in your memory. What did it sell or ask you to do? Did the ad use positive or negative associations to change your behavior? What language was used to convey the advertiser's message?

There Will Come Soft Rains

RAY BRADBURY

I n the living room the voice-clock sang, *Tick-tock, seven o'clock, time to get up, time to get up, seven o'clock!* as if it were afraid that nobody would. The morning house lay empty. The clock ticked on, repeating and repeating its sounds into the emptiness. *Seven-nine, breakfast time, seven-nine!*

In the kitchen the breakfast stove gave a hissing sigh and ejected from its warm interior eight pieces of perfectly browned toast, eight eggs sunnyside up, sixteen slices of bacon, two coffees, and two cool glasses of milk.

"Today is August 4, 2026," said a second voice from the kitchen ceiling, "in the city of Allendale, California." It repeated the date three times for memory's sake. "Today is Mr. Featherstone's birthday. Today is the anniversary of Tilita's marriage. Insurance is payable, as are the water, gas, and light bills."

Somewhere in the walls, relays clicked, memory tapes glided under electric eyes.

Eight-one, tick-tock, eight-one o'clock, off to school, off to work, run, run, eight-one! But no doors slammed, no carpets took the soft tread of rubber heels. It was raining outside. The weather box on the front door sang quietly: "Rain, rain, go away; rubbers, raincoats for today . . ." And the rain tapped on the empty house, echoing.

Diction What attitude or feelings do the words *hissing* and *ejected* suggest?

Outside, the garage chimed and lifted its door to reveal the waiting car. After a long wait the door swung down again.

At eight-thirty the eggs were **shriveled** and the toast was like stone. An aluminum wedge scraped them into the sink, where hot water whirled them down a metal throat which digested and flushed them away to the distant sea. The dirty dishes were dropped into a hot washer and emerged[1] twinkling dry.

Nine-fifteen, sang the clock, *time to clean.*

Out of warrens[2] in the wall, tiny robot mice darted. The rooms were acrawl with the small cleaning animals, all rubber and metal. They thudded against chairs, whirling their mustached runners, kneading the rug nap, sucking gently at hidden dust. Then, like mysterious invaders, they popped into their burrows. Their pink electric eyes faded. The house was clean.

Ten o'clock. The sun came out from behind the rain. The house stood alone in a city of rubble and ashes. This was the one house left standing. At night the ruined city gave off a radioactive glow which could be seen for miles.

Ten-fifteen. The garden sprinklers whirled up in golden founts, filling the soft morning air with scatterings of brightness. The water pelted windowpanes, running down the **charred** west side where the house had been burned evenly free of its white paint. The entire west face of the house was black, save for five places. Here the silhouette in paint of a man mowing a lawn. Here, as in a photograph, a woman bent to pick flowers. Still farther over, their images burned on wood in one titanic instant, a small boy, hands flung into the air; higher up, the image of a thrown ball, and opposite him a girl, hands raised to catch a ball which never came down.

---

1 When the dishes *emerged*, they came out of the dishwasher.

2 *Warrens* are the burrows, or little holes, that animals such as mice dig out and live in.

Vocabulary

shriveled (shriv′əld) *adj.* shrunken and wrinkled

charred (chärd) *adj.* burned

The five spots of paint—the man, the woman, the children, the ball—remained. The rest was a thin charcoaled layer.

The gentle sprinkler rain filled the garden with falling light.

Until this day, how well the house had kept its peace. How carefully it had inquired, "Who goes there? What's the password?" and, getting no answer from lonely foxes and whining cats, it had shut up its windows and drawn shades in an old-maidenly preoccupation with self-protection which bordered on a mechanical paranoia.[3]

It quivered[4] at each sound, the house did. If a sparrow brushed a window, the shade snapped up. The bird, startled, flew off! No, not even a bird must touch the house!

The house was an altar with ten thousand attendants, big, small, servicing, attending, in choirs. But the gods had gone away, and the ritual of the religion continued senselessly, uselessly.

Twelve noon.

A dog whined, shivering, on the front porch.

The front door recognized the dog voice and opened. The dog, once huge and fleshy, but now gone to bone and covered with sores, moved in and through the house, tracking mud. Behind it whirred angry mice, angry at having to pick up mud, angry at **inconvenience.**

For not a leaf fragment blew under the door but what the wall panels flipped open and the copper scrap rats flashed swiftly out. The offending dust, hair, or paper, seized in miniature steel jaws, was raced back to the burrows. There, down tubes which fed into the cellar, it was dropped into the sighing vent of an incinerator which sat like evil Baal[5] in a dark corner.

Interpret Author's Meaning
What happened to the family?

---

3 **Preoccupation** is an extreme concern with an object or activity. **Paranoia** is the mental state of being extremely suspicious and afraid of others.

4 When the house **quivered,** it shook slightly or trembled.

5 An **incinerator** is a kind of furnace for burning trash. **Baal** was a god worshipped in ancient times.

Vocabulary ....

inconvenience (in´kən vēn´yəns) *n.* something that causes difficulty, discomfort, or bother

The dog ran upstairs, hysterically[6] yelping to each door, at last realizing, as the house realized, that only silence was here.

It sniffed the air and scratched the kitchen door. Behind the door, the stove was making pancakes which filled the house with a rich baked odor and the scent of maple syrup.

The dog frothed at the mouth, lying at the door, sniffing, its eyes turned to fire. It ran wildly in circles, biting at its tail, spun in a **frenzy,** and died. It lay in the parlor for an hour.

Two o'clock, sang a voice.

Delicately sensing decay at last, the regiments[7] of mice hummed out as softly as blown gray leaves in an electrical wind.

Two-fifteen.

The dog was gone.

In the cellar, the incinerator glowed suddenly and a whirl of sparks leaped up the chimney.

Two thirty-five.

Bridge tables sprouted from patio walls. Playing cards fluttered onto pads in a shower of pips. Martinis manifested[8] on an oaken bench with egg-salad sandwiches. Music played.

But the tables were silent and the cards untouched.

At four o'clock the tables folded like great butterflies back through the paneled walls.

Four-thirty.

The nursery walls glowed.

Animals took shape: yellow giraffes, blue lions, pink antelopes, lilac panthers cavorting[9] in crystal substance.

Diction What does this description tell you about the dog?

Interpret Author's Meaning By describing how the house responds to the death of the dog, what might Bradbury be saying about living in a world of machines?

---

6 To behave **hysterically** is to be very upset and out of control emotionally.

7 **Regiments** are groups of soldiers.

8 **Pips** are the small printed dots or symbols that show a playing card's value. **Martinis** are alcoholic drinks. When the drinks **manifested,** they suddenly appeared.

9 When the animals are **cavorting,** they are running and playing.

Vocabulary

frenzy (fren′ zē) *n.* a state of wild, intense emotion or excitement

Domestic Kitchen.
Connie Hayes.

The walls were glass. They looked out upon color and fantasy. Hidden films clocked through well-oiled sprockets, and the walls lived. The nursery floor was woven to resemble a crisp, cereal[10] meadow. Over this ran aluminum roaches and iron crickets, and in the hot still air butterflies of delicate red tissue wavered among the sharp aromas of animal spoors![11] There was the sound like a great matted yellow hive of bees within a dark bellows, the lazy bumble of a purring lion. And there was the patter of okapi[12] feet and the murmur of a fresh jungle rain, like other hoofs, falling upon the summer-starched grass. Now the walls dissolved into distances of parched weed, mile on mile, and warm endless sky. The animals drew away into thorn brakes and water holes.

It was the children's hour.

Five o'clock. The bath filled with clear hot water.

Six, seven, eight o'clock. The dinner dishes manipulated[13] like magic tricks, and in the study a *click.* In the metal stand opposite the **hearth** where a fire now blazed up warmly, a cigar popped out, half an inch of soft gray ash on it, smoking, waiting.

---

10 A *cereal* meadow is a grassy field.

11 *Spoors* are animal droppings.

12 The African *okapi* is like a giraffe, but small and short-necked.

13 Here, *manipulated* means "moved around."

Diction What happens in the nursery? Why do you think Bradbury includes this description?

Visual Vocabulary

A **hearth** is a floor of a fireplace that often extends out into a room.

Nine o'clock. The beds warmed their hidden circuits, for nights were cool here.

Nine-five. A voice spoke from the study ceiling:

"Mrs. McClellan, which poem would you like this evening?"

The house was silent.

The voice said at last, "Since you express no preference, I shall select a poem at random." Quiet music rose to back the voice. "Sara Teasdale.[14] As I recall, your favorite. . . ."

There will come soft rains and the smell of the ground,
And swallows circling with their shimmering sound;

And frogs in the pools singing at night,
And wild plum trees in tremulous white;[15]

Robins will wear their feathery fire,
Whistling their **whims** *on a low fence-wire;*

And not one will know of the war, not one
Will care at last when it is done.

Not one would mind, neither bird nor tree,
If mankind perished utterly;[16]

And Spring herself, when she woke at dawn
Would scarcely know that we were gone.

The fire burned on the stone hearth and the cigar fell away into a mound of quiet ash on its tray. The empty chairs faced each other between the silent walls, and the music played.

At ten o'clock the house began to die.

The wind blew. A falling tree bough crashed through the kitchen window. Cleaning solvent,[17] bottled, shattered over the stove. The room was ablaze in an instant!

Diction Bradbury chooses the word *die* instead of a synonym such as *perish* or *expire*. What effect does his word choice have?

---

14 ***Sara Teasdale,*** a twentieth-century American poet, often wrote about the beauty of nature.

15 The plum trees, full of white blossoms, are shaking (***in tremulous white***).

16 ***Perished utterly*** means "died out completely."

17 A ***solvent*** is a mixture of liquid chemicals that would burn easily.

"Fire!" screamed a voice. The house lights flashed, water pumps shot water from the ceilings. But the solvent spread on the linoleum, licking, eating, under the kitchen door, while the voices took it up in chorus: "Fire, fire, fire!"

The house tried to save itself. Doors sprang tightly shut, but the windows were broken by the heat and the wind blew and sucked upon the fire.

The house gave ground as the fire in ten billion angry sparks moved with flaming ease from room to room and then up the stairs. While scurrying water rats squeaked from the walls, pistoled their water, and ran for more. And the wall sprays let down showers of mechanical rain.

But too late. Somewhere, sighing, a pump shrugged to a stop. The quenching rain ceased. The reserve water supply which had filled baths and washed dishes for many quiet days was gone.

The fire crackled up the stairs. It fed upon Picassos and Matisses in the upper halls, like delicacies,[18] baking off the oily flesh, tenderly crisping the canvases into black shavings.

---

18 **Picassos** and **Matisses** are paintings by twentieth-century artists Pablo Picasso and Henri Matisse. In a poetic image, the narration suggests that the burning paintings are **delicacies,** or delicious things for the fire to eat.

Legato, 1983. Jeremy Annett. Oil on hardboard. Private Collection.

Now the fire lay in beds, stood in windows, changed the colors of drapes!

And then, reinforcements.

From attic trapdoors, blind robot faces peered down with faucet mouths gushing green chemical.

The fire backed off, as even an elephant must at the sight of a dead snake. Now there were twenty snakes whipping over the floor, killing the fire with a clear cold venom[19] of green froth.

But the fire was clever. It had sent flame outside the house, up through the attic to the pumps there. An explosion! The attic brain which directed the pumps was shattered into bronze shrapnel[20] on the beams.

The fire rushed back into every closet and felt of the clothes hung there.

The house shuddered, oak bone on bone, its bared skeleton cringing from the heat, its wire, its nerves revealed as if a surgeon had torn the skin off to let the red veins and capillaries quiver in the scalded air. Help, help! Fire! Run, run! Heat snapped mirrors like the first brittle winter ice. And the voices wailed, Fire, fire, run, run, like a tragic nursery rhyme, a dozen voices, high, low, like children dying in a forest, alone, alone. And the voices fading as the wires popped their sheathings like hot chestnuts. One, two, three, four, five voices died.

In the nursery the jungle burned. Blue lions roared, purple giraffes bounded off. The panthers ran in circles, changing color, and ten million animals, running before the fire, vanished off toward a distant steaming river. . . .

Ten more voices died. In the last instant under the fire avalanche, other choruses, oblivious,[21] could be heard announcing the time, playing music, cutting the lawn by remote-control mower, or setting an umbrella frantically out and in, the slamming and opening front door, a thousand things happening, like a clock shop when each clock strikes the hour insanely before or after the other, a scene of maniac confusion, yet unity; singing, screaming,

Diction In what ways does Bradbury give the house and the fire human qualities?

Interpret Author's Meaning Consider what happens to the animals in the nursery. What might this event symbolize?

---

19 **Venom** is a poisonous fluid produced by an animal such as a snake.

20 Here, **shrapnel** refers to bits of torn metal blown around by the explosion.

21 People who are **oblivious** do not notice what is happening around them.

House with Electrical Symbols. Chris Spollen.

a few last cleaning mice darting bravely out to carry the horrid ashes away! And one voice, with sublime disregard[22] for the situation, read poetry aloud in the fiery study, until all the film spools burned, until all the wires withered and the circuits cracked.

The fire burst the house and let it slam flat down, puffing out skirts of spark and smoke.

In the kitchen, an instant before the rain of fire and timber, the stove could be seen making breakfasts at a psychopathic[23] rate, ten dozen eggs, six loaves of toast, twenty dozen bacon strips, which, eaten by fire, started the stove working again, hysterically hissing!

The crash. The attic smashing into kitchen and parlor. The parlor into cellar, cellar into sub-cellar. Deep freeze, armchair, film tapes, circuits, beds, and all like skeletons thrown in a cluttered mound deep under.

Diction In what way are these items like skeletons?

Smoke and silence. A great quantity of smoke.

Dawn showed faintly in the east. Among the ruins, one wall stood alone. Within the wall, a last voice said, over and over again and again, even as the sun rose to shine upon the heaped rubble and steam:

"Today is August 5, 2026, today is August 5, 2026, today is . . ." 🕯

Interpret Author's Meaning Why do you think Bradbury ends the story in this way?

---

22 *Sublime disregard* is a lack of attention to something because one is intellectually or spiritually above it.

23 Here, *psychopathic* means "insane" or "crazy."

After You Read

Respond and Think Critically

1. Why is the house empty? [Recall]

2. What are some of the things the house protects itself from? [Identify]

3. Why is the dog thin and sick? Explain. [Infer]

4. What can you tell about the people who lived in the house? Use details from the story to support your answer. [Infer]

5. Which technology in the house do you find most believable? Which technology do you think could not exist? Explain. [Evaluate]

6. **BQ** BIG Question What is Bradbury's message in this short story? [Conclude]

TIP

Inferring
To answer question 3, think about the clues the author gives you. Combine the clues with your own experience to answer the question.

- Where does the dog first appear in the story?
- What does it do when it enters the house?
- Why does it scratch at the kitchen door?

 FOLDABLES **Study Organizer** Keep track of your ideas about the **BIG Question** in your unit Foldable.

You're the Critic

Bradbury: What Kind of Writer Is He?

Ray Bradbury is known as a science fiction writer, but his work appeals to a much larger audience. Read these excerpts about the author's work.

"After each story ends, there remain several memorable incidents, each wrapped around an intriguing idea about the nature of life, what it means to be fully human."

—The Virginian-Pilot

"There is simply no ready label for a writer who mixes poetry and mythology with fantasy and technology to create literate tales of suspense and social criticism."

—salon.com

Group Activity Discuss the following questions. Refer to the excerpts and use evidence from the story to support your answers.

1. What do you find most memorable about "There Will Come Soft Rains"? What is Bradbury saying about human nature in this story?

2. How effectively does Bradbury mix poetry, fantasy, and technology in this story? Is the story suspenseful? Explain.

1. Bradbury describes the cleaning robots as "mysterious invaders." What does the word *invaders* mean? What connotation, or implied meaning, does this word have?

2. Bradbury uses words such as *regiments, reinforcements,* and *shrapnel* in the story. How would you characterize these words? How do these word choices reflect the theme of the story?

Review: Simile

As you learned on page 203, a **simile** is a type of figurative language. A simile is a figure of speech in which *like* or *as* is used to compare seemingly different things.

3. Recall this sentence from the story: "At four o'clock the tables folded like great butterflies back through the paneled walls." How are the tables like butterflies?

4. In his description of the destruction of the fire, Bradbury writes "the wires popped their sheathings like hot chestnuts." What does this simile mean?

Reading Strategy
Interpret Author's Meaning

5. The house was designed to care for its owners, but it could not protect them from nuclear warfare. What is Bradbury saying about humans and machines?

6. Why does Bradbury include the poem by Sara Teasdale? How does the poem relate to the story?

Vocabulary Practice

Match each boldfaced vocabulary word with a word from the right column that has the same meaning. Two of the words in the right column will not have matches. Then write a sentence for each vocabulary word, or draw or find a picture that represents the word.

1. **shriveled**
2. **charred**
3. **inconvenience**
4. **frenzy**
5. **whims**

a. raw
b. nuisance
c. withered
d. saturated
e. impulses
f. uproar
g. scorched

Example:
shriveled

Sentence: Raisins are dry, shriveled grapes.

Academic Vocabulary

In the story, a voice asks which poem Mrs. McClellan would like to hear. When it gets no response, the voice says, "Since you express no preference, I shall select a poem at **random**." Using context clues, try to figure out the meaning of the word *random*. Check your guess in a dictionary.

LOG ON Literature Online

Selection Resources For Selection Quizzes, eFlashcards, and Reading-Writing Connection activities, go to glencoe.com and enter QuickPass code GL27534u6.

Respond Through Writing

Persuasive Essay

Argue a Position Ray Bradbury presents a world in which advances in technology have a major impact on humans' lives. In a short essay, argue whether such progress is good or bad.

Understand the Task When you choose a side and explain why you feel a certain way, you are **arguing a position.** In a **persuasive essay,** you try to influence your readers to agree with your perspective and ideas.

Prewrite Begin by organizing your thoughts about the advantages and disadvantages of technological progress. Be sure to support your position with evidence, or facts and examples. Make a graphic organizer like the one below for both sides of the argument to decide which position you think is stronger. Think of as many reasons and supporting facts and examples as you can to defend your position.

> **Position:**
> Progress is good.

> **Reason:**
> More free time
> **Supporting Evidence:**
> Computers help people find information faster.

> **Reason:**
> **Supporting Evidence:**

Draft As you begin writing, pay attention to the order of your arguments. For example, you may decide to give one example or piece of evidence to support your position. After this you may present a possible counterargument, or opposing point of view, along with your response to it. Then you may address another point, its counterargument, and your response. This sentence frame may help you think of counterarguments and responses:

Some people may say that _____, but I think that _____.

Revise After you have written your first draft, read it to determine whether your position has enough support. Persuasive writers often build an argument from its weakest point to its strongest point. Look for ways to include persuasive techniques, such as emotional appeals.

Edit and Proofread Proofread your paper, correcting any errors in spelling, grammar, and punctuation. See the Word Bank in the side column for words you may use in your persuasive essay.

GA Performance Standards

For page 853

ELA7W2c Produce a multi-paragraph persuasive essay that describes the points in support of the proposition, employing well-articulated, relevant evidence.

> **Word Bank**
>
> The following are some useful words that you might want to include in your essay. Check their meanings in a dictionary first to make sure you use them correctly.
>
> **advantage**
> **benefits**
> **complex**
> **disadvantage**
> **expense**
> **improve**
> **quality**
> **valuable**

Before You Read

Missing! and *Birdfoot's Grampa*

Connect to the Article and the Poem

Have you ever watched a spider spin a web, a bird build a nest, or an ant carry a piece of food? How much attention do you pay to nature's small creatures?

Partner Talk With a partner, talk about the natural world around you. Are there small creatures you'd miss if they disappeared? What are they, and why would you miss them?

Build Background

Joseph Bruchac, the author of the poem "Birdfoot's Grampa," writes that Native Americans believe that humans have "a special mission" on Earth "to maintain the natural balance." The informational article "Missing!" describes how a change in temperature is harmful to Costa Rica's wildlife.

- Costa Rica is a tropical country in Central America.

- With mountains, forests, and two coastlines, Costa Rica has a great variety of plant and animal life.

- The Monteverde (mon´ tə vār´ dē) Cloud Forest Reserve is in Costa Rica. It is a protected area for plants and wildlife and is home to hundreds of species of plants, birds, and other animals.

- About 25 percent of the land in Costa Rica is protected, including national parks and private reserves.

Vocabulary

vapor (vā´ pər) *n.* a substance suspended in the air, as steam or fog (p. 856).
The smog was a noticeable vapor above the city.

droplets (drop´ litz) *n.* tiny amounts of liquid (p. 857).
The rain fell in droplets that stung her face.

Meet the Authors

Claire Miller

Nature Lover Claire Miller writes for *Ranger Rick,* a children's nature magazine published by the National Wildlife Federation. She says, "No matter where you live, there's lots to discover right outside your door."

Joseph Bruchac

The Good Mind A member of the Abenaki tribe, Joseph Bruchac proudly bears his Native American name, *Gahnegohheyoh,* which means "the good mind." Bruchac is an award-winning author of more than 20 books and a professional teller of traditional Native American stories.

 Literature Online

Author Search For more about Claire Miller and Joseph Bruchac, go to glencoe.com and enter QuickPass code GL27534u6.

Set Purposes for Reading

BQ BIG Question

As you read, ask yourself, what messages are the authors of "Missing!" and "Birdfoot's Grampa" trying to convey to readers?

Literary Element Description

Description is writing that creates an impression of a setting, a person, an animal, an object, or an event. Details in a description help readers see, hear, smell, taste, and feel what the author writes about.

In the informational article "Missing!", the description of the cloud forest in Costa Rica includes details that help you imagine how the clouds form and how they affect the area's frogs. These details help the author convey the ways that global warming is threatening wildlife.

As you read, ask yourself, how does each author's use of vivid verbs and adjectives help convey his or her purpose for writing?

Reading Skill Identify Problems and Solutions

Authors often organize the information in their articles by using a problem-and-solution structure. When you **identify problems and solutions,** you examine a text to understand a conflict, or problem, and how to solve it.

Identifying problems and solutions helps you understand what's happening in a text, why it's happening, and what is being done or what could be done about it. To identify problems and solutions as you read, think about these questions:

- What is the author concerned about? Remember that complicated issues can have more than one problem.

- What is the solution or solutions? Look for words such as *need, attempt, help, can,* and *will* to locate any solutions.

As you read, fill in a graphic organizer like the one below.

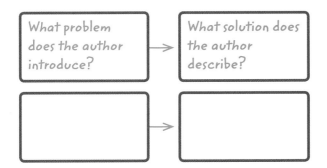

GA Performance Standards

For pages 854–861

ELA7R1c For informational texts, apply knowledge of common organizational structures and patterns.

TRY IT

Identify Problems and Solutions Think of a problem that you see every day in your neighborhood or at school. What is the problem? Can you think of possible solutions?

MISSING!

Claire Miller

The frog population in Costa Rica is declining. Scientists search for answers.

The cloud-covered mountains of Costa Rica are home to a variety of frogs. Many live in the Monteverde Cloud Forest Reserve. Over the years, cloud coverage has changed in the region. Now, some of the forest's frogs have disappeared, and the changing clouds may be part of their problem.

Super Soakers Unlike humans, frogs don't drink water. Instead, they absorb it through their skin. Most of it soaks through a "seat patch" on their bottoms when they sit on moist ground.

In the Monteverde Cloud Forest Reserve, the frogs have depended on the clouds that hang around the mountains to keep the forest floor wet and the mountain streams flowing. Where do the clouds come from?

When Earth's water evaporates from oceans, lakes, or puddles, it changes from liquid to water **vapor.** This water

Identify Problems and Solutions What is the problem in the Monteverde Cloud Forest Reserve?

Vocabulary

vapor (vā′pər) *n.* a substance suspended in the air, as steam or fog

vapor rises when heated by the sun. Strong winds can also blow it upward.

In Monteverde, the water vapor would often rise until it ran into cold air around the mountaintops. This cold air condensed[1] the vapor into liquid water **droplets.** The droplets then clumped together to make up a cloud.

Clouds are the form that water takes right before it returns to Earth as rain, snow, sleet, or hail. In Monteverde, when clouds blanketed the mountain, the droplets gathered to make the little pools of water that the frogs need.

These days, the clouds often form high in the sky instead of down on the mountains of Monteverde. As a result, the forest floor is drier than it once was. So what's causing this high cloud formation?

In recent years, the air temperature in Monteverde has increased. Often the air around the mountaintops is too warm to condense the water vapor. So the water vapor keeps rising until it forms clouds high above the mountains. At the same time, the land below dries out. So the frogs (and their cousins, the toads) have a hard time finding the water they need on the forest floor.

Turning Up the Heat Most scientists believe that people are causing many places on Earth to get warmer, including Monteverde. They call it global warming.

People often add to global warming by burning fuels such as oil, natural gas, and coal. These fuels power almost everything we plug in or drive. As the fuels are burned, a gas called carbon dioxide is given off. Carbon dioxide occurs naturally in our atmosphere.[2] It helps to keep Earth warm by holding in the sun's heat. But having too much carbon dioxide in the air is like throwing a heavy blanket around the planet—it keeps in too much of the sun's heat, and the world gets warmer.

Description Which words in the author's description help you visualize how clouds formed around the mountaintops?

Identify Problems and Solutions How do the bold subheads in this article help you locate the problems and solutions?

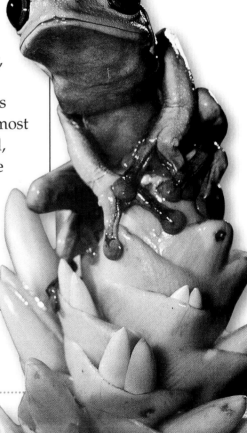

---

1 When water vapor has *condensed,* it has come together to make drops of liquid water.

2 The *atmosphere* is the mixture of gases that surrounds Earth.

droplets (drop′litz) *n.* tiny amounts of liquid

Missing Toad Alan J. Pounds is a scientist who has lived and worked in the Monteverde Cloud Forest Reserve for 24 years—and he's noticed a change in cloud cover and frog populations. "In the early 1980s, there were hundreds of golden toads," he says. "But by 1989, people found only a few of them, and since then, we haven't seen any!"

High cloud formation caused by global warming is a serious problem. And according to Pounds, it adds to a growing list of troubles that the wildlife of Monteverde is faced with. "The frogs and other wild animals have to cope with many problems, such as habitat[3] loss and disease. But when global warming is added to all these problems, it may push them over the edge to extinction."[4]

You Can Help It's too late to save the extinct golden toads, but there are things that you and your family can do to keep the world from getting warmer. For starters, encourage your family to use the car less. Also, turn off the lights and appliances[5] that you aren't using. All these things burn fuel and contribute to global warming. By becoming an Earth-friendly family, you'll help wildlife all around the world! ⌁

Identify Problems and Solutions What does the author suggest that families do to prevent global warming?

---

3   To *cope* means "to deal with and try to overcome." A *habitat* is a plant or animal's home, or a place where it naturally lives and grows.

4   *Extinction* is the act of wiping out of existence.

5   *Appliances* are machines or devices for household use that run on electricity.

Birdfoot's Grampa

Joseph Bruchac

The old man
must have stopped our car
two dozen times to climb out
and gather into his hands
5   the small toads blinded
by our lights and leaping,
live drops of rain.

The rain was falling,
a mist about his white hair
10   and I kept saying
you can't save them all,
accept it, get back in
we've got places to go.

But, leathery hands full
15   of wet brown life,
knee deep in the summer
roadside grass,
he just smiled and said
they have places to go to
20   *too.*

Description How does the description of the old man help you see and feel the scene?

BQ **BIG Question**

What lesson does this poem share with readers?

After You Read

Respond and Think Critically

1. In "Birdfoot's Grampa," why does the old man stop the car "two dozen times"? [Recall]

2. According to the article "Missing!" why are frogs and toads disappearing in the Monteverde Cloud Forest Reserve? [Summarize]

3. Think about what you learned in "Missing!" What can the presence of frogs and toads tell people about the health of the climate? [Infer]

4. According to "Missing!" how can you, the reader, help reduce global warming? Give specific examples. [Analyze]

5. Think about the old man in "Birdfoot's Grampa." Why does he want to save the toads? [Conclude]

6. **BQ** **BIG Question** What do "Missing!" and "Birdfoot's Grampa" tell you about how human activity affects other creatures? [Analyze]

Vocabulary Practice

On a separate sheet of paper, write the vocabulary word that correctly completes each sentence. If none of the words fits the sentence, write "none."

vapor   **droplets**

1. At the end of the long hike, Rebecca's face was covered with _____ of sweat.

2. All through the _____, the fragrance of flowers in bloom filled the air.

3. When the snow melted in spring, the ground was covered with deep _____ of watery mud.

4. The pavement was so hot that the rain turned into _____ only minutes after it fell on the blacktop.

Academic Vocabulary

The author of "Missing!" explains that human activities, such as burning fuels to power cars and appliances, have serious **environmental** effects. In the preceding sentence, *environmental* means "related to the natural world" or "the conditions that affect the lives of plants, animals, and people." Think about how people treat the natural world where you live. What environmental effects do these behaviors have?

TIP

Inferring
To answer question 3, you have to use your knowledge and clues from the article to make a good guess. Here are some tips to help you infer.

- Think about what the article says affects the temperature of Earth.

- Recall what frogs and toads need to survive.

FOLDABLES Study Organizer Keep track of your ideas about the **BIG Question** in your unit Foldable.

 Literature Online

Selection Resources
For Selection Quizzes, eFlashcards, and Reading-Writing Connection activities, go to glencoe.com and enter QuickPass code GL27534u6.

1. In "Missing!" what significant change in the Monteverde Cloud Forest Reserve does the author describe? How does the description help you understand the change?

2. In what way does the description of jumping toads in lines 5–7 of "Birdfoot's Grampa" appeal to the senses?

3. In "Birdfoot's Grampa," what does the second stanza tell you about the speaker of the poem?

Review: Alliteration

As you learned on page 190, poets use **alliteration,** or the repetition of consonant sounds at the beginnings of words, to stress certain words and ideas.

4. Read these lines from "Birdfoot's Grampa":

> the small toads blinded
> by our lights and leaping,
> live drops of rain.

What sounds are repeated? What effect does the alliteration have?

Reading Skill
Identify Problems and Solutions

5. Think about the problems faced by the frogs and toads in "Missing!" and by the toads in "Birdfoot's Grampa." How are their problems similar? What makes their problems different?

Grammar Link

Tricky Subjects and Verbs In most sentences, the **subject** comes before the **verb.** There are two main exceptions.

Questions In many questions, all or part of the verb comes before the subject.

> <u>Do</u> the speaker and the old man <u>have</u> places to go?
> *helping verb / subject / main verb*

To make it easier to find the subject and verb, turn the question into a statement.

> The speaker and the old man <u>do have</u> places to go.

Here/There The words *here* and *there* cannot be subjects. To find the subject of a sentence that begins with *here* or *there,* omit the word. Find the verb; then ask yourself, who or what _____?

> ~~There~~ <u>are</u> <u>clouds</u> above the mountains of Monteverde.
> There <u>are</u> <u>clouds</u> above the mountains of Monteverde.

Practice On a separate sheet of paper, copy each sentence. Underline the subject once and the verb twice.

1. Where do the clouds come from?

2. There are things that you and your family can do to keep Earth from getting warmer.

3. Here are some endangered frogs.

Research and Report

Internet Connection Use the Internet to research other works by Joseph Bruchac that might interest you or your classmates. Make an annotated list of Bruchac's works. In a sentence or two, explain what kind of work it is (for example, a poem or a story), what the work is about, and where online you learned about it.

Comparing Literature

Echo and Narcissus and *Orpheus, the Great Musician*

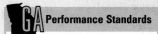
Performance Standards

For pages 862–873

ELA7R1d For literary texts, analyze recurring and similar themes across a variety of selections, distinguishing theme from topic.

BQ BIG Question

As you read these two myths, think about the life lessons that myths teach.

Literary Element Theme

You've learned that the **theme** of a literary work is its message about life. In the myths you are about to read, the themes are implied, or hinted at. Therefore, you must think about the details and the events in the stories to figure out the themes.

Myths are traditional stories that often involve gods, goddesses, and heroes. Many myths attempt to explain a natural or historic event or the origin of a belief or custom. The themes in myths are usually universal, meaning that they deal with concerns that all people experience. As you read, look for the theme of each myth.

Reading Skill Compare and Contrast

Remember that when you compare and contrast, you look for similarities and differences. Comparing and contrasting the themes of several selections can help you understand important life lessons. Comparing and contrasting can also help you analyze recurring themes across different literary works.

On the following pages, you'll compare and contrast the myth "Echo and Narcissus" and the myth "Orpheus, the Great Musician." Use a comparison chart like the one below to record the details and the theme of each myth.

	Details from the Myth	Theme of the Myth
"Echo and Narcissus"		
"Orpheus, the Great Musician"		

Meet the Authors

Roger Lancelyn Green

British author Roger Lancelyn Green was born in 1918. He died in 1987.

Olivia Coolidge

Olivia Coolidge is recognized for her biographies and historical fiction. She was born in 1908.

 Literature Online

Author Search For more about Roger Lancelyn Green and Olivia Coolidge, go to glencoe.com and enter QuickPass code GL27534u6.

ECHO AND NARCISSUS

Retold by Roger Lancelyn Green

Up on the wild, lonely mountains of Greece lived the Oreades,[1] the nymphs or fairies of the hills, and among them one of the most beautiful was called Echo. She was one of the most talkative, too, and once she talked too much and angered Hera, wife of Zeus, king of the gods.

When Zeus grew tired of the golden halls of Mount Olympus, the home of the immortal gods, he would come down to earth and wander with the nymphs on the mountains. Hera, however, was jealous and often came to see what he was doing. It seemed strange at

Comparing Literature

The author begins by telling you about Echo's flaw—she talks too much. How might this detail influence the theme of the myth?

---

1 Oreades (ôr´ ē ad´ ēz)

first that she always met Echo, and that Echo kept her listening for hours on end to her stories and her gossip.

But at last Hera realized that Echo was doing this on purpose to detain[2] her while Zeus went quietly back to Olympus as if he had never really been away.

"So nothing can stop you talking?" exclaimed Hera. "Well, Echo, I do not intend to spoil your pleasure. But from this day on, you shall be able only to repeat what other people say—and never speak unless someone else speaks first."

Hera returned to Olympus, well pleased with the punishment she had made for Echo, leaving the poor nymph to weep sadly among the rocks on the mountainside and speak only the words which her sisters and their friends shouted happily to one another.

She grew used to her strange fate after a while, but then a new misfortune befell her.

There was a beautiful youth called Narcissus,[3] who was the son of a nymph and the god of a nearby river. He grew up in the plain of Thebes[4] until he was sixteen years old and then began to hunt on the mountains toward the north where Echo and her sister Oreades lived.

As he wandered through the woods and valleys, many a nymph looked upon him and loved him. But Narcissus laughed at them scornfully, for he loved only himself.

Farther up the mountains Echo saw him. And at once her lonely heart was filled with love for the beautiful youth, so that nothing else in the world mattered but to win him.

Now she wished indeed that she could speak to him words of love. But the curse which Hera had placed upon her tied her tongue, and she could only follow wherever he went, hiding behind trees and rocks, and feasting her eyes vainly[5] upon him.

Comparing Literature

What might Hera's punishment of Echo have taught the Greeks about their gods?

---

2 To **detain** is to hold back or delay.

3 Narcissus (när sis′ əs)

4 Thebes (thēbz)

5 Something that is done **vainly** is done uselessly or without result.

One day Narcissus wandered farther up the mountain than usual, and all his friends, the other Theban youths, were left far behind. Only Echo followed him, still hiding among the rocks, her heart heavy with unspoken love.

Presently Narcissus realized that he was lost, and hoping to be heard by his companions, or perhaps by some mountain shepherd, he called out loudly:

"Is there anybody here?"

"Here!" cried Echo.

Narcissus stood still in amazement, looking all around in vain. Then he shouted, even more loudly:

"Whoever you are, come to me!"

"Come to me!" cried Echo eagerly.

Still no one was visible, so Narcissus called again:

"Why are you avoiding me?"

Echo repeated his words, but with a sob in her breath, and Narcissus called once more:

"Come here, I say, and let us meet!"

"Let us meet!" cried Echo, her heart leaping with joy as she spoke the happiest words that had left her lips since the curse of Hera had fallen on her. And to make good her words, she came running out from behind the rocks and tried to clasp her arms about him.

But Narcissus flung the beautiful nymph away from him in scorn.

"Away with these embraces!" he cried angrily, his voice full of cruel contempt. "I would die before I would have you touch me!"

Narcissus. Peter Paul Rubens. Oil on canvas. Museum Boymans van Beuningen, Rotterdam, The Netherlands.

"I would have you touch me!" repeated poor Echo.

"Never will I let you kiss me!"

"Kiss me! Kiss me!" murmured Echo, sinking down among the rocks, as Narcissus cast her violently from him and sped down the hillside.

"One touch of those lips would kill me!" he called back furiously over his shoulder.

"Kill me!" begged Echo.

And Aphrodite,[6] the goddess of love, heard her and was kind to her, for she had been a true lover. Quietly and painlessly, Echo pined away and died. But her voice lived on, lingering among the rocks and answering faintly whenever Narcissus or another called.

"He shall not go unpunished for this cruelty," said Aphrodite. "By scorning poor Echo like this, he scorns love itself. And scorning love, he insults me. He is altogether eaten up with self-love . . . Well, he shall love himself and no one else, and yet shall die of unrequited[7] love!"

It was not long before Aphrodite made good her threat, and in a very strange way. One day, tired after hunting, Narcissus came to a still, clear pool of water away up the mountainside, not far from where he had scorned Echo and left her to die of a broken heart.

With a cry of satisfaction, for the day was hot and cloudless, and he was parched[8] with thirst, Narcissus flung himself down beside the pool and leaned forward to dip his face in the cool water.

Comparing Literature

What message about love does this meeting between Echo and Narcissus convey?

Narcissus (N. Tazetta), 1833. P.J. Redoute.

---

6 Aphrodite (af′rə dī′tē)

7 *Unrequited* love is not returned in kind.

8 Something that is *parched* is very hot and dry.

What was his surprise to see a beautiful face looking up at him through the still waters of the pool. The moment he saw, he loved—and love was a madness upon him so that he could think of nothing else.

"Beautiful water nymph!" he cried. "I love you! Be mine!"

Desperately he plunged his arms into the water—but the face vanished and he touched only the pebbles at the bottom of the pool. Drawing out his arms, he gazed intently[9] down and, as the water grew still again, saw once more the face of his beloved.

Poor Narcissus did not know that he was seeing his own reflection, for Aphrodite hid this knowledge from him—and perhaps this was the first time that a pool of water had reflected the face of anyone gazing into it.

Narcissus seemed enchanted by what he saw. He could not leave the pool, but lay by its side day after day looking at the only face in the world which he loved—and could not win—and pining just as Echo had pined.

Slowly Narcissus faded away, and at last his heart broke.

"Woe is me for I loved in vain!" he cried.

"I loved in vain!" sobbed the voice of Echo among the rocks.

"Farewell, my love, farewell," were his last words, and Echo's voice broke and its whisper shivered into silence: "My love . . . farewell!"

So Narcissus died, and the earth covered his bones. But with the spring, a plant pushed its green leaves through the earth where he lay. As the sun shone on it, a bud opened and a new flower blossomed for the first time—a white circle of petals round a yellow center. The flowers grew and spread, waving in the gentle breeze which whispered among them like Echo herself come to kiss the blossoms of the first Narcissus flowers. ❧

Comparing Literature

Narcissus has an experience of love that is much like Echo's. What message does this myth convey about the effect that love can have on a person?

---

9 To gaze *intently* is to look at something with great concentration.

ORPHEUS, THE GREAT MUSICIAN

Retold by Olivia Coolidge

In the legend of Orpheus,[1] the Greek love of music found its fullest expression. Orpheus, it is said, could make such heavenly songs that when he sat down to sing, the trees would crowd around to shade him. The ivy and vine stretched out their tendrils. Great oaks would bend their spreading branches over his head. The very rocks would edge down the mountainsides. Wild beasts crouched harmless by him, and nymphs[2] and woodland gods would listen to him, enchanted.

Orpheus himself, however, had eyes for no one but the nymph Eurydice.[3] His love for her was his

---

1 Orpheus (ôr′fē əs)

2 **Nymphs** are goddesses of nature who are usually young and beautiful and live in forests, mountains, or rivers.

3 Eurydice (yoo rid′ə sē)

inspiration, and his power sprang from the passionate longing that he knew in his own heart. All nature rejoiced with him on his bridal day, but on that very morning, as Eurydice went down to the riverside with her maidens to gather flowers for a bridal garland, she was bitten in the foot by a snake, and she died in spite of all attempts to save her.

Orpheus was inconsolable.[4] All day long he mourned his bride, while birds, beasts, and the earth itself sorrowed with him. When at last the shadows of the sun grew long, Orpheus took his lyre[5] and made his way to the yawning cave which leads down into the underworld, where the soul of dead Eurydice had gone.

Even gray Charon, the ferryman of the Styx, forgot to ask his passenger for the price of crossing. The dog Cerberus, the three-headed monster who guards Hades' gate, stopped full in his tracks and listened motionless until Orpheus had passed. As he entered the land of Hades, the pale ghosts came after him like great, uncounted flocks of silent birds. All the land lay hushed as that marvelous voice resounded across the mud and marshes of its dreadful rivers. In the daffodil fields of Elysium, the happy dead sat silent among their flowers. In the farthest corners of the place of punishment, the hissing flames stood still. Accursed Sisyphus,[6] who toils eternally to push a mighty rock uphill, sat down and knew not he was resting. Tantalus, who strains forever after visions of cool water, forgot his thirst and ceased to clutch at the empty air.

The pillared[7] hall of Hades opened before the hero's song. The ranks of long-dead heroes who sit at Hades' board looked up and turned their eyes away from the pitiless form of Hades and his pale, unhappy queen. Grim and unmoving sat the dark king of the dead on

Comparing Literature

What does Orpheus's action tell you about the effect of love?

---

4 A person who is **inconsolable** is grief-stricken and cannot be comforted.

5 A **lyre** is a stringed musical instrument, similar to a small harp.

6 Charon (kār′ ən); Styx (stiks); Cerberus (sur′ bər əs); Hades (hā′ dēz); Elysium (i liz′ ē əm); Sisyphus (sis′ ə fəs); Tantalus (tant′ əl əs)

7 **Pillared** means "having pillars, or columns."

his ebony throne, yet the tears shone on his rigid cheeks in the light of his ghastly[8] torches. Even his hard heart, which knew all misery and cared nothing for it, was touched by the love and longing of the music.

At last the minstrel[9] came to an end, and a long sigh like wind in pine trees was heard from the assembled ghosts. Then the king spoke, and his deep voice echoed through his silent land. "Go back to the light of day," he said. "Go quickly while my monsters are stilled by your song. Climb up the steep road to daylight, and never once turn back. The spirit of Eurydice shall follow, but if you look around at her, she will return to me."

Orpheus turned and strode from the hall of Hades, and the flocks of following ghosts made way for him to pass. In vain he searched their ranks for a sight of his lost Eurydice. In vain he listened for the faintest sound behind. The barge of Charon sank to the very gunwales[10] beneath his weight, but no following passenger pressed it lower down. The way from the land of Hades to the upper world is long and hard, far easier to descend than climb. It was dark and misty, full of strange shapes and noises, yet in many places merely black and silent as the tomb. Here Orpheus would stop and listen, but nothing moved behind him. For all he could hear, he was utterly alone. Then he would wonder if the pitiless Hades were deceiving him. Suppose he came up to the light again and Eurydice was not there! Once he had charmed the ferryman and the dreadful monsters, but now they had heard his song. The second time his spell would be less powerful; he could never go again. Perhaps he had lost Eurydice by his readiness to believe.

Every step he took, some instinct told him that he was going farther from his bride. He toiled up the path in reluctance[11] and despair, stopping, listening, sighing,

Comparing Literature
What message does the myth tell about the power of love?

---

8 Something that is **_ghastly_** is horrible or dreadful.

9 In ancient times, a **_minstrel_** provided musical entertainment.

10 **_Gunwales_** are the upper edges of the sides of a ship or boat.

11 **_Reluctance_** is unwillingness or hesitation.

Cerberus, Three-headed Dog
Guarding the Gates to Hades.
William Blake. Tate Gallery,
London.

taking a few slow steps, until the dark thinned out into grayness. Up ahead a speck of light showed clearly the entrance to the cavern.

At that final moment Orpheus could bear no more. To go out into the light of day without his love seemed to him impossible. Before he had quite ascended,[12] there was still a moment in which he could go back. Quick in the grayness he turned and saw a dim shade at his heels, as indistinct as the gray mist behind her. But still he could see the look of sadness on her face as he sprung forward saying, "Eurydice!" and threw his arms about her. The shade dissolved in the circle of his arms like smoke. A little whisper seemed to say "Farewell" as she scattered into mist and was gone.

The unfortunate lover hastened back again down the steep, dark path. But all was in vain. This time the

Comparing Literature

What might Eurydice's disappearance have taught the ancient Greeks?

---

12 *Ascended* means "moved upward."

ghostly ferryman was deaf to his prayers. The very wildness of his mood made it impossible for him to attain the beauty of his former music. At last, his despair was so great that he could not even sing at all. For seven days he sat huddled together on the gray mud banks, listening to the wailing of the terrible river. The flitting ghosts shrank back in a wide circle from the living man, but he paid them no attention. Only he sat with his eyes on Charon, his ears ringing with the dreadful noise of Styx.

Orpheus arose at last and stumbled back along the steep road he knew so well by now. When he came up to earth again, his song was pitiful but more beautiful than ever. Even the nightingale who mourned all night long would hush her voice to listen as Orpheus sat in some hidden place singing of his lost Eurydice. Men and women he could bear no longer, and when they came to hear him, he drove them away. At last the women of Thrace, maddened by Dionysus and infuriated by Orpheus's contempt, fell upon him and killed him. It is said that as the body was swept down the river Hebrus,[13] the dead lips still moved faintly and the rocks echoed for the last time, "Eurydice." But the poet's eager spirit was already far down the familiar path.

In the daffodil meadows he met the shade of Eurydice, and there they walk together, or where the path is narrow, the shade of Orpheus goes ahead and looks back at his love. ❧

Orpheus and Eurydice at the Gates of the Underworld, maiolica plate, c.1515. Nicola Pellipario of Urbino (fl.1510-42). Museo Correr, Venice.

---

13 Thrace (thrās); Dionysus (dī′ ə nī′ səs); Hebrus (hē′ brəs)

Comparing Literature

BQ BIG Question

Now use the unit Big Question to compare and contrast "Echo and Narcissus" and "Orpheus, the Great Musician." With a group of classmates, discuss questions such as,

- What do these two stories have in common?

- What lesson does each character learn about love?

Support each answer with evidence from the readings.

Literary Element Theme

Use the details you wrote in your chart to think about the themes of "Echo and Narcissus" and "Orpheus, the Great Musician." With a partner, answer the following questions.

1. In what ways are the themes different in "Echo and Narcissus" and "Orpheus, the Great Musician"? Discuss details from the myths that show these differences. For example, you might look at the different ways that characters respond to love and the outcomes that result from the characters' actions.

2. What are the similarities between the themes in "Echo and Narcissus" and "Orpheus, the Great Musician"? Consider the importance of love in each of the myths.

Write to Compare

In one or two paragraphs, explain how these two myths teach lessons about love. You might focus on these ideas as you write.

- Summarize how each of the characters feels. How do they show their love?

- Include details about the fates of the four main characters (Echo, Narcissus, Orpheus, and Eurydice). Which characters are happiest in the end?

- Explain how the similarities and differences in the myths affect your understanding of the theme of each myth.

Writing Tip

Make Clear Comparisons As you revise your paragraphs, make sure that your ideas follow one another in a logical order. Check your writing to be certain that you are comparing and contrasting the same aspects of the four characters.

Selection Resources
For Selection Quizzes, eFlashcards, and Reading-Writing Connection Activities, go to glencoe.com and enter QuickPass code GL27534u6.

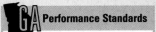
GA Performance Standards

For pages 874–879

ELA7W2b Demonstrate competence in a variety of genres. Produce writing that develops a controlling idea that conveys a perspective on the subject.

Expository Essay

What is the last story that you listened to, read, or saw performed? Chances are you then shared that story with someone else. In this workshop, you will write an expository essay that will help you think about the Unit 6 Big Question: Why Share Stories?

Review the writing prompt, or assignment, below. Then read the Writing Plan. It will tell you what you will do to write your expository essay.

Writing Assignment

An expository essay informs, explains, or does both. Write an expository essay informing your readers about the role of stories in our world. The audience, or those reading your essay, should be your classmates and teacher.

Prewrite

Think about the stories in this unit and what they might signify about the role of stories. For example, what might be the message about stories in "The Bird Like No Other"? Consider these questions: Do the general purposes and messages of stories vary across cultures? How does the way a story is told—through a play or a movie, in a book, on the radio, or in person—affect the story itself?

Gather Ideas

Think about the reasons people share stories. To get ideas, review the stories in this unit and in other units. Then think about stories that you have listened to, read, or seen as movies or plays. Take notes as you think about these stories and about stories that you yourself have written or told.

Choose an Angle

Choose the angle, or the particular approach, that you want to use to give information about or explain the role of storytelling in our world.

Partner Talk With a partner, discuss your angle. Explain to your partner your view of the role of storytelling. Listen to your partner's view. Ask questions about each other's angles. Write a thesis statement for your essay that incorporates your angle.

The role of storytelling in our world is _____, and it is important because it _____.

Writing Plan

- **Present the thesis, or main idea, of the essay in the introduction.**
- **Organize the essay in an effective and appropriate pattern.**
- **Include specific examples to support and clarify ideas.**
- **Use language techniques to maintain reader interest.**
- **Conclude by linking back to the thesis of the essay.**

Prewriting Tip

Thesis Statement Your thesis may be stated directly or implied. For purposes of clarity, it is usually best to write out the thesis and refer to it as you write, even if it will be only implied in your final essay.

Get Organized

Use a web to organize the structure of your essay: thesis (top circle), body paragraph topics (middle circles), and details (bottom circles).

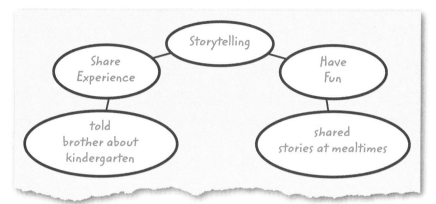

Draft

Get It On Paper

- Begin with something that will interest your audience, such as an anecdote about sharing stories. Connect it to your thesis.
- For each topic in your web, write a sentence explaining the role of storytelling in relation to your angle. Then add a specific example to support the topic.
- End by reconnecting with your thesis.
- Read what you've written and add more information if you need to.

Develop Your Draft

1. State your **thesis** in your introduction.

> Storytelling lets us share experiences and have fun while doing so.

2. Organize body paragraphs effectively. Begin each body paragraph with a **topic sentence** that states the main idea of the paragraph.

> Our lives are full of new experiences, and, by sharing our stories, we are able to help each other face these experiences more confidently.

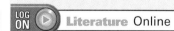

Writing and Research
For prewriting, drafting, and revising tools, go to glencoe.com and enter QuickPass code GL27534u6.

3. Include **examples** that support and clarify your main ideas.

> My mom helped me get over stage fright by telling me about the first time she was in a play.

4. Use **interesting language** to keep the attention of your readers.

> My brother eagerly waited for dinner every night to hear another story.

5. Restate your thesis in your **conclusion.** If you began with an anecdote or a story, end by referencing that item again.

> By sharing my stories I helped my brother, and he helped his friend.

Apply Good Writing Traits: Ideas

When you write, you use smaller ideas to build your big, or main, ideas. Sharing your ideas is the point of writing; you must write clearly so that readers can easily understand your ideas.

Read the paragraph below from Dorothy West's short story "The Bird Like No Other." How does West's writing help you understand her message?

> Whatever Aunt Emily was doing, Colby knew, she would stop what she was doing. Wherever she was, she would start for the porch, so that by the time Colby pounded up the stairs, she would be sitting on her old porch glider, waiting for him to fling himself down beside her and cool his hot anger in her calm.

As you draft your essay, focus your writing on a single narrow topic. Your topic should be specific so that you can write about a few details in depth.

Analyze a Student Model

When my little brother was about to start kindergarten, he was nervous. I wanted to make him feel better, so I told him about all my fun kindergarten experiences. As I shared my stories with my brother, he began to feel less nervous and more excited about school. I told him a story every night at dinner. Soon our whole family was happily sharing school stories.

Through this experience, I learned an important lesson about the role of storytelling. Storytelling lets us share experiences and have fun while doing so.

Our lives are full of new experiences, and, by sharing our stories, we are able to help each other face these experiences more confidently. I used storytelling to help my brother feel prepared for school. My mom helped me get over stage fright by telling me about the first time she was in a play. Before my first airplane ride, my dad read me a story about a girl taking her first airplane ride. The plane, bumping slightly and creaking, didn't frighten me because I knew what to expect.

Sharing stories is fun whether you are the storyteller or the listener. My brother eagerly waited for dinner every night to hear another story. I enjoyed remembering stories that would entertain him. Storytelling entertains us when we are sitting around a fire, riding in the car, or enjoying lunch with friends.

Waiting proudly for the bus on his first day, my brother felt ready. His best friend stood nervously beside us. My brother reassured him, "Don't worry. Today is going to be great! I'll tell you all about kindergarten." By sharing my stories I helped my brother, and he helped his friend. From my seat in the back of the bus, I heard my brother and his friend laughing. I smiled because I knew they were having fun sharing my stories. Storytelling helps us connect with each other and makes our days a little brighter.

Thesis in Introduction

A thesis should clearly state your main idea.

Organization

Begin each body paragraph with a topic sentence that states the main idea of the paragraph.

Examples Used as Support

Use interesting facts, anecdotes, and details to support your main ideas.

Interesting Language

Replace abstract and general words with specific words.

Link to Thesis in Conclusion

Restate your main idea in different words in your conclusion.

Remember that word choice
helps you express your
ideas. Choose interesting
and precise words that will
help readers understand
your meaning.

Revise

Now it's time to revise your draft so your ideas really shine. Revising is what makes good writing great, and great writing takes work!

Peer Review Trade drafts with a partner. Use the chart below to review your partner's draft by answering the questions in the *What to do* column. Talk about your peer review after you have glanced at each other's drafts and written answers to the questions. Next, follow the suggestions in the *How to do it* column to revise your draft.

Revising Plan

What to do	How to do it	Example
Does your thesis clearly address the role of storytelling?	Reread your thesis. Make sure that your angle on the role of storytelling is clear.	~~I like to tell stories.~~ ₗStorytelling lets us share experiences and have fun while doing so.
Is your essay organized in an effective and appropriate pattern?	Organize each body paragraph around one main idea that supports your thesis. Start each paragraph with a topic sentence.	Our lives are full of new experiences, and, ₗby sharing our stories, we are able to help each other face these experiences more confidently.
Do you include examples to support and clarify your main ideas?	Choose interesting examples to support your main ideas. Make sure that the connection between your examples and your main ideas is clear.	ₗMy mom helped me get over stage fright by telling me about the first time she was in a play.
Do you use interesting language?	Use interesting words that clearly express your ideas. Be sure to use only words that you understand.	My brother ₗeagerly waited for dinner every night to hear another story.
Do you link your conclusion to your thesis and introduction?	Restate your thesis in different words to conclude your essay. If you included an anecdote or a story in your introduction, reference it again.	~~In conclusion, I enjoy stories.~~ ₗStorytelling helps us connect with each other and makes our days a little brighter.

Edit and Proofread

For your final draft, read your essay one sentence at a time. The Editing and Proofreading Checklist inside the back cover of this book may help you spot errors. Use the proofreading symbols to mark needed changes. Then make corrections.

Grammar Focus: Participial Phrases

To vary your sentence structure, use participial phrases. A participial phrase is a group of words that includes a participle and other words that complete its meaning. A participial phrase at the beginning of a sentence is always set off by a comma. Participial phrases in other places may or may not need commas. If the phrase is necessary to identify the modified word, it should not be set off with commas. If the phrase simply gives additional information about the modified word, it should be set off with commas. Below are examples of problems with participial phrases and possible solutions from the Workshop Model.

Problem: The introductory participial phrase in this sentence is not set off by a comma.

Waiting proudly for the bus on his first day my brother felt ready.

Solution: Use a comma to set off the introductory participial phrase.

Waiting proudly for the bus on his first day, my brother felt ready.

Problem: The nonessential participial phrase in this sentence is not set off by commas.

The plane bumping slightly and creaking didn't frighten me because I knew what to expect.

Solution: Use commas to set off the nonessential participial phrase.

The plane, bumping slightly and creaking, didn't frighten me because I knew what to expect.

Present

It's almost time to share your writing with others. Write your essay neatly in print or cursive on a separate sheet of paper. If you have access to a computer, type your essay on the computer and check spelling. Save your document to a disk, and print it out.

Grammar Tip

Remember that a phrase is a group of words that acts in a sentence as a single part of speech. A clause is a group of words that has a subject and a predicate. A dependent clause is used as part of a sentence. An independent clause can stand alone.

Presenting Tip

Publishing Make an extra copy of your essay to share with someone who appreciates stories.

Literature Online

Writing and Research For editing and publishing tools, go to glencoe.com and enter QuickPass code GL27534u6.

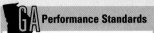
Performance Standards

For page 880

ELA7LSV1i Volunteer contributions and respond when directly solicited by teacher or discussion leader.

Speaking, Listening, and Viewing Workshop

Active Listening and Note-Taking

What Is It?

A **group discussion** is three or more people sharing their thoughts about a topic. When you use **active listening,** you focus on what the speaker is saying.

Why Is It Important?

Group discussion allows you to stretch your thinking. You may hear others saying what you couldn't put into words. Active listening allows you to understand others' thoughts and ideas.

How Do I Do It?

Follow these tips to be an active listener:

- Make eye contact with the speaker and focus on the words being spoken. Clear your mind of other thoughts, such as your after-school plans.

- Connect what you hear to your own knowledge and experience.

- **Take notes** as the person speaks to make sure you are actively listening. If there's something you don't understand, write down questions to get more information about it from the speaker.

- Review your notes soon after the speaker is finished, and fill in any gaps.

- Compare notes with a classmate to see if you understood the speaker's message about and attitude toward the subject.

Follow these tips for group discussion:

- Take part in the conversation! It's your job to contribute your thoughts to the discussion. Don't let the group down.

- Be respectful. Don't interrupt other people when they are speaking. If you disagree with someone, simply say what you think and give your reasons. Try to understand other points of view.

- When someone criticizes your ideas, listen quietly. Give the criticism careful thought before you respond.

- Stay on topic. Don't bring up unrelated stories.

- If you are the discussion leader, make sure everyone takes part. If someone hasn't talked in a while, ask for that person's thoughts.

Speaking, Listening, and Viewing For project ideas, templates, and presentation tips, go to glencoe.com and enter QuickPass code GL27534u6.

Unit Challenge

Answer the Big Question

In Unit 6, you explored the Big Question through reading, writing, speaking, and listening. Now it's time for you to answer the Big Question by completing one of the Unit Challenges below.

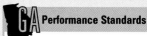

GA Performance Standards

For page 881

ELA7W2b Demonstrate competence in a variety of genres. Produce writing that develops a controlling idea that conveys a perspective on the subject.

WHY Share Stories?

Use the notes you took in your Unit 6 **Foldable** to complete your Unit Challenge.

Before you present your Unit Challenge, be sure to complete the following steps. Use this first plan if you choose to assemble a list of multimedia that you think are best for students your age.

On Your Own Activity: Assemble a Multimedia List

❏ Brainstorm a list of your favorite books, songs, movies, TV shows, and stories.

❏ Ask yourself these questions about each work on the list:

- Would most people my age enjoy this? Why or why not?
- Does this have an important message for people my age?
- Would parents or teachers object to anything about this?

❏ Cross off works that do not belong on the list.

❏ Make sure your list contains at least ten works and that it represents a good selection of different kinds of media.

Use this second plan if you choose to write a story review that explains why a story is or is not worth sharing with other students your age.

Group Activity: Write a Story Review

❏ As a group, choose a story from the unit that you like or dislike.

❏ Discuss what story elements you especially like or dislike.

❏ Begin your review by stating whether you like or dislike the story.

❏ Give a few reasons for your position, using examples from the text as evidence to support your argument.

❏ Conclude by stating why the story is or is not worth sharing.

❏ Have a group member present the review to your classmates.

Independent Reading

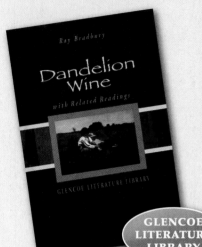

GLENCOE
LITERATURE
LIBRARY

Fiction

To read more about the Big Question, choose one of these books from your school or local library.

Dandelion Wine
by Ray Bradbury

For twelve-year-old Douglas Spaulding, summer is a magical experience, and the summer of 1928 is no exception. From getting brand-new sneakers to picking dandelions with his grandfather, Douglas shares the essence of what summer is to a young boy.

The People Could Fly: American Black Folktales

retold by Virginia Hamilton

In this collection of twenty-four folktales, Virginia Hamilton retells stories once told by enslaved people, including animal tales, tall tales, supernatural stories, and tales of freedom.

Where Angels Glide at Dawn: New Stories from Latin America

edited by Lori M. Carlson and Cynthia L. Ventura

A variety of voices and styles share the richness of Latin American culture in this collection of ten stories. Through tales of traditions, lifestyles, and social and political unrest, this book introduces readers to people of Cuba, El Salvador, Mexico, Panama, and Puerto Rico.

On Her Way: Stories and Poems About Growing Up Girl

edited by Sandy Asher

Whether traveling west in a wagon train or overcoming terrible illness, the girls in this collection of stories and poems face life's challenges with strength and courage.

Nonfiction

Taking Flight: My Story by Vicki Van Meter

by Vicki Van Meter with Dan Gutman

Before she turned thirteen, Vicki Van Meter had piloted flights across the United States and the Atlantic Ocean. Read to find out how her discipline, drive, and desire to soar led her to heights she hardly dreamed possible.

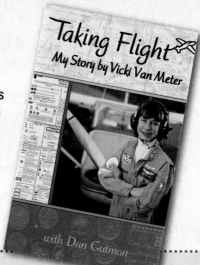

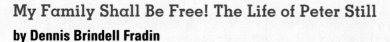

Shipwrecked! The True Adventures of a Japanese Boy

by Rhoda Blumberg

Shipwrecked on an island and rescued by American whalers, Manjiro Nakahama's adventures take him around the globe and back again. After becoming the first Japanese person to set foot in the United States, Nakahama returns to Japan and becomes an honored samurai.

My Family Shall Be Free! The Life of Peter Still

by Dennis Brindell Fradin

Born on a slave plantation around 1800, Peter Still was more than 40 years old when he bought his freedom and, amazingly, reunited with the mother and siblings he thought he'd lost forever.

 Create a Book Cover

Create a book cover for the book you read. Your cover should be engaging and convey something important about the book without giving too much away. Make sure your cover is eye catching and gets others interested in reading the book. Ask a classmate who has read the book to critique the cover you created.

Assessment

READING

Read the passage and answer the questions. Write your answers on a separate sheet of paper.

---

from **The Wonder Years**

Episode 1: "The Wonder Years" by Neal Marlens and Carol Black

[Exterior. Day. Bus stop.
KEVIN and PAUL stand beside one another at the bus stop. WAYNE and others are there.]

KEVIN: *[To PAUL.]* Don't worry about it, you look fine.

PAUL: Let me see our class schedule one more time.

KEVIN: No.

NARRATOR: He was gonna have to get a grip on himself. This was the junior high bus stop and if we were gonna hold our own with the older kids we were gonna have to act mature. We seemed to have something of a height disadvantage, but we did our best to fit in.

[KEVIN and PAUL stick their tongues out, mimicking the older kids. They spot WINNIE who is walking toward the bus stop.]

NARRATOR: What an incredible stroke of luck, a new kid. A helpless waif would be even more lost than we were, a helpless waif in fishnet tights and gogo boots.

WINNIE: Hi Kevin. Hi Paul.

PAUL: *[Amazed.]* Winnie Cooper?

WINNIE: Gwendolyn. I don't want to be called Winnie anymore, my real name is Gwendolyn.

NARRATOR: Well, there was no question now, we were entering <u>uncharted</u> territory. Even the familiar was cloaked in the vestments of the devil. Junior high school was a whole new ball of wax.

[Later that day.
Interior. Day. Cafeteria.
KEVIN and PAUL carry their trays and look for a table to sit at in the cafeteria.]

NARRATOR: Lunch, at last, something I figured even I couldn't screw up.

PAUL: Where do you want to sit?

KEVIN: Anywhere. Let's just sit here.

[KEVIN and PAUL sit down at a table.]

NARRATOR: A suburban junior high school cafeteria is like a microcosm of the world. The goal is to protect yourself, and safety comes in groups. You have your cool kids, you have your smart kids, you have your greasers, and in those days, of course, you had your hippies. In fact, in junior high school, who you are is defined less by who you are than by who's the person sitting next to you—a sobering thought.

KEVIN: *[To PAUL.]* Try to look like you're having fun.

[WINNIE approaches the table at which KEVIN and PAUL are sitting.]

WINNIE: Hi. Do you guys mind if I sit with you?

KEVIN: Sure, Winnie.

NARRATOR: We were on our way. Our group was forming. And Winnie, I mean, Gwendolyn, was not <u>chopped liver</u>. Who knows, maybe we even had an outside chance to become the cool seventh grade group, if we could just remain inconspicuous until we picked up a few more members.

[WAYNE, at another table with friend STEVE, spots KEVIN, PAUL and WINNIE and approaches them.]

WAYNE: Hey Steve, it looks like my baby brother and his girlfriend have found each other.

KEVIN: She's not my girlfriend.

WAYNE: *[To WINNIE.]* He thinks you are so cute.

KEVIN: I don't think she's cute.

WAYNE: He wants to give you a big wet kiss.

[WAYNE makes a sucking noise.]

WAYNE: He told me.

KEVIN: You liar, I never said that! I don't want to kiss her, I don't even like her!

[KEVIN picks up his apple and walks briskly to exit the cafeteria.]

1. Based on the dialogue and narration in this scene, Kevin and Paul could BEST be described as

   A. popular.

   B. confident.

   C. excellent students.

   D. uncertain and nervous.

2. Which information about Winnie is revealed by the stage directions?

   A. Kevin thinks she is cute.

   B. She is wearing gogo boots.

   C. She meets Kevin and Paul in the cafeteria.

   D. She wants to be called Gwendolyn.

3. What is foreshadowed when the narrator says they might become popular "if we could just remain inconspicuous"?

   A. Kevin and Paul will become very popular.

   B. Kevin will spill his drink on the table.

   C. The boys will get into a fight with older kids.

   D. Something will happen to make them conspicuous.

4. The sentence "Even the familiar was cloaked in the vestments of the devil" is an example of

   A. a simile.

   B. a metaphor.

   C. alliteration.

   D. onomatopoeia.

5. In this teleplay, Kevin is characterized mainly by

   A. what others say about him.

   B. the actions of others.

   C. his own words.

   D. his own actions.

6. In this passage, *uncharted* means the same as

   A. unknown.

   B. unimportant.

   C. comfortable.

   D. entertaining.

7. The narrator says, "In fact, in junior high school, who you are is defined less by who you are than by who's the person sitting next to you—a sobering thought." What is the tone of this remark?

    A. thoughtful

    B. cheerful

    C. uncertain

    D. rude

8. The narrator's remark ". . . and in those days, of course, you had your hippies" shows that the action probably takes place

    A. around the 1940s.

    B. around the 1970s.

    C. in the early 2000s.

    D. in the present day.

9. At the end of the scene, Kevin says, "I don't even like her!" because

    A. he is embarrassed.

    B. he does not like Winnie.

    C. he wants to play "hard to get."

    D. he knows that Paul has a crush on Winnie.

10. The narrator uses the phrase *not chopped liver* to mean that Gwendolyn is

    A. stuck up, not a humble person.

    B. irritating, not easy to be around.

    C. important, not someone to overlook.

    D. new to the group, not an old member.

11. Which word below BEST describes the mood of this passage?

    A. sad

    B. inspirational

    C. pessimistic

    D. amusing

12. Which sentence below BEST sums up the theme of this passage?

    A. Girls are big trouble.

    B. Kevin and Paul meet Winnie at the bus stop.

    C. New situations can be difficult and embarrassing.

    D. Family members sometimes get on each other's nerves.

LOG ON ▶ **Literature** Online

Standards Practice For more standards practice, go to glencoe.com and enter QuickPass code GL27534u6.

ENGLISH/LANGUAGE ARTS

Choose the best answer for each question. Write your answers on a separate sheet of paper.

1. Which sentence below is written incorrectly?

   A. The drama club students want to produce a play.

   B. Finding a good script is their problem.

   C. We would like you're opinion about a good play.

   D. It's important for everyone to agree on a script.

2. Which sentence below uses verb tenses consistently?

   A. People have watched television, and they have known we need a good script.

   B. People watch television, and they will know we need a good script.

   C. People watched television, and they have known we need a good script.

   D. People have watched television, and they know we need a good script.

3. Which sentence below is a compound sentence?

   A. I thought of a good play, and others had ideas also.

   B. Some of the plays are not appropriate, however.

   C. Please come to a meeting and share your advice.

   D. Everyone would appreciate your help.

4. In which sentence below is the subject-verb agreement correct?

   A. Where is such scripts and how do we order them?

   B. Where is such scripts and how does we order them?

   C. Where are such scripts and how do we order them?

   D. Where are such scripts and how does we order them?

5. How should the punctuation be corrected in the sentence below?

   > "Who would like to be actors or stagehands in the play," Mindy asked.

   A. Add a comma after *actors*.

   B. Change the comma after *play* to a question mark.

   C. Add a comma after *Who*.

   D. Change the period after *asked* to a question mark.

6. Which sentence below contains an error?

   A. The school theater holds several hundred people.

   B. Audiences allways enjoy comedies on stage.

   C. Let's serve refreshments during intermission.

   D. Our play will definitely be a big success.

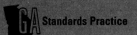

WRITING

Read your assigned topic in the box below. Use one piece of paper to jot down your ideas and organize your thoughts. Then neatly write your essay on another sheet of paper.

Expository Writing Topic

Writing Situation

New students at your school find their first few days difficult. Your principal wants experienced students to offer advice to new students. The advice should help the new students do things such as find classrooms, learn routines, and meet teachers and students.

Directions for Writing

Write an essay for a new students that explains what they should know on the first day at your school. Include specific information that would make the students' life easier.

Writing Checklist

☐ Focus on a single topic.

☐ Organize your main points in a clear, logical order.

☐ Support your ideas or viewpoints with details and examples.

☐ Use precise, vivid words.

☐ Vary the length and structure of your sentences.

☐ Use clear transition words to connect ideas.

☐ Correct any errors in spelling, capitalization, punctuation, and usage.

Reference Section

Literary Terms Handbook

A

Act A major unit of a drama. A play may be subdivided into several acts. Many modern plays have two or three acts. A short play can be composed of one or more scenes but only one act.

See also SCENE.

Alliteration The repetition of consonant sounds, usually at the beginnings of words or syllables. Alliteration gives emphasis to words. For example,

Over the <u>c</u>obbles he <u>c</u>lattered and <u>c</u>lashed

Allusion A reference in a work of literature to a well-known character, place, or situation in history, politics, or science or from another work of literature, music, or art.

Analogy A comparison between two things, based on one or more elements that they share. Analogies can help the reader visualize an idea. In informational text, analogies are often used to explain something unfamiliar in terms of something known. For example, a science book might compare the flow of electricity to water moving through a hose. In literature, most analogies are expressed in metaphors or similes.

See also METAPHOR, SIMILE.

Anecdote A brief, entertaining story based on a single interesting or humorous incident or event. Anecdotes are frequently biographical and reveal some aspect of a person's character.

Antagonist A person or force that opposes the protagonist, or central character, in a story or a drama. The reader is generally meant not to sympathize with the antagonist.

See also CONFLICT, PROTAGONIST.

Anthropomorphism Representing animals as if they had human emotions and intelligence. Fables and fairy tales often contain anthropomorphism.

Aside In a play, a comment made by a character that is heard by the audience but not by the other characters onstage. The speaker turns to one side, or "aside," away from the other characters onstage. Asides are common in older plays—you will find many in Shakespeare's plays—but are infrequent in modern drama.

Assonance The repetition of vowel sounds, especially in a line of poetry.

See also RHYME, SOUND DEVICES.

Author's purpose The intention of the writer. For example, the purpose of a story may be to entertain, to describe, to explain, to persuade, or a combination of these purposes.

Autobiography The story of a person's life written by that person. *Rosa Parks: My Story*, by Rosa Parks with Jim Haskins, is an example of autobiography.

See also BIOGRAPHY, MEMOIR.

B

Ballad A short musical narrative song or poem. Folk ballads, which usually tell of an exciting or dramatic episode, were passed on by word of mouth for generations before being written down. Literary ballads are written in imitation of folk ballads.

See also NARRATIVE POETRY.

Biography The account of a person's life written by someone other than the subject. Biographies can be short or book-length.

See also AUTOBIOGRAPHY, MEMOIR.

C

Character A person in a literary work. (If a character is an animal, it displays human traits.) Characters who show varied and sometimes contradictory traits are called **round.** Characters who reveal only one personality trait are called **flat.** A **stereotype** is a flat character of a familiar and often-repeated type. A **dynamic** character changes during the story. A **static** character remains primarily the same throughout the story.

Characterization The methods a writer uses to develop the personality of the character. In **direct characterization,** the writer makes direct statements about a character's personality. In **indirect characterization,** the writer reveals a character's personality through the character's words and actions and through what other characters think and say about the character. These techniques are frequently blended, as in the characterization of the two boxers in Piri Thomas's story "Amigo Brothers."

Climax The point of greatest emotional intensity, interest, or suspense in a narrative. Usually the climax comes at the turning point in a story or drama, the point at which the resolution of the conflict becomes clear. The climax in O. Henry's "After Twenty Years" occurs when Bob discovers that the man he thinks is Jimmy Wells is actually someone else.

Comedy A type of drama that is humorous and has a happy ending. A heroic comedy focuses on the exploits of a larger-than-life hero. In American popular culture, comedy can take the form of a scripted performance involving one or more performers—either as a skit that is part of a variety show, as in vaudeville, or as a stand-up monologue.

See also HUMOR.

Conflict The central struggle between opposing forces in a story or drama. An **external conflict** exists when a character struggles against some outside force, such as nature, society, fate, or another person. An **internal conflict** exists within the mind of a character who is torn between opposing feelings or goals.

See also ANTAGONIST, PLOT, PROTAGONIST.

Consonance A pleasing combination of sounds, especially in poetry. Consonance usually refers to the repetition of consonant sounds in stressed syllables.

See also SOUND DEVICES.

D

Description Writing that seeks to convey the impression of a setting, a person, an animal, an object, or an event by appealing to the senses. Almost all writing, fiction and nonfiction, contains elements of description.

Details Particular features of things used to make descriptions more accurate and vivid. Authors use details to help readers imagine the characters, scenes, and actions they describe.

Dialect A variation of language spoken by a particular group, often within a particular region. Dialects differ from standard language because they may contain different pronunciations, forms, and meanings.

Dialogue Conversation between characters in a literary work.

See also MONOLOGUE.

Drama A story intended to be performed by actors on a stage or before movie or TV cameras. Most dramas before the modern period can be divided into two basic types: tragedy and comedy. The script of a drama includes dialogue (the words the actors speak) and stage directions (descriptions of the action and scenery).

See also COMEDY, TRAGEDY.

E

Essay A short piece of nonfiction writing on a single topic. The purpose of the essay is to communicate an idea or opinion. A **formal essay** is serious and impersonal. An **informal essay** entertains while it informs, usually in a light, conversational style.

Exposition The part of the plot of a short story, novel, novella, or play in which the characters, setting, and situation are introduced.

Extended metaphor An implied comparison that continues through an entire poem.

See also METAPHOR.

F

Fable A short, simple tale that teaches a moral. The characters in a fable are often animals who speak and act like people. The moral, or lesson, of the fable is usually stated outright.

Falling action In a play or story, the action that follows the climax.

See also PLOT.

Fantasy A form of literature that explores unreal worlds of the past, the present, or the future.

Fiction A prose narrative in which situations and characters are invented by the writer. Some aspects of a fictional work may be based on fact or experience. Fiction includes short stories, novellas, and novels.

See also NOVEL, NOVELLA, SHORT STORY.

Figurative language Language used for descriptive effect, often to imply ideas indirectly. Expressions of figurative language are not literally true but express some truth beyond the literal level. Although it appears in all kinds of writing, figurative language is especially prominent in poetry.

See also ANALOGY, FIGURE OF SPEECH, METAPHOR, PERSONIFICATION, SIMILE, SYMBOL.

Figure of speech Figurative language of a specific kind, such as **analogy, metaphor, simile,** or **personification.**

First-person narrative. *See* POINT OF VIEW.

Flashback An interruption in a chronological narrative that tells about something that happened before that point in the story or before the story began. A flashback gives readers information that helps to explain the main events of the story.

Folklore The traditional beliefs, customs, stories, songs, and dances of the ordinary people (the "folk") of a culture. Folklore is passed on by word of mouth and performance rather than in writing.

See also FOLKTALE, LEGEND, MYTH, ORAL TRADITION.

Folktale A traditional story passed down orally long before being written down. Generally the author of a folktale is anonymous. Folktales include animal stories, trickster stories, fairy tales, myths, legends, and tall tales.

See also LEGEND, MYTH, ORAL TRADITION, TALL TALE.

Foreshadowing The use of clues by an author to prepare readers for events that will happen in a story.

Free verse Poetry that has no fixed pattern of meter, rhyme, line length, or stanza arrangement.

See also RHYTHM.

G

Genre A literary or artistic category. The main literary genres are prose, poetry, and drama. Each of these is divided into smaller genres. For example, **prose** includes fiction (such as novels, novellas, short stories, and folktales) and nonfiction (such as biography, autobiography, and essays). **Poetry** includes lyric poetry, dramatic poetry, and narrative poetry. **Drama** includes tragedy, comedy, historical drama, melodrama, and farce.

H

Haiku Originally a Japanese form of poetry that has three lines and seventeen syllables. The first and third lines have five syllables each; the middle line has seven syllables.

Hero A literary work's main character, usually one with admirable qualities. Although the word hero is applied only to males in traditional usage (the female form is heroine), the term now applies to both sexes.

See also LEGEND, MYTH, PROTAGONIST, TALL TALE.

Historical fiction A novel, novella, play, short story, or narrative poem that sets fictional characters against a historical backdrop and contains many details about the period in which it is set.

See also GENRE.

Humor The quality of a literary work that makes the characters and their situations seem funny, amusing, or ludicrous. Humorous writing can be as effective in nonfiction as in fiction.

See also COMEDY.

I

Idiom A figure of speech that belongs to a particular language, people, or region and whose meaning cannot be obtained, and might even seem ridiculous, by joining the meanings of the words composing it. You would be using an idiom if you said you *caught* a cold.

Imagery Language that emphasizes sensory impressions to help the reader of a literary work see, hear, feel, smell, and taste the scenes described in the work.

See also FIGURATIVE LANGUAGE.

Informational text This type of nonfiction writing conveys facts and information without introducing personal opinion.

Irony A form of expression in which the intended meaning of the words used is the opposite of their literal meaning. **Verbal irony** occurs when a person says one thing and means another—for example, saying "Nice guy!" about someone you dislike. **Situational irony** occurs when the outcome of a situation is the opposite of what was expected.

L

Legend A traditional story, based on history or an actual hero, that is passed down orally. A legend is usually exaggerated and gains elements of fantasy over the years. Stories about Daniel Boone and Davy Crockett are American legends.

Limerick A light, humorous poem with a regular metrical scheme and a rhyme scheme of *aabba*.

See also HUMOR, RHYME SCHEME.

Local color The fictional portrayal of a region's features or peculiarities and its inhabitants' distinctive ways of talking and behaving, usually as a way of adding a realistic flavor to a story.

Lyric The words of a song, usually with a regular rhyme scheme.

See also RHYME SCHEME.

Lyric poetry Poems, usually short, that express strong personal feelings about a subject or an event.

M

Main idea The most important idea expressed in a paragraph or an essay. It may or may not be directly stated.

Memoir A biographical or autobiographical narrative emphasizing the narrator's personal experience during a period or at an event.

See also AUTOBIOGRAPHY, BIOGRAPHY.

Metaphor A figure of speech that compares or equates seemingly unlike things. In contrast to a simile, a metaphor implies the comparison instead of stating it directly; hence, there is no use of connectives such as *like* or *as*.

See also FIGURE OF SPEECH, IMAGERY, SIMILE.

Meter A regular pattern of stressed and unstressed syllables that gives a line of poetry a predictable rhythm. For example, the meter is marked in the following lines from "The Courage That My Mother Had," by Edna St. Vincent Millay:

> The golden brooch my mother wore
> She left behind for me to wear. . . .

See also RHYTHM

Monologue A long speech by a single character in a play or a solo performance.

Mood The emotional quality or atmosphere of a story or poem.

See also SETTING.

Myth A traditional story of unknown authorship, often involving goddesses, gods, and heroes, that attempts to explain a natural phenomenon, a historic event, or the origin of a belief or custom.

N

Narration Writing or speech that tells a story. Narration is used in prose fiction and narrative poetry. Narration can also be an important element in biographies, autobiographies, and essays.

Narrative poetry Verse that tells a story.

Narrator The person who tells a story. In some cases the narrator is a character in the story.

See also POINT OF VIEW.

Nonfiction Factual prose writing. Nonfiction deals with real people and experiences. Among the categories of nonfiction are biographies, autobiographies, and essays.

See also AUTOBIOGRAPHY, BIOGRAPHY, ESSAY, FICTION.

Novel A book-length fictional prose narrative. The novel has more scope than a short story in its presentation of plot, character, setting, and theme. Because novels are not subject to any limits in their presentation of these elements, they encompass a wide range of narratives.

See also FICTION.

Novella A work of fiction shorter than a novel but longer than a short story. A novella usually has more characters, settings, and events and a more complex plot than a short story.

O

Onomatopoeia The use of a word or a phrase that actually imitates or suggests the sound of what it describes.

See also SOUND DEVICES.

Oral tradition Stories, knowledge, customs, and beliefs passed by word of mouth from one generation to the next.

See also FOLKLORE, FOLKTALE, LEGEND, MYTH.

P

Parallelism The use of a series of words, phrases, or sentences that have similar grammatical form. Parallelism emphasizes the items that are arranged in the similar structures.

See also REPETITION.

Personification A figure of speech in which an animal, object, or idea is given human form or characteristics.

See also FIGURATIVE LANGUAGE, FIGURE OF SPEECH, METAPHOR.

Plot The sequence of events in a story, novel, or play. The plot begins with **exposition,** which introduces the story's characters, setting, and situation. The plot catches the reader's attention with a **narrative hook.** The **rising action** adds complications to the story's conflict, or problem, leading to the **climax,** or point of highest emotional pitch. The **falling action** is the logical result of the climax, and the **resolution** presents the final outcome.

Plot twist An unexpected turn of events in a plot. A surprise ending is an example of a plot twist.

Poetry A form of literary expression that differs from prose in emphasizing the line as the unit of composition. Many other traditional characteristics of poetry—emotional, imaginative language; use of metaphor and simile; division into stanzas; rhyme; regular pattern of stress, or meter—apply to some poems.

Point of view The relationship of the narrator, or storyteller, to the story. In a story with **first-person point of view,** the story is told by one of the characters, referred to as "I." The reader generally sees everything through that character's eyes. In a story with a **limited third-person point of view,** the narrator reveals the thoughts of only one character, but refers to that character as "he" or "she." In a story with an **omniscient point of view,** the narrator reveals the thoughts of several characters.

Propaganda Speech, writing, or other attempts to influence ideas or opinions, often through the use of stereotypes, faulty generalizations, logical fallacies, and/or emotional language.

Props Theater slang (a shortened form of *properties*) for objects and elements of the scenery of a stage play or movie set.

Prose Writing that is similar to everyday speech and language, as opposed to poetry. Its form is based on sentences and paragraphs without the patterns of rhyme, controlled line length, or meter found in much poetry. Fiction and nonfiction are the major categories of prose. Most modern drama is also written in prose.

See also DRAMA, ESSAY, FICTION, NONFICTION.

Protagonist The central character in a story, drama, or dramatic poem. Usually the action revolves around the protagonist, who is involved in the main conflict.

See ANTAGONIST, CONFLICT.

Pun A humorous play on two or more meanings of the same word or on two words with the same sound. Puns often appear in advertising headlines and slogans—for example, "Our hotel rooms give you suite feelings."

See also HUMOR.

R

Refrain A line or lines repeated regularly, usually in a poem or song.

Repetition The recurrence of sounds, words, phrases, lines, or stanzas in a speech or piece of writing. Repetition increases the feeling of unity in a work. When a line or stanza is repeated in a poem or song, it is called a refrain.

See also PARALLELISM, REFRAIN.

Resolution The part of a plot that concludes the falling action by revealing or suggesting the outcome of the conflict.

Rhyme The repetition of sounds at the ends of words that appear close to each other in a poem. **End rhyme** occurs at the ends of lines. **Internal rhyme** occurs within a single line. **Slant rhyme** occurs when words include sounds that are similar but not identical. Slant rhyme usually involves some variation of **consonance** (the repetition of consonant sounds) or **assonance** (the repetition of vowel sounds).

Rhyme scheme The pattern of rhyme formed by the end rhyme in a poem. The rhyme scheme is designated by the assignment of a different letter of the alphabet to each new rhyme. For example, one common rhyme scheme is *ababcb*.

Rhythm The pattern created by the arrangement of stressed and unstressed syllables, especially in poetry. Rhythm gives poetry a musical quality that helps convey its meaning. Rhythm can be regular (with a predictable pattern or meter) or irregular, (as in free verse).

See also METER.

Rising action The part of a plot that adds complications to the problems in the story and increases reader interest.

See also FALLING ACTION, PLOT.

S

Scene A subdivision of an act in a play. Each scene takes place in a specific setting and time. An act may have one or more scenes.

See also ACT.

Science fiction Fiction dealing with the impact of real science or imaginary superscience on human or alien societies of the past, present, or future. Although science fiction is mainly a product of the twentieth century, nineteenth-century authors such as Mary Shelley, Jules Verne, and Robert Louis Stevenson were pioneers of the genre.

Screenplay The script of a film, usually containing detailed instructions about camera shots and angles in addition to dialogue and stage directions. A screenplay for an original television show is called a teleplay.

See also DRAMA.

Sensory imagery Language that appeals to a reader's five senses: hearing, sight, touch, taste, and smell.

See also VISUAL IMAGERY.

Sequence of events The order in which the events in a story take place.

Setting The time and place in which the events of a short story, novel, novella, or play occur. The setting often helps create the atmosphere or mood of the story.

Short story A brief fictional narrative in prose. Elements of the short story include **plot, character, setting, point of view, theme,** and sometimes **symbol** and **irony**.

Simile A figure of speech using *like* or *as* to compare seemingly unlike things.

See also FIGURATIVE LANGUAGE, FIGURE OF SPEECH.

Sound devices Techniques used to create a sense of rhythm or to emphasize particular sounds in writing. For example, sound can be controlled through the use of **onomatopoeia, alliteration, consonance, assonance,** and **rhyme.**

See also RHYTHM.

Speaker The voice of a poem—sometimes that of the poet, sometimes that of a fictional person or even a thing. The speaker's words communicate a particular tone or attitude toward the subject of the poem.

Stage directions Instructions written by the dramatist to describe the appearance and actions of characters, as well as sets, costumes, and lighting.

Stanza A group of lines forming a unit in a poem. Stanzas are, in effect, the paragraphs of a poem.

Stereotype A character who is not developed as an individual but as a collection of traits and mannerisms supposedly shared by all members of a group.

Style The author's choice and arrangement of words and sentences in a literary work. Style can reveal an author's purpose in writing and attitude toward his or her subject and audience.

Suspense A feeling of curiosity, uncertainty, or even dread about what is going to happen next. Writers increase the level of suspense in a story by giving readers clues to what may happen.

See also FORESHADOWING, RISING ACTION.

Symbol Any object, person, place, or experience that means more than what it is. **Symbolism** is the use of images to represent internal realities.

T

Tall tale A wildly imaginative story, usually passed down orally, about the fantastic adventures or amazing feats of folk heroes in realistic settings.

See also FOLKLORE, ORAL TRADITION.

Teleplay A play written or adapted for television.

Theme A literary work's overall message about life or human nature. Some works have a **stated theme,** which is expressed directly. More frequently works have an **implied theme,** which is revealed gradually through other elements such as plot, character, setting, point of view, symbol, and irony.

Third-person narrative *See* POINT OF VIEW.

Title The name of a literary work.

Tone The attitude of the narrator toward the subject, ideas, theme, or characters. A factual article would most likely have an objective tone, while an editorial on the same topic could be argumentative or satiric.

Tragedy A play in which the main character suffers a downfall. That character often is a person of dignified or heroic stature. The downfall may result from outside forces or from a weakness within the character, which is known as a tragic flaw.

V

Visual imagery Details that appeal to the sense of sight.

Voice An author's distinctive style or the particular speech patterns of a character in a story.

See also STYLE, TONE.

Reading and Thinking with Foldables®

by Dinah Zike, M.Ed., Creator of Foldables®

Using Foldables Makes Learning Easy and Enjoyable

Anyone who has paper, scissors, and maybe a stapler or some glue can use Foldables in the classroom. Just follow the illustrated step-by-step directions.

Foldable for Units 1 and 3

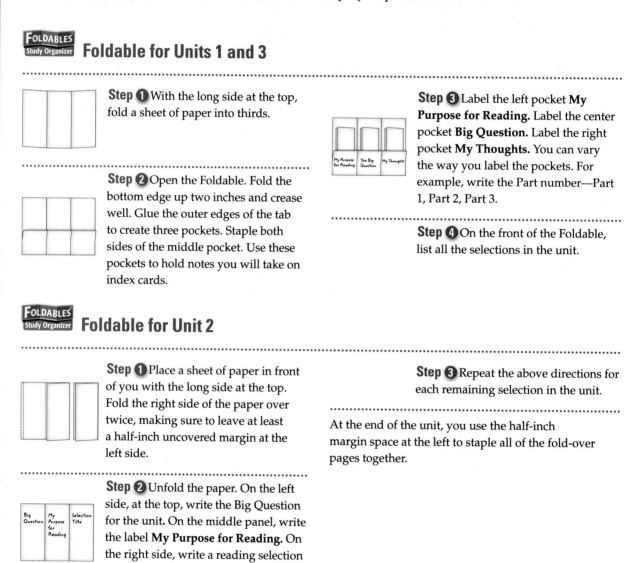

Step ❶ With the long side at the top, fold a sheet of paper into thirds.

Step ❷ Open the Foldable. Fold the bottom edge up two inches and crease well. Glue the outer edges of the tab to create three pockets. Staple both sides of the middle pocket. Use these pockets to hold notes you will take on index cards.

Step ❸ Label the left pocket **My Purpose for Reading.** Label the center pocket **Big Question.** Label the right pocket **My Thoughts.** You can vary the way you label the pockets. For example, write the Part number—Part 1, Part 2, Part 3.

Step ❹ On the front of the Foldable, list all the selections in the unit.

Foldable for Unit 2

Step ❶ Place a sheet of paper in front of you with the long side at the top. Fold the right side of the paper over twice, making sure to leave at least a half-inch uncovered margin at the left side.

Step ❷ Unfold the paper. On the left side, at the top, write the Big Question for the unit. On the middle panel, write the label **My Purpose for Reading.** On the right side, write a reading selection title.

Step ❸ Repeat the above directions for each remaining selection in the unit.

At the end of the unit, you use the half-inch margin space at the left to staple all of the fold-over pages together.

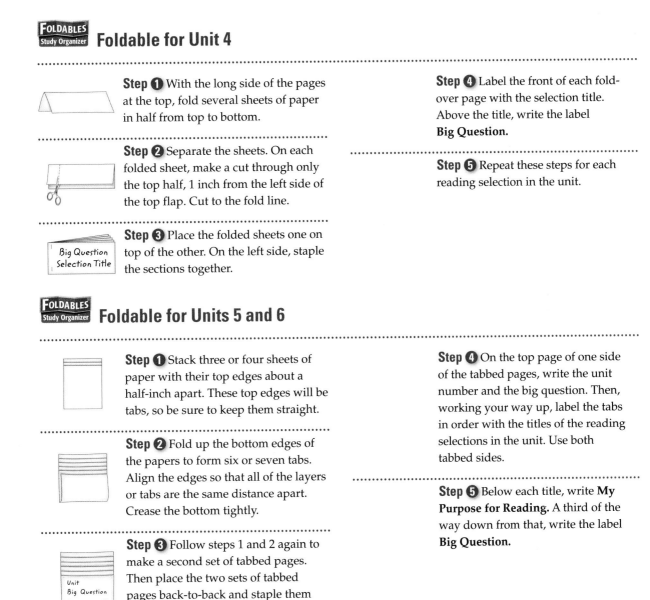

FOLDABLES Study Organizer **Foldable for Unit 4**

Step ❶ With the long side of the pages at the top, fold several sheets of paper in half from top to bottom.

Step ❷ Separate the sheets. On each folded sheet, make a cut through only the top half, 1 inch from the left side of the top flap. Cut to the fold line.

Step ❸ Place the folded sheets one on top of the other. On the left side, staple the sections together.

Big Question
Selection Title

Step ❹ Label the front of each fold-over page with the selection title. Above the title, write the label **Big Question.**

Step ❺ Repeat these steps for each reading selection in the unit.

FOLDABLES Study Organizer **Foldable for Units 5 and 6**

Step ❶ Stack three or four sheets of paper with their top edges about a half-inch apart. These top edges will be tabs, so be sure to keep them straight.

Step ❷ Fold up the bottom edges of the papers to form six or seven tabs. Align the edges so that all of the layers or tabs are the same distance apart. Crease the bottom tightly.

Step ❸ Follow steps 1 and 2 again to make a second set of tabbed pages. Then place the two sets of tabbed pages back-to-back and staple them together at the bottom.

Unit
Big Question

Step ❹ On the top page of one side of the tabbed pages, write the unit number and the big question. Then, working your way up, label the tabs in order with the titles of the reading selections in the unit. Use both tabbed sides.

Step ❺ Below each title, write **My Purpose for Reading.** A third of the way down from that, write the label **Big Question.**

Functional Documents

Business Letter

In the business world, in school, and even at home, there are many standard types of documents that serve specific functions. Understanding these forms of writing will help you to be a better communicator in your everyday life.

The following business letter uses modified block style.

(1) 10 Pullman Lane
Cromwell, CT 06416
January 16, 2009

(2) Mr. Philip Fornaro
Principal
Cromwell School
179 West Maple St.
Cromwell, CT 06416

(3) Dear Mr. Fornaro:

(4) My friends and I in the seventh grade at Brimmer Middle School feel that there is not enough to do in Cromwell during the winter vacation week. Some students can afford to go away for vacation. Many families, however, cannot afford to go away, or the parents have to work.

(5) I would like to suggest that you keep the Brimmer Middle School gym open during the vacation week. If the gym were open, the basketball teams could practice. The fencing club could meet. We could meet our friends there instead of going to the mall.

(6) Thanks for listening to my request. I hope you will think it over.

(7) Sincerely,
Kim Goodwin
Kim Goodwin

(1) In the heading, write your address and the date on separate lines.

(2) In the inside address, write the name and address of the person to whom you are sending the letter.

(3) Use a colon after the greeting.

(4) In your introduction, say who you are and why you are writing.

(5) In the body of your letter, provide details concerning your request.

(6) Conclude by restating your purpose and thanking the person you are writing to.

(7) In the closing, use *Sincerely, Sincerely yours,* or *Yours truly* followed by a comma. Include both your signature and your printed or typed name.

Job Application

When applying for a job, you usually need to fill out a job application. Read the form carefully before beginning to fill it out. Write neatly and fill out the form completely, providing all information directly and honestly. If a question does not apply to you, indicate that by writing *n/a*, short for "not applicable." Keep in mind that you will have the opportunity to provide additional information in your résumé, in your letter of application, or during the interview process.

Please type or print neatly in blue or black ink.

Name: _____ Today's date: _____

Address: _____

Phone #: _____ Birth date: _____ Sex: ___ Soc. Sec. #: _____

Job History (List each job held, starting with the most recent job.)

1. Employer: _____ Phone #: _____

Dates of employment: _____

Position held: _____

Duties: _____

2. Employer: _____ Phone #: _____

Dates of employment: _____

Position held: _____

Duties: _____

Education (List the most recent level of education completed.)

_____

_____

Personal References:

1. Name: _____ Phone #: _____

Relationship: _____

2. Name: _____ Phone #: _____

Relationship: _____

1 The application provides specific instructions.

2 All of the information requested should be provided in its entirety.

3 The information should be provided neatly and succinctly.

4 Experience should be stated accurately and without embellishment.

Activity

Complete a copy of the above application thoroughly. Fill out the application as if you were actually applying for the job. Be sure to pay close attention to the guidelines mentioned above.

Writing a Memo

A memo, or memorandum, is a brief, efficient way of communicating information to another person or group of people. It begins with a header that provides basic information. A memo does not have a formal closing.

TO: *Brimmer Banner* newspaper staff
FROM: Paul Francis
SUBJECT: Winter issue
DATE: January 18, 2009

Articles for the winter issue of the *Brimmer Banner* are due by February 1. Please see Terry about your assignment as soon as possible! The following articles or features have not yet been assigned:

Cafeteria Mess: Who Is Responsible?
Teacher Profile: Mr. Jinks, Ms. Magee
Sports roundup

Using Electronic Business Correspondence

Imagine that you ordered a game through a company's Web site. When you tried playing the game, you found that it didn't work well. You could send a letter to the company you bought the game from explaining your problem. But it's easier and faster to send an e-mail. Any business that operates on the Internet has a way for customers to reach them—either a hyperlink "button" that will take you to customer service, or an e-mail address such as *service@ gamecorp.com.*

Here are a few hints for effective business e-mails.

- Your e-mail window includes an area for the subject of your message. Think carefully and make your subject as clear and concise as possible. In a business e-mail you'll want your recipient to know right away your purpose for writing.

- Reread your message carefully before hitting the Send button. Check your grammar and spelling. Then double-check your spelling by using the spell-checker program on your computer.

- Your e-mail program probably offers options for how to send a message—for example: plain text, rich text, or HTML. If your letter contains some formatting (like italics or boldface) or special characters (such as a cursive typeface that looks like handwriting), choose rich text or HTML to avoid losing your formatting.

Technical Writing

Technical writing involves the use of very specific vocabulary and a special attention to detail. The purpose of technical writing is to describe a process clearly enough so that the reader can perform the steps and reach the intended goal, such as installing software, connecting a piece of equipment, or programming a device.

Instructions for Connecting DVD Player to HDTV

Your DVD player can be connected to an HDTV using RCA cables or, if available, an HDMI cable.

Connecting with RCA Cables

Step 1: Insert the ends of the red, white, and yellow cables into the jacks labeled "AUDIO/VIDEO OUT." ❶ Be sure to match the color of the cable with the color of the jack.

❷ **Step 2:** Insert the other ends of the RCA cables into the jacks labeled "AUDIO/VIDEO IN" on your HDTV. These are usually located on the side or the back of the television. Again, be sure to match the color of the cable with the color of the jack.

Connecting with HDMI Cable

Step 1: Insert one end of the HDMI cable into the HDMI port located on the back of the DVD player.

Step 2: Insert the other end of the HDMI cable into the HDMI port on your HDTV.

❸ **Note:** Your television may have more than one HDMI port. If so, be sure that you set your television to the correct input when viewing.

❶ Uses specific language to clearly describe the process

❷ Lists each step individually

❸ Brings attention to possible variations the reader may encounter

Activity

Choose a device that you own or have access to, such as an mp3 player or a cell phone. Write brief step-by-step directions on how to perform a specific function on the device, so that someone else can follow your instructions and perform the function successfully.

Writing Handbook

Research Report Writing

When you write a research report, you explore a topic by gathering factual information from several different resources. Through your research, you develop a point of view or draw a conclusion. This point of view or conclusion becomes the main idea, or thesis, of your report.

Select a Topic

Because a research report usually takes time to prepare and write, your choice of topic is especially important. Follow these guidelines.

- Brainstorm a list of questions about a subject you would like to explore. Choose one that is neither too narrow nor too broad for the length of paper you will write. Use that question as your topic.

- Select a topic that genuinely interests you.

- Be sure you can find information on your topic from several different sources.

Do Research

Start by looking up your topic in an encyclopedia to find general information. Then find specific information in books, magazines, and newspapers, on CD-ROMs and the Internet, and from personal interviews when this seems appropriate. Use the computerized or card catalog in the library to locate books on your topic. Then search for up-to-date information in periodicals (magazines) or newspapers and from electronic sources, such as CD-ROMs or the Internet. If you need help in finding or using any of these resources, ask the librarian.

As you gather information, make sure each source you use relates closely to your topic. Also be sure that your source is reliable. Be extra careful if you are using information from the Internet. If you are not sure about the reliability of a source, consult the librarian or your teacher.

Internet Research

In order to conduct research on the Internet, you will need to use a search engine, a tool that allows you to use keywords to find information on the World Wide Web. There are many different search engines on the Internet, but most of them operate similarly.

First, open a search engine. Somewhere near the top you'll find a white box that you can type into. Next to it will be a button that in most search engines says "Search." Try searching for Web sites about protecting animals in the wild. For keywords, try: "endangered wildlife." The quotation marks tell the search engine to look for the whole phrase rather than for each word by itself. Click on the Search button and the engine will provide you with a list of sites that include the phrase "endangered wildlife." Visit a few of these sites by clicking on the underlined titles.

As you conduct your Internet search, you may want to narrow your search to something more specific, such as "wildlife preserves." Try different keywords to come up with additional sites dealing with your topic. Most search engines also have an advanced search feature, which allows you be even more specific about your search.

Since there is such a huge amount of information on the Internet, you will have to visit many sites and evaluate which ones have the information you need, based on relevance and appropriateness.

Exercise:

Conduct an Internet search using the word "cooking" as a keyword. How many sites do you find? Now do a search to find a recipe for your favorite dessert. Think of exact phrases you could place in quotes to narrow your search.

Make Source Cards

In a research report, you must document the source of your information. To keep track of your sources, write the author, title, publication information, and location of each source on a separate index card. Give each source card a number and write it in the upper right-hand corner. These cards will be useful for preparing a bibliography.

Sample Source Card

❶ Douglas, Marjory Stoneman   **❷** 15
    ❸ **Everglades: River of Grass.**
    ❹ **Marietta, Georgia: Mockingbird**
      Books, 1986. ❺

❻ Carrollton Public Library   **❼** 654.3 S2

❶ Author   **❺** Date of publication

❷ Source number   **❻** Location of source

❸ Title   **❼** Library call number

❹ City of publication/
    Publisher

Take Notes

As you read, you encounter many new facts and ideas. Taking notes will help you keep track of information and focus on the topic. Here are some helpful suggestions:

- Use a new card for each important piece of information. Separate cards will help you to organize your notes.

- At the top of each card, write a key word or phrase that tells you about the information. Also, write the number of the source you used.

- Write only details and ideas that relate to your topic.

- Summarize information in your own words.

- Write down a phrase or a quote only when the words are especially interesting or come from an important source. Enclose all quotes in quotation marks to make clear that the ideas belong to someone else.

This sample note card shows information to include.

Sample Note Card

❶ Functions of Wetlands   **❷** 15
Besides furnishing a home for a variety of wildlife, the wet, spongy soil of wetlands maintains the level of the water table.
p. 79 **❸**

❶ Write a key word or phrase that tells you what the information is about.

❷ Write the source number from your source card.

❸ Write the number of the page or pages on which you found the information.

Develop Your Thesis

As you begin researching and learning about your topic, think about the overall point you want to make. Write one sentence, your *thesis statement*, that says exactly what you plan to report on.

Sample Thesis Statement

Everglades National Park is a beautiful but endangered animal habitat.

Keep your thesis in mind as you continue to do research and think about your topic. The thesis will help you determine what information is important. However, be prepared to change your thesis if the information you find does not support it.

Write an Outline

When you finish taking notes, organize the information in an outline. Write down the main ideas that you want to cover. Write your thesis statement at the beginning of your outline. Then list the supporting details. Follow an outline form like the one below.

❶ Everglades National Park is a beautiful but endangered animal habitat.

    I.   Special aspects of the Everglades

        ❷ A. Characteristics of wetlands

        B. Endangered birds and other animals

    II. Pressures on the Everglades

        A. Florida agriculture

        B. Carelessness of visitors

    III. How to protect the Everglades

        A. Change agricultural practices

        B. Educate park visitors

            ❸ 1. Mandatory video on safety for individuals and environment

            2. Instructional reminders posted throughout the park

❶ The thesis statement identifies your topic and the overall point you will make.

❷ If you have subtopics under a main topic, there must be at least two. They must relate directly to your main topic.

❸ If you wish to divide a subtopic, you must have at least two divisions. Each must relate to the subtopic above it.

Document Your Information

You must document, or credit, the sources of all the information you use in your report. There are two common ways to document information.

Avoiding Plagiarism

Plagiarism is the act of presenting an author's words or ideas as if they were your own. This is not only illegal, it is also unethical. You must credit the source not only for material directly quoted but also for any facts or ideas obtained from the source. See the Media Workshop on Media Ethics (p. 625) for more information.

Footnotes

To document with footnotes, place a number at the end of the information you are documenting. Number your notes consecutively, beginning with number 1. These numbers should be slightly raised and should come after any punctuation. The documentation information itself goes at the bottom of the page, with a matching number.

In-text number for note:

The Declaration of Independence was read in public for the first time on July 6, 1776.[3]

Footnote at bottom of page:

   [3] John Smith, <u>The Declaration of Independence</u> (New York: DI, 2001) 221.

Parenthetical Documentation

In this method, you give the source for your information in parentheses at the end of the sentence where the information appears. You do not need to give all the details of the source. Just provide enough information for your readers to identify it. Here are the basic rules to follow.

- Usually it is enough to give the author's last name and the number of the page where you found the information.

   The declaration was first read in public by militia colonel John Nixon (Smith 222).

- If you mention the author's name in the sentence, you do not need to repeat it in the parentheses.

  According to Smith, the reading was greeted with wild applause (224).

- If your source does not identify a particular author, as in a newspaper or encyclopedia article, give the first word or two of the title of the piece.

The anniversary of the reading was commemorated by a parade and fireworks ("Reading Celebrated").

Full information on your sources goes in a list at the end of your paper.

Bibliography or Works Cited

At the end of your paper, list all the sources of information that you used in preparing your report. Arrange them alphabetically by the author's last name (or by the first word in the title if no author is mentioned) as shown below. Title this list *Works Cited.* (Use the term *bibliography* if all your sources are printed media, such as books, magazines, or newspapers.)

Works Cited **1**

2 Bertram, Jeffrey. "African Bees: Fact or Myth?" *Orlando Sentinel* 18 Aug. 1999: D2.

3 Gore, Rick. "Neanderthals." <u>National Geographic.</u> January 1996: 2–35. **8**

4 Gould, Stephen J. <u>The Panda's Thumb.</u> New York: W. W. Norton & Co., 1982.

5 "Governor Chiles Vetoes Anti-Everglades **9** Bills–5/13/98." <u>Friends of the Everglades.</u> May 1998. 26 Aug 1998 <http://www.everglades.org/pressrel_may28.htm>.

6 "Neanderthal man." <u>The Columbia Encyclopedia.</u> 5th Edition. New York: Columbia University Press, 1993.

7 Pabst, Laura (Curator of Natural History Museum), Interview. March 11, l998.

1 Indent all but the first line of each item.

2 Newspaper article

3 Magazine article

4 Book with one author

5 On-line article

6 Encyclopedia

7 Interview

8 Include page numbers for a magazine article but not for a book, unless the book is a collection of essays by different authors.

9 Include database (underlined), publication medium (online), computer service, and date of access.

Presenting

For readers to fully appreciate your writing, it is very important that you present it neatly, effectively, and according to the needs of your audience and the purpose of your writing. The following standard is how you should format most of your formal school papers.

Formatting your text

- The standard typeface setting for most school papers is Courier 12 point.

- Double-space your work so that it is easy to read.

- Leave one-inch margins on all sides of every page.

- Include the page number in the upper right-hand corner of each page.

- If you are including charts, graphs, maps, or other visual aids, consider setting them on their own page. This will allow you to show the graphic at a full size that is easy to read.

Exercise:

Look in the library or on the Internet to find style guides for various types of writing, such as short stories or magazine articles. Assess which format is right for your piece of writing and apply it.

Using a Computer for Writing

Using Word Processing Software

A word processor is a digital tool that lets you move your words and ideas around until you find the best way to present them. Each type of word processing software is a bit different, but they all help you plan, draft, revise, edit, and present properly formatted documents.

Menus, Toolbars, and Rulers

Open a word processing document. At the top of your screen, locate the menu bar, one or more toolbars, and a ruler.

Menu Bar Menus help you perform important processes. The Edit menu, for example, allows you to copy, paste, and find text within your document.

Toolbars There are two basic types of tools. **Function tools** perform some kind of computer function, like printing a document or checking its spelling. **Formatting tools** are used to change the way a document looks—for example, changing its font (typeface) or paragraph style.

Ruler The ruler looks like a measuring stick with little markers at each end. These markers control the margins of your document. Try changing the margins on your document. You can also put tabs on the ruler so that you can use the tab key on your keyboard to send your cursor to those positions.

Exercise

Use the menu, toolbars, and ruler to properly format your document according to the guidelines on p. R17.

Multimedia Presentations

You can use digital technology, such as a computer with presentation software, to create a multimedia presentation of your work. Adding pictures, video, and sound to your presentation can attract and hold your audience's attention. However, it is important that you understand the rules and laws about using other people's creations in your work. See the Media Workshop on Media Ethics (p. 625) for more information.

Slides

In a multimedia presentation, each screen a viewer sees is called a slide. Generally, a slide consists of text—not too much of it—and an image of some kind. Each slide should be limited to a single idea with a few supporting details. Because you want to get your point across quickly, it's important that you choose your images and words carefully. An Internet search engine can help you find downloadable images to use in your presentation. Most computer images have the file extension "gif" or "jpeg."

Video

For some types of presentations, adding video can have a big impact. For example, if you're presenting a report on an actor, what better way

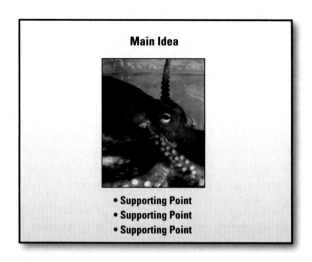

Main Idea

- **Supporting Point**
- **Supporting Point**
- **Supporting Point**

to illustrate his or her style than with movie clips? You can record video clips from your TV or downloaded them from the Internet. Most movie files have the extensions "avi," "mov," or "mpeg."

You can add your images and video clips to your presentation using the Insert menu in your presentation software. Also, most presentation software has a "wizard" or templates that will help you put together your multimedia presentation.

Exercise:

Working with a partner, choose a movie or television show as the basis for a complete multimedia presentation. Include in your presentation at least six slides with pictures and text and two video clips. Don't forget about media ethics, and be careful not to plagiarize as you choose media for your presentation.

Databases

An electronic database is a software program that allows you to organize, store, and retrieve information. Data is organized into a table of columns and rows. Each single piece of information is called a field.

Once the information is in your database, you can recall it in a number of useful ways. For example, you can arrange an address-book database to show you all the names of people who live in a certain city or zip code.

Exercise:

Create a database of your research materials for a current or upcoming report. Enter fields for authors, titles, types of media, and keywords of what useful information was found in each. Practice organizing the database in different ways. For example, organize your database to show how many magazine articles you used in your research.

Field Columns (Categories)

Record

Name	Address	City	State	Zip
Brown, Katie	12814 South Emerald	Chicago	IL	60601
Hauser, Sam	63 Taylor	Stamford	CT	06904
Marmalard, Greg	1001 Porterhouse	Laredo	TX	78040
O'Hare, Megan	140 Blossom	Shaker Heights	OH	44118
Trumbull, Ellen	302 St. Nicolas	Darien	CT	06820

Field

Language Handbook

Grammar Glossary

This glossary will help you quickly locate information on parts of speech and sentence structure.

A

Absolute phrase. *See* Phrase.

Abstract noun. *See* Noun chart.

Action verb. *See* Verb.

Active voice. *See* Voice.

Adjective A word that modifies a noun or pronoun by limiting its meaning. Adjectives appear in various positions in a sentence. **(The gray cat purred. The cat is gray.)**

Many adjectives have different forms to indicate degree of comparison. **(short, shorter, shortest)**

> The positive degree is the simple form of the adjective. **(easy, interesting, good)**

> The comparative degree compares two persons, places, things, or ideas. **(easier, more interesting, better)**

> The superlative degree compares more than two persons, places, things, or ideas. **(easiest, most interesting, best)**

> A predicate adjective follows a linking verb and further identifies or describes the subject. **(The child is happy.)**

> A proper adjective is formed from a proper noun and begins with a capital letter. Many proper adjectives are created by adding these suffixes: -an, -ian, -n, -ese, and -ish. **(Chinese, African)**

Adjective clause. *See* Clause chart.

Adverb A word that modifies a verb, an adjective, or another adverb by making its meaning more specific. When modifying a verb, an adverb may appear in various positions in a sentence. **(Cats generally eat less than dogs. Generally, cats eat less than dogs.)** When modifying an adjective or another adverb, an adverb appears directly before the modified word. **(I was quite pleased that they got along so well.)** The word not and the contraction -n't are adverbs. **(Mike wasn't ready for the test today.)** Certain adverbs of time, place, and degree also have a negative meaning. **(He's never ready.)**

Some adverbs have different forms to indicate degree of comparison. **(soon, sooner, soonest)**

> The comparative degree compares two actions. **(better, more quickly)**

> The superlative degree compares three or more actions. **(fastest, most patiently, least rapidly)**

Adverb clause. *See* Clause chart.

Antecedent. *See* Pronoun.

Appositive A noun or a pronoun that further identifies another noun or pronoun. **(My friend Julie lives next door.)**

Appositive phrase. *See* Phrase.

Article The adjective a, an, or the.

> Indefinite articles **(a and an)** refer to one of a general group of persons, places, or things. **(I eat an apple a day.)**

> The definite article **(the)** indicates that the noun is a specific person, place, or thing. **(The alarm woke me up.)**

Auxiliary verb. *See* Verb.

B

Base form. *See* Verb tense.

C

Clause A group of words that has a subject and a predicate and that is used as a sentence or part of a sentence. Clauses fall into two categories: main clauses, which are also called independent clauses, and subordinate clauses, which are also called dependent clauses.

Types of Subordinate Clauses

Clause	Function	Example	Begins with . . .
Adjective clause	Modifies a noun or pronoun	Songs that have a strong beat make me want to dance.	A relative pronoun such as which, who, whom, whose, or that
Adverb clause	Modifies a verb, an adjective, or an adverb	Whenever Al calls me, he asks to borrow my bike.	A subordinating conjunction such as after, although, because, if, since, when, or where
Noun clause	Serves as a subject, an object, or a predicate nominative	What Philip did surprised us.	Words such as how, that, what, whatever, when, where, which, who, whom, whoever, whose, or why

A main clause can stand alone as a sentence. There must be at least one main clause in every sentence. **(The rooster crowed, and the dog barked.)**

A subordinate clause cannot stand alone as a sentence. A subordinate clause needs a main clause to complete its meaning. Many subordinate clauses begin with subordinating conjunctions or relative pronouns. **(When Geri sang her solo, the audience became quiet.)** The chart on this page shows the main types of subordinate clauses.

Collective noun. *See* Noun chart.

Common noun. *See* Noun chart.

Comparative degree. *See* Adjective; Adverb.

Complement A word or phrase that completes the meaning of a verb. The four basic kinds of complements are direct objects, indirect objects, object complements, and subject complements.

A direct object answers the question What? or Whom? after an action verb. **(Kari found a dollar. Larry saw Denise.)**

An indirect object answers the question *to whom, for whom, to what,* or *for what* after an action verb. **(Do me a favor. She gave the child a toy.)**

An object complement answers the question *what* after a direct object. An object complement is a noun, a pronoun, or an adjective that completes the meaning of a direct object by identifying or describing it. **(The director made me the understudy for the role. The little girl called the puppy hers.)**

A subject complement follows a subject and a linking verb. It identifies or describes a subject. The two kinds of subject complements are predicate nominatives and predicate adjectives.

A predicate nominative is a noun or pronoun that follows a linking verb and tells more about the subject. **(The author of "The Raven" is Edgar Allan Poe.)**

A predicate adjective is an adjective that follows a linking verb and gives more information about the subject. **(Ian became angry at the bully.)**

Complex sentence. *See* Sentence.

Compound preposition. *See* Preposition.

Compound sentence. *See* Sentence.

Compound-complex sentence. *See* Sentence.

Conjunction A word that joins single words or groups of words.

A coordinating conjunction **(and, but, or, nor, for, yet, so)** joins words or groups of words that are equal in grammatical importance. **(David and Ruth are twins. I was bored, so I left.)**

Correlative conjunctions **(both . . . and, just as . . . so, not only . . . but also, either . . . or, neither . . . nor, whether . . . or)** work in pairs to join words and groups of words of equal importance. **(Choose either the muffin or the bagel.)**

A subordinating conjunction **(after, although, as if, because, before, if, since, so that, than, though, until, when, while)** joins a dependent idea or clause to a main clause. **(Beth acted as if she felt ill.)**

Conjunctive adverb An adverb used to clarify the relationship between clauses of equal weight in a sentence. Conjunctive adverbs are used to replace and **(also, besides, furthermore, moreover)**; to replace but **(however, nevertheless, still)**; to state a result **(consequently, therefore, so, thus)**; or to state equality **(equally, likewise, similarly)**. **(Ana was determined to get an A; therefore, she studied often.)**

Coordinating conjunction. *See* Conjunction.

Correlative conjunction. *See* Conjunction.

D

Declarative sentence. *See* Sentence.

Definite article. *See* Article.

Demonstrative pronoun. *See* Pronoun.

Direct object. *See* Complement.

E

Emphatic form. *See* Verb tense.

F

Future tense. *See* Verb tense.

G

Gerund A verb form that ends in -ing and is used as a noun. A gerund may function as a subject, the object of a verb, or the object of a preposition. **(Smiling uses fewer muscles than frowning. Marie enjoys walking.)**

Gerund phrase. *See* Phrase.

I

Imperative mood. *See* Mood of verb.

Imperative sentence. *See* Sentence chart.

Indicative mood. *See* Mood of verb.

Indirect object. *See* Complement.

Infinitive A verb form that begins with the word to and functions as a noun, an adjective, or an adverb. **(No one wanted to answer.)** Note: When to precedes a verb, it is not a preposition but instead signals an infinitive.

Infinitive phrase. *See* Phrase.

Intensive pronoun. *See* Pronoun.

Interjection A word or phrase that expresses emotion or exclamation. An interjection has no grammatical connection to other words. Commas follow mild ones; exclamation points follow stronger ones. **(Well, have a good day. Wow!)**

Interrogative pronoun. *See* Pronoun.

Intransitive verb. *See* Verb.

Inverted order In a sentence written in inverted order, the predicate comes before the subject. Some sentences are written in inverted order for variety or special emphasis. **(Up the beanstalk scampered Jack.)** The subject also generally follows the predicate in a sentence that begins with here or there. **(Here was the solution to his problem.)** Questions, or interrogative sentences, are generally written in inverted order. In many questions, an auxiliary verb precedes the subject, and the main verb follows it. **(Has anyone seen Susan?)** Questions that begin with who or what follow normal word order.

Irregular verb. *See* Verb tense.

L

Linking verb. *See* Verb.

M

Main clause. *See* Clause.

Mood of verb A verb expresses one of three moods: indicative, imperative, or subjunctive.

The indicative mood is the most common. It makes a statement or asks a question. **(We are out of bread. Will you buy it?)**

The imperative mood expresses a command or makes a request. **(Stop acting like a child! Please return my sweater.)**

The subjunctive mood is used to express, indirectly, a demand, suggestion, or statement of necessity **(I demand that he stop acting like a child. It's necessary that she buy more bread.)** The subjunctive is also used to state a condition or wish that is contrary to fact. This use of the subjunctive requires the past tense. **(If you were a nice person, you would return my sweater.)**

N

Nominative pronoun. *See* Pronoun.

Noun A word that names a person, a place, a thing, or an idea. The chart on this page shows the main types of nouns.

Noun clause. *See* Clause chart.

Noun of direct address. *See* Noun chart.

Number A noun, pronoun, or verb is singular in number if it refers to one; plural if it refers to more than one.

O

Object. *See* Complement.

P

Participle A verb form that can function as an adjective. Present participles always end in -ing. **(The woman comforted the crying child.)** Many past participles end in -ed. **(We bought the beautifully painted chair.)** However, irregular verbs form their past participles in some other way. **(Cato was Caesar's sworn enemy.)**

Passive voice. *See* Voice.

Past tense. *See* Verb tense.

Perfect tense. *See* Verb tense.

Personal pronoun. *See* Pronoun, Pronoun chart.

Types of Nouns

Noun	Function	Example
Abstract noun	Names an idea, a quality, or a state	independence, energy
Collective noun	Names a group of things or persons	herd, troop, crowd, class
Common noun	Names a general type of person, place, thing, or idea	musician, city, building
Compound noun	Is made up of two or more words	checkerboard, parking lot, mother-in-law
Noun of direct address	Identifies the person or persons being spoken to	Maria, please stand.
Possessive noun	Shows possession, ownership, or the relationship between two nouns	my friend's room, my friend's brother
Proper noun	Names a particular person, place, thing, or idea	Cleopatra, Italy, Christianity

Phrase A group of words that acts in a sentence as a single part of speech.

An absolute phrase consists of a noun or pronoun that is modified by a participle or participial phrase but has no grammatical relation to the complete subject or predicate. **(The vegetables being done, we finally sat down to eat dinner.)**

An appositive phrase is an appositive along with any modifiers. If not essential to the meaning of the sentence, an appositive phrase is set off by commas. **(Jack plans to go to the jazz concert, an important musical event.)**

A gerund phrase includes a gerund plus its complements and modifiers. **(Playing the flute is her hobby.)**

An infinitive phrase contains the infinitive plus its complements and modifiers. **(It is time to leave for school.)**

A participial phrase contains a participle and any modifiers necessary to complete its meaning. **(The woman sitting over there is my grandmother.)**

A prepositional phrase consists of a preposition, its object, and any modifiers of the object. A prepositional phrase can function as an adjective, modifying a noun or a pronoun. **(The dog in the yard is very gentle.)** A prepositional phrase may also function as an adverb when it modifies a verb, an adverb, or an adjective. **(The baby slept on my lap.)**

A verb phrase consists of one or more auxiliary verbs followed by a main verb. **(The job will have been completed by noon tomorrow.)**

Positive degree. *See* Adjective.

Possessive noun. *See* Noun chart.

Predicate The verb or verb phrase and any objects, complements, or modifiers that express the essential thought about the subject of a sentence.

A simple predicate is a verb or verb phrase that tells something about the subject. **(We ran.)**

A complete predicate includes the simple predicate and any words that modify or complete it. **(We solved the problem in a short time.)**

A compound predicate has two or more verbs or verb phrases that are joined by a conjunction and share the same subject. **(We ran to the park and began to play baseball.)**

Predicate adjective. *See* Adjective; Complement.

Predicate nominative. *See* Complement.

Preposition A word that shows the relationship of a noun or pronoun to some other word in the sentence. Prepositions include about, above, across, among, as, behind, below, beyond, but, by, down, during, except, for, from, into, like, near, of, on, outside, over, since, through, to, under, until, with. **(I usually eat breakfast before school.)**

A compound preposition is made up of more than one word. **(according to, ahead of, as to, because of, by means of, in addition to, in spite of, on account of) (We played the game in spite of the snow.)**

Prepositional phrase. *See* Phrase.

Present tense. *See* Verb tense.

Progressive form. *See* Verb tense.

Pronoun A word that takes the place of a noun, a group of words acting as a noun, or another pronoun. The word or group of words that a pronoun refers to is called its antecedent. **(In the following sentence, Mari is the antecedent of she. Mari likes Mexican food, but she doesn't like Italian food.)**

A demonstrative pronoun points out specific persons, places, things, or ideas. **(this, that, these, those)**

An indefinite pronoun refers to persons, places, or things in a more general way than a noun does. **(all, another, any, both, each, either, enough, everything, few, many, most, much, neither, nobody, none, one, other, others, plenty, several, some)**

An intensive pronoun adds emphasis to another noun or pronoun. If an intensive pronoun is omitted, the meaning of the sentence will be the same. **(Rebecca herself decided to look for a part-time job.)**

An interrogative pronoun is used to form questions. **(who? whom? whose? what? which?)**

A personal pronoun refers to a specific person or thing. Personal pronouns have three cases: nominative, possessive, and objective. The case depends upon the function of the pronoun in a sentence. The first chart on this page shows the case forms of personal pronouns.

A reflexive pronoun reflects back to a noun or pronoun used earlier in the sentence, indicating that the same person or thing is involved. **(We told ourselves to be patient.)**

A relative pronoun is used to begin a subordinate clause. **(who, whose, that, what, whom, whoever, whomever, whichever, whatever)**

Proper adjective. *See* Adjective.

Proper noun. *See* Noun chart.

R

Reflexive pronoun. *See* Pronoun.

Relative pronoun. *See* Pronoun.

S

Sentence A group of words expressing a complete thought. Every sentence has a subject and a predicate. Sentences can be classified by function or by structure. The second chart on this page shows the categories by function; the following subentries describe the categories by structure. See also Subject; Predicate; Clause.

Personal Pronouns

Case	Singular Pronouns	Plural Pronouns	Function in Sentence
Nominative	I, you, she, he, it	we, you, they	subject or predicate nominative
Objective	me, you, her, him, it	us, you, them	direct object, indirect object, or object of a preposition
Possessive	my, mine, your, yours, her, hers, his, its	our, ours, your, yours, their, theirs	replacement for the possessive form of a noun

Types of Sentences

Sentence Type	Function	Ends with ...	Examples
Declarative sentence	Makes a statement	A period	I did not enjoy the movie.
Exclamatory sentence	Expresses strong emotion	An exclamation point	The books are already finished!
Imperative sentence	Expresses a request or a demand	A period or an exclamation point	Please come to the party. Stop!
Interrogative sentence	Asks a question	A question mark	Is the composition due today?

A simple sentence has only one main clause and no subordinate clauses. **(Alan found an old violin.)** A simple sentence may contain a compound subject or a compound predicate or both. **(Alan and Teri found an old violin. Alan found an old violin and tried to play it. Alan and Teri found an old violin and tried to play it.)** The subject and the predicate can be expanded with adjectives, adverbs, prepositional phrases, appositives, and verbal phrases. As long as the sentence has only one main clause, however, it remains a simple sentence. **(Alan, rummaging in the attic, found an old violin.)**

A compound sentence has two or more main clauses. Each main clause has its own subject and predicate, and these main clauses are usually joined by a comma and a coordinating conjunction. **(Cats meow, and dogs bark, but ducks quack.)** Semicolons may also be used to join the main clauses in a compound sentence. **(The helicopter landed; the pilot had saved four passengers.)**

A complex sentence has one main clause and one or more subordinate clauses. **(Since the movie starts at eight, we should leave here by seven-thirty.)**

A compound-complex sentence has two or more main clauses and at least one subordinate clause.
(If we leave any later, we may miss the previews, and I want to see them.)

Simple predicate. *See* Predicate.

Simple subject. *See* Subject.

Subject The part of a sentence that tells what the sentence is about.

A simple subject is the main noun or pronoun in the subject. **(Babies crawl.)**

A complete subject includes the simple subject and any words that modify it. (The man from New Jersey won the race.) In some sentences, the simple subject and the complete subject are the same. **(Birds fly.)**

A compound subject has two or more simple subjects joined by a conjunction. The subjects share the same verb. **(Firefighters and police officers protect the community.)**

Subjunctive mood. *See* Mood of verb.

Subordinate clause. *See* Clause.

Subordinating conjunction. *See* Conjunction.

Superlative degree. *See* Adjective; Adverb.

T

Tense. *See* Verb tense.

Transitive verb. *See* Verb.

V

Verb A word that expresses action or a state of being. **(cooks, seem, laughed)**

An action verb tells what someone or something does. Action verbs can express either physical or mental action. **(Crystal decided to change the tire herself.)**

A transitive verb is an action verb that is followed by a word or words that answer the question What? or Whom? **(I held the baby.)**

An intransitive verb is an action verb that is not followed by a word that answers the question What? or Whom? **(The baby laughed.)**

A linking verb expresses a state of being by linking the subject of a sentence with a word or an expression that identifies or describes the subject. **(The lemonade tastes sweet. He is our new principal.)** The most commonly used linking verb is be in all its forms **(am, is, are, was, were, will be, been, being).** Other linking verbs include appear, become, feel, grow, look, remain, seem, sound, smell, stay, taste.

An auxiliary verb, or helping verb, is a verb that accompanies the main verb to form a verb phrase. **(I have been swimming.)** The forms of be and have are the most common auxiliary verbs: **(am, is, are, was, were, being, been; has, have, had, having).** Other auxiliaries include can, could, do, does, did, may, might, must, shall, should, will, would.

Verbal A verb form that functions in a sentence as a noun, an adjective, or an adverb. The three kinds of verbals are gerunds, infinitives, and participles. See Gerund; Infinitive; Participle.

Verb tense The tense of a verb indicates when the action or state of being occurs. All the verb tenses are formed from the four principal parts of a verb: a base form **(talk)**, a present participle **(talking)**, a simple past form **(talked)**, and a past participle **(talked)**. A regular verb forms its simple past and past participle by adding -ed to the base form. **(climb, climbed)** An irregular verb forms its past and past participle in some other way. **(get, got, gotten)**

In addition to present, past, and future tenses, there are three perfect tenses.

The present perfect tense expresses an action or condition that occurred at some indefinite time in the past. This tense also shows an action or condition that began in the past and continues into the present. **(She has played the piano for four years.)**

The past perfect tense indicates that one past action or condition began and ended before another past action started. **(Andy had finished his homework before I even began mine.)**

The future perfect tense indicates that one future action or condition will begin and end before another future event starts. Use will have or shall have with the past participle of a verb. **(By tomorrow, I will have finished my homework, too.)**

The progressive form of a verb expresses a continuing action with any of the six tenses. To make the progressive forms, use the appropriate tense of the verb be with the present participle of the main verb. **(She is swimming. She has been swimming.)**

The emphatic form adds special force, or emphasis, to the present and past tense of a verb. For the emphatic form, use do, does, or did with the base form. **(Toshi did want that camera.)**

Voice The voice of a verb shows whether the subject performs the action or receives the action of the verb.

A verb is in the active voice if the subject of the sentence performs the action. **(The referee blew the whistle.)**

A verb is in the passive voice if the subject of the sentence receives the action of the verb. **(The whistle was blown by the referee.)**

Troubleshooter

Use the Troubleshooter to recognize and correct common writing errors.

Sentence Fragment

A sentence fragment does not express a complete thought. It may lack a subject or verb or both.

Problem: Fragment that lacks a subject

The lion paced the floor of the cage. Looked hungry. frag

Solution: Add a subject to the fragment to make a complete sentence.

The lion paced the floor of the cage. He looked hungry.

Problem: Fragment that lacks a predicate

I'm painting my room. The walls yellow. frag

Solution: Add a predicate to make the sentence complete.

I'm painting my room. The walls are going to be yellow.

Problem: Fragment that lacks both a subject and a predicate

We walked around the reservoir. Near the parkway. frag

Solution: Combine the fragment with another sentence.

We walked around the reservoir near the parkway.

Tip: When subject and verb are separated by a prepositional phrase, check for agreement by reading the sentence without the prepositional phrase.

Run-on Sentence

A run-on sentence is two or more sentences written incorrectly as one sentence.

Problem: Two main clauses separated only by a comma

Roller coasters make me dizzy, I don't enjoy them. run-on

Solution A: Replace the comma with a period or other end mark. Start the second sentence with a capital letter.

Roller coasters make me dizzy. I don't enjoy them.

Solution B: Replace the comma with a semicolon.

Roller coasters make me dizzy; I don't enjoy them.

Problem: Two main clauses with no punctuation between them

Acid rain is a worldwide problem there are no solutions in sight. run-on

Solution A: Separate the main clauses with a period or other end mark. Begin the second sentence with a capital letter.

Acid rain is a worldwide problem. There are no solutions in sight.

Solution B: Add a comma and a coordinating conjunction between the main clauses.

Acid rain is a worldwide problem, but there are no solutions in sight.

Problem: Two main clauses with no comma before the coordinating conjunction

Our chorus has been practicing all month but we still need another rehearsal. run-on

Solution: Add a comma before the coordinating conjunction.

Our chorus has been practicing all month, but we still need another rehearsal.

Lack of Subject-Verb Agreement

A singular subject calls for a singular form of the verb. A plural subject calls for a plural form of the verb.

Problem: A subject that is separated from the verb by an intervening prepositional phrase

The two policemen at the construction site looks bored. agr

The members of my baby-sitting club is saving money. agr

Solution: Make sure that the verb agrees with the subject of the sentence, not with the object of the preposition. The object of a preposition is never the subject.

The two policemen at the construction site look bored.

The members of my baby-sitting club are saving money.

Tip: When subject and verb are separated by a prepositional phrase, check for agreement by reading the sentence without the prepositional phrase.

Problem: A sentence that begins with **here** or **there**

Here come the last bus to Pelham Heights. agr

There is my aunt and uncle. agr

Solution: In sentences that begin with *here* or *there,* look for the subject after the verb. Make sure that the verb agrees with the subject.

Here comes the last bus to Pelham Heights.

There are my aunt and uncle.

Problem: An indefinite pronoun as the subject

Each of the candidates are qualified. agr

All of the problems on the test was hard. agr

Solution: Some indefinite pronouns are singular; some are plural; and some can be either singular or plural, depending on the noun they refer to. Determine whether the indefinite pronoun is singular or plural, and make sure the verb agrees with it.

Each of the candidates is qualified.

All of the problems on the test were hard.

Problem: A compound subject that is joined by **and**

Fishing tackle and a life jacket was stowed in the boat. agr

Peanut butter and jelly are delicious. agr

Solution A: If the compound subjects refer to different people or things, use a plural verb.

Fishing tackle and a life jacket were stowed in the boat.

Solution B: If the parts of a compound subject name one unit or if they refer to the same person or thing, use a singular verb.

Peanut butter and jelly is delicious.

Problem: A compound subject that is joined by **or** or **nor**

Either my aunt or my parents plans to attend parents' night. agr

Neither onions nor pepper improve the taste of this meatloaf. agr

Solution: Make the verb agree with the subject that is closer to it.

Either my aunt or my parents plan to attend parents' night.

Neither onions nor pepper improves the taste of this meatloaf.

Incorrect Verb Tense or Form

Verbs have different tenses to show when the action takes place.

Problem: An incorrect or missing verb ending

The Parks Department install a new water fountain last week. tense

They have also plant flowers in all the flower beds. tense

Solution: To form the past tense and the past participle, add -ed to a regular verb.

The Parks Department installed a new water fountain last week.

They have also planted flowers in all the flower beds.

Problem: An improperly formed irregular verb

Wendell has standed in line for two hours. tense

I catched the fly ball and throwed it to first base. tense

Solution: Irregular verbs vary in their past and past participle forms. Look up the ones you are not sure of.

Wendell has stood in line for two hours.

I caught the fly ball and threw it to first base.

Problem: Confusion between the past form and the past participle

The cast for The Music Man has began rehearsals. tense

Solution: Use the past participle form of an irregular verb, not its past form, when you use the auxiliary verb *have*.

The cast for The Music Man has begun rehearsals.

Problem: Improper use of the past participle

Our seventh grade drawn a mural for the wall of the cafeteria. tense

Solution: Add the auxiliary verb have to the past participle of an irregular verb to form a complete verb.

Our seventh grade has drawn a mural for the wall of the cafeteria.

Tip: Because irregular verbs vary, it is useful to memorize the verbs that you use most often.

Incorrect Use of Pronouns

The noun that a pronoun refers to is called its antecedent. A pronoun must refer to its **antecedent** clearly. Subject pronouns refer to subjects in a sentence. Object pronouns refer to objects in a sentence.

Problem: A pronoun that could refer to more than one antecedent

Gary and Mike are coming, but he doesn't know the other kids. ant

Solution: Substitute a noun for the pronoun to make your sentence clearer.

Gary and Mike are coming, but Gary doesn't know the other kids.

Problem: Object pronouns as subjects

Him and John were freezing after skating for three hours. pro

Lori and me decided not to audition for the musical. pro

Solution: Use a subject pronoun as the subject part of a sentence.

He and John were freezing after skating for three hours.

Lori and I decided not to audition for the musical.

Problem: Subject pronouns as objects

Ms. Wang asked Reggie and I to enter the science fair. pro

Ms. Wang helped he and I with the project. pro

Solution: Use an object pronoun as the object of a verb or a preposition.

Ms. Wang asked Reggie and me to enter the science fair.

Ms. Wang helped him and me with the project.

Incorrect Use of Adjectives

Some adjectives have irregular forms: comparative forms for comparing two things and superlative forms for comparing more than two things.

Problem: Incorrect use of good, better, best

Their team is more good at softball than ours. adj

They have more better equipment too. adj

Solution: The comparative and superlative forms of good are better and best. Do not use more or most before irregular forms of comparative and superlative adjectives.

Their team is better at softball than ours.

They have better equipment too.

Problem: Incorrect use of bad, worse, worst

The flooding on East Street was the baddest I've seen. adj

Mike's basement was in badder shape than his garage. adj

Solution: The comparative and superlative forms of bad are worse and worst. Do not use more or most or the endings -er or -est with bad.

The flooding on East Street was the worst I've seen.

Mike's basement was in worse shape than his garage.

Problem: Incorrect use of comparative and superlative adjectives

The Appalachian Mountains are more older than the Rockies. adj

Mount Washington is the most highest of the Appalachians. adj

Solution: Do not use both -er and more or -est and most at the same time.

The Appalachian Mountains are older than the Rockies.

Mount Washington is the highest of the Appalachians.

Incorrect Use of Commas

Commas signal a pause between parts of a sentence and help to clarify meaning.

Problem: Missing commas in a series of three or more items

Sergio put mustard catsup and bean sprouts on his hot dog. com

Solution: If there are three or more items in a series, use a comma after each one, including the item preceding the conjunction.

Sergio put mustard, catsup, and bean sprouts on his hot dog.

Problem: Missing commas with direct quotations

"A little cold water" the swim coach said "won't hurt you." com

Solution: The first part of an interrupted quotation ends with a comma followed by quotation marks. The interrupting words are also followed by a comma.

"A little cold water," the swim coach said, "won't hurt you."

Problem: Missing commas with nonessential appositives

My sneakers a new pair are covered with mud. com

Solution: Determine whether the appositive is important to the meaning of the sentence. If it is not essential, set off the appositive with commas.

My sneakers, a new pair, are covered with mud.

Incorrect Use of Apostrophes

An apostrophe shows possession. It can also indicate missing letters in a contraction.

Problem: Singular possessive nouns

A parrots toes are used for gripping. poss

The bus color was bright yellow. poss

Solution: Use an apostrophe and an *s* to form the possessive of a singular noun, even one that ends in *s*.

A parrot's toes are used for gripping.

The bus's color was bright yellow.

Problem: Plural possessive nouns ending in -*s*

The visitors center closes at five o'clock. poss

The guide put several tourists luggage in one compartment. poss

Solution: Use an apostrophe alone to form the possessive of a plural noun that ends in s.

The visitors' center closes at five o'clock.

The guide put several tourists' luggage in one compartment.

Problem: Plural possessive nouns not ending in -s

The peoples applause gave courage to the young gymnast. poss

Solution: Use an apostrophe and an s to form the possessive of a plural noun that does not end in s.

The people's applause gave courage to the young gymnast.

Problem: Possessive personal pronouns

Jenny found the locker that was her's; she waited while her friends found their's. poss

Solution: Do not use apostrophes with possessive personal pronouns.

Jenny found the locker that was hers; she waited while her friends found theirs.

Incorrect Capitalization

Proper nouns, proper adjectives, and the first words of sentences always begin with a capital letter.

Problem: Words referring to ethnic groups, nationalities, and languages

Many canadians in the province of quebec speak french. cap

Solution: Capitalize proper nouns and adjectives that refer to ethnic groups, nationalities, and languages.

Many Canadians in the province of Quebec speak French.

Problem: Words that refer to a family member

Yesterday aunt Doreen asked me to baby-sit. cap

Don't forget to give dad a call. cap

Solution: Capitalize words that are used as part of or in place of a family member's name.

Yesterday Aunt Doreen asked me to baby-sit.

Don't forget to give Dad a call.

Tip: Do not capitalize a word that identifies a family member when it is preceded by a possessive adjective: My father bought a new car.

Problem: The first word of a direct quotation

The judge declared, "the court is now in session." cap

Solution: Capitalize the first word in a direct quotation.

The judge declared, "The court is now in session."

Tip: If you have difficulty with a rule of usage, try rewriting the rule in your own words. Check with your teacher to be sure you understand the rule.

Troublesome Words

This section will help you choose between words and expressions that are often confusing or misused.

accept, except

Accept means "to receive." *Except* means "other than."

Phillip walked proudly to the stage to accept the award.

Everything fits in my suitcase except my sleeping bag.

affect, effect

Affect is a verb meaning "to cause a change in" or "to influence." *Effect* as a verb means "to bring about or accomplish." As a noun, *effect* means "result."

Bad weather will affect our plans for the weekend.

The new medicine effected an improvement in the patient's condition.

The gloomy weather had a bad effect on my mood.

ain't

Ain't is never used in formal speaking or writing unless you are quoting the exact words of a character or a real person. Instead of using *ain't*, say or write *am not, is not, are not*; or use contractions such as *I'm not, she isn't*.

The pizza is not going to arrive for another half hour.

The pizza isn't going to arrive for another half hour.

a lot

The expression *a lot* means "much" or "many" and should always be written as two words. Some authorities discourage its use in formal writing.

A lot of my friends are learning Spanish.

Many of my friends are learning Spanish.

all ready, already

All ready, written as two words, is a phrase that means "completely ready." *Already,* written as one word, is an adverb that means "before" or "by this time."

By the time the fireworks display was all ready, we had already arrived.

all right, alright

The expression *all right* should be written as two words. Some dictionaries do list the single word *alright* but usually not as a preferred spelling.

Tom hurt his ankle, but he will be all right.

all together, altogether

All together means "in a group." *Altogether* means "completely."

The Minutemen stood all together at the end of Lexington Green.

The rebel farmers were not altogether sure that they could fight the British soldiers.

among, between

Use *among* for three or more people, things, or groups. Use *between* for two people, things, or groups.

Mr. Kendall divided the jobs for the car wash among the team members.

Our soccer field lies between the gym and Main Street.

amount, number

Use *amount* with nouns that cannot be counted. Use *number* with nouns that can be counted.

This recipe calls for an unusual amount of pepper.

A record number of students attended last Saturday's book fair.

bad, badly

Bad is an adjective; it modifies a noun. *Badly* is an adverb; it modifies a verb, an adjective, or another adverb.

The badly burnt cookies left a bad smell in the kitchen.

Joseph badly wants to be on the track team.

beside, besides

Beside means "next to." *Besides* means "in addition to."

The zebra is grazing beside a wildebeest.

Besides the zoo, I like to visit the aquarium.

bring, take

Bring means "to carry from a distant place to a closer one." *Take* means "to carry from a nearby place to a more distant one."

Please bring a bag lunch and subway money to school tomorrow.

Don't forget to take your art projects home this afternoon.

can, may

Can implies the ability to do something. *May* implies permission to do something.

You may take a later bus home if you can remember which bus to get on.

Tip: Although *can* is sometimes used in place of *may* in informal speech, a distinction should be made when speaking and writing formally.

choose, chose

Choose means "to select." *Chose*, the past tense of *choose*, means "selected."

Dad helped me choose a birthday card for my grandmother.

Dad chose a card with a funny joke inside.

doesn't, don't

The subject of the contraction *doesn't* (*does not*) is the third-person singular (*he* or *she*). The subject of the contraction *don't* (*do not*) is I, *you, we,* or *they.*

Tanya doesn't have any tickets for the concert.

We don't need tickets if we stand in the back row.

farther, further

Farther refers to physical distance. *Further* refers to time or degree.

Our new apartment is farther away from the school.

I will not continue this argument further.

fewer, less

Fewer is used to refer to things or qualities that can be counted. *Less* is used to refer to things or qualities that cannot be counted. In addition, *less* is used with figures that are regarded as single amounts.

Fewer people were waiting in line after lunch.

There is less fat in this kind of peanut butter.

Try to spend less than ten dollars on a present. [The money is treated as a single sum, not as individual dollars.]

good, well

Good is often used as an adjective meaning "pleasing" or "able." *Well* may be used as an adverb of manner telling how ably something is done or as an adjective meaning "in good health."

That is a good haircut.

Marco writes well.

Because Ms. Rodriguez had a headache, she was not well enough to correct our tests.

in, into

In means "inside." *Into* indicates a movement from outside toward the inside.

Refreshments will be sold in the lobby of the auditorium.

The doors opened, and the eager crowd rushed into the auditorium.

it's, its

Use an apostrophe to form the contraction of *it is*. The possessive of the personal pronoun *it* does not take an apostrophe.

It's hard to keep up with computer technology.

The computer industry seems to change its products daily.

lay, lie

Lay means "to place." *Lie* means "to recline."

I will lay my beach towel here on the warm sand.

Help! I don't want to lie next to a hill of red ants!

learn, teach

Learn means "to gain knowledge." *Teach* means "to give knowledge."

I don't learn very quickly.

My uncle is teaching me how to juggle.

leave, let

Leave means "to go away." *Let* means "to allow." With the word *alone,* you may use either *let* or *leave.*

Huang has to leave at eight o'clock.

Mr. Davio lets the band practice in his basement.

Leave me alone. Let me alone.

like, as

Use *like*, a preposition, to introduce a phrase of comparison. Use *as*, a subordinating conjunction, to introduce a subordinate clause. Many authorities believe that *like* should not be used before a clause in formal English.

Andy sometimes acts like a clown.

The detective looked carefully at the empty suitcase as she examined the room.

Tip: *As* can be a preposition in cases like the following: *Jack went to the costume party as a giant pumpkin.*

loose, lose

Loose means "not firmly attached." *Lose* means "to misplace" or "to fail to win."

If you keep wiggling that loose tooth, you might lose it.

raise, rise

Raise means to "cause to move up." *Rise* means "to move upward."

Farmers in this part of Florida raise sugarcane.

The hot air balloon began to rise slowly in the morning sky.

set, sit

Set means "to place" or "to put." *Sit* means "to place oneself in a seated position."

I set the tips of my running shoes against the starting line.

After running the fifty-yard dash, I had to sit down and catch my breath.

than, then

Than introduces the second part of a comparison. *Then* means "at that time" or "after that."

I'd rather go to Disney World in the winter than in the summer.

The park is too crowded and hot then.

their, they're

Their is the possessive form of *they*. *They're* is the contraction of *they are*.

They're visiting Plymouth Plantation during their vacation.

to, too, two

To means "in the direction of." *Too* means "also" or "to an excessive degree." *Two* is the number after one.

I bought two tickets to the concert.

The music was too loud.

It's my favorite group too.

who, whom

Who is a subject pronoun. *Whom* is an object pronoun.

Who has finished the test already?

Mr. Russo is the man to whom we owe our thanks.

who's, whose

Who's is the contraction of *who is*. *Whose* is the possessive form of *who*.

Who's going to wake me up in the morning?

The policeman discovered whose car alarm was making so much noise.

Mechanics

This section will help you use correct capitalization, punctuation, and abbreviations in your writing.

Capitalization

Capitalizing Sentences, Quotations, and Salutations

Rule: A capital letter appears at the beginning of a sentence.

Example: *Another gust of wind shook the house.*

Rule: A capital letter marks the beginning of a direct quotation that is a complete sentence.

Example: *Sabrina said, "The lights might go out."*

Rule: When a quoted sentence is interrupted by explanatory words, such as she said, do not begin the second part of the sentence with a capital letter.

Example: *"There's a rainbow," exclaimed Jeffrey, "over the whole beach."*

Rule: When the second part of a quotation is a new sentence, put a period after the explanatory words; begin the new part with a capital letter.

Example: *"Please come inside," Justin said. "Wipe your feet."*

Rule: Do not capitalize an indirect quotation.

Example: *Jo said that the storm was getting worse.*

Rule: Capitalize the first word in the salutation and closing of a letter. Capitalize the title and name of the person addressed.

Example: *Dear Dr. Menino*

Dear Editor

Sincerely

Capitalizing Names and Titles of People

Rule: Capitalize the names of people and the initials that stand for their names.

Example: *Malcolm X; J. F. K.; Robert E. Lee; Queen Elizabeth I*

Rule: Capitalize a title or an abbreviation of a title when it comes before a person's name or when it is used in direct address.

Example: *Dr. Salinas,* "Your patient, Doctor, is waiting."

Rule: Do not capitalize a title that follows or is a substitute for a person's name.

Example: *Marcia Salinas is a good doctor. He asked to speak to the doctor.*

Rule: Capitalize the names and abbreviations of academic degrees that follow a person's name. Capitalize Jr. and Sr.

Example: *Marcia Salinas, M.D.; Raoul Tobias, Attorney; Donald Bruns Sr.; Ann Lee, Ph.D.*

Rule: Capitalize words that show family relationships when used as titles or as substitutes for a person's name.

Example: *We saw Uncle Carlos.*

She read a book about Mother Teresa.

Rule: Do not capitalize words that show family relationships when they follow a possessive noun or pronoun.

Example: *Your brother will give us a ride.*

I forgot my mother's phone number.

Rule: Always capitalize the pronoun I.

Example: *After I clean my room, I'm going swimming.*

Capitalizing Names of Places

Tip: Do not capitalize articles and prepositions in proper nouns: *the Rock of Gibraltar, the Statue of Liberty.*

Rule: Capitalize the names of cities, counties, states, countries, and continents.

Example: *St. Louis, Missouri; Marin County; Australia; South America*

Rule: Capitalize the names of bodies of water and other geographical features.

Example: *the Great Lakes; Cape Cod; the Dust Bowl*

Rule: Capitalize the names of sections of a country and regions of the world.

Example: *East Asia; New England; the Pacific Rim; the Midwest*

Rule: Capitalize compass points when they refer to a specific section of a country.

Example: *the Northwest; the South*

Rule: Do not capitalize compass points when they indicate direction.

Example: *Canada is north of the United States.*

Rule: Do not capitalize adjectives indicating direction.

Example: *western Utah*

Rule: Capitalize the names of streets and highways.

Example: *Dorchester Avenue; Route 22*

Rule: Capitalize the names of buildings, bridges, monuments, and other structures.

Example: *Sears Tower; Chesapeake Bay Bridge*

Capitalizing Other Proper Nouns and Adjectives

Rule: Capitalize the names of clubs, organizations, businesses, institutions, and political parties.

Example: *Houston Oilers; the Food and Drug Administration; Boys and Girls Club*

Rule: Capitalize brand names but not the nouns following them.

Example: *Zippo brand energy bar*

Rule: Capitalize the names of days of the week, months, and holidays.

Example: *Saturday; June; Thanksgiving Day*

Rule: Do not capitalize the names of seasons.

Example: *winter; spring; summer; fall*

Rule: Capitalize the first word, the last word, and all important words in the title of a book, play, short story, poem, essay, article, film, television series, song, magazine, newspaper, and chapter of a book.

Example: *Not Without Laughter; World Book Encyclopedia; "Jingle Bells"; Star Wars; Chapter 12*

Rule: Capitalize the names of ethnic groups, nationalities, and languages.

Example: *Latino; Japanese; European; Spanish*

Rule: Capitalize proper adjectives that are formed from the names of ethnic groups and nationalities.

Example: *Shetland pony; Jewish holiday*

Punctuation

Rule: Use a period at the end of a declarative sentence.

My great-grandfather fought in the Mexican Revolution.

Rule: Use a period at the end of an imperative sentence that does not express strong feeling.

Please set the table.

Rule: Use a question mark at the end of an interrogative sentence.

How did your sneakers get so muddy?

Rule: Use an exclamation point at the end of an exclamatory sentence or a strong imperative.

How exciting the play was!
Watch out!

Using Commas

Rule: Use commas to separate three or more items in a series.

> **The canary eats bird seed, fruit, and suet.**

Rule: Use commas to show a pause after an introductory word and to set off names used in direct address.

> **Yes, I offered to take care of her canary this weekend.**

> **Please, Stella, can I borrow your nail polish?**

Rule: Use a comma after two or more introductory prepositional phrases or when the comma is needed to make the meaning clear. A comma is not needed after a single short prepositional phrase, but it is acceptable to use one.

> **From the back of the balcony, we had a lousy view of the stage.**

> **After the movie we walked home. (no comma needed)**

Rule: Use a comma after an introductory participle and an introductory participial phrase.

> **Whistling and moaning, the wind shook the little house.**

Rule: Use commas to set off words that interrupt the flow of thought in a sentence.

> **Tomorrow, I think, our projects are due.**

Rule: Use a comma after conjunctive adverbs such as however, moreover, furthermore, nevertheless, and therefore.

> **The skating rink is crowded on Saturday; however, it's the only time I can go.**

Rule: Use commas to set off an appositive if it is not essential to the meaning of a sentence.

> **Ben Wagner, a resident of Pittsfield, won the first round in the golf tournament.**

Rule: Use a comma before a conjunction (*and, or, but, nor, so, yet*) that joins main clauses.

> **We can buy our tickets now, or we can take a chance on buying them just before the show.**

Rule: Use a comma after an introductory adverb clause.

> **Because I stayed up so late, I'm sleepy this morning.**

Rule: In most cases, do not use a comma with an adverb clause that comes at the end of a sentence.

> **The picnic will be canceled unless the weather clears.**

Rule: Use a comma or a pair of commas to set off an adjective clause that is not essential to the meaning of a sentence.

> **Tracy, who just moved here from Florida, has never seen snow before.**

Rule: Do not use a comma or pair of commas to set off an essential clause from the rest of the sentence.

> **Anyone who signs up this month will get a discount.**

Rule: Use commas before and after the year when it is used with both the month and the day. If only the month and the year are given, do not use a comma.

> **On January 2, 1985, my parents moved to Dallas, Texas.**

> **I was born in May 1985.**

Rule: Use commas before and after the name of a state or a country when it is used with the name of a city. Do not use a comma after the state if it is used with a ZIP code.

> **The area code for Concord, New Hampshire, is 603.**

> **Please forward my mail to 6 Madison Lane, Topsham, ME 04086**

Rule: Use commas or a pair of commas to set off an abbreviated title or degree following a person's name.

> **The infirmary was founded by Elizabeth Blackwell, M.D., the first woman in the United States to earn a medical degree.**

Rule: Use a comma or commas to set off *too* when *too* means "also."

We, too, bought groceries, from the new online supermarket.

Rule: Use a comma or commas to set off a direct quotation.

"My nose," exclaimed Pinocchio, "is growing longer!"

Rule: Use a comma after the salutation of a friendly letter and after the closing of both a friendly letter and a business letter.

Dear Gary,
Sincerely,
Best regards,

Rule: Use a comma when necessary to prevent misreading of a sentence.

In math, solutions always elude me.

Using Semicolons and Colons

Rule: Use a semicolon to join the parts of a compound sentence when a coordinating conjunction, such as *and, or, nor,* or *but,* is not used.

Don't be late for the dress rehearsal; it begins at 7 o'clock sharp.

Rule: Use a semicolon to join parts of a compound sentence when the main clauses are long and are subdivided by commas. Use a semicolon even if these clauses are already joined by a coordinating conjunction.

In the gray light of early morning, on a remote airstrip in the desert, two pilots prepared to fly on a dangerous mission; but accompanying them were a television camera crew, three newspaper reporters, and a congressman from their home state of Nebraska.

Rule: Use a semicolon to separate main clauses joined by a conjunctive adverb. Be sure to use a comma after the conjunctive adverb.

We've been climbing all morning; therefore, we need a rest.

Rule: Use a colon to introduce a list of items that ends a sentence. Use words such as *these, the following,* or *as follows* to signal that a list is coming.

Remember to bring the following items: a backpack, a bag lunch, sunscreen, and insect repellent.

Rule: Do not use a colon to introduce a list preceded by a verb or preposition.

Remember to bring a backpack, a bag lunch, sunscreen, and insect repellent. (No colon is used after bring.)

Rule: Use a colon to separate the hour and the minutes when you write the time of day.

My Spanish class starts at 9:15.

Rule: Use a colon after the salutation of a business letter.

Dear Dr. Coulombe:
Director of the Personnel Dept.:

Using Quotation Marks and Italics

Rule: Use quotation marks before and after a direct quotation.

"Curiouser and curiouser," said Alice.

Rule: Use quotation marks with both parts of a divided quotation.

"This gymnastics trick," explained Amanda, "took me three months to learn."

Rule: Use a comma or commas to separate a phrase such as *she said* from the quotation itself. Place the comma that precedes the phrase inside the closing quotation marks.

"I will be late," said the cable technician, "for my appointment."

Rule: Place a period that ends a quotation inside the closing quotation marks.

Scott said, "Thanks for letting me borrow your camping tent."

Rule: Place a question mark or an exclamation point inside the quotation marks when it is part of the quotation.

"Why is the door of your snake's cage open?" asked my mother.

Rule: Place a question mark or an exclamation point outside the quotation marks when it is part of the entire sentence.

How I love "The Pit and the Pendulum"!

Rule: Use quotation marks for the title of a short story, essay, poem, song, magazine or newspaper article, or book chapter.

short story: "The Necklace"
poem: "The Fish"
article: "Fifty Things to Make from Bottlecaps"

Rule: Use italics or underlining for the title of a book, play, film, television series, magazine, newspaper, or work of art.

book: *To Kill a Mockingbird*
magazine: *The New Republic*
painting: *Sunflowers*

Rule: Use italics or underlining for the names of ships, trains, airplanes, and spacecraft.

ship: *Mayflower*
airplane: *Air Force One*

Using Apostrophes

Rule: Use an apostrophe and an s ('s) to form the possessive of a singular noun.

my brother's rock collection
Chris's hat

Rule: Use an apostrophe and an s ('s) to form the possessive of a plural noun that does not end in s.

the geese's feathers
the oxen's domestication

Tip: If a thing is owned jointly by two or more individuals, only the last name should show possession: *Mom and Dad's car.* If the ownership is not joint, each name should show possession: *Mom's and Dad's parents are coming for Thanksgiving.*

Rule: Use an apostrophe alone to form the possessive of a plural noun that ends in s.

the animals' habitat
the instruments' sound

Rule: Use an apostrophe and an s ('s) to form the possessive of an indefinite pronoun.

everyone's homework
someone's homework

Rule: Do not use an apostrophe in a possessive pronoun.

The dog knocked over its dish.
Yours is the best entry in the contest.
One of these drawings must be hers.

Rule: Use an apostrophe to replace letters that have been omitted in a contraction.

it + is = it's
can + not = can't
I + have = I've

Rule: Use an apostrophe to form the plural of a letter, a figure, or a word that is used as itself.

Write three 7's.
The word is spelled with two m's.
The sentence contains three and's.

Rule: Use an apostrophe to show missing numbers in a year.

the class of '02

Using Hyphens, Dashes, and Parentheses

Rule: Use a hyphen to show the division of a word at the end of a line. Always divide the word between its syllables.

With the new recycling program, more residents are recycling their trash.

Tip: One-letter divisions (for example, *e-lectric*) are not permissible. Avoid dividing personal names, if possible.

Rule: Use a hyphen in a number written as a compound word.

He sold forty-six ice creams in one hour.

Rule: Use a hyphen in a fraction.

> **We won the vote by a two-thirds majority.**
> **Two-thirds of the votes have been counted.**

Rule: Use a hyphen or hyphens in certain compound nouns.

> **great-grandmother**
> **merry-go-round**

Rule: Hyphenate a compound modifier only when it precedes the word it modifies.

> **A well-known musician visited our school.**
> **The story was well written.**

Rule: Use a hyphen after the prefixes *all-, ex-,* and *self-* when they are joined to any noun or adjective.

> **all-star**
> **ex-president**
> **self-conscious**

Rule: Use a hyphen to separate any prefix from a word that begins with a capital letter.

> **un-American**
>
> **mid-January**

Rule: Use a dash or dashes to show a sudden break or change in thought or speech.

> **Daniel—he's kind of a pest—is my youngest cousin.**

Rule: Use parentheses to set off words that define or helpfully explain a word in the sentence.

> **The transverse flute (transverse means "sideways") is a wind instrument.**

Abbreviations

Rule: Abbreviate the titles *Mr., Mrs., Ms.,* and *Dr.* before a person's name. Also abbreviate any professional or academic degree that follows a name. The titles *Jr.* and *Sr.* are not preceded by a comma.

> **Dr. Stanley Livingston (doctor)**
> **Luisa Mendez, M.A. (Master of Arts)**
> **Martin Luther King Jr.**

Rule: Use capital letters and no periods with abbreviations that are pronounced letter by letter or as words. Exceptions are *U.S.* and *Washington, D.C.,* which do use periods.

NAACP	**National Association for the Advancement of Colored People**
UFO	**unidentified flying object**
MADD	**Mothers Against Drunk Driving**

Rule: With exact times use A.M. (*ante meridiem,* "before noon") and P.M. (*post meridiem,* "after noon"). For years use B.C. (before Christ) and, sometimes, A.D. (*anno Domini,* "in the year of the Lord," after Christ).

> **8:15 A.M.**   **6:55 P.M.**
>
> **5000 B.C.**   **A.D. 235**

Rule: Abbreviate days and months only in charts and lists.

> **School will be closed on**
> **Mon., Sept. 3**
> **Wed., Nov. 11**
> **Thurs., Nov. 27**

Rule: In scientific writing abbreviate units of measure. Use periods with English units but not with metric units.

> **inch(es) in.**   **yard(s) yd.**
>
> **meter(s) m**   **milliliter(s) ml**

Rule: On envelopes only, abbreviate street names and state names. In general text, spell out street names and state names.

> **Ms. Karen Holmes**
> **347 Grandville St.**
> **Tilton, NH 03276**
>
> **Karen lives on Grandville Street in Tilton, New Hampshire.**

Writing Numbers

Rule: In charts and tables, always write numbers as numerals. Other rules apply to numbers not in charts or tables.

Student Test Scores

Student	Test 1	Test 2	Test 3
Lai, W.	82	89	94
Ostos, A.	78	90	86

Rule: Spell out a number that is expressed in one or two words.

We carried enough supplies for twenty-three days.

Rule: Use a numeral for a number of more than two words.

The tallest mountain in Mexico rises 17,520 feet.

Rule: Spell out a number that begins a sentence, or reword the sentence so that it does not begin with a number.

One hundred forty-three days later the baby elephant was born.

The baby elephant was born 143 days later.

Rule: Write a very large number as a numeral followed by the word *million* or *billion.*

There are 15 million people living in or near Mexico City.

Rule: Related numbers should be written in the same way. If one number must be written as a numeral, use numerals for all the numbers.

There are 365 days in the year, but only 52 weekends.

Rule: Spell out an ordinal number (first, second).

Welcome to our fifteenth annual convention.

Rule: Use words to express the time of day unless you are writing the exact time or using the abbreviation A.M. or P.M.

My guitar lesson is at five o'clock. It ends by 5:45 P.M.

Rule: Use numerals to express dates, house and street numbers, apartment and room numbers, telephone numbers, page numbers, amounts of money of more than two words, and percentages. Write out the word *percent.*

August 5, 1999

9 Davio Dr.

Apartment 9F

24 percent

Spelling

The following rules, examples, and exceptions can help you master the spelling of many words.

Spelling *ie* and *ei*

Put *i* before *e* except when both letters follow *c* or when both letters are pronounced together as an *a* sound.

believe	sieve	weight
receive	relieve	neighborhood

It is helpful to memorize exceptions to this rule. Exceptions include the following words: *species, science, weird, either, seize, leisure,* and *protein.*

Spelling unstressed vowels

Notice the vowel sound in the second syllable of the word *won-d_r-ful.* This is the unstressed vowel sound; dictionary respellings use the schwa symbol (ə) to indicate it. Because any of several vowels can be used to spell this sound, you might find yourself uncertain about which vowel to use. To spell words with unstressed vowels, try thinking of a related word in which the syllable containing the vowel sound is stressed.

Unknown Spelling	Related Word	Word Spelled Correctly
wond_rful	wonder	wonderful
fort_fications	fortify	fortifications
res_dent	reside	resident

Suffixes and the silent *e*

For most words with silent *e*, keep the *e* when adding a suffix. When you add the suffix *-ly* to a word that ends in *l* plus silent *e*, drop the *-le*. Also drop the silent *e* when you add a suffix beginning with a vowel or a *y*.

wise + ly = wisely

peaceful + ly = peacefully

skate + ing = skating

gentle + ly = gently

There are exceptions to the rule, including the following:

awe + ful = awful

judge + ment = judgment

true + ly = truly

noise + y = noisy

dye + ing = dyeing

mile + age = mileage

Suffixes and the final *y*

When you are adding a suffix to words ending with a vowel + *y*, keep the *y*. For words ending with a consonant + *y*, change the *y* to *i* unless the suffix begins with *i*. To avoid having two *i*'s together, keep the *y*.

enjoy + ment = enjoyment

merry + ment = merriment

display + ed = displayed

lazy + ness = laziness

play + ful = playful

worry + ing = worrying

Note: For some words, there are alternate spellings:

sly + er = slyer or slier

shy + est = shyest or shiest

Adding prefixes

When you add a prefix to a word, do not change the spelling of the word.

un + done = undone

re + schedule = reschedule

il + legible = illegible

semi + sweet = semisweet

Doubling the final consonant

Double the final consonant when a word ends with a single consonant following one vowel and the word is one syllable, or when the last syllable of the word is accented both before and after adding the suffix.

sit + ing = sitting

rub + ing = rubbing

commit + ed = committed

confer + ed = conferred

Do not double the final consonant if the suffix begins with a consonant, if the accent is not on the last syllable, or if the accent moves when the suffix is added.

cancel + ing = canceling

commit + ment = commitment

travel + ed = traveled

defer + ence = deference

Do not double the final consonant if the word ends in two consonants or if the suffix begins with a consonant.

climb + er = climber

nervous + ness = nervousness

import + ance = importance

star + dom = stardom

When adding *-ly* to a word that ends in *ll*, drop one *l*.

hill + ly = hilly   **full + ly = fully**

Forming compound words

When forming compound words, keep the original spelling of both words.

home + work = homework

scare + crow = scarecrow

pea + nut = peanut

Forming Plurals

General Rules for Plurals		
If the noun ends in...	**Rule**	**Example**
s, ch, sh, x, or *z*	add *-es*	loss→losses, latch→latches, box→boxes, bush→bushes, quiz→quizzes
a consonant + *y*	change *y* to *i* and add *-es*	ferry→ferries, baby→babies, worry→worries
a vowel + *y*	add *-s*	chimney→chimneys, monkey→monkeys, toy→toys
a vowel + *o*	add *-s*	cameo→cameos, radio→radios, rodeo→rodeos
a consonant + *o*	add *-es* but sometimes add *-s*	potato→potatoes, echo→echoes photo→photos, solo→solos
f or *ff*	add *-s* but sometimes change *f* to *v* and add *-es*	proof→proofs, bluff→bluffs sheaf→sheaves, thief→thieves, hoof→hooves
lf	change *f* to *v* and add *-es*	calf→calves, half→halves, loaf→loaves
fe	change *f* to *v* and add *-s*	knife→knives, life→lives

Special Rules for Plurals

Rule	Example
To form the plural of most proper names and one-word compound nouns, follow the general rules for plurals.	Jones→Joneses, Thomas→Thomases, Hatch→Hatches
To form the plural of hyphenated compound nouns or compound nouns of more than one word, make the most important word plural.	credit card→credit cards mother-in-law→mothers-in-law district attorney→district attorneys
Some nouns have irregular plural forms and do not follow any rules.	man→men, foot→feet, tooth→teeth
Some nouns have the same singular and plural forms	deer→deer, species→species, sheep→sheep

Speaking, Listening, and Viewing Handbook

A large part of the school day is spent either listening or speaking to others. By becoming a better listener and speaker, you will know more about what is expected of you, and understand more about your audience.

Speaking Effectively

- Speak slowly, clearly, and in a normal tone of voice. Raise your voice a bit, or use gestures to stress important points.

- Pause a few seconds after making an important point.

- Use words that help your audience picture what you're talking about. Visual aids such as pictures, graphs, charts, and maps can also help make your information clear.

- Stay in contact with your audience. Make sure your eyes move from person to person in the group you're addressing.

Speaking informally

Most oral communication is informal. When you speak casually with your friends, family, and neighbors, you use informal speech. Human relationships depend on this form of communication.

- Be courteous. Listen until the other person has finished speaking.

- Speak in a relaxed and spontaneous manner.

- Make eye contact with your listeners.

- Do not monopolize a conversation.

- When telling a story, show enthusiasm.

- When giving an announcement or directions, speak clearly and slowly. Check that your listeners understand the information.

Presenting an oral report

The steps in preparing an oral report are similar to the steps in the writing process. Complete each step carefully and you can be confident of presenting an effective oral report.

Steps in preparing an Oral Report	
Prewriting	• Determine your purpose and audience. • Decide on a topic and narrow it.
Drafting	• Make an outline. • Fill in the supporting details. • Write the report.
Revising and Editing	• Review your draft. • Check the organization of ideas and details. • Reword unclear statements.
Practicing	• Practice the report aloud in front of a family member. • Time the report. • Ask for and accept advice.
Presenting	• Relax in front of your audience. • Make eye contact with your audience. • Speak slowly and clearly.

Practice

Pretend that you have been invited to give an oral report to a group of fifth graders. Your report will tell them what to expect and how to adjust to new conditions when they enter middle school. As you plan your report, keep your purpose and your audience in mind. Include lively descriptions and examples to back up your suggestions and hold your audience's attention. As you practice giving your report, be sure to give attention to your body language as well as your vocal projection. Ask a partner to listen to your report to give you feedback on how to improve your performance. Do the same for your partner after listening to his or her report.

Listening Effectively

Listening to instructions in class

Some of the most important listening in the school day involves listening to instructions. Use the following tips to help you.

- First, make sure you understand what you are listening for. Are you receiving instructions for homework or for a test? What you listen for depends upon the type of instructions being given.

- Think about what you are hearing, and keep your eyes on the speaker. This will help you stay focused on the important points.

- Listen for keywords, or word clues. Examples of word clues are phrases such as above all, most important, or the three basic parts. These clues help you identify important points that you should remember.

- Take notes on what you hear. Write down only the most important parts of the instructions.

- If you don't understand something, ask questions. Then if you're still unsure about the instructions, repeat them aloud to your teacher to receive correction on any key points that you may have missed.

Interpreting nonverbal clues

Understanding nonverbal clues is part of effective listening. Nonverbal clues are everything you notice about a speaker except what the speaker says. As you listen, ask yourself these questions:

- Where and how is the speaker standing?

- Are some words spoken more loudly than others?

- Does the speaker make eye contact?

- Does he or she smile or look angry?

- What message is sent by the speaker's gestures and facial expression?

Practice

Work with a partner to practice listening to instructions. Each of you should find a set of directions for using a simple device–for example, a mechanical tool, a telephone answering machine, or a DVD player. Study the instructions carefully. If you can bring the device to class, ask your partner to try to use it by following your step-by-step instructions. If you cannot have the device in class, ask your partner to explain the directions back to you. Then change roles and listen as your partner gives you a set of directions.

Viewing Effectively

Critical viewing means thinking about what you see while watching a TV program, newscast, film, or video. It requires paying attention to what you hear and see and deciding whether information is true, false, or exaggerated. If the information seems to be true, try to determine whether it is based on a fact or an opinion.

Fact versus opinion

A fact is something that can be proved. An opinion is what someone believes is true. Opinions are based on feelings and experiences and cannot be proved.

Television commercials, political speeches, and even the evening news contain both facts and opinions. They use emotional words and actions to persuade the viewer to agree with a particular point of view. They may also use faulty reasoning, such as linking an effect with the wrong cause. Think through what is being said. The speaker may seem sincere, but do his or her reasons make sense? Are the reasons based on facts or on unfair generalizations?

Commercials contain both obvious and hidden messages. Just as you need to discover the author's purpose when you read a writer's words, you must be aware of the purpose of nonverbal attempts to persuade you. What does the message sender want, and how is the sender trying to influence you?

For example, a magazine or TV ad picturing a group of happy teenagers playing volleyball on a sunny beach expresses a positive feeling. The advertiser hopes viewers will transfer that positive feeling to the product being advertised—perhaps a soft drink or a brand of beachwear. This technique, called transfer, is one of several propaganda techniques regularly used by advertisers to influence consumers.

Following are a few other common techniques.

Testimonial—Famous and admired people recommend or praise a product, a policy, or a course of action even though they probably have no professional knowledge or expertise to back up their opinion.

Bandwagon—People are urged to follow the crowd ("get on the bandwagon") by buying a product, voting for a candidate, or whatever else the advertiser wants them to do.

Glittering generalities—The advertiser uses positive, good-sounding words (for example, *all-American* or *medically proven*) to impress people.

Practice

Think of a television commercial that you have seen often or watch a new one and take notes as you watch it. Then analyze the commercial.

- What is the purpose behind the ad?
- What is expressed in written or spoken words?
- What is expressed nonverbally (in music or sound effects as well as in pictures and actions)?
- What methods does the advertiser use to persuade viewers?
- What questions would you ask the advertiser if you could?
- How effective is the commercial? Why?

Working in Groups

Working in a group is an opportunity to learn from others. Whether you are planning a group project (such as a class trip) or solving a math problem, each person in a group brings specific strengths and interests to the task. When a task is large, such as planting a garden, a group provides the necessary energy and talent to get the job done.

Small groups vary in size according to the nature of the task. Three to five students is a good size for most small-group tasks. Your teacher may assign you to a group, or you may be asked to form your own group. Don't work with your best friend if you are likely to chat too much. Successful groups often have a mix of student abilities and interests.

Individual role assignments give everyone in a group something to do. One student, the group recorder, may take notes. Another may lead the discussion, and another report the results to the rest of the class.

Roles for a Small Group	
Reviewer	Reads or reviews the assignment and makes sure everyone understands it
Recorder 1 (of the process)	Takes notes on the discussion
Recorder 2 (of the results)	Takes notes on the final results
Reporter	Reports results to the rest of the class
Discussion leader	Asks questions to get the discussion going; keeps the group focused
Facilitator	Helps the group resolve disagreements and reach a compromise

For a small group of three or four students, some of these roles can be combined. Your teacher may assign a role to each student in your group. Or you may be asked to choose your own role.

Tips for working in groups

- Review the group assignment and goal. Be sure that everyone in the group understands the assignment.

- Review the amount of time allotted for the task. Decide how your group will organize its time.

- Check that all the group members understand their roles in the group.

- When a question arises, try to solve it as a group before asking a teacher for help.

- Listen to other points of view. Be respectful as you point out mistakes a speaker might have made.

- When it is your turn to talk, address the subject and help the project move forward by building on the ideas of the previous speaker.

Glossary/Glosario

This glossary lists the vocabulary words found in the selections in this book. The definition given is for the word as it is used in the selection; you may wish to consult a dictionary for other meanings of these words. The key below is a guide to the pronunciation symbols used in each entry.

Pronunciation Key					
a	at	**ō**	hope	**ng**	sing
ā	ape	**ô**	fork, all	**th**	thin
ä	father	**oo**	wood, put	**th**	this
e	end	**ōō**	fool	**zh**	treasure
ē	me	**oi**	oil	**ə**	ago, taken, pencil,
i	it	**ou**	out		lemon, circus
ī	ice	**u**	up	**′**	primary stress
o	hot	**ū**	use	**′**	secondary stress

English

A

accusations (ak′ yə zā′ shəns) *n.* statements that suggest someone has done wrong; **p. 807**

arid (ar′ id) *adj.* extremely dry; **p. 688**

aromas (ə rō′ məz) *n.* pleasing smells or scents; **p. 513**

assurance (ə shoor′ əns) *n.* a guarantee, or certainty; **p. 539**

avidly (av′ id lē) *adv.* eagerly; enthusiastically; **p. 724**

B

balmy (bä′ mē) *adj.* mild; soothing; **p. 653**

banished (ban′ ishd) *v.* forced to leave a country or community; **p. 10**

barbarians (bär bār′ ē əns) *n.* people from a culture that others see as uncivilized; **p. 777**

bartered (bär′ tərd) *v.* traded without using money; **p. 693**

Español

A

accusations/acusaciones *n.* aserciones que sugieren que alguien ha hecho mal; **p. 807**

arid/árido *adj.* extremadamente seco; **p. 688**

aromas/aromas *n.* olores agradables; **p. 513**

assurance/seguridad *n.* garantía o certidumbre; **p. 539**

avidly/ávidamente *adv.* con ganas o entusiasmo; **p. 724**

B

balmy/balsámico *adj.* suave; relajante; **p. 653**

banished/desterrado *v.* obligado a salir de un país o una comunidad; **p. 10**

barbarians/bárbaros *n.* gente de una cultura que otros perciben como incultos o no civilizados; **p. 777**

bartered/trocó *v.* cambió sin usar dinero; **p. 693**

benefactors (ben′ ə fak′ tərz) *n.* people who help, especially by giving money or gifts; **p. 100**

C

campus (kam′ pəs) *n.* the land and buildings of a school; **p. 117**

charred (chärd) *adj.* burned; **p. 843**

chivalry (shiv′ əl rē) *n.* the customs of medieval knighthood; **p. 213**

circulation (sur′ kyə lā′ shən) *n.* the sharing of printed materials, such as books and newspapers, among readers; **p. 645**

civic (siv′ ik) *adj.* having to do with a city or citizenship; **p. 484**

coincidence (kō in′ si dəns) *n.* a situation in which two or more events that seem related accidentally occur at the same time; **p. 476**

commended (kə mend′ ed) *v.* expressed approval of; **p. 15**

commotion (kə mō′ shən) *n.* noisy confusion; **p. 14**

conceded (kən sēd′ ed) *v.* admitted as true; **p. 650**

conspirator (kən spir′ ə tər) *n.* a person who secretly plans with others to do something evil or illegal; **p. 300**

converging (kən′ vurj′ ing) *v.* coming together at a place or point; **p. 822**

conviction (kən vik′ shən) *n.* a firmness of belief or opinion; **p. 116**

cope (kōp) *v.* to deal with or try to overcome difficulties; **p. 676**

courtship (kôrt′ ship′) *n.* the act, process, and time period that leads up to mating between animals; **p. 292**

cowered (kou′ ərd) *v.* crouched or drawn back in fear; **p. 43**

crucial (krōō′ shəl) *adj.* extremely important; **p. 539**

cultivated (kul′ tə vā′ tid) *adj.* prepared for growing plants and free from weeds; **p. 43**

benefactors/benefactores *n.* gente que ayuda, especialmente por ofertas de dinero o regalos; **p. 100**

C

campus/campus *n.* la tierra y los edificios de una escuela; **p. 117**

charred/carbonizado *adj.* quemado; **p. 843**

chivalry/caballería *n.* las costumbres de los caballeros medievales; **p. 213**

circulation/circulación *n.* compartir materiales impresos, como libros y periódicos, entre lectores; **p. 645**

civic/cívil *adj.* relacionado con una ciudad o la ciudadanía; **p. 484**

coincidence/coincidencia *n.* situación en la que dos o más eventos que parecen relacionados ocurren por casualidad al mismo tiempo; **p. 476**

commended/comendó *v.* expresó aprobación de; **p. 15**

commotion/conmoción *n.* confusión ruidosa; **p. 14**

conceded/concedió *v.* admitió como verdad; **p. 650**

conspirator/conspirador *n.* alguien que hace planes secretos con otros para hacer algo malo o ilegal; **p. 300**

converging/convergiéndose *v.* juntándose en un lugar o punto; **p. 822**

conviction/convicción *n.* firmeza de opinión o creencia; **p. 116**

cope/contender *v.* bregar con o intentar superar dificultades; **p. 676**

courtship/cortejo *n.* acto, proceso y periodo de tiempo que termina con el apareamiento de animales; **p. 292**

cowered/se agachó *v.* se encogió o retrocedió por miedo; **p. 43**

crucial/crucial *adj.* extremadamente importante; **p. 539**

cultivated/cultivado *adj.* preparado para las plantas y libre de hierbas malas; **p. 43**

D

debris (də brē′) *n.* remains of something destroyed; **p. 251**

deception (di sep′ shən) *n.* that which fools or misleads; **p. 618**

deprived (di prīvd′) *v.* taken away, removed; **p. 182**

desolate (des′ ə lit) *adj.* lifeless or empty; **p. 688**

devastated (dev′ əs tā′ did) *v.* caused great pain, damage, or destruction; overwhelmed; **p. 229**

devastating (dev′ əs tāt′ ing) *adj.* causing a lot of pain, damage, or destruction; overwhelming; **p. 22**

diploma (di plō′ mə) *n.* a certificate indicating that a person has graduated from a school or a program; **p. 270**

disastrous (di zas′ trəs) *adj.* awful, terrible; **p. 650**

discredited (dis kred′ it′ id) *v.* refused to accept as true or accurate; caused to be doubted or disbelieved; **p. 234**

discreetly (dis krēt′ lē) *adv.* in a manner showing good judgment; **p. 428**

disrespect (dis′ ri spekt′) *n.* rudeness or lack of respect; **p. 78**

disrupted (dis rupt′ ed) *v.* interrupted; **p. 251**

disruptions (dis rup′ shənz) *n.* unwanted breaks or interruptions; **p. 405**

droplets (drop′ litz) *n.* tiny amounts of liquid; **p. 857**

E

eavesdrop (ēvz′ drop′) *v.* to listen secretly to a private conversation; **p. 475**

eclipse (i klips′) *n.* the partial or complete hiding from view of the sun or moon by another object in space; **p. 776**

ecstatic (ek stat′ ik) *adj.* overwhelmed with joy or delight; **p. 722**

embarked (em bärkd′) *v.* made a start; **p. 378**

emphasis (em′ fə sis) *n.* special weight or importance; **p. 646**

D

debris/escombros *n.* los restos de algo destruido; **p. 251**

deception/decepción *n.* lo que engaña o distrae; **p. 618**

deprived/deprivó *v.* quitó, eliminó; **p. 182**

desolate/desolado *adj.* vacío o sin vida; **p. 688**

devastated/devastado *v.* que ha sufrido un gran dolor, daño o destrucción; abrumado; **p. 229**

devastating/devastador *adj.* que causa mucho dolor, daño o destrucción; abrumado; **p. 22**

diploma/diploma *n.* certificado que indica que alguien se ha graduado de una escuela o un programa; **p. 270**

disastrous/desastroso *adj.* horrible, terrible; **p. 650**

discredited/desacreditado *v.* no aceptado como cierto o preciso; considerado dudosos o no creíble; **p. 234**

discreetly/discretamente *adv.* de manera que demuestra buen juicio; **p. 428**

disrespect/falta de respeto *n.* no mostrar la cortesía adecuada; **p. 78**

disrupted/desbarató *v.* interrumpió; **p. 251**

disruptions/perturbaciones *n.* complicaciones o ínterrupciones no deseadas; **p. 405**

droplets/gotas *n.* cantidades pequeñas de líquido; **p. 857**

E

eavesdrop/escuchar a escondidas *v.* escuchar secretamente una conversación privada; **p. 475**

eclipse/eclípse *n.* ocultamiento parcial o completo de la vista del sol o la luna por otro objeto en el espacio; **p. 776**

ecstatic/extático *adj.* asombrado con placer o alegría; **p. 722**

embarked/se embarcó en *v.* comenzó; **p. 378**

emphasis/énfasis *n.* importancia o peso especial; **p. 646**

ensure (en shoor´) *v.* to guarantee or make certain; **p. 538**

epithet (ep´ ə thet´) *n.* a descriptive word or phrase used with or in place of a name; **p. 300**

evading (i vād´ ing) *adj.* keeping away or avoiding; **p. 32**

excavated (eks´ kə vāt´ əd) *adj.* uncovered or removed by digging; unearthed; **p. 612**

excess (ek´ ses) *adj.* more than usual or necessary; **pp. 212, 421**

explicit (eks plis´ it) *adj.* clearly expressed or revealed; **p. 825**

F

facility (fə sil´ ə tē) *n.* something, such as a building, built to serve a particular purpose; **p. 490**

fanfare (fan´ fār´) *n.* a short tune sounded by bugle, trumpets, or other brass instruments; **p. 776**

ferocity (fə ros´ ə tē) *n.* a wild fierceness; **p. 115**

festive (fes´ tiv) *adj.* joyful; suitable for a celebration; **p. 705**

forfeit (fôr´ fit) *v.* to lose or lose the right to something; **p. 485**

frenzy (fren´ zē) *n.* a state of wild, intense emotion or excitement; **p. 845**

futile (fū´ til) *adj.* useless, hopeless, ineffective; **p. 313**

G

grievous (grē´ vəs) *adj.* very serious; **p. 630**

H

habitual (hə bich´ o͞o əl) *adj.* regular; usual; done out of habit; **p. 196**

haughtily (hô´ tə lē) *adv.* in a way that shows too much pride in oneself and scorn for others; **p. 10**

hysteria (his ter´ ē ə) *n.* overwhelming fear or emotion; **p. 253**

I

ignorant (ig´ nər ənt) *adj.* without an education or knowledge; **p. 270**

ensure/asegurar *v.* guarantizar o hacer seguro; **p. 538**

epithet/epíteto *n.* palabra o frase descriptiva usada con o en lugar de un nombre; **p. 300**

evading/evasivo *adj.* que elude o evita; **p. 32**

excavated/excavado *adj.* descubierto o sacado por cavar; desenterrado; **p. 612**

excess/exceso *adj.* más que la cantidad normal; **pp. 212, 421**

explicit/explícito *adj.* claramente expresado o revelado; **p. 825**

F

facility/facilidad *n.* algo, como un edificio, construido para servir un propósito en particular; **p. 490**

fanfare/fanfarria *n.* una canción breve tocada por clarín, trompetas o otros instrumentos de metal; **p. 776**

ferocity/ferocidad *n.* fiereza salvaje; **p. 115**

festive/festivo *adj.* feliz; apto para una celebración; **p. 705**

forfeit/echar a perder *v.* perder el derecho a algo, como penalización; **p. 485**

frenzy/frenesí *n.* estado de emoción o excitación intensa y violenta; **p. 845**

futile/fútil *adj.* inútil; sin esperanzas; no effectivo; **p. 313**

G

grievous/grave *adj.* muy serio; **p. 630**

H

habitual/habitual *adj.* regular; usual; hecho por costumbre; **p. 196**

haughtily/con altivez *adv.* de manera que demuestra demasiado orgullo personal y desdén hacia otros; **p. 10**

hysteria/histeria *n.* miedo o emoción abrumador; **p. 253**

I

ignorant/ignorante *adj.* sin educación o conocimiento; **p. 270**

illuminated (i loo′ mə nāt id) *adj.* lit up; **p. 424**

immobilized (i mō′ bə līzd′) *v.* made unable to move; fixed in place; **p. 612**

implies (im plīz′) *v.* suggests without directly stating; **p. 235**

improbable (im prob′ ə bəl) *adj.* not likely; **p. 423**

improvised (im′ prə vīzd′) *v.* invented, composed, or did without preparation; **p. 27**

inconvenience (in′ kən vēn′ yəns) *n.* something that causes difficulty, discomfort, or bother; **p. 844**

inevitably (i nev′ ə tə blē) *adv.* in a way that cannot be avoided or prevented; **p. 499**

infinite (in′ fə nit) *adj.* extremely great; having no limits or end; **p. 706**

infinity (in fin′ ə tē) *n.* an unlimited amount of time or space; **p. 797**

initiative (i nish′ ə tiv) *n.* the action of taking the first step; **p. 836**

inscription (in skrip′ shən) *n.* something written or carved on a surface as a lasting record; **p. 520**

instill (in stil′) *v.* to put in gradually, little by little; **p. 803**

integrity (in teg′ rə tē) *n.* honesty; sincerity; **p. 300**

intricate (in′ tri kit) *adj.* complicated; **p. 196**

ironically (ī ron′ i klē) *adv.* in a way that is different from what would be expected; **p. 497**

L

lacquer (lak′ ər) *n.* a liquid that is poured on wood or metal and dries to form a shiny coat; **p. 137**

lapses (laps′ əs) *n.* interruptions, pauses; **p. 187**

legacy (leg′ ə sē) *n.* anything received from an ancestor or a previous time; **p. 305**

legitimate (li jit′ ə mit) *adj.* authentic or genuine; **p. 816**

M

majority (mə jôr′ ə tē) *n.* the most of a group; **p. 196**

illuminated/iluminado *adj.* lleno de luz; **p. 424**

immobilized/inmobilizado *v.* incapaz de moverse; fijo en un solo lugar; **p. 612**

implies/ímplica *v.* sugiere algo sin decirlo dírectamente; **p. 235**

improbable/improbable *adj.* poco probable; **p. 423**

improvised/improvizó *v.* inventó, compusó o hizo sin preparación; **p. 27**

inconvenience/inconveniencia *n.* algo que causa dificultad, incomodidad o molestia; **p. 844**

inevitably/inevitablemente *adv.* de manera que no se puede evadir o prevenir; **p. 499**

infinite/infinito *adj.* extremadamente enorme o grande; sin límite o fin; **p. 706**

infinity/infinidad *n.* cantidad sin límite de tiempo o espacio; **p. 797**

initiative/iniciativa *n.* capacidad de tomar el primero paso en o comenzar una actividad o proceso; **p. 836**

inscription/inscripción *n.* algo escrito o tallado en una superficie para crear un récord permanente; **p. 520**

instill/inculcar *v.* instalar gradualmente, poco a poco; **p. 803**

integrity/integridad *n.* honestidad; sinceridad; **p. 300**

intricate/intricado *adj.* complicado; **p. 196**

ironically/irónicamente *adv.* en una manera diferente de lo que se espera; **p. 497**

L

lacquer/laca *n.* líquido que se emite en madera o metal y que seca para formar una capa brillante; **p. 137**

lapses/lapsos *n.* interrupciones, pausas; **p.187**

legacy/legado *n.* todo lo recibído de un antepasado o de un tiempo anterior; **p. 305**

legitimate/legítimo *adj.* auténtico o genuino; **p. 816**

M

majority/mayoría *n.* más de la mitad de un grupo; **p. 196**

maneuvered (mə nōō′ vərd) *v.* guided with skill and design; **p. 187**

maximum (mak′ sə məm) *n.* greatest possible amount or number; **p. 646**

melancholy (mel′ ən kol′ e) *n.* sadness; depression; **p. 629**

merge (murj) *v.* to join together so as to become one; unite; **p. 499**

misery (miz′ ər ē) *n.* extreme unhappiness; despair; **p. 678**

mistrusted (mis trust′ ed) *v.* regarded with suspicion or doubt; **p. 130**

moderately (mod′ ər it lē) *adv.* to a limited degree; **p. 200**

N

novelty (nov′ əl tē) *n.* something new and unusual; **p. 97**

O

obligation (ob′ lə gā′ shən) *n.* something a person must do because of laws or duty; **p. 558**

obscure (əb skyoor′) *adj.* not clearly seen; remote; **p. 380**

omen (ō′ mən) *n.* a sign or an event thought to foretell good or bad fortune; **p. 138**

optimistic (op′ tə mis′ tik) *adj.* believing that things will turn out for the best; hopeful; **p. 558**

P

pageant (paj′ ənt) *n.* a show or exhibition; **p. 564**

painstaking (pānz′ tā king) *adj.* requiring close, careful labor or attention; **p. 618**

parasites (par′ ə sīts′) *n.* plants or animals that live in or on other plants or animals and that get all they need from their hosts and provide nothing in return; **p. 293**

passionately (pash′ ə nit lē) *adv.* enthusiastically, intensely; **p. 183**

perpetual (pər pech′ ōō əl) *adj.* constant; unceasing; **p. 26**

maneuvered/manejó *v.* guió con habilidad y preparación; **p. 187**

maximum/máximo *n.* el número o la cantidad más grande posible; **p. 646**

melancholy/melancolía *n.* tristeza, depresión; **p. 629**

merge/fusionar *v.* combinar para que se crea una sola cosa; unir; **p. 499**

misery/miseria *n.* tristeza profunda; desesperación; **p. 678**

mistrusted/desconfió *v.* miró con sospecha o duda; **p. 130**

moderately/moderadamente *adv.* hasta cierto punto limitado; **p. 200**

N

novelty/novedad *n.* algo nuevo y poco ordinario; **p. 97**

O

obligation/obligación *n.* algo que una persona debe hacer por ley o deber; **p. 558**

obscure/oscuro *adj.* no visto claramente; remoto; **p. 380**

omen/agüero *n.* una seña o evento que se cree que indicará buena o mala fortuna; **p. 138**

optimistic/optimista *adj.* cuando cree que las cosas terminarán para el bien; esperanzador; **p. 558**

P

pageant/desfile *n.* una exhibición o presentación; **p. 564**

painstaking/afanoso *adj.* que requiere labor o atención preciso y cuidadoso; **p. 618**

parasites/parásitos *n.* plantas o animales que viven en plantas o animales y que consumen lo que necesitan de sus huéspedes sin darles nada en cambio; **p.293**

passionately/apasionadamente *adv.* intensamente; con entusiasma; **p. 183**

perpetual/perpétuo *adj.* constante; sin cesar; **p. 26**

perspective (pər spek´ tiv) *n.* the ability to see things in their relative, or comparative, importance; **p. 564**

policy (pol´ ə sē) *n.* a guideline for actions or decisions; **p. 476**

pragmatic (prag mat´ ik) *adj.* concerned with practical results; **p. 309**

predator (pred´ ə tər) *n.* an animal that kills and eats other animals; **p. 292, 618**

predominantly (pri dom´ ə nənt´ lē) *adv.* mainly; mostly; **p. 484**

prolong (prə lông´) *v.* to lengthen in time; **p. 381**

prosperous (pros´ pər əs) *adj.* having wealth or good fortune; successful; **p. 92**

provisions (prə vizh´ ənz) *n.* food or supplies; **p. 94**

provoked (prə vōkd´) *v.* brought out some action or emotion; **p. 485**

punctuated (pungk´ chōō āt´ ed) *v.* emphasized; **p. 564**

R

rebellion (ri bel´ yən) *n.* uprising; organized resistance to government or another authority; **p. 629**

reflective (ri flek´ tiv) *adj.* showing serious and careful thinking; thoughtful; **p. 798**

refugee (ref´ ū jē´) *n.* a person who leaves his or her homeland because of danger or persecution and seeks safety in another place; **p. 681**

rehabilitation (rē´ hə bil´ ə tā´ shən) *n.* the act of restoring to good health or useful activity; **p. 646**

replenished (ri plenh´ ishd) *v.* replaced something that has been used; **p. 693**

requirement (ri kwīr´ mənt) *n.* something that is necessary; a demand or a condition; **p. 539**

residential (rez´ ə den´ shəl) *adj.* related to homes; **p. 250**

restless (rest´ lis) *adj.* nervous, unable to keep still; **p. 40**

ritual (rich´ ōō əl) *n.* a set routine; **p. 80**

perspective/perspectiva *n.* la capacidad de ver las cosas en su importancia relativa o comparada con otras cosas; **p. 564**

policy/política *n.* una pauta o guía de reglas para acciones o decisiones; **p. 476**

pragmatic/pragmático *adj.* referido a resultados prácticas; **p. 309**

predator/predador *n.* animal que mata y come otros animales; **p. 292**

predominantly/predominantemente *adv.* principalmente, mayoritariamente; **p. 484**

prolong/prolongar *v.* hacer durar más en tiempo; **p. 381**

prosperous/próspero *adj.* tener riqueza o buena fortuna; exitoso; **p. 92**

provisions/provisiones *n.* recursos necesarios, especialmente comida; **p. 94**

provoked/provocó *v.* incitó o causó alguna acción o emoción; **p. 485**

punctuated/acentuado *v.* enfatizado; **p. 564**

R

rebellion/rebelión *n.* uprising; resistencia organizada en contra del gobierno u otra autoridad; **p. 629**

reflective/reflexivo *adj.* que demuestra pensamiento serio y cuidadoso; meditabundo; **p. 798**

refugee/refugiado *n.* persona que deja su tierra natal a causa de peligro o persecución y busca seguridad en otro lugar; **p. 681**

rehabilitation/rehabilitación *n.* acto de recuperar la salud o una vida útil; **p. 646**

replenished/reabasteció *v.* repuso algo que se había usado; **p. 693**

requirement/requisito *n.* algo que es necesario; una condición o exigencia; **p. 539**

residential/residencial *adj.* relacionado con las casas; **p. 250**

restless/agitado *adj.* nervioso, incapaz de mantenerse quieto; **p. 40**

ritual/ritual *n.* una rutina establacida; **p. 80**

revelation (rev′ ə lā′ shən) *n.* information that is new, especially surprising, or valuable; **p. 806**

revenue (rev′ ə nōō′) *n.* income; money taken in by a government or a business; **p. 786**

S

satchel (sach′ əl) *n.* a carrying bag, often having a shoulder strap; **p. 513**

shriveled (shriv′ əld) *adj.* shrunken and wrinkled; **p. 843**

simultaneously (sī′ məl tā′ nē əs lē) *adv.* at the same time; **p. 183**

soberly (sō′ bər lē) *adv.* very seriously; **p. 838**

solitude (sol′ ə tōōd′) *n.* the state of being alone or separate from others; **p. 378**

specified (spes′ ə fīd′) *v.* explained or described in detail; **p. 499**

speculation (spek′ yə lā′ shən) *n.* the act of forming an opinion or conclusion based on guesswork; **p. 422**

standstill (stand′ stil) *n.* a stop in motion or progress; **p. 78**

stark (stärk) *adj.* plain; harsh, grim, or severe; **p. 705**

subtle (sut′ əl) *adj.* characterized by cleverness; having a faint, delicate quality; **p. 707**

summit (sum′ it) *n.* the top, or highest point; **p. 563**

supervision (sōō′ pər vizh′ ən) *n.* the act of watching or directing others; **p. 76**

suppresses (sə pres′ es) *v.* puts down or stops; **p. 214**

survival (sər vī′ vəl) *n.* the continuation of life; **p. 291**

T

tact (takt) *n.* the ability to handle people or situations without causing bad feelings; **p. 722**

tolerate (tol′ ə rāt′) *v.* to endure; put up with; **p. 227**

revelation/revelación *n.* información que se descubre, especialmente sorprendente o valorable; **p. 806**

revenue/ingresos *n.* dinero adquirido por un gobierno o un negocio; **p. 786**

S

satchel/maletín *n.* bolsa para llevar, muchas veces con correa; **p. 513**

shriveled/marchitado *adj.* encogido y arrugado; **p. 843**

simultaneously/simultáneamente *adv.* al mismo tiempo; **p. 183**

soberly/sobriamente *adv.* muy seriamente; **p. 838**

solitude/soledad *n.* estado de estar solo o separado de otros; **p. 378**

specified/especificó *v.* explicó o describió en detalle; **p. 499**

speculation/especulación *n.* acto de formar una opinión o conclusión basada en adivinación; **p. 422**

standstill/paralización *n.* una detención en el movimiento o progreso; **p. 78**

stark/escueto *adj.* sencillo; agreste, feo o severo; **p. 705**

subtle/sútil *adj.* caracterizado por ingeniosidad; con una calidad delicada y apenas visible; **p. 707**

summit/cima *n.* la cumbre, el punto más alto; **p. 563**

supervision/supervisión *n.* la acción de observar o controlar a otras personas; **p. 76**

suppresses/suprime *v.* sofoca o detiene; **p. 214**

survival/sobrevivencia *n.* la continuación de la vida; **p. 291**

T

tact/tacto *n.* la capacidad de tratar con personas o situaciones sin provocar sentimientos malos; **p. 722**

tolerate/tolerar *v.* soportar; aguantar; **p. 227**

U

ultimately (ul′ tə mit lē) *adv.* in the end; finally; **p. 719**

uncommitted (un′ kə mit′ id) *adj.* not having or showing a particular opinion, view, or course of action; **p. 835**

undoubtedly (un dou′ tid lē) *adv.* without a question, definitely; **p. 15**

V

valiant (val′ yənt) *adj.* brave; courageous; **p. 51**

vapor (vā′ pər) *n.* a substance suspended in the air, as steam or fog; **p. 856**

vegetation (vej′ ə tā′ shən) *n.* plant life; **p. 689**

vicinity (vi sin′ ə tē) *n.* the area around a certain place; **p. 196**

vile (vīl) *adj.* very bad; unpleasant; foul; **p. 479**

violates (vī′ ə lāts′) *v.* treats without proper respect or breaks a law or regulation; **p. 538**

vulnerable (vul′ nər ə bəl) *adj.* capable of being damaged or wounded; easily hurt; **p. 236**

W

warrant (wôr′ ənt) *n.* a written document giving permission to do a search or seize a person or property; **p. 819**

wary (wār′ ē) *adj.* cautious; on the alert; **p. 24**

whereupon (hwār′ ə pôn) *conj.* at which time; after which; **p. 128**

whiff (hwif) *n.* a slight smell or odor; **p. 513**

whims (wimz) *n.* sudden or unexpected ideas; **p. 847**

whimsical (hwim′ zi kəl) *adj.* full of odd or lighthearted ideas; **p. 402**

wholeheartedly (hōl′ här′ tid lē) *adv.* completely; sincerely; **p. 377**

withdrawn (with drôn′) *adj.* shy, quiet, or unsociable; **p. 478**

woe (wō) *n.* great sadness or suffering; great trouble or misfortune; **p. 835**

wrought (rôt) *v.* worked; made; created; **p. 250**

U

ultimately/últimamente *adv.* al final; finalmente; **p. 719**

uncommitted/no comprometido *adj.* no ligado a una opinión, perspectiva o curso de acción en particular; **p. 835**

undoubtedly/indudablemente *adv.* sin duda, definitivamente; **p. 15**

V

valiant/valiente *adj.* valeroso; con coraje; **p. 51**

vapor/vapor *n.* sustancia suspendida en el aire; **p. 856**

vegetation/vegetación *n.* vida vegetal; **p. 689**

vicinity/vecindad *n.* la zona alrededor de un cierto lugar; **p. 196**

vile/vil *adj.* muy malo; desagradable; sucio; **p. 479**

violates/viola *v.* trata sin respeto correcto o rompe la ley o una regla; **p. 538**

vulnerable/vulnerable *adj.* sensible al daño o a las heridas; que resulta lastimado con sensibilidad; **p. 236**

W

warrant/orden judicial (de registro o arresto) *n.* documento escrito que autoriza una búsqueda o detención de una persona o propiedad; **p. 819**

wary/cauto *adj.* prudente; alerto; **p. 24**

whereupon/entonces *conj.* en aquel momento; después de lo cual; **p. 128**

whiff/tufo *n.* leve aroma o olor; **p. 513**

whims/caprichos *n.* ideas repentinas o inesperadas; **p. 847**

whimsical/antojadizo *adj.* con muchas ideas extrañas o poco profundas; **p. 402**

wholeheartedly/incondicionalmente *adv.* completamente, sinceramente; **p. 377**

withdrawn/retirado *adj.* reservado, quieto, o poco sociable; **p. 478**

woe/pena *n.* gran tristeza o sufrimiento; gran dificultad o mala fortuna; **p. 835**

wrought/forjó *v.* laboró; hizo; creó; **p. 250**

Academic Word List

To succeed academically in middle school and high school and prepare for college, it is important to know academic vocabulary—special terms used in classroom discussion, assignments, and tests. These words are also used in the workplace and among friends to share information, exchange ideas, make decisions, and build relationships. Research has shown that the words listed below, compiled by Averil Coxhead in 2000, are the ones most commonly used in these ways. You will encounter many of them in the *Glencoe Literature* program. You will also focus on specific terms in connection with particular reading selections.

Note: The lists are ordered by frequency of use from most frequent to least frequent.

List One

analysis
approach
area
assessment
assume
authority
available
benefit
concept
consistent
constitutional
context
contract
create
data
definition
derived
distribution
economic
environment
established
estimate
evidence
export
factors
financial
formula
function
identified
income
indicate
individual
interpretation
involved
issues
labor
legal
legislation
major
method
occur
percent
period
policy
principle
procedure
process
required
research
response
role
section
sector
significant
similar
source
specific
structure
theory
variables

List Two

achieve
acquisition
administration
affect
appropriate
aspects
assistance
categories
chapter
commission
community
complex
computer
conclusion
conduct
consequences
construction
consumer
credit
cultural
design
distinction
elements
equation
evaluation
features
final
focus
impact
injury
institute
investment
items
journal
maintenance
normal
obtained
participation
perceived
positive
potential
previous
primary
purchase
range
region
regulations
relevant
resident
resources
restricted
security
select
site
sought
strategies
survey
text
traditional
transfer

List Three

alternative
circumstances
comments
compensation
components
consent
considerable
constant
constraints
contribution

convention
coordination
core
corporate
corresponding
criteria
deduction
demonstrate
document
dominant
emphasis
ensure
excluded
framework
funds
illustrated
immigration
implies
initial
instance
interaction
justification
layer
link
location
maximum
minorities
negative
outcomes
partnership
philosophy
physical
proportion
published
reaction
registered

reliance
removed
scheme
sequence
sex
shift
specified
sufficient
task
technical
techniques
technology
validity
volume

List Four

access
adequate
annual
apparent
approximated
attitudes
attributed
civil
code
commitment
communication
concentration
conference
contrast
cycle
debate
despite
dimensions
domestic
emerged

error
ethnic
goals
granted
hence
hypothesis
implementation
implications
imposed
integration
internal
investigation
job
label
mechanism
obvious
occupational
option
output
overall
parallel
parameters
phase
predicted
principal
prior
professional
project
promote
regime
resolution
retained
series
statistics
status
stress

subsequent
sum
summary
undertaken

List Five

academic
adjustment
alter
amendment
aware
capacity
challenge
clause
compounds
conflict
consultation
contact
decline
discretion
draft
enable
energy
enforcement
entities
equivalent
evolution
expansion
exposure
external
facilitate
fundamental
generated
generation
image
liberal

license
logic
marginal
medical
mental
modified
monitoring
network
notion
objective
orientation
perspective
precise
prime
psychology
pursue
ratio
rejected
revenue
stability
styles
substitution
sustainable
symbolic
target
transition
trend
version
welfare
whereas

List Six

abstract
accurate
acknowledged
aggregate

allocation
assigned
attached
author
bond
brief
capable
cited
cooperative
discrimination
display
diversity
domain
edition
enhanced
estate
exceed
expert
explicit
federal
fees
flexibility
furthermore
gender
ignored
incentive
incidence
incorporated
index
inhibition
initiatives
input
instructions
intelligence
interval
lecture

migration
minimum
ministry
motivation
neutral
nevertheless
overseas
preceding
presumption
rational
recovery
revealed
scope
subsidiary
tapes
trace
transformation
transport
underlying
utility

List Seven

adaptation
adults
advocate
aid
channel
chemical
classical
comprehensive
comprise
confirmed
contrary
converted
couple
decades

definite
deny
differentiation
disposal
dynamic
eliminate
empirical
equipment
extract
file
finite
foundation
global
grade
guarantee
hierarchical
identical
ideology
inferred
innovation
insert
intervention
isolated
media
mode
paradigm
phenomenon
priority
prohibited
publication
quotation
release
reverse
simulation
solely
somewhat

submitted
successive
survive
thesis
topic
transmission
ultimately
unique
visible
voluntary

List Eight

abandon
accompanied
accumulation
ambiguous
appendix
appreciation
arbitrary
automatically
bias
chart
clarity
conformity
commodity
complement
contemporary
contradiction
crucial
currency
denote
detected
deviation
displacement
dramatic
eventually

exhibit
exploitation
fluctuations
guidelines
highlighted
implicit
induced
inevitably
infrastructure
inspection
intensity
manipulation
minimized
nuclear
offset
paragraph
plus
practitioners
predominantly
prospect
radical
random
reinforced
restore
revision
schedule
tension
termination
theme
thereby
uniform
vehicle
via
virtually
visual
widespread

List Nine

accommodation
analogous
anticipated
assurance
attained
behalf
bulk
ceases
coherence
coincide
commenced
concurrent
confined
controversy
conversely
device
devoted
diminished
distorted
duration
erosion
ethical
format
founded
incompatible
inherent
insights
integral
intermediate
manual
mature
mediation
medium
military
minimal
mutual
norms
overlap
passive
portion
preliminary
protocol
qualitative
refine
relaxed
restraints
revolution
rigid
route
scenario
sphere
subordinate
supplementary
suspended
team
temporary
trigger
unified
violation
vision

List Ten

adjacent
albeit
assembly
collapse
colleagues
compiled
conceived
convinced
depression
encountered
enormous
forthcoming
inclination
integrity
intrinsic
invoked
levy
likewise
nonetheless
notwithstanding
odd
ongoing
panel
persistent
posed
reluctant
so-called
straightforward
undergo
whereby

Index of Skills

Literary Concepts

Act 792, 795, R1

Alliteration 190, 193, 388, 397, 399, 665, 861, R1, R7

Allusion 547, 552, R1

Analogy 609, 623, R1, R3

Anecdote 495, 503, R1

Antagonist R1

Anthropomorphism R1

Appeal to
authoritay 534
emotion 534, 537
ethics 534, 537
logic 534, 537

Argument 534, 535, 537, 541

Aside R1

Assonance 604, 607, R1, R6, R7

Audience 534

Author's perspective 554, 560

Author's purpose 211, 218, 317, 383, 560, 641, 647, R1

Autobiography R1

Ballad R1

Biography R1

Boldfaced terms 220

Cause-and-effect text structure 220, 223, 290, 298

Character 84, 91, 103, 122, 156, 792, 829, R1, R7
cast of 792
dynamic R1
flat 91, 122, R1
main 91, 156
minor 91, 156
round 91, 122, R1
static R1

Characterization 84, 104, 106, 125, 133, 189, 409, 511, 523, R1
direct 84, 85, 104, 125, 511, R1
indirect 84, 85, 104, 125, 189, 409, 511, R1

Chronological order 220, 223

Classification text structure 290

Climax 73, 85, 91, 769, 792, 793, R2, R5

Comedy R2

Compare-and-contrast text

structure 220, 223

Conflict 19, 58, 73, 84, 156, 157, 284, 288, 324, 331, 473, 481, 672, 675, 683, 769, 828, R2, R5
external 19, 156, 157, 284, 324, 473, 675, 828, R2
internal 19, 156, 157, 284, 324, 473, 675, 828, R2

Connotation 298, 841

Consonance 604, 607, R2, R6, R7

Deck 144, 240, 384, 527

Denotation 298, 841

Description 113, 122, 133, 218, 685, 697, 855, 861, R2

Details R2
sensory 113, 123, 156, 157

Dialect R2

Dialogue 84, 157, 277, 283, 438, 792, 829, R2

Diction 249, 261, 298, 357, 727, 841, 852

Drama R2, R3

Essay 534, R2
formal R2
informal R2
persuasive 534

Evidence 534, 535

Exposition 73, 85, 91, 769, 792, 793, R2, R5

Extended metaphor 711, R2

Fable 86, 89, R2

Falling action 73, 85, 91, 769, 792, 793, R2, R5

Fantasy R3

Fiction R3

Figurative language 203, 205, 388, R3

Figure of speech R3

First-person narrative R3

Flashback 831, 839, R3

Folklore R3

Folktale R3

Footnotes 220

Foreshadowing 179, 189, 813, R3

Free verse 363, 367, R3

Genre 2, 172, 350, 466, 598, 758, R3

Graphics 220

Haiku R3

Hero R3

Historical fiction R3

Humor 401, 409, 503, R3

Idiom 388, 727, R4

Imagery 113, 133, 358, 361, 367, 388, 505, 508, 683, R4
sensory R6
visual R7

Informational text 220, R4

Irony 401, 656, 658, R4
situational 656, R4
verbal 656, R4

Legend 627, 635, R4

Limerick R4

Line 354, 357, 388

Local color R4

Lyric R4

Lyric poetry R4

Main idea R4

Memoir R4

Metaphor 203, 207, 388, 396, 671, 711, R3, R4
extended 711, R2

Meter 388, 413, 417, R4

Monologue R4

Mood 195, 201, 432, 811, R4

Motivation 433, 438, 523, 635

Myth R4

Narration R4

Narrative hook R5

Narrative poetry 61, 69, R4

Narrator 9, 17, 35, 84, 155, 157, 493, 672, R5

Nonfiction R5

Novel R5

Novella R5

Onomatopoeia 388, R5, R7

Oral tradition 627, R5

Order of importance 220

Parallelism R5

Personification 388, 567, 569, 671, R3, R5

Persuasive technique 534

Photographs 240, 527, 712

Plot 19, 35, 58, 61, 73, 83, 84, 85, 91, 156, 157, 672, 769, 792, 829,

Vocabulary

Academic Vocabulary 34, 58, 68, 89, 122, 188, 206, 218, 260, 274, 282, 287, 316, 356, 366, 372, 382, 395, 409, 417, 431, 437, 480, 492, 503, 522, 541, 551, 559, 606, 623, 634, 664, 670, 682, 697, 710, 726, 788, 810, 828, 852, 860

Affix 262

Antonyms 296

Base word 262

Connotation 368

Context clues 70

Denotation 368

Dictionary Skills 659

Etymology 790

Idioms 509

Multiple-meaning words 368

Prefix 262, 532

Root 262

Suffix 262

Synonyms 296

Thesaurus 659

Word origins 790

Word parts 262

Writing

Analyzing

  a model 157, 335, 451, 583, 743, 877

  sound devices 418

Arguing a position 542, 853

Argument 581, 583

Audience 333, 335

  convincing an 410

Autobiographical narrative 123

Bibliography R17

  formatting of R17

Blurb 143, 569, 658

Brainstorming 61, R14

Brochure 332, 339

Call to action 582

Character 156, 829

  main 156

  minor 156

Chronological order 239

Compare and contrast 624

point of view 624

Comparing 153, 331, 447, 579, 737, 873

Conclusion 450, 451, 504, 583, 876, 877

Conflict 156, 157

  external 156

  internal 156

Conventions 334

Counterarguments 582, 583

Database, electronic R18

  data R19

  field R19

Description 123, 698

Descriptive writing 383, 392, 508, 523

Details 219, 447, 579

  sensory 123, 156, 157

  supporting 335

Dialogue 157, 159, 829

Diction 261

Dictionary 193, 297, 582, 624, 671, 829, 852

Direct quotations 219

Documenting information 504, R16

  bibliography R17

  footnotes R16

  note cards R15

  source cards R15

  parenthetical documentation R16, R17

  works cited R17

Drafting 59, 123, 155, 219, 275, 333, 410, 418, 449, 504, 542, 581, 624, 698, 740, 829, 853, 875

  tips 156, 334, 450, 582, 740, 876

Editing 59, 123, 159, 219, 275, 337, 410, 418, 453, 504, 542, 585, 624, 698, 745, 829, 853, 879

  tips 159

Essay 463

  expository 275, 418, 624, 829, 874

  persuasive 542, 580, 853

Evidence 450, 582, 583

Examples 451, 876, 877

Expository writing 275, 418, 448, 624, 829, 874

Fictional narrative 169, 889

Figurative language 207, 481, 665

Footnotes R16

Formatting text R17

  margins R17

  standard typeface R17

  visual aids R17

Free-verse poem 367

Functional documents 332

  business letter R10

  e-mail R12

  instructions R13

  job application R11

  letter R10

  memo R12

  technical writing R13

Haiku 361

Handbook 161

Ideas 876

Imagery 133, 367, 523

Interesting language 876, 877

Internet research R14

  keywords R14

  search engines R14

Interview 749

Investigating names 504

Journal 17, 83, 106, 202, 239, 264, 399, 457, 532, 839

Letter 201, 301, 565, 647, 747

  persuasive 565, 595

Logical order 743

Main idea 219

Map 246

Multimedia presentations R18

  slides R18

  video R18, R19

Narrative 154

  autobiographical 123

  fictional 169, 889

Narrator 155, 157

Note cards R15

Note-taking 239, 332, 448, 739, 874, R15

Organization 156, 334, 335, 450, 451, 581, 875, 877

Outline 449, 504, 581, 740, R16

  subtopics R16

Research, Test-Taking, and Study Skills

Interdisciplinary Activities

Index of Authors and Titles

Acknowledgments

Unit 1

"Wise Old Woman" from *Sea of Gold* by Yoshiko Uchida. Copyright © 1965 by Yoshiko Uchida. Reprinted by permission of the Bancroft Library, University of California at Berkeley.

"We Are All One" from *The Rainbow People* by Laurence Yep. Text copyright © 1989 by Laurence Yep. Used by permission of HarperCollins Publishers.

"The Rider" from *Fuel* by Naomi Shihab Nye (BOA Editions, 1998). Reprinted by permission of the author.

Unit 2

"An Hour with Abuelo" from an *Island Like You: Stories of the Barrio* by Judith Ortiz Cofer. Scholastic Inc./Orchard Books. Copyright © 1995 by Judith Ortiz Cofer. Reprinted by permission.

"Aunty Misery" by Judith Ortiz Cofer. Reprinted by permission of the author.

Unit 3

"From Blossoms" from *Rose* by Li-Young Lee. Copyright © 1986 by Li-Young Lee. Reprinted by permission of BOA Editions, Ltd.

"A Crush" from *A Couple of Kooks and Other Stories About Love* by Cynthia Rylant. Scholastic Inc./Orchard Books. Copyright © 1990 by Cynthia Rylant. Reprinted by permission.

"My First Memory (of Librarians)" from *Acolytes* by Nikki Giovanni. Copyright © 2007 by Nikki Giovanni. Reprinted by permission of HarperCollins Publishers.

Unit 4

"old age sticks" Copyright © 1958, 1986, 1991 by the Trustees for the E.E. Cummings Trust, from *Complete Poems: 1904-1962* by E.E. Cummings, edited by George J. Firmage. Used by permission of Liveright publishing Corporation.

From "Should Naturalized Citizens be President?" by John Yinger and Matthew Spalding. Published in *The New York Times Upfront,* February 4, 2005. Copyright © 2005 Scholastic Inc. Reprinted by permission.

"Without Commercials" from *Horses Make a Landscape Look More Beautiful,* copyright © 1984 by Alice Walker, reprinted by permission of Harcourt, Inc.

"Heroes" by Erma Bombeck (August 2, 1981). Reprinted with permission by The Aaron Priest Literary Agency, Inc.

"Home" from *Maud Martha* by Gwendolyn Brooks. Reprinted by consent of Brooks Permissions.

Unit 5

"If I can stop one heart from breaking" and "I stepped from plank to plank" reprinted by permissions of the publishers and the Trustees of Amherst College from *The Poems of Emily Dickinson,* Thomas H. Johnson, ed., Cambridge, Mass.: The Belknap Press of Harvard University Press, copyright © 1951, 1955, 1979, 1983 by the President and Fellows of Harvard College.

"Rosa" from *On the Bus with Rosa Park,* W.W. Norton & Co., Inc. Copyright © 1999 by Rita Rove. Reprinted by permission of the author.

"Almost Ready" from *Slow Dance Heartbreak Blues* by Arnold Adoff. Text copyright © 1995 by Arnold Adoff. Used by permission of HarperCollins Publishers.

From *The Adventures of Marco Polo* by Russell Freedman. Scholastic Inc./Arthur A. Levine Books. Copyright © 2006 by Russell Freedman. Reprinted by permission.

"Saturday, May 2, 1992," "Sunday May 3, 1992," "Tuesday May 5, 1992," "Thursday May 7, 1992," "Wednesday May 13, 1992," from *Zlata's Diary* by Zlata Filipovic, translated by Christina Pribichevich-Zoric, copyright © 1994 Editions Robert Laffont/Fixot. Used by permission of Viking Penguin, a division of Penguin Group (USA) Inc.

"The Teacher Who Changed My Life" by Nicholas Gage. Reprinted by permission of the author.

"How I Learned English" by Gregory Djanikian. Reprinted by permission of the author.

Unit 6

From "Missing: The Frog Population in Costa Rica is Declining. Scientists Search for Answers" by Claire Miller. Published in *Scholastic Superscience Red,* October 18, 2005. Copyright © 2005 by Scholastic, Inc. Reprinted by permission.

"Birdfoot's Grampa" from *Entering Onondaga* by Joseph Bruchac. Copyright © 1975 by Joseph Bruchac. Reprinted by permission of Barbara S. Kouts.

"Narcissus" from *Tales the Muses Told* by Roger Lancelyn Green, published by The Bodley Head. Reprinted by permission of The Random House Group, Ltd.

From *Greek Myths* by Olivia Coolidge. Copyright © 1949, and renewed 1977 by Olivia E. Coolidge. Adapted and reprinted by permission of Houghton Mifflin Company. All rights reserved.

Photography

1 Peter Griffith/Masterfile; **3** Brand X Pictures; **4** Martin Jacobs/FoodPix/Jupiter Images; **5** Todd Davidson/Illustration Works/CORBIS; **6** Getty Images; **7** Jessie Coates/SuperStock; **8** Yoshiko Uchida. Photograph by George Fry. Yoshiko Uchida photograph collection, BANC PIC 1986.059:269—PIC The Bancroft Library, University **10** Asian Art Museum of San Francisco, The Avery Brundage Collection, B76 D3; **12** The British Museum; **18** Photo by Ken Miller; **20** Joe McBride/CORBIS; **21** Mike Powell/Getty Images; **25** Bill Angresano; **28** Fratelli Alinari/SuperStock; **30** Christie's Images; **32** Getty Images; **38** Hulton Archive/Getty Images; **40** (t)Private Collection/ Bridgeman Art Library, (b)Gareth Byrne/Alamy Images; **42** (t)Jennie Lewis/Alamy Images, (b)Victoria & Albert Museum, London/Art Resource, NY; **44** Private Collection/©Look and Learn/Bridgeman Art Library; **46 52** Bibliotheque Nationale, Paris, Archives Charmet/Bridgeman Art Library; **56** Dorling Kindersley/PunchStock; **57** (t)Getty Images, (b)POPPERFOTO/Alamy Images; **60** E.O. Hoppe/Time & Life Pictures/Getty Images; **63** Jamie Wyeth; **64** Fine Art Photographic Library/CORBIS; **71** The Grand Design/SuperStock; **72** Rene Saldana; **74** Private Collection/Bridgeman Art Library; **77** Kelly Brooks/ Illustration Works/CORBIS; **80** Alamy Images;

81 Private Collection/Bridgeman Art Library; **86** Alinari/Art Resource, NY; **87 88** From Aesop's Fables ©2000 by Jerry Pinkney. Used with permission of Chronicle Books LLC, San Francisco. Visit ChronicleBooks.com; **90** Miriam Berkley; **92 93** Christie's/SuperStock; **94** Brand X Pictures/ PunchStock; **95** Stockdisc/PunchStock; **101** Schalkwijk/Art Resource, NY; **104** Dan Addison/U. Va. Public Affairs; **105** National Portrait Gallery, Smithsonian Institution/Art Resource, NY; **107** (inset)Courtesy American Library Association, Bettmann/CORBIS; **108** The publisher wishes to thank The National Association for the Advancement of Colored People for authorizing the use of this photograph **109** AP Photos; **110** Bettmann/CORBIS; **111** The Mukashi Collection; **112** Courtesy Gary Soto; **114** Mark Gervase/Getty Images; **117** Alamy Images; **118** SuperStock/SuperStock; **121** Getty Images; **124** Schomburg Center for Research in Black Culture, The New York Public Library, Astor, Lenox and Tilden Foundation; **126** Gift of Helen Farr Sloan, ©1998 Board of Trustees, National Gallery of Art, Washington, DC.; **128** Doug Martin; **129** Smithsonian American Art Museum, Washington, DC/ Art Resource, NY; **131** Hampton University Museum, Hampton, VA; **134** Courtesy Scholastic Books; **136** Brand X Pictures/PunchStock; **137** Brand X Pictures/ PunchStock; **138** (t)Burstein Collection/CORBIS, (b)Alamy Images; **139** (l)Christie's Images, (r)Brand X Pictures/PunchStock; **140** akg–images; **141 142** Brand X Pictures/PunchStock; **145** AP Images; **146 148** William F. Cambell; **150** Gerardo Somoza/ CORBIS; **151** Richard Hamilton Smith/CORBIS; **152** Elizabeth Barakah Hodges/SuperStock; **156** ©King Features Syndicate, Inc. Reprinted with special permission.; **162 163** Eclipse Studios; **170–171** PhotoAlto/SuperStock; **173 175** Private Collection/ Christian Pierre/SuperStock; **177** Jane Wooster Scott; **178** AP Images; **180** Stockbyte/Getty Images; **181** Hulton Archive/Getty Images; **182** Stockbyte/ Getty Images; **185** Private Collection/Bridgeman Art Library; **187** Stockbyte/Getty Images; **190** Alice Ochs/Getty Images; **191 192** Shel Silverstein; **194** Bettmann/CORBIS; **196** Art Resource, NY; **198** Doug Martin; **199** San Diego Museum of Art (Gift of Anne R. and Amy Putnam); **202** Tony Getsug; **204** Carl Schneider/Getty Images; **206** Comstock/Alamy

Nicholas Gage, (r)3CD; **722** (t)courtesy Nicholas Gage, (b)3CD; **724** J. Noelker/The Image Works; **725** (l)Eddie Adams, (r)3CD; **728** Courtesy Stanford University News Service; **729** Christie's Images; **731** City of Sacramento Archives and Museum Collection; **732** Private Collection/Bridgeman Art Library; **735** Comstock/Alamy Images; **736** Owen Franken/CORBIS; **742** ©King Features Syndicate, Inc. Reprinted with special permission.; **748 749** Eclipse Studios; **756–757** Peter Griffith/Masterfile; **760** Patti Mollica/SuperStock; **763** Private Collection/Bridgeman Art Library; **765–767** Thayer Allyson Gowdy; **770** Newberry Library/SuperStock; **772** PhotoDisc/Alamy Images; **774** Private Collection/Bridgeman Art Library; **776** Ilene MacDonald/Alamy Images; **779 781** Private Collection/Bridgeman Art Library; **784** Newberry Library/SuperStock; **791** Private Collection/Bridgeman Art Library; **794** Bettmann/CORBIS; **797** JUPITERIMAGES/Brand X/Alamy Images; **800** Fine Arts Museums of San Francisco; **804** Car Culture/Getty Images; **807** SuperStock, Inc./SuperStock; **815** Yale University Art Gallery/Art Resource, NY; **818** Peter Jacobs, NY; **826** age fotostock/SuperStock; **827** (t)Getty Images, (c)Image Ideas, (r b) The McGraw-Hill Companies;

830 Richard Howard/Time & Life Pictures/Getty Images; **833** Private Collection/Bridgeman Art Library; **834** Stella Jones Gallery, New Orleans, LA; **837** SuperStock; **838** Louise Freshman Brown/SuperStock; **840** Jean-Claude Amiel/Kipa/CORBIS; **842** John Wilkes/Getty Images; **846** (t)Connie Hayes/Stock Illustration Source/Getty Images, (bkgd)John Wilkes/Getty Images, (b)JG Photography/Alamy Images; **848** Private Collection/Bridgeman Art Library/Getty Images, (bkgd)John Wilkes/Getty Images; **850** Stock Illustration/Getty Images, (bkgd)John Wilkes/Getty Images; **851** Getty Images; **854** Martin Benjamin; **856 857** Michael Fogden/Animals Animals; **858** Michael and Patricia Fogden/CORBIS; **859** Michael P. Gadomski/Photo Researchers; **861** Michael Fogden/Animals Animals; **863** Mary Evans Picture Library/Edwin Wallace; **865** The Granger Collection; **866** Bridgeman Art Library/SuperStock; **868** Erich Lessing/Art Resource, NY; **871** The Art Archive/Tate Gallery, London/Eileen Tweedy; **872** Museo Correr, Venice/Bridgeman Art Library; **876** Images.com/CORBIS; **882** (tl bl br)Eclipse Studios, (tr)The McGraw-Hill Companies; **883** Eclipse Studios; **R18** (l)The McGraw-Hill Companies, (r)CORBIS.